ACM SIGSOFT Software Engineering Notes

Volume 22, Number 6, November 1997

Simultaneously publishe

Lecture Notes in Computer Science Vol. 1301

Mehdi Jazayeri   Helmut Schauer (Eds.)

Software Engineering –
ESEC/FSE '97

6th European Software Engineering Conference
Held Jointly with the
5th ACM SIGSOFT Symposium
on the Foundations of Software Engineering
Zurich, Switzerland, September 22-25, 1997
Proceedings

Software Engineering Notes (ISSN 0163-5948) is
published six times a year in January, March, May,
July, September, and November by ACM, 1515
Broadway, New York, NY 10036. Periodicals postage
paid at New York, NY 10001 and additional mailing
offices. POSTMASTER: Send address changes to
Software Engineering Notes, ACM, 1515 Broadway,
New York, NY 10036.

 Springer    SIGSOFT

Series Editors

Gerhard Goos, Karlsruhe University, Germany

Juris Hartmanis, Cornell University, NY, USA

Jan van Leeuwen, Utrecht University, The Netherlands

Volume Editors

Mehdi Jazayeri
Technische Universität Wien, Institut für Informationssysteme
Argentinierstr. 8/184-1, A-1040 Wien, Austria
E-mail: jazayeri@tuwien.ac.at

Helmut Schauer
University of Zürich, Department of Computer Science
Winterthurer Strasse 190, CH-8057 Zürich, Switzerland
E-mail: schauer@ifi.unizh.ch

Cataloging-in-Publication data applied for

Die Deutsche Bibliothek - CIP-Einheitsaufnahme

Software engineering : proceedings / ESEC/FSE '97, 6th European
Software Engineering Conference held jointly with the 5th ACM
SIGSOFT Symposium on the Foundations of Software Engineering,
Zurich, Switzerland, September 22 - 25, 1997. Mehdi Jazayeri ;
Helmut Schauer (ed.). - Berlin ; Heidelberg ; New York ; Barcelona ;
Budapest ; Hong Kong ; London ; Milan ; Paris ; Santa Clara ;
Singapore ; Tokyo : Springer, 1997
    (Lecture notes in computer science ; Vol. 1301)
    ISBN 3-540-63531-9

CR Subject Classification (1991): D.2, D.1, D.3, K.6, C.3

ISSN 0302-9743
ISBN 3-540-63531-9 Springer-Verlag Berlin Heidelberg New York

© Springer-Verlag Berlin Heidelberg 1997
Printed in Germany

Typesetting: Camera-ready by author
SPIN 10546309   06/3142 – 5 4 3 2 1 0   Printed on acid-free paper

Foreword

For the first time, this year the European Software Engineering Conference (ESEC) and the ACM SIGSOFT Symposium on the Foundations of Software Engineering (FSE) are being held together in one place. Each of these conferences has a rich tradition of its own. ESEC started in 1987 and FSE in 1993. From the beginning, these two conferences have shared a common focus on a highly technical program. This focus limits the size of the conferences but also results in a conference environment that encourages stimulating discussions and exchange of information and experiences. It is this shared vision that motivated the holding of the joint meeting this year. The city of Zurich offers a wonderful setting for this meeting to take place and for the first ever FSE in Europe. For all practical purposes we have treated the joint meeting as one single conference with one integrated program.

The program committee selected 27 papers out of the 194 submitted. The submissions came from all continents and the accepted papers are from eleven countries. Selection of papers was made strictly based on technical quality and not on any geographical or other distribution. The papers cover a broad range of topics: software architecture, software process, configuration management and process tools, empirical studies, system modeling, testing, decomposition and distribution, program analysis, and formal analysis. The topics range from traditional ones such as testing and formal analysis to emerging issues such as software architecture and code mobility. We have invited several distinguished researchers to make keynote presentations: Dave Parnas, Barry Bochm, and John Rushby. A special session on software engineering education contains invited presentations by Tom Maibaum (the university view) and Jürgen Uhl (the industry view). The program also contains a special session on software engineering education and a panel discussion on "Old problems, new problems, and unsolved problems in software engineering."

To complement the technical program, we have organized a set of pre- and post-conference tutorials. The tutorial program, in fact, is much larger and broader than previous years at either ESEC or FSE. The goal of enlarging the tutorial program is to help the community cope with the rapid expansion of our field. To enable intensive discussion of focused topics of current interest, we have also arranged three post-conference workshops on components, reengineering, and code mobility.

The program and the proceedings are the result of the effort of many people. First, I would like to thank all the authors who submitted their work to the conference and the program committee who did the selecting of the final program. Shari Pfleeger was not officially on the program committee but reviewed almost twenty papers. Renate Kainz and Doris Fisar helped tremendously with the administration of the program committee meeting in Vienna. Georg Trausmuth and Markus Schranz helped with various aspects of the meeting and computer management of the papers and the reviews. Dino Mandrioli put a great tutorial program together, much larger and broader than previous years. Georg Trausmuth handled the poster and demo sessions. I would like to especially thank Martin Glinz for a tireless, thorough, and meticulous job of local organization. He was always available to do all the many tasks that popped up here and there. The final decision to have a joint meeting was made after many discussions led by Lori Clarke representing FSE and Michel Lemoine representing ESEC. The executive chair, Helmut Schauer, facilitated the organisation of the conference in Zurich.

It has been an honor and a pleasure to assemble this program and these proceedings. I hope that this volume gives the reader a sense of the excitement of the state of research in software engineering and the lively ambience of the ESEC and FSE conferences. I also hope that you enjoy the conference in the pleasant environment offered by Zurich.

Vienna, June 1997   Mehdi Jazayeri

Program Committee

PROGRAM CHAIR

Mehdi Jazayeri, Technische Universität Wien (Austria)

EXECUTIVE CHAIR

Helmut Schauer, Universität Zürich (Switzerland)

TUTORIALS CHAIR

Dino Mandrioli, Politecnico di Milano (Italy)

POSTERS AND DEMONSTRATIONS CHAIR

Georg Trausmuth, Technische Universität Wien (Austria)

LOCAL ORGANIZATION CHAIR

Martin Glinz, Universität Zürich (Switzerland)

FINANCIAL CHAIR

Walter Bischofberger, TakeFive Software AG (Switzerland)

MEMBERS

V. Ambriola (Italy)
A. Bertolino (Italy)
W. Bischofberger (Switzerland)
P. Botella (Spain)
R. Conradi (Norway)
J. C. Derniame (France)
F. De Paoli (Italy)
A. Di Maio (Belgium)
A. Finkelstein (United Kingdom)
A. Fuggetta (Italy)
D. Garlan (USA)
C. Ghezzi (Italy)
M. Glinz (Switzerland)
V. Gruhn (Germany)
K. Inoue (Japan)
G. Kappel (Austria)
R. Kemmerer (USA)
R. Klösch (Austria)
J. Kramer (United Kingdom)

P. Kroha (Germany)
J. Kuusela (Finland)
A. van Lamsweerde (Belgium)
G. Leon (Spain)
B. Magnusson (Sweden)
H. Mössenböck (Austria)
H. Müller (Canada)
O. Nierstrasz (Switzerland)
H. Obbink (Netherlands)
J. Palsberg (USA)
W. Schäfer (Germany)
W. Scherlis (USA)
M. Sitaraman (USA)
I. Sommerville (United Kingdom)
S. D. Swierstra (Netherlands)
F. van der Linden (Netherlands)
S. Vignes (France)
J. Welsh (Australia)

Table of Contents

Processes

Configuration and Process Tools

Formal Analysis

Panel Session

Chair: Mehdi Jazayeri (Technische Universität Wien, Austria)

Software Engineering: An Unconsummated Marriage
(Extended Abstract)

David Lorge Parnas, P.Eng

Software Engineering Research Group
Communications Research Laboratory
Department of Electrical and Computer Engineering
McMaster University, Hamilton, Ontario, Canada L8S 4K1

When the first conference on "Software Engineering" was held, under NATO sponsorship three decades ago in Munich, the vast majority of Engineers ignored it. Electrical Engineers were obviously interested in building computers, but they regarded programming those computers as something to be done by others, often scientists who wanted the numerical results, or mathematicians who were interested in numerical methods. Programming was not viewed as engineering, but as a trivial task, akin to using a calculator. An engineer might have to perform such a task in order to get numerical results needed for some other task, but their real job was the other task.

The organisers of the first Software Engineering conferences saw things differently. Knowing that the engineering profession has always been very protective of its legal right to control the use of the word "engineer", they chose the title of the conference to provoke the interest of engineers. Those who organised and attended the conference had recognised four important facts:

1 The mathematicians recognised that programming wasn't really mathematics. They were not adding to our understanding of the properties of mathematical structures; they were building useful products, many of which would be used by others.

2. The scientists recognised that programming itself wasn't really science. They were not adding to mankind's knowledge of the world. Although the programs that they wrote might be used for scientific purposes, writing the programs was building a product, often one that would be used by others.

3. Building products to be used by others was engineering. The profession of engineering was invented, and given legal standing as a self-regulating profession, so that "customers" could know who was qualified to build technical products.

4. The software being built was not very good; it was becoming a major source of problems for those who owned and used it. This was the beginning of the "software crisis", a silly phrase that we still hear today. The problems were exactly those that you would expect if you allow products to be built by people who think that building products is not their "real job" and who were not prepared for this job by a professional education.

The organisers did not succeed in provoking the interest of engineers. Communication between those who study software and those who work as engineers has not been effective. Today, the majority of Engineers understand very little about the science of programming or the mathematics that one needs to analyse a program.

On the other hand, the scientists who study programming understand very little about what it means to be an engineer, why we have such a profession, how the profession is organized, or the things engineers learn during their education. In spite of this mutual ignorance, many of today's engineers spend much of their time writing and using software, and an increasing number of people trained in computer science or mathematics pontificate about "what engineers do". The purpose of this talk is to discuss both fields and attempt explain each to the other.

1 Why is engineering an organised profession?

Bridges can collapse and engines can explode. In the past, many people presented themselves as qualified to design, and direct the construction of, those products, but did not have the requisite knowledge and mathematical ability. The public, governments, and other potential customers wanted to be able to assess the qualifications of those offering their services. Potential customers did not have the knowledge necessary to make the judgement. The solution was to establish an association of Engineers with the power to license their colleagues. Each newly recognised Engineer could become a member of the association and participate in the evaluate of future candidates.

This solution has been adopted in many jurisdictions. Generally, legislation states that nobody may practice engineering or claim to be an engineer unless they have been recognised as qualified by becoming a member of the association of "Professional Engineers". The associations are obligated, by the same legislation, to make sure that all of its members are qualified to practice, that they are aware of their professional responsibilities, and that others who are qualified to practice will be able to enter the association. This is difficult task has been taken seriously by the associations with which I am familiar.

These associations have set up:

- a registration system to verify the qualifications of individuals,
- an accreditation system for institutions to certify appropriate programmes,
- a way of keeping Engineers conscious of their great responsibilities, by discussing difficult cases and providing expert ethical advice.

2 Why do we need "Software Engineering"?

Today, where bridges, engines, aircraft, power plants and medical devices are designed and/or controlled by software, the problems that led to the establishment of the engineering profession are now found in the field of software design. Many people present themselves as qualified to build software, but their products are full of problems. Few people receive an education that prepares them to develop robust and reliable software, and the general public has no way to evaluate the qualifications of those who present themselves as qualified experts.

Just as Chemical Engineering is a marriage of the science of chemistry with a lot of Engineering areas such as thermodynamics, mechanics, and fluid dynamics, the

Software Engineering field should be a marriage of the science of software with the older knowledge of the engineering profession.

The members of the Software Engineering profession, should know that subset of Computer Science that is relevant to software design, but they must also share the knowledge about design, mathematics, and other sciences that are traditionally known by Engineers. Over the years Engineering has split into a number of distinct specialities, each characterised by a distinct area of engineering science, but all sharing certain fundamental knowledge that is useful in all areas of Engineering. It is time that another such speciality, Software Engineering be identified and defined.

3 Issues worth discussing

The talk will discuss:

- Why there are no software engineers today,
- Why we have a software science and what it includes,
- The difference between an Engineering style of education and common Computer Science programmes,
- The differences between the Computer Science viewpoint and the Engineering viewpoint,
- The role of mathematics in Software Engineering,
- Some contrasts between Engineering Mathematics and Mathematics in Computer Science,
- Important parts of Computer Science that Engineers don't know,
- Engineering concepts outside conventional Computer Science that should be known to Software Engineers,
- What Engineering tells us about how to document software systems,
- Dilemmas faced by the Professional Engineer who uses software in professional practice,
- The "Professional Practice Exam" for the year 2001,
- Replacing disclaimers by warranties.

4 How to consummate the marriage

There are many important differences between the classical fields of Engineering and the new one that we are meeting to discuss. However, we will argue that there are more similarities than differences, and that Software Engineering is better understood as a branch of Engineering than as a branch of Computer Science. It is essential that those in "Software Engineering" learn more about classical Engineering and that those in classical Engineering recognise Software Engineering as a new branch of their profession.

Subtypes for Specifications*

John Rushby

Computer Science Laboratory, SRI International,
Menlo Park, CA 94025, USA

Abstract. Specification languages are best used in environments that provide effective theorem proving. Having such support available, it is feasible to contemplate that typechecking can use the services of the theorem prover. This allows interesting extensions to the type systems provided for specification languages. I describe one such extension called "predicate subtyping" and illustrate its utility as mechanized in PVS.

1 Introduction

For programming languages, type systems and their associated typecheckers are intended to ensure the absence of certain undesirable behaviors during program execution [2]. The undesired behaviors generally include untrapped errors such as adding a boolean to an integer, and may (e.g., in Java) encompass security violations. If the language is "type safe," then all programs that can exhibit these undesired behaviors will be rejected during typechecking.

Execution is not a primary concern for specification languages, but type-checking can still serve to reject specifications that are erroneous or undesirable in other ways. A minimal expectation for specifications is that they should be consistent: an inconsistent specification is one from which some statement and its negation can both be derived; such a specification necessarily allows *any* property to be derived and thus fails to say anything useful at all. The first systematic type system (now known as the "Ramified Theory of Types") was developed by Russell [15] to avoid the inconsistencies in naive set theory, and a simplified form of this system (the "Simple Theory of Types," due to Ramsey [13] and Church [4]) provides the foundation for most specification languages based on higher-order logic. If a specification uses no axioms, typechecking with respect to such a type system guarantees consistency. The consistency of axioms cannot be checked algorithmically in general, so the best that a typechecker can do in the presence of axioms is to guarantee "conservative extension" of the non-axiomatic part of the specification (i.e., roughly speaking, that it does not introduce any new inconsistencies).

Since their presence weakens the guarantees provided by typechecking, it is desirable to limit the use of axioms and to prefer those parts of the specification

* This work was supported by the Air Force Office of Scientific Research, Air Force Materiel Command, USAF, under contract F49620-95-C0044 and by the National Science Foundation under contract CCR-9509931.

language for which typechecking ensures conservative extension. Unfortunately, those parts are usually severely limited in expressiveness and convenience, often being restricted to quantifier-free (though possibly recursive) definitions that have a strongly constructive flavor; such specifications may resemble implementations rather than statements of required properties, and proofs about them may require induction rather than ordinary quantifier reasoning. Thus, a very worthwhile endeavor in design of type systems for specification languages is to increase the expressiveness and convenience of those constructions for which typechecking can guarantee conservative extension, so that the drawbacks to a definitional style are reduced and resort to axioms is needed less often.

In developing type systems for specification languages, we can consider some design choices that are not available for programming languages. In particular, a specification language will usually be part of an environment that includes an effective theorem prover, so it is feasible to contemplate that typechecking can rely on general theorem proving, and not be restricted to the trivially decidable properties that are appropriate for programming languages.

"Predicate subtypes" are one example of the opportunities that become available when typechecking can use theorem proving.[2] I am an enthusiastic user of predicate subtypes—I consider them the most useful innovation I have encountered in type systems for specification languages—and the purpose of this paper is to share my enthusiasm. I will do so using simple examples to explain what predicate subtypes are, and to demonstrate their utility in a variety of situations.

2 Predicate Subtypes

A predicate subtype is, as its name suggests, a subtype characterized by some predicate or property. For example, the natural numbers are a subtype of the integers characterized by the predicate "greater than or equal to zero." Predicate subtypes can help make specifications more succinct by allowing information to be moved into the types, rather than stated repeatedly in conditional formulas. For example, instead of

$\forall (i, j : int) : i \geq 0$ and $j \geq 0 \supset i+j \geq i$

we can say

$\forall (i, j : nat) : i+j \geq i$

because $i \geq 0$ and $j \geq 0$ are recorded in the types for i and j.

Theorem proving can be required in typechecking some constructions involving predicate subtypes. For example, if half is a function that requires an even number (defined as one equal to twice some integer) as its argument, then the formula

$\forall (i : int) : half(i+i+2) = i+1$

---

[2] Another is consistency checking for tabular specifications [11].

is well-typed only if we can prove that the integer expression i+i+2 satisfies the predicate for the subtype even—that is, if we can discharge the following proof obligation.

$$\forall(\texttt{i:int}): \exists(\texttt{j:int}): \texttt{i+i+2} = 2\times\texttt{j}$$

Predicate subtypes seem a natural idea and their existence, in inchoate form, is often assumed by those learning formal specifications. To my knowledge, however, they are supported only by the Nuprl [5] and PVS [12] verification systems. Predicate subtypes arose independently in these two systems (in PVS they came from its predecessor, EHDM, whence they were introduced from the ANNA notation [9] by Friedrich von Henke, who was involved in the design of both), and there are differences in their uses and mechanization. In Nuprl, all typechecking relies on theorem proving, whereas in PVS, there is a clear distinction between conventional typechecking (which is performed algorithmically), and the proof obligations (they are called Typecheck Correctness Conditions, or TCCs) engendered by certain uses of predicate subtyping.

The circumstances in which proof obligations are generated, and other properties of predicate subtypes are described in the remainder of this paper. The examples use PVS notation, which is briefly introduced in the following section.

PVS Notation for Predicate Subtypes

PVS is a higher-order logic in which the simple theory of types is augmented by dependent types and predicate subtypes. Built-in types include Boolean (bool), and various numeric types, such as real, integer (int) etc. Type constructors include functions, tuples, records, and abstract data types (freely generated recursive types) such as trees and lists. A large collection of standard theories is provided in libraries and the PVS "prelude" (which is a built-in library). The PVS system includes an interactive theorem prover that can be customized with user-written "strategies" (similar to tactics and tacticals in LCF-style provers), and that provides rather powerful automation in the form of decision procedures (e.g., for ground equality and linear arithmetic over both integers and reals) integrated with a rewriter [10,14]. As noted, some constructions involving predicate subtypes generate TCCs (proof obligations); often, these can be discharged automatically using strategies provided for that purpose but, in other cases, the user must develop suitable proofs interactively. Proof of TCCs can be postponed, but the system keeps track of all undischarged proof obligations and flags affected theories and theorems as incomplete.

Functions (and predicates, which are simply functions with range type bool) can be defined using λ-notation, so that the predicate that recognizes even integers can be written as follows (it is a PVS convention that predicates have names ending in "?").[3]

---

[3] For ease of reading, I am using the typeset rendition of PVS here; PVS can generate this automatically using its LaTeX-printer. PVS uses the Gnu Emacs editor as a front end and its actual input is presented in ASCII.

```
even?: [int→bool] = λ(i:int): ∃(j:int): i = 2×j
```

However, the following "applicative" form is exactly equivalent and is generally preferred.

```
even?(i:int): bool = ∃(j:int): i=2×j
```

The discipline of types ensures that the principle of comprehension is sound in higher-order logic: that is, predicates and sets can be regarded as essentially equivalent. PVS therefore also allows set notation for predicates, so that the following definition is equivalent to the previous two.

```
even?: [int→bool] = {i:int | ∃(j:int): i=2×j}
```

Viewed as a predicate, the test that an integer x is even is written even?(x); viewed as a set it is written x ∈ even?.

Predicates induce a subtype over their domain type; this subtype can be specified using set notation, or by enclosing a predicate in parentheses. Thus, the following are all equivalent, and denote the type of even integers.

```
even: TYPE = (even?)
even: TYPE = (λ(i:int): ∃(j:int): i=2×j)
even: TYPE = ({i:int | ∃(j:int): i=2×j})
even: TYPE = {i:int | ∃(j:int): i=2×j}
```

3 Discovering Errors with Predicate Subtypes

PVS makes no *à priori* assumptions about the cardinality of the sets that interpret its types: they may be empty, finite, or countably or uncountably infinite. When an uninterpreted constant is declared, however, we need to be sure that its type is not empty (otherwise we have a contradiction). This cannot be checked algorithmically when predicate subtypes are involved, so an "existence TCC" is generated that obliges the user to prove the fact.[4] Thus the constant declaration

```
x: even
```

generates the following proof obligation.

```
x_TCC1: OBLIGATION (∃(x: even): TRUE);
```

The existence TCC is a potent detector of erroneous specifications when higher (i.e., function and predicate) types are involved, as the following example demonstrates.

Suppose we wish to specify a function that returns the minimum of a set of natural numbers presented as its argument. Definitional specifications for this

---

[4] If the constant is interpreted (e.g., x: even = 2), then the proof obligation is to show that its value satisfies the corresponding predicate (e.g., ∃ (j: int): 2 = 2×j).

function are likely to be rather unattractive—certainly involving a recursive definition and possibly some concrete choice about how sets are to be represented. An axiomatic specification, on the other hand, seems very straightforward: we simply state that the minimum is a member of the given set, and no larger than any other member of the set. In PVS this could be written as follows.

```
min(s: setof[nat]): nat                                                    1

simple_ax: AXIOM ∀(s: setof[nat]): min(s) ∈ s
                 ∧ ∀(n: nat): n ∈ s ⊃ min(s) ≤ n
```

Here, the first declaration gives the "signature" of the function, stating that it takes a set of natural numbers as its argument and returns a natural number as its value. The axiom `simple_ax` then formalizes the informal specification in the obvious way, and seems innocuous enough. However, as many readers will have noticed, this axiom harbors an inconsistency: it states that the function returns a member of its argument s—but what if s is empty?

How could predicate subtypes alert us to this inconsistency? Well, as noted earlier, sets and predicates are equivalent in higher-order logic, so that a set s of natural numbers is also a predicate on the natural numbers, and thereby induces the predicate subtype (s) comprising those natural numbers that satisfy (or, viewed as a set, are members of) s. Thus we can modify the signature of our min function to specify that it returns, not just a natural number, but one that is a member of the set supplied as its argument.[5]

```
min(s: setof[nat]): (s)
```

Now this declaration is asserting the existence of a function having the given signature and, in higher-order logic, functions are just constants of "higher" type. Because we have asserted the existence of a constant, we need to ensure that its type is nonempty, so PVS generates the following TCC.

```
min_TCC1: OBLIGATION ∃(x: [s: setof[nat] → (s)]): TRUE
```

Inspection, or fruitless experimentation with the theorem prover, should convince us that this TCC is unprovable and, in fact, false.[6] We are thereby led to the realization that our original specification is unsound, and the min function must not be required to return a member of the set supplied as its argument when that set is empty.

---

[5] This is an example of a "dependent" type: it is dependent because the *type* of one element (here, the range of the function) depends on the *value* of another (here, the argument supplied to the function). Dependent typing is necessary to derive the full utility of predicate subtyping.

[6] A function type is nonempty if its range type is nonempty, or if both its domain and range types are empty. Here the domain type is nonempty (be careful not to confuse emptiness of the domain *type*, setof[nat], with emptiness of the *argument* s), so we need to be sure that the range type, (s), is also nonempty—which it is not, when s is empty.

We have a choice at this point: we could either return to the original signature for the `min` function in [1] and weaken its axiom appropriately, or we could strengthen the signature still further so that the function simply cannot be applied to empty sets. The latter choice best exploits the capabilities of predicate subtyping, so that is the one I will use. The predicate that tests a set of natural numbers for nonemptiness is written `nonempty?[nat]` in PVS, so the type of nonempty sets of natural numbers is written `(nonempty?[nat])`, and the strict signature for a `min` function can be specified as follows.

```
min(s: (nonempty?[nat])): (s)
```

This declaration generates the following TCC

```
min_TCC1: OBLIGATION ∃(x: [s: (nonempty?[nat]) → (s)]): TRUE
```

which can be discharged by instantiating with the choice function for nonempty types that is built-in to PVS.[7]

With its signature taken care of, we can now return to the axiom that specifies the essential property of the `min` function. First, notice that the first conjunct in the axiom `simple_ax` shown in [1] is unnecessary now that this constraint is enforced in the range type of the function. Next, notice that the implication in the second conjunct can be eliminated by changing the quantification so that n ranges over only members of s, rather than over all natural numbers. This leads to the following simpler axiom.

```
strict_ax. AXIOM ∀(s.(nonempty?[nat])), (n.(s)):  min(s) ≤ n
```

Satisfied that this specification is correct (as indeed it is), we might be tempted to make the "obvious" next step and define a `max` function dually.

```
max(s: (nonempty?[nat])): (s)
max_ax: AXIOM ∀(s:(nonempty?[nat])), (n:(s)):  max(s) ≥ n
```

This apparently small extension introduces another inconsistency: for what if the set s is infinite? Infinite sets of natural numbers have a minimum element, but not a maximum. Let us see how predicate subtypes could help us avoid this pitfall.

Using predicate subtyping, we can eliminate the axiom `max_ax` and add the property that it expresses to the range type of the `max` function as follows.

```
max(s: (nonempty?[nat])): { x: (s) | ∀(n: (s)): x ≥ n }                    2
```

This causes PVS to generate the following TCC to ensure nonemptiness of the function type specified for `max`.

```
max_TCC1: OBLIGATION
      ∃(x1: [s: (nonempty?[nat]) → {x: (s) | ∀(n: (s)): x ≥ n}]): TRUE
```

---

[7] Choice functions are discussed later, in Section 4.

The following three proof commands

```
(INST + "λ(s:(nonempty?[nat])): choose({x:(s) | ∀(n:(s)):x ≥ n})")
(GRIND :IF-MATCH NIL)
(REWRITE "forall_not")
```

reduce this to the following proof goal.

```
[-1]      x!1 ≥ 0                                                    3
[-2]      s!1(x!1)
  |-------
{1}       ∃(x:(s!1)):∀(n:(s!1)):x ≥ n
```

This is a "sequent," which is the manner in which PVS presents the intermediate stages in a proof. In general, there will be a collection of "antecedent" formulas (here two) above the sequent line (|-------), and a collection (here, only one) of "conclusions" below; the sequent is true if the conjunction of formulas above line implies the disjunction of formulas below. PVS proof commands, which are given in Lisp syntax, transform the current sequent in some way (or generate multiple subgoal sequents); the three shown earlier respectively instantiate an existentially quantified variable (INST), perform Skolemization, definition expansion, and invoke decision procedures (GRIND; s!1 and x!1 are the Skolem constants corresponding to the quantified variables s and x in the original formula), and apply a rewrite rule (REWRITE; the rule concerned comes from the PVS prelude and changes a ∀...NOT... above the line into an ∃... below the line, which makes it easier to read). Once again, inspection, or fruitless experimentation with the theorem prover, should persuade us that the goal ③ is unprovable (it is asking us to prove that any nonempty set of natural numbers has a largest element) and thereby reveals the flaw in our specification.

The flaw revealed in max might cause us to examine a specification for min given in the same form as ②, in order to check that it does not have the same problem. This specification generates a TCC that reduces to a goal similar to ③ (with ≤ substituted for ≥ in the conclusion) but, unlike the max case, this goal is true, and can be proved by appealing to the well-foundedness of the less-than ordering on natural numbers.

With the significance of well-foundedness now revealed to us, we might attempt to specify a generic min function: one that is defined over any type, with respect to a well-founded ordering on that type.

```
minspec[T: TYPE,   <: (well_founded?[T])]: THEORY                    4
BEGIN
   IMPORTING equalities[T]

   min((s:(nonempty?[T]))): { x:(s) | ∀(i:(s)):x < i ∨ x = i }

END minspec
```

This specification introduces a general min function in the context of a theory parameterized by an arbitrary (and possibly empty) type T, and a well-founded ordering < over that type. Observe that the specification has been adjusted a little to separate the < and = cases that were combined into ≤ for the special case of natural numbers.

Typechecking this specification results in the following TCC, requiring us to demonstrate that the function type asserted for min is nonempty.

```
min_TCC1: OBLIGATION                                                      5
    ∃(x1: [s: (nonempty?[T]) → {x: (s) | ∀(i: (s)): x < i ∨ x = i}]): TRUE
```

We begin the proof by instantiating the formula with the (built-in) choice function choose, applied to the predicate {x: (s) | ∀(i: (s)): x<i ∨ x=i} that appears as the range type.

```
(INST + "λ(s: (nonempty?[T])): choose({x: (s) | ∀(i: (s)): x<i ∨ x=i})")
```

This discharges the original proof obligation, but choose requires its argument to be nonempty, so the prover generates a new TCC subgoal to establish this fact.

```
min_TCC1 (TCC):                                                           6

    |--------
{1}     ∀(s: (nonempty?[T])):
                nonempty?⌈(s)⌉({x: (s) | ∀(i: (s)): x < i ∨ x = i})
```

This is asking us to demonstrate the existence of a minimal element for any nonempty set s. Now the type specified for < requires it to be a well-founded ordering, and we can introduce this knowledge into the proof by the command (TYPEPRED "<"). The command (GRIND :IF-MATCH NIL) then instructs the prover to expand definitions and perform other simplifications, and to Skolemize quantifiers of universal force but not to attempt to instantiate those of existential force. This produces the following simplified sequent.

```
{-1}    s!1(x!1)
{-2}    ∀(p: pred[T]):
            (∃(y: T): p(y))
                ⊃ (∃(y: (p)): (∀(x: (p)): (NOT x < y)))
{-3}    ∀(x: (s!1)): NOT ∀(i: (s!1)): x < i ∨ x = i
    |--------
```

Here, the formula {-2} is expressing the well-foundedness of <; instantiating the variable p with s!1 and using the GRIND command yields the following subgoal (this is one of two subgoals generated; the other is trivial).

```
{-1}    s!1(y!1)
[-2]    s!1(x!1)
{-3}    ∀(x: (s!1)): (NOT x < y!1)
[-4]    ∀(x: (s!1)): NOT ∀(i: (s!1)): x < i ∨ x = i
    |--------
```

Instantiating the x of [-4] with y!1 and using GRIND once more (this time allowing it to instantiate quantifiers of existential force), produces the following sequent.

```
{-1}      s!1(i!1)
[-2]      s!1(y!1)
[-3]      s!1(x!1)
  |-------
{1}       y!1 < y!1
{2}       y!1 < i!1
{3}       y!1 = i!1
```

For the specialized min function on natural numbers, the decision procedures completed the proof at this point, but here we recognize that this goal is not true in general, and we need the additional assumption that the relation < be trichotomous (which it is on the natural numbers). Once again, predicate subtypes have led us to discover an error in our specification. We can exit the prover, modify the specification [4] to stipulate that the theory parameter < must be of type well_ordered?[T] (a well-ordering is one that is well-founded and trichotomous) and rerun the proof of the TCC. This time we are successful.

Given the generic theory, we can recover min on the natural numbers by the instantiation min[nat, <]. Because of the subtype constraint specified for the second formal parameter to the theory, PVS generates a TCC requiring us to establish that < on the natural numbers is a well-ordering. This is easily done, but min[nat, >] correctly generates a false TCC (this theory instantiation is equivalent to our previous attempt to specify a max function on the naturals). However, the TCC for min[{ i: int | i < 0 }, >] (i.e., the max function on the negative integers) is true and provable.

The examples in this section illustrate how a uniform check for nonemptiness of the type declared for a constant leads to the discovery of several quite subtle errors in the formulation of an apparently simple specification. I have found the same benefit to accrue in larger specifications.

4   Automating Proofs with Predicate Subtypes

A couple of the proofs in the previous section used the "choice function" choose. PVS actually has two choice functions defined in its prelude. The first, epsilon, is simply Hilbert's ε operator.

```
epsilons [T: NONEMPTY_TYPE]: THEORY
BEGIN
  p: VAR setof[T]

  epsilon(p): T

  epsilon_ax: AXIOM (∃x: x ∈ p) ⊃ epsilon(p) ∈ p
END epsilons
```

Given a set p over a nonempty type T, epsilon(p) is some member of p, if any such exist, otherwise it is just some value of type T. (The VAR declaration for p simply allows us to omit its type from the declarations where it is used; PVS formulas are implicitly universally quantified over their free variables.)

If p is constrained to be nonempty, then we can give the following specification for an epsilon_alt function, which is simply epsilon specialized to this situation (note that T does not need to be specified as NONEMPTY_TYPE in this case).

```
choice [T: TYPE]: THEORY
  p: VAR (nonempty?[T])

  epsilon_alt(p): T

  epsilon_alt_ax: AXIOM epsilon_alt(p) ∈ p
END choice
```

The new choice function epsilon_alt is similar to the built-in function choose, but if we return to the proof of min_TCC1 (recall ⑤) but use epsilon_alt in place of choose, we find that in addition to the subgoal ⑥, we are presented with the following.

```
                                                          7
  |-------
[1]    ∀(s: (nonempty?[T])): ∀(i: (s)):
    epsilon_alt[(s)]({x: (s) | ∀(i: (s)): x < i ∨ x = i}) < i
    ∨ epsilon_alt[(s)]({x: (s) | ∀(i: (s)): x < i ∨ x = i}) = i
```

This subgoal is requiring us to prove that the value of epsilon_alt satisfies the predicate supplied as its argument; it can be discharged by appealing to epsilon_alt_ax, but the proof takes several steps and generates a further subgoal that is similar to ⑥ (and proved in the same way). How is it that the choice function choose avoids all this work that epsilon_alt seems to require?

The explanation is found in the definition of choose.

```
p: VAR (nonempty?[T])

choose(p): (p)
```

This very economical definition uses a predicate subtype to specify the property previously stated in epsilon_alt_ax: namely, that the value of choose(p) is a member of p.[8] But because the fact is stated in a subtype and is directly bound to the range type of choose, it is immediately available to the theorem prover—which is therefore able to discharge the equivalent to ⑦ internally.

Whereas the previous section demonstrated the utility of predicate subtypes in detecting errors in specifications, this example demonstrates their utility in

---

[8] The full definition is actually choose(p): (p) = epsilon(p); this additionally specifies that choose(p) returns the same value as epsilon(p), which is useful in specifications that use both epsilon and choose.

improving the automation of proofs. When properties are specified axiomatically, it can be quite difficult to automate selection and instantiation of the appropriate axiom during a proof (unless they have special forms, such as rewrite rules). Properties expressed as predicate subtypes on the type of a function are, however, intimately bound to that function, and it is therefore relatively easy for a theorem prover to locate and instantiate the property automatically.

5 Enforcing Invariants with Predicate Subtypes

Consider a specification for a city phone book. Given a name, the phone book should return the set of phone numbers associated with that name; there should also be functions for adding, changing, and deleting phone numbers. Here is the beginning of a suitable specification in PVS, giving only the basic types, and a function for adding a phone number p to those recorded for name n in phone book B.

```
names, phone_numbers: TYPE
phone_book: TYPE = [names → setof[phone_numbers]]
B: VAR phone_book
n : VAR names
p: VAR phone_numbers

add_number(B, n, p): phone_book = B WITH [(n) := B(n)∪{p}]
...
```

Here, the WITH construction is PVS notation for function overriding: B WITH [(n) := B(n)∪{p}] is a function that has the same values as B, except that at n it has the value B(n)∪{p}.

Now suppose we wish to enforce a constraint that the sets of phone numbers associated with different names should be disjoint. We can easily do this by introducing the unused_number predicate and modifying the add_number function as follows.

```
unused_number(B, p): bool = ∀(n: names): NOT p ∈ B(n)        8

add_number(B, n, p): phone_book =
  IF unused_number(B, p) THEN B WITH [(n) := B(n)∪{p}] ELSE B ENDIF
```

If we had specified other functions for updating the phone book, they would have to be modified similarly.

But where in this modified specification does it say explicitly that different names must have disjoint sets of phone numbers? And how can we check that our specifications of the updating functions preserve his property? Both deficiencies are easily overcome with a predicate subtype: we simply change the type phone_book to the following.

```
phone_book: TYPE ={ B: [ names → setof[phone_numbers]] |        9
                  ∀(n, m: names): n ≠ m ⊃ disjoint?(B(n),B(m)) }
```

This states exactly the property we require. Furthermore, typechecking the specification [8] now causes the following proof obligation to be generated.

```
add_number_TCC1: OBLIGATION                                          10
   ∀(B, n, p): unused_number(B, p)
       ⊃ ∀(r, m: names): r ≠ m
          ⊃ disjoint?(B WITH [(n) := B(n)∪{p}](r),
                      B WITH [(n) := B(n)∪{p}](m))
```

This requires us to prove that a phone_book B (having the disjointness property), will satisfy the disjointness property after it has been updated by the add_number function. This proof obligation is discharged by three commands to the PVS theorem prover.

Had there been other updating functions, similar proof obligations would have been generated automatically for them, too. This kind of proof obligation arises for the same reason as the one in [2]: a value of the parent type has been supplied where one of a subtype is required, so a proof obligation is generated to establish that the value satisfies the predicate of the subtype concerned. Here, the body of the definition given for add_number in [8] has type [names → setof[phone_numbers]], which is the parent type given for phone_book in [9], and so the proof obligation [10] is generated to check that it satisfies the appropriate predicate.

Observe how this uniform check on the satisfaction of predicate subtypes automatically generates the proof obligations necessary to ensure that the functions on a data type (here, phone_book) preserve an invariant. In the absence of such automation, we would have to formulate the appropriate proof obligations manually (a tedious and error-prone process), or construct a proof-obligation generator for this one special purpose. (The FDM system of the early 1980s had such a proof-obligation generator as its core element [7].) In the following section, I show how the same mechanism can alleviate difficulties caused by partial functions.

6   Avoiding Partial Functions With Predicate Subtypes

Functions are primitive and total in higher-order logic, whereas in set theory they are constructed as sets of pairs and are generally partial. There are strong advantages in theorem proving from adopting the first approach: it allows use of congruence closure as a decision procedure for equality over uninterpreted function symbols, which is essential for effective automation. On the other hand, there are functions, such as division, that seem inherently partial and cause difficulty to this approach. One way out of the difficulty is introduce some artificial value for undefined terms such as $x/0$, but this is clumsy and has to be done carefully to avoid inconsistencies. Another approach introduces "undefined" as a truth value; more sophisticated approaches use "free logics" in which quantifiers range only over defined terms. Both these approaches have the disadvantage of using nonstandard logics, with attendant difficulties. These problems have led some to argue that the discipline of types can be too onerous in a specification language, and that untyped set theory is a better choice [8].

Predicate subtypes offer another approach that I find preferable to the alternatives. Many partial functions become total if their domains are specified with sufficient precision; applying a function outside its domain then becomes a type error, rather than something that has to be dealt with in the logic. Predicate subtypes provide the tool necessary to specify domains with suitable precision.

For example, division is a total function if it is typed so that its second argument must be nonzero. In PVS this can be specified as follows.

```
nonzero_real: TYPE = { x: real | x ≠ 0 }
/: [ real, nonzero_real → real ]
```

Now consider the following formula.

```
test: THEOREM ∀(x, y:real): x ≠ y ⊃ (x-y)/(y-x) = -1                    11
```

Subtraction is closed on the reals, so x-y and y-x are both reals. The second argument to the division function is required to have type nonzero_real; real is its parent type, so we have the proof obligation (y-x) ≠ 0, which is not true in general. However, the antecedent to the implication in 11 will be false when x = y, rendering the theorem true independently of the value of the improperly typed application of division. This leads to the idea that the proof obligation should take account of the context in which the application occurs, and should require only that the application is well-typed in circumstances where its value matters. In this case, a suitable, and easily proved, proof obligation is the following.

```
test_TCC1: OBLIGATION ∀(x, y: real): x ≠ y ⊃ (y - x) ≠ 0
```

This is, in fact, the TCC generated by PVS from the formula 11. PVS imposes a left-to-right evaluation order, and generates TCCs under the logical context accumulated in that order. This is sound, but conservative. For example, PVS generates the unprovable TCC (y - x) ≠ 0 for the following, logically equivalent, reformulation of the formula in 11.

```
test: THEOREM ∀(x, y:real): (x-y)/(y-x) = -1 ∨ x=y
```

Since most specifications are written to be read from left to right (for the convenience of human readers), this conservatism is seldom a problem in practice.

Another example of a partial function is the subp "challenge" from Cheng and Jones [3]. This function on integers is given by

$$subp(i, j) = \textbf{if } i = j \textbf{ then } 0 \textbf{ else } subp(i, j + 1) + 1 \textbf{ endif}$$

and is undefined if $i < j$ (when $i \geq j, subp(i, j) = i - j$).

The challenge is easily handled using dependent predicate subtyping to require that the second argument is no greater than the first.

```
subp((i:int), (j:int | j ≤ i)): RECURSIVE int =
   IF i = j THEN 0 ELSE subp(i, j+1) + 1 ENDIF
MEASURE i-j
```

This generates the following proof obligation from the occurrence of j+1 in the recursive call; it is is discharged automatically by the PVS decision procedures.

```
subp_TCC2: OBLIGATION
   ∀(i: int, j: int | j ≤ i): NOT i = j ⊃ j + 1 ≤ i
```

Two other proof obligations are generated by this example: one to ensure that i-j in the MEASURE satisfies the predicate for nat, and another to establish termination using this measure. These are also discharged automatically by the PVS decision procedures.

In my experience, use of predicate subtypes to render functions total is not onerous, and contributes clarity and precision to a specification; it also provides potent error detection. Regarding the latter, the Z/EVES system [16] provides "domain checking" for Z specifications and has reportedly found errors in every Z specification examined in this way. (Domain checking is similar to the use of predicate subtypes described in this section, but lacks the more general benefits of predicate subtyping.)

7   Comparison with Subtypes in Programming Languages

Subtypes are often used in type systems for programming languages to account for issues arising in object-oriented programs [2]. In particular, a record type A that contains fields in addition to those of a record type B is regarded as a subtype of B. A function type A is regarded as a subtype of a function type B if the range type of A is a subtype of that of B ("covariance") and if its domain type is a supertype of that of B ("contravariance"). These "structural" subtypes are rather different to predicate subtypes. I know of no programming language that provides predicate subtypes, although the annotations provided for "extended static checking" (proving the absence of runtime errors such as array bound violations) [6] have some similarities. Bringing the benefits of predicate subtyping to programming languages seems a worthwhile research endeavor.

Conversely, I know of no specification language that provides structural subtyping, still less combines it with predicate subtyping. There are some difficulties (e.g., preserving a simple treatment of equality) in the presence of contravariant subtyping over functions, and integration of the two styles of subtyping presents an interesting research challenge. PVS does extend subtyping covariantly over the range types of functions (e.g., [nat → nat] is a subtype of [nat → int]) and over the positive parameters to abstract data types (e.g., list of nat is a subtype of list of int), but requires equality on domain types. However, PVS also provides type "conversions" that can automatically restrict, or (less automatically) expand the domain of a function; these allow, for example, a set of int to be provided where a set of nat is expected (or vice-versa). We do expect to add some structural subtyping (e.g., for records) to PVS in future.

8 Conclusion

I have illustrated a few circumstances where predicate subtypes contribute to the clarity and precision of a specification, to the identification of errors, and to the automation provided in analysis of specifications and in theorem proving. There are many more circumstances where predicate subtypes provide benefit (for example, going higher-order, the injections and surjections are subtypes of the functions with the same arity; declaring a function as an injection in PVS will therefore generate the proof obligation to show that it is one-to-one), and they have been used to excellent effect by several users of PVS. I hope that the examples provided here will have persuaded you of the utility of predicate subtyping and may lead you to adopt a language that provides them, or to incorporate them in your own favorite language.

Acknowledgments

PVS and its mechanisms for predicate subtyping were developed by Sam Owre and Natarajan Shankar; I am merely an enthusiastic and grateful user of the system. This paper draws freely on their knowledge and insights.

References

Papers by SRI authors are generally available from http://www.csl.sri.com/fm.html.

[1] Rajeev Alur and Thomas A. Henzinger, editors. *Computer-Aided Verification, CAV '96*, volume 1102 of *Lecture Notes in Computer Science*, New Brunswick, NJ, July/August 1996. Springer-Verlag.

[2] Luca Cardelli. Type systems. In *Handbook of Computer Science and Engineering*, chapter 103, pages 2208–2236. CRC Press, 1997. Available at http://www.research.digital.com/SRC.

[3] J. H. Cheng and C. B. Jones. On the usability of logics which handle partial functions. In Carroll Morgan and J. C. P. Woodcock, editors, *Proceedings of the Third Refinement Workshop*, pages 51–69. Springer-Verlag Workshops in Computing, 1990.

[4] A. Church. A formulation of the simple theory of types. *Journal of Symbolic Logic*, 5:56–68, 1940.

[5] R. L. Constable, S. F. Allen, H. M. Bromley, W. R. Cleaveland, J. F. Cremer, R. W. Harper, D. J. Howe, T. B. Knoblock, N. P. Mendler, P. Panangaden, J. T. Sasaki, and S. F. Smith. *Implementing Mathematics with the Nuprl Proof Development System*. Prentice-Hall, Englewood Cliffs, NJ, 1986.

[6] David L. Detlefs. An overview of the Extended Static Checking system. In *First Workshop on Formal Methods in Software Practice (FMSP '96)*, pages 1–9, San Diego, CA, January 1996. Association for Computing Machinery.

[7] Richard A. Kemmerer. Verification assessment study final report. Technical Report C3-CR01-86, National Computer Security Center, Ft. Meade, MD, 1986. 5 Volumes (Overview, Gypsy, Affirm, FDM, and EHDM). US distribution only.

19

[8] Leslie Lamport and Lawrence C. Paulson. Should your specification language be typed? SRC Research Report 147, Digital Systems Research Center, Palo Alto, CA, May 1997. Available at http://www.research.digital.com/SRC.

[9] David C. Luckham, Friedrich W. von Henke, Bernd Krieg-Brückner, and Olaf Owe. *ANNA: A Language for Annotating Ada Programs*, volume 260 of *Lecture Notes in Computer Science*. Springer-Verlag, 1987.

[10] S. Owre, S. Rajan, J.M. Rushby, N. Shankar, and M.K. Srivas. PVS: Combining specification, proof checking, and model checking. In Alur and Henzinger [1], pages 411–414.

[11] Sam Owre, John Rushby, and N. Shankar. Integration in PVS: Tables, types, and model checking. In Ed Brinksma, editor, *Tools and Algorithms for the Construction and Analysis of Systems (TACAS '97)*, volume 1217 of *Lecture Notes in Computer Science*, pages 366–383, Enschede, The Netherlands, April 1997. Springer-Verlag.

[12] Sam Owre, John Rushby, Natarajan Shankar, and Friedrich von Henke. Formal verification for fault-tolerant architectures: Prolegomena to the design of PVS. *IEEE Transactions on Software Engineering*, 21(2):107–125, February 1995.

[13] F. P. Ramsey. The foundations of mathematics. In D. H. Mellor, editor, *Philosophical Papers of F. P. Ramsey*, chapter 8, pages 164–224. Cambridge University Press, Cambridge, UK, 1990. Originally published in *Proceedings of the London Mathematical Society*, 25, pp. 338–384, 1925.

[14] John Rushby. Automated deduction and formal methods. In Alur and Henzinger [1], pages 169–183.

[15] Bertrand Russell. Mathematical logic as based on the theory of types. In Jean van Heijenoort, editor, *From Frege to Gödel*, pages 150–182. Harvard University Press, Cambridge, MA, 1967. First published 1908.

[16] Mark Saaltink. The Z/EVES system. In *ZUM '97: The Z Formal Specification Notation; 10th International Conference of Z Users*, volume 1212 of *Lecture Notes in Computer Science*, pages 72–85, Reading, UK, April 1997. Springer-Verlag.

The views and conclusions contained herein are those of the author and should not be interpreted as necessarily representing the official policies or endorsements, either expressed or implied, of the Air Force Office of Scientific Research or the U.S. Government.

Developing Multimedia Applications with the WinWin Spiral Model

Barry Boehm, Alex Egyed, USC-Center for Software Engineering

Julie Kwan, USC University Libraries

Ray Madachy, USC-CSE and Litton Data Systems

Abstract

Fifteen teams recently used the WinWin Spiral Model to perform the system engineering and architecting of a set of multimedia applications for the USC Library Information Systems. Six of the applications were then developed into an Initial Operational Capability. The teams consisted of USC graduate students in computer science. The applications involved extensions of USC's UNIX-based, text-oriented, client-server Library Information System to provide access to various multimedia archives (films, videos, photos, maps, manuscripts, etc.).

Each of the teams produced results which were on schedule and (with one exception) satisfactory to their various Library clients. This paper summarizes the WinWin Spiral Model approach taken by the teams, the experiences of the teams in dealing with project challenges, and the major lessons learned in applying the Model. Overall, the WinWin Spiral Model provided sufficient flexibility and discipline to produce successful results, but several improvements were identified to increase its cost-effectiveness and range of applicability.

1. Introduction

At the last two International Conferences on Software Engineering, three of the six keynote addresses identified negotiation techniques as the most critical success factor in improving the outcome of software projects. Tom DeMarco stated that "how the requirements were negotiated is far more important than how the requirements were specified" [DeMarco, 1996]. In discussing "Death March" projects, Ed Yourdon stated that "Negotiation is the best way to avoid Death March projects," [Yourdon, 1997]. Mark Weiser concluded that "Problems with reaching agreement were more critical to his projects' success than such factors as tools, process maturity, and design methods" [Weiser, 1997].

At the USC Center for Software Engineering, we have been developing a negotiation-based approach to software system requirements engineering, architecting, development, and management. It is based on three primary foundations:

- Theory W, a management theory and approach. It is based on making winners of all of the system's key stakeholders as a necessary and sufficient condition for project success [Boehm-Ross, 1989].
- The WinWin Spiral Model, an extension to the Spiral Model of the software process. It is described further below.

- The WinWin groupware tool for facilitating distributed stakeholders' negotiation of mutually satisfactory (WinWin) system specifications [Boehm et al., 1995; Horowitz et al., 1997].

2. The WinWin Spiral Model

The original spiral model [Boehm, 1988] uses a cyclic approach to develop increasingly detailed elaborations of a software system's definition, culminating in incremental releases of the system's operational capability. Each cycle involves four main activities:

- Elaborate the system or subsystem's product and process objectives, constraints, and alternatives.
- Evaluate the alternatives with respect to the objectives and constraints. Identify and resolve major sources of product and process risk.
- Elaborate the definition of the product and process.
- Plan the next cycle, and update the life-cycle plan, including partition of the system into subsystems to be addressed in parallel cycles. This can include a plan to terminate the project if it is too risky or infeasible. Secure the management's commitment to proceed as planned.

The Spiral Model has been extensively elaborated (e.g., SPC, 1994]), and successfully applied in numerous projects (e.g., [Royce, 1990], [Frazier-Bailey, 1996]). However, some common difficulties have led to some further extensions to the model.

One difficulty involves answering the question, "Where do the elaborated objectives, constraints, and alternatives come from?" The WinWin Spiral Model resolves this difficulty by adding three activities to the front of each spiral cycle, as illustrated in Figure 1 [Boehm-Bose, 1994].

- Identify the system or subsystem's key stakeholders.
- Identify the stakeholders' win conditions for the system or subsystem.
- Negotiate win-win reconciliations of the stakeholders' win conditions.

Figure 1. The WinWin Spiral Model

2. Identify Stakeholders' win conditions

3. Reconcile win conditions. Establish next level objectives, constraints, alternatives

1. Identify next-level Stakeholders

7. Review, commitment

4. Evaluate product and process alternatives. Resolve Risks

6. Validate product and process definitions

5. Define next level of product and process - including partitions

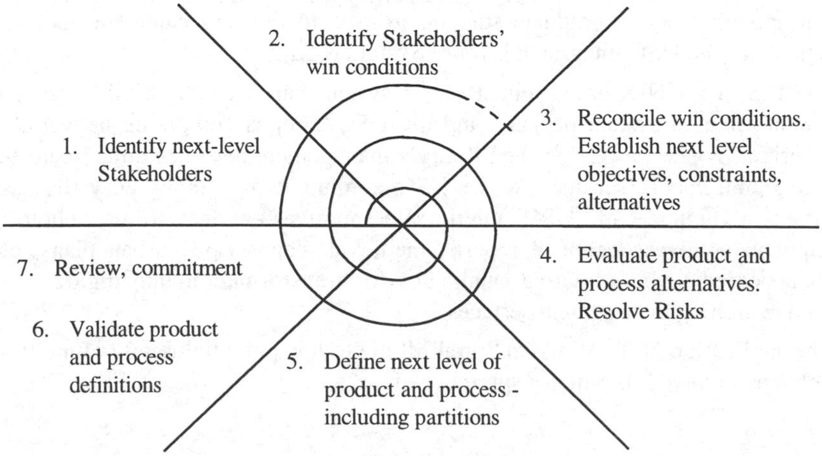

In an experiment involving a bootstrap application of the WinWin groupware system to the definition of an improved version of itself, we found that these steps indeed produced the key product and process objectives, constraints, and alternatives for the next version [Boehm et al, 1994]. The overall stakeholder WinWin negotiation approach is similar to other team approaches for software and system definition such as CORE [Mullery, 1979], gIBIS [Conklin-Begeman, 1991], GRAIL [Dardenne et al., 1993], Tuiqiao [Potts-Takahashi, 1993], Participatory Design and JAD [Carmel et al., 1993]. Our primary distinguishing characteristic is the use of the stakeholder win-win relationship as the success criterion and organizing principle for the software and system definition process. Our negotiation guidelines are based on the Harvard Negotiation Project's techniques [Fisher-Ury, 1981].

2.1. Process Anchor Points

Another difficulty in applying the Spiral Model across an organization's various projects is that the organization can be left with no common reference points around which to organize its management procedures, cost and schedule estimates, etc. In the process of working out this difficulty with our COCOMO II cost model industry and government Affiliates (see Acknowledgments), we found a set of three process anchor points which could be related both to the completion of spiral cycles and to the organization's major decision milestones. Two of these, the Life Cycle Objectives (LCO) and Life Cycle Architecture (LCA) milestones, are elaborated in Table 1. The third, the Initial Operational Capability (IOC), is summarized in Table 2. These anchor points are further elaborated and related to WinWin Spiral Model cycles in [Boehm, 1996]. We also found that the LCO and LCA milestones are highly compatible with the use of the successful Architecture Review Board practice pioneered by AT&T and Lucent Technologies [AT&T, 1993].

3. Applying the WinWin Spiral Model

New software process models generally take years to validate. The Spiral Model was originated in 1978, first tried on a 15-person internal TRW project in 1980-82 [Boehm et al, 1982], and only in 1988-92 scaled up to a 100-person contract project [Royce, 1990] and fully-documented method [SPC, 1994]. For the WinWin Spiral Model, we were fortunate to find a family of multimedia applications upon which to test the model: a set of graduate student projects to develop candidate multimedia extensions for the USC Integrated Library System (ILS).

The ILS is a UNIX-based, client-server system based on the SIRSI commercial library information system package and the USC campus computing network. The ILS is primarily text-based, but the Library's management has been quite interested in providing multimedia services to the USC community. Exploratory discussions identified a number of USC multimedia archives--student films, photo and stereopticon archives, technical reports, medieval manuscripts, urban plans, etc.— which appeared to be attractive candidates for transformation into digitized, user-interactive archive management services.

The application of the WinWin Spiral Model to this potential family of multimedia applications involved four major spiral cycles:

Table 1. Contents of LCO and LCA Milestones

Milestone Element	Life Cycle Objectives (LCO)	Life Cycle Architecture (LCA)
Definition of Operational Concept	• Top-level system objectives and scope • System boundary • Environment parameters and assumptions • Evolution parameters • Operational concept • Operations and maintenance scenarios and parameters • Organizational life-cycle responsibilities (stakeholders)	• Elaboration of system objectives and scope by increment • Elaboration of operational concept by increment
Definition of System Require-ments	• Top-level functions, interfaces, quality attribute levels, including: • Growth vectors • Priorities • Stakeholders' concurrence on essentials	• Elaboration of functions, interfaces, quality attributes by increment • Identification of TBDs (to-be-determined items) • Stakeholders' concurrence on their priority concerns
Definition of System and Software Architecture	• Top-level definition of at least one feasible architecture • Physical and logical elements and relationships • Choices of COTS and reusable software elements • Identification of infeasible architecture options	• Choice of architecture and elaboration by increment • Physical and logical components, connectors, configurations, constraints • COTS, reuse choices • Domain-architecture and architectural style choices • Architecture evolution parameters
Definition of Life-Cycle Plan	• Identification of life-cycle stakeholders • Users, customers, developers, maintainers, interoperators, general public, others • Identification of life-cycle process model • Top-level stages, increments • Top-level WWWWWHH* by stage	• Elaboration of WWWWWHH* for Initial Operational Capability (IOC) • Partial elaboration, identification of key TBDs for later increments
Feasibility Rationale	• Assurance of consistency among elements above • Via analysis, measurement, prototyping, simulation, etc. • Business case analysis for requirements, feasible architectures	• Assurance of consistency among elements above • All major risks resolved or covered by risk management plan

* WWWWWHH: Why, What, When, Who, Where, How, How Much

Table 2. Contents of the Initial Operational Capability (IOC) Milestone

The key elements of the IOC milestone are:
- Software preparation, including both operational and support software with appropriate commentary and documentation; data preparation or conversion; the necessary licenses and rights for COTS and reused software, and appropriate operational readiness testing.
- Site preparation, including facilities, equipment, supplies, and COTS vendor support arrangements.
- User, operator and maintainer preparation, including selection, teambuilding, training and other qualification for familiarization usage, operations, or maintenance.

- Cycle 0 (Summer 1996): Determining feasibility of an appropriate family of multimedia applications (project family LCO milestone);
- Cycle 1 (Fall 1996): Determining feasibility of individual applications (project LCO);
- Cycle 2 (Fall 1996): Achieving a feasible LCA project milestone for each application;
- Cycle 3 (Spring 1997): Achieving a workable project IOC for each application.

3.1. Cycle 0: Project Family Life Cycle Objectives

During 1993-96, the USC-CSE experimented with teaching the WinWin Spiral Model in its core 100-student MS-level software engineering course, using representative but hypothetical applications. In 1995-96, the application was a hypothetical advanced library application: a selective dissemination of information system using a form of "push" technology. Some of the library staff, primarily Kwan (then Director of the Science and Engineering Library, and Denise Bedford (then ILS Project Manager), detected an unusually high level of student interest in library operations resulting from this assignment. They followed up with the instructor (Boehm) to determine whether all of this student energy and talent could be channeled toward developing useful USC Library applications.

CSE had been looking for such a source of new applications, so in Summer 1996, Kwan, Bedford, Boehm, and Egyed (the prospective teaching assistant for the 1996-97 software engineering course), explored each other's win conditions to determine whether a feasible set of life-cycle objectives for a family of USC Library applications could be identified. The most feasible applications area turned out to be the exploratory multimedia applications. Table 3 summarizes the win conditions for the

Table 3. Primary Stakeholder Win Conditions

Library Information Technology and Users	Library Operations and Users	Center for Software Engineering
• Accelerated transition to digital library capabilities; Dean's vision • Evaluation of emerging multimedia archiving and access tools • Empowering library multimedia users • Enhancing library staff capabilities in high-performance online library services • Leveraging limited budget for advanced applications	• Continuity of service • No disruption of ongoing transition to SIRSI-based Library Information System • Operator career growth opportunities • No disruption of USC Network operations and services • More efficient operations via technology	• Similarity of projects (for fairness, project management) • Reasonable match to WinWin Spiral Model • 15-20 projects at 5-6 students per team • Meaningful LCA achievable in 1 semester • Meaningful IOC achievable in 2 semesters • Adequate network, computer, infrastructure resources

Figure 2. Example Library Multimedia Problem Statements

Problem Set #2: Photographic Materials in Archives

Jean Crampon, Hancock Library of Biology and Oceanography

There is a substantial collection of photographs, slides, and films in some of the Library's archival collections. As an example of the type of materials available, I would like to suggest using the archival collections of the Hancock Library of Biology and Oceanography to see if better access could be designed. Material from this collection is used by both scholars on campus and worldwide. Most of the Hancock materials are still under copyright, but the copyright is owned by USC in most cases.

Problem Set #8: Medieval Manuscripts

Ruth Wallach, Reference Center, Doheny Memorial Library

I am interested in the problem of scanning medieval manuscripts in such a way that a researcher would be able to both read the content, but also study the scribe's hand, special markings, etc. A related issue is that of transmitting such images over the network.

Problem Set #9: Formatting Information

Caroline Sisneros, Crocker Business Library

Increasingly the government is using the WWW as a tool for dissemination of information. Two much-used sites are the Edgar Database of Corporate Information (http://www.sec.gov/edgarhp.htm) and the Bureau of the Census (http://www.census.gov). Part of the problem is that some of the information (particularly that at the EDGAR site) in only available as ASCII files. For information that is textual in nature, while the files can be cleaned up, formatting of statistical tables is often lost in downloading, e-mailing, or transferring to statistical programs. And while this information is useful for the typical library researcher, who usually have a very distinct information need, the investment in what it would take to put this information is a usable format is often too much trouble.

Problem Set #13: Moving Image Archive

Sandra Joy Lee, Moving Image Archive, School of Cinema/TV

The USC Moving Image Archive houses USC student film and video productions dating from the1930s to current productions in the School of Cinema-Television. Moving image materials in multiple formats, specialized viewing equipment, limited storage space, and complex access needs create challenges that may be solved with new computer technologies. Fifteen movie clips (.mov format), each approximately 45 minutes in length, over 100 digital film stills (.gif format), and textual descriptions of the films will be made available to students wishing to explore this project.

three primary stakeholders: the Library information technology community, including its users; the Library operational community, including its users; and the Center for Software Engineering.

As indicated in Table 3, the *Library information technology community* was energized by the vision of the new Dean of the University Libraries, Dr. Jerry Campbell, to accelerate the Libraries' transition to digital capabilities. A new dedicated computer-interactive facility, the Leavey Library, and the transition to the SIRSI client-server library information system were whetting users' appetites for advanced applications. However, there was little budget for evaluating emerging multimedia technology and developing exploratory applications.

The *Library operations community* and its users were already undergoing a complex transition to the new SIRSI system. They were continually on the lookout for new technology to enhance their operations, but also highly sensitive to the risks of disrupting continuity of service, and limited in their resources to experiment in new areas.

The *Center for Software Engineering* had a large pool of talent to develop exploratory applications, if the applications could fit within the constraints of student courses. These included not only schedule and computer resource constraints (e.g., 10 megabytes of disk storage per student), but also constraints on fairness of grading and available instructor and teaching assistant time, which translated into the need for a family of highly similar (but not identical) projects.

During Summer 1996, Kwan and Bedford identified a set of candidate Library multimedia projects and clients, and provided brief summaries of each. Examples are shown in Figure 2. Successful convergence on the project-family LCO milestone was achieved by an exchange of memoranda between the Library and the CSE. A memo from Boehm to Charlotte Crockett, Director of the Leavey Library, summarized the proposed set of projects, the potential Library costs and risks and how they would be addressed, and the envisioned Library benefits in terms of their win conditions. A memo to Boehm from Lucy Wegner, the Library's interim Assistant Dean for Information Technology, provided specific constraints under which the Library would participate (e.g., no disruption of Library services; no interference with other librarian responsibilities; use of only the Library's test LIS host, only after LIS testing was complete; no advance commitments to use the results or to continue into product development in Spring 1997).

3.2. Cycle 1: Individual Application Life Cycle Objectives

Figure 3 shows the multimedia archive project guidelines as provided to the Library staff during Cycle 0 and provided to the students on the first day of class, August 28, 1996. The guidelines provided about 2 ½ weeks for the students to organize into teams, and 11½ weeks to complete the LCO and LCA milestones.

Figure 3. Multimedia Archive Project Guidelines

Project Objectives

Create the artifacts necessary to establish a successful life cycle architecture and plan for adding a multimedia access capability to the USC Library Information System. These artifacts are:

1. An Operational Concept Definition
2. A System Requirements Definition
3. A System and Software Architecture Definition
4. A Prototype of Key System Features
5. A Life Cycle Plan
6. A Feasibility Rationale, assuring the consistency and feasibility of items 1-5

Team Structure

Each of the six team members will be responsible for developing the LCO and LCA versions of one of the six project artifacts. In addition, the team member responsible for the Feasibility Rationale will serve as Project Manager with the following primary responsibilities:

1. Ensuring consistency among the team members' artifacts (and documenting this in the Rationale).
2. Leading the team's development of plans for achieving the project results, and ensuring that project performance tracks the plans.

Project Approach

Each team will develop the project artifacts concurrently, using the WinWin Spiral approach defined in the paper "Anchoring the Software Process." There will be two critical project milestones: the Life Cycle Objectives (LCO) and Life Cycle Architecture (LCA) milestones summarized in Table 1.

The LCA package should be sufficiently complete to support development of an Initial Operational Capability (IOC) version of the planned multimedia access capability by a CS577b student team during the Spring 1997 semester. The Life Cycle Plan should establish the appropriate size and structure of such a team.

WinWin User Negotiations

Each team will work with a representative of a community of potential users of the multimedia capability (art, cinema, engineering, business, etc.) to determine that community's most significant multimedia access needs, and to reconcile these needs with a feasible implementation architecture and plan. The teams will accomplish this reconciliation by using the USC WinWin groupware support system for requirements negotiation. This system provides facilities for stakeholders to express their Win Conditions for the system; to define Issues dealing with conflicts among Win Conditions; to support Options for resolving the Issues; and to consummate Agreements to adopt mutually satisfactory (win-win) Options.

There will be three stakeholder roles:

- Developer: The Architecture and Prototype team members will represent developer concerns, such as use of familiar packages, stability of requirements, availability of support tools, and technically challenging approaches.
- Customer: The Plan and Rationale team members will represent customer concerns, such as the need to develop an IOC in one semester, limited budgets for support tools, and low-risk technical approaches.
- User: The Operational Concept and Requirements team members will work with their designated user-community

representative to represent user concerns, such as particular multimedia access features, fast response time, friendly user interface, high reliability, and flexibility of requirements.

Major Milestones

September 16	---	All teams formed	October 14	---	WinWin Negotiation Results
October 21,23	---	LCO Reviews	October 28	---	LCO Package Due
November 4	---	Feedback on LCO	December 6	---	LCA Package Due, Individual Critique

Individual Project Critique

The project critique is to be done by each individual student. It should be about 3-5 pages, and should answer the question, "If we were to do the project over again, how would we do it better - and how does that relate to the software engineering principles in the course?"

In addition, the projects were provided with guidelines for developing each of the five documents indicated in the Product Objectives of Figure 3, including approximate page budgets for the LCO and LCA version of the documents. They were also provided with guidelines and an example of a multimedia archive prototype, and a domain model for a typical information archive extension (Figure 4). The domain model identifies the key stakeholders involved in such systems, and such key concepts as the system boundary: the boundary between the system being developed and its environment.

The course lectures followed the WinWin Spiral Model in beginning with overviews of the project artifacts and how they fit together, and with key planning and

Figure 4. Information Archive Extension Domain Model

1. **System Block Diagram:**
   This diagram shows the usual block diagram for extensions providing access to new information archive assets from an existing information archive (IA) System:

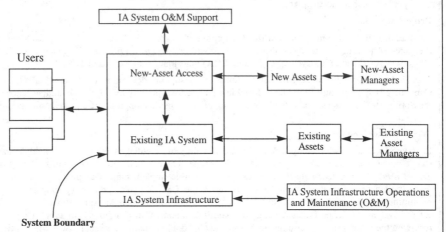

The system boundary focuses on the automated applications portion of the operation, and includes such entities as users, operators, maintainers, assets, and infrastructure (campus networks, etc.) as part of the system environment. The diagram abstracts out such capabilities as asset catalogues and direct user access to O&M support and asset mangers.

2. **Some Stakeholder Roles and Responsibilities**

2.1 Asset Managers. Furnish and update asset content and catalogue descriptors. Ensure access to assets. Provide accessibility status information. Ensure asset-base recoverability. Support problem analysis, explanation, training, instrumentation, operations analysis.

2.2 Operators. Maintain high level of system performance and availability. Accommodate asset and services growth and change. Protect stakeholder privacy and intellectual property rights. Support problem analysis, explanation, training, instrumentation, operations analysis.

2.3 Users. Obtain training. Access system. Query and browse assets. Import and operate on assets. Establish, populate, update, and access asset-related user files. Comply with system policies. Provide feedback on usage.

2.4 Application Software Maintainer. Perform corrective, adaptive and perfective (tuning, restructuring) maintenance on software. Analyze and support prioritization of proposed changes. Plan design, develop, and verify selected changes. Support problem analysis, explanation, training, instrumentation, operations analysis.

2.5 Service providers (e.g. network, database, or facilities management services). Similar roles and responsibilities to Asset Managers under 2.1

organizing guidelines. The project teams were self-selected; a key risk management emphasis was on the risk of forming teams with incompatible people and philosophies. As a result, there were relatively few personnel problems during this phase, compared with previous offering of the course. Later lectures provided more detail on the artifacts, plus guest lectures from Kwan and others on Library operations and the SIRSI system, and from experts in such areas as user interface design and multimedia system architecting.

The Fall 1996 course ended up with 86 students. Most were in 6-person teams. To accommodate special cases, including roughly 25 off-campus students, there were 2 teams with four students, one with five, and one with seven, for a total of 15 teams. The course ended up with 12 Library multimedia applications to be architected. Table 4 lists these, and indicates which three applications were done by two teams, and also which were implemented directly (*) by five of the six teams in Spring 1997, and which were combined into a single implementation by the sixth team (**).

Table 4. Library Multimedia Applications

Team	Application	Client
* 1.	Stereoscopic Slides	John Ahouse
**2.	Latin American Pamphlets	Barbara Robinson
**3,5.	EDGAR Corporate Data	Caroline Cisneros
**4.	Medieval Manuscripts	Ruth Wallach
* 6,10.	Hancock Photo Archive	Jean Crampon
7.	ITV Courseware Delivery	Julie Kwan
**8,11.	Technical Reports Archives	Charles Phelps
**9.	CNTV Moving Image Archive	Sandra Joy Lee
12.	Student Access to Digital Maps	Julie Kwan
*13.	LA Regional History Photos	Dace Taube
14.	Korean-American Museum	Ken Klein
15.	Urban Planning Documents	Robert Labaree

* - Combined in Spring 1997   ** - Implemented in Spring 1997

Each project's LCO cycle was focused by the use of the USC-CSE WinWin groupware system for requirements negotiation [Boehm et al, 1995; Horowitz et al, 1997]. "The WinWin User Negotiations" section of Figure 3 summarizes the WinWin artifacts and the stakeholder (developer, customer, and user) roles to be played by the various project team members. To minimize the impact on Library operations, the user artifacts were entered by the student Operational Concept and Requirements team members, rather than the librarians themselves.

Besides support for entering, refining, and negotiating Win Conditions, Issues, Options, and Agreements, WinWin includes a Domain Taxonomy to aid in organization, navigation, and terminology control of these artifacts. Table 5 shows the domain taxonomy for multimedia archive systems furnished to the teams, along with guidelines for relating the taxonomy elements to the requirements specification elements needed for the LCO package.

Table 5. Multimedia Archive Domain Taxonomy

1. Operational Modes
   1.1 Classes of Service (research, education, general public)
   1.2 Training
   1.3 Graceful Degradation and Recovery
2. Capabilities
   2.1 Media Handled
      2.1.1 Static (text, images, graphics, etc.)
      2.1.2 Dynamic (audio, video, animation, etc.)
   2.2 Media Operations
      2.2.1 Query, Browse
      2.2.2 Access
      2.2.3 Text Operations (find, reformat, etc.)
      2.2.4 Image Operations (zoom in/out, translate/rotate, etc.)
      2.2.5 Audio Operations (volume, balance, forward/reverse, etc.)
      2.2.6 Video/Animation Operations (speedup/slowdown, forward/reverse, etc.)
      2.2.7 Adaptation (cut, copy, paste, superimpose, etc.)
      2.2.8 File Operations (save, recall, print, record, etc.)
      2.2.9 User Controls
   2.3 Help
   2.4 Administration
      2.4.1 User Account Management
      2.4.2 Usage Monitoring and Analysis
3. Interfaces
   3.1 Infrastructure (SIRSI, UCS, etc.)
   3.2 Media Providers
   3.3 Operators
4. Quality Attributes
   4.1 Assurance
      4.1.1 Reliability/Availability
      4.1.2 Privacy/Access Control
   4.2 Interoperability
   4.3 Usability
   4.4 Performance
   4.5 Evolvability/Portability
   4.6 Cost/Schedule
   4.7 Reusability
5. Environment and Data
   5.1 Workload Characterization
6. Evolution
   6.1 Capability Evolution
   6.2 Interface and Technology Evolution
   6.3 Environment and Workload Evolution

The taxonomy serves as a requirements checklist and navigation aid:
- The taxonomy elements map onto the Requirements Description table of contents in the Course Notes.
- Every WinWin stakeholder artifact should point to at least one taxonomy element (modify elements if appropriate).
- Every taxonomy element should be considered as a source of potential stakeholder win conditions and agreements.

Figure 5 shows two examples of Win Condition artifacts from the Moving Image Archive (student films) team. It shows how the artifacts are related to each other (the Referenced By entries) and to the domain taxonomy elements (the Taxonomy Element entries), plus additional information on the artifact's owner, priority, status, etc. It also shows how the Comments field is used by the team members in clarifying concepts, removing inconsistencies, and informally exploring negotiated agreements.

The WinWin negotiation period took longer than expected. Complexities in scaling up the tool to 15 on-campus/off-campus teams caused difficulties, and the teams needed to simultaneously learn enough about WinWin, team operations, and the library multimedia applications domain to succeed. As a result, the deadlines for

Figure 5. Example WinWin Artifacts

• ID: arucker-WINC-6
• Owner: arucker
• Role: user
• Creation_Date: 10/15/96 12:25
• Revision_Date: 10/15/96 12:25
• Name: View holdings
• Body: The system should be capable of showing the different types of media holdings (production notebook, vhs, 16mm film, etc) that are available for a particular movie.
• Priority: High
• Status: Active
• State: Covered
• Taxonomy Elements: 3.2.1 Query
• Taxonomy Elements: 3.2.2 Browse
• ReferencedBy: arucker-AGRE-2, LinkFromAgre,Passed
• Comments :
firouzta 10/16/96 07:52
I am not clear on this win condition. Does this mean that for the material that is not digitized, the system should only present information on the type of the media on which the material is stored? Or, is it that all material, digitized or not, has information on other types of media that the material is stored on, and the system will provide the user with this information?
arucker 10/16/96 12:51
It means that for each movie, the system will provide information about the various types of media that the movie is stored on.
• ID: arucker-WINC-7
• Owner: arucker
• Role: user
• Creation_Date: 10/16/96 13:00
• Revision_Date: 10/17/96 13:13
• Name: Online Request
• Body: The system should allow online requests of movies from the Moving Image Archive.
• Priority: Medium
• Status: Active
• State: Covered
• Taxonomy Elements: 3.2.1 Query
• Taxonomy Elements: 3.2.2 Browse
• ReferencedBy: arucker-AGRE-1, LinkFromAgre,Passed
• Comments :
arucker 10/16/96 16:30
I'm not sure which item of the taxonomy this should refer to.
firouzta 10/16/96 21:05
2.2.1 and 2.2.2

completing the WinWin package and the LCO package were moved back a week. Fortunately, the LCO packages were good enough that the LCA cycle could be compressed by a week.

All 15 of the project LCO packages were delivered on time with respect to the revised schedule. Their degree of completeness was generally appropriate for an LCO package, but the components often had serious inconsistencies in assumptions, relationships, and terminology. Most teams had planned time for members to review each others' artifacts, but this time was generally spent finishing up one's own artifacts. Some concepts caused problems for many teams: the nature of the system boundary; organizational relationships; and the primary focus of the life-cycle plan (development of the Initial Operational Capability). These were then discussed further in the course lectures.

3.3. Cycle 2. Individual Application Life Cycle Architectures

All 15 of the project LCA packages were delivered on time, including the prototypes, which were demonstrated to the instructors and librarian clients in two special half-day sessions. The documentation packages had effectively fixed the problems surfaced in the LCO packages but had additional challenges in accommodating the new user insights stimulated by the prototypes.

Although the librarians crated the problem statement and participated in the requirements negotiation with the student teams and with various stages of the prototype, the final prototype presentations yielded insightful surprises. Caroline Sisneros, the librarian who proposed the Edgar corporate data problem was "blown way" with the resultant product which built upon the seemingly simple text formatting problem and delivered a one-stop Java site which synthesized several kinds of business information. She commented in her evaluation memo "[The team] obviously looked beyond the parameters of the problem and researched the type of information need the set of data meets. My interactions with the team were minimal, not because of any difficulty, but because as a group they had a synergy and grasped the concepts presented to them. The solution the team came up with was innovative, with the potential to be applied to other, similar problems."

The library clients were generally very satisfied with the value added relative to their time invested. Sandra Joy Lee, the proposer for the Digital Moving Image Archive, commented "They were very instrumental in the discovery of solutions that did not demand too much staff time from my office. In short order, they solved all the problems with creativity and technical sophistication."

The projects also surmounted a number of challenges characteristic of real-world projects. The Library Information System test server continued to be needed for the LIS cutover, and was therefore unavailable to the project prototypes. There were delays in arranging for a suitable alternative Web server for developing prototypes. At times librarians were unavailable to provide inputs on critical decisions, leading to extra rework. Inevitable personnel conflicts arose among the 15 teams. However, the WinWin Spiral Process provided an appropriate mix of flexibility and discipline to enable the projects to adapt to these challenges while staying on schedule. In particular, the use of risk management and a continuously-evolving Top 10 Risk Item list for prioritizing team effort [Boehm,1991] helped the teams focus their effort on the most critical success factors for their projects.

With respect to the LCO-LCA process, the student critiques provided a number of areas for future improvement. The WinWin groupware tool helped with team building and feature prioritization, but people needed more preliminary training and experience in its use. It was also cumbersome to modify groups of WinWin artifacts. Several items, particularly the prototyping capabilities, should have been provided and employed earlier. The prototypes helped a great deal in clarifying and stabilizing the librarians' requirements; they could have helped even more if available during the initial WinWin requirements negotiation process.

Although it was strongly emphasized during the initial lectures, students felt that an even stronger emphasis was needed on the risks of forming teams with personality conflicts and critical-skill shortfalls. The strong focus on the six specific team member roles was good in ensuring that each product component was successfully generated, but it caused difficulties in keeping all the team members apprised of issues and developments with the other components. Consistency management of partially redundant components (operational concept, requirements, architecture) became particularly difficult, especially in adapting to change. There was strong consensus that smaller teams and fewer, better-integrated components would have been more effective.

Another difficulty involved consistency maintenance among the multiple views. The various product views required were synthesized from multiple sources: the [Sommerville, 1996] course textbook, evolving commercial standards [IEEE-EIA, 1995], and object-oriented methods, particularly [Booch, 1994] and [Rumbaugh et al. 1991]. The views included system block diagrams, requirements templates, usage scenarios, physical architecture diagrams, class hierarchies, object interaction diagrams, data flow diagrams, state transition diagrams, data descriptions, and requirements traceability relations. Each had its value, but the overall set was both an overkill and was weakly supported by integrated tools. We plan on using a more concise and integrated set of views next year, based on the Rational Unified Modeling Language and toolset [Booch-Jacobson-Rumbaugh, 1997].

3.4. Cycle 3: Development of Initial Operational Capabilities

The transition from an LCO/LCA phase with 86 students, 15 teams, and 12 applications to an IOC phase with 28 students, 6 teams, and 8 applications caused a number of challenges. Only one team retained the majority of their LCO/LCA participants for their IOC phase. The other teams had to work with a mix of participants with varying project backgrounds.

Even more challenging was the integrating of teams who had produced different LCA artifacts for the same application: the two EDGAR Corporate Data teams and the two Technical Reports teams. In two cases, the instructors had to persuade students to join different teams rather than continuing to fight about whose architecture was best. Other conflicts developed within teams where some team members had extensive LCA experience on the application and others had none (in one case, the experienced members exploited the less experienced members; in another case, vice versa).

Other challenges included a change of instructor (Boehm to Madachy), a change of process model (spiral to risk-driven waterfall), and documentation approach (laissez-faire to everything-on-the-Web). Also, there were infrastructure surprises: the SIRSI server and the SIRSI-related search engine were expected to be available for Cycle 3, but were not.

Nonetheless, each of the projects successfully delivered their IOC packages of code, life cycle documentation, and demonstrations on time. A major reason was the strong emphasis on risk management, which enabled teams to depart from a pure waterfall approach to resolve whatever critical risk items surfaced. An example of one of the teams' initial Top-N risk item lists is shown as Table 6. Risks were prioritized by assessments of their risk exposure (probability-of-loss times magnitude-of-loss), and reassessed weekly with respect to changes in criticality and progress in risk resolution. As indicated in Table 6, a key strategy was design-to-schedule: identifying a feasible core capability and optional features to be implemented as schedule permitted.

In the student critiques for Cycle 3, the most common suggestion for *course improvement* was to provide a solid DBMS and search engine (13 of 28) critiques). The next highest was again to reduce the quantity and redundancy of the documentation (9 of 28 critiques). Project timesheets indicated that total documentation-related effort (requirements, plans, design, product documentation) during Cycle 3 was 47% of the total, with two projects as high as 54% and 60%.

Other common suggestions (appearing in 6 to 8 critiques) were for better

Table 6. Example Top-N Risk Item List

Risk	Risk Aversion Options	Risk Monitoring
1. Changes of requirements from previous semester.	Option 1: Propose a solution for the system (describing the requirements in details) to the users and having them commit to the requirements. Option 2: Adopt an incremental approach to the development by building a prototype first.	Option 1: Once committed, the requirements must be closely monitored. Changes to requirements must be thoroughly assessed and if excessive, they should be defer till later. Option 2: This has an impact on the schedule and hence close monitoring on progress and effort are required.
2. Tight Schedule	Study the requirements carefully so as not to overcommit. Descope good-to-have features if possible. Concentrate on core capabilities.	Close monitoring of all activities is necessary to ensure that schedule are met.
3. Size of project	If requirements are too excessive, descope good-to-have features and capabilities out of the project. Identify the core capabilities to be built.	
4. Finding a search engine	Conduct a software evaluation of search engine. Have team members actively source for free search engines and evaluate them. Determine the best for the project.	Have team members submit evaluation report and conduct demos so that an informed decision can be made.
5. Required technical expertise lacking	Identify the critical and most difficult technical areas of the project and have team members look into them as soon as possible.	Monitor the progress of these critical problems closely. If need be, seek external help.

documentation guidelines, better match of course notes and lectures to project activities, more timely feedback on intermediate products, more disk space, better tools (scanning, HTML conversion, CM) and more training on key Web skills. The most common suggestions for *project improvement* were improved intra-team communication (8 critiques), early error elimination (7), improved client communication (5), and improved on/off-campus team coordination (5). We are using these insights to improve the organization of next year's projects.

From the client standpoint, all of the librarian participants had been very pleased with the prototype demonstration and LCA packages, and were fully supportive of continuing work with their student teams during the second semester. However, the second semester had a smaller enrollment since it was not a required course as during the first semester. Consequently, only six projects were continued during the IOC phase due to the reduction in the number of teams. The LCA projects performed by the continuing students then directed the choice of continuing projects rather than any priority views of the librarians.

The librarians' involvement with the student teams during the second semester was, for the most part, qualitatively and quantitatively different than during the preceding semester. Major system requirements had already been negotiated, but there were typically a few new requirements when the project was taken on by newly reconstituted project teams whose views added subtle differences to the original concepts. Nonetheless, the time required for the librarians' participation was not as extensive as during the preceding semester with the exception of one team. The LAPIS project faced another challenge, having technical problems with scanning and OCR of sample documents until just before the final IOC demonstration. Consultation with a faculty member who uses these technologies for his research in machine translation indicated that the types of documents used, given their historic type fonts, represented a separate OCR research problem in itself; the faculty member was then able to help the project implement a fallback solution.

With one exception, the librarians were delighted with the final IOC presentations. The skillful integration of the requirements and functionality of finished products was evident to all. Kwan noted in her evaluation memo "The interaction between the student teams and the librarians produced obvious differences in products designed for different users. For example, the technical reports interface mirrored the technical nature of the type of material included and expected future users of the system while the moving image archive interface reflected the needs and interests of a very different clientele." Barbara Robinson, who proposed LAPIS (Latin American Pamphlet Information System), saw the project as a means for the international community of Latin Americanists to preserve fragile material, a difficult conservation issue for the community; after the IOC delivery, she prepared a proposal to expand the project for full-scale implementation.

The one exception project was the attempt to integrate the three photographic-image application (stereoscopic slides, Hancock photo archive, LA regional history photos) into a single application. The short schedule required the team to patch together pieces of the three architectures and user interfaces. Some features of the result were good (e.g., a colored-glasses stereo capability with good resolution), but none of the clients were enthusiastic about implementing the results. The other five application are either being adopted or extended for possible adoption by the Library elements.

The librarians expressed in their evaluations that working with Theory W and WinWin philosophy made it easy for them to "think big" about their projects. The negotiation process, however, made it possible for the teams and librarians to agree mutually on a feasible set of deliverables for the final IOC products during the academic session. And, although the time commitment was not great, participation in this project allowed the librarians to focus a part of their time and thinking on multimedia applications and software engineering. One of the greatest advantages for the librarians involved was to become more familiar with digital library issues and the software engineering techniques which are involved in their implementation.

Further details on the project processes and artifacts can be found in their USC-CSE Web pages:

'http://sunset.usc.edu/classes/cs577a' and 'http://sunset.usc.edu/classes/cs577b.'

4. Conclusions

We had a number of hypotheses we wished to test with respect to the use of the WinWin Spiral Model for multimedia applications or other similar applications. Unfortunately, considerations of stakeholder satisfaction (successful applications for the library clients; fairness of grading for the students) conflict with the most rigorous forms of experimental design. For example, having some teams operate in a contract-oriented, adversarial, waterfall-model mode would have been a better test of the relative benefits of using the WinWin Spiral Model. However, given available experience, it did not seem feasible or fair to consign some projects to use such a mode.

Modulo these caveats, here are the main hypotheses we wished to test, and a summary of the best evidence we can provide about them.

Hypothesis 1. Teams can use the WinWin Spiral Model to simultaneously develop the components of a consistent and feasible LCA package for a new multimedia application in 11 weeks. Each of the 15 LCA teams delivered their packages on time, and satisfied an extensive set of grading criteria covering each LCA component the conceptual integrity of the integrated package, and client evaluations of the prototypes.

Hypothesis 2. Using two (LCO and LCA) spiral cycles to develop the LCA package was feasible and value-adding. Feasibility of two cycles is covered under Hypothesis 1. Based on the results of the LCO reviews, using a single spiral cycle would have produced less satisfactory results in about half of the projects. Several projects produced unbalanced detail in either the archiving or the query/browsing part of their LCO packages; the LCA cycle enabled than to balance their architecture packages. On the other hand, using three cycles would have left insufficient time to both produce and coordinate three sets of artifacts.

Hypothesis 3. The Library clients will see enough prospective value in the LCA packages to decide to continue as many as possible into full-scale development. There were more than enough clients for the six project teams available in Spring

1997. Perhaps erroneously, we tried to have one project team address all three image-archive applications. Some additional LCA packages (historical maps, urban plans) had considerable client interest but could not be pursued.

Hypothesis 4. The LCA packages would be adequate to ensure satisfactory IOC development in 11 weeks. Again, all six teams completed full IOC packages on time. The projects having the most difficulties were the ones which started with two LCA packages for the same application (startup difficulties) or with LCA packages for three separate image archive applications (conceptual integrity difficulties).

Hypothesis 5. The WinWin Spiral approach will produce wins for the stakeholders. Five of the six completed projects had highly enthusiastic clients who are continuing with the applications developed. The sixth IOC product's clients did not wish to continue with the product developed, but were receptive to another try. The preponderance of the student critiques indicated that the experience had been valuable and career-enhancing. Even the documentation overkill was considered by some students as good preparation for many industrial projects with similar overkill.

Hypothesis 6. The WinWin Spiral approach will be flexible enough to adapt to real-world conditions. Section 3 summarized many real-world conditions (pleasant and unpleasant surprises with COTS packages; unavailability of expected infrastructure packages and library information system expertise; personnel complications and changes) to which the projects were successfully able to adapt. More formal or contract-oriented approaches would not have been able to accommodate the necessary change processing in the short times available for architecting and development.

Hypothesis 7. The WinWin Spiral approach will efficiently use the developers' time. As indicated under Hypothesis 6, the approach avoided some inefficiencies. However, as implemented, it had some significant inefficiencies in document overkill and multiple-view coordination. Next year's projects will have less redundant and voluminous documentation, an integrated toolset (the Rational ROSE system and its associated packages), and smaller development teams.

Hypothesis 8. The WinWin tool outputs can transition smoothly into requirements specifications. This had been a problem in previous uses of WinWin. Mapping the WinWin domain taxonomy onto the table of contents of the requirements specification, and requiring the use of the domain taxonomy as a checklist for developing WinWin Agreements, effectively focused stakeholder negotiations and facilitated transitioning WinWin Agreements into requirements specifications. The manual transition engendered some inefficiencies; we are exploring automated aids for the transition.

Hypothesis 9. The WinWin approach will improve developer-client relations. In terms of the fear, uncertainty, and doubt often exhibited by clients toward new applications, the Library clients exhibited virtually no fear, considerable uncertainty, and some doubt about going forward with the projects, as indicated by the project conditions stipulated by the Library memo (Section 3.1). By the LCA milestone, as indicated by a meeting between the computer science principals and Dean Campbell and the Library principals, the uncertainty and doubt about working with the student teams had been replaced by enthusiasm and considerable trust (although a good deal of uncertainty remained about the applications' technical parameters). This growth of enthusiasm and trust continued through the development period, and has led to a mutual commitment to pursue further projects in 1997-98. The ability of the WinWin approach to foster trust was consistent with earlier experiences [Boehm-Bose,1994].

Bottom Line:

Overall, the projects' results indicate that the WinWin Spiral Model is a good match for multimedia applications, and likely for other applications with similar characteristics (rapidly moving technology; many candidate approaches; little user or developer experience with similar systems; premium on rapid completion). It provides sufficient flexibility to adapt to the accompanying risks and uncertainties, and the discipline to maintain focus on achieving its anchor-point milestones. Finally, it provides the means for growing trust among stakeholders, enabling them to evolve away from adversarial contract-oriented system development approaches toward mutually supportive and cooperative approaches.

5. Acknowledgments

This research is sponsored by DARPA through Rome Laboratory under contract F30602-94-C-0195 and by the Affiliates of the USC Center for Software Engineering: Aerospace Corp., Air Force Cost Analysis Agency, Allied Signal, Bellcore, Boing, Electronic Data Systems, E-Systems, GDE Systems, Hughes Aircraft, Interactive Development Environments, Institute for Defense Analysis, Jet Propulsion Laboratory, Litton Data Systems, Lockheed Martin, Loral Federal Systems, MCC, Motorola, Network Programs, Northrop Grumman, Rational Software, Science Applications International, Software Engineering Institute, Software Productivity Consortium, Sun Microsystems, TI, TRW, USAF, Rome Laboratory, US Army Research Laboratory, and Xerox. We also thank Denise Bedford, Anne Curran, Ellis Horowitz, Ming June Lee, Bill Scheding, Archita Shah, and Nirat Shah for support in key areas.

6. References

[AT&T, 1993]. "Best Current Practices: Software Architecture Validation," AT&T, Murray Hill, NJ 1993.

[Boehm, 1988]. B. W. Boehm, "A Spiral Model of Software Development and Enhancement," Computer, May 1988, v. 21 no. 5, pp. 61-72.

[Boehm, 1991]. B. W. Boehm, "Software Risk Management: Principles and Practices," IEEE Software, January 1991, pp. 32-41.

[Boehm, 1996] B.W. Boehm, "Anchoring the Software Process," IEEE Software, July 1996, v.13 no.4, pp.73-82.

[Boehm et. al., 1982]. B. W. Boehm, J. F. Elwell, A. B. Pyster, E.D. Stuckle, and R. D. Williams, "The TRW Software Productivity System," Proceedings, 6th International Conference on Software Engineering, ACM/IEEE, September 1982, pp. 148-156.

[Boehm et al., 1994]. B.W. Boehm, P Bose, E. Horowitz,, M.J. Lee, "Software Requirements As Negotiated Win Conditions", Proceedings of ICRE, April 1994, pp.74-83.

[Boehm et al., 1995]. B.W. Boehm, B. K. Clark, E. Horowitz, R. Madachy, R.W. Selby, and C. Westland, "Cost Models for Future Software Processes: COCOMO 2.0," Annals of Software Engineering, 1995, v.1, pp. 57-94.

[Boehm-Bose, 1994]. B.W. Boehm and P. Bose, "A Collaborative Spiral Software Process Model Based on Theory W," Proceedings, 3rd International Conference on the Software Process, Applying the Software Process, IEEE, Reston, Va. October 1994.

[Boehm-Ross, 1989]. B.W. Boehm and R. Ross "Theory W Software Project Management: Principles and Examples," IEEE Transactions on Software Engineering, July 1989, pp.902-916.

[Booch, 1994]. G. Booch , Object-Oriented Analysis and Design, 2nd Edition, Benjamin/Cummings Publishing, 1994.

[Booch-Jacobson-Rumbaugh, 1997]. G. Booch, I. Jacobson, J. Rumbaugh, "The Unified Modeling Language for Object-Oriented Development," Documentation set, version 1.0, Rational Software Corporation, 1997.

[Carmel et al., 1983]. E. Carmel, R. Whitaker, and J. George, " PD and Joint Application Design: A Transatlantic Comparison," Comm. ACM, June 1993, pp. 40-48.

[Conklin-Begeman, 1988]. J. Conklin and M. Begeman, "gIBIS: A Hypertext Tool for Exploratory Policy Discussion," ACM Trans. OIS, October 1988, pp.303-331.

[Dardenne et al., 1993] A. Dardenne, S. Fickas, and A. van Lamsweerde, "Goal-Directed Concept Acquisition in Requirement Elicitation," Proceedings, IWSSD 6, IEEE, October 1991, pp. 14-21.

[DeMarco, 1996]. T. DeMarco, "The Role of Software Development Methodologies: Past, Current and Future," Keynote Address, ICSE 18, IEEE/ACM, March 1996, pp. 2-4.

[Finkelstein et al., 1991]. A Finkelstein, J. Kramer, B. Nusibeh, L Finkelstein, and M. Goedicke, "Viewpoints: A Framework for Integrating Multiple Perspectives in System Development," International J. Software Engineering and Knowledge Engineering, March 1992, pp. 31-58.

[Fisher-Ury, 1981]. R. Fisher, W. Ury, Getting to Yes, Penguin Books, 1981.

[Frazier-Bailey, 1996]. T. P. Frazier, J.W. Bailey, "The costs and benefits of domain-oriented software reuse: Evidence from the STARS demonstration projects," IDA Paper P-3191, Institute for Defense Analysis, 1996.

[Horowitz et al., 1997]. Horowitz, E. "WinWin Reference Manual: A System for Collaboration and Negotiation of Requirements", Center for Software Engineering, University of Southern California Technical Report, Los Angeles, CA 90089-0781, 1997.

[IEEE-EIA, 1995]. Trial Use Standard J-STD-016-1995, "Software Development", formerly known as IEEE 1498/EIA 640.

[Mullery, 1979]. G. Mullery, "CORE: A Method for Controlled Requirements Specification," Proceedings, ICSE 4, IEEE, Septmember 1979, pp. 126-135.

[Potts-Takahashi, 1993]. C. Potts and K. Takahashi, "An Active hypertext for System Requirements," Proceedings, IWSSD 7, IEEE, December 1993, pp. 62-68.

[Royce, 1990]. W.E. Royce, "TRW's Ada Process Model for Incremental Development of Large Software Systems," Proceedings, ICSE 12, IEEE/ACM, March 1990, pp. 2-11.

[Rumbaugh et. al., 1991]. J. Rumbaugh, M. Blaha, W. Premerlani, F. Eddy, and W. Lorensen, Object-Oriented Modeling and Design, Prentice Hall, 1991.

[Sommerville, 1996]. I. Sommerville, Software Engineering, Addison-Wesley, 5th Edition, 1996.

[SPC, 1994]. Software Productivity Consortium, "Process Engineering with the Evolutionary Spiral Process Model," SPC-93098-CMC, version 01.00.06, Herndon, Virginia, 1994.

[Weiser, 1997]. M. Weiser, "Software Engineering that Matters to People," Keynote Address, ICSE 97, IEEE/ACM, May 1997.

[Yourdon, 1997]. E. Yourdon, "'Death March' Projects," Keynote Address, ICSE 97, IEEE/ACM, May 1997.

What We Teach Sofware Engineers in the University: Do We Take *Engineering* Seriously?

One Academic('s) View of Software Engineering Education

TSE Maibaum[1]
email: tsem@doc.ic.ac.uk

Abstract

Software Engineering, as a discipline in its own right, is reaching the end of its third decade. As such, we might legitimately be expecting that Software Engineering curricula will reflect some level of maturity, both with respect to the conception of software as an artefact and with respect to the incorporation of effective engineering principles. I will argue that this is simply not the case and further that the trend may well be the opposite of what engineers from traditional disciplines might respect.

1.   Introduction

The discipline of software engineering is now reaching the end of its third decade. Having been flattered into giving my views, as an academic, of software engineering education, I began to analyse consciously my feelings of unease concerning this topic. Over many years, I have actively attempted to understand how the fruits of my research (and that of others) in formal methods could be realised in applicable engineering practice. This has lead me to consider the differences between mathematics, science and engineering and to try to place software engineering within this spectrum ([Maibaum 86, 94]).

In the sequel, I will argue that:

• software engineering *is* an engineering discipline

• software engineering *is* different from traditional engineering disciplines in certain crucial ways

• software engineering curricula fail to meet the requirements of engineering education as commonly conceived by conventional engineers

---

[1] Department of Computing, Imperial College, 180 Queen's Gate, London SW7 2BE. UK; tel: ++44 171 593 8274 fax: ++441715818024

The rationale for the above assertions is fundamentally straightforward. That software engineering is an engineering discipline is a simple consequence of the fact that ([Rogers, p51])

"engineering refers to the practice of organising the design and construction of any artifice which transforms the physical world around us to meet some recognised need."

Engineering is different from science and mathematics. The differing objectives and methodologies of the three disciplines induce important differences in practice. Moreover, they induce significant differences in the education of practitioners. Finally, conventional engineers are taught the principles of the 'devices'[2] they use in designing artefacts, as well as the systematic design principles to be used in building instances of such devices. I contend that modern software engineering curricula do not take cognisance of these foundations and design methods; nor do they provide the software engineer with the formal tools[3] for analysis and prediction required by engineers for the design of devices[4]. See also [Parnas].

The view taken above is negative; however, I firmly believe that software engineering curricula *could* reflect the engineering principles in which I firmly believe. We could populate a software engineering curriculum with material reflecting this appropriate foundational material and systematic design principles, in spite of the relative immaturity of the subject and the underlying computer science. It is simply[5] a matter of will for software engineering academics and software engineering practitioners who recognise the importance and applicability of engineering principles in the construction of software artefacts.

---

[2] See below for an explanation of this terminology as an aspect of the organisation of engineering design disciplines.

[3] Here, 'formal' is used in the sense of 'based on mathematical or scientific principles' and not simply restricted to its meaning as part of the phrase 'formal methods'.

[4] Furthermore, there are serious implications of this for software engineering research, but the present paper will not emphasise these.

[5] For those that do not recognise it, this is a typical example of English understatement!

2.   What Engineering Is

In preparing to write this paper, I read a very illuminating book by[6] Walter G. Vincenti called "What Engineers Know and How They Know It" ([Vincenti]). In his introductory chapter, he argues the case for engineering being different, in epistemological terms and, consequently as *praxis*, from science or even applied science: "In this view, technology, though it *may apply* science, is not the same as or entirely *applied* science" ([Vincenti, p4]). In "The Nature of Engineering", GFC Rogers argues that engineering is indeed different from science. He argues this view based on what he calls "the teleological distinction" concerning the *aims* of science and technology:

"In its effort to explain phenomena, a scientific investigation can wander at will as unforeseen results suggest new paths to follow. Moreover, such investigations never end because they always throw up further questions. The essence of technological investigation is that they are directed towards serving the process of designing and manufacturing or constructing particular things whose purpose has been clearly defined. We may wish to design a bridge that uses less material, build a dam that is safer, improve the efficiency of a power station, travel faster on the railways, and so on. A technological investigation is in this sensemore prescribed than a scientific investigation. It is also more limited, in that it may end when it has led to an adequate solution of a technical problem. The investigation may be restarted if there is renewed interest in the product, either because of changing social or economic circumstances or because favourable developments in a neighbouring technology make a new advance possible. On the other hand, it may come to a complete stop because the product has been entirely superseeded by something else that will meet humanity's changing needs rather better."

He makes a further claim: "Because of its limited purpose, a technological explanation will certainly involve a level of approximation that is certainly unacceptable in science." We shall see later the implications of this approximative approach to software engineering and to its teaching.

Going back to the distinctions between the aims of science and engineering, we have, again from [Rogers, p55],

"We have seen that in one sense science progresses by virtue of discovering circumstances in which a hitherto acceptable hypothesis is falsified, and that scientists actively pusue this situation. Because of the catastrophic consequences of engineering failures - whether it be human catastrophy for the customer or economic catastrophy for the firm - engineers and technologists must try to avoid falsification of their

---

[6] I would like to thank William Newman of Rank Xerox Laboratories, Cambridge, for bringing this thoroughly enjoyable work to my attention.

theories. Their aim is to undertake sufficient research on a laboratory scale to extend the theories so that they cover the foreseeable changes in the variables called for by a new conception. The scientist seeks revolutionary change - for which he may receive a Nobel Prize. The engineer too seeks revolutionary conceptions by which he can make his name, but he knows his ideas will not be taken upunless they can be realised using a level of technology not far removed from the existing level."

So science *is* different from engineering. Proceeding on this basis, we can ask ourselves what the *praxis* of engineering is (and ignore the specifics of scientific *praxis*). Vincenti defines engineering activities in terms of design, production and operation of artefacts. Of these, design and operation are highly pertinent to software engineering , while it is often argued that production plays a very small role, if any, in the *praxis* of software engineering. In the context of discussing the focus of engineers' activities, he then talks about *normal design* as comprising "the improvement of the accepted tradition or its application under 'new or more stringent conditions'" ([Constant]). He goes on to say: "The engineer engaged in such design knows at the outset how the device in question works, what are its customary features, and that, if properly designed along such lines, it has good likelihood of accomplishing the desired task." (See [Vincenti, p7].)

In [Jackson], Michael Jackson discusses this concept of 'normal design', although he does not use this phrase himself:

1   "   In this context, design innovation is exceptional. Only once in a thousand car designs does the designer depart from the accepted structures by an innovation like front-wheel drive or a transversely positioned engine. True, when a radical innovation proves successful it becomes a standard design choice for later engineers. But these design choices are then made at a higher level than that of the working engineer: the product characteristics they imply soon become well understood, and their selection becomes as much a matter of marketing as of design technology. Unsuccessful innovations - like the rotary internal combustion engine - never become established as possible design choices."

2   "An engineering handbook is not a compendium of fundamental principles; but it does contain a corpus of rules and procedures by which it has been found that those principles can be most easily and effectively applied to the particular design tasks established in the field. The outline design is already given, determined by the established needs and products."

3   "The methods of value are micro-methods, closely tailored to the tasks of developing particular well-understood parts of particular well-understood products."

Another important aspect of engineering design is the organising principle of hierarchical design: "Design, apart from being normal or radical, is also multilevel and hierarchical. Interesting levels of design exist, depending on the nature of the immediate design task, the identity of some component of the device, or the engineering discipline required."[7]   An implied, but not explicitly stated view of engineering design is that engineers normally design *devices* as opposed to *systems*. A device, in this sense, is an entity whose design principles are well defined, well structured and subject to *normal* design principles.   A system, in this sense, is an entity which lacks some important characteristics making normal design possible. "Systems are assemblies of devices brought together for a collective purpose"([Vincenti, p201]). Examples of the former given by Vincenti are aeroplanes, electric generators, turret lathes; examples of the latter are airlines, electric-power systems and automobile factories. The software engineering equivalent of devices may include compilers, relational databases, PABXs, etc. Software engineering examples of systems may include air traffic control systems, mobile telephone networks, etc. It would appear that systems become devices when their design attains the status of being *normal*. That is, the level of creativity required in their design becomes one of systematic choice, based on well defined analysis, in the context of standard definitions and criteria developed and agreed by engineers.

Let us now considern the particular characteristics of software engineering as a discipline. we want to address the question: Is the knowledge used by software engineers different in character from that used by engineers from the conventional disciplines? The latter are underpinned not just by mathematics, but also by some physical science(s) - providing models of the world in terms of which artefacts must be understood. (The discussion above illustrates this symbiosis.) We might then ask ourselves about the nature of the mathematics and science underlying software engineering. It is not surprising, perhaps, that the mathematics underlying software engineering is formal logic. It can also be seen as the science underlying software engineering, although one might distinguish computational logic and theoretical computer science, as distinct from logic itself, as being this 'science'[8].

Logic is the mathematics of concepts and abstractions. Software engineering may be distinguished from other engineering disciplines because the artefacts constructed by the latter are physical, whereas those constructed by the former are conceptual. (After all, a program is not the printout, nor is it the physical state of some part of the memory of some computer. These are all representations of the program, in the same

---

[7] It is quite clear from the engineering literature that engineering normally involves the use of multiple technologies. The observation that software engineering requires knowledge of other domains an that its teaching should be application oriented is not as perspicacious as its proponents would have us believe. This is part of the essence of engineering, whatever the 'discipline'.

[8] This is not to say that elements of conventional engineering disciplines are not also useful for software engineers. See [Parnas] for a discussion of this.

way that '2', '10', 'II', ... are all representations of a particular integer - a purely conceptual entity.) Hence, there should be no surprise in the close connection between logic and software engineering. It is clear that the important symbiotic relationship between analysis, physics and engineering that we have experienced over more than 200 years will be repeated in the next century between logic, theoretical computer science and software engineering.

There are some interesting and significant differences between the two kinds of mathematics and engineering mentioned above. One of these is that the 'real world' acts as a (physical) constraint on the construction of (physical) artefacts in a way which is more or less absent in the science and engineering of concepts and abstractions. There seems to be a qualitative difference in the dimensions of the design space for software engineering as a result.

The engineering of concepts and abstractions predates the existence of computers. Philosophical logicians, particularly, have engaged in it for some time. An obvious example, of which I have some knowledge, is deontic logic, originally developed to study legal reasoning, particularly as pertaining to concepts of duty, obligation and prohibition. What distinguishes the theoretical computer science and software engineering dependence on logic is the day to day invention of theories by engineers and the problems of size and structure introduced by the nature of the artefacts with which we are dealing in software engineering.

Now, what distinguishes the mathematics of theoretical computer science from that of (formal methods and) software engineering should be analogous to the difference between conventional mathematics and its application and use in engineering. Let us examine one well developed technology where we might expect this distinction to manifest itself.

Program construction from a specification has a well understood underlying mathematics developed over the last 25 years. (We are restricting our attention to sequential programs. Concurrency and parallelism are much less mature topics.) We might expect to find a CAD tool for program construction analogous to the 'poles and canvas' model used in in electronics for the design of filters. Instead, what we find is just a relaxation on the exhaustiveness requirement, ie we can leave out mathematical steps (proofs of lemmas) on the assumption that they can be filled in if necessary. Where is the abstract model (analogous to the 'poles and canvas' one) which encapsulates the mathematics and constrains manipulation in a (mathematicallyscientifically) sensible manner?

The underlying model used by the rigorous programmer (ie the software engineer) is exactly the same as that used by the theoretician. As the only real difference is that the assumption that mathematical steps may be omitted, based on the educated guess of the engineer that the omissions could actually be corrected if this proved necessary (- no pun intended!), it may be asserted that this requires the engineer to be a better mathematician than the theoretician! This is clearly very different from the experience of the conventional engineer. We may thus begin to question the thrust of much software engineering research over the last decade.

In conclusion, software engineering *is* an engineering discipline, but it has a special character of its own which distinguishes it from other engineering disciplines. Hence, the curriculum of software engineering is not simply subsumed as a speciality within some existing discipline. To put in context the remarks in the next section on software engineering and its teaching, we should first examine what Vincenti calls 'categories of [engineering] knowledge'. These comprise:

1. Fundamental design concepts

2. Criteria and specifications

3. Theoretical tools

4. Quantitative data

5. Practical considerations

6. Design instrumentalities

Fundamental design concepts include the *operational principle* of their device. According to Michael Polamyi (as per [Vincenti]), this means knowing for a device "how its characteristic parts....fulfil their special functions in combining to an overall operation which achieves the purpose". A second principle taken for granted is the *normal configuration* for the device, ie the commonly accepted arrangement of the constituent parts of the device. These two principle (and possibly others) provide a framework within which normal design takes place.

Criteria and specifications allow the engineer using a device with a given operational principle and normal configuration to "translate general, qualitative goals couched in concrete technical terms" ([Vincenti, p211]). That the development of such criteria may be problematic is clear.[9] However, the development and acceptance of such criteria is an inherent par of the development of engineering disciplines.

---

[9] I have long been puzzled by the seemingly intractable problems of systematising knowledge about the "ilities" of software engineering: usability, portability, dependability, etc. So much so, that I began to accept the possibility that these qualitative concepts were inherently uncharacterisable. Vincenti's book discusses at length such an "ility" relates to aeroplane design and called *flying qualities*. These "comprise those qualities characteristics of an aircraft that govern the ease and

Engineers require *theoretical tools* to underpin their work. These include intellectual concepts for thinking about design as well as mathematical methods and theories for making design calculations. Both conceptual tools and mathematical tools may be devised specifically for use by the engineer and be of no particular use or value to a scientist/mathematician. Again, [Jackson] states: "The methods of value are micro-methods, closely tailored to the tasks of developing particular well understood parts of particular well understood products. ...[T]he most useful context for the precision and reliability that formality can offer is in sharply focused micro-methods, supporting specialised small-scale tasks of analysis and detailed design." [10]

Engineers also use *quantitative data,* often the result of empirical observations, as well as tabulations of values of functions used in mathematical models. A good example in software engineering of this thoroughness in providing data useful for design is the work of Knuth on sorting and searching. There are also *practical considerations* in engineering. These are not usually subject to systematisation in the sense of the categories above, but reflect pragmatic concerns. For example, a designer will want to make use of various trade-offs in the design of devices which are the result of general knowledge about the device, its use, its context, etc.

Design instrumentalities include "the procedures, ways of thinking, and judgmental skills by which it is done" ([Vincenti, p220]). This is clearly what the Capability Maturity model has in mind when it refers to will defined and repeatable processes in software engineering ([SEI]).

3. The Status of Software Engineering Education

If we take the above characterisation of engineering and engineering knowledge and apply it to software engineering curricula, we quickly come to realise that the latter do not generally transmit knowledge and skills which prepare our students to be professional engineers. The material presented in these programmes falls far short of conveying any of the categories of knowledge described above. Most of the material presented in such courses either suffers from confusing craftsmanship and engineering

---

precision with which a pilot is able to perform the task of controlling the vehicle". It was one of the triumphs of aeronautical engineering between the world Wars that they "translate[d] an amorphous, qualitative design problem into a quantitatively, specifiable problem susceptible of realistically attainable solutions." See [Vincenti, Chap 3]

[10] Jackson is discussing formal methods and arguing, persuasively, that universalist views of formal methods are misguided (*my* word) and that their obvious role is in micro-methods".

or does not take cognisance of the differences between mathematics/science and engineering.

In relation to the difference between craftsmanship and engineering, the following discussion may be helpful ([Carvalho et al]). The problem is that, without a formal representation of the objects, rules, and guidelines involved in an engineering process, this chain is nothing but a set of prescriptive and descriptive rules. Therefore, a method built upon this basis does not possess the "exactness" and "inferential (analytical) power" that are components of every mature engineering process.

To illustrate the limitation we refer to, let us consider the difference between *valid generalizations* and *scientific theories*. A valid generalization is usually a regularity observed in Nature. Such a generalization could be so valid and so general that we can use it for, say, practical craftsmanship. For instance, the knowledge that iron dilates with increasing temperature allowed our ancestors, 3000 years ago, to protect wooden wheels with iron belts by the simple device of making a belt a little smaller than the appropriate size, hitting it, putting it around the wooden wheel and waiting until it became cold and contracted again, thus fastening onto the wheel. A software engineering example is the instruction in structured programming that one should not use "goto"s. But, with this simple knowledge we can only achieve such simple kinds of things. By developing laws explaining natural phenomena, ie scientific theories, and by using an appropriate calculus, we can predict complex phenomena and we are able to do it in a very precise way - so precise that we were able, for instance, to launch a space vehicle such as the Voyager and calculate its trajectory with a precision such as to use the gravitational attraction of Jupiter to impel it out of the solar system some years after launch. This kind of prediction involves an underlying calculus with a well defined set of inference and deductive rules.

As to engineering versus science/mathematics, we start by quoting again from [Jackson]. "...formalisation in traditional engineering is applied locally to well-understood characteristics. The context for applying the formalism is almost fixed, and the calculations to be made are almost standardised." It is hard to see how this criteria is realised in most foundational software engineering courses. I agree with [Parnas] that software engineering should be based on traditional engineering education.

An anecdote based on personal experience can be used to illustrate the point. For the past two years I have been responsible for teaching our third year software engineering course at Imperial College. It is one of two compulsory courses for all computing students in their third year and it follows first and second year courses on programming, program and systems design, discrete mathematics and logic, and program specification and verification. The aim of the course is to convey to students the ideas of modelling, measurement and quality and the role of testing in relation to these. The course illustrates the ideas positively (from science and traditional engineering and a few examples of software engineering) and negatively (with a multitude of examples from software engineering , beginning with function points!) Although some students responded constructively to the material, most students could not see the relevance of mathematical, scientific and engineering principles and practices to their work. I do not feel that this response was sue purely to the inadequacies of my teaching. It confirms a serious deficiency from the point of view of engineering, in the attitudes, concepts and skills which we inculcate in them.

Parnas (in [Parnas]) sees a trend in which new and topical computer science material supplants traditional and valuable elements of computer science, let alone engineering curricula. We can also observe that many software engineering programmes are shying further and further away from mathematics requirements on entry. There is generally a feeling that the subject of software engineering is becoming less and less 'technical'. I am often not so impressed by what new graduates and PhDs have accomplished as disturbed by large gaps in the knowledge. Many colleagues share the concern. [It may simply be a historical accident that early members of the computer science/software engineering community had training in the mature fields of science, engineering and mathematics, thus bringing with them the sound methodologies associated with these fields, whereas today we have many staff who are the products of computer science or software engineering curricula.

Much of the discussion of software engineering research and education takes place in the context of the so-called software crisis. in his typically entertaining and challenging style, Wlad Turski in a talk given at our Imperial College alumnus meeting three years ago, made a plausible case for software engineering being no different from other engineering disciplines in generating the occasional large disasters. He claimed that there is no software crisis, but in fact the IT industry has managed to produce lots of systems which work well. Tony Hoare has echoed this view in more recent talks and papers (eg, at ICSE18 last year). On the other hand, anyone who uses software systems or applications expresses dissatisfaction at a level which is infinitesimal compared to those held in relation to products of more traditional disciplines. This points not only to the immaturity of the discipline, but also to irresponsibility on the part of industry in accepting different (and lower) standards for the production of software than they would for any other class of artefact. Sometimes this might be taken for a *lack* of standards. It is often reflected in the personnel practices of these organisations, where scientific or engineering skills are not important criteria for employment of software development. Many of the demands from industry for "skills" which their ideal graduate should possess are in the category of technicians' skills and not related to engineering education as engineers would recognise it. So, industry also has a role to play in reforming our view of software engineering and software engineering education. In those countries where professional institutions accredit chartered engineers, they too have a role in assuring that important engineering principles are reflected in the design of curricula and that the appropriate categories of engineering knowledge are properly represented.

Software engineering education has a long way to go if we wish to see its content reflecting adequately the engineering content of its (admittedly) immature state of development. We have a lot to learn and absorb from the example of our more conventional relations in engineering.

4.   References

[BCS/IEE]   *A Report on Undergraduate Curricula for Software Engineering*, Institution of Electrical Engineers, London, 1989.

[Carvalho et al]   S Carvalho, J Fiadeiro, A Haeberer, H Haeusler andT Maibaum, Project ARTS: Towards a Mature Software Engineering Discipline, submitted for publication, 1997.

[CMM]   MC Paulk et al, Capability Maturity Model for Software, Version 1.1, Technical report CMU/SEI-93-TR-24, Software Engineering Institute, 1993.

[Constant]   EW Constant, *The Origins of the Turbojet Revolution*, The Johns Hopkins University press, 1982.

[Finkelstein]   A Finkelstein, European Computing Curricula: a Guide and Comparative analysis, *The Computer Journal*, Vol 36, No 4, 299-319, 1993.

[Finkelstein et al] A Finkelstein, J Kramer, S abramsky, K Broda, S Drossopoulou and S Eisenbach, An Integrated Engineering Study Scheme in Computing, *The Computer Journal*, Vol 36, No 4, 320-334, 1993.

[Jackson]   MA Jackson, private communication: a draft of a foreword to a collection of papers on formal methods technology transfer, 1997.

[Maibaum 86] TSE Maibaum, Rôle of Abstraction in Program Development (invited paper), in *Information Processing '86*; H-J Kugler ed, North Holland, 1986.

[Maibaum 94] TSE Maibaum, Taking More of the Soft out of Software Engineering (Keynote address), in *Proceedings of 7th International Workshop on Software Specification and Design*, 1993, IEEE Press,

[Parnas]   DL Parnas, Education for Computing Professionals, *IEEE Computer*, Vol 23, No 1, 17-23, 1990.

[Rogers]   GFC Rogers, *The Nature of Engineering*, The Macmillan Press Ltd, 1983.

[Vincenti]   WG Vincenti, *What Engineers Know and How They Know It*, The Johns Hopkins University press, 1990.

What we Expect from Software Engineers in the Industry

- Abstract -

Dr. Jürgen Uhl
Principal, Object Technology Practice
IBM Informationssysteme GmbH

Expectations, or better, requirements on software engineers depend on the category of project in which they work. In many application development or system integration projects, which today probably employ the majority of the software engineering community, requirements as expressed by project managers are mostly concrete and short term, like skills in development environments, a particular methodology, database systems, or specific application components. With today's rapid change in these systems, all we can expect from the basic education of software engineers is that it gives them the ability to quickly adopt to such new environments.

Looking closer, it is not really the skills for a particular tool or component which makes a project successful but rather the knowledge of common software engineering principles. Unfortunately, neither industry nor academia have developed and agreed on such principles to the degree achieved by other engineering disciplines. Therefore, teaching is often limited to a meta level like "what makes a software engineering methodology" and that's probably what we need to put more focus on in education.

On the other hand, there are a couple of aspects that software engineering education should pay more attention to. First there is the aspect of (re-)using rather than building. Masters curricula in computer science still seem to teach a lot more of "how do I build a compiler, database system, transaction monitor, networking system, ...?" rather than "how do I use all these systems to build applications?" or "how do I build application frameworks" rather than "how do I (re-)use application frameworks to assemble applications?". The latter often have a lot more to do with organization and economics which is another underdeveloped aspect in software engineering education. Second, there is the issue of scale which in fact is hard to teach theoretically. Software engineers need to get a feeling for what huge transaction rates, huge databases, huge projects or huge reliability requirements mean, what specific problems occur in addition to the smaller scale and which measures are needed to keep the efforts at least linear.

The presentation will sketch typical industry scenarios from software engineering in commercial application development, research and development labs and outline the expectations on software engineers in these domains.

Security Issues in Distributed Software

Richard A. Kemmerer

Reliable Software Group, Department of Computer Science
University of California, Santa Barbara, CA 93106

Abstract: As more business activities are being automated and an increasing number of computers are being used to store vital and sensitive information the need for secure computer systems becomes more apparent. This need is even more apparent as the systems and applications are being distributed and access is via an insecure network. The security of these systems can be achieved only through systematic design; they can not be achieved through haphazard seat-of-the-pants methods.

This paper introduces some known threats to secure distributed computing, discusses some of the current approaches to achieving security in these systems, and demonstrates further problems. Most of the discussion centers around web-based computing.

1 Introduction

The growth of the Internet and the World Wide Web (www) during the past few years has been phenomenal. Today the web is being used by millions of people to obtain information and conduct commerce both locally and throughout the world. It is considered to be a platform for building distributed applications. This evolution is made possible by browsers with processing capabilities and by programming languages that allow web designers to embed real programs into HyperText Markup Language (HTML) documents. The problem is that today's web browsers are insecure, and the security and privacy of the individuals using these browsers is in danger of being compromised. With the increased use of applets, which are downloaded programs that automatically run on the user's system when the web page is downloaded (possibly without the user even noticing), the threat is even greater. Downloading and executing code from anywhere on the Internet brings security problems along with it. A systematic and thorough analysis of security flaws in browsers and related technology is necessary to reach a sufficient level of confidence that no security breaches will result from running applets downloaded from an untrusted source.

By developing a set of *security properties* for secure browsers, designers will be able to choose the properties that they wish to include in their browser. As with any design choice, this will depend on how the goals of security and privacy interact with other goals for the browser, such as efficiency and user friendliness. It is expected, however, that the public pressure for more secure browsers will increase as more vulnerabilities are disclosed. Another approach to secure browsing is the development of *secure user procedures* that will assure the security and privacy of the user doing the browsing. These can be as simple as having the browser list the applets on a page and wait for a user response before running the page or as complex as using public key encryption and digital signatures to assure that a page is from an approved server. With this approach the user would be given the choice as to how much risk he/she is willing to accept as a tradeoff against efficiency or user friendliness.

To determine these properties and procedures it is necessary to study the known weaknesses in existing browsers and the attacks that have exercised these weaknesses. It is also necessary to analyze the possible countermeasures to these attacks. This paper concentrates on web-based computing as one aspect of secure distributed computing. In discussing secure web-based computing, however, other distributed software security issues will also be raised.

The next section presents the necessary background information to discuss web-based computing. It includes the definition of security properties, a brief overview of the Java and JavaScript languages, and an even briefer introduction to browsers. This is followed by a discussion of some of the currently available browser security options and current approaches to assuring Java applet security. Section 4 summarizes some known browser attacks and countermeasures to the attacks. The final section presents some conclusions on the value of analyzing web browser attacks and deterrents.

2 Background

2.1 Computer Security

Computer security is an area that is growing in importance as more business applications are being automated and more vital and sensitive information is being stored in computers. The term *computer security* means the protection of resources (including data and programs) from accidental or malicious disclosure, modification, or destruction. In addition, the system resources must also be protected (i.e., system services should not be denied). These computer security properties are usually referred to as confidentiality, integrity, and availability. More precisely:

> *Confidentiality* ensures that sensitive information is not disclosed to unauthorized recipients.
>
> *Integrity* ensures that data and programs are modified or destroyed only in a specified and authorized manner.
>
> *Availability* ensures that the resources of the system will be usable whenever they are needed by an authorized user.

The degree to which each of these properties is needed varies from application to application. For instance, the defense industry is primarily interested in confidentiality. In contrast, the banking industry is primarily interested in integrity, and the telephony industry may value availability most. The exact requirements that are needed for a particular system or application are expressed in the security policy for that system or application.

2.2 Java and JavaScript

The *Java Language* is a general-purpose object-oriented language that was introduced by Sun Microsystems in 1995 [GJS 96]. One of the major design goals for Java was portability. The result is that not only the Java source code, but also the binary code is executable on all processors. This is accomplished by compiling the source code into platform independent bytecode, which is then run by the Java virtual machine.

Some of the features of the Java language that make it simpler and supposedly more secure are that it is strongly typed, there are no preprocessor statements (like C's #define and #include), there are no pointers, no global variables, and no global functions. Java also has automatic garbage collection. By keeping the language simple and without many of the error prone features, such as multiple inheritance, it is expected that Java will be more secure.

Java code was designed to run on any client; therefore, compiled Java programs are network and platform independent. *Java applets* are Java programs that are intended to run on a Java virtual machine running in a user's browser. A special tag in a downloaded HTML file tells a web server to download the bytecode for a Java applet. The most popular web browsers, such as Netscape Navigator and Microsoft Explorer, include support for the execution of applets. Applets can be used for implementing small stand-alone applications, as well as for implementing clients of client/server applications.

The *Java Virtual Machine* is emulated in software and can run on numerous platforms [LY 96]. It could also be compiled or implemented directly in microcode or hardware, but currently it is mostly emulated in software. The virtual machine deals with class files, which contain Java virtual machine instructions, a symbol table, and a few other necessary items. Java virtual machine instructions are all one byte long and are therefore called *bytecodes*. Bytecodes can also be generated from other high level languages, such as Ada or C, or they could be generated manually.

When Java classes are downloaded from the network it is necessary to use a class loader. Java supplies an abstract *ClassLoader* Class for this purpose. Because abstract classes cannot be used directly, each browser needs to declare a subclass of this class for downloading classes. The main function of a class loader is converting the array of bytes that is downloaded from the net to an instance of class Class. That is, the array of bytes must be translated to the structure of a class. The ClassLoader method that actually does the conversion is defineClass. Every class object contains a reference to the class loader that defined it.

JavaScript is an object-based scripting language that has been specifically designed by Netscape to embed executable statements (scripts) into HTML pages. JavaScript resembles Java, but without Java's static typing and strong type checking. Scripts are embedded directly into an HTML page and interpreted by the browser. By invoking JavaScript functions, it is possible to perform actions (such as playing an audio file, executing an applet, or sending an e-mail message) in response to a user opening or exiting a page.

2.3 Browsers

Both Netscape Navigator 3.01 and Microsoft Explorer 3.02 support the execution of Java applets and JavaScript. Their implementations of the Java virtual machine and the JavaScript interpreter differ, but they support the requirements of these languages. Moreover, they both support the "cookie" technology, which was developed by Netscape to make up for the stateless nature of web communications. A cookie is a small piece of information that is stored by the browser on server request and that can be sent to the server at any time. A browser is sent a request to set a cookie the first time it asks the server for an HTML page. Cookies are useful to maintain related information during long browsing sessions, such as maintaining shopping baskets and remembering configuration preferences. Although cookies have been introduced to improve the quality of the service provided by the web, they can also be exploited for malicious purposes.

3 Browser Security Options

Both Netscape Navigator 3.01 and Microsoft Explorer 3.02 give the user options to increase the security of the browser. These options are:
 - the option to turn the execution of Java and/or JavaScript on or off. This enables the user to trade the convenience of these languages for the security of not running any outside program in the user's machine.
 - the option of alerting the user before accepting a cookie and before sending a form in an insecure environment. This lets the user choose whether to continue the operation or not.
 - certificates and digital signatures. These currently are not widely used, but they are likely to be used more in the future.
 - Netscape Navigator has an option to alert the user before sending forms by e-mail.
 - Microsoft Explorer allows the user to set three levels of security (high, medium, low) against active contents (which is Microsoft's term for Java and JavaScript).

As mentioned above, Java applets are designed to be downloaded from the web and to be run directly by a Java virtual machine within a browser. Since applets are automatically run by the browser just by accessing a web page that contains a reference to the applet, security concerns should be alleviated before users can be expected to accept the concept of running applets from untrusted sources. That is, special security measures should be taken to protect against security, privacy, and denial of service threats.

Because the Java language does not place security limits on downloaded applets and applets can be generated from other high level languages, it is necessary for the browser that contains the Java virtual machine to limit the downloaded applet. These limitations normally are not placed on applets loaded from the local file system, however, because the local host is trusted.

To address the security of downloaded applets existing applet viewers (including web browsers such as Netscape Navigator 2.0) impose the following restrictions on downloaded applets [CW 96]:
- An applet is prevented from reading or writing files on the host that is executing it.
- An applet can make network connections only to the host that it came from.
- An applet cannot start any program on the host that is executing it.
- An applet is prevented from loading libraries or defining native methods.
- An applet can read only a restricted set of system properties. In particular, it can read the file separator (e.g., "/"), the path separator (e.g., ":"), the line separator, the Java class version number, the Java vendor-specific string and URL, the Java version number, and finally the operating system name and architecture.

The idea is that by placing these limitations on downloaded applets the applets are effectively placed in a "sandbox". The applet may do whatever it wants inside the sandbox, but it is limited as to what it can do on the outside.

The Java virtual machine also limits the name space of downloaded applets. When a Java virtual machine tries to load a class from a source other than the local host machine a class loader, which cannot be overridden by the downloaded applet, is invoked. The class loader sets up a separate naming environment to accommodate the source. This will assure that name clashes don't occur between the names in this source and the names in classes loaded from other sources. Bytecode loaded from the local file system is set up in the system name space, which is shared by all other name spaces. The system name space is always searched first to prevent system classes from being overridden.

After the name space is set up, the class loader calls a *bytecode verifier* to assure that the bytecode has proper structure. This is necessary because the bytecode could have been generated by an incorrect Java compiler, by a compiler altered to skip the compile time checks, or by a nonJava compiler. The bytecode also could have been altered after it was produced. The bytecode is verified in four passes and is claimed to satisfy the following conditions if it passes the verification.
- The downloaded bytecode has the proper format for a class file
- All "final" classes are not subclassed, and all "final" methods are not overridden.
- Every class except Object must have a superclass.
- All variables and method references have legal names and types.
- Methods are called with the appropriate arguments.
- Variables are assigned values of the appropriate type.
- There are no stack overflows or underflows.
- All objects on the stack are of the appropriate type.

When the bytecode has been verified it is allowed to run on the host machine.

4 Browser Attacks

The use of the world wide web and web browsers has spread to most every segment of society. However, the web browsers in use today were initially built with little concern for security. As is often the case, the developers appear to have had a naive view of security. As a result, there have been many published browser attacks. Most of these have fixes, but new attacks are constantly being discovered. The attacks on browsers vary in sophistication and in the amount of resources that the attacker needs to carry out the attack. In this section a few representative attacks are presented.

One of the simplest forms of browser attacks and also one of the hardest to stop is a denial of service attack, which uses Java features to exhaust the host system or prevent the use of some feature. Obvious examples of this attack are busy-waiting to consume cpu cycles and allocating memory until all of the available memory is exhausted. Other attacks in this category lock a class to prevent access to particular resources (e.g., locking the InetAddress class in Netscape blocks host name lookups). The reason that the denial of service attacks are difficult to stop is that there is no regulation of how much of a resource an applet can consume. That is, an applet is either given as much as it wants or it is given nothing. More information on this attack can be found in [DFW 96].

Another simple attack deals with the use of cookies to keep track of a user's activities, which is a privacy violation. This attack is described in [Ste 97] and reports a real situation that has been set up by DoubleClick Corporation.

A more sophisticated attack is the Domain Name Server attack. This attack assumes that the attacker has control of a DNS, which a trusting host (or even a firewall) uses to validate a server address. In this attack the applet requests a connection to the server by using its name. The malicious domain name server returns another address that corresponds to another machine other than the one requested by the applet (e.g., the attacker's machine). The browser is then viewing a page different than what it thinks. Netscape fixed this problem in Navigator 2.01 and 2.02 by looking up the IP address for each site processed and by refusing to listen to (possibly false) updates to that address [Ros 96].

Another interesting attack is the net spoofing attack. It assumes that the attacker has a way to make the user connect to the attacker machine, which delivers rewritten pages in such a way that each URL refers to the attacker machine. The attacker machine works as a "man in the middle." This requires the attacker to have control such that everything that the browser thinks it is sending to the web actually goes to the attacker machine. The attacker may then forward the request to the real machine and relay the results back to the victim, while making copies of the interesting parts before passing them on. This attack is fully described in [FBD 96].

Most of the attacks that have appeared in the literature rely either on bugs in the browser implementation, assumptions about what capabilities the attacker has, or language errors. Many of these attacks have already been thwarted with countermeasures.

Recently, the Reliable Software group at the UCSB carried out a number of experimental attacks that were based on features of the browser or of the language exploited. In particular, the JavaScript capability of sending e-mail from within a script, the Java capability of opening a new window and downloading a new HTML page in it, and the object-oriented nature of Java that associates every applet with a thread have been exploited. These experiments demonstrate that even a good implementation can lead to an insecure environment if it is possible to combine "features" that have been designed independently of each other. These experiments led to the definition of two new attacks. One attack is to build dossiers on Internet users, which is a privacy violation. The second deals with confidentiality; its goal is to steal access information, such as a user's PIN. These experiments are described in detail in [DPS 97].

5 Conclusion

Properties for secure browsers as well as procedures for secure browsing need to be developed. Both are important, for sometimes by following secure procedures one can work as securely with a less secure browser as with a browser with a higher level of security assurance. That is, there may be many tradeoffs between implementing secure features and enforcing the user to follow secure browsing procedures. By analyzing and categorizing browser attacks and countermeasures the needed features and procedures can be better understood.

References

[CW 96]   Mary Campione and Kathy Walrath, The Java Tutorial: Object-Oriented Programming for the Internet, ISBN 0-201-63454-6, The Java Series, Addison-Wesley, 1996. (http://java.sun.com/tutorial/index.html)

[DFW 96]   Drew Dean, Edward W. Felten, and Dan S. Wallach, "Java Security: From HotJava to Netscape and Beyond," *Proceedings of the 1996 IEEE Symposium on Security and Privacy*, Oakland, California, May 1996. (http://www.cs.princeton.edu/sip/pub/secure96.html)

[DPS 97]   Flavio De Paoli, Andre L. dos Santos, and Richard A. Kemmerer, "Vulnerability of 'Secure' Web Browsers," *Proceedings of the National Information Systems Security Conference*, Baltimore, Maryland, October 1997.

[FBD 96]   Edward W. Felten, Dirk Balfanz, Drew Dean, and Dan S. Wallach, Web Spoofing: An Internet Con Game, Technical Report 540-96, Dept. of Computer Science, Princeton University, December 1996. (http://www.cs.princeton.edu/sip/pub/spoofing.html)

[GJS 96]   James Gosling, Bill Joy, and Guy Steele, *The Java Language Specification*, ISBN 0-201-63451-1, The Java Series, Addison Wesley, 1996. http://www.nge.com/home/java/spec10/index.html

[LY 96]   Tim Lindholm and Frank Yellin, *The Java Virtual Machine Specification*, ISBN 0-201-63452-X, The Java Series, Addison Wesley, 1996.

[MRR 97]   D. Martin, S. Rajagopalan and A. Rubin, "Blocking Java Applets at the Firewall", in the *Proceedings of the Internet Society Symposium on Network and Distributed System Security*, February 1997.

[Ros 96]   Jim Roskind, Navigator 2.02 Security-Related FAQ, May 1996.
            http://home.netscape.com/newsref/std/java_security_faq.html

[Ste 97]   Lincoln D. Stein, WWW Security Faq, version 1.3.7, March 30, 1997.
            (http://www.genome.wi.mit.edu/WWW/faqs/www-security-faq.html)

A Framework for Classifying and Comparing Architecture Description Languages

Nenad Medvidovic and Richard N. Taylor

Department of Information and Computer Science
University of California, Irvine
Irvine, California 92697-3425, U.S.A.
{neno,taylor}@ics.uci.edu

Abstract. Software architectures shift developers' focus from lines-of-code to coarser-grained architectural elements and their interconnection structure. Architecture description languages (ADLs) have been proposed as modeling notations to support architecture-based development. There is, however, little consensus in the research community on what is an ADL, what aspects of an architecture should be modeled in an ADL, and which ADL is best suited for a particular problem. Furthermore, the distinction is rarely made between ADLs on one hand and formal specification, module interconnection, simulation, and programming languages on the other. This paper attempts to provide an answer to these questions. It motivates and presents a definition and a classification framework for ADLs. The utility of the definition is demonstrated by using it to differentiate ADLs from other modeling notations. The framework is used to classify and compare several existing ADLs.[1]

Keywords: software architecture, architecture description languages, definition, classification, comparison

1 Introduction

Software architecture research is directed at reducing costs of developing applications and increasing the potential for commonality between different members of a closely related product family [GS93, PW92]. Software development based on common architectural idioms has its focus shifted from lines-of-code to coarser-grained architectural elements (software components and connectors) and their overall interconnection structure. To support architecture-based development, formal modeling notations and analysis and development tools that operate on architectural specifications are needed. Architecture description languages (ADLs) and their accompanying toolsets have been proposed as the answer. Loosely defined, "an ADL for software applications focuses on the high-level structure of the overall application rather than the implementation details of any specific source module" [Ves93]. ADLs have recently become an area of intense research in the software architecture community [GPT95, Gar95, Wolf96].

A number of ADLs have been proposed for modeling architectures both within a particular domain and as general-purpose architecture modeling languages. Examples specifically considered in this paper are Aesop [GAO94], MetaH [Ves96], LILEANNA [Tra93], ArTek [TLPD95], C2 [MTW96, MORT96, Med96], Rapide [LKA+95, LV95], Wright [AG94a, AG94b], UniCon [SDK+95], Darwin [MDEK95, MK96], and SADL [MQR95]. Recently, initial work has been done on an architecture interchange language, ACME [GMW95, GMW97], which is intended to support mapping of archi-

---

[1] This material is based upon work sponsored by the Air Force Materiel Command, Rome Laboratory, and the Advanced Research Projects Agency under contract number F30602-94-C-0218. The content of the information does not necessarily reflect the position or policy of the Government and no official endorsement should be inferred.

tectural specifications from one ADL to another, and hence enable integration of support tools across ADLs.[2]

There is, however, still little consensus in the research community on what an ADL is, what aspects of an architecture should be modeled by an ADL, and what should be interchanged in an interchange language [MTW96]. For example, Rapide may be characterized as a general-purpose system description language that allows modeling of component interfaces and their externally visible behavior, while Wright formalizes the semantics of architectural connections. Furthermore, the distinction is rarely made between ADLs on one hand and formal specification, module interconnection (MIL), simulation, and programming languages (PL) on the other. Indeed, for example, Rapide can be viewed as both an ADL and a simulation language, while Clements contends that CODE [NB92], a parallel programming language, is also an ADL [Cle96a].

Several researchers have attempted to shed light on these issues, either by surveying what they consider existing ADLs [KC94, KC95, Cle96a, Ves93] or by listing "essential requirements" for an ADL [LV95, SDK+95, SG94, SG95]. Each of these attempts furthers our understanding of what an ADL is; however, for various reasons, each ultimately falls short in providing a compelling answer to the question.

This paper builds upon the results of these efforts. It is further influenced by insights obtained from studying individual ADLs, relevant elements of languages commonly not considered ADLs (e.g., PLs), and experiences and needs of an ongoing research project, C2. The paper presents a definition and a relatively concise classification framework for ADLs: an ADL must explicitly model *components*, *connectors*, and their *configurations*; furthermore, to be truly usable and useful, it must provide *tool support* for architecture-based development and evolution. These four elements of an ADL are further broken down into their constituent parts.

The remainder of the paper is organized as follows. Section 2 motivates our definition and taxonomy of ADLs. Section 3 demonstrates the utility of the definition by determining whether several existing notations are ADLs. Sections 4-7 describe the elements of components, connectors, configurations, and tool support, respectively, and assess the above ADLs based on these criteria. Conclusions round out the paper.

2 ADL Classification and Comparison Framework

Any effort such as this one must be based on discoveries and conclusions of other researchers in the field. For that reason, we closely examined ADL surveys conducted by Kogut and Clements [KC94, KC95, Cle96a] and Vestal [Ves93]. We also studied several researchers' attempts at identifying essential ADL characteristics and requirements: Luckham and Vera [LV95], Shaw and colleagues [SDK+95], Shaw and Garlan [SG94, SG95], and Tracz [Wolf97]. As a basis for architectural interchange, ACME [GMW95, GMW97] gave us key insights into what needs to remain constant across ADLs. Finally, we built upon our conclusions from an earlier attempt to shed light on the nature and needs of architecture modeling [MTW96].[3]

Individually, none of the above attempts adequately answers the question of what an ADL *is*. Instead, they reflect their authors' views on what an ADL *should have* or

---

[2] Although ACME is not an ADL, it contains a number of ADL-like features. We include it in the paper in order to highlight the difference between an ADL and an interchange language.

[3] Due to space constraints, details of these approaches are omitted. They are provided in [Med97].

should be able to do. However, a closer study of their various collections of features and requirements shows that there is a common theme among them, which is used as a guide in formulating this framework for ADL classification and comparison. To a large degree, this taxonomy reflects features supported by existing ADLs. In certain cases, also included are those characteristics typically not supported by ADLs, but which have been identified as important for architecture-based development.

To properly enable further discussion, several definitions are needed. There is no standard definition of architecture, but we will use as our working definition the one provided by Garlan and Shaw [GS93]:

> *[Software architecture is a level of design that] goes beyond the algorithms and data structures of the computation: designing and specifying the over-all system structure emerges as a new kind of problem. Structural issues include gross organization and global control structure; protocols for communication, synchronization, and data access; assignment of functionality to design elements; physical distribution; composition of design elements; scaling and performance; and selection among design alternatives.*

An *ADL* is a language that provides features for modeling a software system's *conceptual* architecture. ADLs provide a concrete syntax and a conceptual framework for characterizing architectures [GMW97]. The conceptual framework typically subsumes the ADL's underlying semantic theory (e.g, CSP, Petri nets, finite state machines).

The building blocks of an architectural description are *components, connectors,* and *architectural configurations.*[4] An *ADL* must provide the means for their *explicit* specification; this enables us to determine whether or not a particular notation is an ADL. In order to infer any kind of information about an architecture, at a minimum, *interfaces* of constituent components must also be modeled. Without this information, an architectural description becomes but a collection of (interconnected) identifiers.

Several aspects of both components and connectors are desirable, but not essential: their benefits have been acknowledged and possibly demonstrated by some ADL, but their absence does not mean that a given language is not an ADL. These features are *interfaces* (for connectors), and *types, semantics, constraints,* and *evolution* (for both). Desirable features of configurations are *understandability, heterogeneity, composition-ality, constraints, refinement and traceability, scalability, evolution,* and *dynamism.*

Finally, even though the suitability of a given language for modeling software architectures is independent of whether and what kinds of tool support it provides, an accompanying toolset will render an ADL both more usable and useful. The kinds of tools that are desirable in an ADL are those for *active specification, multiple views, analysis, refinement, code generation,* and *dynamism.*

This framework is depicted in Fig. 1. It is intended to be extensible and modifiable, which is crucial in a field that is still largely in its infancy. The features of a number of surveyed languages are still changing (e.g., SADL, ACME, C2, ArTek). Moreover, work is being continuously done on extending tool support for all ADLs. Sections 4-7 elaborate further on components, connectors, configurations, and tool support in ADLs. They motivate the taxonomy and compare existing ADLs based on their level of support of the different categories.[5]

---

[4] "Architectural configurations" will, at various times, be referred to as "configurations" or "topologies."

[5] Due to space restrictions, the comparison of ADLs in Sections 4-7 is limited to a representative subset of the languages whenever possible. A complete comparison of existing ADLs is given in [Med97].

```
ADL
    Architecture Modeling Features
        Components
            Interface
            Types
            Semantics
            Constraints
            Evolution
        Connectors
            Interface
            Types
            Semantics
            Constraints
            Evolution
        Architectural Configurations
            Understandability
            Compositionality
            Heterogeneity
            Constraints
            Refinement and traceability
            Scalability
            Evolution
            Dynamism
    Tool Support
        Active Specification
        Multiple Views
        Analysis
        Refinement
        Code Generation
        Dynamism
```

Figure 1. ADL classification and comparison framework. Essential modeling features are bolded.

3 Differentiating ADLs from Other Languages

In order to clarify what *is* an ADL, it may be useful to point out several notations (*e.g.*, high-level design notations, MILs, PLs, OO modeling notations, and formal specification languages) that, though similar, are *not* ADLs according to our definition.

The requirement to model *configurations* explicitly distinguishes ADLs from some high-level design languages. Existing languages that are commonly referred to as ADLs can be grouped into three categories based on how they model configurations:

* *implicit configuration languages* model configurations implicitly through interconnection information that is distributed across definitions of individual components and connectors;
* *in-line configuration languages* model configurations explicitly, but specify component interconnections, along with any interaction protocols, "in-line;"
* *explicit configuration languages* model both components and connectors separately from configurations.

The first category, implicit configuration languages, are, by definition given in this paper, *not* ADLs, although they may serve as useful tools in modeling certain aspects of architectures. Two examples of such languages are LILEANNA and ArTek. In LILEANNA, interconnection information is distributed among *with* clauses of individual packages, package bindings (*view* construct), and compositions (*make*). In ArTek, there is no configuration specification; instead, each connector specifies component ports to which it is attached.

The focus on conceptual architecture and explicit treatment of *connectors* as first-class entities differentiate ADLs from MILs [DK76, PN86], PLs, and OO notations and languages (e.g., Unified Method [BR95]). MILs typically describe the *uses* relationships among modules in an *implemented* system and support only one type of connection [AG94a, SG94]. PLs describe a system's implementation, whose architecture is typically implicit in subprogram definitions and calls. Explicit treatment of connectors also distinguishes ADLs from OO languages, as demonstrated in [LVM95].

It is important to note, however, that there is less than a firm boundary between ADLs and MILs. Certain ADLs, e.g., Wright and Rapide, model components and connectors at a high level of abstraction and do not assume or prescribe a particular relationship between an architectural description and an implementation. We refer to these languages as *implementation independent*. On the other hand, several ADLs, e.g., Uni-Con and MetaH, require a much higher degree of fidelity of an architecture to its implementation. Components modeled in these languages are directly related to their implementations, so that a module interconnection specification may be indistinguishable from an architectural description in such a language. These are *implementation constraining* languages.

An ADL typically subsumes a formal semantic theory. That theory is part of an ADL's underlying framework for characterizing architectures; it influences the ADL's suitability for modeling particular kinds of systems (e.g., highly concurrent systems) or particular aspects of a given system (e.g., its static properties). Examples of formal specification theories are Petri nets [Pet62], Statecharts [Har87], partially-ordered event sets [LVB+93], communicating sequential processes (CSP) [Hoa85], model-based formalisms (e.g., *CH*emical *A*bstract *M*achine [IW95], Z [Spi89]), algebraic formalisms (e.g., Obj [GW88]), and axiomatic formalisms (e.g., Anna [Luc87]).

Of the above-mentioned formal notations, Z has been demonstrated appropriate for modeling only certain aspects of architectures, such as architectural style rules [AAG93, MTW96]. Partially-ordered event sets, CSP, Obj, and Anna have already been successfully used by existing modeling languages (Rapide, Wright, and LILEANNA, respectively). Modeling capabilities of the remaining three, Petri nets, Statecharts, and CHAM are somewhat similar to those of ADLs. Although they do not express systems in terms of components, connectors, and configurations per se, their features may be cast in that mold and they may be considered ADLs in their existing forms. In the remainder of this section we will discuss why it would be inappropriate to do so.[6]

3.1 Petri Nets

Petri net places can be viewed as components maintaining state, transitions as components performing operations, arrows between places and transitions as simple connectors, and their overall interconnection structure as a configuration. Petri nets mandate that processing components may only be connected to state components and vice-versa. This may be an unreasonable restriction. Overcoming it may require some creative and potentially counterintuitive architecting. A bigger problem is that Petri nets do not model component interfaces, i.e., they do not distinguish between different types of tokens. If we think of tokens as messages exchanged among components, this is a crucial shortcoming. Colored Petri nets [Jen92, Jen94] attempt to remedy this problem by allowing different types of tokens. However, even they explicitly model

---

[6] These three notations represent only a small subset of ADL-like formal specification languages. They are used here to draw attention to what differentiates them from ADLs and to outline heuristics for determining whether a potential candidate is indeed an ADL according to our definition. These heuristics can then be used in the future to evaluate other notations as possible ADLs.

only the interfaces of state components (places), but not of processing components (transitions). Therefore, Petri nets violate the definition of ADLs.

3.2 Statecharts

Statecharts is a modeling formalism based on finite state machines (FSM), which provides a state encapsulation construct, support for concurrency, and broadcast communication. To compare Statecharts to an ADL, the states would be viewed as components, transitions among them as simple connectors, and their interconnections as configurations. However, Statecharts does not model architectural configurations explicitly: interconnections and interactions among a set of concurrently executing components are implicit in *intra*-component transition labels. In other words, as was the case with LILEANNA and ArTek, the topology of an "architecture" described as a Statechart can only be ascertained by studying its constituent components. Therefore, Statecharts is not an ADL.

3.3 CHAM

In the CHAM approach, an architecture is modeled as an abstract machine fashioned after chemicals and chemical reactions. A CHAM is specified by defining molecules, their solutions, and transformation rules that specify how solutions evolve. An architecture is then specified with processing, data, and connecting elements. The interfaces of processing and connecting elements are implied by (1) their topology and (2) the data elements their current configuration allows them to exchange. The topology is, in turn, implicit in a solution and transformation rules. Therefore, even though CHAM can be used effectively to prove certain properties of architectures, without additional syntactic constructs it does not fulfill the requirements to be an ADL.

4 Components

A component is a unit of computation or a data store. Therefore, components are loci of computation and state [SDK+95]. A component in an architecture may be as small as a single procedure (e.g., MetaH *procedures*) or as large as an entire application (e.g., hierarchical components in C2 and Rapide or *macros* in MetaH). It may require its own data and/or execution space, or it may share them with other components.

Each surveyed ADL models components in one form or another. In this section, we present the aspects of components that need to be modeled in an ADL and assess existing ADLs with respect to them.

4.1 Interface

A component's interface is a set of interaction points between it and the external world. An interface specifies the services (messages, operations, and variables) a component provides. In order to be able to adequately reason about a component and its encompassing architecture, ADLs also typically provide facilities for specifying component needs, i.e., services required of other components in the architecture. Interfaces also enable a certain, though limited, degree of reasoning about component semantics.

All surveyed ADLs support specification of component interfaces. They differ in the terminology and the kinds of information they specify. For example, each interface point in MetaH, ACME, Aesop, and Wright is a *port*. On the other hand, in C2, the entire interface is provided through a single port; individual interface elements are *messages*. In UniCon, an interface point is a *player*, and in Rapide a *constituent*.

4.2 Types

Software reuse is one of the primary goals of architecture-based development [BS92, GAO95, MOT96]. Since architectural decomposition is performed at a level of abstraction above source code, ADLs can support reuse by modeling abstract components as types and instantiating them multiple times in an architectural specification. Abstract component types can also be parameterized, further facilitating reuse.[7]

All of the surveyed ADLs distinguish component types from instances. MetaH and UniCon support only a predefined set of types. Three ADLs make explicit use of parameterization: ACME, Darwin, and Rapide.

4.3 Semantics

Modeling of component semantics enables analysis, constraint enforcement, and mappings of architectures across levels of abstraction. Several languages do not model component semantics beyond interfaces. SADL and Wright focus on other aspects of architectural description (connectors and refinement), although, in principle, Wright allows specification of component functionality in CSP.

Underlying semantic models vary across those ADLs that do support specification of component semantics. For example, Rapide uses partially ordered event sets (posets), while Darwin uses π-calculus [MPW92]. MetaH and UniCon supply certain kinds of semantic information in property lists, e.g., specification of event traces in UniCon to describe component semantics. MetaH also uses an accompanying language, ControlH, for modeling algorithms in the guidance, navigation, and control domain [BEJV94].

4.4 Constraints

A constraint is a property of or assertion about a system or one of its parts, the violation of which will render the system unacceptable to one or more stakeholders [Cle96b]. In order to ensure adherence to intended component uses, enforce usage boundaries, and establish intra-component dependencies, constraints on them must be specified. Constraints may be defined in a separate constraint language or using the notation of the given ADL and its underlying semantic model.

All surveyed languages restrict component usage via interfaces. Specification of semantics further constrains internal elements of a component. Several ADLs provide additional means for specifying constraints on components: Wright specifies protocols of interaction with a component for each port; Rapide uses an algebraic language to specify constraints on the abstract state of a component; MetaH and UniCon constrain specification, implementation, and usage of components by specifying their non-functional attributes; SADL and Aesop provide and enforce stylistic invariants.

4.5 Evolution

As design elements, components evolve. ADLs should support component evolution through subtyping and refinement. Only a subset of existing ADLs provide this support. Even within those ADLs, evolution support is limited and often relies on the chosen implementation language. The remainder of the ADLs view and model components as inherently static.

---

[7] A detailed discussion of the role of parameterization in reuse is given in [Kru92].

Rapide supports inheritance. MetaH and UniCon define component types by enumeration, allowing no subtyping, and hence no evolution. ACME supports structural subtyping via its *extends* feature, while Aesop supports behavior preserving subtyping to create substyles. C2 provides a more advanced subtyping and type checking mechanism, described in [MORT96].

5 Connectors

Connectors are architectural building blocks used to model interactions among components and rules that govern those interactions. Unlike components, connectors might not correspond to compilation units in implemented systems. They may be separately compilable message routing devices, or shared variables, table entries, buffers, instructions to a linker, dynamic data structures, procedure calls, initialization parameters, client-server protocols, pipes, etc. [GMW95, SDK+95].

Surveyed ADLs model connectors in many forms. Languages such as C2, Wright, UniCon, ACME, and SADL model them explicitly and refer to them as *connectors*. In Rapide and MetaH they are *connections*, modeled in-line, and cannot be named, subtyped, or reused. Rapide does allow abstracting away complex connection behavior into a "connector component." Connectors in Darwin are *bindings* and are also specified in-line. In this section, we present the aspects of connectors that we believe need to be modeled in an ADL and compare existing ADLs with respect to them.

5.1 Interface

In order to enable proper connectivity of components and their communication in an architecture, a connector should export as its interface those services it expects. Therefore, a connector's interface is a set of interaction points between it and the components attached to it. It enables reasoning about the well-formedness of a configuration.

Only those ADLs that model connectors explicitly support specification of connector interfaces. Wright, Aesop, ACME, and UniCon refer to connector interface points as *roles*. Explicit connection of component ports (players in UniCon) and connector roles is then required in an architectural configuration. In C2, on the other hand, a connector's interface is modeled with *ports* and is determined by (potentially dynamic) interfaces of its attached components. This added flexibility may prove a liability when analyzing for interface mismatches between communicating components.

5.2 Types

Architecture-level communication is often expressed with complex protocols. To abstract away these protocols and make them reusable, ADLs should model connectors as types. This is typically done in two ways: as extensible type systems defined in terms of communication protocols and independent of implementation, or as enumerated types based on their implementation mechanisms.

Only ADLs that model connectors as first-class entities distinguish connector types from instances. This excludes MetaH, Rapide, and Darwin. Wright, ACME, C2, and Aesop base connector types on protocols. SADL and UniCon, on the other hand, only allow prespecified, though extensible, sets of connector types.

5.3 Semantics

To perform analyses of component interactions, consistent refinements across levels of abstraction, and enforcement of interconnection and communication constraints, architectural descriptions should provide connector protocol and transaction semantics. It is interesting to note that languages that do not model connectors as first-class objects, e.g., Rapide, may model connector semantics, while some ADLs that do model connectors explicitly, such as C2, do not provide means for defining their semantics.

ADLs generally use a single semantic model for both components and connectors. For example, Rapide uses posets, and Wright models connector *glue* with CSP. As was the case with its components, UniCon allows specification of semantic information for connectors in property lists.

5.4 Constraints

In order to ensure adherence to interaction protocols, establish intra-connector dependencies, and enforce usage boundaries, connector constraints must be specified. With the exception of C2, ADLs that model connectors as first-class objects constrain their usage via interfaces. Wright further constrains connectors by specifying protocols for each role, while UniCon restricts the types of players that can serve in a given role using the *Accept* attribute. C2 restricts the number of component ports that may be attached to each connector port (one). ADLs that specify connections in-line (e.g., Rapide, MetaH, and Darwin) place no such constraints on them.

5.5 Evolution

Component interactions are governed by complex and changing protocols. Maximizing connector reuse is achieved by modifying or refining existing connectors. ADLs can support connector evolution with subtyping and refinement.

ADLs that do not model connectors as first-class objects also provide no facilities for their evolution. Others currently only focus on component evolution (C2) or provide a predefined set of connector types with no evolution support (UniCon). Wright does not facilitate connector subtyping, but supports type conformance, where a role and its attached port may have behaviorally related, but not necessarily identical, protocols. Aesop and SADL provide more extensive support for connector evolution. Aesop supports behavior preserving subtyping, while SADL supports refinements of connectors across styles and levels of abstraction.

6 Configurations

Architectural configurations, or topologies, are connected graphs of components and connectors that describe architectural structure. This information is needed to determine whether: appropriate components are connected, their interfaces match, connectors enable proper communication, and their combined semantics result in desired behavior. In concert with models of components and connectors, descriptions of configurations enable assessment of concurrent and distributed aspects of an architecture, e.g., potential for deadlocks and starvation, performance, reliability, security, etc. Configurations also enable analyses for adherence to design heuristics and style constraints.

6.1 Understandable Specifications

A major role of architectures is to facilitate understanding of systems at a high level of abstraction. Therefore, ADLs must model structural information with simple and understandable syntax, where system structure is clear from a configuration specification alone.

Configuration descriptions in *in-line configuration ADLs*, such as Rapide, Darwin, and MetaH, tend to be encumbered with connector details, while *explicit configuration ADLs*, such as UniCon, ACME, Wright, SADL, and C2 have the best potential to facilitate understandability of architectural structure.

Several languages provide both a graphical and textual notation. Graphical specification provides another way of achieving understandability. However, this is only the case if there is a precise relationship between the graphical description and the underlying model. UniCon, MetaH, Aesop, C2, Rapide, and Darwin, support such "semantically sound" graphical notations, while ACME, SADL, and Wright do not.

6.2 Compositionality

Architectures may be required to describe software systems at different levels of detail, where complex behaviors are either explicitly represented or abstracted away into single components and connectors. An ADL may also need to support situations in which an entire architecture becomes a single component in another, larger architecture. Therefore, support for compositionality, or hierarchical composition, is crucial.

Several ADLs provide explicit features to support hierarchical composition: MetaH macros, ACME templates and rep-maps, composite elements in Darwin and UniCon, internal component architecture in C2, and Rapide and SADL maps. Other ADLs, such as Wright, allow hierarchical composition in principle, but provide no specific constructs to support it.

6.3 Heterogeneity

A goal of architectures is to facilitate development of large systems, with components and connectors of varying granularity, implemented by different developers, in different programming languages, and with varying OS requirements. It is therefore important that ADLs provide facilities for architectural specification and development with heterogeneous components and connectors.

ADLs may be tightly tied to a particular formal modeling or implementation language, or they may support multiple such languages. Some ADLs fail to maximize reuse by supporting only certain types of components and connectors. For example, UniCon can use existing filters and sequential files, but not spreadsheets or constraint solvers. Most surveyed ADLs support modeling of both fine- and coarse-grain components. At one extreme, *computations* in UniCon or *procedures* in MetaH describe a single operation, while the other can be achieved by hierarchical composition, discussed above. Finally, MetaH requires that each component contain a loop with a call to a predeclared procedure to periodically dispatch a process. Any existing components have to be modified to include this construct.

6.4 Constraints

Constraints that depict desired dependencies among components and connectors in a configuration are as important as those specific to individual components and connectors. Many global constraints are derived from or directly dependent upon local constraints. For example, performance of a system will depend upon the performance of each individual element.

Only a handful of ADLs provide facilities for global constraint specification. Aesop, SADL, and C2 specify stylistic invariants. Aesop and SADL allow specification of invariants corresponding to different styles, while in C2 they refer to a single

70

(C2) style and are therefore fixed. Refinement maps in SADL and Rapide constrain valid configuration refinements. Rapide's timed poset constraint language can be used to constrain configurations. Finally, MetaH allows explicit constraint of *applications*[8] with non-functional attributes.

6.5 Refinement and Traceability

ADLs provide expressive and semantically elaborate facilities for specifying architectures. However, an ADL must also enable correct and consistent refinement of architectures to executable systems and traceability of changes across levels of refinement. This may very well be the area in which existing ADLs are most lacking.

Several languages enable system generation directly from architectural specifications; these are typically the *implementation constraining languages* (see Section 3). Both UniCon and MetaH allow specification of source files that corresponds to given architectural elements. There are several problems with this approach: the assumption that the relationship between architectural elements and those of the resulting implementation is 1-to-1 may be unreasonable; there is also no guarantee that specified source modules will correctly implement the desired behavior or that future changes to those modules will be traced back to the architecture and vice versa.

Only SADL and Rapide support refinement and traceability. Both provide refinement maps for architectures at different abstraction levels. SADL uses the maps to correctly refine architectures across styles, while Rapide generates comparative simulations of architectures at different abstraction levels. Both languages thus provide the means for tracing decisions across levels of architectural specification.[9]

6.6 Scalability

Architectures are intended to support large-scale systems. For that reason, ADLs must support specification and development of systems that may grow in size. Objectively evaluating an ADL's support for scalability is difficult, but certain heuristics can be of help.

One way of supporting scalability is through hierarchical composition, discussed in Section 6.2. Furthermore, it is generally easier to expand architectures described in *explicit configuration ADLs* (e.g., C2, UniCon) than *in-line configuration ADLs* (e.g., Rapide): connectors in the latter are described solely in terms of the components they connect; adding new components may require modification of existing connectors.

ADLs, such as C2, that allow a variable number of components to be attached to a connector are better suited to scaling up than those, such as Wright or ACME, which specify the exact number of components a connector can handle. UniCon allows architects to either specify the maximum number roles in a connector or leave it unbounded.

Note that these are heuristics and should not be used as the only criteria in excluding a candidate ADL from consideration. For example, both Wright and Rapide have been highlighted as examples of ADLs lacking scalability features, yet they have both been used to specify architectures of large, "real world" systems [All96, LKA+95].

---

[8] MetaH applications specify architectures containing both hardware and software elements of a system.
[9] [Med97] discusses in detail the drawbacks of each approach and motivates a hybrid approach.

6.7 Evolution

Architectures evolve to reflect evolution of a single software system; they also evolve into families of related systems. ADLs need to augment evolution support at the level of components and connectors with features for incremental development and support for system families.

Incrementality of an architectural configuration can be viewed from two different perspectives. One is its ability to accommodate addition of new components. Issues inherent in doing so were discussed above and the arguments applied to scalability also largely apply to incrementality.

Another view of incrementality is an ADL's support for incomplete architectural descriptions. Most existing ADLs and their supporting toolsets have been built to prevent precisely these kinds of situations. For example, UniCon, and Rapide compilers and constraint checkers raise exceptions if such situation arise. Thus, an ADL, such as Wright, which focuses its analyses on information local to a connector is better suited to accommodate incremental specification than, e.g., SADL, which is very rigorous in its refinement of *entire* architectures.

Another aspect of evolution is support for application families. In [MT96], we showed that the number of possible architectures in a component-based style grows exponentially as a result of a linear expansion of a collection of components. All such architectures may not belong to the same logical family. Therefore, relying on component and connector evolution mechanisms is insufficient. Aesop, and, more recently, ACME and Wright have provided support for system families.

6.8 Dynamism

Explicit modeling of architectures is intended to support development and evolution of large and potentially long-running systems. It may be necessary to evolve such systems during execution. Configurations exhibit dynamism by allowing replication, insertion, removal, and reconnection of architectural elements or subarchitectures.

The majority of existing ADLs view configurations statically. The exceptions are Darwin, Rapide, and C2. Darwin allows runtime replication of components via *dyn*amic instantiation, as well as deletion and rebinding of components by interpreting Darwin scripts. Rapide's *where* clause supports a form of architectural rewiring at runtime. Finally, C2's architecture construction notation supports insertion, removal, and rewiring of elements in an architecture at runtime [Med96].

7 Tool Support for ADLs

A major impetus behind developing languages for architectural description is that their formality renders them suitable for manipulation by software tools. The usefulness of an ADL is directly related to the kinds of tools it provides to support architectural design, evolution, refinement, constraints, analysis, and executable system generation.

The need for tool support in architectures is well recognized. However, there is a definite gap between what is identified as desirable by the research community and the state of the practice. While every surveyed ADL provides some tool support, they tend to focus on a single area, such as analysis or refinement, and direct their attention to a particular technique (e.g., Wright's analysis for deadlocks), leaving other facets unexplored. This is the very reason ACME has been proposed as an architecture interchange language: to enable interaction and cooperation among different ADLs' toolsets and thus fill in these gaps. This section surveys the tools provided by different ADLs, attempting to highlight the biggest shortcomings.

7.1 Active Specification

Only a handful of existing ADLs provide tools that support active specification of architectures. In general, such tools can be proactive or reactive. UniCon's graphical editor is proactive; it invokes the language processor's checking facilities to *prevent* errors during design. Reactive specification tools detect *existing* errors. They may either only inform the architect of the error or also force him to correct it before moving on. An example of the former is C2's Argo design environment [RR96], and of the latter MetaH's graphical editor.

7.2 Multiple Views

When defining an architecture, different stakeholders may require different views of the architecture. Customers may be satisfied with a "boxes-and-lines" description; developers may want detailed component and connector models; managers may require a view of the corresponding development process.

Several ADLs (e.g., Rapide, UniCon, Aesop, MetaH, Darwin, and C2) support two basic views of an architecture: textual and graphical. UniCon, MetaH, and Aesop further distinguish different types of components and connectors iconically, while Darwin and C2, for example, do not. Each of these ADLs allows both top-level and detailed views of composite elements.

Support for other views is sparse. C2 provides a view of the development process that corresponds to the architecture [RR96]. Rapide and C2 allow visualization of an architecture's execution behavior by building a simulation and providing tools for viewing and filtering events generated by the simulation.

7.3 Analysis

Architectural descriptions are often intended to model large, distributed, concurrent systems. Evaluating properties of such systems upstream, at architectural level, can substantially lessen the costs of any errors.

The types of analyses for which an ADL is well suited depend on its underlying semantic model. For example, Wright, which is based on CSP, analyzes individual connectors for deadlocks. MetaH and UniCon both support schedulability analysis by specifying non-functional properties, such as criticality and priority. SADL can establish relative correctness of two architectures with respect to a refinement map. Rapide's and C2's event monitoring and filtering tools also facilitate analysis of architectures. C2 uses critics to establish adherence to style rules and design guidelines.

Language parsers and compilers are another kind of analysis tools. Parsers analyze architectures for syntactic correctness, while compilers establish semantic correctness. All of the surveyed languages have parsers. UniCon, MetaH, and Rapide also have compilers, which enable these languages to generate executable systems from architectural descriptions. Wright uses FDR [For92], a model checker, to establish type conformance.

Another aspect of analysis is enforcement of constraints. Parsers and compilers enforce constraints implicit in types, non-functional attributes, component and connector interfaces, and semantic models. Rapide's constraint checker also analyzes the conformance of a Rapide simulation to formal constraints defined in the architecture.

7.4 Refinement

The importance of supporting refinement of architectures across styles and levels of detail was argued in Section 6.5 and, more extensively, in [MQR95] and [Gar96]. Refining architectural descriptions is a complex task whose correctness cannot always be guaranteed by formal proof, but adequate tool support can give us increased confidence in this respect.

Only SADL and Rapide provide tool support for refinement of architectures. SADL requires manual proofs of mappings of constructs between an abstract and a concrete style. Such a proof need be performed only once, after which SADL provides a tool that checks whether two architectural descriptions adhere to the mapping.

Rapide's event pattern mappings ensure behavioral consistency between architectures. Maps are used to verify that the events generated by simulating an architecture satisfy constraints in the architecture to which it is mapped.

7.5 Code Generation

The ultimate goal of software design and modeling is to produce the executable system. An elegant and effective architectural model is of limited value unless it can be converted into a running application. Doing so manually may result in many problems of consistency and traceability between an architecture and its implementation. It is, therefore, desirable, if not imperative, for an ADL to provide code generation tools.

A large number of ADLs, but not all, do so. Aesop generates C++ code, MetaH - Ada, UniCon - C, and C2 - Java, C++, and Ada. Rapide can construct executable systems in C, C++, Ada, VHDL, and Rapide. On the other hand, SADL, ACME, and Wright are used strictly as modeling notations and provide no code generation support.

7.6 Dynamism

Given that the support for modeling dynamism in existing ADLs is limited, it is of no surprise that tool support for dynamism is not very prevalent. Rapide can model only planned modifications at runtime; its compilation tools ensure that all possible configuration alternatives are enabled. C2's *ArchShell* tool [Ore96, MOT97], on the other hand, currently enables arbitrary interactive construction, execution, and runtime-modification of C2-style architectures implemented in Java. Darwin supports both planned (the *dyn* construct) and unplanned runtime changes (interpretation of Darwin scripts)

8 Conclusions and Future Work

Classifying and comparing any two languages objectively is a difficult task. For example, a PL, such as Ada, contains MIL-like features and debates rage over whether Java is "better" than C++ and why. On the other hand, there exist both an exact litmus test (Turing completeness) and a way to distinguish different kinds of PLs (imperative vs. declarative vs. functional, procedural vs. OO). Similarly, formal specification languages have been grouped into model-based, state-based, algebraic, axiomatic, etc. Until now, however, no such definition or classification existed for ADLs.

The main contribution of this paper is just such a definition and classification framework. The definition provides a simple litmus test for ADLs that largely reflects community consensus on what is essential in modeling an architecture: an architectural description differs from other notations by its *explicit* focus on connectors and architectural configurations. We have demonstrated how the definition and the accompanying framework can be used to determine whether a given notation is an ADL and, in the process, discarded several notations as potential ADLs. Some (LILEANNA and ArTek) may be more surprising than others (Petri nets and Statecharts), but the same criteria were applied to all.

Of those languages that passed the litmus test, several straddled the boundary by either modeling their connectors in-line (*in-line configuration ADLs*) or assuming a bijective relationship between architecture and implementation (*implementation constraining ADLs*). We have discussed the drawbacks of both categories. Nevertheless, it should be noted that, by simplifying the relationship between architecture and implementation, *implementation constraining ADLs* have been more successful in generating code than "mainstream" (*implementation independent*) ADLs. Thus, for example, although C2 is implementation independent, we assumed this 1-to-1 relationship in building the initial prototype of our code generation tools [MOT97].

Finally, neither the definition nor the accompanying framework have been proposed as immutable laws on ADLs. Quite the contrary, we expect both to be modified and extended in the future. We are currently considering several issues: providing a clearer distinction between descriptive languages (e.g., ACME) and those that primarily provide semantic modeling (e.g., Wright); distinguishing style- or domain-specific ADLs from "general purpose" ADLs; and expanding the "top" level of the framework to include criteria such as support for system families, openness, and extensibility. We have also had to resort to heuristics and subjective criteria in comparing ADLs at times, indicating areas where future work should be concentrated. However, what this taxonomy provides is an important first attempt at answering the question of what an ADL is and why, and how it compares to other ADLs. Such information is needed both for evaluating new and improving existing ADLs, and for targeting architecture interchange efforts more precisely.

9 References

[AAG93]   G. Abowd, R. Allen, and D. Garlan. Using Style to Understand Descriptions of Software Architecture. In *Proceedings of the First ACM SIGSOFT Symposium on the Foundations of Software Engineering*, pages 9-20, Los Angeles, CA, December 1993.

[AG94a]   R. Allen and G. Garlan. Formal Connectors. Technical Report, CMU-CS-94-115, Carnegie Mellon University, March 1994.

[AG94b]   R. Allen and G. Garlan. Formalizing Architectural Connection. In *Proceedings of the Sixteenth International Conference on Software Engineering*, pages 71-80, Sorrento, Italy, May 1994.

[All96]   R. Allen. HLA: A Standards Effort as Architectural Style. In A. L. Wolf, ed., *Proceedings of the Second International Software Architecture Workshop (ISAW-2)*, pages 130-133, San Francisco, CA, October 1996.

[BEJV94]   P. Binns, M. Engelhart, M. Jackson, and S. Vestal. Domain-Specific Software Architectures for Guidance, Navigation, and Control. To appear in *International Journal of Software Engineering and Knowledge Engineering*, January 1994, revised February 1995.

[BR95]   G. Booch and J. Rumbaugh. *Unified Method for Object-Oriented Development*. Rational Software Corporation, 1995.

[BS92]   B. W. Boehm and W. L. Scherlis. Megaprogramming. In *Proceedings of the Software Technology Conference 1992, pages 63-82*, Los Angeles, April 1992. DARPA.

[Cle96a]   P. C. Clements. A Survey of Architecture Description Languages. In *Proceedings of the Eighth International Workshop on Software Specification and Design*, Paderborn, Germany, March 1996.

[Cle96b]   P. C. Clements. Succeedings of the Constraints Subgroup of the EDCS Architecture and Generation Cluster, October 1996.

[DK76]   F. DeRemer and H. H. Kron. Programming-in-the-large versus Programming-in-the-small. *IEEE Transactions on Software Engineering*, pages 80-86, June 1976.

[For92]   *Failures Divergence Refinement: User Manual and Tutorial*. Formal Systems (Europe) Ltd., Oxford, England, October 1992.

[GAO94]   D. Garlan, R. Allen, and J. Ockerbloom. Exploiting Style in Architectural Design Environments. In *Proceedings of SIGSOFT'94: Foundations of Software Engineering*, pages 175–188, New Orleans, Louisiana, USA, December 1994.

[GAO95]   D. Garlan, R. Allen, and J. Ockerbloom. Architectural Mismatch, or, Why It's Hard to Build Systems out of Existing Parts. In *Proceedings of the 17th International Conference on Software Engineering*, Seattle, WA, April 1995.

[Gar95]   D. Garlan, editor. *Proceedings of the First International Workshop on Architectures for Software Systems*, Seattle, WA, April 1995.

[Gar96]   D. Garlan. Style-Based Refinement for Software Architecture. In A. L. Wolf, ed., *Proceedings of the Second International Software Architecture Workshop (ISAW-2)*, pages 72-75, San Francisco, CA, October 1996.

[GMW95]   D. Garlan, R. Monroe, and D. Wile. ACME: An Architectural Interconnection Language. Technical Report, CMU-CS-95-219, Carnegie Mellon University, November 1995.

[GMW97]   D. Garlan, R. Monroe, and D. Wile. ACME: An Architecture Description Interchange Language. Submitted for publication, January 1997.

[GPT95]   D. Garlan, F. N. Paulisch, and W. F. Tichy, editors. *Summary of the Dagstuhl Workshop on Software Architecture*, February 1995. Reprinted in ACM Software Engineering Notes, pages 63-83, July 1995.

[GS93]   D. Garlan and M. Shaw. *An Introduction to Software Architecture: Advances in Software Engineering and Knowledge Engineering*, volume I. World Scientific Publishing, 1993.

[GW88]   J. A. Goguen and T. Winkler. Introducing OBJ3. Technical Report SRI-CSL-88-99. SRI International, 1988

[Har87]   D. Harel. Statecharts: A Visual Formalism for Complex Systems. *Science of Computer Programming*, 1987.

[Hoa85]   C. A. R. Hoare. *Communicating Sequential Processes*. Prentice Hall, 1985.

[IW95]   P. Inverardi and A. L. Wolf. Formal Specification and Analysis of Software Architectures Using the Chemical Abstract Machine Model. *IEEE Transactions on Software Engineering*, pages 373-386, April 1995.

[Jan92]   K. Jensen. *Coloured Petri Nets: Basic Concepts, Analysis Methods, and Practical Use*. Volume 1: Basic Concepts. *EATCS Monographs on Theoretical Computer Science*, Springer-Verlag, 1992.

[Jen94]   K. Jensen. *An Introduction to the Theoretical Aspects of Coloured Petri Nets*. In J. W. de Bakker, W. P. De Roever, and G. Rozenberg, eds., volume 803 of *A Decade of Concurrency, Lecture Notes in Computer Science*, pages 230-272, Springer-Verlag, 1994.

[KC94]   P. Kogut and P. Clements. Features of Architecture Description Languages. Draft of a CMU/SEI Technical Report, December 1994.

[KC95]   P. Kogut and P. Clements. Feature Analysis of Architecture Description Languages. In *Proceedings of the Software Technology Conference (STC'95)*, Salt Lake City, April 1995.

[Kru92]   C. W. Krueger. *Software reuse*. Computing Surveys, pages 131-184, June 1992.

[LKA+95]   D. C. Luckham, J. J. Kenney, L. M. Augustin, J. Vera, D. Bryan, and W. Mann. Specification and Analysis of System Architecture Using Rapide. *IEEE Transactions on Software Engineering*, pages 336-355, April 1995.

[Luc87]   D. Luckham. *ANNA, a language for annotating Ada programs: reference manual*, volume 260 of *Lecture Notes in Computer Science*. Springer-Verlag, Berlin, 1987.

[LV95]   D. C. Luckham and J. Vera. An Event-Based Architecture Definition Language. *IEEE Transactions on Software Engineering*, pages 717-734, September 1995.

[LVB+93]   D. C. Luckham, J. Vera, D. Bryan, L. Augustin, and F. Belz. Partial Orderings of Event Sets and Their Application to Prototyping Concurrent, Timed Systems. *Journal of Systems and Software*, pages 253-265, June 1993.

[LVM95]   D. C. Luckham, J. Vera, and S. Meldal. Three Concepts of System Architecture. Unpublished Manuscript, July 1995.

[Med96]   N. Medvidovic. ADLs and Dynamic Architecture Changes. In A. L. Wolf, ed., *Proceedings of the Second International Software Architecture Workshop (ISAW-2)*, pages 24-27, San Francisco, CA, October 1996.

[Med97]   N. Medvidovic. A Classification and Comparison Framework for Software Architecture Description Languages. Technical Report, UCI-ICS-97-02, University of California, Irvine, January 1997.

[MDEK95]   J. Magee, N. Dulay, S. Eisenbach, and J. Kramer. Specifying Distributed Software Architectures. In *Proceedings of the Fifth European Software Engineering Conference (ESEC'95)*, Barcelona, September 1995.

[MK96]   J. Magee and J. Kramer. Dynamic Structure in Software Architectures. In *Proceedings of ACM SIGSOFT'96: Fourth Symposium on the Foundations of Software Engineering (FSE4)*, pages 3-14, San Francisco, CA, October 1996.

[MOT96]   N. Medvidovic, P. Oreizy, and R. N. Taylor. Reuse of Off-the-Shelf Components in C2-Style Architectures. In *Proceedings of the 1997 Symposium on Software Reusability (SSR'97)*, pages 190-198, Boston, MA, May 17-19, 1997. Also in *Proceedings of the 1997 International Conference on Software Engineering (ICSE'97)*, pages 692-700, Boston, MA, May 17-23, 1997.

[MORT96]   N. Medvidovic, P. Oreizy, J. E. Robbins, and R. N. Taylor. Using object-oriented typing to support architectural design in the C2 style. In *Proceedings of ACM SIGSOFT'96: Fourth Symposium on the Foundations of Software Engineering (FSE4)*, pages 24-32, San Francisco, CA, October 1996.

[MPW92]   R. Milner, J. Parrow, and D. Walker. *A Calculus of Mobile Processes, Parts I and II*. Volume 100 of *Journal of Information and Computation*, pages 1-40 and 41-77, 1992.

[MQR95]   M. Moriconi, X. Qian, and R. A. Riemenschneider. Correct Architecture Refinement. *IEEE Transactions on Software Engineering*, pages 356-372, April 1995.

[MT96]   N. Medvidovic and R. N. Taylor. Reusing Off-the-Shelf Components to Develop a Family of Applications in the C2 Architectural Style. In *Proceedings of the International Workshop on Development and Evolution of Software Architectures for Product Families*, Las Navas del Marqués, Ávila, Spain, November 1996.

[MTW96]   N. Medvidovic, R. N. Taylor, and E. J. Whitehead, Jr. Formal Modeling of Software Architectures at Multiple Levels of Abstraction. In *Proceedings of the California Software Symposium 1996*, pages 28-40, Los Angeles, CA, April 1996.

[NB92]   P. Newton and J. C. Browne. The CODE 2.0 Graphical Parallel Programming Language. In *Proceedings of the ACM International Conference on Supercomputing*, July 1992.

[Ore96]   Peyman Oreizy. Issues in the Runtime Modification of Software Architectures. Technical Report, UCI-ICS-96-35, University of California, Irvine, August 1996.

[PC94]   P. Kogut and P. Clements. Features of Architecture Description Languages. Draft of a CMU/SEI Technical Report, December 1994.

[Pet62]   C. A. Petri. Kommunikationen Mit Automaten. PhD Thesis, University of Bonn, 1962. English translation: Technical Report RADC-TR-65-377, Vol.1, Suppl 1, Applied Data Research, Princeton, N.J.

[PN86]   R. Prieto-Diaz and J. M. Neighbors. Module Interconnection Languages. *Journal of Systems and Software*, pages 307-334, October 1989.

[PW92]   D. E. Perry and A. L. Wolf. Foundations for the Study of Software Architectures. *ACM SIGSOFT Software Engineering Notes*, pages 40-52, October 1992.

[RR96]   J. E. Robbins and D. Redmiles. Software architecture design from the perspective of human cognitive needs. In *Proceedings of the California Software Symposium (CSS'96)*, Los Angeles, CA, USA, April 1996.

[SDK+95]   M. Shaw, R. DeLine, D. V. Klein, T. L. Ross, D. M. Young, and G. Zelesnik. Abstractions for Software Architecture and Tools to Support Them. *IEEE Transactions on Software Engineering*, pages 314-335, April 1995.

[SG94]   M. Shaw and D. Garlan. Characteristics of Higher-Level Languages for Software Architecture. Technical Report, CMU-CS-94-210, Carnegie Mellon University, December 1994.

[SG95]   M. Shaw and D. Garlan. *Formulations and Formalisms in Software Architecture*. Springer-Verlag Lecture Notes in Computer Science, Volume 1000, 1995.

[Spi89]   J. M. Spivey. *The Z notation: a reference manual*. Prentice Hall, New York, 1989.

[TLPD95]   A. Terry, R. London, G. Papanagopoulos, and M. Devito. The ARDEC/Teknowledge Architecture Description Language (ArTek), Version 4.0. Technical Report, Teknowledge Federal Systems, Inc. and U.S. Army Armament Research, Development, and Engineering Center, July 1995.

[Tra93]   W. Tracz. LILEANNA: A Parameterized Programming Language. In *Proceedings of the Second International Workshop on Software Reuse*, pages 66-78, Lucca, Italy, March 1993.

[Ves93]   S. Vestal. A Cursory Overview and Comparison of Four Architecture Description Languages. Technical Report, Honeywell Technology Center, February 1993.

[Ves96]   S. Vestal. MetaH Programmer's Manual, Version 1.09. Technical Report, Honeywell Technology Center, April 1996.

[Wolf96]   A. L. Wolf, editor. *Proceedings of the Second International Software Architecture Workshop (ISAW-2)*, San Francisco, CA, October 1996.

[Wolf97]   A. L. Wolf. Succeedings of the Second International Software Architecture Workshop (ISAW-2). *ACM SIGSOFT Software Engineering Notes*, pages 42-56, January 1997.

Applying Static Analysis to Software Architectures

Gleb Naumovich, George S. Avrunin, Lori A. Clarke and Leon J. Osterweil

email: {**naumovic|avrunin|clarke|ljo**} **@cs.umass.edu**
Laboratory for Advanced Software Engineering Research
Computer Science Department
University of Massachusetts
Amherst, Massachusetts 01003

Abstract. In this paper we demonstrate how static concurrency analysis techniques can be used to verify application-specific properties of an architecture description. Specifically, we use two concurrency analysis tools, INCA, a flow equation based tool, and FLAVERS, a data flow analysis based tool, to detect errors or prove properties of a WRIGHT architecture description of the gas station problem. Although both these tools are research prototypes, they illustrate the potential of static analysis for verifying that architecture descriptions adhere to important properties, for detecting problems early in the lifecycle, and for helping developers understand the changes that need to be made to satisfy the properties being analyzed.

1 Introduction

With the advent of improved network technology, distributed systems are becoming increasingly common. Such systems are more difficult to reason about than sequential systems because of their inherent nondeterminism. In recognition of this, software architecture research is attempting to define architecture description languages to help developers describe distributed system designs. These high-level descriptions allow developers to focus on structural, high-level design issues before lower level details are addressed, thereby helping to discover areas of high risk and to address these risks as early in the lifecycle as possible. To be truly beneficial, developers should be given tools to help them reason about their architecture descriptions, to help them discover problems as early as possible, and to help them verify that desired properties would indeed be maintained by these designs as well as by any systems correctly derived from these designs. It has been demonstrated that detecting errors early in the lifecycle [3] greatly reduces the cost of fixing those errors. Architecture description languages combined with appropriate analysis tools could therefore be an important means for reducing costs and improving reliability.

A number of architecture description languages have been developed, such as WRIGHT [2], Rapide [13], Darwin [14, 15], and UniCon [20]. There has also been some work on validating aspects of architecture designs. Using architectures specified in UniCon, for instance, developers can estimate local timing information and use those estimates to check time-dependent properties with the RMA real-time analysis tool [12]. Another approach is to use model-theoretic proof techniques to verify conformance of elaborated architecture descriptions to higher-level architecture designs [14, 18]. Developers using the Rapide architecture description language can simulate executions of the system and verify that the traces of those executions conform to high-level specifications of the desired behavior [13]. Although one would expect the number of traces through an architecture description to be much less than the number of possible executions in the corresponding software system, for most interesting systems there are still far too many such traces to explore them all. Thus, this is basically a sampling technique, and while it increases confidence in the architecture, it does not verify that all executions conform to the specifications. Another validation approach that has been explored is the use of static analysis techniques to verify general properties of architecture descriptions. When successful, this type of analysis does verify that all possible executions conform to the specification. Allen and Garlan [1] use the static analysis tool FDR [7] to prove freedom from deadlock as well as compatibility between the components and connectors in an architecture description. These are general properties that are desirable for all architecture descriptions.

The primary goal of this work is to investigate the applicability of existing static analysis techniques for verifying *application-specific properties* of architectures. We investigate one example architecture, a WRIGHT description of the gas station problem, and illustrate the kinds of properties that can be verified and the kinds of errors that can be found early in the lifecycle. Two versions of a WRIGHT architecture specification of the gas station example were graciously provided to us by David Garlan. We applied two static analysis tools: INCA, which is based on flow equations, and FLAVERS, which is based on data flow analysis. Both of these tools are research prototypes that illustrate the potential for static analysis to verify that architecture descriptions adhere to important properties, to detect problems early in the lifecycle, and to help developers understand the changes that need to be made to satisfy the properties being analyzed.

The next section gives a high-level overview of the two static analysis tools used in this case study. Section 3 gives a brief description of the gas station problem and the WRIGHT specification of the problem. Section 4 introduces the properties we selected to prove about this architecture and describes the analysis process and the results of that process. Section 5 summarizes the overall results, describes the benefits of this approach, and points out some interesting directions for future research.

2 Tools Used

A number of automated static concurrency analysis techniques have been proposed. They span such approaches as reachability analysis (e.g. [11, 21, 8]), symbolic model checking [4, 17], flow equations [5], and data flow analysis [6, 16]. The goal of this work is to demonstrate the applicability of static analysis techniques to architecture descriptions but not, at least at this point in time, to determine which approach might be best. Thus, we selected two different static analysis tools, based on fundamentally different approaches, with which we have considerable expertise. One tool, INCA [5], is based on flow equations, and the other, FLAVERS [6], is based on data flow analysis. Both these tools can be used to check whether all executions of a concurrent system satisfy a property, such as the mutually exclusive use of some resource. Although these tools use different approaches, they both are *conservative* in that if they determine that a property holds, it is guaranteed to hold for all executions. When the tools fail to prove that a property holds, however, this may be because the system does indeed violate the property or it may be because the analysis, in order to assure conservativeness and improve efficiency, has over-approximated the executable behavior of the system. Thus, when a property fails to hold, the results are *inconclusive* and usually require further investigation. A brief description of each of these tools is given here.

Inequality Necessary Conditions Analysis (INCA) derives a set of necessary conditions for the existence of an execution violating the property. In INCA, the sequential processes making up the concurrent system are translated into finite state automata (FSAs) from which necessary conditions, expressed as linear inequalities on the occurrences of transitions in those automata, are derived. These inequalities reflect certain kinds of compatibility conditions among the executions of the individual processes that must be satisfied in an execution of the full program. The violation of the property is also expressed as inequalities in terms of occurrences of the FSA transitions. The consistency of the resulting system of linear inequalities is checked using standard integer linear programming (ILP) techniques. This approach is inherently compositional, in the sense that the inequalities are generated from the automata corresponding to the individual processes, rather than from a single automaton representing the full concurrent system. Thus, INCA avoids considering the state space of the full system. The size of the system of inequalities is essentially linear in the number of processes in the system. Furthermore, the use of properly chosen cost functions in solving the ILP problems can guide the search for a solution. ILP is itself an *NP*-hard problem in general, and the standard techniques for solving ILP problems (branch-and-bound methods) are potentially exponential. In practice, however, the ILP problems generated from concurrent systems have large, totally unimodular subproblems and seem particularly easy to solve. Experience suggests that the time to solve these problems grows approximately quadratically with the size of the system of inequalities (and thus with the number of processes in the system).

The FLow Analysis for VERifying Software (FLAVERS) static analysis tool employs data flow analysis to verify that a model of the system must always be consistent with a property. In FLAVERS, the control flow graph representation of each sequential process, annotated with events of interest, is composed into a trace flow graph, which explicitly represents the communications among the distributed processes as well as the interleavings of events among those processes. The node size of the trace flow graph is at worst quadratic, and for all practical examples we considered it is sub-linear, in the number of program instructions. The properties to be checked are translated into a finite state automaton, where the transitions are annotated with the appropriate events of interest. Using a data flow analysis algorithm that is $O(N^2 S)$, where N is the node size of the trace flow graph and S is the state size of the automaton, FLAVERS determines whether the sequences of events that can be observed on system executions are accepted by the language of the automaton. If at the terminal node of the flow graph all event sequences are in the language of the property, we know that the property holds on all executions of the system. When some event sequences are in the language of the property and some are not, the results of the analysis are inconclusive, since it has to be determined whether the event sequences that violate the property happen on any real executions of the system. FLAVERS offers a means to deal with inconclusive results by allowing the analyst to add additional constraints, in the form of finite state automata, which limit the behaviors represented by the task flow graph. For example, a constraint can model the behavior of a single variable in the system. This additional information about the system restricts the data propagation through the flow graph during the analysis, thereby improving the accuracy of the analysis.

INCA and FLAVERS are based on very different analysis techniques, although both avoid enumerating the total state space of a distributed system. In addition, both techniques have been used to prove a wide range of properties of distributed systems. Because of this and our expertise with these tools, we chose them for our initial exploration of analyzing application-specific properties of architectures.

3 Architecture Specification of the Gas Station Example

The Gas Station system [9] models a self-serve gas station. This example has been widely studied by the static analysis research community. It has also been used in the software architecture community, and was the example provided to us by Garlan. In the general case, this system consists of n customers who come to a gas station to obtain gas for their vehicles, m cashiers who sell the gas, and p pumps that discharge the gas. The customers pay the cashiers (and get change in some versions), who order the pumps to discharge gas. We consider a specific instance of this system, with two customers, one cashier, and one pump. Garlan gave us WRIGHT specifications for two versions of this system.

WRIGHT formally describes architectures as collections of *components*, which represent computation units in the system, and *connectors*, which represent the means of information exchange among the components. Each component and connector is augmented with specifications that permit one to characterize the behavior of the components and their interactions. For a component the specification consists of a number of *ports*, and a *computation*. Each port represents a number of interactions in which the component may participate. In other words, a port partially describes the interface of the component, taking the point of view of the connector or connectors that communicate with this component through this port. The computation describes the internal functionality of the component. A connector is represented by a set of *roles* specifying the interface of this connector and the *glue* that specifies how the interactions actually take place. A system specification is composed of a set of component and connector type definitions, as described above, a set of instantiations of specific objects of these types, and *attachments*. Attachments specify which components are linked to which connectors. WRIGHT uses CSP [10] to describe the behavior of roles, ports, computations, and glues.

Figure 1 shows the WRIGHT specification for the first version of the Gas Station. This architecture describes three types of components and three types of connectors for communications between the customers and the cashier, the cashier and the pump, and the customers and the pump. The concrete instantiation of this architecture contains four components, Customer1, Customer2, Cashier, and Pump and

Component Customer
    Port Pay = $\overline{\text{pay!x}}$ → Pay
    Port Gas = $\overline{\text{take}}$ → pump?x → Gas
    Computation = $\overline{\text{Pay.pay!x}}$ → $\overline{\text{Gas.take}}$ → Gas.pump?x → Computation
Component Cashier
    Port Customer1 = pay?x → Customer1
    Port Customer2 = pay?x → Customer2
    Port Topump = $\overline{\text{pump!x}}$ → Topump
    Computation = Customer1.pay?x → $\overline{\text{Topump.pump!x}}$ → Computation
        $\lceil\rceil$ Customer2.pay?x → $\overline{\text{Topump.pump!x}}$ → Computation
Component Pump
    Port Oil1 = take → $\overline{\text{pump!x}}$ → Oil1
    Port Oil2 = take → $\overline{\text{pump!x}}$ → Oil2
    Port Fromcashier = pump?x → Fromcashier
    Computation = Fromcashier.pump?x →
        (Oil1.take → $\overline{\text{Oil1.pump!x}}$ → Computation)
        $\lceil\rceil$ (Oil2.take → $\overline{\text{Oil2.pump!x}}$ → Computation)
Connector Customer_Cashier
    Role Givemoney = $\overline{\text{pay!x}}$ → Givemoney
    Role Getmoney = pay?x → Getmoney
    Glue = Givemoney.pay?x → $\overline{\text{Getmoney.pay!x}}$ → Glue
Connector Customer_Pump
    Role Getoil = $\overline{\text{take}}$ → pump?x → Getoil
    Role Giveoil = take → $\overline{\text{pump!x}}$ → Giveoil
    Glue = Getoil.take → $\overline{\text{Giveoil.take}}$ → Giveoil.pump?x → $\overline{\text{Getoil.pump!x}}$ → Glue
Connector Cashier_Pump
    Role Tell = $\overline{\text{pump!x}}$ → Tell
    Role Know = pump?x → Know
    Glue = Tell.pump?x → $\overline{\text{Know.pump!x}}$ → Glue
Instances
    Customer1: Customer
    Customer2: Customer
    cashier: Cashier
    pump: Pump
    Customer1_cashier: Customer_Cashier
    Customer2_cashier: Customer_Cashier
    Customer1_pump: Customer_Pump
    Customer2_pump: Customer_Pump
    cashier_pump: Cashier_Pump
Attachments
    Customer1.Pay as Customer1_cashier.Givemoney
    Customer1.Gas as Customer1_pump.Getoil
    Customer2.Pay as Customer2_cashier.Givemoney
    Customer2.Gas as Customer2_pump.Getoil
    cashier.Customer1 as Customer1_cashier.Getmoney
    cashier.Customer2 as Customer2_cashier.Getmoney
    cashier.Topump as cashier_pump.Tell
    pump.Fromcashier as cashier_pump.Know
    pump.Oil1 as Customer1_pump.Giveoil
    pump.Oil2 as Customer2_pump.Giveoil

Fig. 1. The WRIGHT Specification of the First Version of the Gas Station

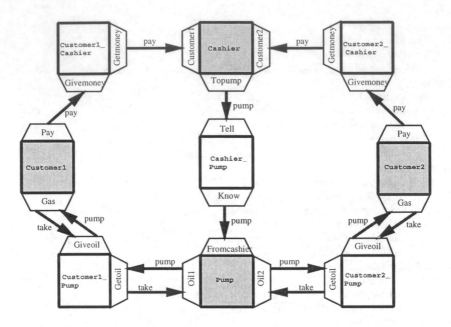

Fig. 2. Gas Station system, version 1

five connectors, `Customer1_cashier`, `Customer2_cashier`, `Cashier_pump`, `Customer1_pump`, and `Customer2_pump`. As shown in Figure 1, each `Customer` component has two ports, where `Pay` specifies the behavior of the Customer as viewed by the `Customer_cashier` connector, and `Gas` specifies the behavior as viewed by the `Customer_pump` connector. The behavior of the `Gas` port consists of repeatedly taking the hose (`take` event) and pumping gas (`pump?x` event). The computation part of `Customer` specifies that a `Customer` does the following sequence of actions repeatedly: pay for gas, take the hose, obtain gas from the pump.

Figure 2 presents an informal diagram of this architecture, with shaded boxes representing WRIGHT components and clear boxes representing WRIGHT connectors. The components' ports and the connectors' roles are shown as trapezoids, and named interactions between the ports and the roles are shown as labeled directed edges. Note that this diagram does not describe the order in which the interactions occur locally to connectors and components, the way the formal WRIGHT specification in Figure 1 does.

In this architecture, the customers repeatedly pay the cashier, then take the hose, and then wait for gas. The cashier, upon receiving a payment, turns the pump on. After a customer takes the hose and the pump receives authorization from the cashier, the pump then discharges the amount of gas, specified by the cashier, to the customer.

This version of the Gas Station is known to have a critical race. Specifically, it is possible for `Customer1` to pay before `Customer2` pays but for `Customer2` to take the hose before `Customer1`, thus getting the amount of gas purchased by `Customer1`.

Component Customer
     Port Pay = $\overline{\text{pay!x}}$ → Pay
     Port Gas = pump?x → Gas
     Computation = $\overline{\text{Pay.pay!x}}$ → Gas.pump?x → Computation

Component Pump
     Port Oil1 = $\overline{\text{pump!x}}$ → Oil1
     Port Oil2 = $\overline{\text{pump!x}}$ → Oil2
     Port Fromcashier = pump?x → Fromcashier
     Computation = Fromcashier.pump1?x →
        $\overline{\text{Oil1.pump!x}}$ → Computation)
       [] Fromcashier.pump2?x → $\overline{\text{Oil2.pump!x}}$ → Computation)

Component Cashier
     Port Customer1 = pay?x → Customer1
     Port Customer2 = pay?x → Customer2
     Port Topump = $\overline{\text{pump1!x}}$ → Topump ⊓ $\overline{\text{pump2!x}}$ → Topump
     Computation = Customer1.pay?x → $\overline{\text{Topump.pump1!x}}$ → Computation
       [] Customer2.pay?x → $\overline{\text{Topump.pump2!x}}$ → Computation

Fig. 3. WRIGHT Components of the Second Version of the Architecture

The second version of the Gas Station removes this race by combining taking the hose and pumping the gas into a single action and by having the cashier tell the pump which customer should get gas. This means that, instead of paying and actively requesting gas by taking the hose, the customers now must pay and wait until the pump contacts them by sending gas. Figure 3 shows the second version of the specification for Customer, Pump, and Cashier components only, since changes to the connectors are trivial. Figure 4 contains the corresponding illustration. Note that the only difference between the diagrams in Figures 2 and 4 is in communications between the ports of the components and the roles of the connectors.

4 Checking Properties of the Gas Station Architecture

The existing versions of INCA and FLAVERS do not accept WRIGHT specifications as input. While it should be relatively straightforward to build front-ends for both tools that would construct the appropriate internal representations directly from WRIGHT, this seemed inappropriate for the initial exploration we had in mind. Both tools accept Ada code as input, so we manually translated the WRIGHT specifications into Ada in order to apply the tools. The close relationship between the concurrency constructs in CSP and Ada made this translation fairly easy. Each component and connector instantiation of the architecture is represented by an Ada task. The "?" and "!" operations of CSP naturally correspond to Ada rendezvous. The non-deterministic and deterministic CSP choice operators are modeled with the Ada select statement.

84

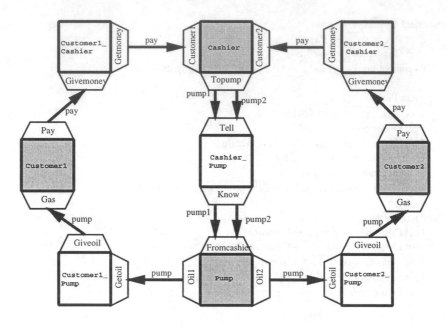

Fig. 4. Gas Station system, version 2

Figure 5 gives the Ada code for the `Customer1` component for the first WRIGHT specification. The assignment statement sets the variable `cash` to the value of a function whose body is not specified; the analysis tools treat this as a nondeterministic assignment. After choosing an amount of gas with this assignment, the `Customer1` task calls the `getmoney_pay` entry of the `Customer1_cashier` task with the parameter `cash`. This rendezvous corresponds to the $\overline{\text{pay}}$!x event. The `Customer1` task then calls the `getoil_take` entry of the `Customer1_pump` task, and then accepts a call at its own `gas_pump` entry. Note that a separate Ada entry exists for each interaction type between a role and a port, the name of the entry being the name of the receiving port or role, to which the name of the interaction is appended via the underscore symbol. For example, the interaction `pump` between the `Gas` port of `Customer1` component and `Customer_cashier` connector corresponds in the Ada version of `Customer1` to the entry named `gas_pump`. The complete Ada code for all versions of the example can be found in [19].

Our goal was to investigate whether existing static concurrency analysis tools could be usefully applied to check application-specific properties of architecture descriptions. Since the gas station is relatively simple, however, we focused on properties that reflect high-level requirements for a self-service gas station. Since we do not have any "official" requirements documents for the gas station, we chose a small number of properties that seemed to us to reflect reasonable requirements. Our goal was simply to explore the applicability of the static analysis tools to architectures; we make no claim that these are the most important or significant requirements.

```
task body Customer1 is
      cash : AMOUNT;
begin
      loop
            cash := Some_Amount;
            Customer1_cashier.getmoney_pay ( cash );
            Customer1_pump.getoil_take;
            accept gas_pump ( gas_amount : in AMOUNT);
      end loop;
end Customer1;
```

Fig. 5. Ada Translation of the Customer Specification

In the remainder of this section, we show how INCA and FLAVERS were used to check several properties of the gas station architectures, identifying certain faults and verifying that modifications to the architectures corrected these faults.

4.1 The Critical Race to the Pump

As mentioned above, the first WRIGHT specification has a critical race, in which one customer pays for gas and the second customer then pays and takes the pump before the first customer gets gas. In this case, the second customer gets the gas paid for by the first customer. The first requirement we considered was that customers get gas in the order in which they pay. We wanted to know whether INCA and FLAVERS could detect the violation of this property in the first WRIGHT version, and whether they could show that the property holds in the second version.

We begin with the first version. The property we want to check is stated in terms of customers paying and getting gas. For the analysis, we must identify locations in the code that correspond to these events. We identified a customer paying with the corresponding rendezvous between the connector task from that customer to the cashier and the cashier task, and the customer getting gas with the rendezvous between the pump task and the connector task from the pump to the customer.

The INCA approach is to produce necessary conditions for an execution of the system that violates the property. We express a violation of the property as an INCA *query*. By symmetry, it is enough to ask for an execution in which Customer2 pays and gets gas while Customer1 has paid but not yet gotten gas. So we wrote a query describing an execution in which a rendezvous between Customer1_cashier and Cashier occurs, followed by a rendezvous between Customer2_cashier and Cashier and a rendezvous between Pump and Pump_Customer2 before the next rendezvous between Pump and Pump_Customer1.

The INCA query we used is shown in Figure 6. This specifies a segment of an execution divided into two intervals. The first interval runs from the beginning of the execution (specified by the :initial keyword) and ends with some rendezvous between Customer1_cashier and Cashier at the customer1_pay entry (specified by the :ends-with keyword and the rend function). This interval is followed immedi-

```
(defquery "race" "nofair"
  (omega-star-less
    (sequence
      (interval :initial t :open t
        :ends-with '(
          (rend "customer1_cashier;cashier.customer1_pay")))
      (interval
        :ends-with '((rend "pump;customer2_pump.getoil"))
        :require '(
          (rend "customer2_cashier;cashier.customer2_pay"))
        :forbid '((rend "pump;customer1_pump.getoil"))))))
```

Fig. 6. INCA Query: Customers Get Gas in the Order They Pay.

ately by a second one ending with a rendezvous between Pump and Customer2_pump at the getoil entry of Customer2_pump. The second interval contains a rendezvous between Customer2_cashier and Cashier at the customer2_pay entry (specified by the :require keyword) and does not contain any rendezvous between Pump and Customer1_pump at the getoil entry (specified by the :forbid keyword).

From the Ada code corresponding to the first WRIGHT specification and this query, INCA generated a system of inequalities. In this case, the system of inequalities had an integer solution, and INCA gave us the behavior of each task corresponding to that solution. From these task behaviors, it is straightforward to construct an execution in which the desired property is violated. To check this property for the second WRIGHT specification, it was necessary to use two queries. (This is due to a technical reason involving certain cycles in the FSAs.) The first query checked that the cashier notifies the pump in the same order as customers pay, and the second query checked that the pump gives gas to the customers in the same order as it is notified by the cashier. The corresponding systems of inequalities were inconsistent, verifying that customers always get gas in the order that they pay with this second architecture.

The FLAVERS analysis is similar. For a FLAVERS analysis, the events of interest are indicated by annotating the Ada code. In this case, we used automatically generated annotations on the accept statements. For example, the "accept gas_pump" statement in the Customer1 task was annotated with the event customer1_gas_pump. We then gave FLAVERS a property specification, in the form of a *quantified regular expression* (QRE), asking whether any execution could generate the sequence of events corresponding to a violation of the property. The QRE we used is shown in Figure 7. It consists of the alphabet, quantifier, and regular expression. The alphabet of the QRE appears in braces and lists all events used for the specification of the property. The alphabet is followed by the "none" quantifier instructing FLAVERS to attempt to verify the property that no execution leads to a sequence of events in the alphabet that lies in the language of the regular expression that follows. In the regular expression, the period stands for the disjunction of all symbols, the asterisk is the transitive closure operator, the notation [-e] stands for the disjunction of all symbols in the alphabet other than e, and the semicolon is the concatenation operator. The language of the regular expression thus

```
{cashier_customer1_pay, cashier_customer2_pay,
customer1_pump_getoil, customer2_pump_getoil}

none

.*;
cashier_customer1_pay;
[-customer1_pump_getoil]*;
cashier_customer2_pay;
[-customer1_pump_getoil]*;
customer2_pump_getoil;
.*
```

Fig. 7. FLAVERS QRE: Customers Get Gas in the Order They Pay.

consists of all strings over the alphabet in which a cashier_customer1_pay occurs, followed by a cashier_customer2_pay and a customer2_pump_getoil before a customer1_pump_getoil occurs.

For the first WRIGHT specification, FLAVERS produces an execution in which the property is violated. For the second specification, FLAVERS verifies that this property holds for all executions.

Thus, both tools were able to detect the fault in the first version of the architecture, show how it occurs, and verify that a modification to the architecture corrects the fault. The remaining properties were checked on this modified version.

4.2 No Free Gas

We next checked the requirement that no customer receives gas without paying for it. This amounts to checking that, in every execution and for each customer, the events of paying for gas and receiving gas strictly alternate, with paying for gas coming first. By symmetry again, it is sufficient to check this for Customer1. We used the same rendezvous corresponding to the events of the customer paying and getting gas as in the previous section.

Using INCA, the standard way to show two events alternate is to use two queries. In this case, the first query describes a prefix of an execution in which the number of times the customer has paid for gas exceeds the number of times it has received gas by at least two. The second query describes a prefix of an execution in which the number of times the customer has received gas is greater than the number of times the customer has paid for gas. (For the complete set of INCA queries and FLAVERS QREs, refer to [19].) INCA reported that the necessary conditions for the existence of such executions were inconsistent. This means that, in every prefix of an execution, the number of times the customer has paid for gas is either equal to the number of times it has received gas or is one greater than the number of times the customer has received gas, showing that the events of paying for gas and receiving it strictly alternate, with paying for gas occurring first.

For FLAVERS, we used a QRE with the same alphabet as the one in Figure 7 and a regular expression requiring the two events to alternate appropriately. Here the regular expression, as opposed to the previous property, specifies what behavior must be observed on all executions. FLAVERS verified that the property holds on all executions.

4.3 Customers Get the Right Amount of Gas

We also checked whether a customer receives the amount of gas that he or she paid for. To facilitate the analysis, we allowed only two amounts (the type AMOUNT in our Ada programs had two values, 1 and 2). We then checked whether it was possible for a customer to pay for one amount of gas and then receive the other amount. By symmetry, it is sufficient to check only for one of the customers paying for one unit of gas and receiving two units.

Our INCA query asked for a prefix of an execution in which the first interval ends with a rendezvous with parameter 1 between Customer1_cashier and Cashier at the customer1_pay entry (the event where the customer pays for one unit of gas) and the second interval ends with a rendezvous with parameter 2 between Pump and Customer1_pump at the getoil entry (the event where the customer receives two units of gas). The second interval was forbidden to contain a rendezvous with parameter 1 between Pump and Customer1_pump at the getoil entry (the event where the customer receives the single unit of gas that was paid for). INCA reported that the system of inequalities it generated was inconsistent, so no such execution could exist. This showed that customers never get the wrong amount of gas.

FLAVERS required additional event annotations to capture the numeric values of parameters that specify amounts of money and gas. Currently these annotations are manually added to the source code of the system under analysis in the form of comments. The QRE for this property specified that on no execution should it be possible that the event of Cashier receiving 1 at its customer1_pay entry is followed by the event of Pump giving 2 to the getoil entry of the Customer1_pump connector before Pump gives 1 to Customer1_pump. FLAVERS verified the property.

4.4 Another Race Condition

In checking the first two properties described earlier, we identified the event of a customer paying for gas with the pay?x action on the cashier's customer port (or, in the Ada code, with the corresponding rendezvous between the connector between the customer and cashier and the cashier task). Similarly, we identified the event of a customer receiving gas with the pump!x action on the pump's oil port (or with the corresponding rendezvous between the pump and the connector between the pump and customer). Viewing events as actions taken by components, we have here taken the viewpoint of the cashier and pump components about when a customer pays or receives gas. But we could just as well take the viewpoint of the customer component. In that case, we would identify the customer paying with the pay!x action on the customer's pay port and receiving gas with the pump?x action on the customer's gas port. The Ada rendezvous corresponding to the first action involves the customer and the Customer_cashier connector; the rendezvous corresponding to the second action involves the Customer_pump connector. In essence, we checked whether the pump "believes" customers get gas in the same order as the cashier "believes" they paid for it. We could also check whether customers believe they get gas in the same order as they believe they paid for it. (Similarly, we could also check whether the pump believes customers get gas in the same order as the customers believe they paid for it, etc.)

To check this property for the second version, we modified the INCA query and FLAVERS QRE described in Section 4.1 to use the rendezvous in the customer task. INCA found a solution to the inequalities and produced the corresponding behavior of each task. These behaviors yield an execution of the system in which the first customer completes the rendezvous with the connector between it and the cashier, followed by the corresponding rendezvous between the second customer and its connector, but the second customer's connector delivers the money to the cashier before the first customer's connector. (A similar race occurs with the connector between the pump and the customers even if the money arrives at the cashier in the correct order.) FLAVERS produced the same execution.

The problem here is that, while communication between a component and a connector is synchronous, the communication between two components mediated by that connector is not. We can think of it as the customer "mailing" the money to the cashier, and the pump similarly "mailing" the gas to the customer—the customer passes the money into the connector, but has no way of knowing when the connector delivers it to the cashier. This is in contrast to the original Ada versions of the gas station presented by Helmbold and Luckham [9], where the communication between customers and the cashier was via direct Ada rendezvous between the two tasks.

In a certain sense, of course, this is not a critical requirement for the gas station, since customers do get the gas they pay for. In a real gas station, though, it would certainly make customers unhappy. We therefore decided to modify the architecture to ensure that customers receive gas in the order they pay, as viewed by the customers themselves. There are a number of ways in which such a modification might be carried out. One would be to use a single connector tying both customers to the cashier, and a single connector from the pump to the two customers. Another would be to add additional connectors from the cashier to the customers and from the customers to the pumps, allowing the components to signal when they had received money or gas. Instead, we chose to keep the basic "boxes and arrows" structure, but to modify the components and connectors so that the connectors signal the component that sends information when that information has been delivered. We did this by adding "callback" and "go_ahead" actions to the communication between the customers and cashier, and between the pump and the customers. The new versions of the customer and cashier tasks and the customer-cashier connectors are shown in Figure 8; the other modifications are similar. Figure 9 illustrates this architecture.

We then analyzed this modified architecture, translating it into Ada in the same way as the first two versions (i.e., with one task for each component and connector, etc.). Now, however, we identified the event of a customer paying for gas with the rendezvous representing the callback from the connector signaling that the money had been delivered to the cashier. As for the previous case, we identified the event of the customer getting gas with the rendezvous between the customer and the customer-pump connector at the customer's Gas_pump entry.

Component Customer
    Port Pay = $\overline{\text{pay}}$!x → callback → Pay
    Port Gas = pump?x → go_ahead → Gas
    Computation = $\overline{\text{Pay.pay}}$!x → Pay.callback → Gas.pump?x → Gas.go_ahead
        → Computation

Component Cashier
    Port Customer1 = pay?x → go_ahead → Customer1
    Port Customer2 = pay?x → go_ahead → Customer2
    Port Topump = $\overline{\text{pump1}}$!x → Topump ⊓ $\overline{\text{pump2}}$!x → Topump
    Computation = Customer1.pay?x → Customer1.go_ahead → $\overline{\text{Topump.pump1}}$!x
        → Computation [] Customer2.pay?x → Customer2.go_ahead
        → $\overline{\text{Topump.pump2}}$!x → Computation

Connector Customer_Cashier
    Role Givemoney = $\overline{\text{pay}}$!x → callback → Givemoney
    Role Getmoney = pay?x → go_ahead → Getmoney
    Glue = Givemoney.pay?x → $\overline{\text{Getmoney.pay}}$!x → $\overline{\text{Givemoney.callback}}$
        → $\overline{\text{Getmoney.go\_ahead}}$ → Glue

Fig. 8. Modified Customer, Cashier, and Customer_cashier with Callback and Go_ahead

For INCA, it was necessary for technical reasons (again involving cycles in the FSAs) to decompose the property into two queries. We first wrote a query to check whether the cashier tells the pump to give gas to the customers in the same order as the customers pay for gas (in terms of the callback rendezvous). INCA verified this property. We then used a query that checked whether customers get gas in the same order as the cashier tells the pump to give it to them. INCA also verified this. Together, these show that customers get gas in the same order as they pay. Using QREs for the same two subproperties, FLAVERS also verified the property.

We also verified the other properties for this version of the architecture, using both INCA and FLAVERS.

4.5 Performance

INCA and FLAVERS are research prototypes, and so the absolute time that analyses of the properties took are indicative of neither the real potential of the tools nor their scalability. However, we briefly discuss these times here to illustrate the current state of the tools. We ran all experiments on a DEC Alpha Station 200 4/233 with 128 megabytes of physical memory. For each of the three versions of the architecture, it took less than 20 seconds for each of the tools to create the appropriate internal representation used by the analyses. INCA took less than two seconds to check each of the properties (less than one second for most properties). FLAVERS, a less mature prototype, took less than 7 minutes to check each of the properties (less than 2 minutes for most properties). A major direction of our ongoing research is investigating these differences in performance.

In addition to the application-specific properties, the tools are also capable of checking general properties. For example, we used INCA to prove the absence of deadlock in

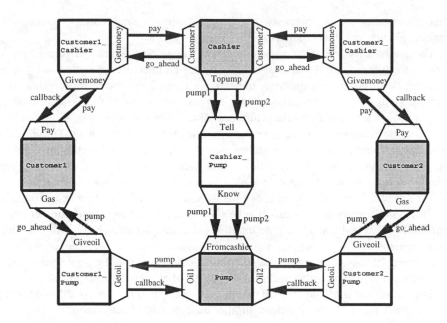

Fig. 9. Gas Station system, version 3

all three versions of the architecture. (The current implementation of FLAVERS cannot check for deadlock.)

5 Conclusions

In this paper, we have shown how existing static analysis tools can be used to check application-specific properties of architecture specifications. The tools were able to detect faults in the specifications, to provide example executions displaying the faults, and to verify that modifications to the specifications correctly removed the faults. Such tools can provide critical early feedback to system architects, helping to reduce the cost and improve the reliability of distributed systems.

While our initial exploration used WRIGHT as the architecture description language and INCA and FLAVERS as the static analysis tools, we see nothing that limits this approach to a particular language or tools. Although the close relation between CSP and Ada made it easy to manually translate the WRIGHT specification into Ada for use with our tools, we expect that the internal representations that static concurrency analysis tools use could be created from most architecture description languages with sufficiently well-defined semantics. Similarly, other static analysis tools capable of formulating and checking application-specific properties, such as SPIN [11] or SMV [17] could be used with architecture specifications.

The static analysis tools automate the checking of properties, but it is still up to the system architect to formulate those properties. As always, this is not straightforward and has to be done carefully. The fact that the tools can provide "counterexamples" when they cannot verify a property can, however, provide important assistance to the architect in understanding complex features of the system.

The preliminary investigation reported here suggests a number of interesting directions for future work. First, analyzing software architectures specified in other architecture description languages may indicate particular language constructs that affect different kinds of static analysis and may suggest extensions to the existing analysis tools or modifications to the architecture description languages in order to achieve improved analysis support. For example, the dynamic features of Darwin [14] might cause difficulties for many static analysis techniques. Another research direction involves the analysis of architectural styles, families of architectures with common structure. Properties proved for an architectural style should hold for instantiations of that style and could be used as constraints to improve the accuracy of analysis of an instantiation of that style. Static analysis tools can also be used to show that an instantiation correctly conforms to a style. Finally, we note that the static analysis tools can be used to show that a refinement or implementation of an architecture has the properties assumed in the architecture description. For instance, the tools could show that the implementation of a connector in a pipe-and-filter architecture actually behaves as it should.

The gas station is a small, but relatively rich, example. The race condition in which one customer takes the pump before another customer has been studied from various standpoints in the static concurrency analysis literature, and the two WRIGHT specifications supplied to us by Garlan were intended to illustrate it. The second race condition, arising from the asynchronous communication between components provided by the connectors in the first two versions of the architecture, does not arise in the Ada implementations of the gas station used in earlier concurrency analysis. The static analysis identified a genuine architectural issue that we, at least, had not expected to encounter. We make no claim, of course, that our third version of the gas station specification is the optimal way to avoid this race, but we believe that the way that the tools detected this unexpected problem and verified that a modification did indeed correct it illustrates the importance of applying static concurrency analysis techniques to architecture descriptions. While analyzing larger and more complex architectures will of course be somewhat harder, the much greater difficulty in understanding those larger and more complex systems makes static analysis even more important.

Acknowledgments

This work was supported in part by the Air Force Materiel Command, Rome Laboratory, and the Advanced Research Projects Agency under Contract F30602-94-C-0137 and in part by the National Science Foundation grant CCR-9407182.

The authors gratefully acknowledge the help of David Garlan in providing WRIGHT specifications for the gas station example.

References

1. R. Allen and D. Garlan. Formalizing architectural connection. In *Proceedings of the 14th International Conference on Software Engineering*, pages 71–80, May 1994.

2. R. Allen and D. Garlan. The WRIGHT architectural specification language. Technical Report CMU-CS-96-TBD, Carnegie Mellon University, School of Computer Science, 1996.

3. B. W. Boehm. Software and Its Impact: A Qualitative Assessment. *Datamation*, pages 48–59, May 1973.

4. J. Burch, E. Clarke, K. McMillan, D. Dill, and L. Hwang. Symbolic model checking: 10^{20} states and beyond. In *Proceedings of the Fifth Annual IEEE Symposium on Logic in Computer Science*, pages 428–439, 1990.

5. J. C. Corbett and G. S. Avrunin. Using integer programming to verify general safety and liveness properties. *Formal Methods in System Design*, 6:97–123, January 1995.

6. M. Dwyer and L. Clarke. Data flow analysis for verifying properties of concurrent programs. In *Proceedings of the Second ACM Sigsoft Symposium on Foundations of Software Engineering*, volume 19, pages 62–75, December 1994.

7. Formal Systems (Europe) Ltd., Oxford, England. *Failures Divergence Refinement: User Manual and Tutorial. 1.2β*, 1992.

8. P. Godefroid and P. Wolper. Using partial orders for the efficient verification of deadlock freedom and safety properties. In *Proceedings of the Third Workshop on Computer Aided Verification*, pages 417–428, July 1991.

9. D. Helmbold and D. Luckham. Debugging Ada tasking programs. *IEEE Software*, 2(2):47–57, March 1985.

10. C. A. R. Hoare. *Communicating Sequential Processes*. Prentice Hall, 1985.

11. G. J. Holzmann. *Design and Validation of Computer Protocols*. Prentice Hall Software Series, 1991.

12. M. H. Klein, T. Ralya, B. Pollak, R. Obenza, and M. Harobur. *A Practitioner's Handbook for Real-Time Analysis: Guide to Rate Monotonic Analysis for Real-Time Systems*. New York: Kluwer-Academic, 1993.

13. D. C. Luckham, L. M. Augustin, J. J. Kenney, J. Veera, D. Bryan, and W. Mann. Specification analysis of system architecture using Rapide. *IEEE Transactions on Software Engineering*, 21(4):336–355, April 1995.

14. J. Magee, N. Dulay, S. Eisenbach, and J. Kramer. Specifying distributed software architectures. In *Proceedings of 5th European Software Engineering Conference*, pages 137–153, September 1995.

15. J. Magee and J. Kramer. Dynamic structure in software architectures. In *Proceedings of the 4th ACM SIGSOFT Symposium on the Foundations of Software Engineering*, pages 3–13, October 1996.

16. S. Masticola and B. Ryder. A model of Ada programs for static deadlock detection in polynomial time. In *Proceedings of the Workshop on Parallel and Distributed Debugging*, pages 97–107. ACM, May 1991.

17. K. L. McMillan. *Symbolic Model Checking*. Kluwer Academic Publishers, Boston, 1993.

18. M. Moriconi, X. Qian, and R. A. Riemenschneider. Correct architecture refinement. *IEEE Transactions on Software Engineering*, 21(4):356–372, April 1995.

19. G. Naumovich, G. S. Avrunin, L. A. Clarke, and L. J. Osterweil. Applying static analysis to software architectures. Technical Report UM-CS-1997-008, University of Massachusetts/Amherst, 1997. (http://laser.cs.umass.edu/abstracts/architecture.html).

20. M. Shaw, R. DeLine, D. V. Klein, T. L. Ross, D. M. Young, and G. Zelesnik. Abstractions for software architecture and tools to support them. *IEEE Transactions on Software Engineering*, 21(4):314–335, April 1995.

21. A. Valmari. A stubborn attack on state explosion. In E. M. Clarke and R. Kurshan, editors, *Computer-Aided Verification 90*, pages 25–41. American Mathematical Society, Providence RI, 1991. Number 3 in DIMACS Series in Discrete Mathematics and Theoretical Computer Science.

Making Design Patterns Explicit in FACE

A Framework Adaptive Composition Environment

Theo Dirk Meijler, Serge Demeyer, Robert Engel

Baan Labs (TDM)[1]

Software Composition Group, University of Berne (SD)[2]

Washington University, Computer Science Department (RE)[3]

Abstract. Tools incorporating design patterns combine the advantage of having a high-abstraction level of describing a system and the possibility of coupling these abstractions to some underlying implementation. Still, all current tools are based on generating source code in which the design patterns become implicit. After that, further extension and adaptation of the software is needed but this can no longer be supported at the same level of abstraction. This paper presents FACE, an environment based on an explicit representation of design patterns, sustaining an incremental development style without abandoning the higher-level design pattern abstraction. A visual composition tool for FACE has been developed in the Self programming language.

Keywords. Frameworks, Design Patterns, Software composition, Visual Composition, Reflection

1 Introduction

Design patterns [4] are gaining more and more attention as a technique for supporting the development and maintenance of object-oriented applications and frameworks. As a result of this success tools are being developed that support software engineers thinking and working at the level of design patterns as well as mapping these abstractions to an underlying implementation. Tools providing such a high level of abstraction for representing and dealing with patterns have indeed been described or have even reached the market (see the "Related Work" section).

Currently these tools generate source code and possibly documentation from the higher-level design pattern abstraction. Although such an approach provides the basic

---

1. Baan Labs, Groot Zonneoord, PO Box 250, NL-6710 BG Ede, The Netherlands. *Tel:* +31 (318) 69.6685. *E-mail*: meijler@research.baan.nl.

2. Institut für Informatik (IAM), Universität Bern, Neubrückstrasse 10, CH-3012 Berne, Switzerland. *Tel:* +41 (31) 631.3314. *Fax:* +41 (31) 631.3965. *E-mail:* demeyer@iam.unibe.ch. *WWW:* http://iamwww.unibe.ch/~demeyer/

3. Department of Computer Science, Washington University, Campus Box 1045, St. Louis, MO 63130, USA. *Tel:* +1 (314) 935 8501. *E-mail:* engel@cs.wustl.edu. WWW: http://siesta.cs.wustl.edu/~engel.

facilities for the initial development phases (i.e., rapid prototyping via code generation and library support), it fails to adequately support an incremental style of programming necessary to build mature frameworks and corresponding applications. The reason is that editing source code — almost inevitable in such an incremental process — breaks the implicit link between the higher abstraction level within the tools and the lower level implementation within the source code. This implies that once the source-code is changed all such tools become useless since changes to the higher-level representation code generation would override the "hand-made" changes. We call this problem the design-implementation gap.

Here we present FACE (Framework Adaptive Composition Environment), an approach that bridges this design-implementation gap by supporting incremental development using frameworks at the abstraction level of design patterns.

A framework is a software artifact that is specifically directed at enabling, through reuse, the easy development of applications in a certain domain. Current object-oriented frameworks, however, are still hard to use for application development, due to their use of subclassing as a specialization mechanism. The developer of the application is expected to have (almost) the same expertise as the person(s) who implemented framework. He has to understand the framework (the superclasses) almost as well as the framework developer does. Moreover, the application developer also uses the same language and tools as the framework developer.

FACE is, in contrast to object-oriented frameworks, an environment where a framework is used, and an application is built, on the basis of an approach that we call "modeling = programming." Application development is a task clearly distinct from framework development. Building an application is done by building a model which is described in terms of modeling primitives that the framework developer has defined. The purpose of this is to let the application developer work at a higher level of abstraction, circumventing the use of subclassing, and preventing, as much as possible the need for coding.

Design patterns are normally seen as micro architectures, reusable pieces of design, that link often occurring problems to a "best-practice" design, where a corresponding implementation is suggested but not enforced. At best a framework is made up of a combination of such micro architectures. In the modeling = programming approach of FACE the level of abstraction of design patterns coincides with the modeling abstractions of the application developer. Thus design patterns provide him with understandable modeling primitives with a hidden — framework specific as we shall see — implementation. Modeling will be a matter of defining the roles and relationships of classes in pattern-specific terms. For example, in the abstract factory pattern (see section 2), a factory class must be specialized by specifying its creation operations and specifying which creation operation instantiates which product class.

The model that must be composed by the application developer will be referred to as a *schema*. It is in general made using four kinds of modeling primitives: 1) classes and the role they play in the pattern, 2) operations and the role they play in the pattern, 3) relationships between classes and/or operations which may be pattern specific, and

4) parameters. Specifying which creation operation instantiates which product class, as mentioned before, is an example of a pattern-specific relationship.

When creating such a schema the application developer is said to *instantiate* the pattern. This goes as follows: A so-called *primal schema* consists of a basic set of abstract classes and their relationships capturing the essence of the micro architecture. This primal schema is cloned to form the *kernel* of the schema. Next, the kernel is extended by defining concrete classes with associated roles and operations, creating corresponding relationships and specifying necessary parameters. Since this must be done correctly, this must conform to a kind of "syntax" of available modeling primitives and how they may be combined. The modeling syntax is furthermore coupled to a semantics such that the run time behavior indeed corresponds to what was intended, e.g., with respect to which operation instantiates which product. We note explicitly that in order to allow for sufficient flexibility we may need to be able to parameterize a schema with source code.

We illustrate the FACE modeling = programming approach in this paper for individual patterns. Since — as in "normal" object-oriented frameworks — the full framework may encompass several design patterns the specialization of the framework goes accordingly: The developer copies a full primal schema to create the kernel schema and extends it. This also includes "non-pattern" specific relationships and classes. We will not further treat this in this paper.

The patterns that are presented here must be seen as "mini-frameworks." The reason being that it is generally known that there is no such thing as a standard implementation for a pattern; it is always fitted to the specific usage. Thus, the realization presented here cannot be simply copied to fit any framework. This is true for primal schema modeling primitives as well as semantics. The patterns have been chosen from the "Design patterns" book design pattern catalogue [4], each having a non-trivial class structure and belonging to a different pattern category, namely the "AbstractFactory" and the "State" pattern.

Although we focus in this paper on explaining and illustrating the programming = modeling concept of FACE through design patterns, and thus basically introduce a framework technology/ methodology, FACE allows (and needs) to let the modeling of the application developer be actively supported by a tool. We shall shortly discuss a prototype implementation of such a tool.

The rest of this paper is organized as follows: In section 2 we give a short description of the Abstract Factory design pattern. In section 5 the same is done for the State design pattern. In section 3 we show an example instantiation of the Abstract Factory design pattern in the FACE approach; in section 6 the same is done for the State pattern. In section 4 we present a *definition* of the Abstract Factory pattern which consists of the *meta-schema* describing the modeling syntax and a primal-schema. In section 7, this is done for the State pattern. In section 8, we show how a run-time meaning is given to schemas that instantiate the State design pattern. In section 9 we discuss how the syntax rules as embodied in the meta-schema are used to support the application developer in creating a correct schema. In section 10 we discuss related work, in section 11 we give a conclusion and discuss future work.

97

2 Short Description of the Abstract Factory Design Pattern

The first example in this paper will be the Abstract Factory design pattern. We refer to
[4] for details. The Abstract Factory design pattern is used when client objects want to
create certain objects (e.g., window objects, scrollbar objects) but the instantiation of
these objects should not commit the client to choosing a specific implementation for
these objects (e.g., either Presentation Manager Window or Motif Window). The basic
idea of the pattern is to delegate the creation to a special factory object upon a client
request. By using polymorphism, the factory object's class determines how the factory
object reacts to a request for a certain object. E.g., when requested to create a window
a MotifWidgetFactory object will return a Motif window, a PMWidgetFactory a PM-
Window.

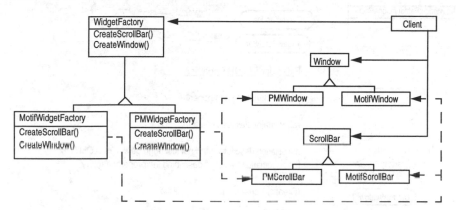

Figure 1. Illustration of the Abstract Factory pattern. We extend the OMT notation
with dashed lines to indicate the relationship between the widget factories and the
classes they relate. Note that this relationship will normally be hidden in the code.

3 Instantiating the Abstract Factory Design Pattern

In FACE, application development and adaptation is done at a higher level of abstraction than that of source code. It is done at the level of schema extension and editing. In
figure 2 we see a diagram of a schema representing a typical instantiation of the Abstract Factory design pattern, corresponding to the example in figure 1.

We first make some remarks about the notation. The concept of a schema in FACE
is related to the concept of a class-diagram in an object-oriented modeling technique
such as OMT, since it intends to show the classes (entities that are or may be instantiated
to run-time objects) and their relations. Thus, it is no surprise that the graphical notation
uses elements similar to those used in class-diagrams of OMT. Standard relationships
like subtyping (which is purely interface based sub-typing) and associations are used in
FACE schemas, and occur in the figure. However as mentioned in the introduction, the
schema for a specific pattern contains pattern specific relationships, in this case which

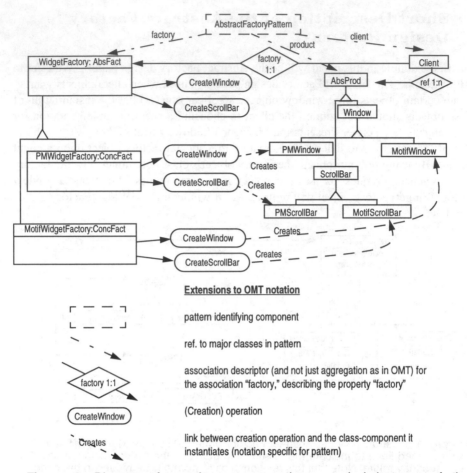

Figure 2. Diagram of a schema representing a typical instance of the AbstractFactory pattern, as corresponding to the example given in section 2.

operation instantiates which class. Such a modeling primitive falls outside the standard OMT modeling and thus has its own notation. Furthermore diamonds have a somewhat changed meaning: Diamonds do not automatically mean aggregation; they mean association. Some of the notational deviations are more conceptual and will be discussed below. We note explicitly that the diagram is meant to describe how a design pattern instantiation can be modeled in FACE. Such a notation might also be used by a corresponding tool, but this is currently not the case.

Before we go into detail regarding the elements and structure of such a schema, we need some special terminology. In general we shall speak of the components of the schema. We shall use the term "class-component"; one of the reasons for this terminology is that, for the application developers, classes in the schema are really black-box components that can only be specialized by means of parameters[1] and relationships. We now list some relevant aspects.

The first relevant aspect is the use of a separate component indicating that the Abstract Factory component has been used. It is also a container since it refers, using references named after the role that they play, to the most important abstract classes of the pattern. The class "AbsProd" in a sense plays a similar role: It is a container for the abstract product classes such as "Window" and "Scrollbar"; this will be used in the copying of the primal schema see section 4.

Secondly, the operations that form the heart of the pattern are promoted into explicit components of the schema, in this case the "create..." operations.

Thirdly, relationships are made explicit that have a context specific run-time meaning. In this case the operation "createWindow" of the class-component "MotifWidgetFactory" has an "instantiates" relationship with the class-component "MotifWindow," indicating that this operation will create instances of that class.

Fourthly, class-components are typed as corresponding to the role they play in the pattern: For example, the class-components "MotifWidgetFactory" and "PMWidgetFactory" are both of the type "ConcFact" (Concrete Factory). This means that they are specialized in a specific way, namely in this case with the set of operations and per operation the link to the class-component that it creates and that this specialization has the corresponding run-time meaning (see section 8).

Finally, we made the association descriptor (as indicated using a diamond in the figure) as a separate independent schema component. One of the parameters of an association descriptor is whether the association is an ownership (and thus aggregation) or otherwise a reference. There are various both conceptual and FACE-implementation technical reasons for this which we will not further discuss.

We stress again that the schema makes only aspects explicit that are relevant: operations of the product classes that do not play a role in this pattern are not shown; internal structure is hidden, since it is of no relevance to the application developer. We thus require that product classes be implemented beforehand, either coming "ready made" with the framework or implemented in a separate coding phase of components.

In section 4, we show how we can define a meta-schema, what kind of elements (what kind of classes, what kind of relationships) a schema may have, and how these may be combined.

4 Framework Specific Definition of the Abstract Factory Pattern

In section 3 we saw that pattern specific class-components were used, and pattern specific relationships (e.g., "creates") between these to form a schema. However, not all combinations of relationships and class-components lead to a correct "well-formed" schema. For example, the "creates" relationship must be made from a create operation to a concrete product class-component, and not to any other kind of class-component. In general, each pattern usage in a framework comes with a specific set of class-com-

---

1. Not shown in this example, parameters may also be procedures, thus allowing, where necessary, for greater flexibility.

ponents and relationships and with rules how these may be combined. This must be expressed in a so-called "meta-schema" to allow FACE to adapt to a specific framework with specific patterns. The meta-schema thus expresses the "modeling syntax" of the schema and will be discussed below. In section 9 we shall see how such a meta-schema may be used to support the application developer in creating a correct schema.

Just as an application developer using standard ("classical") source code level application development starts from the set of abstract classes, the application developer in FACE does not start from scratch, but starts from a kernel schema, a schema that only contains the identifying component and the abstract class-components and their relationships, and adds concrete class-components and their relationships to this kernel. Therefore, a pattern definition not only encompasses the meta-schema (that defines how the kernel schema may be extended), but also a template for the kernel schema. This template is called the "primal schema." These two together are represented together in figure 3.

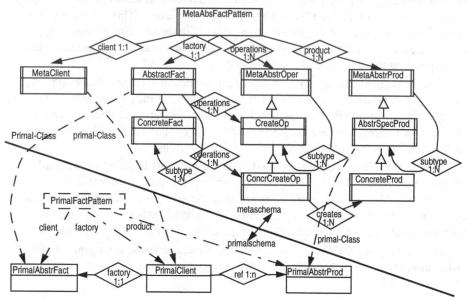

Figure 3. Abstract factory pattern definition as consisting of the meta-schema, and the primal-schema. The two are separated by a slash. Metaclass-components are indicated with double lines at the sides. These define classes of class-components, e.g., all Concrete Widget class components in figure 5 are instance of "ConcreteFact." Association descriptors are again indicated by diamonds. Dashed lines are used to link a metaclass-component to its primal class-component.

The figure illustrates that the syntax rules themselves are also embodied as a schema, the "meta-schema." This allows for the similar treatment of schemas and metaschemas by tools (see section 9). The class-components in this meta-schema are called metaclass-components, the reason being that instances of a metaclass-component are class-components. The structural relationship between a metaclass-component and its instances is the same as between a class-component and its instances (see section 3). Thus, a meta-class component defines the existence and possible use of a certain type of special purpose class-components. In figure 3, for example, "ConcreteFact" defines the type of those class-components that correspond to factory objects. These class-components have "ConcFact" written behind their name in figure 2.

Most of the relationships between metaclass-components is via association descriptors as these were also described in section 3. These describe what kinds of structures are allowed in the schema. For instance the "creates" association descriptor between "ConcrCreateOp" and "ConcreteProd" describes that an operation such as "CreateWindow" has an explicit reference to the class-component that will be created by this operation (which must be a concrete product class-component). Through the "operations" association descriptor between "AbstractFact" and "CreateOp" is stated that Factories have these special kind of "creating" operations.

In figure 3 we also see the primal schema. This schema is copied, and used as the kernel for the rest of the schema development when the application developer instantiates "MetaAbsFactPattern." In order to make the primal schema relatively general, "PrimalClient" is given an association with "PrimalAbstrProd" so that the Client object may refer to any kind of product.

5 Short Description of the State Design Pattern

The next example in this paper will be the State design pattern. We refer to [4] for details. The state design pattern is used when an object has to exhibit state dependent behavior, that is, dependent on its state the object reacts differently to the same requests for operation execution. The solution the pattern offers is illustrated in figure 4 for an object p that has to implement the "TCP" network protocol. The object delegates requests that have to be handled state dependently to another object (the state object). It changes state by exchanging that object.

The TCP network protocol implementation that is an example of the use of the state pattern is taken from [5]. The solution is somewhat different from the standard solution [4] in that, instead of the context object (here called a "protocol" object) directly reacting to messages, and delegating these to its state object, there will be a request object[1] that represents the operation to be executed. The protocol handles the request by giving it a reference to the state object and sending it the message "apply." The request then sends the corresponding message to the state object. In this way the protocol class can be generally applied in any use of the pattern, independent of what kind of operation requests may need to be handled.

6 Instantiating the State Design Pattern

In figure 5 a schema for a particular instantiation of the state design pattern is represented. This diagram is again close to a class-diagram, as in the example for the Abstract-Factory pattern (figure 2), it contains much more pattern specific information, so that it

---

1. In [5] this is called a messenger object. We follow however the general terminology in [4].

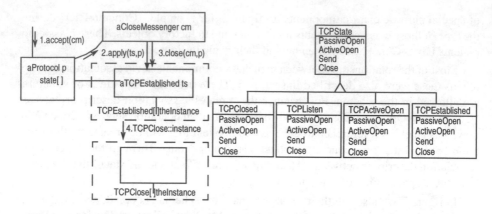

Figure 4. Solution to implementing the state design pattern as used by Hueni et.al.[5]. Left: An object p refers in its property "state" to one of the state objects. Each of these state objects is a "singleton" instance of the classes given at the right side. The figure shows a typical sequence of messages. The class hierarchy at the right side shows that each state object is an instance of the abstract class TCPState, which defines the basic messages that can be sent in each state. Each of the subclasses specifically defines the behavior of the object for each of these states for each of these commands. A fully implemented protocol needs more states. Only subclasses are shown for states needed to establish a connection and for the closed state. Note that we shall call "messengers" as used in [5] "requests" in the text.

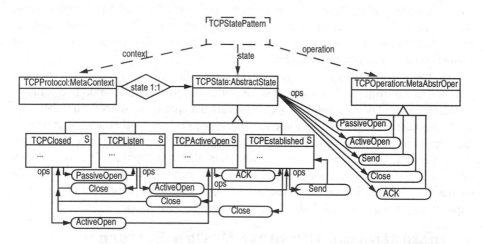

Figure 5. Diagram representing a schema that instantiates the state design pattern. In this case a realization of the TCP Protocol modeled in state pattern specific terms. The rectangles with a line in them are class-components. Class-components labelled with "S" represent concrete States. Ovals are again operations. The ones used to link two concrete state class-components are also called "transition descriptors." An arrows that links two concrete state class-components via a transition descriptor represents: when the operation named in the descriptor is applied to an instance of that class-component, the next state will be the one which the arrow points to.

describes in sufficient detail what the run-time system should do. Particularly, the enrichment encompasses:

- The use of framework (pattern) specific component types in the schema: for example all the concrete class-components that represent a state are of the type "ConcreteState." This corresponds to a generic implementation. Another example are the transition descriptors like "Close," "Send" that describe the links between the ConcreteState class-components.

- The use of framework (pattern) specific relationships between components of the schema: In particular, the links between ConcreteState class-components (as qualified by the transition descriptor) represent corresponding state transitions. The name of the transition descriptor corresponds to the operation that invokes this transition

- The transition descriptor may be parameterized with extra information that describes what else should happen in a state transition. Two such parameters are pre- and post- transition procedures, e.g. used for measuring response times. This is not shown.

- A pattern specific identifying component "TCPStatePattern" identifies the fact that the pattern is used; it is a container in the sense that it refers to all the major (abstract) class-components that play a role in the pattern.

As in figure 2, association descriptors are used here. For instance, the association descriptor between TCPProtocol and TCPState, describes that instances of TCPProtocol contain a reference to a state object. The association descriptor is thus a general component that can be used in any schema.

7 Framework-specific Definition of the State Pattern

Figure 6 illustrates how the state pattern may be defined as a meta-schema and linked to that a primal schema. Again the meta-schema embodies the rules for correctly creating schemas for this pattern and the primal schema defines the basic abstract class-structure that the application developer will use to extend. This primal schema is copied as a whole when the application developer instantiates the "MetaStatePattern."

We note again:

- In the meta-schema metaclass-components specify what kind of class-components may occur, e.g., all the concrete State classes such as "TCPClosed," "TCPListen" etc. are instances of ConcreteState, all transition descriptors are instance of "MetaTransDescr." Association descriptors specify what kind of relationships these components may have, e.g., the association descriptor "operations" of ConcreteState describes that a ConcreteState class-components can have operations of the type "MetaTransDescr," i.e., transition descriptors.

- Through the correspondence between meta-class components and primal classes, the correspondence between the meta-schema and the primal schema is made. In general, when the developer instantiates a metaclass-component, the resulting class-component is a copy of the primal-class of the metaclass-component. For

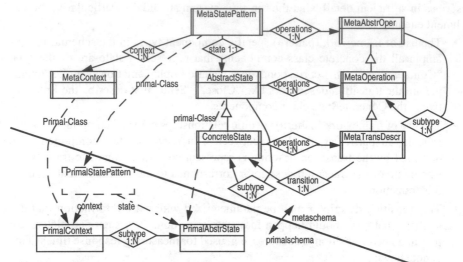

Figure 6. Meta-component structure for the state composition pattern. Metaclass-components are indicated with double lines at the sides. Association descriptors are again indicated by diamonds. See further the text and the explanation of figure 5 Note that since "MetaTransDescr" is a subtype of "MetaOperation," transition descriptors, which are instances of MetaTransDescr are really operation descriptors.

MetaStatePattern, the whole structure consisting of PrimalStatePattern, Primal-Context and PrimalState is copied, since PrimalContext and PrimalState are structurally contained by PrimalStatePattern.

8 Realizing the Run-Time Meaning of the Class-Composition.

The idea of using schemas to describe applications has been described so far in an implementation independent way. One of the major questions is how the parameterization and linking of class-components and relationship components may lead to the corresponding run-time behaviour of the objects, and how we would allow such a correspondence to be easily (or as easy as possible) set up by the framework developer.

Basically two approaches are possible: a compiled approach in which "real" classes in standard object-oriented technology are generated from a schema or an interpreted approach in which the schema is represented explicitly (or "reified") at run-time and the run-time software adapts its behavior to this information. Due to a greater simplicity and run-time configurability we have currently only applied the second approach. The first approach leads to more efficient execution, but this has not been a major concern so far.

In the second approach the schema is represented explicitly at run-time as objects that represent the class-components and relationships. This is quite natural, since the schema will normally be created interactively as an object structure by the application developer anyway. The class-components are thus run-time represented as objects but they function as classes, in the sense that they can be requested for instances. When requested for instances, they will return an instance object (either by copying a prototype that they carry or by calling a constructor). The instance objects will have a generic implementation, implemented in the underlying object-oriented language[1]. The implementation is generic in the sense that these instance objects will query the objects in the schema to adapt their behaviour to the parameters. Such a query will be called an "upcall." The class-component in its role of run-time accessible object thus implements behaviour to answer these queries.

We describe in further detail how the state class-components and their linking via transition descriptors determine the behaviour of the corresponding instances at runtime (figure 7).

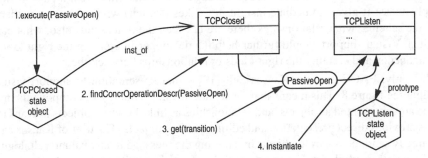

Figure 7. Object interaction for making a state object execute a transition diagram: The state object does an up-call to its class-component, in this case to "TCPClosed." "TCPClosed" finds the concrete operation descriptor for "PassiveOpen." The state object retrieves the information from this object, especially the reference to the next class-component, being "TCPListen." The state object asks it for instantiation. "TCPListen" returns its prototype. This instance is returned to the calling protocol object.

Assume that the TCP-Protocol object p refers through its state property to an instance of the state class-component "TCPClosed" and it has to handle a request that is an instance of "PassiveOpen." The default behaviour of the protocol object is (as described in section 2), to send the message "apply" to the request, together with a reference to the state object. As a result (this is shown in figure 7) the request will send the message "execute" to the state object, with the name "PassiveOpen" as a parameter. The state object will query its class-component "TCPClosed" for the transition descriptor using the upcall message "findConcrOperationDescr." TCPClosed will return the transition descriptor. This descriptor is queried for its parameters. The object will query the transition descriptor for the transition target. It will return a reference to the class-component "TCPListen." The state object will ask "TCPListen" for an instance ("TCPListen" has only one instance). This instance will be returned to the protocol object, that will change the value of its "state" property to refer to this other state object.

---

1. This underlying language can be anything: so far, implementations have been done in Self and C++.

9 Using a Meta-schema to Drive the Visual Composition Environment

So far we have shown through examples how a schema contains information for modeling a pattern in pattern specific terms, and how a meta-schema contains the modeling syntax for this. A FACE editing tool can actively support the application developer in modeling schemas correctly. Such a tool can be generic since it will be driven by the meta-schema.

It was suggested in section 1, and it is only natural, that the application developer should have *visual* support in creating and editing the schema. This strengthens the idea of explicitness: It gives immediate insight in (makes explicit) what components there are in the schema, what relationships there are between them, and thus also, what can be edited. Visual support should further help the developer in creating the right kinds of components, and creating the right kinds of relationships between them.

Currently, FACE uses the Kansas-Self [19] visual presentation to support visual modeling see figure 8. This means that (as mentioned in section 8) all components in a schema are represented as objects, and relationships as links between objects in Kansas. Kansas provides direct presentation and editing of these objects. The user of Kansas can also directly send messages to objects by entering the message in an evaluator dialogue box of the presented object. For example, the user can instantiate a meta-class component by directly sending the message "instantiate" to the object that represents it. To support meta-schema driven modeling only those meta-class components that need to be instantiated are presented, other information in the meta-schema is not shown. Relations between class-components are created by first using Kansas support to create a link between the objects that present those, and then sending a message to an object that represents the link to create the relationship; in doing so, a test will be made on basis of the meta-schema if the relationship is correct, otherwise it will be denied.

One could say that this is the "poor-man's solution" of visual support; there are no "tailor made" presentations for schemas such as the ones shown in the figures in this paper, and the developer is not helped in performing a certain sequence of actions. We admit this but on the other hand we assert that it provides a proof of concept as it contains all the elements presented in this paper. Creating instances of a class or meta-class component, corresponds to copying the prototype it carries as described in section 8, which is again natural in Self. Using the schemas to determine run-time behaviour following the principle described in section 8 is no problem in the Kansas environment. Furthermore we assert that fancier presentations will not change the principle of supporting the developer in creating the correct components and relationships.

The principle of checking relationships that the developer attempts to create on the basis of the meta-schema is as follows: The system is implemented in such a way that for an attempted relationship (e.g., "creates" between the "CreateWindow" operation of "PMWidgetFactory" and the "PMWindow" product class in figure 2) the corresponding association descriptor can be found (in this case the "creates" association descriptor as presented in figure 3). This association descriptor is queried by the method that checks the attempt. A check is made whether the target of the link is an instance of the

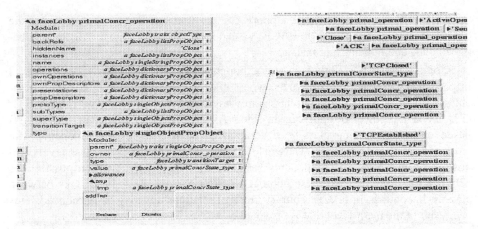

Figure 8. Snapshot of FACE Class-composition as made available through Kansas: Each class-component is represented by an object. Each property, e.g., "transitionTarget" (corresponding to the "transition" property described in figure 6) is itself represented by an object. Linking the tmp attribute of that object to another object corresponds to "attempting" to make the link between the owner of the property object and the other object, in this case the link is attempted between a concrete operation component for the transition 'Close' for the "transitionTarget" property to a concrete state class-component, namely the one that represents TCPClosed. By requesting evaluation of "addTmp" (push the "Evaluate" button) the composition will be made if it is a correct link, as is the case here.

meta-class component that the association descriptor points to or of one of its subtypes. If this check returns true, the attempt succeeds. In this example, "PMWindow" is an instance of "ConcreteProd," so the attempt succeeds.

10 Related work

The idea of actively supporting design patterns is finding its way into CASE tools. A first commercial product supporting patterns is Objectif [12]. A more experimental approach is described by Pagel & Winter [15]. These kinds of tools focus on helping the framework designer: patterns are mainly used to support the design of the framework architecture. Code can be generated, but this is not the main goal of these tools.

Closer to our work is work is work described by Soukop [19] and Sommerlad, et.al. [17], which supports application developers. Basically these tools provide quite extensive code generation. In the case of Soukop, it is quite clear that the developer has to further adapt the classes after code has been generated and that thus the link between the higher abstraction (which are basically only macros) and the code will further be lost (this was called the design-implementation gap problem in the introduction). In the work of Sommerlad et.al, it is not clear whether the higher abstraction level allows for adding code, and thus precludes having to change generated code. We assume that they have the same design -implementation problem. They certainly have the problem that creating framework-specific support is a heavy burden on the framework developer. In FACE, no tool extension or adaptation is needed: only the adaptation or extension of meta-schemas.

Vista [11] is a visual tool that supports composition, and that can be adapted to the composition rules. In contrast to FACE, Vista does not support a precise distinction between class components and instances.

Composition at the level of classes (although not visually supported) is encountered in particular in "generic" constructs, where classes can be parameterized with other classes, such as in the template classes in C++. The Standard Template Library STL [13] shows the power of applying this idea. Also the work of Batory et. al. [1][2] is based on parameterizing class-level components with class-level components. The work of McGee and Kramer on Darwin [10] represents another form of class-level composition: Links between components basically describe communication possibilities between the instances. All these approaches offer a fixed meaning to links between classes. In contrast, in FACE arbitrary kinds of relationships may be introduced. This is a result of the meta-level that is provided.

In this respect, our work has roots in the area of open programming languages such as CLOS[6], and in Open Implementations[16]. Open programming languages such as CLOS reify their software components (classes), but the reification is not "black-box" the reification is quite complex, and it is difficult to create "drastically" different components because of the intricate cooperation between all parts of the reified class.

The way in which we use reification and reflection is close to the model of Klas and Neuhold [7]. Their model also allows one to introduce new kinds of relationships. They focus on adaptive data models for databases systems, less on frameworks and application development. We feel that our model is simpler and therefore easier to understand and use.

Steyaert et. al. [20] have described how the use of a meta-level interface could be applied to provide powerful configuration capabilities for user interface builders. Also, using reflection, new kinds of components could be described using the composition environment itself. However, the way in which they open up the framework and corresponding visual composition seems to be restricted: They do not describe mechanisms for introducing new component cooperation forms in the framework.

The work of Lieberherr et. al.[8][9] on adaptive programming also shows how useful it is to have programs that adapt to the class-structure. They focus on adaptiveness of traversal operations. We think that our approach is broader. It may also cover traversal adaptiveness (but we still have to prove that), although it is, of course, not as well "tuned" for that.

11 Conclusion and Further work

In most software development environments, there is a gap between the design level, where new CASE tools may let the designer represent the system in terms of design patterns, and the implementation level, where the developer works at the level of source code. In working at the implementation level the connection with the higher-level concepts is either implicit or only available in terms of documentation, so that adapting and extending a system in agreement with the chosen design patterns is not actively supported. We call this problem the design-implementation gap. We have shown in this paper how to represent software as a "model" at the high-level abstraction of design patterns, while still capturing enough information for running the application. We have thus presented a "modeling = programming" approach. Basically, the model (called a "schema") makes explicit all the information that the application developer may want to see and/or change. Such information is normally implicit in source code, such as the roles of classes and relation between the classes. All other implementation information remains implicit. Furthermore we have shown that a visual composition tool, for which FACE currently implements a simple solution, can help the developer to create and adapt these models correctly according to the pattern specific syntax rules.

By illustrating such a modeling = programming approach for design patterns, we imply that the same approach will carry over to full frameworks consisting of several patterns and other components and relationships. Still, how this would work is outside the scope of this paper. We stress furthermore that we have focussed on raising the abstraction level to the level of design patterns, not on making instantiations of design patterns into modeling "molecules" that can be reused blindly in any framework. The reason is that each framework applies design patterns in a specific way.

FACE is a framework adaptive "environment." It can be adapted to different frameworks and in more restrained sense to the patterns in the framework by means of a meta-schema and generic software that implements the semantics of a schema. We have shown how this may be done. It is our hypothesis that due to this technology the gain of simpler application development is not lost by the effort setting up and adapting such a "modeling = programming" framework and that this approach will thus be an attractive alternative to "standard" object-oriented framework technology. This still needs to be proven.

Future work will be in two directions:

- Using FACE for re-engineering purposes [19]: discovering patterns, anti-patterns, the relationships between classes etc. and representing this in FACE schemas; afterwards, improve system design by applying restructuring transformations based on design patterns.
- Applying FACE to real world frameworks. Interesting questions will be, how complex meta-schemas will become. We want to investigate whether we can uncouple patterns (similar as described by Soukop [19]) so that the reuse and merging of patterns will be easy.

Acknowledgements

We thank Dirk Riehle for his first reviews; Tamar Richner, Robb Nebbe, Oscar Nierstrasz and many others for their helpful comments and corrections. This work has been carried out at the Software Composition Group, University of Berne, and funded by the Swiss National Science Foundation under Project no. 2000-46947.96.

References

[1]   Don Batory and Sean O'Malley, "The Design and Implementation of Hierarchical Software Systems With Reusable Components," *ACM Transactions on Software Engineering and Methodology*, October 1992.

[2]   Don Batory, Vivek Singhal, Jeff Thomas, Sankar Dasari, Bart Geraci and Marty Sirkin, "The GenVoca Model of Software-System Generators," *IEEE Software*, Sept. 1994, pp. 89-94.

[3]   Serge Demeyer, Stéphane Ducasse, Robb Nebbe, Oscar Nierstrasz and Tamar Richner, "Using Restructuring Transformations to Reengineer Object-Oriented Systems," Submitted to WCRE'97. Available from the SCG-website (http://iamwww.unibe.ch/~famoos/).

[4]   Erich Gamma, Richard Helm, Ralph Johnson and John Vlissides, *Design Patterns*, Addison Wesley, Reading, MA, 1995.

[5]   Hermann Hueni, Ralph E. Johnson and Robert Engel, "A Framework for Network Protocol Software," *Proceedings OOPSLA'95, ACM SIGPLAN Notices*, to appear.

[6]   Gregor Kiczales, Jim des Rivières and Daniel G. Bobrow, *The Art of the Metaobject Protocol*, MIT Press (Ed.), 1991.

[7]   Wolfgang Klas, E.J. Neuhold and Michael Schrefl, "Metaclasses in VODAK and their Application in Database Integration," *Arbeitpapiere der GMD*, no. 462, 1990.

[8]   Christina V. Lopes, Karl J. Lieberherr, "AP/S++: Case-Study of a MOP for Purposes of Software Evolution," *Proceedings Reflection '96*, to appear.

[9]   Karl J. Lieberherr, Ignacio Silva-Lepe, Cun Xiao, "Adaptive object-oriented programming using graph-based customization," Commun *of the ACM*, Vol 37, no. 5, May 1993, pp 94-101.

[10]   Jeff Magee, Naranker Dulay and Jeffrey Kramer, "Structuring Parallel and Distributed Programs," *Proceedings of the International Workshop on Configurable Distributed Systems*, London, March 1992.

[11]   Vicki de Mey, "Visual Composition of Software Applications," *in [14]*, pp. 275-303.

[12]   Microtool homepage: http://www.microtool.de/

[13]   David R. Musser and Atul Saini, *STL Tutorial and Reference Guide*, Addison-Wesley, 1996.

[14]   Oscar Nierstrasz and Dennis Tsichritzis (Ed.), *Object-Oriented Software Composition*, Prentice Hall, 1995.

[15]   Bernd-Uwe Pagel, Mario Winter, "Towards Pattern-Based Tools," *EuroPLoP Preliminary Conference Proceedings*, July 1996

[16]   Ramana Rao, "Implementational Reflection in Silica," *Proceedings ECOOP '91*, P. America (Ed.), LNCS 512, Springer-Verlag, Geneva, Switzerland, July 15-19, 1991, pp. 251-267.

[17]   Albert Schappert, Peter Sommerlad and Wolfgang Pree, "Automated Support for Software Development with Frameworks," *Proceedings SSR'95 ACM SIGSOFT Symposium on Software Reusability*, 1995.

[18]   Randall B. Smith and David Ungar, "Programming as an Experience: The Inspiration for Self," *Proceedings ECOOP'95*, W. Olthoff (Ed.), LNCS 952, Springer-Verlag, Aarhus, Denmark, August 1995, pp. 303-330.

[19]   Jiri Soukop, "Implementing Patterns," *Pattern Languages of Program Design*, Addison Wesley 1995, Chapter 20.

[20]   Patrick Steyaert, K. De Hondt, S. Demeyer, N. Boyen and M. de Molder, "Reflective User Interface Builders," *Proceedings Meta'95*, C. Zimmerman (Ed.), 1995.

TTM15 - A Large Multi-site Improvement Project

Graham Allen, Leighton Davies, Göran Lindmark
Ericsson Telecom AB
Tellusborgsvägen 83-87
S-126 25 Stockholm
Sweden
+46-8-7190000
etxt.etx{grah,davs,lima}@memo.ericsson.se

Even-André Karlsson
Q-Labs AB
Ideon Research Park
S-223 70 Lund
Sweden
+46-46-182999
Even-Andre.Karlsson@q-labs.se

Abstract

Ericsson is committed to provide world class products to it's customers. As our products are more and more dependent on software we have taken on a corporate goal to build a world class software organisation. This has lead to several local and global improvement initiatives. In this article we describe one of the improvement projects, TTM15 within Ericsson's business unit for fixed telecommunication networks. What is unique with this project is the size and distribution of the target organisation. This has given many organisational challenges, but also opportunities in synergy effects, peer networks and learning from each other. This article describes the goals, organisation, content experiences and current status of the project.

Keywords

Process improvement, incremental development, team work, reviews, process adherence, GQM, CMM

1. Introduction

"Today a large part of Ericsson's profits and development costs emanate from software. It is very important to Ericsson to build a world-class software organisation"—Lars Ramqvist, CEO of the Ericsson group.

This challenge has been picked up all over Ericsson, and many corporate and local improvement initiatives are ongoing, e.g. policy deployment and CMM [1, 2], and local improvement work piloted in smaller projects, e.g. [3,4]. This has also lead Ericsson to set up very high quality goals, i.e. a 50% reduction in the number of customer reported faults each year. When we realise the current quality of telecommunication software, e.g. availability, these are goals that only a world-class software organisation can achieve. The TTM15 (Time To Market 15 months) improvement project is one major initiative within Ericsson's business unit for fixed telecommunication networks, BUX, to meet this challenge.

The goals which the TTM15 improvement project should support were:

- Lead-time: 15 months from Toll Gate 1 (frozen requirements) to Toll Gate 4 (delivered to first customer).
- Quality: 0.1 faults pr. KNCSS (1000 non commented source statements) during the first 6 months in operation.
- Size: All projects should be less than 500.000 man hours.
- Frequency: Each product line shall have a new release every 6-9 months.

These goals were valid for all development projects starting in 1996. This was the situation which faced the TTM15 improvement project in the middle of 1995. Thus the purpose of the TTM15 project was to

- Select, prepare and support a set of process improvements that could help the involved organisations and development projects to reach the TTM15 goals.

To fully understand the organisation of the TTM15 project we need to look at the situation for the target organisation, BUX.

BUX is responsible for developing the AXE 10 applications for fixed telecommunication networks, i.e. the large local and transit exchanges. BUX is operating in the following environment:

- Software development projects in BUX are distributed, with design spread over 20 local design centres (LDC's) in 4 continents. This is a strategic advantage for Ericsson having core technical competence close to the customer.
- Standard software projects in BUX are large, not unusually in the range of 1 million man-hours.
- BUX's customers also need local adaptations of the standard software to accommodate national standards and features. Thus the standard version developed is adapted by marked projects.
- The LDC's involved in the development have a large amount of autonomy, e.g. software quality responsibility and market authority.

The status within BUX development at the start of the TTM15 project can be summarised as follows:

- Many local design centres have very good software development practices in different areas, but we need to speed up the transfer of practices between the local design centres.
- A joint effort between the large development projects and local improvement initiatives is necessary to give the full effect.

The most unique aspect of the TTM15 project compared to other improvement project is the distribution, i.e. how we speed up the transfer of best practices between LDC's through competence teams and in co-operation with large target projects.

The rest of this article is organised as follows:

- Section 2 describes the organisation and process of the TTM15 project. The TTM15 project was set up to support the development and implementation of a set of improvements in this distributed organisation.
- Section 3 describes each of the improvement areas. These improvement areas were selected to support the target projects and involved LDC's to reach their quality and lead time goals.
- In section 4 we discuss the measurement program used to evaluate the effect of these improvements on the project goals.
- Section 5 contains an evaluation of the results/ current status and some discussion on the experiences from the organisation of TTM15.
- Section 6 concludes the article and points out directions for future improvements within BUX.

2. Process and Organisation

In this section we discuss the process and organisation that we have used in the TTM15 project. It is organised onto three parts:

- Design criteria giving the rationales behind the process and organisation.
- Organisation and process describing the initiation, preparation, support, and completion phases of the TTM15 project.
- Local activities and financing are discussed at the end.

2.1 Design Criteria

The following design criteria were used when we initiated and planned the TTM15 project:

- Involvement of LDC's and target projects. The LDC's and target projects needed to be involved throughout the selection and preparation to ensure the local commitment to take on the improvements.
- Balance between centralised and decentralised. There needed to be a balance between work done centrally and what is done locally. The advantage of gathering competence centrally was the synergy effect and competence network, but these people need always to be in touch with the local needs.
- Synergy with local improvement initiatives. The improvements could not be taken out of the blue, we needed to build on best practices which had worked in other smaller environments, and build on local initiatives.
- Timing with target projects. The preparation and support of the improvements had to be just in time for the target projects. Too early and there would be no receiver and too late and they couldn't change anything.
- Incremental preparation of implementation. The preparation of the material to support the improvements had to be done incrementally with effective feedback mechanisms from the LDC's and development projects to adjust to their needs.
- Involvement of experts and standard process owners. BUX is working in an environment with Ericsson standardised development and project management processes. We need to involve the standard process owners in our improvements, so that work done was in line with these processes, and that improvements could easily be transferred into the standard processes.

In summary we worked with the philosophy that improvements had to involve the entire organisation. Thus as well as a demand for improvements from BUX management there had also to be a push for improvements from practitioners (developers and local project management, both technical and administrative), where they could contribute so that their ideas and best practices were taken into account and used.

2.2 Organization and Process

This section describes the initiation, preparation, support and conclusion phases of the TTM15 project.

Initiation

The project was initiated in the spring of 1995. A three day TTM workshop was planned for September, and an invitation to send 2-3 key practitioners was given to the 20 LDC involved in the next major BUX project.

In the invitation the LDC's were recommended to prepare before coming to the workshop. This preparation consisted of an analysis of the current strengths and problems, i.e. what was keeping the LDC back from reaching their full potential in major projects, and proposals for possible improvements to reach this potential. This input was then brought by the LDC representatives into the workshop.

The TTM workshop was run by a trained facilitator with about 55 participants. The purpose was to reach agreement on some key problems that needed to be addressed. As output, 3-8 possible process improvements as solutions to these key problems were expected. We ended up with the following five improvement areas which are described in section 3:

- Team work
- Reviews and inspections
- Incremental development
- Methods, tools and training
- Customer focus and project information

Based on the output from the workshop requirements specifications for each of the selected improvement areas were written. Best practices from both within and outside Ericsson related to these improvement areas were collected. With this compiled material the LDC's were visited to ensure commitment for the improvements, present the overall plan, and recruit persons to work with preparation, implementation and support of the improvement areas.

Preparation

The preparation phase of the project started with a TTM15 kick-off in December 1995 where all candidates for working with the improvement areas were invited. The purpose was to form "competence teams" around each of the improvement areas. These teams would consist of representatives from LDC's with experiences within the improvement area, relevant standard process owners and process improvement experts. Each team consisted of 4-6 persons. This set up is shown in the left part of the figure. (Props is Ericsson's project management process and Medax is the AXE 10 development process.)

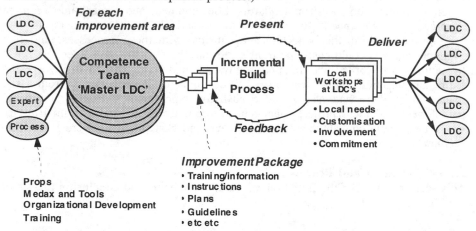

Each team then took on the preparation of an improvement package to satisfy the requirement specification from the workshop. The team members worked about 40-80% of their time with TTM15 during the preparation phase. The rest of the time they spent on local activities at their LDC. The TTM15 work was divided between the following types of activities:

- Competence team work, either individually or in the team. Each team decided on an LDC where to hold the meetings. This ensured that the project remained decentralised and that we were able to work closely with the LDC's with best practices.
- 3 "common workshops" where we brought all the teams together to present and discuss each others work. This was important to keep the material consistent, and also for everyone to be aware of what was going on in the other teams. As each team member also was regarded as an ambassador for the

entire TTM15 project, it was important to ensure this knowledge. In the composition of the teams we also tried as far as possible to get people from all LDC's involved in some team.
- Local workshops at the LDC's where the material was presented and discussed to ensure that local needs were taken into account as well as involvement and commitment to take on the improvement package. Two of these workshops were held, one mainly to present the planned and draft material, and the second was used to give more in depth training and preparation for the target project participants. The first of these local workshops was done by a cross functional team of one person per improvement area. This also ensured the communication across teams.

The specific support package developed by each team will be discussed under the improvement areas in section 3.

Support
During execution we mainly used two types of support activities:
- Visits to the LDC's by the competence team members to support the local implementation.
- Experience exchange meetings where we gathered the local responsible for one improvement area to exchange experiences and strengthen their network.

In addition to these team specific activities we had common workshops to evaluate and compare the progress for the whole TTM15 project. These events were also used to analyse the measurements (see section 4).

Completion
The TTM15 project finished by the end of 1996, completing the active support to the LDC's of the new techniques. The material and training were transferred to permanent line organisations. Some of the LDC's (The Netherlands for incremental development, United Kingdom for review, inspections and Finland for team work, and the line organisation for process support to projects in Sweden for Methods, Tools and Training) have taken on a "master" role within the BUX organisation being responsible for the further development and spreading of their improvement area. Each competence team was responsible for identifying the proper maintainer of what they had produced, and ensure that they took on this responsibility.

A small amount of effort was also allocated to do the final analysis of the measurements as the main target projects for TTM15 reach completion during 1997, and have been six months in operation during 1998.

Local activities and financing
We worked throughout TTM15 to involved the LDC's actively. This was achieved in several ways:
- The improvement areas were generated by the LDC's themselves.
- The improvements were implemented by people from the LDC's.
- We visited the LDC's repeatedly to ensure that we met their needs.
- A responsible for each improvement area was appointed at each LDC.
- Each person within each competence team was responsible for 3-4 LDC's which they visited and followed up concerning their improvement area.
- Each competence team prepared a recommended local implementation plan for their area which helped the responsible at the LDC to implement the

improvements. Local adaptations of this plan was supported by the competence team member.

- CMM like capabilities were produced for each of the improvement areas which the LDC's used to check their implementation.

Thus TTM15 consisted of activities on four different levels:

- The TTM15 project where we had the overall schedule and common workshops etc.
- Competence team activities which produced the improvement package including promoting and supporting this at the LDC's.
- LDC level which was responsible for implementing the improvements with support of their dedicated competence team member.
- Development project level where these improvements were put into use.

Financing of the TTM15 project was divided into 3 parts, based on the levels above; the first two levels were financed by BUX centrally, the third level was financed by the LDC's own improvement budget, and the last was financed by the development projects. We think that this division of cost was important, as our experience is that you put much higher requirements on something you pay for than something you get for free or is paid to do.

The schedule for TTM15 was so that we were about 2-3 months ahead of our main target project. This allowed us to have the material ready, but still be so close in time that we addressed the people really involved in the target project.

3 Improvement Areas

This section gives a short overview of the improvement areas that were developed in TTM15. The five areas selected at the TTM workshop in September 1995 were:

- Team work
- Reviews and inspections
- Incremental development
- Methods, tools and training
- Customer focus and project information

All these areas had given considerable improvements in other parts of Ericsson, so they were well tried. We tried to reuse as much as possible of the existing material, adapting and extending it to the needs of BUX. Note that the major content of these improvements were not so much technical, but rather organisational. We were quite convinced that we had not reached the limit for what we can achieve within the current development environment, thus substantial improvements could result from how we organise the work and enforcing already good practices.

In addition to the five improvement areas above, we also decided to implement a measurement program. This is further described in section 4.

In the rest of this section we will give a short overview of each of the improvement areas, i.e.:

- What is it?
- Purpose and benefits
- What was provided by the competence team?

At the end of this section we make some comparison between the areas.

3.1 Team Work
What is it?
A team is a group (3-6 people) working interdependently over a limited period of time (6-16 weeks) to achieve a common goal.
What does it mean for teams and management?
- To get high performance teams we need a focus on team assignment, team planning, commitment between team, project and line, as well as effective means for the teams to follow up and report on their work.
- High performing teams also means working closer together. This requires more focus on and training in social skill both for the teams and management.

Purpose and benefits:
- Higher motivation through more autonomy, authority and less isolated work.
- Easier to manage as the team takes over some of the planning and detailed work allocation.
- Faster competence build-up as team members learn from each other
- Better quality since four eyes see better than two, and the team members are dependent on the quality of each others work.

What was provided?
- Material:
  - Management guidelines to form, initiate and monitor teams.
  - Team work processes and guidelines supporting the team members to work effectively in teams.
- Team coach course (11 days) for one team coach from each LDC. The team coach learns to coach teams, and can also give the following courses at the LDC:
  - Team work overview (1 hour)
  - Team member course (2-3 days) consisting of team building theory and exercises (soft skills) as well as the team work processes and guidelines.
  - Management course (1 day) going through the management guidelines and preparing management for their changed role.

The team coach course was developed in co-operation with Ericsson's Management and Organisational Development unit and the guidelines are an extension of material developed at Ericsson in Canada.

3.2 Reviews and Inspections
What is it?
Reviews and inspections are different kinds of activities to ensure the quality of the work, i.e.
- Inspections is the traditional end of work inspection or Fagan inspection. This has since long been in place in Ericsson. Our contribution was to enhance it with the latest improvements implemented at Ericsson in Norway and Untied Kingdom which was based on the work of Tom Gilb [5].
- 1/3 presentation is an informal presentation by the author of a document after 1/3 of the estimated time/effort for doing the document is used. The participants in the 1/3 presentation are those affected by the document, e.g. those who made the input documents, those who shall use it and other technical experts. It is also recommended to have those who shall do the final inspection present. The purpose is to discover misunderstandings and provide feedback to the author as early as possible. The time 1/3 was chosen as this is

when most people have a clear grip of the problem and some ideas about solutions, but have not put to much work into it. Good suggestions or misunderstandings can easily be taken into account. The 1/3 presentation is also an excellent opportunity to check the original estimates and goals for the work.

- Frequent reviews (team reviews) are reviews where what has been produced since last time is checked, usually just within the team. The purpose is to find faults as early as possible and to keep the amount to review each time down. Some organisations have implemented this as a 3-1-1 scheme, i.e. 3 days of work, 1 day of review preparation and 1 day of review and planning.

Purpose and benefits

- Better quality is the main purpose of reviews and inspections. We want to focus on finding the fault as early after it is introduced as possible. This is why we not only focus on the end of work inspection when the document is completed.
- Competence transfer is also a very important benefit of reviews and inspections, the feedback from peers critically reading your work is invaluable for improving.

What was provided?

- Concept clarification and work instructions for the different reviews and inspections.
- Planning and follow up guidelines for what, when and how to plan the different types of reviews and inspections. This contains recommendations on which reviews and inspections to use for which type of documents as well as standard preparation and review rates.
- Check lists for common faults and rule sets per document.
- Review and inspection champion training, where each LDC is given the opportunity to send people to a trainer course to become trainers at their LDC. These trainers are supported by the competence team when they do their first course locally.

The review and inspection champion training was developed in co-operation with the Ericsson training department based on best practices from many Ericsson design centres, among them United Kingdom, Norway, Denmark and Erisoft (Sweden).

3.3 Incremental Development

What is it?

Incremental development means to split the project into several interdependent increments which can be done in sequence as illustrated below (the phase names are taken from AXE 10's development model). Note that this figure only shows

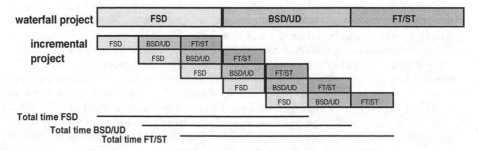

the part of the development process spanned by the increments, there must be activities to define the requirements and increments up front as well as some final activities before the complete system is delivered to the customer.

Purpose and benefits

- Shorter lead-time through concurrent engineering, as we see from the figure we achieve both a shorter total lead time, as well a longer lead time for each phase. This requires of course more people over the shorter time as the total amount of effort is constant. Planning the increments so that there can be a continuous and smooth growth of functionality is of course crucial and not trivial [6].
- Faster feedback and learning as we can learn from each increment. Incremental development will speed up the learning process in the organisation significantly.
- More fine grained and concrete control through both planning the increments, and being able to follow up and see concrete results earlier and faster.
- Higher motivation for developers as they see results of and get feedback from their work faster. They also have a chance to improve in the same project based on the feedback from early increments. We have also found increments very valuable in getting new people up to speed.

What was provided?

- Support for selection and planning of increments for development projects, consisting of:
  - General presentation on incremental development and experience from other projects
  - Workshops during feasibility of development projects both on subproject and main project level to determine increments.
- Preparation for the organisation to execute the project in increments, this consisted of guidelines and a one day workshop which was conducted at all LDC's:
  - Incremental development–Guidelines and experiences (2 hour presentation)
  - Incremental development with the project management process PROPS (1 hour presentation.)
  - Incremental development with current development processes and tools (1 hour presentation)
  - Workshop: How can the LDC take advantage of incremental development (4 hours)

The guidelines were developed in close co-operation with the standard process owners. The general guidelines were based on experiences from several other projects using incremental development within Ericsson, in particular at Ericsson in Norway, Australia and the Netherlands.

3.4 Methods, Tools and Training
What is it?

Methods, tools and training is mainly an increased focus on process adherence. BUX has well defined organisation wide processes, the problem is that a lot of people are new and they are not familiar enough with all the processes. What we focus on is just in time training through process kick-offs before each phase. Here a process overview is given together with hints and common pitfalls. At the end of the phase an evaluation meeting is held to collect input to continuously improve the kick-offs and the processes.

Purpose and benefits
- Less confusion and rework since people know what to do. This will again lead to higher quality and shorter lead-time.

What was provided??
The main output was a course package for the local process support person at each LDC. This consisted of:
- Guidelines and training for performing process kick-off and evaluation (1 day)
- Material and training for process kick-off content (process overview) (2-3 days). This course covered all the material, but at the LDC the local process support person only selected the relevant parts for each kick-off.

A Process game was also used as a complement to the ordinary training. In this game the players simulate a development project with all different activities and the documents to be produced.

The course was developed in co-operation with Ericsson training in Ireland, who are doing introductory courses on the process. Ideas were also used from Ericsson in Norway who had used process kick-offs and process evaluations for several years.

3.5 Customer Focus and Project Information

What is it?
- Ensure that all project participants have a clear view of why things are done relating back to the needs of the final customer.
- Ensure that all project participants understand their part in the project and how they are contributing to the whole.

Purpose and benefits
- Simple solutions to meet customer needs
- Focus on the right activities
- Finding faults before the customer does

What was planned to be provided?
- A set of project ground rules—expected behaviour
- Information strategy in project
- Customer focus activities
    - Visibility of customers at interfaces, e.g. at the completion of each increment
    - Planning customer involvement
    - A stronger network for market projects
- A set of training courses
    - Why customer focus?
    - Market situation for AXE 10
    - Development project and its value to the customers
    - Human skills—relating of customer involvement

These aspects were influenced by ideas from Ericsson in Australia who had worked very hard to get each individual person in the organisation to focus on the needs of the end customer.

Note that due to a lack of resources and commitment, only a fraction of the above requirements were achieved.

3.6 Comparison of improvement areas

The organisation of these improvement areas had a lot in common, e.g.:

- The goal was to enhance and support the LDC's capabilities within each area.
- Training for local coaches/trainers/champions was used heavily. TTM15 was a project, and the capabilities needed to be transferred to the line.
- Regular visits by competence team members to support the implementation at each LDC.
- Regular experience exchange seminars within each area during the development project to build network and learn from each other.
- Focus on the target development project but the improvements were used in all projects starting in 1996
- Close connection to standard process owners and training organisations.

There are however slight, but important differences mostly to take into account the division of authority between the development projects and the LDC's.

- Incremental development has a quite strong project focus, as it is up to the project to determine the increments. This is also partly the case for customer focus and project information.
- Team work is another extreme where it is up to each LDC to implement it as the autonomy of each LDC requires them to decide how to organise the work internally.
- Methods, tools and training is also mostly a local responsibility—they should deliver competent resources to the projects, although the projects decide on any adaptations of the standard processes.
- Reviews and inspections is a mixture of responsibility as the line is responsible for the quality of what they deliver, but it is partly up to the project to plan and allow enough time for reviews and inspections.

This division of responsibility was the reason that there were slight differences in the approaches to implementation of the different improvement areas, i.e. incremental development was working much closer with the development project, whereas team work, methods, tools and training, and reviews and inspections were preparing local trainers at the LDC which could adapt the general material to local needs.

4 Measurements

TTM15 was a major improvement initiative, and we wanted to quantify which effects it had on our goals of lead time and quality. To achieve this we decided to incorporate a measurement program based on the Goal-Question-Metrics (GQM) approach [7] to try to follow up the improvement areas and their effect on the goals of the development projects. Note that Ericsson already had in place a system to track productivity, quality and lead-time (PQT) of software projects. In the rest of this section we will briefly discuss the measurement area in the same format as the improvement areas. It was organised very similarly with a competence team.

What is it?

It is a measurement programme aiming at following up:

- The overall goals, i.e. on quality and lead-time.
- The use of the five TTM15 improvement areas, i.e. to what degree they were implemented.

- The performance of each of the TTM15 improvement areas, and their aggregated impact on the overall goals.

Since a lot of measurements were already in place in BUX we focused on using these existing measurements instead of creating too many new ones.

Purpose and benefits
- Provide insight for management, both at each LDC, project and BUX level
- Quantify the effect of each improvement to help us select and spread good practices
- Feedback and a better baseline for future improvements

What was provided?
- A GQM plan and a measurement plan to follow up the goals of quality and lead-time and the five improvement areas. Each improvement area was followed up both regarding to what extent it was actually implemented, and which effect it had on the goals.
- Training for the measurement responsible at each LDC
- Support for analysis of the measurements

The GQM team worked closely with the competence teams to develop the GQM plan and measurement plan for each area, and the improvement areas also participated in the analysis of the results.

The GQM work used experiences from a similar measurement programme in the GSM-mobile switch development organisation within Ericsson [4].

5 Current Status and Experiences

The current status of TTM15 project (June 1997):
- All planned material has been produced, except for customer focus and project information where we had a lack of resources.
- The first groups of team coaches, local process support persons, and review and inspection champions have been trained with good results. About 20-30 people from different LDC's attended each of the courses. Local implementation activities were conducted in LDC's with the support of the competence teams. The provided improvement have been actively used in about half of the LDC's. The preliminary quality figures from the main target project which are good, indicating that we can reach the quality goal.
- Increments in the main target project were planned and the organisation has been prepared to execute the project in increments. About 20 LDC's were visited and about 300 people given the training on incremental development. The project is now in the later stages of testing of the third and last increment, and is projected to reach the lead-time goal.
- Measurement responsibles are being trained and the GQM and measurement plans adapted to local needs. We have had the first analysis session with the development project to interpret the results. Unfortunately only four LDC's are fully participating in the measurement programme due to lack of resources, although many more are providing parts of the information. This reduces the effectiveness of the analysed results.

In general we evaluate the TTM15 project as a success, even if we did not achieve a 100% implementation throughout all LDC's. This is did not surprise us as:
- TTM15 was the first global improvement project within the BUX organisation, thus this type of project was new to all involved.

- TTM15 was only one of many competing improvement initiatives, both on corporate Ericsson level and locally, thus some LDC's chose to focus on other improvements.

5.1 Positives
The following factors were a key to the implementation of TTM15:
- A long term goal and plan, as described in detail in section 2, a TTM15 project management dedicated to follow it through, and BUX management commitment to the project.
- Involvement of the LDC as well as the target development project throughout the TTM15 project. We have not mentioned the target development project that much, but key people from that project were involved from the selection of the improvements at the first workshop in September 1995. The focus on a clear target project was crucial as it gave a concrete goal for the improvements.
- Reuse of best practices from within Ericsson, both inside and outside BUX. This allowed us to produce much more and better material than otherwise. The acceptance of the changes were also easier when we know that they had been used successfully before, even on a smaller scale.
- Synergy with content of ongoing local and central improvement activities, thus the LDC's saw TTM15 as a way to work faster with their own problems and solutions by co-operating with others. This is not surprising as it were the LDC's which selected the improvement areas in the first TTM workshop.
- Delegation of responsibility to the competence teams, where each competence team was responsible for the successful implementation of their area.
- Involvement of process improvement experts which had experiences from introduction of similar improvements in other parts of Ericsson. There was one such person in each competence team. This helped the other team members, which were not so experienced in change management and technology transfer.
- The involvement of standard process owners to ensure the compatibility with their work, and to ensure that the results were taken care of after TTM15.

5.2 Opportunities for Improvement
There are a few things that we could have been better at:
- LDC management involvement and control. We should have been better at involving the LDC management in the control and follow-up of the TTM15 project. We tried this, but these are busy people which are hard to get involved. A meeting every 4 months with BUX and LDC management to review the progress and future plans would have been ideal.
- Support for local implementation at the LDC. As mentioned in section 1 there are several improvement initiatives ongoing at Ericsson at the moment, and the message is often confusing for each individual LDC. We tried to do something about this by documenting and explaining how the five TTM15 improvements connected and supported the two other main initiatives, CMM and policy deployment. Another problem was that each improvement area within TTM15 had different contact persons at the LDC. This was important to get as many persons involved as possible—and the improvement areas were to some extent addressing different parts of the organisation, e.g. incremental development was mainly up to the project manager, technical co-ordinator and

test leader, team work was the responsibility of line management, measurements for the quality co-ordinator, etc. an advantage for many LDC's to have a dedicated change facilitator allocated at the LDC during the implementation of TTM15. This person would need to know the TTM15 and the other improvement programs as well as the local organisation. Such a person could do the important job of explaining, initiating, synchronising and supporting the local implementations.

6 Conclusion and further work

In this article we have described the organisation, content and current status of the TTM15 improvement project within Ericsson's business unit for fixed telecommunication networks. We still have a long way to go before we have completed these improvements, but we are confident that we are on the right track. In this improvement project we emphasised the use of in house experiences and competence. This has been intentional—we have a lot to learn from each other, and we need to build a stronger improvement network in the BUX organisation.

A TTM12 project with new improvement areas is already underway, and we are discussing future plans for a more long term (3-5 years) systematic approach to software improvements, which can better integrate the different programs in combinations with individual development opportunities for our employees.

Acknowledgement

Göran Olsson for supporting the TTM15 project, Per Lidzén and Monika Swensson for initiating the TTM workshop, and all other involved in TTM15 at Ericsson and Q-Labs.

References

1. M. Paulk, B. Curtis, M. Chrissis and C. Weaver, "Capability Maturity Model for Software (Version 1.1)", CMU/SEI-93-TR-024
2. "Ericsson finds CMM powerful model for process improvement", http://www.esi.es/Publications/Improve/I596/profile.html
3. Øyvind Johansen and Even-André Karlsson, "Experiences from using Cleanroom at Ericsson in Arendal, Norway", 2st European Industrial Symposium on Cleanroom Software Engineering, 27-29 Mar. 1995, Berlin
4. H. Hientz, G. Smith, A. Gustavsson, P. Isacsson and C. Mattsson, "Systematic Process Improvement in a Multi-Site Software Development Project", Proceedings of the 21st Annual Software Engineering Workshop, December 1996, Goddard Space Flight Center, Maryland, SEL-96-002
5. Tom Gilb and Dorothy Graham, Software Inspections, Addison Wesley, 1993
6. Even-André Karlsson, "A construction planning process", 3rd annual International Conference on Cleanroom Software Engineering Practices, 9-11 October 1996, College Park, Maryland, USA
7. Victor R. Basili, "Software Modeling and Measurement: The Goal/Question/Metric Paradigm", CS-TR-2956, 1992. Computer Science Technical Report Series. University of Maryland, College Park. MD.

Change Management Needs
Integrated Process and Configuration Management

Gregor Joeris

Intelligent Systems Department, Center for Computing Technology
University of Bremen, P.O. Box 330 440, D-28334 Bremen
joeris@informatik.uni-bremen.de

Abstract. Change management is a core problem of software development. Management of changes means managing the process of change as well as managing all artifacts of an evolving software system. Both challenges have been focused extensively in the field of software process modeling and software configuration management, respectively. In this paper, we motivate that change management needs an integrated approach to process and configuration management. A fundamental prerequisite to provide such a comprehensive support is the integration of the underlying representation formalism of process and version models. To cope with this problem, we propose a conceptual framework to provide a common conceptual basis of process and version modeling concepts and identify the requirements for comprehensive process support for change management. Furthermore, we classify and evaluate different approaches of how to integrate process and version models from a conceptual point of view.

1. Introduction

Change management is one of the core problems of software development. Management of changes to any software document means (1) managing the process of change as well as (2) managing all artifacts of an evolving software system. Both aspects serve as motivation for an integrated modeling approach to support process and configuration management in a process-centered software engineering environment (PSEE):

(1) Focusing the *software development process* has been always a core challenge of software engineering. At the beginning, very coarse-grained and informal descriptions of the software process in terms of life-cycle models were considered and have been criticized ever since. In the last decade, the explicit and unambiguous specification and continuous improvement of processes were recognized as a key factor for successful completion of software projects ([CFFS92]).

The software process is characterized - like every engineering process - by the complexity of both, the product and the process, and the dynamically changing environment in which the process takes place. Thus, *feedbacks*[1] and changes occur in all life cycle phases. Though many process modeling languages (PML) were developed and feedbacks in the software process have been recognized as an important factor of *software process technology* (SPT) (cf. [Dow87]), most PMLs provide only poor concepts for managing the process of change. Moreover, most existing PMLs lack integration of version and configuration modeling mechanisms into the overall representation formalism.

(2) Software configuration management (SCM) has been identified as a major part of a well defined software development and maintenance process ([Hum89]). SCM deals with controlling the evolution of complex software systems and supports both, technical development as well as management of the evolution of software systems ([Fei91, CoWe97]):

The *technical view* of SCM provides mechanisms and functions to control versions of software objects, to build derived versions, and to construct consistent software configurations. On a technical level, it supports performing changes by different mechanisms like workspace control, long transactions, or sub-databases. Many version models and concepts have been proposed ([CoWe97, Cag95]). But all of them lack sophisticated process support, although some process-oriented features were sometimes added. Currently, process support is of growing interest in software configuration management (cf. [Est95, MiCl96, EDA97, Leb97]).

The *management view* of SCM focuses on the organizational and administrative aspects of SCM. As part of the overall management of a software project, SCM provides methods to handle change requests, and to perform changes in a controlled manner by introducing well-defined change processes. Furthermore, it supports monitoring the status of the software components.

It seems that SCM provides all concepts and techniques for a methodical approach to change management. Moreover, change management seems to be just another notion of SCM. But, a detailed and comprehensive process support for implementation and management of changes is not given. On the technical level, support for process automation is sometimes provided to build derived objects and to trigger procedures before or after a SCM activity is done. On the other hand, the management view of SCM considers only very coarse-grained and informal process descriptions with all the drawbacks of such models. Thus, there is a gap of process support between the technical and the management view of SCM.

We believe that an integrated approach to process and configuration management can bridge this gap and is the basis for comprehensive change management support provided by a PSEE. The prerequisite of such an approach is the integration of the underlying process and version modeling formalisms. This paper aims at providing a conceptual framework for the integration of process and version models. It identifies

---

[1] The term feedback is used as a generic term to denote deviations from a linear progression of a process. Similar terms are 'iteration', 'repetition', or 'rework' (cf. [Dow87]).

the core problems and requirements for integrated representation formalisms. In particular, it focuses on the capabilities needed for comprehensive process support for change management. Furthermore, we use the framework to classify approaches of how to integrate process and version models on a conceptual level.

Section 2 introduces the conceptual framework for integration of process and version models and relates it to other work on conceptual frameworks. Further, it describes the main integration aspects of an integrated representation formalism. Section 3 characterizes change processes and outlines the main requirements for integrated process and configuration management in order to support change management. In section 4 existing process and version models are classified and evaluated using the proposed framework. Finally, section 5 gives a short conclusion.

2. Conceptual Integration Framework

2.1 Objectives of the Conceptual Framework and Related Work

Several conceptual and terminological frameworks have been proposed in the field of software process technology for different purposes (e.g., [CFFS92], [FeHu93], [Lon93], [CFF93], [CoLi95]). Some aim at providing an unambiguous and generally accepted terminology, some characterize and clarify the basic challenges, requirements and concepts, and some are designed for comparison and evaluation of existing approaches. All of them provide valuable knowledge for an essential understanding about the software process and are fruitful for developing both, a sophisticated theory and technology concerning software processes. In relation to our conceptual framework, the following work is of particular interest:

In [CFF93], a framework for evolving software processes is introduced. Process change and the process of process evolution is a specific topic concerning changes which is not focused on in this paper. Some requirements of evolving processes may be adopted and adapted for handling general changes of software documents.

Conradi and Liu discuss in [CoLi95] whether a process modeling language should be designed by using one or many languages for the different sub-models of a process model. They define four classes of PML design approaches. Furthermore, they distinguish six core process elements (activities, artifacts, production tools, roles, humans, model evolution) and take versioning as a non-core element into account. The aim of the paper is to clarify the basic concepts, functionality and tool architecture of a PSEE with respect to the various PML design approaches. A deep consideration of integration aspects for process and version models is not provided.

Our conceptual framework takes only a subset of the software process modeling domain into account, namely the process space, the product and version space, and the work environment which are introduced below. Thus, it neither claims to be a general framework for software process technology, nor is it intended to provide a precise terminology. Rather, the aim of our conceptual framework is to integrate concepts from software process technology and SCM to provide the conceptual basis for studying change processes and to identify the integration dimensions of process and version models. Thus, it claims to be adequate for clarifying and improving the understanding of the interdependencies between modeling concepts of these research areas. Moreover, it serves as the basis for the characterization of different integration aspects and is used for the evaluation and classification of existing approaches.

Interrelationships between process and configuration management have been discussed by the SCM community mainly with respect to cooperation support (e.g. [GCCM95, EDA97]) or low-level process control and automation rather than focusing on all integration aspects. A deep consideration of these interrelationships, particularly with high-level process concept, is currently of growing interest.

2.2 Fundamentals of the Conceptual Framework

With the intention of considering process and version modeling formalisms in mind, we have to deal with different terminologies from SPT and SCM. In particular, a *process model* usually combines descriptions of different perspectives of a process, namely activities, artifacts, resources, organizational units, and execution behavior (cf. [CFFS92, Lon93]), but the artifact (sub)model of existing PMLs takes only the product space into account. On the other hand, a *version model* consists of a *product space* which describes the software documents[2] and their relationships and a *version space* which identifies and organizes the object's versions.

In order to define a common terminological basis and to avoid this overlapping meaning of process and version model, we adopt and integrate the basic notions from SPT and SCM: First, we adopt the notions repository, product, version, and workspace from SCM as defined below. Next, we use the notion process space to denote the active parts of a process and hence use it in a restricted sense rather than covering all aspects of a process.

Our framework is based on the notions of process space, product space and version space. Figure 1 illustrates these perspectives and their interdependencies and additionally shows the resource and organization perspectives which will be disregarded in the following. All these spaces together define the modeling scope of an integrated representation formalism. Moreover, Figure 1 illustrates the work environment which defines the virtual world in which processes are performed by agents. The building blocks of the framework are defined as follows and their integration aspects are discussed in the following sub-section.

The *process space* defines what tasks have to be done and how these tasks may be accomplished in terms of a partially ordered set of process steps. Furthermore, it specifies the dynamic execution behavior (execution states, control and data flow) of process instances. With respect to change management we emphasize two aspects, namely (a) different forms of feedbacks and change processes and (b) process support for SCM as part of a change process is needed on a low-level of abstraction for the technical side as well as on a high-level of abstraction for the management side.

---

[2] We use the notions document, artifact, and software object synonymously throughout this paper and use change as a general term for modification of any software document.

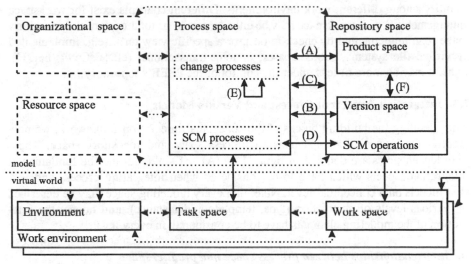

Fig. 1. Overview of the conceptual framework

The *repository space* consists of the *product space* and *version space* and provides the fundamental procedures for defining, identifying and accessing of versions, variants, and configurations ([CoWe97]). The *product space* describes the structure of a software product without taking versioning into account. It defines the composition of software documents/objects and their dependencies. Software objects are coarse-grained units which have an internal fine-grained structure. The *version space* defines how versions are represented and managed. In general, version representations may be classified into state-oriented versioning and change-oriented versioning. The internal representation is encapsulated by basic operations for retrieving and constructing of versions. Note, that we do not subsume capabilities for low-level process control under the repository space which are often associated with SCM (cf. [Leb94]). To provide an orthogonal and well-defined conceptual framework, these capabilities are part of the process space.

The *work environment* provides the virtual environment in which an agent (human or machine) perform its activities. It is divided into the workspace, task space, and the technical and organizational environment: The *workspace* provides all software documents that the agent needs to do the work including temporary results. The *task space* contains the personal work list, provides enactment support (guidance, enforcement, automation) and handles process feedback information [DoFe94]. Thus, the task space is the activity-oriented equivalent to the data-oriented notion workspace. Finally, the technical and organizational *environment* is derived from the resource model and organization model and should be customized to the user-specific needs. E.g. it provides uniform invocation of tools.

The work environment controls and maintains the task and workspaces in conjunction with the process and configuration management services and allows for interoperability among different work environments. Different concepts exist for workspace management: E.g., a workspace may be either a partial or total copy of the repository space (e.g. implemented by check-in/out), or a specific view on it (e.g. implemented by virtual file systems, sub-databases, or long transactions) (cf. [EsCa94, Fei91]). Thus, it may be more or less under the control of the PSEE's repository.

2.3 Integration Aspects of Process and Version Models

After defining the building blocks of the conceptual integration framework, we now identify the interrelationships between process space and repository space. These interdependencies are denoted in figure 1 by (A) - (F). We outline the fundamental integration aspects which have to be considered when integrating process and version models on a conceptual level. Note, that every modeling space may be described on various levels of abstraction (type, template and instance), and hence, the integration of the modeling elements have to be considered on every level.

A. *Interrelationships between process space and product space*
a) *Interdependencies between process and product structure:* The process and product structure, i.e. the (de)composition of processes/documents and their (static) dependencies, have great interdependencies. E.g. the software architecture determines a lot of tasks to be accomplished and module dependencies define data and control flow dependencies. Managing these interdependencies is fundamental for an integrated modeling approach and in conjunction with the management of design decisions the basis for impact analysis.

b) *Formal input/output-relationship:* From a functional point of view, a process takes software objects as inputs and produces new or modified objects as output. From the product point of view, software documents are used, created and modified by operations or processes. In any case, there is a (static) relationship between the abstract process definition and product definition that determines which kind of input and output a process may consume or produce, respectively. This relationship further determines several properties of the actual dataflow (see below) and is more complex than in conventional programming languages: (1) kind of parameter (input, output, in/out), (2) kind of data passing (original, copy, reference), (3) kind of access (exclusive, shared, read-only, write), (4) cardinality of parameter (optional or mandatory, unique or multiple values), and (5) parameter type (restricted by document/object type and/or by a document specified in the product space which acts as a placeholder for the actual version).

B. *Interrelationships between process space and version space*
a) *Actual data flow:* Different kinds of actual data passing and access have to be taken into account. In particular, several versions may be passed between running activities. Thus, the actual data flow has to take versioning into account. In general, the logical data flow of the process space must be separated from the physical passing of versions using workspace management capabilities in order to realize different data flow scenarios (e.g. push vs. pull).

b) *Interdependencies between the version state and the process' execution behavior:* As the product structure influences the process structure, the actual version state may affect the execution behavior of a process. E.g. a process must not be started if the version is not approved. Furthermore, version state transition may be associated with specific activities.

c) *Concurrency control:* Processes which operate concurrently on the same version have to be coordinated using an adequate control mechanism which depends on the employed workspace management approach. This implicit coordination provided by a SCM system may affect the scheduling of processes under the control of a process engine which is in charge of explicit coordination of activities.

C. Interrelationships between process space and repository space

a) *Reflexivity:* Obviously, process specifications are documents; due to several reasons process models will evolve in time. Thus, process models are part of the repository space and will be under version control. Moreover, the process of process (model) changes (usually referred to as meta process) is defined in the process space. Therefore, process representation formalisms have to provide reflective features [BaFu93]. Note, that for the sake of readability this reflexivity relation was not accurately illustrated in figure 1.

D. Interrelationships between change processes and SCM operations

a) *Integration of basic SCM operations in the process space:* A version model defines not only the structure of the product and version space. It also provides basic operations to build up and modify these spaces (e.g. retrieving and constructing of versions, building of derived objects). These basic procedures have to be integrated into the general PML used for the process space.

b) *Support for general SCM processes:* For managing changes, process support is needed for SCM activities on different levels of abstraction (see Sec. 3.2).

E. Intrarelationships in the process space

a) *Correlation of change processes:* Many separately and independently initiated but correlated change processes which concern similar problems have to be synchronized during execution and may have to be joined together.

b) *Transactional and non-transactional* activities have to be integrated following different strategies of how to react on changes.

F. Interrelationships between product space and version space: The integration of product space and version space is essential for a versioned repository. In particular, construction of configurations and building of derived objects have to be investigated with respect to change management. In this paper we do not further address this topic. For a comprehensive overview see [CoWe97].

3. Process Support for Change Management

SCM deals with changes on both, technical and management level, but it lacks comprehensive process support for software engineers and managers, as mentioned in the introduction. In the following, we focus on changes from a process-oriented view in order to outline the main requirements of an integrated approach to process and configuration management. First, we focus on feedbacks in a software process from a technical point of view. Next, we describe the process support needed for SCM activities. Finally, we briefly sketch the cooperation support needed for actors who perform changes.

3.1 Feedbacks and Change Processes

The notion feedback was employed to subsume notions like backtracking, repetition, iteration, rework and so on (cf. [Dow87]). This variety of notions already shows that there will be no general concept for handling changes in a PSEE. The following list gives an overview of such situations (cf. [HKNW96]) and defines some of the above mentioned notions:

- *Loops*: predefined repetition with defined exit condition until an accurate result is accomplished; no analyzing or planning phase. Example: combination of manual and automatic process steps until an accurate result is accomplished
- *Rework*: predictable or unpredictable repetition of finished tasks or activities reusing the previous process and resources; additionally, a change request is documented, analyzed and authorized and the change will be validated and approved following general configuration management policies (cf. [Hum89]); but, no planning of activities and resources is needed. Example: iteration of coding, testing and reviewing a software module due to error correction
- *New process*: instead of repetition of the previous process, a new process is instantiated for implementing and managing the change which consists of analysis and authorization of change, planning the activities for change, implementation and approval; the process may be as complex as the overall development process. Example: modification of a system which does not fulfill the user's needs.
- *Reaction*: reaction to change requests and adaptation of previous results during enactment by the agent who currently performs the task (simultaneous engineering). Example: during module implementation new features may be added.
- *Backtracking/Rollback*: undoing previous actions and proceeding differently which is useful for automated process steps with transactional semantics.
- *Prototyping*: predefined iterations of processes on type level with corresponding iterated evolution of actual process instances and their results.

Furthermore, the situations of feedbacks in the software process sketched above are even more complicated since many possibly dependent or overlapping feedbacks may occur concurrently. Process support for feedbacks have to take this diversity of change situations into account. Thus, the core requirement with respect to the process modeling and enacting capabilities of a PML is the *adaptability* of the execution behavior specification which includes:

- *Modeling and initiating of feedbacks*: Flexible modeling mechanisms have to be provided in order to determine the target of a feedback and to define how to react to this situation. In particular, predefined control flow constructs like loops have to be combined with ad hoc decisions where to restart a process. Instead of reactivation of finished activities, in some situations new activities have to be dynamically initiated and integrated into the process for handling the changes.
- *Impact analysis and consequences*: After initiating a feedback, we have to consider who is potentially affected, what could be the consequences, and how should one react. E.g. transactional activities should be aborted whereas human activities may be suspended or even informed.
- *Managing the flow of change:* When actual changes are done, we have to decide when these changes should be propagated to the affected process steps. E.g., to support simultaneous engineering, this can be done before the activity is finished. Thus, advanced data and control flow mechanisms are needed and have to be integrated with workspace management services for propagation. Furthermore, changes may lead to on-the-fly modifications of the planned activities.

The need for a flexible and adaptable execution behavior induces further requirements. We emphasize the following three derived requirements: (1) On-the-fly modifications and local customization of enacting process instances to react to unforeseen situations (cf. [CFF93]), (2) coordination and joining of correlated change processes, and (3) support for transactional workflows ([GHS95]).

3.2 Process Support for Configuration Management

For change management, process support for SCM activities are needed on a low-level of abstraction for the technical side as well as on a high-level of abstraction for the management side. To bridge this gap we need capabilities for:

a) *Process control and process automation*: the process space should be able to control the basic SCM operations, i.e. who, when and where changes can be made (e.g. in conjunction with a role concept modeled in the resource space); moreover, mechanisms for automatically triggering actions should be provided and integrated in the overall process modeling capabilities, e.g., for building derived objects, for constructing or updating a workspace, etc.

b) *Integration of management processes and technical processes*: processes for implementation of changes have to be integrated with management processes of SCM like change request authorization or approval of changes. This requires special modeling features (reflexivity, see section 2.3) and monitoring capabilities. Furthermore, product-centered processes based on state-transition diagrams for controlling the product life-cycle have to be supported (cf. [EDA97]).

c) *Modeling of global SCM policies*: establishing and controlling general SCM policies (e.g. for quality assurance) and customization to the organization's existing policies require modeling capabilities for global process rules or constraints

Furthermore, rather to provide traceability only for the version history, an integrated approach has to be extended to include the process history as well.

3.3 Work Environment Support for Performing Changes

Support for performing changes has to deal with the trade-off of "sharing vs. isolation" ([Cag95]). On the one hand, software engineers want to perform changes isolated from influences of other changes as much as possible. On the other hand, they want to be notified about all changes which affect their work and want to obtain these new results as early as possible. Thus, the right degree of cooperation between various work environments defined as inter work environment data exchange is essential. We need support for both, controlled cooperation and free cooperation:

Controlled cooperation support deals with notification of changes and propagation of intermediate and final results. It may be explicitly controlled on process level by passing of intermediate results or may be implicitly controlled on data level by extended transaction protocols with relaxed isolation properties depending on the applied workspace management concept. Furthermore, we have to distinguish between simultaneous changes of versions of dependent objects and concurrent changes to the same version of an object. The latter further requires reconciliation of concurrently changed versions.

Free cooperation support deals with direct interaction among engineers which is not fully controlled by the process engine or repository (e.g. shared applications, video conferencing, etc.). The concept of shared workspaces seems to be a good approach in this direction: On process level, we can control which activities may share parts of their workspaces, whereas the actual data interchange is managed by the actors (cf. [EDA97]). Finally, we need synchronization mechanisms to integrate synchronous cooperating activities into a predefined workflow on process level.

Another important service of work environment management is the configuration of the workspace which has to support some form of '*recovery*' for change management: To implement a change, the old work environment must be re-established and adapted, i.e. at least old and new input versions, the previously produced results, and the modified task description or the change request have to be provided.

4. Classification of Process and Version Model Integration

Representation formalisms of both, process and version models vary between several paradigms (cf. [FNK94], [CoWe97]). Thus, existing approaches of integrating process and version models can only be compared and classified on an abstract and conceptual level. To achieve this goal, we apply meta modeling techniques in conjunction with our conceptual framework, i.e. we neglect all details and use an ER-like notation to sketch a model of the underlying concepts which will be embedded in the conceptual framework. In addition, we give examples and briefly evaluate some of the few existing integrated approaches to process and configuration management and point out their strengths and weaknesses. Most of them are descended from configuration management systems extended by process-oriented features.

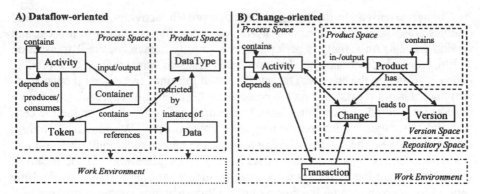

Fig. 2. Activity-centered integration approaches

First of all, we distinguish between activity- and product-centered integration approaches. Furthermore, we divide the activity-centered approaches into dataflow-oriented and change-oriented, illustrated in Figure 2. The product-centered approaches are classified into product-state-based and object-based approaches, illustrated in Figures 3.

4.1 Activity-centered Integration

A) Dataflow-oriented: The dataflow-oriented approach is based on activities and information flows between them. Furthermore, it is characterized by a clear separation of processes and products. In the process model, the dataflow is represented by tokens which refer to any product or data item and hence abstract from their representation, as illustrated in Figure 2. Thus, no assumption is made about the underlying object model so that every object model (versioned or not) may be integrated. Another advantage is that feedbacks and change processes can be supported on a high-level of abstraction. On the other hand, only a very loose-coupled integration can be achieved. E.g., since versioning cannot be presumed, dataflow and execution behavior do not take versioning into account. Moreover, most often only poor work environment and cooperation support is provided by this approach.

Examples of this approach are Petri-net based or activity-centered process management approaches like *Spade* [BFGL94] or DYNAMITE [HJKW96]. The latter is particularly designed to cope with the dynamic nature of software processes, and provides some remarkable capabilities to support change processes. It provides specific mechanisms for feedback handling and supports cooperation on process level by passing of intermediate results between running activities. The involved tasks of a feedback and the produced results are versioned within the process model so that traceability and reestablishing of the work environment is guaranteed. The integration with a version and resource model is currently investigated (cf. [HKNW96]).

B) Change-oriented: In the change-oriented approach, activities, transactions, and changes are closely interrelated and are the basis for the integration of process and version models. An activity is performed in a (mostly human-centered) transaction within the work environment. The transaction leads to some change of a product which is related to the activity. The actual flow of information between the work environments is not represented on the process level. Rather, this approach is based on support for controlled cooperative work between activities which determine the content and topology of the corresponding work environments. Whereas the activities define the context, the underlying SCM system is in charge of providing version and workspace control capabilities and of supporting cooperative work on the technical level. Its strength lies in the good cooperation support and its weakness is the little support for coordination on the process level. Obviously, this approach fits very well to change-oriented version models and hence allows for tightly integrated version and process modeling formalism as well. However, the systems which follow this approach most often support integration only on a technical level so that only a loose integration on a conceptual level is achieved (e.g., *EPOS* [Con+94], *COO* [God+96], *ClearGuide* [Leb97]) or have very limited process management capabilities (e.g., *Asgard* [MiCl96]).

4.2 Product-centered Integration

C) Product-state-centered: The product-state-centered approach to integrate process capabilities into configuration management focuses mainly on controlling the product life-cycle and on a low-level process functionality based on state transitions and event/trigger mechanisms, as illustrated in Figure 3. Usually, there is no (high-level) notion of an activity. Thus, the work environment consists only of the workspace which is managed by the SCM system. Event/trigger mechanisms may well support low-level process functionality. But they are not suitable as a general process modeling formalism, because they are difficult to understand for humans, the execution is hard to control, and high-level concepts for process specifications are missing [BEM94].

Most SCM-systems fall into this class. E.g., *ClearCase* [Leb94] provides a process *control* toolset which supports access control, event recording and dynamic policy enforcement based on triggers. However, ClearCase does not offer any comprehensive process modeling and enacting capabilities.

The problems of the low-level process formalisms may be reduced by a process formalism which hides the low-level event/trigger definitions: *Adele-Tempo* [EsCa94, BEM94] is a SCM-system which provides process functionality based on a trigger mechanism. On top of this, the process formalism Tempo was proposed which is based on the role concept. A process type is defined as a set of objects playing a role. Thus, this formalism is again product-centered. It supports actor assignment to activities but lacks modeling information and control flows of processes. Comprehensive process support is therefore missing.

Another approach of integrating high-level process support for SCM systems and in particular for the Adele system is *APEL* [EDA97]. This approach is mainly

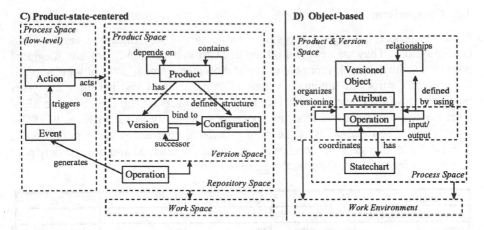

Fig. 3. Product-centered integration approaches

based on activities (following the change-oriented approach), but also integrates product-state-based aspects. It provides comprehensive process and cooperation support. Unfortunately, enactment is not provided on this high-level of abstraction but needs compilation to the Adele language, i.e. to event/trigger rules.

D) Object-based: The object-based approach is adapted from object-oriented modeling techniques which are applied for process and configuration management. In this approach, software objects are the building blocks of the model. They define the structure of the product space, organize their own versioning, and specify operations which may be performed on an object. Further, the execution behavior is specified by a statechart variant which defines the coordination of the object's operations. Operations and their coordination specifications form the process space which overlaps the product and version space. In this approach, product-state- and structure-based aspects are integrated best. Moreover, SPM and SCM concepts are integrated on a high level of abstraction. However, we believe that an approach that is exclusively based on objects has its limitations for a general PML. The intrinsic subordination of activities to software objects or documents and the implicit representation of information flows are strong weaknesses. But, an enhancement of such an approach which defines and integrates different object classes for processes, artifacts and their versions etc. whose behavior are coordinated by message/event passing seems to be a promising approach (cf. [Joe97]).

ESCAPE+ [NSS96] and *SOCCA* [EnGr94] follow this approach. SOCCA does not explicitly take versioning into account, whereas ESCAPE+ extends its predecessor ESCAPE [Jun95] of version concepts.

4.3 Comparison

From the process management point of view, most PMLs disregard versions and configurations. They are designed on top of SCM systems and hence are integrated only on a technical level. From the configuration management point of view, support for process control and automation may be found in SCM systems for a few years based on "low-level" mechanisms like rules and triggers. Integration of more high-level process modeling and enacting concepts is currently investigated in the SCM community. The capabilities of the most promising approaches are summarized in Table 1. Note, that these approaches are not dataflow-oriented and provide only poor support for feedback handling on the process level.

Requirement	EPOS	Adele/Tempo	APEL	ESCAPE
Integration Aspects				
structural integration	by planning	no	no	inherent
input/output relationship	alternate task and data net	implicit,	in/out parameter + dataflow dependencies	derived from object relation
behavioral integration	based on attributes	ECA-rules on attributes	local STDs	inherent (statecharts)
scheduling & concurrency control	not integrated	implicit	(yes)	implicit
SCM operations	(no)	yes	(no)	yes
general SCM processes	yes	(no)	yes	(no)
joining of correlated processes	no	no	no	no
Int. WE support				
controlled cooperation	cooperating transactions	role collaboration	various cooperation policies	cooperation patterns
free cooperation	WE overlaps	public areas	public areas	no

Table 1: Integrated SPM and SCM support provided by different systems

5. Conclusion

Integration of process and configuration management support is of growing interest. We have addressed this topic by focusing changes and change processes. A fundamental prerequisite to provide such a comprehensive support in a PSEE is the integration of the underlying representation formalism of processes and versions to obtain explicit descriptions of the process and repository space. Due to the diversity of the existing modeling languages for processes and versions, integration of these formalisms is a great challenge. To cope with this problem, a common conceptual basis of process and version modeling concepts and elements is needed. In this paper, we have proposed a first approach to such a conceptual framework which adopts and integrates generally used notions of SPT and SCM, and is based on the notions of process space, product space, version space and work environment. We have tried to outline the interdependencies between process and version models on a high-level of abstraction and to identify the basic requirements for an integrated approach.

An important issue discussed in this paper is the classification of how to integrate process and version models. Based on the fundamental distinction of activity-centered and product-centered integration, four classes have been identified, namely the dataflow-oriented, the change-oriented, the product-state-based, and the object-based approach. Every approach has its specific strengths and weaknesses.

We hope that the material presented in this paper will be fruitful to support future work on this challenge. Still much work has to be done in this direction. First, it is an open issue whether the development of a comprehensive PML leads to one large language or to several separated but well integrated sub-PMLs (cf. [CoLi95]). Second, the interdependencies between process and version models must be discussed in more detail. E.g., the consequences of specific representation paradigms like state-oriented vs. change-oriented version models on the integration with process concepts have to be considered. Furthermore, we have to focus on the impact of different concepts for workspace management on an integrated approach. Third, SCM functionality for building derived version and constructing configurations which may be provided by version rules have to be considered in a more comprehensive version of the framework. Finally, the framework has to be extended to explicitly describe the interrelationships between process and version models on the different level of abstraction (type, template, instance level).

Acknowledgments
I am grateful to Bernhard Westfechtel for fruitful comments on this paper.

References

[BaFu93] Bandinelli, S.; Fugetta, A.: "Computational Reflection in Software Process Modeling: the SLANG Approach", in *Proc. of the 15th Int. Conf. on Software Engineering*, IEEE Computer Society Press, 1993; pages 144-154.

[BEM94] Belkhatir, N.; Estublier, J.; Melo, W.L.: "ADELE-TEMPO: An Environment to Support Process Modelling and Enaction", in [FKN94], pages 187-222.

[BFGL94] Bandinelli, S.; Fuggetta, A.; Ghezzi, C.; Lavazza, L.: "SPADE: An Environment for Software Process Analysis, Design, and Enactment", in [FKN94]; pages 223-248.

[Cag95] Cagan, M.: "Untangling Configuration Management", in [Est95]; pages 35-52.

[CFFS92] Conradi, R.; Fernström, C.; Fuggetta, A.; Snowdon, R.: "Towards a Reference Framework for Process Concepts", in *Software Process Technology - Second European Workshop EWSPT'92*, LNCS 635, Springer, Berlin, 1992; pages 3-17.

[CFF93]   Conradi, R.; Fernström, C.; Fugetta, A.: "A Conceptual Framework for Evolving Software Processes", in *ACM SIGSOFT Software Engineering Notes*, 18(4), Oct. 1993; pages 26-34.

[CoLi95]   Conradi, R; Liu, Ch.: "Process Modelling Languages: One or Many?", in *Software Process Technology - Fourth European Workshop EWSPT'95*, LNCS 913, Springer, Berlin, 1995; pages 98-118.

[Con+94]   Conradi, R. et al.: "EPOS: Object-Oriented Cooperative Process Modelling" In [FKN94]; pages 33-70.

[CoWe97]   Conradi, R.; Westfechtel, B.: "Version Models for Software Configuration Management", to appear in *Computing Surveys*, 1997

[DoFe94]   Dowson, M.; Fernström, Ch.: "Towards Requirements for Enactment Mechanisms", in *Software Process Technology - Third European Workshop EWSPT'94*, LNCS 772, Springer, Berlin, 1994; pages 90-106.

[Dow87]   Dowson, M.: "Iteration in the Software Process", in *Proc. of the 9th Int. Conf. on Software Engineering*, IEEE Computer Society Press, 1987; pages 36-39.

[EnGr94]   Engels, G.; Groenewegen, L.: "SOCCA: Specification of Coordinated and Cooperative Activities", in [FKN94], pages 71-102.

[EDA97]   Estublier, J.; Dami, S.; Amiour, M.: "High Level Process Modeling for SCM Systems", in *Software Configuration Management - ICSE'97 SCM-7 Workshop*, LNCS 1235, Springer, Berlin, 1997; pages 81-97.

[EsCa94]   Estublier, J.; Casallas, R.: "The Adele Configuration Manager", in [Tic94], pages 99-130.

[Est95]   Estublisher, J. (ed.): "Software Configuration Management - ICSE SCM-4 and SCM-5 Workshops, Selected Papers". LNCS 1005, Springer, Berlin, 1995.

[FeHu93]   Feiler, P.H.; Humphrey, W.S.: "Software Process Development and Enactment: Concepts and Definitions", in *Proc. of the 2nd Int. Conf. on the Software Process*, IEEE Computer Society Press, 1993; pages 28-40.

[Fei91]   Feiler, P.H.: "Configuration Management Models in Commercial environments". Technical Report CMU/SEI-91-TR-7, Software Engineering Institute, Carnegie Mellon University, Pittsburgh, 1991.

[FKN94]   Finkelstein, A.; Kramer, J.; Nuseibeh, B.: "Software Process Modelling and Technology". Research Studies Press, Chichester, 1994.

[GCCM95]   Godart, C.; Canals, G.; Charoy, F.; Molli, P.: "About some relationships between configuration management, software process and cooperative work: the *COO* Environment", in [Est95]; pages 173-178.

[God+96]   Godart, C.; Canals, G.; Charoy, F.; Molli, P.; Skaf, H.: "Designing and Implementing *COO*: Design Process, Architectural Style, Lessons Learned", in *Proc. of the 18th Int. Conf. on Software Engineering*, IEEE Computer Society Press, 1996, pages 342-352.

[GHS95]   Georgakopoulos, D.; Hornick, M.; Shet, A.: "An Overview of Workflow Management: From Process Modeling to Workflow Automation Infrastructure". *Distributed and Parallel Databases*, 3(2), April 1995; pages 119-153.

[HJKW96] Heimann, P.; Joeris, G.; Krapp, C.-A.; Westfechtel, B.: "DYNAMITE: Dynamic Task Nets for Software Process Management", in *Proc. of the 18th Int. Conf. on Software Engineering*, IEEE Computer Society Press, 1996, pages 331-341.

[HKNW96] Heimann, P.; Krapp, C.-A.; Nagl, M.; Westfechtel, B.: "An Adaptable and Reactive Project Management Environment", in Nagl, M. (ed.) *Building Tightly Integrated Software Development Environments: The IPSEN Approach*, LNCS 1170, Springer, Berlin, 1996; pages 504-534.

[Hum89]   Humphrey, W.: "Managing the Software Process". Addison-Wesley, Readings, Massachusetts, 1989.

[Joe97]   Joeris, G.: "Cooperative and Integrated Workflow and Document Management for Engineering Applications", to appear *in Proc. of the DEXA'97 Workshop on Scientific Workflows*, IEEE Computer Society Press, 1997.

[Jun95]   Junkermann, G.: "A Grapical Language for Specification of Software Processes", Dissertation at the University Dortmund, Germany, 1995 (in german).

[Leb94]   Leblang, D.B.: "The CMChallenge: Configuration Management that Works", in [Tic94], pages 1-37.

[Leb97]   Leblang, D.B.: "Managing the Software Development Process with ClearGuide", in *Software Configuration Management - ICSE'97 SCM-7 Workshop*, LNCS 1235, Springer, Berlin, 1997; pages 67-80

[Lon93]   Lonchamp, J: "A Structured Conceptual and Terminological Framework for Software Process Engineering", in *Proc. of the 2nd Int. Conf. on the Software Process*, IEEE Computer Society Press, 1993; pages 41-53.

[MiCl96]   Micallef, J.; Clemm, G.: "The Asgard System: Activity-Based Configuration Management", in *Software Configuration Management - ICSE'96 SCM-6 Workshop*, LNCS 1167, Springer, Berlin, 1996; pages 175-186.

[NSS96]   Neumann, O.; Sachweh, S.; Schäfer, W.: "A High-Level Object-Oriented Specification Language for Configuration Management and Tool Integration", in *Software Process Technology - Fifth European Workshop EWSPT'96*, LNCS 1149, Springer, Berlin, 1996; pages 137-143.

[Tic94]   Tichy, W. (ed.): "Configuration Management". John Wiley & Sons, New York, 1994.

The Design of a Next-Generation Process Language*

Stanley M. Sutton, Jr. and Leon J. Osterweil

Department of Computer Science
University of Massachusetts
Amherst, MA 01003-4610

Abstract. Process languages remain a vital area of software process research. Among the important issue for process languages are semantic richness, ease of use, appropriate abstractions, process composability, visualization, and support for multiple paradigms. The need to balance semantic richness with ease of use is particularly critical.

JIL addresses these issues in a number of innovative ways. It models processes in terms of steps with a rich variety of semantic attributes. The JIL control model combines proactive and reactive control, conditional control, and more simple means of control-flow modeling via step composition and execution constraints. JIL facilitates ease of use through semantic factoring, the accommodation of incomplete step specifications, the fostering of simple sub-languages, and the ability to support visualizations. This approach allows processes to be programmed in a variety of terms, and to a variety of levels of detail, according to the needs of particular processes, projects, and programmers.

1   Introduction

Process language research was an early emphasis of software process studies. It has remained vital for several reasons. First, no language has gained general acceptance or widespread use. This is not just a linguistic problem, as the use of languages depends also on organizational, methodological, and technological support. Second, first-generation languages generally have obvious limitations. This is in part because many of these languages were based on existing paradigms that were not particularly well adapted to the domain of software process [11, 24, 33, 26, 15, 4, 25]. Finally, research in other areas of software process has affected our ideas about what can and should be done with process languages. In this paper we report on the design of a "next-generation" process language that is intended to capitalize on lessons learned from first-generation languages, overcome limitations of those languages, and explore issues emerging from ongoing process research.

Section 2 identifies our primary language design goals, which are based on our experience with first-generation process languages. Section 3 describes the

---
* This work was supported in part by the Air Force Materiel Command, Rome Laboratory, and the Advanced Research Projects Agency under Contract F30602-94-C-0137.

design of JIL, our next-generation process language, including examples based on the Booch object-oriented design process. Section 4 discusses the multi-modal interpretation of JIL programs. An assessment of the JIL approach is presented in Section 5, and our status is discussed in Section 6.

2 Language Design Goals

Process programming proposes that it is feasible and valuable to represent software processes using programs written in compilable, executable coding languages [28, 29]. Our experience with APPL/A [33] has validated this proposal. We now take many properties of coding languages as fundamental to representing software processes, including formal syntax, well-defined semantics, executability, analyzability, object management, and consistency management. These issues have been the focus of much previous work (e.g., [31, 23, 11, 24, 6, 12, 33]), and they should continue to be addressed by second-generation process languages. Our focus here, however, is on the issues outlined below.

2.1 Semantic Richness

Software processes are multi-faceted and technically challenging applications. To support this domain, a process programming language must provide many kinds of interrelated semantics. This pressure for semantic richness is reflected in first-generation process languages. Many of these are based on extensions of conventional programming languages or paradigms, including functional languages ([11, 26]), rule based or reactive languages ([24, 23, 12, 6]), imperative languages ([33]), and Petri nets ([4, 15]). Conversely, where process languages have neglected certain areas of semantics (e.g., reflexivity, resource modeling), process programs have suffered. Process language semantics must be both rich and rigorous. They must cover an adequate range of process semantics, and they must do so with appropriate models that support reasoning about processes.

2.2 Ease of Use

Ease of use is an important requirement for process programming languages because the individuals and organizations responsible for defining software processes are often not experienced at programming. The semantic richness of process languages means, however, that significant software engineering skills are required to program in them effectively. This is an impediment to the widespread adoption of process languages. A key issue for process languages is thus balancing the need for technical rigor with this need for ease of use.

2.3 Appropriate Abstractions

The clear and concise representation of software processes requires appropriate kinds and levels of abstraction. The development and maintenance of process programs is complicated if the user must construct process-specific abstractions from lower-level abstractions, as with process languages that are based on general-purpose programming languages (e.g., APPL/A). Process programming languages should provide built-in concepts and constructs that map naturally into the software process domain. (Languages that do this with varying degrees of success include MVP-L [30], ProcessWeaver [18], LOTOS [31], and Oikos [27].)

2.4 Composability

Programming of software processes in general is difficult. Thus it is important to be able to readily compose larger processes out of smaller components and to support reuse-based process programming. Also, the ability to program processes by composing elements having different language paradigms or representing different semantic aspects would introduce additional flexibility and incrementality into process program development. Composition is also recognized as important in the subject-oriented view of object-oriented programming [19].

2.5 Clarity through Visualization

Many first-generation process languages are textual. A few process languages support graphical representations of process control (e.g., Slang [3], Melmac [15], Process Weaver [18], and Hakoniwa [22]). Visual process representations greatly aid understanding and communication of some processes. Simple ideas are often most simply represented visually, and this can aid greatly in process design and verification. On the other hand, more complex and dynamic process structures may be easier to express in textual languages, since visual representations can become cluttered and unwieldy and often tolerate ambiguity in order to cultivate simplicity of expression. Thus, strictly visual representations are likely to be unsuitable for complex processes in general (especially if they are complex enough to support process execution [17]). In light of these tradeoffs, our goals for a second-generation process language give top priority to the expressive power afforded by textual languages, while supporting the use of visual representations where they are workable.

2.6 Multiple Paradigms

In our opinion, one of the most useful features of APPL/A is its incorporation of triggers into a largely imperative language (Ada). We relied heavily on this combination of proactive and reactive control in our process programming. Some combination of these two types of control is also found in many other process languages (e.g., Adele [6],AP5 [11], EPOS [13], HFSP [26, 36], Marvel [24], Merlin [23], and ProcessWeaver [18]). ALF [10] is another process project that is explicitly multi-paradigmatic in combining proactive and reactive control along with preconditions and postconditions, and Pleiades demonstrates that multiple paradigms are also important in software object management [37]. And multiple paradigms have also been found useful in requirements specification [14]. In most process languages, however, one control paradigm typically predominates while the other is secondary. Thus, many languages primarily support one style of programming (such as rule-based programming in Merlin or Marvel, or functional programming in HFSP, among others). Our experience and observations suggest that emphasizing one paradigm becomes problematic when another paradigm is more natural for a particular process. Thus, one of our goals is to support multiple paradigms without favoring any of them.

3   Design of JIL

In this section we discuss the design of JIL, emphasizing process steps, the control paradigm, and exception handling. Examples are based on a process for software design following the principles of Booch Object-Oriented Design [8].

3.1   Process Steps

The central construct in JIL is the *step*. A JIL step is intended to represent a step in a software process. A JIL program is a composition of steps, each of which may contain a set of subunits (representing different aspects of the step) and supplementing units (such as separate procedures and packages). The elements of a step specification represent kinds of semantics that are important to process definition, analysis, understanding, and execution. Briefly, the elements include:

- *Objects and declarations*: The parameters and local declarations for software artifacts used in the step
- *Resource requirements*: Specifications of resources needed by the step, including people, software, and hardware
- *Substep set*: The substeps of a step (which are themselves steps)
- *Step constraints*: Restrictions or prescriptions on the relative execution order of substeps
- *Proactive control specification*: An imperative specification of the order in which substeps are to be executed (direct invocation)
- *Reactive control specification*: A reactive specification of the conditions or events in response to which substeps are to be executed (indirect invocation)
- *Preconditions, constraints, postconditions*: Define artifact consistency conditions that must be satisfied (respectively) prior to, during, and subsequent to the execution of the step
- *Exception handlers*: Handlers for local exceptions, including handlers for consistency violations (e.g., precondition violations)

An example of a JIL step specification is shown in Figure 1. This specification represents the first step in a (simplified) Booch Object-Oriented Design process [8]. The step specification has a template-like syntax (i.e., it is composed of various fields). The substeps are listed within the specification. The proactive control specification (Section 3.2), reactive control specification (Section 3.2), and exception handlers (Section 3.3) are all contained in separate, named subunits. The preconditions and postconditions are defined in separate units (see

```
STEP Identify_Classes_And_Object IS
    OBJECTS:  Reqts_Spec:
                  Requirements_Specification.Specification_Type;

    DECLARATIONS:  Class_Candidate_List, Object_Candidate_List:
                  Booch_Product_Definition.Name_List;

    -- Substeps
    STEPS:  Browse_Requirements,
            Extract_Class_Candidates,
            Identify_Classes,
            Extract_Object_Candidates,
            Identify_Objects,
            Edit_Class_Object_Dictionary;

    -- Proactive control specification   [Separate subunit--see Figure 2]
    ACTIVITY:  Identify_Classes_And_Objects_Activity;

    -- Reactive control specification   [Separate subunit--see Figure 3]
    REACTIONS:  Identify_Classes_And_Objects_Reactions;

    PRECONDITIONS:                     -- [Separate package]
        FROM Requirements_Consistency_Conditions USE
            Passed_Review(Reqts_Spec);

    POSTCONDITIONS:       -- [Separate package]
        FROM Booch_Product USE
            Unique_Name_Per_Class(Booch_Product.Class_Diagram);
            Every_Object_Has_A_Class(Booch_Product.Object_Diagram,
                              Booch_Product.Class_Diagram);
            ...

    -- Exception handlers [Separate subunit--see Figure 5]
    HANDLERS:  Handle_Class_And_Object_Errors;
END Identify_Classes_And_Objects;
```

Fig. 1. Example of a JIL step specification.

Section 3.2). Some parts of the step specification are unspecified. An example of a possible step constraint is shown later (Section 3.2). Some general comments on the language follow before specific features are discussed in more detail.

As the division of elements in a step specification may suggest, JIL is a *factored* language. That is, it provides independent representations for independent semantics, insofar as possible. This has several consequences. First, the various aspects of a step can be specified relatively independently of one another. For example, the substeps for a step can be given without indicating any proactive or reactive control flow, and control flow can be specified without regard to resources or preconditions and postconditions. (The elements of a step are not entirely independent, however. For example, consistency conditions will typically reference objects used by the step, and control specifications must refer to the substeps of the step.) Second, the relative independence of elements in the step specification allows steps to be defined using just a subset of the elements (in other words, many elements are optional). This promotes flexibility in process specification, since just those elements that are relevant to a particular purpose need be used. However, this imposes additional requirements on process interpretation, since various kinds and combinations of elements may be present in a step. Implications for interpretation are discussed in Section 4.

3.2 Control Paradigm

JIL affords a unique variety of control paradigms that enable alternative approaches to specifying process control flow. The JIL control paradigm is characterized by three primary features:

- The combination of proactive and reactive control, the value of which was demonstrated by first-generation process languages.
- The integration of preconditions and postconditions, which have also been widely used.
- The ability to specify loosely organized processes without requiring detailed programming.

Particularly important, though, is the flexibility that JIL affords in the use of these control paradigms. Any or all may be used within a single program (each step interpreted independently according to the elements it contains). Additionally, elements may be combined in a single step (which is interpreted according to the particular combination of elements). These different aspects, and the resulting interpretation paradigm, are discussed below.

Proactive Control The proactive control specification of a JIL step provides a context in which the execution of substeps can be imperatively programmed. The step specification designates a separate subunit to represent the proactive control specification for the step. This has two parts, a specification and body. The specification lists the entry calls and signals that can be received by the executing instance of the proactive part of the step. (These support interprocess communication.) The body provides the imperative code that controls the execution of substeps. The syntax of the imperative code is based on Ada, including loop and conditional commands, entry-call accept statements, and a new `parallel` command with mandatory and optional branches. (Space limitations preclude presentation of an extensive example here, but see [35]).

An explicit "invoke" command is used to distinguish substep invocation from ordinary procedure invocation. A substep can be invoked as a "subprocess" or "process." In the former case, the substep executes as a child process of the calling step; in the latter case, the substep executes as an independent process (i.e., as a separately invoked program). Subprocesses, in turn, can be invoked synchronously, like a procedure call, or asynchronously, as a parallel thread of control (like an Ada task).

Reactive Control The step specification also designates a separate subunit for the specification of reactions to events. The JIL event model recognizes and defines four types of events related to product state, process state, resource state, and exceptions (Table 1). Most first-generation process languages focus on events of one kind (e.g., product state events in APPL/A, AP5, and Marvel; process events in Adele). The definition of an event kind corresponding to exceptions is an important feature of JIL in that it allows for a generalization of the exception handling model (described in Section 3.3). The reactions triggered in response to these events can include commands of the same sorts as used in the proactive control specification; in particular, substeps can be invoked reactively.

Event Category	Examples
Product state events	Artifact updates
	Artifact state transitions
Process state events	Control events (e.g., step invocation)
	Signals (explicitly generated)
Resource state events	Resource access
	Resource access conflicts
Exceptions	Runtime exceptions
	Consistency violations (e.g., of preconditions)

Table 1. Categories of events in JIL.

An example reactive control specification is shown in Figure 2. This figure shows two types of reactions. The first is to a process event, the termination of the substep Identify Objects. The reaction is to restart the step if the class diagram is still being modified (since those modifications may outdate the object diagram). The second is to an update of the requirements, upon which the work of this step depends. The reaction is to terminate the current step.

Preconditions and Postconditions A step may have preconditions and postconditions. These are defined in separate packages that may be shared by multiple steps. The conditions are intended to help control the execution of the step according to varying aspects of product, process, and resource state.[2] (*Con-*

---

[2] Process and resource states are also accessed implicitly in the step specification through the step constraints and resource requirements, respectively.

```
REACTIONS Identify_Classes_And_Objects_Reactions IS
-- Reactions for Booch Process Step Identify_Classes_And_Objects
BEGIN
     REACT TO COMPLETION OF Identify_Objects BY
          IF NOT Complete(Identify_Classes) THEN
               INVOKE SUBPROCESS Identify_Objects;
          END IF;
     END REACT;

     REACT TO UPDATE OF Reqts_Spec BY
          TERMINATE Identify_Classes_And_Objects;
     END REACT;
END Identify_Classes_And_Objects_Reactions;
```

Fig. 2. Example of a JIL reactive control specification.

straints can also be specified for a step. Constraints are syntactically like pre-conditions and postconditions, but they are enforced during the execution of the step. Constraints thus support intra-step consistency, while preconditions and postconditions support inter-step consistency.)

As the default, a step should not execute unless its preconditions are satisfied, and it should not terminate normally unless its postconditions are satisfied. However, we believe that this model is too restrictive for software processes in general; thus JIL includes several generalizations and extensions of it.

One generalization is that steps may be granted *variances* that allow them to be initiated before their preconditions are verified or to terminate before their postconditions are verified. Variances may be granted in cases where the conditions cannot be evaluated (e.g., due to contention for objects or other resources) or where there is good reason for overriding the programmed condition [32]. The granting of variances is supported through a runtime service.

A second generalization is that alternative responses may be made when violations occur. For example, when a step violates a postcondition the step may be aborted and its inconsistent results discarded. Alternatively, the step may be terminated abnormally but its results retained; this would interrupt the normal flow of the process but avoid the loss of work. In other cases, it may be more desirable to allow the step to terminate normally while leaving the product in an inconsistent state. This would allow the process to continue normally but with the product in need of some repair (this is somewhat analogous to the approach to handling inconsistency described in [2]). The coding of such approaches is done in the exception handlers (Section 3.3).

At present, we are using Pleiades [37] as our product definition language and Pleiades constraints as our primary form of preconditions and postconditions. Pleiades generates an Ada package specification and the constraints represent arbitrary Ada functions. Other invokable functions (e.g., independently defined functions in Ada) may also be used as preconditions or postconditions.

Loose Process Organization The proactive and reactive control specifications allow the flow of control within a step to be programmed in great detail. The preconditions and postconditions allow for further fine-grained conditional control. However, it is not always necessary in JIL to specify process control flow in great detail; it is often only necessary to indicate the composition of steps from substeps. This is important because it allows the execution agent (e.g., a human developer) to determine the order in which to attempt to execute the substeps (although preconditions and postconditions may restrict what the user can actually do). If appropriate, simple control relations among the substeps of a step can be specified using the step constraint functions. These are comparable to the control specifications of ALF [10], which represent path expressions [9].

An example of a step constraint specification is shown in Figure 3. This constraint allows the extraction of class and object candidates to proceed in parallel, followed by the identification of classes and objects in parallel. (Additional step constraint functions include Unordered (arbitrary sequence), Any (nondeterministic), and Alternate (choice).) If step constraints are given along with an activity specification, then the step constraints are used to constrain the programmed behavior of the activity (violation of a step constraint by the activity leading to an exception). If step constraints are given without an activity specification, they are used instead to drive the execution of substeps according to the indicated control pattern.

```
STEP CONSTRAINTS Restrict_Identify_Classes_And_Objects IS BEGIN
    Ordered(Parallel(Extract_Class_Candidates,
                     Extract_Object_Candidates),
            Parallel(Identify_Classes,
                     Identify_Objects));
END STEP CONSTRAINTS Restrict_Identify_Classes_And_Objects;
```

Fig. 3. Example of step-ordering constraints.

3.3 Exception Handling

Two main models of exception handling have been used in first-generation process programming languages (and in programming languages generally). These may be characterized as block-oriented and rule-based. The block-oriented model is represented by Ada and C++ and was used in APPL/A [33]. In this approach, an exception handling block is attached to the scope in which the exception may occur. This approach is especially appropriate for process-specific exception handling, where different occurrences of the exception should be handled in context sensitive ways. It is cumbersome, though, when the exception must be handled in a uniform way, regardless of where it arises. The alternative model is rule-based exception handling, in which exceptions trigger exception-handling rules. The consistency rules of AP5 [11] and Marvel [24] are examples. This approach is ideally suited to the case in which an exception can be handled uniformly regardless of where it originates, but it is much more cumbersome when exceptions must be handled according to the context in which they arise.

Exception handling in JIL combines these complementary approaches to exception handling. Global exception handling is provided through the reactive control mechanism, in which exceptions are treated like "normal" events outside the process in which they occur. This allows one process to react in a normal way to an exception in another process. Local exception handling can be provided for a step through exception handlers. An example is shown in Figure 4, in which each **handle** statement represents an exception-handling block.

The exceptions shown in Figure 4 correspond to violations of preconditions and postconditions. The handling takes a variety of forms showing some of the possibilities for terminating or continuing the step. The ABORT command terminates the step abnormally, either with or without raising an exception. The TERMINATE command terminates the step normally. The REDO command terminates the current execution of the step and begins another. The AWAIT REPAIR command suspends the execution of the step pending the repair of the failed condition. The repair must be effected by some other step, which may be invoked, for example, as a reaction to the condition violation. Two compound forms of the handle statement are the HANDLE UNLESS (not shown) and HANDLE UNTIL. These allow for the specification of primary and secondary handling actions; the primary action is taken, respectively, unless some given condition is met or until some given deadline is reached, in which case the secondary action is performed.

As with the variety of control models, the combination of local and global exception handling contributes to semantic richness and availability of alternative paradigms. It also allows flexibility that can contribute to ease of use.

3.4 Other Features

As noted, we are using the Pleiades [37] language to define our products and product consistency conditions. Pleiades provides several high-level type constructors that are especially appropriate for software products, including graphs, relations and relationships, and sequences.

A resource model and resource specification language are under development. The model includes both project-oriented and system-oriented representations of resources, including categories of human, software, and hardware resources. We believe that this model will be more general than those typically used in software systems and software processes to date.

Process state has been recognized as an important consideration in process control, management, and evaluation [20, 3, 12]. We plan to have the JIL runtime system maintain key components of the process state automatically. Addition-

```
HANDLER Handle_Class_And_Object_Errors IS
BEGIN
    HANDLE FAILURE OF Requirements_Specification_Not_Empty
    AS PRECONDITION BY
        ABORT RAISE Requirements_Error;
    END HANDLE;

    HANDLE FAILURE OF No_Duplicate_Class_Names
    AS POSTCONDITION BY
        REDO STEP;
    END HANDLE;

    HANDLE FAILURE OF Every_Object_Has_A_Class
    AS POSTCONDITION BY
        AWAIT REPAIR;
    UNTIL Deadline(Identify_Classes_And_Objects) THEN
        ABORT;
    END HANDLE;
END Handle_Class_And_Object_Errors;
```

Fig. 4. Example of JIL exception handlers.

ally, the JIL event model defines events related to changes in process state; these can be used to trigger reflexive reactions.

The investigation of transaction modeling, including consistency management, was a major theme of APPL/A. In JIL, for simplicity and naturalness, steps provide a framework for defining units of concurrency control, atomicity, and consistency. However, for flexibility, as in the APPL/A model, these properties can be relaxed for a given step. Thus, for example, a step may be serializable without being atomic. Additionally, artifacts can be accessed in shared modes to allow collaborative work. Collaboration is further supported through an agenda management system, which allows group agendas and shared agenda items.

4 The Interpretation of JIL Programs

The interpretation of JIL programs is itself a process, for which the Julia environment provides an execution engine. Since JIL interpretation is a process, the JIL interpreter is itself a process program. This program provides an operational specification of JIL semantics. To bootstrap our execution capabilities, we are programming a preliminary "level 0" JIL interpreter in Ada. Using that, we plan to program more sophisticated and flexible interpreters in JIL. This will provide us with a basis for experimentation with alternative interpretation strategies and also with alternative language semantics.

A full treatment of Julia is beyond the scope of this paper (but see [34]). To illustrate the Julia philosophy and approach, we elaborate here on one key issue in the interpretation of JIL, namely multi-modal interpretation.

JIL offers great flexibility in specifying process control flow, particularly for substep invocation. Such flexibility imposes a corresponding requirement for flexibility on the JIL interpreter. Depending on the elements present in a step specification, the step is interpreted in one of several modes. The choice of mode is determined primarily by three elements in the step specification:

- *Commands*: These include both proactive commands (activity specifications) and reactive commands (reactions). Substeps can be invoked by both.
- *Execution constraints*: These constrain the execution of substeps invoked by other means (e.g., commands), but they can also be interpreted directly to drive substep invocation.
- *Substep preconditions and postconditions*: These guard the execution of individual substeps invoked by other means, but they can also provide a basis for inferring when substeps may be automatically invoked.

The presence or absence of these elements in various combinations dictate various modes of interpretation. Table 2 summarizes the combinations that determine particular modes; the modes are described briefly below.

Programmed A step that has any command elements (activity specification or reactions) is interpreted in the programmed mode. In this mode it is assumed that substeps of the step are invoked by commands in the proactive or reactive parts of the step. (The programmed mode thus supports any combination of proactive and reactive styles of programming, without any preference for either.) If substeps have preconditions or postconditions, these guard the substeps invoked via commands. If execution constraints are also present, then the programmed substep invocations must conform to the constraints at runtime or an exception is raised. In both cases, programmed control flow is locally constrained.

Guided A step with execution constraints but no commands or substep conditions is interpreted in the guided mode. In this mode, the execution constraints are interpreted as a specification of an order for automatic invocation of substeps.

Step Features			Interpretation Mode
Commands	Step Constraints	Substep Conditions	
Present	(Secondary)	(Secondary)	Programmed
Absent	Present	Absent	Guided
Absent	Absent	Present	Inferred
Absent	Present	Secondary	Guided/Guarded
Absent	Secondary	Present	Inferred/Constrained
Absent	Absent	Absent	Unconstrained

Table 2. Summary of applicability of JIL interpretation modes.

Inferred A step with substep pre- and postconditions but no commands or execution constraints is interpreted by inference. In this mode, the conditions are used to infer an order for the automatic invocation of substeps.

Guided/Guarded and Inferred/Constrained A step may lack commands but have both execution constraints and substep conditions. For such cases, there are two possible modes of interpretation. In the guided/guarded mode, the execution constraints are given priority and used to determine which substeps to invoke; the substep conditions are used to guard the invocations as in the programmed mode. In the inferred/constrained mode, the substep conditions are given priority and used to infer which substeps to invoke; inferences are subject to runtime checking of the execution constraints, as in the programmed mode. The choice between the guided/guarded and inferred/constrained modes cannot be based just on the presence or absence of elements in a step specification. A default mode may be stipulated, but the alternative can be allowed via interpreter directives.

Unconstrained The simplest mode of interpretation is the unconstrained, in which a step has substeps but lacks commands, execution constraints, or substep conditions. In this case the steps are invoked automatically in some nondeterministic order, possibly in parallel.

JIL programs can be composed of steps with heterogeneous interpretation modes. The availability of multiple interpretation modes addresses the needs for semantic richness and alternative paradigms. The ability to specify process control flow in greater or lesser detail facilitates flexibility and ease of use.

5 Discussion

Fundamental Requirements JIL is a formally defined, executable programming language with semantics are based on Ada, APPL/A, and Pleiades. This directly supports the fundamental goals described in the introduction to Section 2. The language will support a variety of kinds of analyses related to control and data flow, concurrency control, exception propagation, resource usage, etc.

Semantic Richness JIL addresses an unusually wide variety of semantic domains, including process control, product artifacts, and project resources. Maintenance of process state will also be supported through the language runtime system. The JIL semantic model builds on important lessons learned from first generation process languages (e.g., in integrating product and process representations, and in combining proactive and reactive control). However, JIL goes beyond first generation languages in several important respects such as the availability of alternative control paradigms, the degree of flexibility in consistency management, and the generality of the exception handling mechanism.

Ease of Use JIL facilitates ease of use in several ways. The allowance for loosely specified process control means that process programs can be constructed and organized simply, without requiring detailed programming. The factoring of step representations into relatively independent elements allows these to be treated more or less individually. Thus specialists in particular domains (e.g., product definition or resource modeling) can work in their areas of expertise without needing a detailed understanding of the whole language. The availability of alternative control models means that programmers can program in styles with which they are most comfortable or that are most appropriate to their process application. Support for visualization of processes and process programs should also facilitate process understanding and definition by technical specialists and non-specialists alike. We are committed to supplying templates, visual icons, and other high-level representations to facilitate the "coding" of JIL programs.

Appropriate Abstractions JIL is at a level of abstraction that is directed to the programming of important aspects of software processes. The central construct in the language is the step abstraction. Specialized step attributes address essential semantics of the process, product, and resource models. Additionally, the variety of control paradigms allows process control flow to be expressed in terms that are appropriate to a specific process or project. Although the language constructs are intended to be especially appropriate for software processes, they are still general purpose. The control model offers high-level control constructs, but imposes no particular control model. The Pleiades type model offers high-level type constructors, but imposes no required product model. This preserves the flexibility to program process-specific semantics in particular process programs.

Composability Composability of JIL programs is provided by the ability to create a process step from existing substeps. It is further supported by the flexible interpretation model, which allows composed substeps to be interpreted in a way appropriate to their individual programming. It is also supported by the ability to attach resource specifications to steps, which enables analysis of their combined resource requirements and allows planning for their integrated execution.

Clarity through Visualization The JIL language is textual, but we hope to provide several sorts of visual windows into JIL programs and processes. We foresee the development of several kinds of adjunct visual programming languages, for example, for composing process steps, organizing control flow of substeps within a step, specifying step execution constraints, associating software objects to steps, associating resources to steps, and so on. Additionally we expect to support visualizations of process execution state (such as those provided by the ProcessWall [21]), resource usage, and other runtime concerns.

Multiple Paradigms JIL is especially rich in alternative control paradigms. It accommodates both simple and completely programmed representations of process control. It combines proactive and reactive mechanisms, and incorporates conditional control. Step execution constraints can be used to guide process execution directly or to constrain execution that is programmed using other mechanisms. JIL also takes advantage of Pleiades support for multiple paradigms for software object management, for example, the alternative views of data structures, and the provision of navigational and associative access to data.

6 Status

We have been experimenting with preliminary versions of the JIL, writing process programs and refining the syntax and semantics. The JIL definition has progressed to a stable initial version with which we are continuing development of process programs, language support technology, and environment infrastructure. We have defined the BNF for the JIL grammar and generated a parser that translates JIL source code into an IRIS [1] internal representation. We are developing an interpreter and a JIL-to-Ada command translator. We are also developing visual language (implemented in Java) for a subset of JIL. Our primary process programming efforts are directed at a design process based on Booch Object Oriented Design [8] and a dataflow-analysis process based on iterative, incremental improvement of analytic accuracy [16].

Acknowledgments

The Julia/JIL project reflects the work of many people. The Julia-to-IRIS translator was built by Peri Tarr. The resource model has been developed by Rodion Podorozhny. The agenda-management system has been programmed by Eric Mc-Call. The Booch product server was programmed in Pleiades by Jin Huang and Arvind Nithrakashyap. Elements of the user interface have been programmed by Sandy Wise. Process programs in JIL have been written by Peri Tarr, Rodion Podorozhny, Jin Huang, Dan Rubenstein, Chris Prosser, and Todd Wright.

References

1. D. Baker, D. Fisher, and J. Shultis. *The Gardens of Iris.* Incremental Systems Corporation, Pittsburgh, PA, 1988.
2. R. Balzer. Tolerating inconsistency. In *Proc. of the 13th Internat. Conf. on Software Engineering*, pages 158 – 165. IEEE, May 1991.
3. S. Bandinelli and A. Fuggetta. Computational reflection in software process modeling: the SLANG approach. In *Proc. of the 15th Internat. Conf. on Software Engineering*, pages 144–154. IEEE, 1993.
4. S. Bandinelli, A. Fuggetta, and S. Grigolli. Process modeling in-the-large with SLANG. In *Proc. of the Second Internat. Conf. on the Software Process*, pages 75–83. IEEE, 1993.
5. N. S. Barghouti. Supporting cooperation in the MARVEL process-centered SDE. In H. Weber, editor, *5th ACM SIGSOFT Symp. on Software Development Environments*, pages 21–31, Tyson's Corner VA, December 1992. ACM Press. Special issue of *Software Engineering Notes*, 17(5), December 1992.

6. N. Belkhatir, J. Estublier, and M. L. Walcelio. ADELE-TEMPO: An environment to support process modelling and enaction. In A. Finkelstein, J. Kramer, and B. Nuseibeh, editors, *Software Process Modelling and Technology*, pages 187 – 222. John Wiley & Sons Inc., 1994.

7. G. A. Bolcer and R. N. Taylor. Endeavors: A process system integration infrastructure. In *Proc. of the Fourth Internat. Conf. on the Software Process*, pages 76 – 85. IEEE, Dec. 1996.

8. G. Booch. *Object-Oriented Analysis and Design with Applications*. The Benjamin/Cummings Publishing Company, Inc., second edition, 1994.

9. R. H. Campbell and A. N. Haberman. The Specification of Process Synchronization by Path Expressions. In *Operating Systems – Proc. of an Int. Symposium, Rocquencourt, France*, volume 16 of *Lecture Notes in Computer Science*, pages 89– 102. Springer, 1974.

10. G. Canals, N. Boudjlida, J.-C. Derniame, C. Godart, and J. Lonchamp. EPOS: Object-oriented cooperative process modelling. In A. Finkelstein, J. Kramer, and B. Nuseibeh, editors, *ALF: A Framework for Building Process-Centred Software Engineering Environments*, pages 153 – 185. John Wiley & Sons Inc., 1994.

11. D. Cohen. *AP5 Manual*. Univ. of Southern California, Information Sciences Institute, March 1988.

12. R. Conradi, C. Fernström, and A. Fuggetta. Concepts for evolving software processes. In A. Finkelstein, J. Kramer, and B. Nuseibeh, editors, *Software Process Modelling and Technology*, pages 9 – 31. John Wiley & Sons Inc., 1994.

13. R. Conradi, M. Hagaseth, J.-O. Larsen, M. N. Nguyên, B. P. Munch, P. H. Westby, W. Zhu, M. L. Jaccheri, and C. Liu. EPOS: Object-oriented cooperative process modelling. In A. Finkelstein, J. Kramer, and B. Nuseibeh, editors, *Software Process Modelling and Technology*, pages 33 – 70. John Wiley & Sons Inc., 1994.

14. R. Darimont and A. van Lamsweerde. Formal refinement patterns for goal-driven requirements elaboration. In *Proceedings of the Fourth ACM SIGSOFT Symp. on the Foundations of Software Engineering*, pages 179–190, Oct. 1996.

15. W. Deiters and V. Gruhn. Managing software processes in the environment melmac. In *Proc. of the Fourth ACM SIGSOFT Symp. on Practical Software Development Environments*, pages 193–205. ACM Press, 1990. Irvine, California.

16. M. B. Dwyer and L. A. Clarke. Data Flow Analysis for Verifying Properties of Concurrent Programs. In *Proceedings of the Second ACM SIGSOFT Symp. on Foundations of Software Engineering, New Orleans*, pages 62–75. ACM Press, December 1994.

17. W. Emmerich, S. Bandinelli, L. Lavazza, and J. Arlow. Fine grained process modelling: An experiment at british airways. In *Proc. of the Fourth Internat. Conf. on the Software Process*, pages 2–12. IEEE, Dec. 1996.

18. C. Fernström. PROCESS WEAVER: Adding process support to UNIX. In *Proc. of the Second Internat. Conf. on the Software Process*, pages 12 – 26, 1993.

19. W. Harrison and H. Ossher. Subject-Oriented Programming: A Critique of Pure Objects. In *Proceedings of the Eighth Annual Conf. on Object-Oriented Programming Systems, Languages, and Applications*, pages 411–428, October 1993. Published as ACM SIGPLAN Notices 28(10).

20. D. Heimbigner. Experiences with an Object-Manager for A Process-Centered Environment. In *Proceedings of the Eighteenth Internat. Conf. on Very Large Data Bases*, Vancouver, B.C., 24-27 August 1992.

21. D. Heimbigner. The ProcessWall: A Process State Server Approach to Process Programming. In *Proc. Fifth ACM SIGSOFT/SIGPLAN Symp. on Software Development Environments*, pages 159–168, Washington, D.C., 9-11 December 1992.

22. H. Iida, K.-I. Mimura, K. Inoue, and K. Torii. Hakoniwa: Monitor and navigation system for cooperative development based on activity sequence model. In *Proc. of the Second Internat. Conf. on the Software Process*, pages 64 – 74. IEEE, 1993.

23. G. Junkermann, B. Peuschel, W. Schäfer, and S. Wolf. MERLIN: Supporting co-operation in software development through a knowledge-based environment. In A. Finkelstein, J. Kramer, and B. Nuseibeh, editors, *Software Process Modelling and Technology*, pages 103 – 129. John Wiley & Sons Inc., 1994.

24. G. E. Kaiser, N. S. Barghouti, and M. H. Sokolsky. Experience with process modeling in the MARVEL software development environment kernel. In B. Shriver, editor, *23rd Annual Hawaii Internat. Conf. on System Sciences*, volume II, pages 131–140, Kona HI, January 1990.

25. G. E. Kaiser, S. S. Popovich, and I. Z. Ben-Shaul. A bi-level language for software process modeling. In W. F. Tichy, editor, *Configuration Management*, number 2 in Trends in Software, chapter 2, pages 39–72. John Wiley & Sons, 1994.

26. T. Katayama. A hierarchical and functional software process description and its enaction. In *Proc. of the 11th Internat. Conf. on Software Engineering*, pages 343 – 353. IEEE, 1989.

27. C. Montangero and V. Ambriola. OIKOS: Constructing process-centered sdes. In A. Finkelstein, J. Kramer, and B. Nuseibeh, editors, *Software Process Modelling and Technology*, pages 33 – 70. John Wiley & Sons Inc., 1994.

28. L. J. Osterweil. A Process-Object Centered View of Software Environment Architecture. In R. Conradi, D. T, and D. Wanvik, editors, *Advanced Programming Environments*, pages 156–174, Trondheim, 1986. Springer-Verlag.

29. L. J. Osterweil. Software processes are software, too. In *Proc. Ninth Internat. Conf. on Software Engineering*. IEEE, 1987.

30. H. D. Rombach and M. Verlage. How to assess a software process modeling formalism from a project member's point of view. In *Proc. of the Second Internat. Conf. on the Software Process*, pages 147 – 159. IEEE, 1993.

31. M. Saeki, T. Kaneko, and M. Sakamoto. A method for software process modeling and description using LOTOS. In *Proc. of the First Internat. Conf. on the Software Process*, pages 90 – 104. IEEE, 1991.

32. S. M. Sutton, Jr. Preconditions, postconditions, and provisional execution in software processes. Technical Report UM-CS-95-77, University of Massachusetts, Computer Science Department, Amherst, MA 01003, August 1995.

33. S. M. Sutton, Jr., D. Heimbigner, and L. J. Osterweil. APPL/A: A language for software-process programming. *ACM Trans. on Software Engineering and Methodology*, 4(3):221–286, July 1995.

34. S. M. Sutton, Jr. and L. J. Osterweil. The design of a next-generation process language. Technical Report UM-CS-96-30, University of Massachusetts, Computer Science Department, Amherst, MA 01003, May 1996. revised January, 1997.

35. S. M. Sutton, Jr. and L. J. Osterweil. Programming parallel workflows in JIL. In *Proceedings of the 9th Internat. Conf. on Parallel and Distributed Computing and Systems*, 1997. To appear.

36. M. Suzuki and T. Katayama. Meta-operations in the process model HFSP for the dynamics and flexibility of software processes. In *Proc. of the First Internat. Conf. on the Software Process*, pages 202 – 217. IEEE, 1991.

37. P. L. Tarr and L. A. Clarke. PLEIADES: An Object Management System for Software Engineering Environments. In *Proceedings of the First ACM SIGSOFT Symp. on the Foundations of Software Engineering*, pages 56–70. IEEE, Dec. 1993.

Software Release Management

André van der Hoek, Richard S. Hall, Dennis Heimbigner, and
Alexander L. Wolf

Software Engineering Research Laboratory
Department of Computer Science
University of Colorado
Boulder, CO 80309 USA
{andre,rickhall,dennis,alw}@cs.colorado.edu

Abstract. A poorly understood and underdeveloped part of the software process is software release management, which is the process through which software is made available to and obtained by its users. Complicating software release management is the increasing tendency for software to be constructed as a "system of systems", assembled from pre-existing, independently produced, and independently released systems. Both developers and users of such software are affected by these complications. Developers need to accurately document complex and changing dependencies among the systems constituting the software. Users will be heavily involved in the location, retrieval, and assembly process of the systems in order to appropriately configure the software to their particular environment. In this paper we identify the issues encountered in software release management, and present an initial set of requirements for a software release management tool. We then describe a prototype of such a tool that supports both developers and users in the software release management process.

1 Introduction

The advent of the Internet and the use of component-based technology have each individually influenced the software development process. The Internet has facilitated geographically distributed software development by allowing improved communication through such tools as distributed CM systems, shared whiteboard systems, and real-time audio and video. Component-based technology has facilitated the construction of software through assembly of relatively large-grained components by defining standards for component interaction such as CORBA [5]. But, it is their combined use that has led to a radically new software development process: increasingly, software is being developed as a "system of systems" by a federated group of organizations.

Sometimes such a process is initiated formally, as when organizations create a virtual enterprise [4] to develop software. The virtual enterprise establishes the rules by which dependencies among the components are to be maintained by the members of the enterprise. Other times it is the connectivity of the Internet that provides the opportunity to create incidental systems of systems.

For example, applications are typically built using public-domain software as major components, such as Tcl/Tk [13] for the graphical user interface. The use of public-domain software creates a dependency that, while less formal than in a virtual enterprise, is no less serious a concern.

In either case, component dependencies create a complex system of systems that in effect is being developed by a distributed and decentralized group of organizations. Given that the components of the system are in general pre-existing, independently produced, and independently released systems themselves, the primary issue involves managing the deployment of the system as a whole. In particular, the following two problems become evident.

1. *To developers of a system of systems, deployment of the system is cumbersome.* The developers must carefully and accurately describe their system, especially in terms of its dependencies on other systems. Of course, this problem occurs not just at the outermost level of system construction, but also at all intermediate levels of a hierarchically structured system.

2. *To users of a system of systems, the task of locating, retrieving, and tracking the various components is complicated and error prone.* A consistent set of components must be retrieved from potentially multiple sources, possibly via multiple methods, and placed within the context of the local environment.

These problems lead to a need for what we term *software release management*, which is the process through which software is made available to and obtained by its users. We have defined such a process and built a specialized tool to support that process. The tool, called SRM (Software Release Manager), is currently in use at the University of Colorado.

SRM is based on two key notions. First, components are allowed to reside at physically separate sites, yet the location of each component is transparent to those using SRM. Second, the dependencies among components are explicitly recorded so that they can be understood by users and exploited by the tool. The tool in particular uses dependency information to automate and optimize the retrieval of the components.

Software release management fits within the larger context of software configuration and deployment, which involves additional tasks such as installation, update, and removal. This larger context is being investigated in our Software Dock project [8]. SRM serves as the release manager in the Software Dock prototype, but is designed to be used independently.

In this paper we further motivate the need for software release management by illustrating how, in a distributed development setting, a lack of appropriate support for software release management leads to difficulties. We then present a set of requirements for a software release management process. Based on these requirements, we describe the functionality of our software release management tool, SRM. We conclude with a look at related work and some directions for the future.

2 A Motivating Example

During the past decade, the Arcadia consortium has developed approximately 50 tools to support various aspects of the software development process [10]. Arcadia's research staff is located at four universities across the US. Typically, each tool is developed, maintained, and released by a single university. Many of the tools, however, are dependent on tools developed at other sites. The maintenance of these dependencies has been largely ad hoc, with no common process or infrastructure in place. Figure 1 shows a graph of the dependencies that existed at one point in time. It illustrates the fact that the dependencies among the tools are very complex, and hardly manageable by a human. In fact, the figure presents only a snapshot of the full dependence graph, since it does not show the evolution of the tools into various versions, each with its own dependencies.

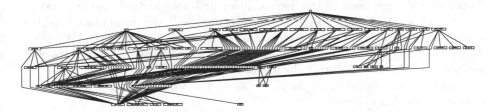

Fig. 1. Dependence Graph of the Arcadia Tools.

Two recent experiences at the University of Colorado clearly show the need for a process and tool to support the management of Arcadia software releases. In the first case, one of the Arcadia tools from a remote site, ProDAG [14], was needed for a project. ProDAG depends on a number of other tools that were also not present at the University of Colorado. Thus, besides ProDAG, each of these other tools and, in turn, the tools upon which they transitively depended, needed to be retrieved and installed. This turned out to be a lengthy and difficult exercise, due to the following reasons.

- *The tools that were needed were distributed from different sites, via different mechanisms.* Typically, FTP sites and/or Web pages were used to provide access to the tools. However, to obtain a different version than the one "advertised", someone responsible for the tool had to be contacted directly.
- *The dependency information was scattered over various sources.* Dependency information for a tool could be found in source files, "readme" documentation files, Web pages, and various other places. Sometimes, dependency information for a single tool could be found in multiple places.
- *The dependency information was incomplete or not even present.* Sometimes the dependency information pointed to a wrong version of a tool, or simply omitted which version of a tool was needed. In other cases, some of the dependencies were not recorded and could only be obtained by explicitly

asking the person responsible for the tool. Finding the right person was not always easy because of changes in personnel and responsibilities.

Consequently, retrieving the correct versions of all tools that ProDAG depended on turned out to take far more time, and far more iterations, than expected.

In the second case, another project was initiated at the University of Colorado that also needed ProDAG. However, the version of ProDAG that was installed previously was not usable due to the following reasons.

- *For a number of tools on which ProDAG depends, new versions had been released that fixed a number of important bugs.* Thus, these versions needed to be obtained and installed.
- *The person who initially installed ProDAG at the University of Colorado had left.* Consequently, we did not know which versions of the underlying tools were installed.

Thus, even though most of the dependencies had not changed and the correct versions of most of the tools were already installed, the combination of the above two problems resulted in a complete re-installation of ProDAG. Of course, during the process of obtaining and installing ProDAG anew, the same problems surfaced as experienced during the initial installation.

Analyzing the cause of all the above problems, we can identify at least two critical issues that surface:

- the existence of complex dependencies among components; and
- the lack of user support for location, retrieval, and tracking of components.

These problems are not unique to the situation in which the Arcadia consortium finds itself. Instead, these problems are fundamental and common to many other instances of software development. As examples, contracting often involves many contractors who independently develop many components constituting one or more software products that are put together by an integrator; large companies often consist of many independently functioning departments, each supported by their own set of software development tools; and companies sometimes form virtual enterprises to create a joint product, assembled from components developed by each company. In all these cases, the relative independence of the participating groups, combined with the need to produce a joint result, creates a situation similar to the one presented above. Components have to be released among groups, systems have to be released to external organizations, many versions of many different components are produced, and, most importantly of all, dependencies among components become increasingly complex.

From the above discussion it should be clear that software release management is an important part of the software development process. Simply making available and retrieving interdependent components individually neither facilitates independent software development nor encourages widespread use of large systems of systems. What is needed is a software release management process that documents the released components, records and exploits the dependencies among the components, and supports the location and retrieval of groups of compatible components.

3   Software Release Management

In the past, when a single organization developed a software system, configuration management systems (e.g., Aide de Camp [16], ClearCase [1], and Continuus [3]) were used to support software release management. Once a software system needed to be released, all components of the release were frozen, labeled, and archived in the configuration management system. Through advertising, potential users were made aware of the release, who then had to contact the development organization to obtain the release.

The advent of the Internet has changed this process dramatically. FTP sites and Web pages allow organizations to make their software available to the whole Internet community, to provide information about their products, and even to distribute both free trial versions and licensed revenue versions of their software. In support of the user, there are now search engines, databases, and indexes that provide a way to locate and retrieve a software system over the Internet.

Notwithstanding the success of this approach to releasing software over the Internet, it is insufficient to support the release of systems of systems. New requirements, from both developers and users of such systems, are laid upon software release management. For developers, a software release management process and support tool should provide a simple way to make software available to potential users. This entails the following requirements.

- *Dependencies should be explicit and easily recorded.* It should be possible for a developer to document dependencies as part of the release process, even if dependencies cross organizational boundaries. Moreover, this description should be directly usable by the release management tool for other purposes.
- *A system should be available through multiple channels.* Once a developer releases a system, the release management tool should automatically make it available via such mechanisms as FTP sites and Web pages.
- *The release process should involve minimal effort on the part of the developer.* For example, when a new version of a system is to be released, the developer should only have to specify what has changed, rather than treating the new version as a completely separate entity.
- *The scope of a release should be controllable.* A developer should be able to specify to whom, and under what conditions, the release is visible. Licensing, access control, and electronic commerce all need to seamlessly interoperate with the software release management process.
- *A history of retrievals should be kept.* This allows developers to track their systems, and to contact users with announcements of new releases, patches, related products, and the like.

For users, a software release management tool should provide an easy way to locate and retrieve components. This leads to the following requirements.

- *Sufficient descriptive information should be available.* Based on this information, a user should be able to easily determine which (versions of) systems are of use.

- *Physical distribution should be hidden.* If desired, a user should be unaware of where components are physically stored.
- *Interdependent systems should be retrievable as a group.* A user should be able to retrieve a system and the systems upon which it depends in one step, rather than having to retrieve each system individually, thus avoiding possible inconsistencies.
- *Unnecessary retrievals should be avoided.* Once a system has been retrieved by a user, the release management tool should keep track of this fact, and not re-retrieve the same system if subsequently requested.

A software release management process and support tool that satisfy these requirements will alleviate the problems evident in our motivating example. They will make it easier for developers to release systems of systems, and for users to efficiently obtain those systems in an appropriate configuration.

4 A Software Release Manager

SRM (Software Release Manager) is a prototype software release management tool that we have developed over the past year. It was designed to explore the issues involved in satisfying the requirements presented in the previous section, and employs a process similar to the traditional "label and archive" paradigm described in the same section. It assumes an archive containing a release is made available to users, and that users are responsible for locating and retrieving these archives. However, SRM enhances this process in two important ways.

- It *structures* the information used in the release management process, and then *uses* this structure in automating much of the process to support developers and users.
- It *hides* physical distribution from its users. In particular, dependencies among components can spread across multiple, physically distributed, organizational boundaries, and both developers and users are capable of accessing the information regarding components in a way transparent to the location of the information.

SRM realizes this process through a four-part architecture: a logically centralized, but physically distributed, release database; an interface to place components into the release database; an interface to retrieve components from the release database; and a retrieve database at each user site to record information about the components already retrieved. This architecture is depicted in Figure 2. Below, we discuss the first three parts of the architecture in detail. The fourth part, the retrieve database, has been superseded by the Software Dock [8] and is not discussed further here.

4.1 The Release Database

The release database is a repository that SRM uses to store the structured information pertaining the releases, as well as the releases themselves. The database

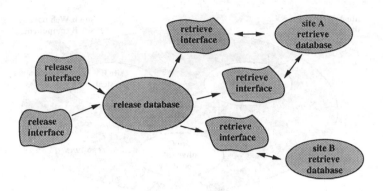

Fig. 2. SRM Architecture.

has been implemented using NUCM, a distributed repository for versioned artifacts [18]. SRM manipulates NUCM in such a way that the release database is
logically centralized, but physically distributed. It is logically centralized in that
it appears to users of SRM as if they are manipulating a single database; all
artifacts from all distributed sites are visible at the same time. It is physically
distributed in that the artifacts are stored in separate repositories spread across
different sites. Each site corresponds to a separate organization contributing components to the release database. In particular, when an organization releases a
component, a copy of the component is stored in a repository that is physically
present at that organization.

Figure 3 illustrates the structure of the release database using a hypothetical
arrangement of release information. As we can see, SRM stores four types of artifacts in a release database: the released components, metadata describing each
component, the dependency information for the components, and Web pages
for each component. Released components and their corresponding Web pages,
which represent the bulk of the data in the repository, are stored at the site
where the components were released. In this way, each site provides the storage
space for its own components. The other artifacts—i.e., the metadata and the
dependency information—are contained in single file that is stored at just one
of the sites. This happens to be site C in Figure 3. We have chosen to centralize
the storage of metadata and dependency artifacts for simplicity reasons. In the
future we plan to explore other, distributed schemes to manage these artifacts.

4.2 The Release Interface

Through the release interface of SRM, developers can *release* a component to
the release database, *modify* a release in the release database, or *withdraw* a
release from the release database. Releases are provided bottom-up with respect
to the dependencies, which is to say that before a component can be released, all

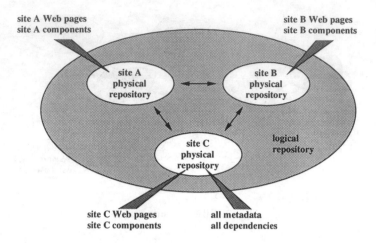

Fig. 3. Release Database Structure.

other components upon which it depends must have been released.[1] The inverse is true for withdrawing a release.

Releasing a Component. To release a component, a developer must provide three pieces of information: metadata describing the component; dependencies of the component on other components; and the source location of the component.

The metadata consists of, among other things, a component name, a component version, contact person for the component, the platform(s) the component runs on, and a detailed description of the component. Based on the metadata information, users that browse the release database can quickly assess the suitability of a particular component.

The second piece of information that a developer must provide describes the first-level, or direct, dependencies of the component on other components. SRM is able to calculate transitive dependencies across multiple components by following paths over first-level dependencies. Figure 4 shows an example of dependency specification. The interface allows for a simple point-and-click selection of first-level dependencies. In this case there are three that have been selected, LPT 3.1, Q 3.3, and TAOS 2.0, highlighted by the dark shading. SRM automatically includes a transitive dependency that it has calculated from previously provided information. In particular, Q 3.3 depends on Arpc 403.4, so this latter system has been highlighted by the lighter shading as a transitive dependency. The combination of the first-level and transitive dependencies is the set of dependencies maintained by SRM for the component being released.

---

[1] In fact, one could provide releases in any order, although it would not be possible to specify some of the dependencies. The missing dependencies could, and should, be added later using the modify operation.

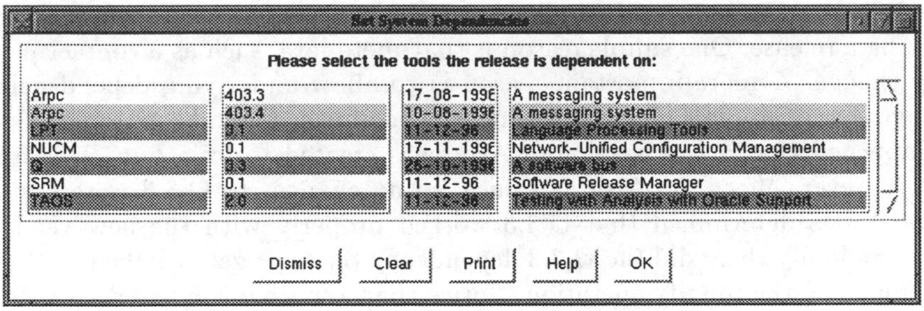

Fig. 4. Specifying Dependencies in SRM.

It should be noted that although some of the components might have been released at other sites, specifying them as a dependency for the component being released is as easy as specifying a locally developed component as a dependency; the release database is transparently distributed. For example, TAOS 2.0 resides at the University of California, LPT 3.1 resides at the University of Massachusetts, and Q 3.3 resides at the University of Colorado.

The third and final piece of information is the source location of a component. SRM assumes that a component release is contained in a single file, such as a TAR file or ZIP archive. Since SRM makes no assumptions about the format of the file, different formats can be used for different components.

SRM stores all metadata, all dependency information, and a copy of the component itself in the release database. Old versions of the component are not removed; the new release will co-exist with the old release. Therefore, the release database becomes a source of historical information about the various released components and their dependencies. In essence, the SRM repository automatically becomes the documentation for the release management process.

One assumption made throughout this process is that components are released through SRM only. However, there may very well be dependencies on components that have been produced by organizations that do not use SRM. For such cases, SRM provides the concept of *foreign* dependencies. A developer who wants to explicitly state that a component is dependent on a foreign dependency (which is the case for SRM itself, since it is built using Tcl/Tk [13]) simply releases two components. First the developer releases Tcl/Tk to SRM, then the developer releases the component that needed to be released in the first place. In both cases the same process is followed, and in both cases the result is the same: a component stored inside SRM that can be used as a dependency and that can be retrieved by users. However, there is one important difference. Instead of providing an archive containing the release, for foreign dependencies a developer specifies a URL through which the component can be retrieved. As opposed to storing the component inside SRM, SRM will maintain and use the given URL transparently to retrieve the component when needed.

Modifying a Release. SRM allows a developer to modify the information describing a release. One simple reason is that metadata, such as a contact person, may change. A more important reason is to allow underlying dependencies to change. For example, Q 3.3 [12], as mentioned above, depends on Arpc 403.4 [9]. It happened that a new version of Arpc was created to fix a bug. This fix did not, however, affect the Arpc interface, so no changes to Q 3.3 were required. Once it was determined that Q 3.3 worked properly with the new version of Arpc, and only then, did the Q 3.3 dependency on Arpc get switched to the new version using the modify operation. Notice that a mechanism based on a default dependency, such as "the latest", would not have worked in this scenario. This is because the dependency would have switched automatically from the old to the new *before* it was verified that the new version was compatible.

Withdrawing a Release. The third operation supported by the release interface allows developers to withdraw components from the release database. This functionality is desired for the obvious reasons. Just one restriction is placed on withdrawal of components, but it is an important one that maintains the integrity of the database: the only components that can be withdrawn are those components upon which there are no dependencies.[2] For example, since Q 3.3 depends on Arpc 403.4, as shown in Figure 4, Arpc 403.4 cannot be withdrawn from the release database. Thus, if a developer indeed wants to withdraw Arpc 403.4, either Q 3.3 needs to be withdrawn first, or the dependencies of Q 3.3 need to be changed to not include Arpc 403.4.

4.3 The Retrieve Interface

Once components have been placed into the release database, the retrieve interface of SRM can be used to retrieve the components from the database. SRM uses information in the release database to support a user in locating and retrieving components. In effect, the retrieve interface forms a bridge between the development environment and the user environment.

The retrieve interface is built as a static, Web-page-based interface because the connectivity of the Internet guarantees widespread access to the release database. Standard Internet browsers, such as Netscape Navigator and Microsoft Explorer, can be used to retrieve components.

Every time a component is released, SRM creates a Web page for that component and updates a main Web page listing all available components. When users want to retrieve a component, they first retrieve the main Web page through their Internet browser. Upon selection of a component from the main Web page, the Web page corresponding to the selected component will be presented to the

---

[2] This rather strong policy can be circumvented by simply modifying the release to have no contents. This crude mechanism maintains the integrity of the database at the same time as it provides developers the flexibility to remove dependent systems, but should only be used in extreme circumstances.

user. The contents of this page is the metadata that were provided upon release of the component. This allows a user to quickly assess the suitability of the various components. In addition, the Web page shows the dependence graph for the component and provides selection buttons to turn off or on dependent components for retrieval. This portion of the interface is shown in Figure 5. In this example, ProDAG is being retrieved, and three of its four dependencies have been selected for retrieval as well.

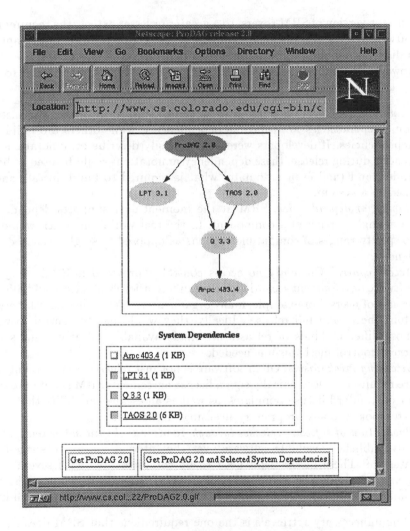

Fig. 5. Portion of an SRM Retrieval Web Page.

A user of the retrieve interface is not aware of the fact that the various components might have originated from several geographically distributed sites. The distribution is hidden within the SRM release database, which silently retrieves the components from the various repositories and ships them back to he user.

Finally, it should be noted that the retrieve interface keeps detailed statistical information about the number of retrievals that have taken place, allowing developers to assess the usage of their components.

5 Requirements Evaluation

The current version of SRM covers, to a greater or lesser extent, the requirements for software release management enumerated in Section 3. Most importantly, it hides distribution and promotes the use of dependency information.

However, we can see places where SRM can be strengthened in order to fully satisfy the requirements.

- *Annotation of dependencies.* Not all dependencies are alike. For instance some dependencies are run-time dependencies, while others are build-time dependencies. If developers were able to easily describe or annotate dependencies during release, these dependency annotations could be used to better understand (and even automate) what is required to build, install, and/or execute a system.
- *Ranges of dependencies.* SRM at the moment only supports dependencies on a single version of a component. In the real world, one often would like to specify ranges of compatible versions as opposed to single version dependencies.
- *Access control.* Currently no access control is provided in SRM. A typical software development scenario involves different levels of release and different groups of users. For example, many organizations like to distinguish between alpha, beta, and full releases. Ideally, they would like to control to whom those different kinds of releases are made available. Clearly, some sort of access control mechanism is needed.
- *Licensing mechanisms.* Often software is not just released to users, but users are required to electronically sign a license agreement. SRM should provide a set of standard license templates, as well as an escape capability that allows it to hook into any proprietary licensing mechanism.
- *Publication of software releases through additional channels.* Currently, SRM only publishes available software over the Internet via a Web-page-based interface. These mechanisms need to be complemented with several other means of publishing a release, such as FTP sites, a developer-controlled mailing list, automatic postings to one or more news groups, and the like.

Avoiding unnecessary retrievals is the one requirement that SRM does not address on its own. Instead, it satisfies this requirement through an integration with the Software Dock, which we describe elsewhere [8].

Despite its current shortcomings, SRM clearly has advantages over the "label and archive" paradigm traditionally used for software release management. We have discussed how SRM improves both the process by which developers make components available to users and the process by which users obtain the components. Besides these two important improvements, however, SRM has another advantage.

In settings where a set of semi-independent groups is cooperating to build one or more software products, such as in all of the cases discussed in Section 2, the old and often ad hoc release management process employed by the various participating groups can be replaced by a single, more disciplined, and unified process employed by all the groups. Each of the groups is still able to use its own development process, its own configuration management system, and its own development tools. But the various mechanisms for release management can be unified under SRM to provide a common point of intersection for the organizations. In this way the various groups are flexibly joined at a high level of abstraction. SRM provides developers a basis for communicating about interdependent components that avoids low-level details of path names, FTP sites, and/or URLs. Moreover, because SRM maintains all versions of all components in its release database, and maintains the status of components located at each site in its retrieve databases, it becomes the language and mechanism for intergroup communication about interdependent components.

6 Related Work

To date, software release management by itself has received very little attention from either the academic or the commercial world. Many of the existing software deployment systems do in fact incorporate some rudimentary form of software release management, but only because it is needed to support their core activities, such as configuration and installation. However, none of these systems have specifically and methodologically tackled the issues of software release management and, therefore, contain deficiencies with respect to software release management. Specifically, most of the deployment systems lack adequate dependency handling, while the ones that do tend to lack distribution. Enhancing these systems with the features explored in SRM, which is the only existing system that fully addresses release management, would result in much more useful and powerful deployment tools.

Below, we discuss a representative sample of the existing deployment systems and relate these systems to SRM.

6.1 20/20's NetInstall

NetInstall [15] is a system that provides automatic installation of software that is published on Web pages. When a user selects a software system, an installation agent is downloaded that installs the desired software system for the user. Although different in focus from SRM, it is relevant because implicit in NetInstall is a release "builder" that creates the appropriate installation agent. Through this release builder the developer is supported in creating a release, while the user is supported by automatic retrieval and installation of the release.

NetInstall differs substantially from SRM in that it focuses on single system delivery, whereas SRM manages the much more complex problem of coordinated releases of systems of systems. In addition, NetInstall does not support publication of the release (i.e., developers have to create Web pages containing installation agents for their systems themselves).

6.2 Marimba's Castanet and Open Software Associates' netDeploy

Marimba's Castanet [11], as well as Open Software Associates' netDeploy [2], provides for automatic software updates once a system has been installed on a site. In essence, these systems mirror software from a single distribution site onto a set of mirror sites, keeping the mirror sites up to date with the distribution site. Both systems provide a "tuner" through which users can select the software that they want to have mirrored onto their site.

In many ways Castanet and netDeploy are similar to SRM; however, there are some important differences. Both systems, similarly to NetInstall, focus on single system settings and neither system is therefore capable of managing dependencies or relating components developed at different sites the way SRM does. In addition, components are continuously and automatically kept up to date by Castanet and netDeploy. Given that new versions of software can be incompatible with existing versions, this can be a frustrating experience for users who depend on a particular version of a software system. SRM will prevent this from happening by placing the user in control of when a new release is retrieved and thus allowing a user to judge, based on the information presented, whether to update the software or not.

6.3 AT&T's ship and Tivoli's TME

AT&T's ship [7] (and similarly Tivoli's TME [17]) is an extensive software deployment system that provides for automatic software installation and update. Unlike SRM, which provides control to both developers and users, ship places all control in the hands of the developer. A developer decides to which sites a release is to be shipped, and then ship takes control of the various user sites and installs the necessary software components there. While doing so, ship maintains small databases of components and versions installed at the user sites. Using the information in these databases, ship can check for necessary components being present at the user sites, and report back to the developer site about whether the installation can be completed or not.

While clearly being more powerful than Castanet and netDeploy, ship still does not address all software release management issues. It suffers from similarities to the old label and archive paradigm: the developer is in control, not the user. Finally, even though ship is capable of handling dependencies, it is only capable of handling dependencies that stem from the same release site. As each release site corresponds to a single organization, this places a serious limitation on the usability of ship that SRM does not possess.

6.4   FreeBSD Porting System

The FreeBSD porting system supports the FreeBSD user community by organizing freely available software into a carefully constructed hierarchy known as the "ports collection". The system uses specialized make [6] macros and variables to enable the building of systems in the hierarchy as well to manage their associated dependencies. It uses various forms of heuristics to determine a site's state and employs the results in building and installing a software package.

SRM is complementary to the FreeBSD porting system. Whereas the emphasis of SRM is on making software systems available to users and facilitating users in obtaining such software systems, the emphasis of FreeBSD is on the build and installation process. It is conceivable that the two systems could cooperate closely to support a user beyond the point where SRM delivers a set of components. FreeBSD would be responsible for receiving the components delivered by SRM and then building and installing the components for the user.

7   Conclusions

The work described here represents a novel approach to the software release process. By means of a software release management system, SRM, a bridge has been built between the development process and the deployment process through which both developers and users are supported. To developers, SRM provides a convenient and uniform way to release interdependent systems to the outside world. To users, SRM provides a way to retrieve these systems through the well-known interface of the Internet. For both, the fact that components are released from various geographically distributed sources is hidden.

The basic concept behind SRM is simple: to provide distribution transparency to the release of interdependent software components. However, its fundamental contribution—the awareness and support of the release management process—is an important one. The software release management process has largely been ignored in the past, but its identification as a major component in the deployment process has led us to develop SRM, a system that better supports the actual process taking place. The key differentiators that provide this support are the following.

- *SRM uses structured information about the release management process to automate much of this process.*
- *SRM hides distribution and decentralization from both developers and users.*
- *SRM places users in control of when deployment of a software system takes place.*

Currently, SRM is in use as the release management system for the software produced by the Software Engineering Research Laboratory at the University of Colorado.[3] Our experiences with initial versions of SRM in this setting have allowed us to evaluate the user interface and functionality provided. Based on

---

[3] See http://www.cs.colorado.edu/users/serl for a pointer to our released software.

the feedback received, many modifications and enhancements have been made to both the interface and functionality, resulting in the system as presented in the previous sections.

Our future plans call for several significant functionality improvements to SRM, including the incorporation of standard licensing templates, a mechanism for annotating dependencies, and access control over releases. In addition, we plan to investigate how different SRM repositories can be federated to form more flexible hierarchies of organization. Finally, we are looking into how SRM can be integrated with other software deployment systems.

Acknowledgments. We thank Jonathan Cook for being a willing first user of SRM, and would like to acknowledge Antonio Carzaniga, Mike Hollis, and Craig Snider for their contributions to the design and implementation of SRM.

This work was supported in part by the Air Force Material Command, Rome Laboratory, and the Advanced Research Projects Agency under Contract Number F30602-94-C-0253. The content of the information does not necessarily reflect the position or the policy of the U.S. Government and no official endorsement should be inferred.

References

1. L. Allen, G. Fernandez, K. Kane, D. Leblang, D. Minard, and J. Posner. ClearCase MultiSite: Supporting Geographically-Distributed Software Development. In *Software Configuration Management: ICSE SCM-4 and SCM-5 Workshops Selected Papers*, 1995.
2. Open Software Associates. OpenWEB netDeploy. Available on the world wide web at *http://www.osa.com/products/openweb/oweb000.htm.*
3. Continuus Software Corporation, Irvine, California. *Continuus Task Reference*, 1994.
4. W.H. Davidow and M.S. Malone. *The Virtual Corporation.* Harper Business, 1992.
5. Digital Equipment Corporation, Hewlett-Packard Company, HyperDesk Corporation, NCR Corporation, Object Design, Inc., and SunSoft, Inc. *The Common Object Request Broker: Architecture and Specification, Version 1.2.* Object Management Group, Framingham, Massachusetts, December 1993.
6. S.I. Feldman. Evolution of Make. In *Proceedings of the International Workshop on Software Versioning and Configuration Control*, pages 413–416, 1988.
7. G. Fowler, D. Korn, H. Rao, J. Snyder, and K.-P. Vo. Configuration Management. In B. Krishnamurthy, editor, *Practical Reusable UNIX Software*, chapter 3. Wiley, New York, 1995.
8. R.S. Hall, D.M. Heimbigner, A. van der Hoek, and A.L. Wolf. An Architecture for Post-Development Configuration Management in a Wide-Area Network. In *Proceedings of the 1997 International Conference on Distributed Computing Systems*, pages 269–278. IEEE Computer Society, May 1997.
9. D.M. Heimbigner. Arpc: An augmented remote procedure call system. Technical Report CU-ARCADIA-100-96, University of Colorado Arcadia Project, Boulder, CO 80309-0430, Revised 19 June 1996. Version 403.4.

10. R. Kadia. Issues Encountered in Building a Flexible Software Development Environment. In *SIGSOFT '92: Proceedings of the Fifth Symposium on Software Development Environments*, pages 169–180. ACM SIGSOFT, December 1992.

11. Marimba. Castanet White Paper. Available on the world wide web at *http://www.marimba.com/developer/castanet-whitepaper.html*.

12. M.J. Maybee, D.M. Heimbigner, and L.J. Osterweil. Multilanguage Interoperability in Distributed Systems. In *Proceedings of the 18th International Conference on Software Engineering*, pages 451–463. Association for Computer Machinery, March 1996.

13. J.K. Ousterhout. *Tcl and the Tk Toolkit*. Addison-Wesley Publishing Company, 1994.

14. D.J. Richardson, T.O. O'Malley, C.T. Moore, and S.L. Aha. Developing and Integrating ProDAG in the Arcadia Environment. In *SIGSOFT '92: Proceedings of the Fifth Symposium on Software Development Environments*, pages 109–119. ACM SIGSOFT, December 1992.

15. 20/20 Software. 20/20 NetInstall. Available on the world wide web at *http://www.twenty.com/Pages/NI/NI.shtm*.

16. Software Maintenance & Development Systems, Inc, Concord, Massachusetts. *Aide de Camp Configuration Management System*, April 1994.

17. Tivoli. Tivoli TME 10 Software Distribution. Available on the world wide web at *http://www.tivoli.com/products/Courier/*.

18. A. van der Hoek, D.M. Heimbigner, and A.L. Wolf. A Generic, Peer-to-Peer Repository for Distributed Configuration Management. In *Proceedings of the 18th International Conference on Software Engineering*, pages 308–317. Association for Computer Machinery, March 1996.

A Contextual Approach for Process-Integrated Tools

Klaus Pohl and Klaus Weidenhaupt

RWTH Aachen, Informatik V, Ahornstraße 55, D-52074 Aachen, Germany
{pohl,weidenh}@informatik.rwth-aachen.de

Abstract: *Research in process-centered environments (PCEs) has focused on project management support and has been dominated by the search for suitable process modelling languages and enactment mechanisms. The consequences of the process orientation on the tools used during process performance, and for offering fine-grained, method-based support to the engineers performing the process have been studied much less.*

In this paper, we discuss the requirements for a tighter integration of interactive engineering tools and present a contextual approach for the process-integration of those tools. To achieve process integration we argue that tools, like processes, should be explicitly defined. The integration of the tool models with the process definitions forms an environment model which is interpreted during tool execution. Based on this interpretation tool behavior is adjusted according to the process definition; i.e. the interpretation empowers the tools to provide fine-grained method-conform process support.

Our approach has been implemented as a reusable object-oriented framework and validated by specializing this framework to develop two prototypical process-integrated environments (PIEs).

1 Introduction

During the last decade a tendency of moving from product-oriented computer supported development environments to process-oriented environments, so-called process-centered environments (PCEs), could be observed. The explicit definition of processes is a prerequisite for easy adaptation to project specific needs and the integration of process changes. In contrast, the process support offered by product-oriented environments is hard-coded, i.e. there exists no explicit process definition. Due to the required re-programming process changes are hard to accomplish.

PCEs can be divided into three conceptually distinguishable domains [1,2]: the modelling, the performance, and the enactment domains. The *modelling domain* comprises all activities for defining and maintaining software process models using a formal language with an underlying operational semantics which enables mechanical interpretation of the models. The *enactment domain* encompasses what takes place in a PCE to support (guide, enforce, control) process performance; this is essentially a mechanical interpretation of the process models by a so-called process engine. The *performance domain* is defined as the set of actual activities conducted by human agents and non-human agents (computers).

Process support provided by PCEs can be characterized by the typical interactions between the three domains: (1) a process model is instantiated, i.e. process parameters like resources and time scheduling are bound to project specific values and passed to the enactment domain; (2) based on the interpretation of the instantiated model, the enactment domain supports, controls, and monitors the activities of the performance domain; (3) the performance domain provides feedback information on current process performance to the enactment domain. This is a prerequisite for adjusting process model enactment to the actual process performance and enabling branches, backtracks, and loops in process model enactment.

Research in the PCE area has focused on *process (project) management support* and has been dominated by the search for suitable process modelling languages and enactment mechanism, i.e. *has focused on the modelling and enactment domains* [3]. It has resulted in a set of mature process modelling languages and enactment mechanism (e.g. [4,5,6,7,8,9]). Although the need for process integration of the tools used to perform the process has been recognized [10,3,11,12,2] the integration of the performance domain, respectively the tools, with the modelling and enactment domains has almost been neglected [3,2,11]. Such an integration is essential if fine-grained, methodical support should be offered to the engineers, e.g. during the creation of a requirements specification or a high/low level design.

The process integration of the tools presented in this paper is based on the assumption that the humans executing the process should play an active role during process execution, i.e. that process execution should not only be dictated by the process enactment mechanism. We argue that *process-integrated tools* are a prerequisite for enabling the user to understand and control process execution and to play a more active role by initiating the execution of predefined method fragments depending on the actual process situation.

In section 2 we elaborate the main requirements to be considered for process-integration of interactive engineering tools. The key ideas for achieving these requirements are sketched in section 3. The consideration of those requirements has led to a significant improvement of our approach for process-integration of tools described in [2]. We now advocate that for achieving process integration the capabilities of the interactive tools should be explicitly defined. The resulting tool models should, in addition, be integrated with the process definitions. Our new contextual approach for defining and integrating tool and process models is outlined in section 4. Our overall approach has been validated by implementing a generic architecture which interprets the integrated model and thereby assures that the engineering environment "behaves" according to the method definitions (section 5).

Finally, we compare our contextual approach for process-integrated tools with other research and existing PCEs (section 6) and provide an outlook to future work (section 7).

2 Requirements for Process-Integrated Tools

In the enactment domain, process definitions are enacted to drive process performance. In the performance domain, tools are used by humans to execute the various process steps and method fragments. Integrating these two domains for providing fine-grained methodical support for the engineers has different facets and requirements which are identified in this section.

A widely adopted view on the tool integration problem has been proposed by Wasserman who distinguishes platform, user interface, data, control, and process integration [10] but, like other authors, does not discuss process integration in depth. The integration between the enactment and performance domain mainly has to cope with data, control, and the process integration aspects. While we share Wasserman's view on data integration and control integration, process integration requires certain features which are not discussed in the literature so far. These requirements are also related to, but significantly more comprehensive than those discussed by [1,13,14,15,16,17] whose analysis is mainly based on the weak integration of the enactment and performance domains in existing PCEs.

2.1 Service Integration

A *tool service* is a functionality provided by a tool which can be accessed (called) from outside, e.g. the creation of a certain artefact, the compilation of the source code, printing or loading a document, etc. Tool services can vary in their complexity. To ensure that the tools of the performance domain can execute the services requested by the enactment mechanism, the tools used must be considered when defining process models.

Current process modelling formalisms lack comprehensive modelling concepts for representing tool resources at the same conceptual level as processes. They offer only limited, low-level constructs for representing service invocation (e.g. black transitions in SPADE [4], the `call`-statement in Marvel [5], or the wrapping techniques for blackbox integration employed in the OZ environment [18]). For exploiting existing tool support in the process definitions the method engineer has to collect information about the available tools, their services and the service invocation (e.g. parameters required) from various sources (e.g. manuals, program documentations, personal knowledge or experience). Considering the heterogeneous environments and work settings which exist today in industry, guaranteeing that the services defined in the process model are correctly mapped to the tool environment used for performing the process is not trivial, especially if a process model is enacted in different environments.

Thus, mechanisms are required which systematically support the method engineer in finding and assigning adequate tool support to certain process steps. If the available tools (e.g. their services, in and out parameters of the services) are defined at a conceptual level the method engineer can be supported in relating the tool services to the process definitions. For example, the tool and process models can be compared and discrepancies, such as lack of sufficient tool functionality or wrong assignments, can be detected.

2.2 Invocation of Method Fragments

On the one hand, methodical support can not be fully predefined due to many criteria not known a priori which influence the actual process performance and/or due to the weak understanding of the steps themselves. The actual process performance is thus often driven by humans which, depending on the process situation, decide what to do next, i.e. process performance depends on intelligent and creative individuals which make the right decisions. It is thus important that the computer based environment does not restrict the humans in their creativity.

On the other hand, there exist method fragments which are well understood, do not depend on unknown criteria and can thus can be predefined [19,2]. To increase the productivity and the quality of the product under development, such methodical knowledge should, whenever possible, be used to guide the engineer. As a consequence, the computer-based environment has to assure that the well understood method fragments are used to guide the user whenever possible.

Process-integrated tools must thus provide means for initiating the execution of predefined method fragments, e.g. by comparing the current process situation with the method fragment definitions.

2.3 Process Sensitive Tools (Informing the User about the Enactment State)

A tight integration between the enactment and performance domains can only be achieved if both domains consider the process status of each other. The enactment domain has to consider current process performance for deducing the process steps to be performed next (section 2.4), whereas the current enactment state has to be reflected in the performance domain. To assure that the user is aware of the current enactment state, the tools must be process sensitive. A process sensitive tool

- adapts its behavior (the user interactions allowed and the services provided) according to the current enactment state and the process definitions. For example, the selectability of product parts may be restricted to the ones allowed in the current state, or the product parts on which a service can be performed are highlighted to draw user attention to them;
- empowers the user to activate predefined method fragments and services provided by other tools. Since process definitions are subject to frequent change, the activation

of predefined method fragments and services should not be hard-coded in the tool. Instead, the activation should be based on the actual process definitions. The tools must be process-aware; i.e. must have knowledge about the actual process definitions.

Supplying the performance domain with knowledge about the enactment state is straight-forward in situations where a particular service has to be performed on a certain product part. In this case, the relevant product parts are passed as parameters of the service request. If there are alternatives among which the user has to choose, the enactment domain must inform the tool about the set of services allowed, the selectable product parts for each service, respectively product part combinations.

2.4 Feedback Information (Informing the Process Engine about Performance State)

For adjusting the enactment state according to the current process performance, the performance domain must provide feedback information about the execution of a particular service by a tool. The data to be exchanged depend on the service executed. Consequently, the feedback data have to be defined as out-parameters for each service type (see service integration above). In addition, information about the current process performance state, e.g. unforeseeable events like a process deviation, has to be provided. This information can either be created by observing (monitoring) activities, or directly provided by the user.

Technically, the distribution of the feedback information has to be enabled by a control integration mechanism.

The problem of gathering feedback information from the performance domain has also been recognized in current approaches. In SPADE [4], for example, a specific Petri-Net construct, the user input place, has been introduced. Message events generated by the tools have to be mapped into tokens of such places. In Provence [20], the enactments mechanism captures events from the performance domain via a monitoring system for operating system traps, e.g. file system accesses. However, mapping performance domain events to feedback information understood by the enactment mechanism is by far not trivial, e.g. to deduce that saving a file in an text editor means that a bug fix in the source file has been completed.

2.5 Synchronization of Enactment and Performance Domain

The definition of a communication protocol and its application within each domain is a prerequisite for synchronizing the process states of both domains. In current PCE approaches, the interaction between the enactment domain and the tools is typically established by an implicit client-server relationship, i.e. the enactment domain acts as a client which requests the execution of a tool service. Conversely, the tool plays the role of a server which executes the service and returns the results (feedback information) to the enactment mechanism. This simple cooperation pattern is sufficient as long as we consider traditional tools which are not process-integrated.

Due to the more active role of process-integrated tools (section 2.2 - 2.4), a more elaborate interaction protocol between the two domains than client-server has to be provided. Such a protocol should, for example, distinguish between different process states like normal process performance, process deviations, the performance of automated services, or user choices.

2.6 Process-Aware Control Integration Mechanism

In contrast to service integration which defines the service interfaces, a control integration mechanism is required for transmitting particular service requests and feedback information between the components of a process-integrated environment. A control integration mechanism is responsible for passing the requested service to a tool which is able to execute the service. To enable correct physical distribution of the service requests and the feedback information provided after service execution, the control integration mechanism has to be aware of the services provided by a particular tool. In addition, service and feedback distribution has to consider relevant knowledge defined in the process model, e.g. if the process model restricts possible allocation of resources needed for performing a service, or if the model explicitly defines the service provider, this has to be considered when distributing a service. Thus, either the control mechanism must be process-aware, i.e. must know the relevant parts of the actual process definition, or the enactment domain must instruct service distribution according to the process definition. In most existing PCEs (e.g. SPADE [4], MELMAC [6], Merlin [21], ProcessWEAVER [9]), neither a process-awareness of the control mechanism nor the ability of the enactment domain to control service distribution is offered.

Existing control integration mechanism like FIELD [22], BMS of HP's Softbench [23], Tooltalk [24], or CORBA [25] provide an excellent foundation for implementing a process-aware control integration mechanism.

3 Key Solution Ideas

Our key solution ideas for fulfilling the requirements discussed in section 2 (see figure 1) are:

- The explicit definition of *tool models* and their integration with process models (section 4). The solution described in this paper extends our previous solution [2] in two main aspects. First, tool models are defined separately from the process models and represent the capabilities of the tools. Secondly, the integration of the tool and process models forms an integrated *environment model* that takes both process and tool support into account. The environment model offers five main advantages: (a) it achieves service integration by uniformly defining the services provided by the tools and by the enactment mechanism; (b) it enables the tool to adapt the user guidance according to the actual method definitions; (c) it defines how objects should be displayed by the tool; (d) it defines the required feedback information for each type of service request; (e) it empowers the tool to support the user in initiating the invocation of predefined method fragments.
- The definition of a comprehensive *communication protocol* as a basis for synchronising

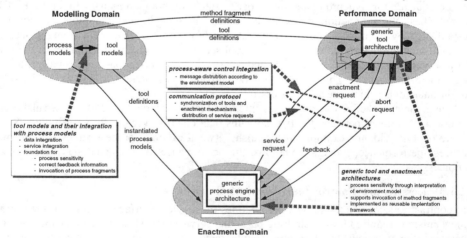

Fig. 1. The Key Solution Ideas.

both domains. The communication protocol extends the conventional client-server relationship between enactment mechanism and tools offered by most PCEs to a more flexible pattern where both domains can play the role of a server and a client, i.e. the enactment domain can request the execution of tool services and the performance domain (tools) can request the enactment of predefined method fragments. The detailed description of the communication protocol can be found in [2];

- The implementation of a *process-aware control integration mechanism* on top of ToolTalk [24], which ensures that service requests are distributed between both domains in accordance with the process definitions.
- The development of *generic architectures* for process-integrated tools and enactment mechanisms (section 5). Both architectures ensure that process performance is in accordance with the environment model and guarantee the synchronization of the enactment and performance domains based on the communication prototcol. The generic tool architecture facilitates the invocation of predefined method fragments and assures that the guidance provided to the user corresponds to the process definition and the actual process situation. The generic enactment architecture handles enactment requests of the performance domain by enacting the requested method fragments and provides means for an easy integration of existing enactment mechanisms.

4 Modelling Tools and Processes

According to the requirements discussed in section 2 there are *three types of services* in process-integrated environments (PIE): automated, guidance and enactment services (section 4.1). Whereas the process model defines when a service should be performed, the tool model defines which services are provided by a particular tool.

In section 4.2 we sketch a *contextual process meta model*, i.e. a process modelling language, which defines an ontology for representing the three service types as well as their situated invocation. We further illustrate the definition of the three service types using the defined ontology.

For representing the services offered by a tool we propose a *tool meta model*, i.e. tool modelling language, which provides additional concepts for defining the capabilities of the tool (section 4.3). The definition of the concepts of the tool meta model was driven by the need for an easy integration with the process meta model.

An integration of the proposed tool and process meta models can be achieved by defining associations between both meta models (section 4.4). Thereby the so called *environment meta model* is formed.

4.1 Requirements for Modelling Concepts

4.1.1 Three Service Types

According to the requirements discussed in section 2 there exist three types of services in a PIE:

- *automated services* which require no user interactions and are executed by the tool according to the service request obtained by the enactment domain;
- *guidance services* which guide the user in making a selection among a set of alternative services and product parts. If the execution of a *guidance service* is requested, the tool must adapt its behavior (the services offered and the product parts displayed at its user interface) according to the process definition and the information obtained with the service request;
- *enactment services* which enable the tools to request the enactment of a predefined method fragment from the enactment domain.

To illustrate the three service types assume a requirements engineering environment consisting of a set of interactive tools.

In this environment the creation of an entity type is an atomic action (*automated service*) provided the Entity Relationship (ER) editor. The refinement of an entity type is defined as *guidance service*. Since the guidance service defines two possible ways for achieving a refinement of an entity type (discrimination of attributes and the specialization (subtyping) of the entity type), the ER editor has to offer these alternatives to the requirements engineer, i.e. the ER editor has to adapt its user interface according to the guidance service definition.

The refinement technique "subtyping" is defined as a method fragment which specifies a set of process steps (services) to be performed in a certain order. If the requirements engineer selects this alternatve, the defined method fragment has to be enacted by the process engine, i.e. the ER editor has to request the execution of the predefined method fragment by the process engine (*enactment service*).

4.1.2 Service Invocation is Situated

The applicability of a particular service depends on the current process situation. A situation is normally regarded as an abstraction of current reality based on observed object states (see [26,2] for details). A simple example for the situated nature of actions is a delete action; if no object (e.g. entity) exists the delete action (e.g. delete entity) can not be applied.

In most situations many services (actions) can be applied. For example, when modelling an ER-diagram you can create an arbitrary new entity, delete one of the entities, define a new attribute and so forth. Consequently, a choice among the allowed services has to be made. As stated in many contributions, such a choice (decision) is always driven by the goal (or set of goals) which the person (or group) tries to achieve (e.g. [27,28,29,30,31]). The decision which service to apply in a given situation can either be predefined in the process model (i.e. the process modeler does not allow any choice) or the decision has to be made by the engineers performing the process (i.e. the process modeler has defined more than one service for a given situation).

To enable the definition of a set of services which can be applied in a given situation, we have to define the situations themselves as objects and provide means to represent the goal the user wants to achieve in a given situation.

4.2 A Contextual Process Meta Model

The contextual process meta model (see upper part of figure 2) described in this section was developed within the NATURE project (see [32,33,19,2] for a detailed description).

A *situation* is built from product parts of the *product* undergoing the development process. An *intention* reflects the goal to be achieved in a given situation. A *context* represents a meaningful relation between a situation and an intention. Thus, the meta model provides concepts for the explicit representation of process situations and the goals to be achieved in such situations. The refinement of the notion of context into executable, choice and plan contexts enables the representation of the three service types which appear in a PIE:

- *Executable contexts* represent the part of the process definition which can be strictly enforced, or even automated, i.e. the user does not have any choice what to do next. An executable context is operationalized by performing the *action* related to this context. Performing the action changes the product and may thus generate new situations. Thus, executable contexts are used to define atomic tool services (automated services);
- *Choice contexts* represent the part of the process definition, in which the user has to make a decision. For each choice context at least two *alternatives* must be defined. An alternative can be another choice, executable, or plan context. For each alternative, *arguments* (pros and/or cons) can be provided to guide the application engineer in

choosing one of the alternatives. Thus, choice contexts are used to define the guidance services.

- *Plan contexts* define a strategy to fulfill a particular intention (goal); i.e. they define a certain order on a subset of arbitrary contexts (plan, choice, and/or executable contexts). A plan context can be supported by forcing the application engineer to deal with the contexts in the order defined by the plan. Thus, plan contexts are used to define enactment services.[1]

4.3 The Tool Meta Model

Representing processes and tools at a conceptual level is a prerequisite for comparing and mapping the services defined in the process definition to the services offered by the tools of the environment. For achieving process-sensitive tools we propose to model tools not only in terms of the services provided (as in most other PCE approaches), but also in terms of their graphical user interface and interaction capabilities. The tool meta model was designed to facilitate an easy integration with the contextual process meta model proposed in section 4.2.

The cornerstone of the tool meta model is the concept *tool category* (see lower part of figure 2). An atomic service (*action*) provided by a tool category is related to the tool category by a *provides_action* association, e.g. the action CreateEntity is related to the ER-editor. For each action the *input* and *output* parameters (*products*) are defined. The modelling of the atomic actions is important for assigning executable contexts to tool categories (section 4.4).

The graphical presentation of the product parts is defined as instantiation of the association *displays* between a graphical shape provided by the tool (modelled as instances of the concept *graphical shape*) and a product part.

Besides the capabilities of a tool for displaying product parts, also the interaction capabilities have to be defined. We assume that each tool enables the selection and de-selection of product parts by default and thus do not model these interactions. In contrast, the *CommandElements* provided by a tool have to be explicitly defined. In our implementation we currently distinguish between three types of such capabilities, namely *PullDownMenu*, *ControlIcons* and *ControlKeys*.

4.4 The Environment Meta Model: Integrating Process and Tool Meta Models

While the process meta model supports the definition of method fragments in terms of executable, choice and plan contexts, the tool meta model is used to define the capabilities of the tools available in the environment. By interrelating the tool and process meta models an integrated meta model, the so called *environment meta model*, is formed which defines how and by which tool a context has to be executed (see dashed lines in figure 2).

To define the tool category responsible for executing a choice or executable context (remember plan contexts are enacted by process engines) the executable and choice contexts defined in the process model must be related to the tool definition. Since the tool meta model was designed with this interrelation in mind, the integration of the tool and process meta models is fairly easy (see figure 2).

Besides the easy integration, the tool and process meta models facilitate consistency check through which a consistent interrelation of both models can be supported.

---

[1] For defining the *control flow* of plan contexts we propose to represent the concepts of the process meta model using an existing process modelling language. For our prototypical environments (section 5) we have chosen the petri-net language SLANG [4] and the imperative language C++ (see [34] for details).

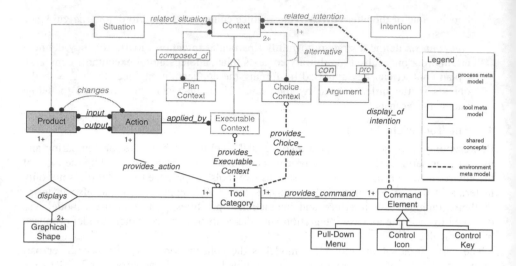

Fig. 2. The Environment Meta Model.

4.4.1 Relating Tool Categories and Executable Contexts

Each executable context defined in the process model has to be associated with the tool category responsible for executing the context. This responsibility is represented as an instance of the association *provides_executable_context*. For example, if the executable context *CreateEntity* is related to a tool category *ER-editor* the ER-editor has to perform the action *A* associated in the process model with this context.

Given an executable context E, the associated action A and a set of tool categories T_1 – T_n, we distinguish between three types of assignment:

- *automated assignment*: If there exists exactly one tool category T_i which offers the required action A this tool category is automatically associated to the executable context E;
- *choice of tool category*: If there exist two or more tool categories T_1 - T_n which offer the required action A the method engineer must relate exactly one tool category with the executable context E;
- *lack of tool support:* If no tool category provides the required action A a new tool action has to be implemented in a tool and defined in the corresponding tool model, or the process model has to be changed.

For each assignment between a tool category and an executable context two consistency checks can be performed to ensure that the input and output defined for the tool action in the tool model correspond with the process model definitions.

C1 *assure that the* output *associations defined in the tool model between the action and the product parts are subsumed by the* change *associations defined for the action in the process model:* Given an action A. Let P_o be the set of product parts related to A in the tool model using *output* associations and P_c the set of product parts related to A in the process model via *change* associations. Then, P_o must be a subset of P_c;

C2 *assure that all product parts defined as* input *for the action are subsumed by the situation of the executable context related to the action:* Given an action A. Let P_i be the set of product parts related to A in the tool model via *input* associations. Let E be the executable context associated to the action A in the process model, S its situation and P_s the set of product parts defined for the situation. Then P_i must be a subset of P_s.

Only if both checks are successful, i.e. if the input and output parameters defined in the tool model correspond with the process definitions, the tool category is assigned to the executable context. Otherwise, the method engineer is informed about the mismatch.

4.4.2 Relating Tool Categories and Choice Contexts

Each choice context has to be related to exactly one tool category by an *provides_choice_context* association. Thereby the tool category assigned to the choice context is made responsible for performing the choice context, i.e. a new guidance service is defined for the tool category.

In addition, for each context C_j defined as alternative of the choice context CC the presentation of the intention I related to the context C_j has to be defined. Since an intention (e.g. the intention *delete*) can be associated with more than one context (e.g. the context *deleteEntity* and *deleteAttribute*) a context dependent presentation of the intention is required. This is achieved by relating the context C_j to at least one command element using the *display_of_intention* association (figure 2).

Like the relation of an executable context to a tool category, also the relation of a choice context to a tool category can be supported by automated consistency checks:

C3 *assure that the tool category can display all intentions associated with the alternatives of the choice contexts:* Given a choice context CC which is related in the process model to a set of alternative contexts CA. For each context $C_x \in CA$, the tool category T associated (using the provides_choice_context association) with the choice context CC must be assigned to at least one command element (via a provides_command association) which is related (using a display_of_intention association) to the context C_x;

C4 *assure that the tool category can display all product parts associated with the situations of all alternative contexts of the choice context:* Given a choice context CC for which a set CA of alternative contexts is defined in the process model and a set of product parts P_{CA} which subsumes all products related to any situation S which is related to a context $C_x \in CA$. If a tool category T is associated to the choice context CC then for all product parts $P_i \in P_{CA}$ a displays relation between P_i, a graphical shape G, and T must exist.

4.5 Environment Meta Model: Summary

In summary, representing both processes and tools at a conceptual level supports the method engineer in assigning the required tool functionality to the method definitions. Moreover, the above mentioned consistency constraint assure correct assignments in the environment model.

Service integration is achieved by the environment model through the relation of executable and choice contexts defined in the process model to the tool definitions.

The *feedback required* after context execution is inherently defined by the context types (in the case of executable contexts as output product types; in the case of choice contexts the contexts as alternatives).

The foundation for the *invocation of method fragments* is established by the fact that a plan context can be related as an alternative to a choice contexts. This makes the tools aware of plan context definitions, i.e. the tools get to know the plan contexts which can be activated in a given process situation (illustrated in section 5.2)

Vice versa, the environment model empowers the enactment domain to invoke the tool responsible for executing a choice or executable context whenever such a context becomes active during the enactment of a plan context.

Last but not least, the definition of the graphical and interaction capabilities for the contexts lays the foundation for the *adaptation of tool behavior* (illustrated in section 5.1).

The interpretation of the environment model at run-time by the three main components of our implementation framework, namely the *tools, the enactment mechanism and the control integration mechanism*, builds the foundation for achieving a process-integrated environment.

5 Implementation and Validation

Based on the contextual process and tool modelling approach outlined in section 4 and the communication protocol defined in [2] we have defined a generic architecture for process-integrated environments which consists of three main components:

- An *enactment architecture* for process engines which interprets the process relevant parts of the environment models. It drives process enactment based on the process knowledge defined in the environment model, deduces the tool category for performing a particular service (context) based on the environment models, handles enactment requests of the performance domain by enacting the requested method fragments, and provides means for an easy integration of existing enactment mechanisms for the interpretation of plan contexts;
- A process-aware control integration mechanism which has been implemented on top of the ToolTalk. It controls message distribution (service requests) based on the interpretation of the environment model.
- A *generic tool architecture* which consists of two major generic subsystems, the *StateManager* and the *ContextManager*. The task of the *StateManager* is to ensure that message exchange with the enactment mechanism is carried out according to the communication protocol. In addition, the StateManager controls and maintains the current state of the tool. State transitions are triggered by user interaction events or the receipt of a message from the enactment domain. The task of the *ContextManager* is assigned to two major subcomponents. The *ContextExecutor* is responsible for adjusting the tool behavior and for providing user guidance according to the environment model (section 5.1). The task of the *ContextMatcher* is to identify predefined method fragments (section 5.2).

All architectural components have been realized as a set of collaborating object-oriented components. The design of the architecture and its implementation is described in detail in [34]. In this paper we focus on the process-sensitivity of the tools and thus sketch the two components of the ContextManager: the ContextExecutor and the ContextMatcher.

5.1 The ContextExecutor

The ContextExecutor controls the execution of choice and executable contexts. Context execution is either initiated by the ContextMatcher or by the StateManager due to the receipt of a context execution message from the enactment domain.

If the execution of an automated service (executable context) is requested, the Context-Executor invokes the tool action associated with the executable context in the environment model, with the situation data as input parameters.

If the execution of a guidance service (choice context) is requested, the ContextExecutor adapts the user interface of the tool according to the definition of the choice context and the current situation data. More precisely, in the command region of the user interface only those menu items and icons are displayed which are associated to an alternative of the choice context. In the product region, all products corresponding to the situation data of the choice context are *highlighted* to draw user attention on them (the entity publication in figure 3). Furthermore, all products which may contribute to a situation of an alternative context are displayed as *selectable* (bright color), whereas all other products part become *unselectable* (e.g. the relationship loaned_by in figure 3).

Thus, all contexts (situations and intensions) defined as alternatives of the choice context are displayed to the engineer. On user request, the ContextExecutor displays the pros and cons for each alternative defined in the model in a special guidance window (not shown in figure 3).

As an example for the adaptation of tool behavior, the right part of figure 3 shows an entity relationship (ER) editor which currently executes the choice context `CC_RefineEntity` with the entity type `publication` as current situation data. There are three alternatives defined for this choice context (see left part of figure 3): (1) the executable context *EC_Create_isA_link* by which an IsA-Link between two selected entity types is created; (2) the executable context *EC_Discriminate_Attribute* for creating a discriminating attribute for the selected entity type; and (3) the plan context *PC_SubtypeEntity* for creating subtypes of the selected entity type.

According to the associations specified between the choice context and the command elements provided by ER editor, the intention of the alternative context `EC_CreateIsALink` appears as menu item in the `edit` pull-down menu and as icon in the icon bar using the bitmap `CreateIsALink.xpm` (see figure 3). Similar, the command elements for the other two alternative contexts of the choice context are retrieved from the environment model and displayed to the user (not illustrated in figure 3).

In the product area, the situation data (the entity type `proceedings` of the choice context `CC_RefineEntity`) is highlighted. According to the environment model, all situations of the three alternatives are only based on entity types (not depicted in figure 3). Consequently, the ContextExecutor has marked all other objects as unselectable (displayed in gray), i.e. only entity types (`book`, `copy_of_publication`, `user`) are selectable (displayed in white).

5.2 The ContextMatcher

During the execution of a choice context the user selects and deselects product parts and command elements. The task of the ContextMatcher is to compare the current state of the user interface (product parts and command elements selected) with the definitions of the contexts defined as alternatives of the currently active choice context. It compares the commands with the intentions of the alternative contexts and the product parts with the situation of the alternative contexts. The matcher currently applies a best fit approach, i.e. it associates a situation slot with the most specific selected product (part).

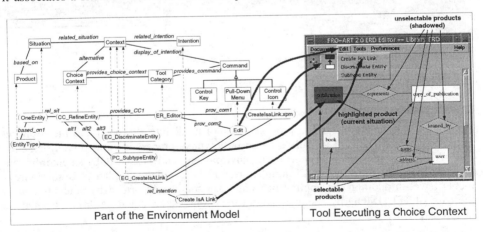

| Part of the Environment Model | Tool Executing a Choice Context |

Fig. 3. Influence of the Environment Model on the Tool Behavior.

Whenever the selected product parts and the intentions match with a context definition, the ContextMatcher requests the activation of the context from the StateManager. If the activated context is a plan context the StateManager sends an enactment request (together with the situation data) to the enactment mechanism.

Note that the detection and activation of a new defined plan, executable or choice context can be achieved by just relating the new context as alternative to a choice context or (only in the case of choice contexts) directly to the tool category. The definition of a new method fragment does not require any reprogramming or adaptation of the tools, since the responsible tool automatically displays the intentions and highlights the products. Moreover, it automatically compares selected intentions and product parts with the new context definition and activates the detected context. For example, if the selected product parts and the selected command element match with a new defined plan context, the enactment of the plan context is initiated by the tool.

In the following we illustrate the invocation of a method fragment (figure 4). The ER editor is in the choice context CC_RefineEntity. The user has selected the two entities publication and journal and the menu command associated with the intention Create IsA Link. The ContextMatcher compares the selected product parts and the intention associated with the selected command element with the context definition subsumed in the environment model. For efficiency reasons the matching is performed whenever a command element (intention) has been selected by the user.

The ContextMatcher detects that the selected items match with the definition of the executable context EC_CreateIsALink defined as alternative of the active choice context (see left part of figure 4).

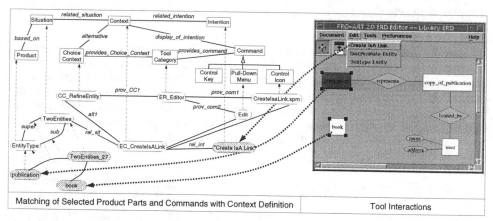

| Matching of Selected Product Parts and Commands with Context Definition | Tool Interactions |

Fig. 4. Matching a Context.

5.3 Validation

We have validated the integrated process and tool modelling approach and the resulting implementation framework by building two prototypical process-integrated environments: PRO-ART 2.0, a requirements engineering environment, and TECHMOD, an environment for supporting the construction of simulation models for chemical plants. Both environments have, in addition, be applied in small case studies performed by students and in the case of TECHMOD by chemical engineers. Conclusions could be drawn from three different perspectives:

Application engineer's view: Most users reported that the fine grained method support provides very helpful guidance. The reflection of the methodical guidance in the behavior of the tools was regarded as a major advantage, especially the adaptation of the user interface according to the method definitions and the support provided for invoking predefined method fragments even if the user is not aware them.

Method engineer's view: It turned out that defining method fragments using the three context types offers significant advantages. First the three context types provide a guideline how to structure method models. Secondly, the method engineer is forced to make decision points explicit (by defining choice contexts), Thirdly, the three context types imply that the tool definitions are considered adequately during process definition. Fourthly, adaptation of method guidance can be achieved by just changing the model definitions and it can be assured that the application engineer is always aware of the actual method definition. This is essential especially in settings, where new methodical knowledge about good process performance is constantly elicited and learned.

Tool builder's view: From this viewpoint, the main result was that the building blocks of the integrated environment meta model were sufficient for defining tools. Moreover, the developers were forced to define process knowledge explicitly in plan contexts instead of embedding it in the tools, i.e. the "process in the tool syndrome" [11] was avoided. The implementation of twelve process-sensitive tools for the two PIEs was significantly facilitated by the generic tool architecture and the reuse of the generic implementation framework.

6 Related Work

Whereas the main focus of our approach is to establish a process integration of the tools used in a PIE, most research contributions do not consider the integration of tools in PCEs although the problems of a-posteriori integration of existing CASE tools have been widely recognized (e.g. [35,11,36,15]). Recent publications therefore argue that "a posteriori tool integration (e.g. by means of wrappers) could be less effective since a tool is still seen as a monolithic 'operator' " [4]. Consequently, existing PCEs do not offer process-integrated tools.

An exception, where partial process-integration of the tools is offered, is the GTSL approach [12] developed within the GOODSTEP project [37] which aims at the *generation* of specific tool services, schemata, and consistency checks from tool specifications which are coupled with process models. This approach mainly provides solutions to the service and data integration problem, but does not provide means for the invocation of method fragments nor for the dynamic adaptation of the tool behavior according to the process definition and the enactment state.

Meta-CASE environments or CASE shells like MetaEdit [38] or Phedias [39] are based on the generation of tools according to a (meta model) specification. They focus mainly on notational and ontological aspects, but lack process-orientation (see also [40]).

Existing process modelling languages almost neglect the definition of tools, although some provide low-level constructs for the invocation of foreign programs like black transitions in SLANG [4], the `call`–Statement in Marvel [5], or the binding of abstract process operators to tools during process instantiation in ALF [41]. On the other hand, control-oriented tool integration approaches like FIELD [22] and its commercial derivatives (such as HP's BMS [23] and Sun's ToolTalk [24]) as well as object-oriented distribution infrastructures like CORBA [25] or OLE [42] store tool (service) descriptions in their message servers/object brokers, but do not consider the process models.

As a consequence, if at all, tool and process models coexist in the message server repository and in the process repository without a systematic approach for assuring consistency.

Many PCE approaches like SPADE [4], Process WEAVER [9], EPOS [43], and Merlin

[21] employ such mechanisms for invoking tool services, although the tool model used by the message server and the process model used by the enactment domain are not systematically integrated. In addition, tool invocation in existing PCEs is restricted to atomic actions while user guidance by adapting the accessible objects and operations through guidance services is not systematically supported; i.e. the tools of these environments are not process-sensitive.

In contrast, our approach takes a different stance on process and tool modelling. Among others, it offers a uniform way to express enactment and tool services by which service and data integration between the enactment and performance domains can be achieved, and the foundation for process-sensitive tools is established.

The FIELD-based Forest environment [44] is an attempt to establish a central description of processes and tools. Forest extends the tool-related message distribution patterns stored in the message server by so-called policy descriptions which can be regarded as primitive process definitions. Although this approach improves the integration of tool and process models it provides no means for establishing process-sensitive tools and for supporting the invocation of method fragments.

In summary, the problem of tool integration in PCEs was recognized and some partial solutions to the problem exist. So far, no comprehensive approach was proposed which establishes process integration of tools and, on the other hand, enables the humans performing the process to play a more active role by initiating the execution of method fragments.

7 Conclusions

Our contextual approach for fine grained and adaptable method support in process centered environments presented in this paper is based on the requirements for the process-integration of interactive engineering tools elaborated in section 2. The consideration of those requirements have led to a significant improvement of our previous solutions for process-integrated tools described in [2].

To meet the requirements we argued that from a modelling perspective *tools should no longer be treated as second class citizens*. Instead tools, as the processes, have to be explicitly defined. We presented a contextual meta model for defining the process (method) support and a *tool meta model* for defining the basic capabilities of the interactive engineering tools used to perform the processes. We then proposed to relate the available tool support with the method definition. The interrelation of the tool and method definitions can be supported by automated consistency checks, e.g. it can be checked if a tool is able to perform the associated services (executable and choice contexts) defined in a method fragment.

The integration of the tool and the method definitions forms an *environment model*. Based on an interpretation of the environment model *process-sensitive tools* are established. The tools are able to *adapt themselves automatically* according to the method definitions. Moreover, the engineering *tools can initiate the enactment of predefined method fragments* by matching user interactions and method definitions.

Our overall approach has been validated by implementing a *generic architecture for process-integrated engineering environments* which consists of three main components (enactment architecture, tool architecture, and process-aware control integration mechanism). Each of these components interprets the environment model and thereby assures that the environment "behaves" according to the method definitions.

These applications have shown that our approach significantly facilitates the adaptation of fine-grained method support to organizational and project specific needs as well as the integration of new method fragments. For example, the approach has proven very useful for defining and enforcing project specific trace services, i.e. to guide the engineers in capturing trace information in accordance to a contract [45].

Future research is concerned with the detection and the execution of choice contexts across tool boundaries. Moreover we plan to validate the TECHMOD environment in an industrial setting and investigate in the generation of basic executable services based on model definitions, like the ones applied in the MetaEdit+ CASE shell [38] or in GTSL [12].

Acknowledgments: The authors like to thank their colleagues R. Klamma, R. Dömges, P. Haumer and M. Jarke for many fruitful discussions and comments on early versions of the paper. Without the enthusiasm of our students S. Brandt, S. Ewald, M. Hoofe, T. Rötschke, K. Schreck, W. Thyen the implementation of the generic architecture and the PRO-ART 2.0 and TECHMOD environments would not have been possible. This work was in part founded by the European Community under ESPRIT Reactive Long Term Research 21.903 CREWS and by the DFG Project 445/5–1 "Prozeßintegration von Modellierungsarbeitsplätzen".

References

[1] M. Dowson. Consistency Maintenance in Process Sensitive Environments. In *Proc. of the Process Sensitive Software Engineering Environments Architectures Workshop*, Boulder, Colorado, USA, Sept. 1992.

[2] K. Pohl. *Process Centered Requirements Engineering*. RSP marketed by J. Wiley & Sons Ltd., England, 1996.

[3] J. Lonchamp. An Assessment Exercise. In A. Finkelstein, J. Kramer, and B. Nuseibeh, editors, *Software Process Modelling and Technology*, pages 335–356. RSP, London, 1994.

[4] S. Bandinelli, E. Di Nitto, and A. Fuggetta. Supporting Cooperation in the SPADE-1 Environment. *IEEE Transactions on Software Engineering*, 12(12):841–865, 1996.

[5] N. Barghouti. Supporting Cooperation in the MARVEL Process–Centered Software Development Environment. In *Proc. of the ACM SIGSOFT/SIGPLAN Software Engineering Symposium on Practical Software Development Environments*, pages 21–31, New York, New York, USA, 1992.

[6] W. Deiters and V. Gruhn. The FUNSOFT Net Approach to Software Process Management. *Intl. Journal of Software Engineering and Knowledge Engineering*, 4(2), 1994.

[7] T. Mochel, A. Oberweis, and V. Sänger. Income/star: The petri net simulation concepts. *Journal of Mathematical Modelling and Simulation in Systems Analysis*, 13:21–36, 1993.

[8] P. Heimann, G. Joeris, C.-A. Krapp, and B. Westfechtel. DYNAMITE: Dynamic Task Nets for Software Process Management. In *Proc. of the 18th Int. Conf. on Software Engineering*, pages 331–341, 1996.

[9] C. Fernström. Process WEAVER: Adding Process Support to Unix. In *Proc. of the 2nd International Conference on Software Processes*, pages 12–26, Los Alamitos, CA, USA, 1993.

[10] A. I. Wasserman. Tool Integration in Software Engineering Environments. In F. Long, editor, *Proc. of the Intl. Workshop on Software Engineering Environments*, pages 137–149, Berlin, Germany, 1990. Springer-Verlag.

[11] C. Montangero. The Process in the Tool Syndrome: is it becoming worse? In *Proc. of the 9th Intl. Software Process Workshop*, pages 53–56, Arlie, Virginia, USA, Oct. 1994. IEEE Computer Society Press.

[12] W. Emmerich. *Tool Construction for Process–Centred Software Development Environments based on Object Databases*. PhD thesis, University of Paderborn, Paderborn, Germany, 1995.

[13] M. Dowson and C. Fernström. Towards Requirements for Enactment Mechanisms. In B. Warboys, editor, *Proc. of the 3rd Europ. Workshop on Software Process Technology*, number 772 in LNCS, pages 90–106, Villard de Lans, Frankreich, Feb. 1994. Springer-Verlag.

[14] C. Fernström. State Models and Protocols in Process Centered Environments. In W. Schäfer, editor, *Proc. of the 8th Intl. Software Process Workshop*, pages 72–77, Wadern, Germany, Mar. 1993. IEEE Computer Society Press.

[15] C. Fernström and L. Ohlsson. Integration Needs in Process-Enacted Environments. In *Proc. of the 1st Intl. Conf. on the Software Process*, pages 142–158, 1991.

[16] I. Thomas and B. A. Nejmeh. Definitions of Tool Integration for Environments. *IEEE Software*, 8(2):29–35, 1992.

[17] ECMA-NIST. *A Reference Model for Frameworks of Software Engineering Environments*. Number TR/55 Version 3. ECMA & NIST, 1993.

[18] G. Valetto and G. E. Kaiser. Valetto, g. and e. kaiser, g. In *Valetto, G. and E. Kaiser, G.*, pages 40–48, July Valetto, G. and E. Kaiser, G.

[19] K. Pohl, R. Dömges, and M. Jarke. Decision Oriented Process Modelling. In *Proc. of the 9th Intl. Software Process Workshop*, pages 124–128, Arlie, Virginia, USA, Oct. 1994. IEEE Computer Society Press.

[20] N. S. Barghouti and B. Krishnamurthy. Using event contexts and matching constraints to monitor software processes. In *Procs 17th Intl. Conf. on Software Engineering, Seattle, Washington, USA*, pages 83–92, May 1995.

[21] G. Junkermann, B. Peuschel, W. Schäfer, and S. Wolf. MERLIN: Supporting Cooperation in Software Development Through a Knowledge–Based Environment. In A. Finkelstein, J. Kramer, and B. Nuseibeh, editors, *Software Process Modelling and Technology*, pages 103–130. RSP, London, 1994.

[22] S. P. Reiss. Connecting Tools Using Message Passing in the FIELD Environment. *IEEE Software*, 4(7):57–67, July 1990.

[23] M. Cagan. The HP SoftBench Environment: An Architecture for a New Generations of Software Tools. *Hewlett–Packard Journal*, 41(3):36–47, June 1990.

[24] SunSoft. The ToolTalk Service (White Paper). Technical report, SunSoft Inc., June 1991.

[25] OMG. *CORBA: Architecture and Specification*. Object Management Group, Inc., 1995.

[26] L. A. Suchmann. *Plans and Situated Actions: The problem of human machine communication*. Press Syndicate of the University of Cambridge, 1987.

[27] R. Stallman and G. Sussman. Forward Reasoning and Dependency-Directed Backtracking in a System for Computer-Aided Circuit Analysis. *Artificial Intelligence*, 9(2):135–196, 1977.

[28] V. Dhar and M. Jarke. On modeling processes. *Decision Support Systems*, (9):39–49, 1993.

[29] C. Potts. A Generic Model for Representing Design Methods. In *Proc. of the Eleventh Intl. Conf. on Software Engineering*, Pittsburgh, PA, May 1989.

[30] G. Fischer. Integrating Construction and Argumentation in Domain-Oriented Design Environments. In *Proc. of the First Intl. Symp. of Requirements Engineering*, page 284, San Diego, CA, Jan. 1993. IEEE Computer Society Press.

[31] M. Jarke, K. Pohl, C. Rolland, and J.-R. Schmitt. Experience-Based Method Evaluation and Improvement: A Process Modeling Approach. In *IFIP WG 8.1 Conference CRIS '94*, Maastricht, Netherlands, 1994.

[32] C. Rolland and N. Prakash. Reusable Process Chunks. In *Proc. of the Intl. Conf. Database and Expert Systems Applications*, Prague, Slovakia, Sept. 1993.

[33] C. Rolland and G. Grosz. A General Framework for Describing the Requirements Engineering Process. In *Proc. of the Intl. Conf. on Systems, Man, and Cybernetics*, San Antonio, Texas, USA, Oct. 1994. IEEE Computer Society Press.

[34] K. Pohl, R. Klamma, K. Weidenhaupt, R. Dömges, P. Haumer, and M. Jarke. A Framework for Process-Integrated Tools. Technical report, RWTH Aachen, 1996.

[35] A. Fuggetta and C. Ghezzi. State of the Art and Open Issues in Process-Centered Software Engineering Environments. *Journal of Systems and Software*, 26:53–60, 1994.

[36] M. Anderson and P. Griffiths. The Nature of the Software Process Modelling Problem is Evolving. In *Proc. of the 3rd European Workshop on Software Process Technology, EWSPT '94*, LNCS 772, pages 31–34, 1994.

[37] GOODSTEP-Team. The GOODSTEP Project: General Object-Oriented Database for Software Engineering Processes. In *Proc. of the Asia-Pacific Software Engineering Conference*, pages 410–420, Tokyo, Japan, 1994.

[38] S. Kelly, K. Lyytinen, and M. Rossi. MetaEdit+ — A Fully Configurable Multi-User and Multi-Tool CASE and CAME Environment. In *Proc. of the 8th Intl. Conference on Advanced Information Systems Engineering*, LNCS 1080, pages 1–21, Heraklion, Crete, Greece, 1996.

[39] X. Wang and P. Loucopoulos. The Development of Phedias: a CASE Shell. In *Proc. 7th. Int. Workshop on CASE, Toronto, Canada*, pages 122 – 131. IEEE Computer Society Press, 1995.

[40] P. Marttiin, K. Lyytinen, M. Rossi, V. Tahvanainen, and J.-P. Tolvanen. Modeling requirements for future CASE: Issues and Implementation Considerations. *Information Resources Management Journal*, 8(1):15–25, 1995.

[41] G. Canals, N. Boudjlida, J.-C. Derniame, C. Godart, and J. Lonchamp. ALF: A Framework for Building Process-Centred Software Engineering Environments. In A. Finkelstein, J. Kramer, and B. Nuseibeh, editors, *Software Process Modelling and Technology*, pages 153–186. RSP, London, 1994.

[42] K. Brockschmidt. *Inside OLE, Second Edition*. Microsoft Press, Redmond WA, 1995.

[43] R. Conradi, M. Hagaseth, J.-O. Larsen, M. Nguyen, B. Munch, P. Westby, W. Zhu, M. Jaccheri, and C. Liu. EPOS: Object–Oriented Cooperative Process Modelling. In A. Finkelstein, J. Kramer, and B. Nuseibeh, editors, *Software Process Modelling and Technology*, pages 33–70. RSP, London, 1994.

[44] D. Garlan and E. Ilias. Low-cost, Adaptable Tool Integration Policies for Integrated Environments. In *Proc. of the 4th ACM SIGSOFT Symposium on Software Development Environments*, volume 15, 1990.

[45] K. Pohl, R. Dömges, and M. Jarke. Towards Method-Driven Trace Capture. In *Proc. of the 9th Intl. Conf. on Advanced Information Systems Engineering*, Barcelona, Spain, June 1997.

Generic Fuzzy Reasoning Nets as a Basis for Reverse Engineering Relational Database Applications

Jens H. Jahnke, Wilhelm Schäfer, Albert Zündorf

AG-Softwaretechnik, Fachbereich 17, Universität Paderborn,
Warburger Str. 100, D-33098 Paderborn, Germany;
e-mail: [jahnke|wilhelm|zuendorf]@uni-paderborn.de
WWW: http://www.uni-paderborn.de/fachbereich/AG/schaefer/index_engl.html

Abstract. Object-oriented technology has become mature enough to satisfy many new requirements coming from areas like computer-aided design (CAD), computer-integrated manufacturing (CIM), or software engineering (SE). However, a competitive information management infrastructure often demands to merge data from CAD-, CIM-, or SE-systems with business data stored in a relational system. One approach for seamless integration of object-oriented and relational systems is to migrate from a relational to an object-oriented system. The first step in this migration process is reverse engineering of the legacy database. In this paper we propose a new graphical and executable language called *Generic Fuzzy Reasoning Nets* for modelling and applying reverse engineering knowledge. In particular, this language enables to define and analyse fuzzy knowledge which is usually all what is available when an existing database schema has to be reverse engineered into an object-oriented one. The analysis process is based on executing a fuzzy petri net which is parameterized with the fuzzy knowledge about a concrete database application.

1   Introduction and Related Work

Object-oriented technology has become mature enough to satisfy many new requirements coming from areas like computer-aided design (CAD), computer-integrated manufacturing (CIM), or software engineering (SE). Those new requirements are not fulfilled by relational technology [LS88, Mai89]. However, a competitive information management infrastructure often demands to merge data from CAD-, CIM-, or SE-systems with business data stored in a relational system. In addition, complex dependencies between those data stored in the different systems might exist and should be maintained. One approach for seamless integration of object-oriented and relational systems is to migrate the data (and the corresponding schema) from a relational to an object-oriented system.

The whole migration process consists of three steps which are (1) the *schema migration process* which maps a relational schema to an equivalent object oriented schema, (2) the *data migration process* which converts extensions of the relational schema to extensions of the object oriented schema and (3) the *application migration process* which creates a new application program using the object oriented database for every application program that uses the legacy database.

This paper focuses on the first step in the migration process, namely the migration of the schema. A major job to do when migrating a schema is to analyse and reverse engineer the schema. This paper proposes a new approach for analysing existing relational schemas in order to reverse engineer them into object-oriented ones.

Analysing an existing database schema means to analyse the schema definition, the application code written in a so-called embedded SQL (Standard Query Language)-language where the embedding language is e.g. C or COBOL, and the available extensions of the schema. This analysis requires to express possibly uncertain assumptions about the schema which is to be reverse engineered. These assumptions may be partly deducable from the schema definitions and in particular the defined integrity constraints or from the SQL-queries within the application code. They may also only be deduced from the currently available schema extensions. Furthermore, an application has been developed incrementally over time by many developers who are sometimes even not accessible any more and who often did not do a good job on documentation. The result is that integrity constraints may even define contradicting constraints.

In order to retrieve an object-oriented schema an analysis tool should help to combine basic assumptions and to investigate their consequences. As many of those assumptions are uncertain, a tool should be able to deduce different possible consequences and their confidences. By supporting an incremental and interactive verification process, the tool should then let the reverse engineer decide finally which is the best alternative to choose.

Existing approaches [DA87,JK90,SK90,And94,PB94,PKBT94,FV95] do not support this kind of reasoning process, since the knowledge about the reverse engineering process is usually not defined explicitly but hard-coded in a batch-oriented analysis tool. One notable exception is an approach which is based on defining the reverse engineering knowledge in terms of PROLOG-rules [SLGC94]. However this approach as well as all others do not support the explicit (and thus easily changeable) definition and analysis of uncertain knowledge.

The next section gives a more detailed example which kind of semantic information we have to derive and which kind of uncertainty we have to deal with. Section 3 then presents our approach how to capture formally and precisely yet intuitively the (uncertain) reverse engineering knowledge about relational databases. Section 4 describes the inference engine which analyses basic facts about the investigated database and which then infers as much semantic information as possible by applying the reverse engineering knowledge described within Section 3. Within this step the inference engine incorporates and verifies interactively added user knowledge. Section 5 concludes with describing the current state of our work.

2 A Motivating Scenario

Due to its simplicity the relational model lacks the expressive power to explicitly represent high level modelling concepts like, e.g. object relationships, aggregation, and inheritance. However, indicators for these concepts are spread all over the application code, the schema and the extension of a legacy relational database. The focus of reverse engineering is to find such indicators in order to recover information about high level modelling concepts. In [FV95] this process is described as *semantic completion* of a relational schema. Consequently, the recovered information which is the result of this process is denoted as the *semantic information* of a relational schema. This semantic information is the basis for a translation of the relational schema into an object-oriented data model, as described in [FV95].

As an illustrating example consider the cutout of a relational database system represented by its schema (Fig. 1), its extension (Fig. 2) and its application code (Fig. 3). The reverse engineered object model for this example is given in OMT-like notation in Fig. 5. In order to be able to produce this object model the semantic information depicted in Fig. 4 has to be deduced from the legacy database. In the following we will explain how this information is retrieved from the sample database.

First we deduce that there may be two different kinds (*variants*) of persons, due to the fact that every person in the sample extension has either a null-value in the AFR column or in the dep column, but there is no person that has both columns with null value. Due to our domain knowledge about the analysed database application, we name the variant with values in the AFR column Developer, while the other variant with dep values is denoted as Manager.

Attribute dep is probably a key of variant Manager, as it is declared as an index and it is not-null in this variant and the functional dependencies to all other attributes in Developer hold in the extension.

```
create table Project (                        create index Person(dep)
    descr varchar(50) not null,
    manager varchar(50),            create table WP(
    size numeric,                       descr varchar(50) not null,
    scheduled datetime)                 proj varchar(50)
                                        dev varchar(50),
create table Person(                     size numeric,
    name varchar(80),                   scheduled datetime,
    email varchar(80),                  foreign key proj references Project(descr))
    dep varcher(80),
    AFR real)
```

Fig. 1: Sample database schema

Furthermore, the first statement in Fig. 3 selects two persons with different name attributes. In [And94] this is called a cyclic exclusion, which serves as an indicator that name is a key of table Person. On the other hand, the second select statement, which gets the AFR value of some entry in table Person with a specific value for name, includes the keyword *distinct*, which is a negative indicator for name being a key

[And94]. Due to our experience, we know that some programmers tend to use the keyword distinct by default even if not necessary. Thus, we resolve the above conflict by assigning a higher weight to the pro argument than to the counter argument.

Person	name	email	dep	AFR
	Steve	snoopy	NULL	1.2
	Brenda	brenda	MW	NULL
	Martin	mksoft	NULL	1.9
	Boris	bumbum	NULL	1.4
	Michael	mike	IS	NULL

...

Project	descr	manager	size	scheduled
	Varlet	Michael	150	05/31/97
	Merlin	Brenda	320	06/01/98
	GEN	Michael	80	02/01/97

...

WP	descr	project	dev	size	scheduled
	Trafo	Varlet	Martin	30	02/01/97
	PE	Merlin	Steve	20	04/01/97
	GUI	GEN	Boris	10	01/01/97
	Ana	Varlet	Martin	12	03/01/97...

Fig. 2: Database extension

```
select * from Person x,y
where (x.AFR>$A) and (y.AFR>$A)
and not (x.name=y.name)
...
select distinct AFR from Person
where name=$N
...
select email from Person,WP
where scheduled<$E and dev=name
...
```

Fig. 3: Application code

From the observation that tables `Project` and `WP` both have attributes `descr`, `size` and `scheduled` with matching types, it is likely that at-a-time these attributes have identical meaning. According to [FV95] attributes with identical meanings are collected in so-called equivalence classes. Normally, this indicates an inclusion dependency (IND) between both sets of attributes. However, this assumption can be disproved by analysing the extension in Fig. 2. In fact, there is no tupel in table `Project` and `WP` with common values in these columns. Therefore, we assume that there is a hidden *domain relation* `Task` for all tupels in `Project` and `WP`. At this, the term domain relation is used as the relational analogy for a superclass in the object oriented data model (cf. [FV95]). The deduced inheritance relationship is characterized by inclusion dependencies (ISA-IND) from `Project` and `WP` to the new domain relation.

Moreover the third statement of Fig. 3 is a strong indicator that attribute `dev` of table `WP` belongs to the same equivalence class as attribute `name` of table `person`, because the statement includes a join of both tables over these attributes. Thus, we conclude that there exists an IND in either direction between these attributes. However, we already know that there are two different variants of `person`, namely `Developer` and `Manager`. Thus, we have to check for both variants, whether the possible INDs can be disproved by a counterexample in the extension. In fact, the assumption of an IND between variant `Manager` and `WP` is refuted by the given extension, while INDs in both directions between variant `Developer` and `WP` are fulfilled.

According to [FV95] we classify the IND going from table `WP` to table `Developer` as a *key-based* IND, as we assumed that the attributes on its right side built a key in table `Developer`. Such an IND represents a referential integrity constraint and is called an R-IND in [FV95]. Consequently, the supposed inverse IND from `Developer` to `WP` is denoted *inversely key-based* but not key-based. Such INDs are classified as so-called

C-INDs, as they reveal a cardinality constraint for the regarded relationship between WP and Developer, i.e. there is at least one tupel in WP for each tupel in Developer. Together, these two inverse INDs are translated into an association between WP and Developer with cardinality 1-n to 0-1 in the object-oriented model (Figure 5).

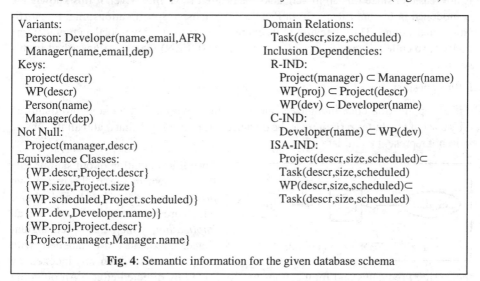

Variants:
Person: Developer(name,email,AFR)
Manager(name,email,dep)
Keys:
project(descr)
WP(descr)
Person(name)
Manager(dep)
Not Null:
Project(manager,descr)
Equivalence Classes:
{WP.descr,Project.descr}
{WP.size,Project.size}
{WP.scheduled,Project.scheduled)}
{WP.dev,Developer.name)}
{WP.proj,Project.descr}
{Project.manager,Manager.name}

Domain Relations:
Task(descr,size,scheduled)
Inclusion Dependencies:
R-IND:
Project(manager) ⊂ Manager(name)
WP(proj) ⊂ Project(descr)
WP(dev) ⊂ Developer(name)
C-IND:
Developer(name) ⊂ WP(dev)
ISA-IND:
Project(descr,size,scheduled)⊂
Task(descr,size,scheduled)
WP(descr,size,scheduled)⊂
Task(descr,size,scheduled)

Fig. 4: Semantic information for the given database schema

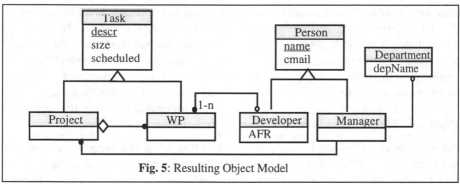

Fig. 5: Resulting Object Model

The reader should note that due to the lack of space we do not present all parts of the sample database that is investigated in order to derive the depicted semantic information. In addition some information like e.g. the names for the variants Developer and Manager cannot be deduced automatically, but has to be added manually.

3   Generic Fuzzy Reasoning Nets

In order to make reverse engineering knowledge about relational databases accessible for a (semi-)automatic analysis process, it has to be specified in a formal representation. Moreover, it is of great importance that this knowledge is easily adaptable. For example, different legacy database applications may provide different sources of information which has to be considered in the reverse engineering process. Furthermore, the credibility of indicators may differ from one to another developer/company depending on the preferred style of programming and the history of the legacy database application.

Coding the reverse engineering knowledge in a programming language like C or C++ is not feasible, since this approach lacks the desired flexibility. Even if this knowledge is modelled in textual rules (e.g. in PROLOG) extensive specifications might be difficult to understand. Thus, because of its expressive power we developed a graphical formalism, so called *Generic Fuzzy Reasoning Nets* (GFRN) which are described in this section.

Let us consider the following reverse engineering rule R:

if the application code includes a select statement with a *distinct* keyword qualified by a set of attributes *a* **then** it can be deduced with certainty ϕ that *a* and all its subsets do not represent candidate keys.

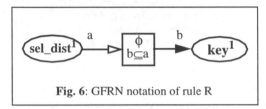

Fig. 6: GFRN notation of rule R

The GFRN notation of our sample rule R is shown in Fig. 6. There are two *predicates*, sel_dist^1 and key^1, which are represented by ovals and an *implication*, which has a rectangular shape. Predicates are labelled with unique names which are indexed by their arity. Predicates and implications are connected by directed edges. An outgoing edge from a predicate to an implication denotes that this predicate is in the antecedent of the implication, while an ingoing edge from an implication to a predicate shows that the predicate is in the implication's consequent. Negations are represented by black arrow heads. Each edge is labelled with a (list of) formal parameter(s), which serves as argument for the participating predicate. Each implication has an associated confidence factor (ϕ). Furthermore, each implication has a set of constraints over the formal parameters of its in- and outgoing edges. In Fig. 6 the implication has only one constraint which specifies parameter b to be a subset of parameter a.

The semantic of a GFRN is formally defined by a translation into weighted formulas in first-order logic: Each predicate is translated in a corresponding predicate symbol. Each implication is translated into a pair $\mathcal{F}^* := (\mathcal{F}, \phi)$, where ϕ is a valuation (usually between 0 and 1) and $\mathcal{F}$ is a closed formula in classical first-order logic[CS80]. The reader should note that in the GFRN language all formal parameters of implications are implicitly quantified with a universal quantifier. For example the implication in Fig. 6 is translated in the following logic formula $\mathcal{F}$:

$\mathcal{F}$: $(\forall a)(\forall b \subseteq a)(sel\_dist(a) \Rightarrow \neg key(b))$

In different approaches to uncertain logic the valuation ϕ can have different semantic. In probabilistic logic [Paa88] ϕ defines a probability measure for the likelihood that $\mathcal{F}$ is fulfilled, while in possibilistic logic[DP88] which is based on the theory of fuzzy sets [Zad78] ϕ represents an upper bound of possibility that $\mathcal{F}$ is true (respectively a lower bound of necessity in necessity valued possibilistic logic [DLP94]).

We choose a possibilistic semantic for ϕ because in our application domain valuations are intuitively chosen by the reverse engineer based on heuristics and assumptions rather than on statistical analysis of precise likelihood measures. Furthermore computation of probabilistic measures is much more expendable, in order to fulfil all axioms of probability theory and as argued we do not need this degree of precision. For a detailed discussion on the pros and cons of probabilistic and possibilistic logic we refer to [DP88].

The knowledge that we used in our reverse engineering scenario (Section 2) is easily modelled in a GFRN as shown in Fig. 7. We already know predicates sel_dist^1 and key^1 from Fig. 6. The fact that a cyclic exclusion might be an indicator for a key constraint is specified by an additional predicate $cycl\_excl^1$ and implication i_2.

According to our experience with legacy database applications we have chosen the confidence of implication i_2 as quite high (0.8) while the confidence of implication i_1 is relatively low (0.3). This is due to our observation that a cyclic exclusion serves as a credible indicator for a key constraint, while the keyword $distinct$ is often used in application code when it is not really needed.

Implication i_{10} specifies with confidence 1 that a supposed key constraint may only exist, if it cannot be disproved by a counterexample in the database extension.

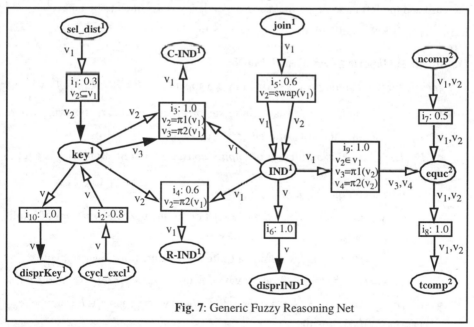

Fig. 7: Generic Fuzzy Reasoning Net

Furthermore, the GFRN includes a predicate $join^1$ which reflects the fact that we are interested in finding joins over attributes of different tables in the application code of the legacy relational database. The argument of predicate $join^1$ is a set of tupels, each tupel representing a pair of compared attributes of both tables. As argued in our reverse engineering scenario such a join statement may reveal an inclusion dependency in one or the other direction between the participating attributes. This is reflected via implication i_5 which has two outgoing edges to predicate IND^1. The right edge is labelled with parameter v_2 which is constrained to be the application of function swap on parameter v_1. Function swap is defined to take a set of pairs and to exchange the element positions of each pair. Consequently, for a given join statement i_5 specifies the conclusion of an IND in both possible directions with a certainty factor of 0.6.

A supposed IND may only reside if it cannot be disproved by an analysis of the extension of the legacy database. This is specified by implication i_6. Moreover, i_9 strictly implies that every pair of attributes in an IND belongs to the same equivalence class. At this, functions π_1 and π_2 stand for the relational projection on the first and the second element in each tupel.

Another heuristical indicator for a possible equivalence of two attributes is the compatibility of their names ($ncomp^2$). Furthermore, it is obvious that equivalent attributes must have compatible types, which is specified through $tcomp^2$ and i_8. The reader should note that due to the application of fuzzy sets in our approach the notion of type and name compatibility is not as strictly defined as in most other approaches.

Finally, implications i_3 and i_4 serve to classify an IND as either an R-IND, if there is a key constraint for the attributes on the right of the inclusion, or a C-IND if this is not the case and the left hand of the inclusion dependency is assumed to be a key.[3]

Formally a GFRN is defined by the following 5-tupel.

Definition 1: Generic Fuzzy Reasoning Net

A *generic fuzzy reasoning net* is defined by a 5-tupel $GFRN:=(P, I, E, F, cf)$, where

- $P = \{p_1^{k1}, p_2^{k2}, ..., p_z^{kz}\}$ is a finite set of unique *predicate symbols*, where $kq \in I\!N$ denotes the arity of predicate symbol p_q^{kq}.

- $I = \{i_1, i_2, ..., i_m\}$ is a finite set of *implications*, each implication $i_g \in I$ is a tupel $i_g = (\iota_g, V_g, K_g)$, with
  - ι_g, a unique *implication identifier*,
  - $V_g = <v_1, v_2, ..., v_f>$, $f \in I\!N^+$, a list of unique *parameter names* of implication i_g,
  - $K_g = \{k_1, k_2, ..., k_s\}$, $s \in I\!N$ is a finite set of *constraints* over V_g, with $k_x = (w, r, f^\mu, <w_1, w_2, ..., w_u>)$ where $w, w_1, ..., w_y \in V_g, r \in \{\in, \subseteq\}$ and $f^\mu \in F$.

- $E = \{e_1, e_2, ..., e_n\}$, $n \in I\!N^+$ is a finite set of *edges*, where each $e_g \in E$ is a tupel $e_g = (\chi_g, l_g, s_g, d_g, A_g)$, with
  - χ_g an unique *identifier*,

---

3. The confidence of implication i_4 has been chosen as 0.6 because according to [FV95] an IND may also represent an inheritance relationship (classified as an ISA-IND), if there exists key constraints for both sides of the IND.

- l_g:$(p_q^{kq},(\iota,V,K)) \in (P \times I)$, a *location*,
- $s_g \in \{+, -\}$, a *sign*,
- $d_g \in \{antecedent,\ consequent\}$, a direction, and
- $A_g = <\alpha_1,\alpha_2,...,\alpha_{kq}>$, an *actualization vector* of e_g where $\alpha_j = \varepsilon$ or $\alpha_j \in V$ for $1 \le j \le kq$.

- $F = \{f_1^{u1}, f_2^{u2}, ..., f_x^{ux}\}$ is a finite set of unique *function symbols*, where $uq \in I\!N$ denotes the arity of function symbol f_q^{uq}.

- *cf:* $I \rightarrow (0, 1]$ is a function that associates real values between 0 and 1 to implications.

4 The Fuzzy Inference Engine

A GFRN solves the problem to represent general reverse engineering knowledge formally but yet intuitively accessible. In order to analyse existing applications this knowledge has to be combined with concrete information about the application's schema, the available extensions, and the available procedural code (cf. the example in Section 2). An inference engine uses the knowledge expressed in a GFRN together with concrete information about an existing application to infer all possible pieces of semantic information about the application (e.g. Fig. 4) together with their confidences. The confidence information is then used by the reverse engineer to decide which are the pieces of semantic information that are used to construct the object-oriented schema.

4.1 Introducing Incomplete Information to the Inference Process

The inference process starts with the defined GFRN and a usually incomplete amount of information about a concrete application. This information is incomplete because it is not feasible to retrieve all facts about the application which may be relevant for deduction *before* the inference process is started. For example it is not practical to determine in advance the set of all possible inter- and intrarelational dependencies that can or cannot be disproved via the extension of a relational database application, since the number of resulting facts grows exponentially with the size of the analysed schema. The only way out is to start inferencing with incomplete information which may be completed depending on the intermediate results during the inference process (as we will illustrate later).

In our approach we will refer to the initial amount of incomplete information as the *premise*, which consists of a set of facts which we call *axioms*. We distinguish three types of axioms which are handled differently during the inference process.

The first type of axioms are so-called *strong* axioms, since they cannot be disproved during the inference process. Typically, strong axioms are automatically retrieved during an initial investigation of the concrete legacy database application. Revisiting the motivating scenario in Section 2 the information that a select-distinct statement and a cyclic join has been found in the application code will be represented in our approach as two strong axioms with confidence 1.

Another type of axioms are called *weak* axioms. Weak axioms stem from the subjective belief of a reengineer that certain facts may be true with a given confidence. As opposed to strong axioms the confidence of weak axioms may be changed during the inference process. For example let us assume that the reengineer in our sample scenario interactively adds the assumption that attribute dev is a key of table WP with his/her subjective confidence of 0.5. Given the available extension in Fig. 2 this assumption has to be refuted during the inference process, as the values of attribute dev are not unique for each tupel in table WP.

Finally, a premise may include a number of *deferred axioms* which are evaluated on an on-demand basis during the inference process. For example, if we consider the GFRN in Fig. 7 it is obvious that axioms over predicates disprIND[1] and tcomp[2] should be defined as deferred, because otherwise, as argued above, there would be an enormous number of strong axioms that would have to be created.

Formally, a premise is defined as follows.

Definition 2: Proposition

Let (P, I, E, F, cf) be a GFRN and U the set of constants in our universe of discourse. A *proposition* d is a tupel $d := (p_q^{kq}, O)$, where

- p_q^{kq} is a predicate symbol,
- $O := <o_1, o_2, ..., o_{kq}>$, is a list of *constants*, $o_i \in U$; $1 \leq i \leq k$.

Any proposition $d := (p_q^{kq}, <o_1, ..., o_{kq}>)$ is said to be in the extend of P ($d \in ext(P)$), iff $p_q^{kq} \in P$.

Definition 3: Premise

A *premise* Z_G over a given GFRN $G := (P, I, E, F, cf)$ is defined as a tupel $Z_G := (A^s_G, A_G^w, A^d_G)$:

- $A^s_G := \{a^s_1, a^s_2, ..., a^s_n\}$, $n \in I\!N^+$ is a finite set of *strong axioms*, while
  $A^w_G := \{a^w_1, a^w_2, ..., a^w_n\}$, $n \in I\!N^+$ is a finite set of *weak axioms*,
  where each $a \in A^s_G \cup A^w_G$ is a tupel $a := (d, s, \phi)$
  - $d \in ext(P)$ is a *proposition*,
  - $s \in \{+, -\}$ is the *sign* of a, and
  - $\phi \in (0, 1]$ is a *confidence*.
- $A^d_G := \{a^d_1, a^d_2, ..., a^d_m\}$, $m \in I\!N^+$ is a finite set of *deferred axioms*,
  where each $a \in A^d_G$ is a tupel $a := (p, s, \phi)$
  - $p \in P$ is a *predicate*,
  - $s \in \{+, -\}$ is the *sign* of a_k, and
  - $\phi : ext(P) \rightarrow (0, 1]$ is a *confidence function*.

4.2 Fuzzy Petri Nets

The requirement to deal with incomplete and inconsistent information demands an inference mechanism that allows for nonmonotonic reasoning. We employ fuzzy petri nets (FPNs) [Loo88,KM96] to execute GFRN specifications as they fulfil the above requirement. A further advantage of this approach is that petri nets are an ideal choice for implementing the proposed inference engine, because they can be evaluated efficiently due to their high degree of structural parallelism and pipelining [KM96].

Generally, a petri net [Pet81] is a directed bipartite graph with active and passive elements. In terms of terminology we follow [KM96] and call active elements *transitions*, while passive elements are referred to as *places*.

Definition 4: Fuzzy Petri Net

Given a finite set of propositions D a *fuzzy petri net* (FPN) is defined by a tupel $FPN := (Pl, Tr, C, D, c, th, m, b)$, where

- $(Pl, Tr; C)$ is a net without isolated elements, with
  - $Pl := \{pl_1, pl_2, ..., pl_{2n}\}$, $n \in \mathbb{N}^+$, is a finite set of *places*,
  - $Tr := \{tr_1, tr_2, ..., tr_x\}$, $x \in \mathbb{N}^+$, is a finite set of *transitions*,
  - $C \subseteq (Pl \times Tr) \cup (Tr \times Pl)$ a *flow relation*.
- $m: Pl \rightarrow [0, 1]$ is a function that associates real values between 0 and 1 to places.
- $b: \{+,-\} \times D \rightarrow Pl$ is a bijective function that associates signed propositions to places.
- $c, th : Tr \rightarrow [0, 1]$ are functions that associate real values between 0 and 1 to transactions.

According to Definition 4 each place pl in an FPN is marked by a real value ($m(pl)$) between 0 and 1. Each proposition is associated with two places in an FPN: The marking of one place represents the fuzzy belief that the proposition is true, and the marking of the other place represents the fuzzy belief that its negation is true. Furthermore, each transition tr has a confidence ($c(tr)$) and a *threshold* ($th(tr)$).

As an example, Fig. 8 shows a transition with k input places. At a certain point in time t we denote the fuzzy beliefs associated to places pl_1 to pl_k with $m_t(pl_1)$ to $m_t(pl_k)$, respectively. In order to determine, whether transition tr_q is enabled the fuzzy AND-operator (which is defined as the minimum function) is applied on the fuzzy beliefs of all its input places. If the result of this operation is greater than the threshold $th(tr_q)$ then tr_q is said to be enabled. In this case tr_q generates a *fuzzy truth token* $ftt_{t+1}(tr_q)$ for its output arcs which computes to the result of the above AND-operation concatenated with the transitions confidence $c(tr_q)$ via another AND-operation. Otherwise $ftt_{t+1}(tr_q)$ is defined to be zero.

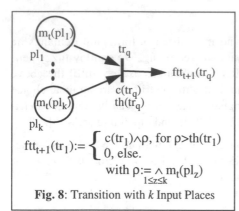

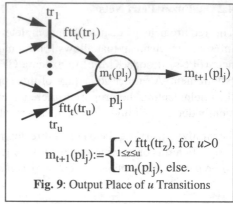

$$ftt_{t+1}(tr_1):= \begin{cases} c(tr_1) \wedge \rho, & \text{for } \rho > th(tr_1) \\ 0, & \text{else.} \end{cases}$$

with $\rho := \bigwedge_{1 \leq z \leq k} m_t(pl_z)$

Fig. 8: Transition with k Input Places

$$m_{t+1}(pl_j):= \begin{cases} \bigvee_{1 \leq z \leq u} ftt_t(tr_z), & \text{for } u > 0 \\ m_t(pl_j), & \text{else.} \end{cases}$$

Fig. 9: Output Place of u Transitions

Fig. 9 shows that given a place pl_j with fuzzy belief $m_t(pl_j)$ in the output of u transitions, the new fuzzy belief $m_{t+1}(pl_j)$ is computed by applying the fuzzy OR-operator (which is defined as the maximum function) over the set of fuzzy truth tokens generated by transitions tr_1 to tr_u. In case there is no transition with pl_j in its output ($u=0$), the fuzzy belief for pl_j remains unaltered.

A major difference of the employed FPN formalism in contrast to classical petri nets is that when an enabled transition fires, tokens are not removed from its input places. On the contrary, input tokens are only copied and remain at there original places. This procedure is necessary for logic inference, since the truth of a proposition may imply the truth of several other conditions. Because of this speciality well-known structural conflicts like deadlocks and traps [Pet81] can not occur in an FPN.

In [Loo88] Looney presents an algorithm for belief evaluation in acyclic fuzzy petri nets. This algorithm is extended in [KM96] for FPNs with arbitrary topology. At-this, evaluation of fuzzy beliefs is carried out by a number of subsequent belief revision steps. In each belief revision step the fuzzy beliefs at all places in the FPN are updated in parallel according to Fig.8 and Fig. 9. The evaluation process terminates when the FPN has reached *steady-state*. This is the case when the most recently performed belief revision step did not cause a change of any fuzzy belief in the entire FPN.

However, some FPN may exhibit sets of places that show periodically oscillation of their fuzzy beliefs over an infinite number of belief revision steps. In this case it is said that *limitcycle* exists at each of these places. The evaluation algorithm presented in [KM96], which is also utilized in our approach, allows for a detection and elimination of limitcycles.

4.3 Expansion and Evaluation of a FPN based on a GFRN

In the following we will explain how a GFRN with a given premise can be executed by expanding and evaluating a fuzzy petri net. Due to the lack of space we will only give an informal description of the inference algorithm. A formal specification of this algorithm using graph rewriting systems is described in [JSZ97].

The inference algorithm has two main phases. In the first phase (expansion), an FPN is created according to the specified GFRN and a given premise. In the second phase (evaluation) fuzzy beliefs are computed until steady-state has been reached.

The expansion phase is performed within three steps. In the first step places for all relevant propositions are created in the FPN. Each proposition in the FPN represents an instance of a certain predicate in the corresponding GFRN with constants as parameters. As defined above, a proposition d is represented by two places: One place $b(+,d)$ carries the fuzzy belief that d is true (we call it the *positive place of d*), while the other place $b(-,d)$ carries the fuzzy belief that d is false (we call it the *negative place of d*).

The first propositions that are created in the FPN are defined by the set of strong and weak axioms in the given premise. Then, iteratively every implication with one or more existing propositions in its antecedent and/or consequent is checked, whether all its formal parameters are completely determined by the actual parameters of these propositions. If this is the case, then all propositions that have not yet been created for this implication are created. Whenever a new proposition has to be created, which is defined by a deferred axiom, the fuzzy belief of this proposition is computed by its confidence function. This expansion step is complete when no further proposition can be created.

In the second expansion step the FPN is completed by creating transitions between positive and negative places of propositions. The instantiation of an implication in a GFRN consists of at least two transitions in the FPN. This is because every implication also implies a contraposition, i.e. from a⇒b we can conclude ¬b⇒¬a. In our approach the contraposition is considered in the inference process, which allows to refute already made assumptions when certain other facts they imply prove to be false.

Let us consider the sample GFRN implication i in Fig. 10 which has two predicates in its antecedent (p_2,p_3) and one predicate in its consequent (p_1).

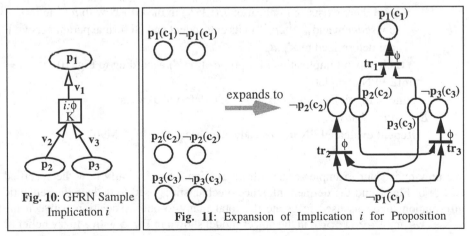

Fig. 10: GFRN Sample Implication i

Fig. 11: Expansion of Implication i for Proposition

The left side of Fig. 11 shows the three pre-existing propositions $(p_1(c_1), p_2(c_2)$ and $p_3(c_3))$. If the formal parameters $v_1,..,v_3$ of implication i are bound to constants $c_1,..,c_3$ such that the constraints K hold, the right side of Fig. 11 shows how implication i is expanded into three transitions with confidence ϕ^4.

At this, transition tr_1 represents the rule $p_2(c_2) \land p_3(c_3) \to p_1(c_1)$ while the contraposition $\neg p_1(c_1) \to \neg(p_2(c_2) \land p_3(c_3))$ is normalized to $\neg p_1(c_1) \land p_3(c_3) \to \neg p_2(c_2)$, represented by transition tr_2 and $\neg p_1(c_1) \land p_2(c_2) \to \neg p_3(c_3)$ represented by transitions tr_3.

Generally, the number of transitions that are created for the contraposition is equal to the number of propositions in the antecedent of the expanded implication.

Finally, the third expansion step removes all ingoing edges from propositions that represent strong or deferred axioms from the FPN. This is done in order to fulfil the requirement of Section 4.1 that during the evaluation phase the beliefs of strong and deferred axioms must not be changed.

The evaluation phase of the inference process starts when the FPN has been completely expanded. In this phase fuzzy beliefs are evaluated at each place in the FPN (according to Fig. 8 and Fig. 9) until steady state has been reached.

The described inference algorithm is given below.

algorithm inference
begin
    Expansion Phase:
        For each (strong and weak) axiom create a new proposition;
        Repeat
            If there exists a set of proposition $d_1..d_n$ with $d_n := (p_n{}^{kn}, O_n)$
                and there exists an implication $i : (\iota, V, K)$ in the GFRN with $p_1{}^{kl} .. p_n{}^{kn}$ in its antecedent or consequent
                and all formal parameters $v \in V$ are determined by $d_1..d_n$
            then expand all propositions in the antecedent and consequent of i.
            If there exists a set of proposition $d_1..d_n$ with $d_n := (p_n{}^{kn}, O_n)$
                and there exists an implication $i : (\iota, V, K)$ in the GFRN with $p_1{}^{kl}$ in its consequent and $p_1{}^{kl} .. p_n{}^{kn}$ in its antecedent and all formal parameters $v \in V$ are determined by $d_1..d_n$
            then expand implication i for proposition d_1 according to Fig. 10
        until FPN complete;
        remove ingoing edges from strong and deferred axioms;
    Evaluation Phase:
        Repeat evaluate FPN **until** steady state according to [KM96]
  end

We now revisit our example scenario from Section 2 to exemplify how the specified GFRN of Fig. 7 and the defined inference mechanism is used to deduce the semantic information that was used to create the total many-to-one association between the classes WP and Developer in the object-model shown in Fig. 5 with a fuzzy belief of 0.6.

---

4. By default the threshold of transitions is set to zero at expansion time. It maybe increased in order to eliminate limitcycles (cf. [KM96]).

For this example we assume that it already has been deduced that table `Person` has the two variants `Developer` and `Manager`. We will use n as an abbreviation for `Developer.name` and d as an abbreviation for `WP.dev`.

At first an initial automatic investigation of the application code in Fig. 3 retrieves the following three facts (cf. Section 2) which serve as strong axioms with fuzzy belief 1:

Strong axioms: $A^s:= \{(\text{cycl\_excl}^1,\{n\},+,1), (\text{sel\_dist}^1,\{n\},+,1), (\text{join}^1,\{(n,d)\},+,1)\}$

Furthermore, the reengineer has a subjective belief that with confidence 0.5 attribute dev is a key of table `WP`. This is represented as a weak axiom.

Weak axiom: $A^w:= \{(\text{key}^1,\{d\},+,0.5)\}$

Moreover, there is an automatic procedure ϕ_1 that computes the fuzzy belief for compatibility of two given attribute types. Finally, we have automatic procedures ϕ_2 and ϕ_3 which try to disprove supposed key- and IND-constraints by finding counterexamples in the available extension. Since we want these three procedures to be executed on an on-demand basis, we define the following deferred axioms.

Deferred axioms: $A^d:= \{(\text{tcomp}^1,+,\phi_1), (\text{disprKey}^1,+,\phi_2),(\text{disprIND}^1,+,\phi_3)\}$

The expansion of the FPN in Fig 12 starts with the instantiation of the strong and weak axioms, i. e. we create places for the propositions *cycl_excl({n})*, *sel_dist({n})*, *join({(n,d)})*, and *Key({d})*.

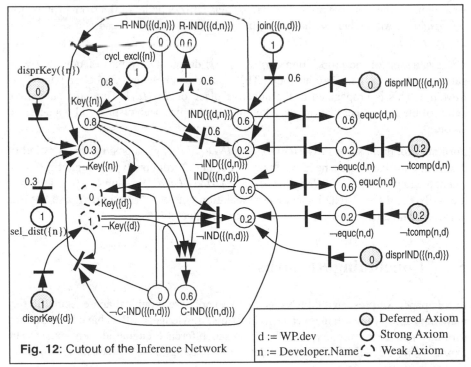

Fig. 12: Cutout of the Inference Network

Within the first expansion step implication i_5 is applied to proposition $join(\{(n,d)\})$. This binds parameter v_1 of implication i_5 to $\{(n,d)\}$. Then the constraint $v_2=swap(v_1)$ binds parameter v_2 to $\{(d,n)\}$. Thus we create places for the two inclusion dependencies $IND(\{(n,d)\})$ and $IND(\{(d,n)\})$. Within the second expansion step implication i_5 creates the transitions $join(\{(n,d)\}) \rightarrow IND(\{(n,d)\}) \wedge IND(\{(d,n)\})$ and $\neg IND(\{(n,d)\}) \rightarrow \neg join(\{(n,d)\})$ and $\neg IND(\{(n,d)\}) \rightarrow \neg join(\{(d,n)\})$. However, the third expansion step removes the latter two transitions because they target a strong axiom.

The just created $IND(\{(n,d)\})$ proposition allows the instantiation of implication i_9. This creates an equivalence class proposition $equc(n,d)$. This in turn enables the expansion of implication i_8 creating proposition $tcomp(n,d)$. Note that $tcomp(n,d)$ is defined by a deferred axiom. In addition, the expansion of implication i_6 creates proposition disprIND($\{(n,d)\}$). Altogether, the inclusion dependency will be verified by analysing the type compatibility of the involved attributes and by searching for a counterexample in the database extension. The remainder of the depicted FPN is expanded analogously.

The evaluation of the expanded FPN starts by assigning the fuzzy beliefs of the strong and weak axioms to the corresponding places. Thus, the depicted propositions $cycl\_excl$, sel_dist, and $join$ get a fuzzy belief of 1. The positive place of $Key(\{d\})$ gets the fuzzy belief 0.5 based on the reverse engineer's decision.

According to Fig. 8 and Fig. 9 the confidence of transition $cycl\_excl(\{n\}) \rightarrow Key(\{n\})$ restricts the maximum fuzzy belief propagated to the positive place of $Key(\{n\})$ to 0.8. Analogously, the negative place of $Key(\{n\})$ gets a fuzzy belief of 0.3 from proposition $sel\_dist(\{n\})$. Altogether, we have a higher belief that attribute name is a key of table Developer.

The evaluation of the proposition $disprKey(\{d\})$ detects two tuples of table WP with value Martin in their dev attribute. This counterexample assigns belief 1 to $disprKey(\{d\})$. This is propagated to the negative place of $Key(\{d\})$. Thus, the subjective belief of the reengineer that dev is a key of table WP has been disproved by a deferred axiom.

Furthermore, propositions $IND(\{(n,d)\})$ and $IND(\{(d,n)\})$ get a positive fuzzy belief of 0.6 from $join((n,d))$ and a negative fuzzy belief of 0.2 from the type compatibility test. Then, the fuzzy beliefs of $R\text{-}IND(\{(d,n)\})$ and $C\text{-}IND(\{(n,d)\})$ compute to 0.6. Together the R-IND and the C-IND indicate an association between Developer and WP that has the cardinalities shown in Fig 5 with a confidence of 0.6.

5   Concluding Remarks

In this paper we presented GFRNs as a new expressive graphical and executable formalism to specify uncertain reverse engineering knowledge. GFRNs have been defined formally and a first prototype of the proposed inference engine already exists. The expressiveness of GFRNs is now validated by applying them to practical examples as part of industrial projects.

We currently develop a GFRN editor that facilitates creation and customization of GFRN specifications. This will be used to build a database of reverse engineering knowledge for relational databases.

A major point is that GFRNs and the corresponding inference engine will not be used as stand alone tools. As soon as the inference engine is integrated into our database migration environment [JSZ96] the user may interactively add and verify assumptions about a database and derive all semantic information necessary for the migration to the object-oriented data model. This enables our migration environment to provide sophisticated support for the entire database migration process.

References

[And94] M. Andersson. Extracting an Entity Relationship Schema from a Relational Database through Reverse Engineering. In *Proc. of the 13th Int. Conference of the Entity Relationship Approach, Manchester*, pages 403–419. Springer, 1994.

[CS80] J. D. Carney and R. K. Scheer. *Fundamentals of Logic*. Macmillan Publishing Co., Inc., 1980.

[DA87] K. H. Davis and A. K. Arora. Converting a Relational Database Model into an Entity-Relationship Model. In *Proc. of the 6th Int. Conference of the Entity Relationship Approach, New York*, pages 271–285. North-Holland, November 1987.

[DLP94] D. Dubois, J. Lang, and H. Prade. *Handbook of Logic in Artificial Intelligence and Logic Programming*, pages 449–403. Clarendon Press, Oxford, 1994.

[DP88] D. Dubois and H. Prade. An introduction to possibilistic and fuzzy logics. In P. Smets, E. H. Mamdani, D. Dubois, and H. Prade, editors, *Non-Standard Logics for Automated Reasoning*, pages 287–326. Academic Press, London, 1988.

[FV95] C. Fahrner and G. Vossen. Transforming Relational Database Schemas into Object-Oriented Schemas according to ODMG-93. In *Proc. of the 4th Int. Conf. of on Deductive and Object-Oriented Databases 1995*, 1995.

[JK90] P. Johannesson and K. Kalman. A method for translating relational schemas into conceptual schemas. In F. H. Lochovsky, editor, *Entity-Relationship Approach to Database Design and Querying*. ERI, 1990.

[JSZ96] J. H. Jahnke, W. Schäfer, and A. Zündorf. A design environment for migrating relational to object oriented database systems. In *Proc. of the 1996 Int. Conference on Software Maintenance (ICSM'96)*. IEEE Computer Society, 1996.

[JSZ97] J. H. Jahnke, W. Schäfer, and A. Zündorf. Specification and implementation of generic fuzzy reasoning nets using programmed graph rewriting systems. Technical report, University of Paderborn, 1997. forthcoming.

[KM96] A. Konar and A. K. Mandal. Uncertainty management in expert systems using fuzzy petri nets. *IEEE Transactions on Knowledge and Data Engineering*, 8(1):96–105, February 1996.

[Loo88] C. G. Looney. Fuzzy petri nets for rule-based decisionmaking. *IEEE Transactions on Systems, Man, and Cybernetics*, 18(1):178–183, February 1988.

[LS88] C. Lewerentz and A. Schürr. GRAS, a management system for graph-like documents. In *Proc. of the 3rd Int. Conf. on Data and Knowledge Bases*. Morgan Kaufmann, 1988.

[Mai89] D. Maier. Making database systems fast enough for CAD applications. In W. Kim and F. H. Lochovsky, editors, *Object-Oriented Concepts, Databases and Applications*, pages 573–582. Addison-Wesley, 1989.

[Paa88] G. Paass. Probabilistic logic. In P. Smets, E. H. Mamdani, D. Dubois, and H. Prade, editors, *Non-Standard Logics for Automated Reasoning*, pages 213–251. Academic Press, London, 1988.

[PB94] W. J. Premerlani and M. R. Blaha. An approach for reverse engineering of relational databases. *Communications of the ACM*, 37(5):42–49, May 1994.

[Pet81] J. L. Peterson. *Petri Net Theory and Modeling of Systems*. Prentice Hall, 1981.

[PKBT94] J-M. Petit, J. Kouloumdjian, J-F. Boulicaut, and F. Toumani. Using queries to improve database reverse engineering. In *Proc. of 13th Int. Conference of ERA, Manchester*, pages 369–386. Springer, 1994.

[SK90] F. N. Springsteel and C. Kou. Reverse Data Engineering of E-R Designed Relational Schemas. In *Proc. of Databases, Parallel Architectures and their Applications*, pages 438–440. Springer, March 1990.

[SLGC94] O. Signore, M. Loffredo, M. Gregori, and M. Cima. Reconstruction of er schema from database applications: a cognitive approach. In *Proc. of 13th Int. Conference of ERA, Manchester*, pages 387–402. Springer, 1994.

[Zad78] L. A. Zadeh. Fuzzy sets as a basis for a theory of possibility. *Fuzzy Sets and Systems*, 1978.

Providing Automated Support
to Deductive Analysis of Time Critical Systems

Andrea Alborghetti, Angelo Gargantini, Angelo Morzenti
Politecnico di Milano, Dipartimento di Elettronica e Informazione
email: [garganti, morzenti]@elet.polimi.it

Abstract

We report on our experience in using a general purpose theorem prover to provide mechanical support to deductive analysis of specifications written in the TRIO temporal logic, and on applying the resulting tool to a widely known case study in the field of time- and safety-critical systems. First, we illustrate the required features for a general purpose theorem prover to satisfy our needs, we provide a rationale for our choice, and we briefly illustrate how TRIO was encoded into the prover's logic. Then we present the case study used to validate the obtained TRIO prover and to assess the overall approach. Finally we discuss the encouraging results of our experiment and provide some technical and methodological suggestions to researchers and practitioners willing to use our tool to analyze TRIO specifications, or aiming at customizing a general purpose theorem prover on any other formal language, especially if based on temporal logics.

Keywords: specification, validation, verification, time and safety critical systems, formal methods, temporal logic, automated theorem proving, case study, experience report.

1. Introduction

The importance of effective procedures for specification, validation, and verification in the development of correct and reliable computer-based systems can hardly be over-emphasized, especially in the case of time- and safety-critical systems. Validation and verification arc most (cost) cffcctive when performed in the initial phases of system development, before the costly phases of design and coding take place [Kem85]. This emphasizes the importance of the notation adopted for carrying out the specification phase, which must support the unambiguous description of the system requirements and at the same time allow for the (possibly automated) analysis of such specifications.

Formal methods (i.e., notations, and associated tools, having a strong mathematical foundation) have since long been considered a promising approach to address the above demands, but at the same time they where the target of many criticisms, especially coming from practitioners who were not convinced of their effectiveness in improving the quality of the developed products and of their overall convenience, notably from an economic viewpoint. In the recent past, however, some sensational failures in computer-based systems occurred (such as the Therac-25 accident, the Pentium bug, or the Arianne rocket fiasco), soon demonstrated to derive from miscarried specification and verification. They provided evidence that the high price of applying formal methods is certainly worth while for the most critical applications.

In the past years a host of formal languages and methods were introduced for the specification and analysis of critical systems, based on mathematical logic, state-transition systems, (process) algebras, etc. [H&M96] but no single language, method, or tool has gained universal acceptance nor has proved to tackle all problems in all application areas. It is now a widespread opinion that every individual notation has its own strong and weak points, and that there exist trade-offs among them.

TRIO, a language and tool set based on temporal logic, was defined and developed at Politecnico di Milano to support the specification, simulation, analysis and verification [MMG92, F&M94, FMM94] of time-critical systems. In particular, in [FMM94] we introduced an axiomatization of the logic that allows the specifier to formally derive properties of real-time systems from their specification in TRIO. We experienced however that formal verification can become difficult and error-prone when performed by hand: the likelihood of introducing errors in proofs, because of overlooked details or implicit, incorrect assumptions, can grow to the point of balancing the benefits of formal proofs. Therefore a strong need arises to provide an automated support to formal derivation. On the other hand, automated theorem proving is a highly specialized research field where very sophisticated techniques are need to obtain that particular combination of power, generality, simplicity, and flexibility needed in practical applications. For these reasons we did not consider undertaking the development from scratch of a new theorem prover for TRIO; rather, we looked for existing tools that could be employed for that purpose.

The present paper reports on our experience in using a general purpose theorem prover to provide a mechanical support to deductive analysis of TRIO specifications, and on applying the resulting tool to a widely known case study in the field of time- and safety-critical systems. In Section 2 we report a brief summary of TRIO. In Section 3 we illustrate the required features for a general purpose theorem prover to satisfy our needs, we provide a rationale for our choice of the PVS proof checker [SOR93], and we briefly illustrate how TRIO was encoded into the prover's logic. Section 4 presents the case study that we used to validate the obtained TRIO prover and to assess the overall approach. The results of our experience, discussed in Sections 5 and 6, are encouraging: proofs can be conducted almost at the same level of abstraction as in informal manual derivation, but now they are "certified" by the tool. On the contrary, one cannot expect, especially for complex proofs, that the prover "does it all by itself": our tool is in fact a proof checker, and the overall line of reasoning in a derivation (which, significantly, constitutes the most creative part) must still be provided by the user.

Altogether, we believe that our work provides evidence of the feasibility of the approach; in the present paper we supply technical and methodological information to researchers and practitioners willing to use our tool to analyze TRIO specifications, or aiming at customizing a general purpose theorem prover on any other formal language, especially if based on temporal logics.

2. TRIO: a Shortest Language Overview

TRIO is a first order logic augmented with temporal operators that allow to express properties whose truth value may change over time. The meaning of a TRIO formula is not absolute, but is given with respect to a current time instant which is left implicit. The basic temporal operator is called Dist: for a given formula W, Dist(W, t) means that W is true at a time instant whose distance is exactly t time units from the current instant, i.e., the instant when the sentence is claimed.

Many other temporal operators can be derived from Dist. In this paper we use the following ones.

$\text{Futr}(F, d)$	$\overset{\text{def}}{=} d \geq 0 \wedge \text{Dist}(F, d)$	future
$\text{Past}(F, d)$	$\overset{\text{def}}{=} d \geq 0 \wedge \text{Dist}(F, -d)$	past
$\text{Lasts}(F, d)$	$\overset{\text{def}}{=} \forall d'(0 < d' < d \rightarrow \text{Dist}(F, d'))$	F holds over a period of length d
$\text{Lasted}(F, d)$	$\overset{\text{def}}{=} \forall d'(0 < d' < d \rightarrow \text{Dist}(F, -d'))$	F held over a period of length d
$\text{Until}(A_1, A_2)$	$\overset{\text{def}}{=} \exists t\ (t > 0 \wedge \text{Futr}(A_2, t) \wedge \text{Lasts}(A_1, t))$	
		A_1 holds until A_2 becomes true
$\text{Alw}(F)$	$\overset{\text{def}}{=} \forall d\ \text{Dist}(F, d)$	F always holds
$\text{AlwF}(F)$	$\overset{\text{def}}{=} \forall d\ (d > 0 \rightarrow \text{Dist}(F, d))$	F will always hold in the future
$\text{AlwP}(F)$	$\overset{\text{def}}{=} \forall d\ (d < 0 \rightarrow \text{Dist}(F, d))$	F always held in the past
$\text{SomP}(A)$	$\overset{\text{def}}{=} \exists d(d < 0 \wedge \text{Dist}(F, d))$	F held sometimes in the past
$\text{Som}(A)$	$\overset{\text{def}}{=} \exists d\ \text{Dist}(F, d)$	Sometimes F held or will hold
$\text{UpToNow}(F)$	$\overset{\text{def}}{=} \exists \delta\ (\delta > 0 \wedge \text{Past}(F, \delta) \wedge \text{Lasted}(F, \delta))$	
		F held for a nonzero time interval that ended at the current instant
$\text{Becomes}(F)$	$\overset{\text{def}}{=} F \wedge \text{UpToNow}(\neg F)$	F holds at the current instant but
		it did not hold for a nonzero interval that preceded the current instant
$\text{LastTime}(F, t)$	$\overset{\text{def}}{=} \text{Past}(F, t) \wedge (\text{Lasted}(\neg F, t))$	
		F occurred for the last time t units ago

Notice that, for the operators expressing a duration over a time interval (for example Lasts), we gave definitions where the extremes of the specified time interval are excluded, i.e. the interval is open. Operators including either one or both of the extremes can be easily derived from the basic ones we listed above. For notational convenience, we indicate inclusion or exclusion of extremes of the interval by appending to the operator's name suitable subscripts, 'i' or 'e', respectively. A few examples regarding the operators Lasts, Lasted, Until, AlwF and SomP follow.

$\text{Lasts}_{ie}(A, d)$	$\overset{\text{def}}{=}$	$\forall d'(0 \leq d' < d \rightarrow \text{Dist}(F, d'))$
$\text{Lasted}_{ii}(A_1, d)$	$\overset{\text{def}}{=}$	$\forall d'(0 \leq d' \leq d \rightarrow \text{Dist}(F, -d'))$
$\text{Until}_{ie}(A_1, A_2)$	$\overset{\text{def}}{=}$	$\exists t\ (t > 0 \wedge \text{Futr}(A_2, t) \wedge \text{Lasts}_{ie}(A_1, t))$
$\text{AlwF}_i(F)$	$\overset{\text{def}}{=}$	$\forall d\ (d \geq 0 \rightarrow \text{Dist}(F, d))$
$\text{SomP}_i(A)$	$\overset{\text{def}}{=}$	$\exists d(d \leq 0 \wedge \text{Dist}(F, d))$

3. Encoding TRIO into the Prover's Logic

The first choice we had to take in providing automatic support to proofs in TRIO was that of a convenient formal theory: an encoding of TRIO formulas and the desired reasoning mechanisms (inference rules) in the language of the automatic tool. In [FMM94] we introduced a Hilbert–like proof system, based on the use of *modus ponens* as the only inference rule, which is known to be well suited for studying the properties of a logic, but not for constructing readable proofs or for automatic theorem proving.

To the purpose of automation, two principal kinds of proof system are used in practice: clausal form coupled with the resolution rule [Wos84], and Gentzen–like systems [Pra65].

Resolution-based procedures find a proof by contradiction, deriving from the premises and the negation of the goal a huge number of consequences, until a contradiction is found. To improve efficiency, formulas are expressed in a very simple and rigid way, as clauses. This reduces the readability, and prevents the user from understanding the proofs or the reasons of their failure. We believe that this way it is not adequate to support validation and verification, where interaction with the user is fundamental.

Gentzen systems, instead, favor the combination of a simple interaction with the prover (to direct the proof in the more complex cases) with automated solving of simpler subgoals by means of decision procedures. Gentzen systems include a set of inference rules that naturally correspond to the meaning of every operator. For instance, the sequent

$$\frac{\Delta \vdash \Gamma, A \qquad \Delta \vdash \Gamma, B}{\Delta \vdash \Gamma, A \wedge B}$$

(where A and B are formulas, Δ and Γ are set of formulas and $\Delta \vdash \Gamma$ means that Γ is deducible from Δ) means that the formula $A \wedge B$ is deducible from a set of hypothesis, if and only if so are both A and B.

This presentation is easily understandable, which helps significantly in designing and examining proofs. Besides, these inference rules can be easily used by a prover to decompose a proof into a tree of subgoals. For instance, the rule above can be used to reduce the deduction of $A \wedge B$ to those of A and B. Furthermore, if a subgoal fails because a counterexample can be found for it, the same counterexample falsifies also the original goal.

For the above reasons, we chose a Gentzen–like axiomatization, augmenting the set of rules for the predicate calculus with those necessary for dealing with temporal aspects. We introduced some basic inference rules for modeling some basic properties of the Dist operator (a brief summary of TRIO is reported in the appendix) such as:

$$\frac{\Delta \vdash Dist(A,0)}{\Delta \vdash A} \qquad\qquad \frac{\Delta \vdash Dist(A,d) \qquad \Delta \vdash Dist(B,d)}{\Delta \vdash Dist(A \wedge B,d)}$$

and the Temporal Translation rule (TT):

$$\frac{Dist(\Delta,d) \vdash Dist(\Gamma,d)}{\Delta \vdash \Gamma}$$

whose intuitive meaning is that a deduction is still valid if looked from a different time instant.

For apparent reasons of cost and reliability, we aimed at encoding TRIO into a logic for which a prover already existed, and at including its proof system in the language of that prover. There exist some well known encoding methods, classified as either *syntactic* or *semantic*.

In the syntactic approach, the *source logic* is encoded into a *base logic*, the latter being used as a logical metalanguage to represent the formulas of the former, together with its inference rules, expressed through proper axioms. This approach is particularly powerful, allowing for the representation of every kind of rule, including the TT rule.

However, it complicates even the simplest proofs, for it forces the user to prove in the base logic that a sequence of steps forms a valid proof of the source logic, so that it is almost unfeasible, unless the prover itself is equipped with some mechanism that facilitates this kind of encoding. There is a wide variety of provers and logical environments, such as Isabelle [Pau90], ICLE [Daw92], Mollusc [Ric93] and others, which provide a facility of this kind, and have been used successfully for encoding in their language several first–order or higher–order logics.

Unfortunately, all these provers lack powerful decision procedures for arithmetic, which are essential when dealing with TRIO, since time is numeric in nature. The only prover we found that uses a Gentzen–like deductive system and applies powerful decision procedures for Presburger arithmetic and other decidable theories is PVS [SOR93], which we adopted for our experiment. Unfortunately, PVS provides no facility for syntactic encoding, so we looked for alternative encoding methods.

In the *semantic* approach the meaning of a formula is expressed in the base logic; this can make the proof of the encoded formula in the base logic very different from that in the source logic. In this way Hoare Logic and RTTL have been encoded within the HOL system [Gor89, CHH93], the Unity logic into the Boyer–Moore prover [Gol90] and the Duration Calculus (DC) within PVS [SS94].

A first choice of a semantic encoding of TRIO in PVS is representing TRIO formulas as functions from a temporal domain to booleans [Jef96]. This would make explicit the current time instant and we experienced that this encoding seriously jeopardizes the readability of proofs. So we looked for a suitable interface to hide the details of the encoding, as in the case of DC [SS94]. Unfortunately, the lack of the necessary documentation on the PVS prover made it difficult for us to build an interface similar to the one available for DC (one of whose constructors was also in the team of PVS developers) and, most important, prevented us from providing reliable estimates of the feasibility of the approach, especially concerning the de-coding from a formula in the internal logic back to TRIO.

For this reason we avoided the construction of an interface by using a suppressed state encoding, that considers TRIO formulas as an uninterpreted type. To provide the usual interpretation to TRIO formulas, we introduce the function *now* from the type TRIO formula to booleans. This function applied to a TRIO formula A has value true iff A is true now. This makes the overall system (PVS prover + axioms that realize the encoding) behave exactly as a TRIO prover that applies our proof system as we described above.

To represent the desired inference rules, we introduced axioms that intuitively explain the meaning of the various operators, stating for example that $now(A \wedge B) = now(A) \wedge now(B)$. Using these axioms and the inference rules of PVS, it was not difficult to implement the desired inference rules for TRIO, through the definition of suitable *strategies*, i.e. rules of the following kind:

$$\frac{\Delta \vdash \Gamma, now(Dist(A,d)) \quad \Delta \vdash \Gamma, now(Dist(B,d))}{\Delta \vdash \Gamma, now(Dist(A \wedge B,d))}$$

These rules also allowed us to encode indirectly the TT rule, which does not seem to be representable directly in PVS, as the system does not provide means to add an external *Dist* operator to *all* formulas of a sequent, as required by the TT rule, in a single derivation step.

4. The Case Study

We validated our approach on the GRC (General Railroad Crossing) problem, which was recently used as a benchmark for languages and tools for critical systems analysis (for a statement of the problem, see the preface of [H&M96]). In the GRC problem several trains travel on railway tracks; a road intersects the tracks, with a bar at the crossing blocking vehicle traffic during train passage. For the sake of simplicity every train travels in the same direction: the case of trains traveling in both directions can be dealt with by symmetry. Two regions R and I, surrounding the crossing, are defined as depicted below.

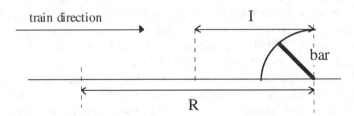

Fig. 1 The topology of the railroad crossing

Any *finite* number of trains can enter or leave any region during any finite time interval. The system must simultaneously ensure that the bar be closed whenever a train is inside region I (*safety* property), and that the bar is down only when strictly necessary (*utility* property).

It takes the train a minimum time d_m and a maximum time d_M to go from the beginning of R to the beginning of I; from h_m to h_M to go from beginning of I to its end ($d_M \geq d_m > 0$ and $h_M \geq h_m > 0$). The bar can be in two stationary positions, *open* or *closed*, or it can be moving up or moving down and is operated through commands *goUp* and *goDown*.

The following predicates formalize train movements.

RI(k)	the k-th train is entering R
II(k)	the k-th train is entering I
IO(k)	the k-th train is leaving I (and therefore R)

They denote *unique events*, i.e., they must satisfy the following axioms (expressed for event E):

$$\forall k\Big(E(k) \rightarrow \big(AlwP(\neg E(k)) \wedge AlwF(\neg E(k))\big)\Big)$$

i.e. E(k) is true at most in a single time instant

$$\forall k\Big(E(k) \wedge k > 1 \rightarrow SomP_i(E(k-1))\Big)$$

i.e. (weak) time monotonicity of parameter k

$$Alw(\neg E(0)) \qquad \text{by convention E(0) never occurs}$$

Informally, RI and IO represent the only input events detected by sensors; the occurrence of output events is *deduced* from the occurrence of the input ones.

Time dependent variables, CRI, CII, and CIO, count the occurrences of the corresponding events RI, II, and IO. These variables are counters, a counter is a time dependent variable, that increases for every occurrence of a given event, starting from a null initial value.

(A1) Counter(C,E) $\overset{\text{def}}{=}$

$$\left(\begin{array}{c} Alw\Big(\forall k\big(k \geq 1 \rightarrow (C = k \leftrightarrow SomP_i(E(k)) \wedge \neg SomP_i(E(k+1)))\big)\Big) \\ \wedge \\ Som\big(C = 0 \wedge AlwP(C = 0)\big) \end{array}\right)$$

i.e., C is a counter for event E if C is always the value of the highest k for which E(k) has occurred.

(A2) Counter(CRI, RI) $\wedge$ Counter(CII, II) $\wedge$ Counter (CIO, IO)

i.e., CRI, CII, and CIO are the counter for events RI, II, and IO, respectively.

The geometry of the region R and the behavior of the trains are formalized below.

$$\forall k\Big(RI(k) \rightarrow \exists t\big(d_m \leq t \leq d_M \wedge Futr(II(k), t)\big)\Big)$$

if the k-th train enters R now, then the k-th train will enter I between d_m and d_M time units in the future

$$\forall k\Big(II(k) \rightarrow \exists t\big(d_m \leq t \leq d_M \wedge Past(RI(k), t)\big)\Big)$$

if the k-th train enters I now, it entered R between d_m and d_M time units in the past

$$\forall k\Big(II(k) \rightarrow \exists t\big(h_m \leq t \leq h_M \wedge Futr(IO(k), t)\big)\Big)$$

if the k-th train enters I, then it will exit R between h_m and h_M time units in the future

$$\forall k \Big(IO(k) \to \exists t \big(h_m \le t \le h_M \wedge \text{Past}(II(k),t) \big) \Big)$$

if the k-th train exits R, then it entered I between d_m and d_M time units in the past

We assume that the bar, after a *goDown* or a *goUp* command (the two commands are mutually exclusive) reaches the final position in γ time units ($\gamma < d_m$ and velocity of motion is equal in the two directions). When the bar is moving upwards an opposite command *goDown* may be issued, causing an immediate change in movement direction.

When the bar in the closed state receives a *goUp* command, it will move upwards for γ time units or until a *goDown* is issued.

(M1) $\text{UpToNow}(closed) \wedge goUp \to \text{Until}_{ie} \big(mvUp, \ goDown \vee \text{Past}(goUp, \gamma) \big)$

A bar in the *up* position that receives a *goDown* command moves for γ and then remains closed until the next *goUp* command.

(M2)
$\text{UpToNow}(up) \wedge goDown \to \text{Lasts}_{ie}(mvDown, \gamma) \wedge \text{Futr}\big(\text{Until}_{ie}(closed, \ goUp), \gamma \big)$

When the bar moving up receives a *goDown* command it inverts its motion, at the same speed reaches again the closed position, and stays there until the next *goUp*.

(M3)
$$\begin{pmatrix} \text{UpToNow}(mvUp) \wedge \\ goDown \wedge \\ \text{LastTime}(goUp, t) \end{pmatrix} \to \begin{pmatrix} \text{Lasts}_{ie}(mvDown, t) \wedge \\ \text{Futr}\big(\text{Until}_{ie}(closed, \ goUp), t \big) \end{pmatrix}$$

After moving up for γ time units, if there is no *goDown* command the bar stays open until the next *goDown* command.

(M4) $\quad\quad \text{Lasted}_{ie}(mvUp, \gamma) \wedge \neg goDown \to \text{Until}_{ie}(open, \ goDown)$

Initially, i.e., before any operation takes place, the bar is open (the bar is installed before any train arrives).

(M5) $\quad\quad \text{AlwP}_i (\neg goDown) \to open$

The bar control strategy computes the number of trains that are possibly in I: whenever it becomes positive a *goDown* command is issued, while whenever it becomes 0 a *goUp* command is issued. Formally, the above train number is CTPI $=_{def}$ past(CRI, d_m) - CRO (d_m in the past operator models maximum speed of trains moving from region R to region I). Let CTPI$_\gamma =_{def}$ past(CRI, d_m-γ) - CRO: CTPI$_\gamma$ account for a forward time shift of γ in issuing the command *goDown* to the bar due to the duration of the bar movement.

The commands issued to the bar are then defined as follows.

(C1) $\quad\quad$ goDown $\leftrightarrow$ Becomes(CTPI$_\gamma$>0)

(C2) $\quad\quad$ goUp $\leftrightarrow$ Becomes(CTPI=0)

These axioms must ensure then safety and utility properties, formalized as follows:

Safety: $(CII > CRO) \rightarrow$ closed

i.e., if the number of trains entered in region I is greater than those who left it, the bar is down.

Utility: $\text{Lasted}_{ii}(CII = CIO, \ \gamma) \wedge \text{Lasts}_{ii}(CII = CIO, \ \gamma + d_M - d_m) \rightarrow$ open

i.e., if the number of trains entered in region I is equal to those who left it, the bar is up (the constants γ and d_M-d_m+γ in the Utility property derive from the delay in bar rising upon train exit and from the conservative advance in bar lowering upon train enter).

5. Analysis of the Case Study

The first verification step consisted of deriving the desired *Safety* and *Utility* properties. Even with the assistance of the prover, the derivation required a great effort; moreover, to facilitate proofs, it was necessary to modify part of the specification, as it often happens in a verification activity.

As an important by-product of verification, we discovered that the strategy for governing the bar was incorrect: it allowed for the passage of a train through the crossing with the bar not closed, thus violating the *Safety* property. This constitutes a typical combination of verification and validation, whereby the requirements are assessed or found inadequate by the process of proving interesting system properties.

5.1 System Validation and Verification

The original control policy was based on the idea that any transition of CTPI from zero to a positive value should be anticipated by a similar transition of CTPIγ taking place γ time units before. Therefore, by axiom C1, when a train is inside region I the bar would be closed and *Safety* guaranteed.

We used the prover to check rigorously this idea, by formalizing the reasoning above through a sequence of lemmas and trying to prove each of them. We then discovered an error, caused by a misunderstanding of the system behavior, when we failed proving the following lemma (L7).

Alw(Becomes(CTPIγ>0)$\leftrightarrow$ Futr(Becomes(CTPIγ > 0,γ))

The proof attempt decomposed the original goal into four separate subgoals, some of which were derived from the specification. However we could not derive the following subgoal:

$\text{Dist}(\text{UpToNow}(CTPI = 0), \ \gamma) \ |- \ \text{UpToNow}(CTPI\gamma = 0), \ \text{Dist}(CTPI = 0, \ \gamma)$

Then we tried to falsify it, starting from a partial model that verified the antecedent and falsified all the consequents, and then trying to complete it respecting the various specification's axioms. This activity led to a counterexample, showed in Fig. 2, that falsified lemma L7 and hence the *Safety* property.

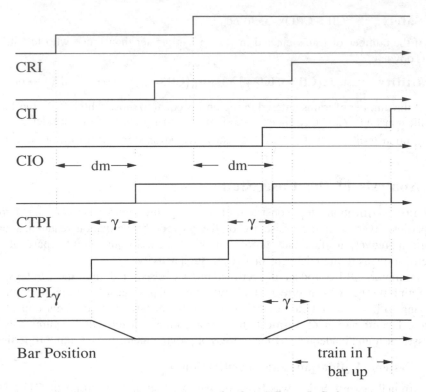

Fig. 2 A counterexample for L7 and Safety

We note that the time spent on the unfeasible proof was very short, since we quickly found the mentioned counterexample. Even more important, both the search of a proof and of a counterexample could be seen as parts of a single process, because every step of the failed proof is, at the same time, a step in the construction of the counterexample. In fact the backward application of an inference rule can be read both as: "To prove the goal I must prove all the subgoals" or "To falsify the goal I can falsify one of the subgoals".

This fact provides important methodological suggestions, for it shows that there exists a systematic way to extract useful indications from the failure of a proof, through the construction of a counterexample.

In our case, the counterexample showed clearly that the problem was originated by the fact that the increment of CTPIγ (used for sending a *goDown* command to the bar) was not necessarily from zero to a positive value, for CTPIγ could have been already positive.

The counterexample suggested also that the problem could simply be avoided by issuing the *goUp* command when CTPIγ, rather than CTPI, becomes zero. Therefore axiom C2 was modified into

$$(C2) \quad goUp \leftrightarrow Becomes(CTPI\gamma = 0)$$

which indeed allowed us to prove both *Safety* and *Utility*.

5.2 Systematic Specifications Support Easy Proofs

Another interesting methodological issue concerns the specification of the bar. One of the key steps in proving the *Safety* property consisted of deriving the following lemma (L6):

$$\text{goDown} \wedge \text{Lasts}_{ii}\left(\neg\text{goUp}, t\right) \wedge t \geq \gamma \to \text{Futr}\left(\text{Lasts}_{ii}\left(\text{closed}, t - \gamma\right), \gamma\right)$$

Unfortunately this property, apparently depending only on the behavior of the bar, was not deducible exclusively from its specification. A simple counterexample can be constructed by considering a situation where the bar is always in the *mvDown* state and the *goDown* command has been issued periodically an infinite number of times in the past.

In practice this counterexample can be excluded based on the control policy and the definition of the counters by showing that there must be a first *goDown*. Nevertheless it showed that the specification was not well modularized. When analyzing properties of a non trivial system, modularity is a key issue for mastering complexity, and therefore, considering that the extra effort required by this deficiency could not be justified, we changed the specification of the bar, to make it more self-contained.

The need for modularity was not the only reason for changing the specification: even if we uncovered all the assumptions adopted in the first version and derived them from the specification of other system components, the particular expression of the axioms M1÷M5 would still hinder the proofs.

In fact, one of the most natural ways to conduct a proof is by analyzing the various possible cases. Of course, the case analysis must be exhaustive: in our example case, we would consider, as the various cases, the possible current system states, using an axiom like Alw(open ∨ closed ∨ mvUp ∨ mvDown) to guarantee the exhaustiveness of the analysis. Unfortunately, from the fact that the bar is in a given state, say open, the axioms do not allow one to draw directly any conclusion on other states. For instance, axiom M1 tells what happens if the bar is closed and a goUp is issued, but the case when the bar is closed and no goUp is issued is not considered explicitly. Similar argument show how difficult it would be to prove the completeness of the specification, i.e., that the desired behavior is specified for every bar state and for every issued command.

To overcome these difficulties we adopted a *state–based* specification of the bar: for each bar state we introduced an axiom describing its starting and ending conditions. For instance, the following axiom is relative to the *open* state (notice that it is structured as a set of nested implications with mutually exclusive premises).

$$\text{Alw}\left(\text{open} \rightarrow \left(\begin{array}{l}\left(\text{AlwP}(\neg\text{goDown}) \rightarrow \text{SomF}\left(\begin{array}{l}\text{AlwP}(\text{open} \wedge \neg\text{goDown}) \\ \wedge \text{ goDown} \wedge \text{mvDown}\end{array}\right)\right) \wedge \\ \neg\text{AlwP}(\neg\text{goDown}) \rightarrow \exists \text{d1, d2} \left[\text{Past}\left(\begin{array}{l}\text{d2} > \text{d1} \wedge \\ \left(\begin{array}{l}\text{UpToNow(mvUp)} \\ \wedge \\ \text{Lasts}_{\text{ie}}(\text{open} \wedge \neg\text{goDown}, \text{d2}) \\ \wedge \\ \text{Futr(goDown} \wedge \text{mvDown}, \text{d2})\end{array}\right)\end{array}\right), \text{d1}\right]\end{array}\right)\right)$$

This new version of the axioms facilitated the proof of desired properties, and increased the confidence in the completeness of the specification. We do not think, however, that it would be a generally adequate solution, since it is not sufficiently readable, nor it is easy to write; moreover, it does not prevent the introduction of inconsistencies.

We then feel that a further step is needed, from purely state–based specifications to tabular specifications, as advocated by [HPSK78] and [HM83]. Applying this idea to the description of the bar, we would obtain a table with a row and a column for each state; a cell contains the condition under which the system moves from the state corresponding to its row to the state of its column. For instance, the row for the *open* state would the following,

	open	closed	mvUp	mvDown
open	¬goDown	–	–	goDown

stating that if the bar is in the *open* state and a *goDown* is issued, it goes into the *mvDown* state; otherwise it remains in the *open* state. This presentation is easy to read and write; moreover, completeness and consistency can be easily guaranteed by simple table inspections. In practice, the conditions that appear in the table can be arbitrarily complex TRIO formulas referring to the past history of the system, which gives enough power to represent more complicated behaviors, as in the case of time-outs

By means of suitable translation rules a set of TRIO axioms could be generated from the tables, to be used in proofs. In general, this could be done in a simple and convenient way in the case of discrete time domains, but not so easily when time was modeled by the set of real numbers.

5.3 Discrete vs. Dense Time Domain

This is only one of the difficulties arising from adopting the set of reals as the temporal domain. For instance we found that, in an informal proof, it was very frequent to use expressions like: "the last time in which A happened" or "the next time in which A will happen". When formalizing these concepts in PVS, it was necessary to prove, for instance, that there really existed a "last" or "next time" in which A happened. To this end, it would have been necessary, first of all, to exclude (or severely limit) the possibility of accumulation points of events, introducing a considerable amount of extra work.

As an example of this kind of complication, to prove the *Safety* property it was necessary to prove the following lemma, called Becomes_CTPIγ.

$$\text{Alw}\Big(\neg\text{CTPI}\gamma = 0 \rightarrow \exists t\big(\text{Past}\big(\text{Becomes}(\neg\text{CTPI}\gamma = 0), t\big) \wedge \text{Lasted}_{ii}\big(\neg\text{CTPI}\gamma = 0, t\big)\big)\Big)$$

This lemma states that, if CTPIγ is positive, there must be a last time in which it became positive (being previously zero), and its correctness should be evident to the reader. Despite this, its proof required the introduction of many other lemmas, requiring almost a third of the total effort necessary to prove the *Safety* property. With a discrete temporal domain, instead, the proof of this lemma would have been straightforward.

Although many of the required lemmas could be exploited also in future proofs, this shows that the higher detail and precision in specifications allowed by modeling time as a continuous set does not come for free, having a negative impact on the complexity of proving even trivial facts. Therefore, one could use a discrete time model as a useful approximation for single-clock systems, keeping the full generality of real-valued time for asynchronous systems where events occur arbitrarily close in time.

5.4 Figures of Total Effort

Concerning the cost of our activity, the proof of the two properties required the introduction of 53 intermediate lemmas, reported in about 1000 pages of proof, generated by the prover (every step is the result of an interaction with the user: intermediate steps done by the prover are not reported), distributed among the various theorems and lemmas.

It is interesting to notice that lemmas concerned with properties of Counters and Events, for a total of 258 pages, are completely reusable without modifications. The percentage of possible reuse could be increased from 26% to 38%, by generalizing some lemmas to cover a broader range of cases.

The total time required for analysis was slightly more than 3 person-months, from the first serious reading of the original specification to the writing of the last page of documentation. The documentation activity took about 3 weeks and produced a 100 pages summary of the proofs.

The rest of the time was spent (i) trying to reach a sufficient understanding of the system behavior, (ii) searching for a way to formalize our reasoning, and (iii) deriving the actual proofs. After a training phase, during which we could hardly produce more than 20 pages of proofs in a day, our productivity increased significantly, reaching a rate of about 100 pages in a day in the last proofs. All the hard work was concentrated in the first two steps, witnessing the adequacy of the tool and of our encoding.

The effort required for the second phase derived mainly from the adoption of real-valued time and from the original description of the bar. In particular, we spent about a week analyzing the specification of the bar and providing an alternative formalization; then, when the alternative was found, half a day sufficed to complete the related proofs. Therefore, we are quite confident that, for adequately trained engineers, the effort should be required mainly by the first phase: understanding the system. This does not mean that proofs would become easy and cheap: it only means that time would be spent more proficiently.

6. Conclusions and Future Developments

We summarize here a few final remarks on the experiment described in the present paper and the lessons we learned from it. Regarding the choice of a formal theory for our logic, we found that Gentzen-like systems favor human reasoning on the proofs; then we chose PVS as a tool for interactive construction of proofs, despite its lack of support to a syntactic encoding, mainly because of its powerful decision procedures.

Overall, our experience can certainly be considered successful. Indeed, the encoding and the theory could be effectively employed, in our case study, to prove system properties and to disprove false conjectures. Moreover, unsuccessful attempts to derive putative theorems led to the construction of counterexamples providing useful indications for the correction of incomplete or inconsistent specifications. This alternation between system specification, validation, and verification constitutes a very useful and effective combination of verification and simulation [M&S96]. During the analysis activity we realized that modeling time as a continuous set leads to significant increase of the complexity of proofs; this however cannon be avoided when modeling asynchronous systems.

On the other hand, the figures presented in the preceding Section 5 show that the definition and utilization of this novel approach to system analysis required a significant effort, in terms of both human and computing resources. Therefore the question arises, as it is often the case with applications of formal methods, whether the obtained results were really worth the required effort, and if this method can usefully be employed in practical, industrially-sized applications.

An impartial judgment on this crucial aspect should consider that a significant part of the effort spent in the investigation of the GRC case study derived from (self)instruction on the PVS tools (that we had never used extensively before) and from gaining experience in the use of the TRIO axiomatization and encoding for deriving system properties. In fact, even if the figures reported in Section 5 on the case study do not include the work to define the encoding of TRIO in PVS, this could be effectively validated only when applied systematically to a realistic example.

We therefore expect significant cost reductions in future applications of the proposed method, deriving from: increased knowledge of both the formal and mathematical aspects of PVS as well as of its most mundane features of the tool, which have a strong impact on its practical usability. Besides, from the development of our case study, we were able to extract some generally useful methodological guidelines. They should lead to the definition and construction of libraries of generic reusable components (PVS parametric theories) supporting the definition of high-level notions (such as states, events, counters, etc.), whose relevant features and properties would be pre-defined and proved in advance.

Even when assuming that all these improvements will be effectively realized and applied, we maintain that the analysis of complex, (time) critical systems, especially when performed by means of formal correctness proofs, is a difficult, costly activity that requires skilled, well trained personnel. In our opinion these methods can therefore be applied with tangible advantages only to the most critical, non-standard kernel components of the developed systems. Recent advances in the technology of theorem provers, proof checkers, model checkers, and simulators, have improved the state of the art and widened their application area, but have not produced, in our view, any dramatic breakthrough.

We intend to pursue the present approach to the specification, validation, and verification of time critical systems along the following lines.

- Development of other case studies of similar size and complexity, to verify our above-reported hypothesis on diminishing costs in successive applications;
- Investigation of alternative, promising approaches to the encoding of TRIO, such as the adoption of a semantic encoding coupled with the construction of a front-end acting as a parser/unparser of the language [SS94];
- Construction of libraries of predefined theories to support reusability, modularization, and bottom-up construction of specifications and proofs;
- Integration of different, complementary tools and methods, in the same line as [Rus96], combining theorem-provers not only with model-checkers, but also with simulators/history-checkers, as advocated by [F&M94, M&S96].

Acknowledgments
We thank Ralph Jeffords for useful suggestions on the encoding of TRIO in PVS, and Dino Mandrioli for his advice on the focus and presentation of this paper.

7. References

[CHH93] R. Cardell–Oliver R. Hale and J. Herbert. "An embedding of Timed Transition Systems in HOL". *Formal Methods in System Design*, August 1993.
[Daw92] Mark Dawson, "The Imperial College Logic Environment". Technical report, imperial College of Science, Technology and Medicine, 1992.
[F&M94] M.Felder, A.Morzenti, "Validating real-time systems by history-checking TRIO specifications", ACM TOSEM-Transactions On Software Engineering and Methodologies, vol.3, n.4, October 1994.
[FMM94] M.Felder, D.Mandrioli, A.Morzenti, "Proving properties of real-time systems through logical specifications and Petri net models", IEEE TSE-Transactions of Software Engineering, vol.20, no.2, Feb.1994, pp.127-141.
[Gol90] D. Goldshlag, "Mechanizing Unity". In M. Broy and C.B. Jones, editors, *Programming Concepts and Methods*, North Holland, 1990.
[Gor89] M.C.J. Gordon, "Mechanizing programming logics in higher–order logic". In G. Birtwistle and P.A. Subrahmanyam, editors, *Current Trends in Hardware verification and Theorem Proving*, Springer–Verlag, New York, 1989.
[H&M96] Heitmeyer C., Mandrioli D. (editors) "Formal Methods for Real-Time Computing", John Wiley & Sons, Series Trends in Software vol. 5, 1996.

[HM83]   Heitmeyer C., McLean J., Abstract requirements specifications: A new approach and its application. IEEE TSE-Transactions of Software Engineering, SE-9, 5, Sept.1983, pp.580-589

[HPSK78] Heninger K., Parnas D.L., Shore J.E., Kallander J.W., Software requirements for the A-7E aircraft. Tech. Rep. 3876, Naval Research Lab., Wash., DC, 1978

[Jef96]   R.D.Jeffords, "Encoding the Real-Time Logic TRIO in PVS", Naval Research Laboratory Research Report, May 1996.

[Kem85]   R.A. Kemmerer, "Testing formal specifications to detect design errors," *IEEE Transactions on Software Engineering*, vol. 11, no. 1, pp. 32-43, January 1985.

[M&S96]   A.K.Mok and D.Stuart, "Simulation vs. Verification: Getting the Best of Both Worlds", Proc. of COMPASS, 11th Annual Conference on Computer Assurance, June 1996, Gaitersburg, MA.

[MMG92] A.Morzenti, D.Mandrioli, C.Ghezzi, "A Model-Parametric Real-Time Logic", ACM TOPLAS-Transactions on Programming Languages and Systems, Vol.14, n.4, October 1992 pp.521-573.

[Pau90]   L. Paulson, "The next 700 theorem provers". In P. Odifreddi, editor, *Logic and Computer Science*, Academic Press, New York, 1990.

[Pra65]   D.Prawitz, "Natural Deduction. A Proof Theoretical Study", Almqvist & Wiksell, Stockholm, 1965.

[Ric93]   B.L. Richards, "Mollusc User's Guide". Technical report, University of Edinburgh, 1993.

[Rus96]   J.Rushby, "Automated Deduction and Formal Methods", Proc. of CAV '96, Springer Verlag LNCS 1102, pp.169-183, July 1996.

[SOR93]   N. Shankar S. Owre and J.M. Rushby. "User guide for the PVS specification and verification system, language and proof checker (beta release)". Computer Science Laboratory, SRI International, Menlo Park, CA 94025, USA, February 1993.

[SS94]   J.U. Skakkebæk and N. Shankar, "Toward a Duration Calculus assistant in PVS", in Willem–Paul de Roever Hans Laangmaack and Jan Vytopil, editors, *Proc. 3rd Int'l Symp. on Formal Techniques in Real–Time and Fault–Tolerant Systems.* Springer–Verlag, 1994.

[Wos84]   Larry Wos, Ross Overbeek, Ezing Lusk and Jim Boyle, "Automated reasoning: introduction and applications", Prentice Hall inc., 1984.

Verification of Liveness Properties Using Compositional Reachability Analysis

Shing Chi Cheung[†]   **Dimitra Giannakopoulou**[‡]   **Jeff Kramer**[‡]

[†]Department of Computer Science, Hong Kong University of Science and Technology, Clear Water Bay, Hong Kong.

[‡]Department of Computing, Imperial College of Science, Technology and Medicine, London SW7 2BZ, UK.

Email: scc@cs.ust.hk, {dg1, jk}@doc.ic.ac.uk

Abstract

The software architecture of a distributed program can be represented by a hierarchical composition of subsystems, with interacting processes at the leaves of the hierarchy. Compositional reachability analysis (CRA) is a promising state reduction technique which can be automated and used to derive in stages the overall behaviour of a distributed program based on its architecture. Conventional CRA however has a limitation. The properties available for analysis after composition and reduction are constrained by the set of actions that remain globally observable. The liveness properties which involve internal actions of subsystems may therefore not be analysed. In this paper, we extend compositional reachability analysis to check liveness properties which may involve actions that are not globally observable. In particular, our approach permits the hiding of actions independently of the liveness properties that are to be verified in the final graph. In addition, it supports the simultaneous checking of multiple properties (both liveness and safety), and identifies those properties that are violated. The effectiveness of the extended technique is illustrated using a case study of a Reliable Multicast Transport Protocol (RMTP) with over 96,000 states and 660,000 transitions.

Keywords

Reachability analysis, compositional verification, distributed computing systems, labelled transition systems, Büchi automata, liveness properties.

1   Introduction

Distributed processing is widely used to provide computing support for diverse applications. Many of these applications are complex and critical; an error can have catastrophic consequences. Behaviour analysis is a useful technique that can help discover defects and check if a program performs as intended.

Static analysis techniques for concurrent and distributed programs can be used to verify two classes of property: *safety* and *liveness* [4]. A *safety* property asserts that the program never enters an undesirable state. For example, mutual exclusion is a safety property which specifies the absence of a program state where a common resource is simultaneously accessed by more than one client. A *liveness* property asserts that a program eventually enters a desirable state. For example, the assertion that a program will eventually close a file after opening it is a liveness property.

In this paper, we focus our discussion on liveness properties which can be specified in terms of *Büchi automata* - finite state machines that accept infinite words [3, 14]. These machines will be referred to as *property automata*. Each property automaton specifies the set of acceptable execution sequences in terms of actions that correspond to a liveness property of interest. For example, the property automaton in Figure 1 asserts the liveness property that a write request will eventually be granted. This is because the automaton accepts an infinite word *w* if and only if the execution of the automaton on *w* contains the acceptance state 0 an infinite number of times. Therefore, this automaton accepts the language (*write_request* request_grant*)$^\omega$, where juxtaposition represents concatenation, and the operators * and $^\omega$ denote finite and infinite repetition accordingly.

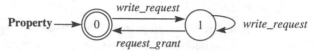

Fig. 1. A property automaton

However, distributed programs are generally complex to analyse. Even for small programs, analysis of their behaviour is tedious without the support of an *effective automated* technique. One approach is to perform analysis in a compositional manner, thus exploiting the design structure (software architecture) of the distributed program [12]. This can be represented by a hierarchical composition of subsystems, with interacting (primitive) processes at the leaves of the hierarchy. Behaviour of a primitive process can be modelled as a *state machine* whose transitions are labelled by the activities it can perform. *Composite processes* appear at the nodes of the hierarchy. Each composite process is a subsystem formed by a collection of processes that can be either primitive or composite. The behaviour of a composite process is derived by composing the behaviours of its immediate children in the hierarchy. Details of the subsystem that are internal to it are then hidden. A minimal state-machine is generated for its abstracted behaviour, corresponding to the behaviour of the subsystem visible to its environment. The global system behaviour is obtained in this way, and can be used for verification.

Promising results have been reported from the use of *Compositional Reachability Analysis (CRA)* to generate a state space graph for a well-structured distributed program [19, 22, 23, 26]. Yeh [25] described several case studies which suggested similar performance between a technique of compositional reachability analysis and that of constraint expressions [5]. Sabnani et al. [22] described an experiment applying compositional reachability analysis to the Q.931 protocol. They found that the intermediate state space graphs generated never exceeded 1,000 states although the global state space graph given by traditional reachability analysis of the protocol contained over 60,000 states. Similar observations have also been made by Tai and Koppol [23]. CRA is particularly suitable for analysing properties of programs which are likely to evolve. It helps localise the effect of change. When changes are applied to a program, only the properties involving those subsystems that are affected by the changes need be re-computed.

The CRA technique however has a limitation. The properties available for analysis after minimisation are constrained by the set of actions that remain globally observable. This poses a severe problem if properties to be checked involve a large set of actions that are not globally observable. Previous work [7] has proposed a mechanism to address this problem during the checking of *safety* properties. In this paper, we extend the CRA technique with a mechanism for the checking of *liveness* properties. The extension allows multiple liveness properties to be validated simultaneously. Liveness properties are violated when some subsystems, within the context of a distributed program, can perform execution sequences not acceptable to the specified property (Büchi) automata. If no violation of liveness properties is detected, the analysis constructs a global LTS *observationally equivalent* [20] to that constructed using conventional CRA techniques; otherwise it indicates which and how liveness properties are violated.

As mentioned, we have adopted the approach which expresses properties as Büchi automata. Büchi automata can be used to express formulae of linear time temporal logic [14]. Fernandez et al. propose a technique to compose the property automata with the system [10]. Godefroid and Holzmann [13] compute the product automaton of the specifications of the system with a Büchi automaton for the negation of a formula of interest. Verification then reduces to checking if the product automaton accepts only the empty set. A similar approach has been proposed by Aggarwal et al. [1]. Their work extends the selection/resolution (S/R) model with acceptance states, adding to it the expressiveness of Büchi automata. However, the issues of compositionality and hiding of internal actions are not addressed in any of the above works.

Recently Bultan et al. have proposed a method for performing compositional analysis of temporal properties expressed in the branching time logic ∀CTL [6]. The method generates counterexamples using a compositional approach. Branches of the intermediate graphs are pruned if they do not provide potential counterexamples for the property under verification. All actions are assumed to be globally observable in the method. The issues of hiding internal actions and incorporating the checking mechanism into the framework of compositional reachability analysis have not been addressed. Moreover, their method can handle a single property at a time. Every change introduced into the system when a violation is detected requires rechecking of all the system properties one by one.

The rest of this paper is structured as follows. Sections 2 and 3 introduce labelled transition systems and present a reliable multicast transport protocol (RMTP) which is used as a case study in our discussion. Section 4 describes compositional reachability analysis and its limitations. Section 5 proposes a technique to overcome these limitations. The technique detects and locates violation of liveness properties related to subsystems. This is followed by a comparison of experimental results and conclusions in Sections 6 and 7, respectively.

2 Labelled Transition Systems

A *labelled transition system* (LTS) can be used to model the behaviour of a synchronous communicating process in a distributed program. An LTS contains all the states the process may reach and all the transitions it may perform. The model has been widely used in the literature for specifying and analysing distributed programs [9, 11, 16, 21, 24]. In the model, communicating processes are synchronised through actions sharing the same labels. For example, let a represent the action in which a machine in a flexible manufacturing system transfers a part to a conveyor belt. The action a occurs only if the machine is ready to hand over the part, and the conveyor belt is simultaneously prepared to receive the part. In terms of LTS, a is modelled as a possible action in the standalone behaviour of both processes. Its execution then requires simultaneous participation from both processes. Formally, an LTS of a process P is a quadruple $< S, A, \Delta, p >$ where

(i) S is a set of states;
(ii) $A = \alpha P \cup \{\tau\}$, where αP is the communicating *alphabet* of P which does not contain the internal action τ;
(iii) $\Delta \subseteq S \times A \times S$, denotes a transition relation that maps from a state and an action onto another state;
(iv) p is a state in S which indicates the initial state of P.

An LTS of $P = < S, A, \Delta, p >$ transits into another LTS of $P' = < S, A, \Delta, p' >$ with an action $a \in A$ if and only if $(p, a, p') \in \Delta$. That is,

$$< S, A, \Delta, p > \xrightarrow{a} < S, A, \Delta, p' > \text{ iff } (p, a, p') \in \Delta.$$

Since there is a one-to-one mapping between a process P and its LTS, we use the terms process and LTS interchangeably. Processes in a distributed program may be composed by operator $\|$, which has similar semantics to those of the composition operator used in CSP [15]. $P1 \| P2$ is the parallel composition of processes $P1$ and $P2$ with synchronisation of the actions common to both of their alphabets and interleaving of the others. Observability of actions in a process can be controlled by a restriction operator $\uparrow$. $P{\uparrow}L$ represents the process projected from P in which actions in A-L are replaced by the internal action τ.

Finally, a liveness property is expressed as a Büchi automaton $B = < S, A, \Delta, q_0, F >$, where S is a finite set of states, A is a set of observable actions, Δ is a set of transitions, q_0 is its initial state, and F is a set of acceptance states. An execution of B on an infinite word $w = a_1 a_2 a_3 \ldots$ over A is an infinite sequence $\sigma = q_0 q_1 q_2 \ldots$ of elements of S, where $(q_{i-1} a_i q_i) \in \Delta$ for every $i > 0$. An execution of B is accepting if it contains some acceptance state of B an infinite number of times. A word w is accepted by B if there exists an accepting execution of B on w.

3 The Reliable Multicast Transport Protocol (RMTP)

To illustrate our approach, we present a Reliable Multicast Transport Protocol (RMTP) as proposed by Lin and Paul [18]. The protocol is designed for applications that cannot tolerate data loss. It provides sequenced, lossless delivery of data from a sender to a group of receivers, at the expense of delay. Reliability is achieved by a periodic transmission of acknowledgement by the receivers (*ACK* packets) and a selective retransmission mechanism by the sender. Scalability is provided by grouping receivers into a hierarchy of local regions, with a *Designated Receiver (DR)* in each of those regions. Receivers in each local region send their ACKs to the corresponding DR, DRs send their ACKs to the higher level DRs or to the sender (see Figure 2), thereby avoiding the ACK-implosion problem. In addition, DRs cache received data and respond to receivers in their local regions, thus decreasing end-to-end latency. The term *Acknowledgement Processor (AP)* is used to denote either a DR or the sender, when referring to them as entities that receive and process ACKs. Receivers which are not designated receivers are referred to as *ordinary receivers*.

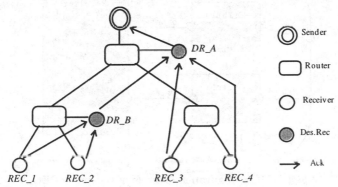

Fig. 2. A multicast tree of receivers

To cater for situations where DRs may fail, receivers use a mechanism to dynamically select the nearest operational AP in the multicast tree. This is the part of the RMTP protocol that our case study focuses on. Dynamic selection of APs is achieved in RMTP by the use of a special packet, called the SND_ACK_TOME (SAT) packet. The sender and all DRs periodically advertise themselves (action *adv*) by multicasting SAT packets along their subtrees. The SAT packets are tagged with the same initial *time-to-live* (TTL) values. Routers decrement the TTL value when forwarding packets. Therefore a larger TTL value indicates a closer proximity in the multicast tree. On receiving an SAT packet, a receiver compares the TTL value associated with the incoming packet with that associated with the AP currently selected. The receiver switches to a new AP if the incoming packet has a larger TTL value. When a receiver fails to receive a new SAT packet from the currently selected AP after a certain period of time, it assumes failure of the AP and initiates another selection cycle.

In our case study, we have modelled this part of the protocol for the configuration depicted in Figure 2. Three processes are associated with both ordinary and designated receivers in the multicast tree, namely the Receiver, Channel, and Watch processes.

Let us consider the ordinary receiver REC_1 in Figure 2 as an example. Figure 3 presents the configuration diagram of REC_1 that encapsulates three processes (shown in the Darwin architectural description language [17]). Communicating actions take place where portals of components (represented as grey dots) are bound together. A portal is an interface instance and has a type that is simply a set of names that refer to actions or events shared between bound components. Interface types in the diagram are defined as follows:

```
interface dr_info {ms_fail; selA; selB; selS;}
interface dr_mes {mesA; mesB; mesS;}
interface fails {failA; failB;}
interface advs {advA; advB; advS;}
```

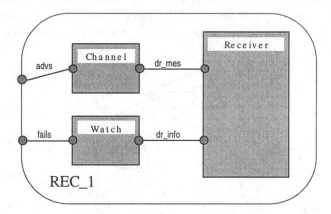

Fig. 3. The configuration diagram of subsystem REC_1

As illustrated in the configuration diagram, REC_1 interacts with other entities in the multicast tree through interfaces *advs* and *fails*, consisting of actions *advA*, *advB*, *advS*, *failA*, and *failB*. For convenience, we use *actX/Y/Z* to stand for the set of actions *actX*, *actY* and *actZ* which share the same prefix *act* in their labels. The behaviour of REC_1 is given by the composite behaviour of its three constituent processes described in terms of LTS as in Figure 4.

The Channel process models a lossy channel, which receives advertisements from the APs above the receiver (actions *advA/B/S*), and transmits them to the Receiver process (actions *mesA/B/S*), or loses them (action *lose*). The specification assumes fair execution in the sense that unfair execution sequences where the Channel keeps losing all messages are refused. The Watch process models the time-out associated with the selection of a new AP. It observes all potential APs for the receiver, and when a failure of the selected AP occurs (actions *failA/B*), it informs the Receiver (actions *ms_fail*) so that the selection procedure is initiated. The receiver then selects as its AP (action *selA/B/S*) the AP whose advertisement it receives first. Selections are modified whenever an advertisement is received from a nearer AP than the one currently selected. In the composite behaviour of the Receiver, Channel and Watch processes, only actions *failA/B*, and *advA/B/S* synchronise with the environment of REC_1 (via its interface portals `fails` and `advs`), so all the remaining actions can be made unobservable, i.e.,

REC_1 = (Channel ‖ Watch ‖ Receiver) ↑ {*failA/B, advA/B/S*}.

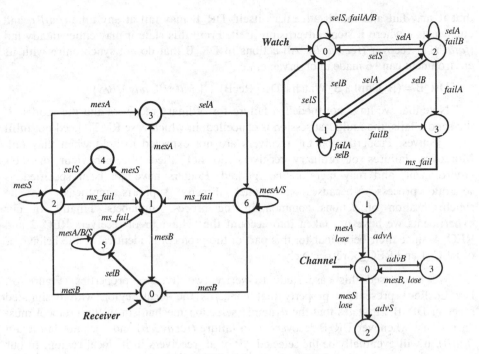

Fig. 4. LTS of the receiver REC_1

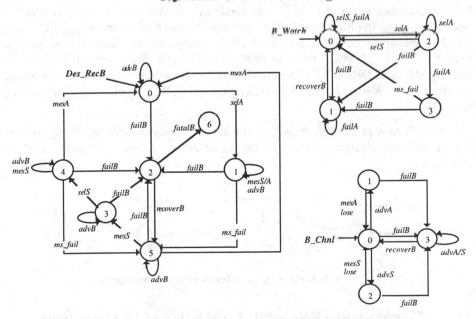

Fig. 5. LTS of the designated receiver DR_B

In Figure 5 we illustrate the behaviour of designated receiver DR_B. DR_B has also been specified in terms of three components. A DR behaves like a receiver, except that it may fail and that it advertises itself. DR_B may fail at any time *(failB)*, and enter a state where it stops advertising itself. From this state it may either fatally fail *(fatalB)* or recover *(recoverB)*. All actions in DR_B that do not synchronise with its environment can be made unobservable, i.e.,

DR_B = (B_Chnl ‖ B_Watch ‖ Des_RecB) ↑ { *failA/B, advA/B/S*}.

Note that we have not modelled failure for ordinary receivers and the sender. If the sender fails, the multicast session is cancelled, in which case RMTP need not fulfil its objectives. Properties on the receivers are not expected to hold when they fail. Moreover, failures of ordinary receivers do not affect the behaviour of their environment, and may therefore be ignored. Routers have not been specified as separate processes because our model directly supports multicast by the synchronisation of actions common in the process alphabets. Finally, in our experiments we have not taken into account the behaviour of receivers REC_2 and REC_4, since their behaviour for this part of the protocol is identical to the behaviour of REC_1 and REC_3, respectively

We have used this case study to verify two liveness properties (Figure 6). Liv_LocReg1 presents a property that concerns the local region with designated receiver DR_B. It states that the dynamic selection mechanism of the protocol must ensure that whenever DR_B recovers from failure *(recoverB)* and does not fail again *(failB)*, it will eventually be the selected AP of all receivers in its local region. In our case study, the latter corresponds to checking that *(selB)* will eventually be performed by REC_1. Since we want to be able to verify this property for the local region, we need to postpone the hiding of actions *selB* and *recoverB* of components REC_1 and DR_B respectively until the next level in the compositional hierarchy, as seen in Figure 9. Property LivRec3 refers to REC_3, and asserts that whenever DR_A is its selected AP and DR_A fails (action *ms_fail* synchronised with its corresponding watch process - Watch3 in Figure 9 - reflects this fact), REC_3 will eventually select a new AP.

We will now proceed to show how the above liveness properties of the protocol can be effectively validated using an enhanced compositional reachability analysis technique.

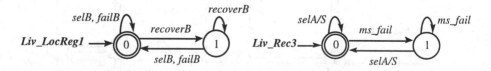

Fig. 6. Liveness properties as property automata

4   Compositional Reachability Analysis and its Limitations

Promising results have been reported in the literature on the use of a compositional approach to derive the overall system behaviour using reachability analysis [22, 23, 26]. In compositional reachability analysis (CRA) techniques, the model of the target system is given as an LTS that describes an abstraction of the system behaviour, according to the requirements of the user. Figure 7 gives an LTS describing the abstracted behaviour of designated receiver DR_A[1]. Action *A.selS* in the figure represents *selS* in designated receiver DR_A. The LTS indicates that the Sender is the only AP selected by DR_A. The selection is performed voluntarily by DR_A upon its recovery from failure.

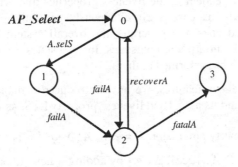

Fig. 7. A global LTS of RMTP

The analysis is performed in two steps. Firstly the RMTP protocol is decomposed into a hierarchy of subsystems that mirrors its multicast tree. Secondly the LTS of the overall system is composed step by step from those of its subsystems in a bottom-up manner. In each intermediate step, the LTS of a subsystem is simplified by hiding internal actions that are not of interest to the global view of the protocol.

The key to the success of CRA techniques is to employ a modular software architecture and hide as many internal actions as possible in each subsystem. The observable behaviour of a subsystem where internal actions have been hidden can in general be represented by a simpler LTS. However, the properties that are available for reasoning in the analysis are then constrained by the set of remaining globally observable actions. For instance, consider the case of liveness property Liv_Rec3 in Figure 6. This property involves actions that are internal to subsystem REC_1. Actions *selA*, *selS*, and *ms_fail* would therefore need to be exposed in the global graph of the system for verifying property Liv_Rec3. However, this compromises the CRA approach. One of the main advantages of CRA is that it offers to the users the possibility of abstracting from the behaviour of subsystems those details in which they are not interested. This should obviously not be made at the expense of the effectiveness of analysis.

In our previous work [7] we describe a technique for making the verification of safety properties independent from the actions that are observable at the global state graph of the system. In this paper, we provide a way of achieving the same goal for the case of liveness properties. Our method achieves this without reducing the advantages that CRA exhibits as compared to traditional reachability analysis. Our experimental results presented in Section 6 demonstrate and confirm this.

---

[1]   This LTS has been constructed automatically by using the TRACTA tool [12].

5   Validation of Liveness Properties

5.1   Specification of Properties

We have incorporated in CRA a mechanism for checking liveness properties. The method exhibits three main desirable features. *Firstly*, it finds a way of making the hiding of actions independent of the liveness properties that are to be checked in the final graph. *Secondly*, it checks simultaneously multiple properties, specifically identifies the violated ones and generates the overall system behaviour. *Thirdly*, it avoids keeping specific information on states. Instead states are differentiated in terms of the actions that can be performed at them.

To achieve the above features, we have introduced a mapping between a given property automaton and its associated liveness property LTS, as in Definition A.

Definition A: A property automaton $P = < S, A, \Delta, q, F>$ is mapped into a liveness property LTS $P' = < S, A \cup \{acc\}, \Delta', q>$ by adding a new globally unique action acc and new transitions such that:

    (i) $acc \notin \alpha A$; and

    (ii) $\Delta' = \Delta \cup \{s \xrightarrow{acc} s \mid s \in F\}$.

Applying the Definition A to the property automata in Figure 6 results in the LTS depicted in Figure 8.

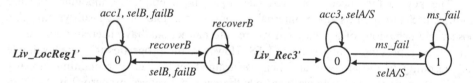

Fig. 8. Liveness properties in ECRA

The mapping identifies the acceptance state of Liv_LocReg1 with its ability to perform the action $acc1$ in Liv_LocReg1'. Transitions, which identify acceptance states, are referred to as acceptance transitions. The use of acceptance transitions removes the need for modelling acceptance states in the LTS model. Storing acceptance states as special states in the analysis process would have required the introduction of specific rules for the minimisation procedure. With the use of acceptance transitions, any two states s and s' of a subsystem *Sys* are considered behaviourally equivalent, if and only if s and s' (or the respective states to which they can unobservably transit) represent the same acceptance status for liveness properties that have been introduced in the subtree rooted at *Sys*. Thus, in our checking mechanism described in the following section, an LTS violates a liveness property iff its minimised equivalent does.

5.2 Checking Properties and Locating Violations

In our Extended Compositional Reachability Analysis (ECRA) technique, every property automaton B is mapped to an LTS B' as described in Definition A. Each B' is included in the compositional hierarchy for composition with the (sub)system for which it expresses some liveness property. CRA is then used to compute the global graph for the system. In our case study for example, the liveness property LTS Liv_Rec3' has been included in the subtree of REC_3 (see Figure 9). REC_3 thus becomes:

(Channel3 ‖ Watch3 ‖ Receiver3 ‖ Liv_Rec3') ↑ {*failA, advA/S, acc3*}.

In ECRA, a process P satisfies the liveness property expressed as a property automaton B if and only if all cycles in $P‖B'$ contain a transition labelled by the acceptance action of B'.[2] For simplicity, the technique assumes fair selection and fair process execution in the modelled systems[3]. For example in a communicating channel, the assumption ignores unfair execution sequences that keep losing messages. It also ignores those situations where a ready process never fires. Under the stated assumption, satisfaction of property B can be reduced to checking the existence of acceptance transitions at *terminal* sets of states of $P‖B'$. A set of states C in an LTS $< S, A, \Delta, p >$ is said to be *terminal* if and only if:

- C is a strongly connected component; and
- C is closed under Δ, i.e., $\forall\, s \in C, (s, a, s') \in \Delta \Rightarrow s' \in C$.

The computation of terminal sets of states in a graph can be performed with complexity linear to the size of a graph [2]. ECRA also keeps track of all acceptance actions that have been introduced in the analysis. Let a be an acceptance action introduced to identify the acceptance states of a property automaton B. Our method concludes that the property B is not satisfied by a system S if $S‖B'$ contains terminal sets of states where a cannot be executed. Since the action a uniquely identifies a property automaton, ECRA specifically indicates which properties cannot be satisfied by the system under analysis.

When analysis uncovers property violations, a useful kind of diagnostic information to provide to the user is a detailed path leading to the violation. In a compositional technique where actions have been hidden at intermediate phases of analysis, abstracted information can be recovered by using hierarchical tracing [27]. When no violation is detected, ECRA removes acceptance transitions from the global state-graph and then minimises it. The minimisation results in an LTS observationally equivalent to the one that would have been obtained if the liveness properties had not been included in the analysis.

---

[2]   This is a mechanism adapted from that described by Gribomont et al [14] and Fernandez et al [10].

[3]   Our analysis technique additionally includes a liveness checking mechanism that does not assume fairness, i.e. for cases where the fairness assumption is too restrictive. Assuming fairness is thus provided as an option in our analysis tools. It is beyond the scope of this paper to describe the latter mechanism.

5.3 Checking the RMTP Protocol

The RMTP protocol as described in section 3 has been used for comparing our method with both traditional Reachability Analysis (RA) and CRA. In the case study, we have assumed that the user wishes to globally expose actions *failA, A.selS, recoverA* and *fatalA*, and therefore observe only part of the behaviour of component DR_A in the system. All remaining actions have been hidden as soon as they were made internal to subsystems.

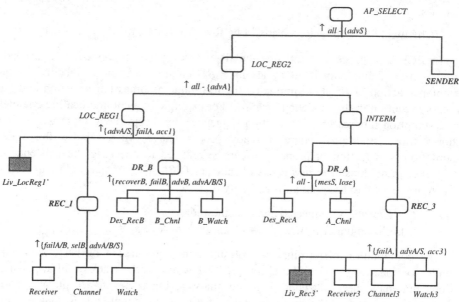

Fig. 9. The compositional hierarchy for the RMTP

The ECRA technique has been applied to the compositional hierarchy that mirrors the RMTP multicast tree of Figure 2, where LTS Liv_LocReg1'and Liv_Rec3' have been introduced as described in section 5.2 (see Figure 9). The global graph thus constructed for AP_SELECT contains 344 states and 2,626 transitions. Property Liv_Rec3'is satisfied. However, the graph contains terminal sets of states where *acc1* cannot be executed. As such, ECRA has identified that the system modelled by our specifications violates Liv_LocReg1, and has returned a trace in the global graph, that leads to a terminal set of states in which *acc1* cannot be performed.

This trace together with the intermediate subsystems obtained have been used for building up the debugging trace «*selB, failB, advA, τ, τ, failA, recoverB, advB, τ*» on the graph of subsystem LOC_REG1 before minimisation. This trace leads LOC_REG1 to a non-acceptance state that forms a terminal singleton of states where the only actions that can be performed are *advA/B/S*. Mapping this trace to REC_1 we obtained trace «*selB, failB, ms_fail, advA, mesA, selA, failA, advB, mesB*» which drives components (Receiver, Channel, Watch) to state (0, 0, 3). In this state of REC_1, both the Receiver and the Watch components are deadlocked, and REC_1 can only perform non-progress cycles where the Channel keeps receiving and losing advertisements. At this stage, it was relatively easy to track down the problem to an omission in the specification of component Watch. When component Watch is in state 3, it is ready to inform the Receiver about the failure of its AP, but is not ready to record a new AP selection by the Receiver. However, the trace obtained illustrates that the Receiver may be at the stage of selecting DR_B due to its proximity in the multicast tree, in which case it is no longer interested in failures of its current AP.

After the addition of transition (3, *selB*, 1) to process Watch (Figure 4), we performed ECRA on the corrected version of the RMTP, obtaining the global graph shown in Figure 10. Having used a compositional approach, we re-computed only those subsystems affected by the change in the specifications. No violation of liveness properties was detected this time. Acceptance transitions may therefore be removed from the global graph, resulting in an LTS that reflects the behaviour of component DR_A in the multicast tree. This LTS may be used to check further behavioural properties, such as the one which asserts that whenever DR_A recovers from failure, it can always select an AP.

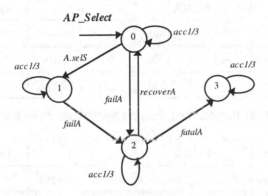

Fig. 10. Global LTS of RMTP obtained by ECRA

5.4 When Fairness Affects Analysis Results

In our case study of the RMTP we have checked if liveness properties Liv_LocReg1 and Liv_Rec3 are satisfied by the protocol. The automaton for Liv_LocReg1 illustrated in Figure 6 will accept any infinite word w that belongs to language $(recoverB^*\ (selB \cup failB))^{\omega}$. However we have observed that under the fairness assumption, property Liv_LocReg1 is trivially satisfied.

Let T be a terminal set of states that violates Liv_LocReg1. It is impossible for a *recoverB* transition to be enabled at any state s of T, as in this case *acc1* will also be enabled at s which contradicts our violation assumption. Since no acceptance transition for Liv_LocReg1 occurs in T, any trace leading to the root of T must contain *recoverB* but not *failB* or *selB*. However *failB* is always a possibility in the behaviour of DR_B after recovery from failure, and therefore $(s, failB, s')$ will be possible for some $s \in T$. As T is a terminal set of states $s' \in T$, and *acc1* is enabled at s' which again contradicts our assumption.

It is clear that the existence of the *failB* transition in Liv_LocReg1 makes the satisfaction of the property trivial under the fairness assumption. In order to avoid the problem, property Liv_LocReg1 was modified to accept language (*recoverB* selB*)$^\omega$, and *fatalB* was removed from the behaviour of DR_B. We conducted our experiments after performing these alterations, and the results confirmed the fact that the protocol does not violate property Liv_LocReg1.

6   Experimental Results

We have analysed the RMTP case study using ECRA, CRA and RA for both the cases of incorrect and correct specifications. We have compared the three techniques in terms of the size of the graphs that they have generated. The experiments were conducted using TRACTA - an environment for analysing behaviour of distributed systems [12]. The results are summarised in Tables 1 and 2.

Incorrect	ECRA		CRA		Traditional RA	
Specification	#states	#trans.	#states	#trans.	#states	#trans.
Largest subsystem	90	370	91	305	not applicable	
Global system	344	2,626	1,291	7,586	96,528	664,416

Table 1: Results for Incorrect Specifications of RMTP

Specification	ECRA		CRA		Traditional RA	
After Correction	#states	#trans.	#states	#trans.	#states	#trans.
Largest subsystem	90	370	91	305	not applicable	
Global system	4	13	1,371	8,035	96,528	672,588

Table 2: Results for Specifications of RMTP After Correction

The size of the graph generated by traditional RA shows that even the part of the RMTP protocol presented is nontrivial to analyse. The results were obtained by excluding from the analysis components REC_2 and REC_4 which exhibit behaviour identical to that of components REC_1 and REC_3, respectively. In the experiments, CRA was found to be more efficient than traditional RA, even with the global exposition of actions involved in the liveness properties of interest. The largest graph generated by CRA is smaller than that by traditional RA by 70 times. This justifies the use of CRA for this verification. However, the advantages that CRA exhibits as compared with traditional RA gradually disappear as the number of actions that need to be globally observable increases.

ECRA, on the other hand, performs better in both cases. In the case where the specification is correct, it reduces the global graph generated by CRA by 300 times, and the one generated by RA by 24,000 times. Moreover, it returns a graph that exposes concisely the system behaviour of interest to the developer. We have to mention here that, in ECRA, although the largest intermediate subsystem in the correct case has the same size as the one in the incorrect case, the size for most of the intermediate subsystems was reduced in the former case.

We have made the following observation in our experiments with ECRA and CRA techniques. Consider subtrees of the compositional hierarchy containing liveness LTSs that involve actions in some set *Actions*. In most cases, for all subsystems in which all members of *Actions* have been exposed by CRA, ECRA performs better or, in the worst case, equally to CRA. An informal explanation for this is that ECRA is a technique that achieves *selective* minimisation when liveness properties are included in the analysis. It inhibits, in the minimisation process, the merging of states that could result in hiding violations in the global graph for the system. It is therefore not expected to increase the size of a graph where observable actions can be used to detect the violation. In the absence of violations, it allows minimisation to proceed to its full effects, as has been shown in Table 2.

7   Conclusion and Future Work

In this paper, we have extended compositional reachability analysis with a mechanism for verifying multiple liveness properties that may involve globally unobservable actions. The mechanism does not require modification of the well-known formalism of LTS, and can be readily integrated in the existing framework of CRA. The integration preserves the existing composition and minimisation procedures of CRA. This has been achieved by avoiding special treatment of acceptance states. Acceptance states are identified with transitions labelled by actions globally unique to the system under analysis. A further advantage is that the approach is complementary to our approach for checking safety properties [7]. Safety properties are specified as property automata which can be composed directly with those specifying liveness properties under the CRA framework. As mentioned, to the best of our knowledge, no similar work provides the possibility of simultaneously checking multiple properties in the framework of CRA. This is particularly so in the presence of action hiding. Solutions that have been proposed compromise one or more desirable features of CRA.

A case study of a reliable multicast transport protocol of over 96,000 states and 660,000 transitions has been used to illustrate our technique and compare it to alternative ways of verifying liveness properties. Promising results have been obtained. The mechanism preserves key desirable features of CRA while enhancing its verification capabilities.

Our experience with the case study has shown that fairness is a very important issue when analysing a system with respect to liveness properties. Assuming strong fairness in our models may result in an insufficient search for property violations. On the other hand, making no fairness assumptions may yield an unnecessarily large number of violations that are of no real interest. We are currently researching into the possibility of achieving a practical solution to this problem.

Further work is needed for providing guidance concerning which actions should be hidden, and where properties should be included, in the compositional hierarchy. This is both a logical decision as to which is the most sensible, and an efficiency decision as to which aids the minimisation automation. Our current work involves further optimisations to the proposed liveness checking mechanism as well as the possibility of adding contextual constraints to it [8]. We are also investigating a method which, after recording the violation on subsystem states, prunes from those subsystems all transitions originating from those states. Finally, we are evaluating the benefits and limitations obtained from automatically generating Büchi automata based on specifications in the linear time temporal logic LTL [14].

Acknowledgements

We gratefully acknowledge helpful discussions with our colleague, Jeff Magee, and the financial support provided by the following grants: the EPSRC Grant GR/J 87022 (TRACTA Project), the EU (ARES Framework IV contract 20477) and British Council UK/HK Joint Research Scheme project JRS96/38.

References

[1]   S. Aggarwal, C. Courcoubetis, and P. Wolper, "Adding Liveness Properties to Coupled Finite-State Machines," *ACM Transactions on Programming Languages and Systems*, vol. 12, no. 2, , 1990.

[2]   A. V. Aho, J. E. Hopcroft, and J. D. Ullman, *Data Structures and Algorithms*: Addison-Wesley, 1983.

[3]   B. Alpern and F. B. Schneider, "Verifying Temporal Properties without Temporal Logic," *ACM Transactions on Programming Languages and Systems*, vol. 11, no. 1, pp. 147-167, 1989.

[4]   G. R. Andrews, *Concurrent Programming - Principles and Practice*: The Benjamin / Cummings Publishing Company Ltd., 1991.

[5]   G. S. Avrunin, U. A. Buy, J. C. Corbett, L. K. Dillon, and J. C. Wileden, "Automated Analysis of Concurrent Systems with the Constrained Expression Toolset," *IEEE Transactions on Software Engineering*, vol. 17, no. 11, pp. 1204-1222, 1991.

[6]   T. Bultan, J. Fischer, and R. Gerber, "Compositional Verification by Model Checking for Counter-Examples," presented at International Symposium on Software Testing and Analysis, San Diego, California, January 1996.

[7]   S. C. Cheung and J. Kramer, "Checking Subsystem Safety Properties in Compositional Reachability Analysis," presented at 18th International Conference on Software Engineering, Berlin, Germany, March 1996.

[8]   S. C. Cheung and J. Kramer, "Context Constraints for Compositional Reachability Analysis," *ACM Transactions on Software Engineering and Methodology*, , October 1996.

[9]   E. M. Clarke, D. E. Long, and K. L. McMillan, "Compositional Model Checking," presented at 4th Annual Symposium on Logic in Computer Science, Pacific Grove, California, June 1989.

[10] H.-C. Fernandez, L. Mounier, C. Jard, and T. Jéron, "On-the-fly Verification of Finite Transition Systems," in *Computer-Aided Verification*, R. Kurshan, Ed.: Kluwer Academic Publishers, 1993.

[11] C. Ghezzi, M. Jazayeri, and D. Mandrioli, *Fundamentals of Software Engineering, Chapter 6*: Prentice-Hall, Inc., 1991.

[12] D. Giannakopoulou, J. Kramer, and S. C. Cheung, "TRACTA: An Environment for Analysing the Behaviour of Distributed Systems," presented at ACM SIGPLAN Workshop on Automated Analysis of Software, Paris, January 1997.

[13] P. Godefroid and G. J. Holzmann, "On the Verification of Temporal Properties," presented at 13th IFIP WG 6.1 International Symposium, on Protocol Specification, Testing, and Verification.

[14] P. Gribomont and P. Wolper, "Temporal Logic," in *From Modal Logic to Deductive Databases*, A. Thayse, Ed.: John Wiley and Sons, 1989.

[15] C. A. R. Hoare, *Communicating Sequential Processes*: Prentice-Hall, 1985.

[16] J. Kemppainen, M. Levanto, A. Valmari, and M. Clegg, ""ARA" Puts Advanced Reachability Analysis Techniques Together," presented at 5th Nordic Workshop on Programming Environment Research, Tampere, Finland, January 1992.

[17] J. Kramer and J. Magee, "Exposing the Skeleton in the Coordination Closet," presented at Coordination '97, Berlin, September 1997.

[18] J. C. Lin and S. Paul, "RMTP: A Reliable Multicast Transport Protocol," presented at IEEE INFOCOMM'96, San Francisco, California, March 1996.

[19] J. Malhotra, S. A. Smolka, A. Giacalone, and R. Shapiro, "A Tool for Hierarchical Design and Simulation of Concurrent Systems," presented at BCS-FACS Workshop on Specification and Verification of Concurrent Systems, Stirling, Scotland, July 1988.

[20] R. Milner, *Communication and Concurrency*: Prentice-Hall, 1989.

[21] A. Rabinovich, "Checking Equivalences Between Concurrent Systems of Finite Agents," presented at 19th International Colloquium on Automata, Languages and Programming, Wien, Austria, July 1992.

[22] K. K. Sabnani, A. M. Lapone, and M. Ü. Uyar, "An Algorithmic Procedure for Checking Safety Properties of Protocols," *IEEE Transactions on Communications*, vol. 37, no. 9, pp. 940-948, September 1989.

[23] K. C. Tai and P. V. Koppol, "Hierarchy-Based Incremental Reachability Analysis of Communication Protocols," presented at IEEE International Conference on Network Protocols, San Francisco, California, October 1993.

[24] A. Valmari. Alleviating State Explosion during Verification of Behavioural Equivalence, Technical Report, A-1992, Department of Computer Science, University of Helsinki, Finland, August 1992.

[25] W. J. Yeh. Controlling State Explosion in Reachability Analysis, Technical Report, SERC-TR-147-P, SERC, Purdue University, December 1993.

[26] W. J. Yeh and M. Young, "Compositional Reachability Analysis Using Process Algebra," presented at Symposium on Testing, Analysis, and Verification (TAV4), Victoria, British Columbia, October 8-10, 1991.

[27] W. J. Yeh and M. Young, "Hierarchical Tracing of Concurrent Programs," presented at 3rd Irvine Software Symposium (ISS'93), Irvine, California, April 1993.

Model Checking Graphical User Interfaces Using Abstractions*

Matthew B. Dwyer, Vicki Carr, Laura Hines

Kansas State University

Abstract

Symbolic model checking techniques have been widely and successfully applied to statically analyze dynamic properties of hardware systems. Efforts to apply this same technology to the analysis of software systems has met with a number of obstacles, such as the existence of non-finite state-spaces. This paper investigates abstractions that make it possible to cost-effectively model check specifications of software for graphical user interface (GUI) systems. We identify useful abstractions for this domain and demonstrate that they can be incorporated into the analysis of a variety of systems with similar structural characteristics. The resulting domain-specific model checking yields fast verification of naturally occurring specifications of intended GUI behavior.

1 Introduction

The majority of modern software applications have a graphical user interface (GUI). These interfaces serve a number of functions including: presentation of information to users, guiding users through interaction with the system, and embodying metaphors for user work processes. One can also view the user interface component of an application as constraining user access to underlying application data and functionality. For example, privacy or security concerns may cause the engineering of user interfaces that assure constrained access to data. Interfaces may also be constructed to assure response to requests in safety-critical contexts. To the extent that GUIs improve human-computer interaction their use in safety-critical applications will increase. In this context, validation of GUI implementations with respect to specifications of their intended behavior will be an increasingly important component of software development efforts.

In this paper, we present an approach to model checking specifications of GUI implementations. Model checking is typically applied to reactive systems [11], and GUI implementations are highly reactive, engaging in an ongoing sequence of

---

*Department of Computing and Information Sciences, 234 Nichols Hall, Manhattan, KS 66506, USA. dwyer@cis.ksu.edu Supported in part by NSF and DARPA under grant CCR-9633388.

interactions with both the end user and the underlying application. Model checking of software systems can be an expensive, and even an intractable, process. Our success in cost-effectively model checking GUI implementations is based on identification and application of domain-specific abstractions of components of system behavior. Graphical user interfaces share a number of common architectural features. Most GUI implementations are constructed using frameworks or toolkits [13] designed to reduce programming effort and increase portability. While there are significant benefits to using a GUI toolkit, their use often results in a complex event-driven software system that bridges the gap between the toolkit and the underlying application. It is the behavior of such event-driven GUI software components that we validate in this paper. To do this, we present abstractions that can be used in the construction of state-transition models of these software systems. We are careful not to "over abstract" the system models, and we formalize this by defining the class of specifications whose model checking results are preserved under each of our abstractions. This assures correctness in verification while enabling significant reduction in the size and complexity of the state-transition models. This allows existing model checking technology, such as SMV [12], to be used to verify specifications of intended system behavior.

Since GUIs are common components of production software systems, we hope that advances in validating such systems will have an impact in practice. We report on our experience validating specifications of GUI behavior for two production systems developed in industry. The specifications we checked were derived from informally stated requirements created by the system developers. We applied a methodology involving identification of instances of abstractions, encoding of abstractions into a state-transition model of a GUI implementation, and model checking specifications derived from system requirements using SMV. The results of this experience are encouraging. We were able to encode abstract state-transition systems for non-finite-state applications and model check properties of those systems in under a minute. While these systems may not be representative of all GUI systems, they do represent a large number of systems being built in industry. We are expanding our use of this approach to additional GUI systems.

The contributions of this paper are an analysis of the GUI software domain, the development of abstractions for model checking GUI software, and an evaluation of the practicality of using those abstractions in model checking production software systems. Our work can be seen as another piece of evidence, along with other case studies [1, 16], in support of research [3, 6, 9] suggesting that abstractions can be used to reduce infinite and large finite-state systems to sizes for which model checking is practical.

2   Background

Existing model checking tools require a specification of system behavior in some form of temporal logic and a state-transition model of the executable behavior of the system being validated. We use SMV [12] as our model checking tool;

this choice dictated both the state-transition and specification languages used and we describe these languages below. We also discuss the role of abstraction in the model checking process.

2.1 SMV Transition Systems

SMV provides a language for programming guarded-transition systems. There are two approaches to writing SMV programs: as a collection of parallel assignment statements to state variables, or as logical formulae that describe state pre and post-conditions. Since we began with GUI implementations, we found the translation to parallel assignment statements more natural, and we will describe the features of SMV we used for our system models.

A transition-system is a collection of SMV MODULEs. Modules define a scope in which state variables and their state transitions can be defined. Within a module, state variables are introduced after a VAR keyword. Variables can be of boolean, enumeration, integer range and fixed array types. Transitions between system states are defined by way of parallel assignment statements using the ASSIGN keyword. For each state variable, v, its initial value is defined by assigning a value to init(v). The value of a state variable in the next step of a system's execution is defined by assigning a value to next(v). In most cases the next state value for a variable is defined in terms of its current value and the values of other state variables. SMV provides the case statement which is a collection of guarded assignments. Figure 2 illustrates a single SMV module.

Taken in total a collection of state variables and next-state assignments form a transition system. The initial state of this system is comprised of the initial states of all variables. The next-state relation for the entire system is the component-wise application of individual next-state assignments. Thus, we can think of a state of an SMV transition system with k state variables as a k-tuple, $(v_1, v_2, \ldots, v_k)$, whose elements are values of the variables. The entire transition system is a directed graph connecting such states whose edges represent legal state transitions.

2.2 Computation Tree Logic (CTL) and $\forall$CTL

Propositional logic specifications use a vocabulary of atomic formula to make statements about system behavior. An *atomic formula* is a *proposition* or its negation. With respect to a transition system, propositions can be defined as relational expressions that test the value of a single state variable against some constant value in its domain.

Atomic formula can be combined into state formula using the usual propositional logic connectives: $\vee$, $\wedge$, $\neg$, and $\rightarrow$. Thus, for example, we could formulate a specification that says $y = 0 \rightarrow x > 1$ and attempt to reason about the validity of that formula at some state during the computation of our system. We can determine the truth or falsity of an atomic formula by looking at the values of state variables corresponding to the system state.

Temporal logics allow us to extend specifications about individual states of our system to describe sequences of states. In computation tree logic (CTL), we are given two path quantifiers **A** and **E** describing whether all or some execution of the system satisfies the balance of the formulae. Under the path quantifiers we have three temporal operators **G**, **F**, and **U** describing the invariance, eventuality, or an interval-like relationship among sub-formulae[1]. A quantifier and temporal operator always appear as a pair in CTL giving six combinations. Formulas built with these operators are themselves state formula. Thus, we can nest temporal operators to produce specifications about patterns of state sequences for a system. For example, a response property stating that any occurrence of a state in which p is valid is followed by a state in which q is valid can be formulated as $\mathbf{AG}(p \rightarrow \mathbf{AF}q)$.

A subset of CTL in which negations only appear in atomic propositions and the only temporal operators are **AG**, **AF**, and **AU** is called ∀CTL. This is a rich and useful specification language that allows one to describe patterns of system behavior that should be true of all computations.

The keyword `SPEC` indicates a CTL specification in an SMV input file. There can be multiple specifications for a given system, and in our experience individual specifications are relatively small. We note that SMV uses an ASCII character set and adopts C-like operator symbols for logical connectives. Thus, the connectives, $\vee$, $\wedge$, $\neg$, and $\rightarrow$, are written as $|$, $\&$, $!$ and $\rightarrow$.

2.3 Model-Checking

Using SMV model checking is a process of comparing a given CTL specification to sequences of transition-system states in order to determine whether the specification holds at the initial state of the system. For our purposes, it is enough to know that algorithms that are linear in the size of both the transition system and specification exist for performing model checking.

The results returned by a run of the SMV model checker indicate either that the specification is true for the transition-system or that it is false. In the case of a false result, SMV produces a *counter-example*; this is a sequence of system states that causes the specification to fail.

Note that SMV model checks a specification and returns the results under the assumption that the state transition model is a faithful description of all and only the executable behaviors of the actual modeled system. If the state transition model errs either by including additional infeasible behavior or by excluding some executable behavior then the results of the model check cannot always be interpreted as statements about the behavior of the actual system.

2.4 Abstractions

We use the terminology of Dams [6] and refer to a transition system that completely describes the behavior of a system we are validating as a *concrete transi-*

---

[1] We avoid the use of the next state operator **X** since abstraction may change the definition of "next" state.

tion system, denoted C; note that the concrete system need not be finite-state. An abstraction is a "simplified representation" of the behavior of some component of the concrete system. Applying a collection of abstractions to the concrete system yields an *abstract transition system*, denoted A.

An important property of an abstraction is the degree to which it preserves the information of a concrete system. Dams [6] discusses two kinds of preservation that can be used in model checking. An abstraction is *strongly* preserving for model checking if every specification that holds on the concrete system also holds on the abstract system and vice versa. An abstraction is *weakly* preserving for model checking if every specification that holds on the concrete system also holds on the abstracted system. It is important to note that when using weakly preserving abstractions false results may indicate a fault in the system under analysis, a mistake in the specification, or imprecision due to the use of abstraction. In practice, counter-examples are crucial in diagnosing which of these three cases has lead to the false result and in giving guidance on how to remediate the problem.

The notion of preservation is dependent on the specification language used. There are two points to be addressed when considering CTL specifications: the path quantifiers and the propositions. We consider path quantifiers because, as Dams [6] points out, some abstractions that are weakly preserving for universal quantification are not weakly preserving for existential quantification. We consider the set of propositions because we want to be able to ask questions about the concrete system, but model check them over the abstract system to find the answer. To do this, we must insure that our specification language has a set of propositions that are defined in both C and A. For state variables that are unabstracted in A the propositions related to those variables carry-over directly from C. For abstracted variables we may also carry-over some propositions. For example, in the string input field abstraction mentioned above, both concrete and abstract versions have propositions that indicate an empty field.

We characterize abstractions in terms of the information they preserve in order to interpret the results returned by a model checker appropriately. As discussed in Section 3, all of our abstractions are at least weakly preserving with respect to $\forall$CTL

As a practical matter, there are two ways we can reduce the size of a transition system: eliminate state variables or decrease the size of state variable domains. We may replace a collection of variables with a single variable whose values abstractly represent the possible values of the original variables. For example, a collection of input fields that are processed as a group may be abstracted to a single variable representing whether all, some, or none of the fields are filled in. Alternately, we may replace a variable that ranges over a large, potentially infinite domain, with a variable that ranges over a small finite domain. For example, an input field of type string may be abstracted to a binary domain representing only whether the field is empty or contains some string. Since the state-space of a transition system can grow exponentially in the number of state variables, even small reductions in system size due to abstraction can lead to dramatic reductions in model checking time.

SMV provides features that support abstractions in state transition systems. When modeling the environment in which a system operates, for example user or hardware inputs, it is often convenient to model environment behavior as non-deterministic. This is common in model checking [1, 16], although it is not usually explicitly described as a weakly preserving abstraction with respect to ∀CTL. SMV provides for fairness constraints via the FAIRNESS keyword. This allows us to encode abstractions that are stronger than non-deterministic behavior which may more accurately describe our system's environment. For example, in a GUI system we may choose to model our end user as repeatedly closing a data file. This might capture our intuitive notion that end users will periodically stop work. This could be expressed as a fairness constraint, e.g., FAIRNESS AF(data=closed), stating that infinitely often the data file will eventually become closed on all computations. SMV allows for an arbitrary CTL formula in fairness constraints, and consequently, we must carefully reason about the extent to which they preserve information in our state-transition system.

3   GUI Abstractions

The selection of abstractions to be used in model checking is based on a number of factors including: possibility of false results due to use of abstraction, run-time performance, and preservation of information relevant for a given specification. Depending on our goals we might choose, for example, to suffer some misleading false results to gain faster run-times. For model checking the most appropriate abstraction might depend on both the system and specification being checked. Our goal, however, is not to find the "best" abstractions, rather we seek abstractions that enable analysis of naturally occurring specifications of GUI behavior in an amount of time that is comparable to current best-practice, i.e., testing. We looked for such abstractions by studying the GUI software domain both in terms of structural features of software systems in the domain and of correctness properties that are common in the domain.

3.1   A Domain Analysis

We developed abstractions, based on common architectural features of GUI systems, that support validation of the kinds of correctness properties that GUI developers are interested in. We are interested in checking correctness properties related to the sequencing of GUI activities, and do not consider the validation of usability, presentation, and other properties of GUI implementations.

Modern GUI implementations are constructed using a framework or toolkit, such as GARNET [13] or Visual Basic[2], that provides a collection of reusable components for implementing common features of a user interface. Traditional GUIs built with such frameworks have the architecture depicted in Figure 1. The framework provides a main *event loop* which continually accepts user input

---

[2] Visual Basic is a trademark of Microsoft Corporation.

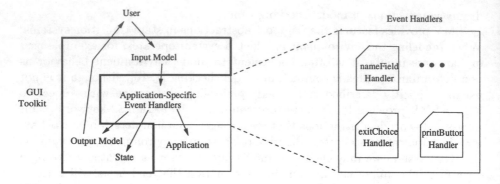

Figure 1: GUI System Architecture

events according to an *input model*. Input events are dispatched to *handler* routines that perform application specific processing, update the GUI *state* and generate user output according to an *output model*. The input and output models control translation of data between internal program encodings, e.g., strings, button identity values, and the graphical depictions presented to the user. These depictions are referred to as *widgets*; there are a variety of different kinds of widgets, such as sliders, toggles, selection boxes, and menus. Our analysis is concerned with the data that is associated with enabling of widgets and input and output events for each widget in a GUI.

A GUI implementation built with such a framework is an event-driven system. The flow of control between event-handlers is due to the activity of the user, but is constrained by handlers enabling and disabling GUI controls. As a practical matter, this implicit flow of control makes it more difficult for developers to understand global system behavior. We can view a collection of GUI event-handlers as a state transition system capable of producing output. The event-handlers encode state and transition information and respond to successive input events by changing state and producing output. Our goal is to produce a faithful model of this transition system on which we can verify specifications of intended GUI behavior. In order to do this, we must be able to define a vocabulary of observable system states or events that can be used to describe both specifications of intent and the GUI system behavior. There are a variety of different kinds of events that one could consider, such as, individual mouse clicks, keystrokes, or the action of dragging a depicted object. Given our focus on reasoning about behavior encoded into application-specific event-handlers we choose to consider enabling and disabling of controls, input events as encoded by the input model for transmission to the handlers and output events as encoded by handlers for transmission to the output model. Clearly, the event-handlers will have non-trivial interaction with the underlying application. We abstract those interactions based on the semantics of GUI event-handler branch tests that use application routine return values. We choose abstractions that allow us to distinguish return values that can affect the sequencing of GUI activities.

In addition to structural properties of GUI software we also consider the specifications that developers are interested in checking. As one might expect there are a wide variety of safety properties that GUI developers might wish to validate. A common property is requiring that a user be validated before being granted access to data; one of the systems considered in Section 4 has such a property. Another class of specifications dictate the conditions under which various GUI controls, e.g., buttons, will be enabled. Response properties are also used, for example, to require that when the help button is pressed eventually a help screen is displayed. There are a variety of specifications that one can formulate for a given informal system requirement. We have found it convenient to distinguish between response specifications that indicate that eventually a desired state will be achieved and those that indicate that a desired state will be achieved before any further GUI activity is allowed. We express the latter using nested U operators in a manner that is similar to bounded-overtaking specifications [11].

The GUI specifications we analyze use only universal quantification, and they all can be written in ∀CTL. It is important to note that we did not start out restricting ourselves to ∀CTL. The specifications that occurred naturally in the validation of the GUI systems we considered happened to lie in this language.

3.2 Abstractions for Model-Checking

Our domain analysis identified opportunities to abstract the behavior of GUI implementations. In the following we describe three abstraction classes in detail: *grouped fields*, *independent subsystems*, and *application state*. We discuss the intuition behind each abstraction, describe how to identify an instance of the abstraction, how to transform a system model to encode the abstraction, and describe the information preserved by the abstraction. The presentation of the abstractions is general as the details of exactly how to identify instances and transform system models will depend on the GUI toolkit and programming language with which the GUI software is implemented.

Grouped Fields are input or output fields that are treated as a single entity from the perspective of the GUI event-handler code. A common example is an address consisting of street number, street name, city, state, country, and zipcode fields. When a group of input (output) fields are read (written) by the same fragment of GUI event-handler code we can apply this abstraction. In addition, we require that all such fields be enabled and disabled as a group. As long as we are not interested in specifications that concern activity in individual fields we can abstract state variables for multiple fields to one or two group state variables; we may need multiple variables to model enabledness of input in addition to input values. The group value variable represents the composite values of the fields; this value is typically abstracted using the application state abstraction. Transitions for input (output) and enabledness of group variables correspond to transitions of the final field of the group undergoing input (output) or a change in enabledness. If a specification refers to no propositions for individual fields of a group then the grouped fields abstraction weakly preserves ∀CTL.

Independent Subsystems occur in GUI implementations just as in other complex software systems. Intuitively, subsystems are independent when their interface is very small. Often times one subsystem will execute without modifying the state of any other subsystem. For example, most online help systems in GUIs will preserve the state of the GUI while the user interacts with the help system and can be effectively abstracted from the analysis of GUI behavior. When no state variables within a given component of a state transition system are used in guard expressions external to that component this indicates a completely independent subsystem. The variables for such a subsystem can be eliminated for specifications that do not contain propositions formed with those variables. If a specification refers to no propositions for internal state variables of an independent subsystem then the independent subsystem abstraction weakly preserves ∀CTL.

Application State consists of both control and data components. Data state information contributes significantly to the overall size of an applications state transition system. In fact, it is often the case that applications have infinite data states. The points at which GUI event-handler code depends on the data values stored in an application are where branch conditions are evaluated. In well-engineered applications, it is often the case that such branch conditions are simple relational expressions involving a few calls on application operations. By abstracting the result values returned by those operations we can represent the behavior of the application without the need to explicitly represent its complete data state. There are a wide variety of situations in which this kind of abstraction can be applied. The abstraction models all possible data values that could appear in the application by allowing the result of any application call in a branch decision to non-deterministically choose any of its possible return values. All data values in the concrete system will be classified as one of these return values by the application call. If a specification refers to propositions for abstracted application data values then the abstraction weakly preserves ∀CTL.

Other Abstractions have been developed that shrink the transition system based on the semantics of GUI input and output models, in the presence of linked GUI objects, when identity of data values is not a concern in specifications, and when uninterruptable sequences of GUI activity can occur; we have left out their description in the interest of space.

These abstractions can be incorporated into a state-transition model of a GUI implementation's behavior. Then, using traditional model checking technology we can check specifications against the abstracted system model. The first two abstractions described above actually preserve more information than is required to weakly preserve ∀CTL. We will often use multiple abstractions for a given system. The resulting abstract transition system will only preserve the information preserved by the weakest abstraction used. Since application state abstraction will almost always be used we end up with transition systems that weakly preserve ∀CTL.

4 Experience

In this section we discuss the application of our approach to two GUI implementations built using Visual Basic. We believe, however, that the approach is more general and that it could be applied to systems built with other GUI toolkits [13]. We first discuss our strategy for building SMV transition systems from GUI code.

4.1 Building GUI Transition Systems

The applications we consider below are essentially database systems with GUI front-ends that constrain access to the underlying data. For such systems, building a concrete transition system to model the underlying database system is not possible since the system is effectively non-finite state. Our approach is to identify abstraction opportunities in the GUI event-handler source code and to encode those abstractions directly into an SMV transition system.

Each GUI widget is represented by a collection of SMV state variables. User controls such as buttons, toggles, and sliders are represented as an SMV module with two variables : representing control enabledness and control value. Enabledness is always a boolean while the control value can have a larger domain, e.g., a slider might be modeled with an integer range. Another common control in a GUI is a choice box, this is a collection of grouped buttons that operate in a mutually exclusive fashion. A choice box requires two state variables representing enabledness of the box and which, if any, of the toggles is pushed. Figure 2 illustrates a module for a button. This module is parameterized by boolean expressions that describe the conditions under which the button should be enabled or disabled. Note that the button will be an SMV process and consequently the FAIRNESS condition is required to insure its progress.

Menus and menu selections are a mechanism for organizing large numbers of controls without using excessive screen space. In modeling their effect on GUI event-handler software we represent the individual selections with variables for enabledness and a boolean selection value.

GUI output is displayed on screens or forms. Screens are bordered areas of the display containing controls, fields, and menus. There can be multiple screens on a display but at most one of them has the user's focus and can accept user input. Given our interest in logical behavior of the GUI software we need only model the in-focus screen. We use a single state variable defined over a set of values that encode screen identity. A special case of screens are forms; these typically occupy the entire screen and consequently the notion of in-focus screen corresponds to current visible form.

```
MODULE button(enable_cond,            Sub cmdSearch_Click ()
              disable_cond)             screen.MousePointer = 11 'Set Hourglass Cursor
VAR                                     frmMain.Enabled = False 'Disable Main Form
  enabled : boolean;
  pushed : boolean;                     'FindFlag indicates the last field changed
ASSIGN                                  Select Case FindFlag
  init(enabled) := 1;                     ...
  next(enabled) :=                        Case 3
    case                                    criteria = "Product_Name like " & ...
      enabled & disable_cond : 0;           dsmsds.FindFirst criteria
      !enabled & enable_cond : 1;           If dsmsds.NoMatch Then
      1 : enabled; - - No change              MsgBox "No Match Found", MB_OK,
    esac;                                               "MSDS System" 'no_match
  init(pushed) := 0;                        Else
  next(pushed) :=                             If count > 1 Then
    case                                        frmGrid.Show 'multiple_matches
      enabled & !pushed : 1;                  Else
      pushed : 0;                               Call fillform 'one_match
      1 : pushed; - - No change               End If
    esac;                                     End If
FAIRNESS                                  End Select
  running                                 screen.MousePointer = 1 'Set Pointer Cursor
                                        End Sub
```

Figure 2: SMV Button Module   MSDS Search Event-Handler

Input data fields, like controls, are modeled by enabledness and value state variables. Output fields are modeled only by a value state variable. In forms-based GUIs for database applications it is often the case that fields on a form correspond to attributes of database records. In this case, GUI event handler code may read and write groups of fields on a form as records in the database are inserted and selected, for example the `fillform` call in Figure 2. This maps naturally onto our grouped fields abstraction, and we use a single, or pair of, state variables for the group.

As discussed in Section 3, we construct transition systems for application behavior based on the semantics of application operations and the use of those operations in GUI event-handler branch expressions. For example, in the MSDS system described below, the Visual Basic code for performing a search by product name is given in Figure 2. The `dsmsds` is the underlying application database for the system. The GUI event-handler executes a search and interprets its result as one of three separate cases: no match found, one match found, and more than one match found. Thus, for the search component of the underlying application we model its behavior as non-deterministically choosing between these three values whenever a search is performed. This is represented with two SMV state variables: one representing the activation and conclusion of a search and the other the result of the search.

We note that translating from an imperative programming language into SMV transition systems requires an inversion of system control. Imperative programs explicitly define sequences of operations that affect the system data state. In guarded-transition systems, the ordering of data state transitions is controlled in a decentralized fashion through the guard expressions on individual state variable transitions. The execution point of a GUI is modeled by a single variable named `control` that is in one of three states: `user`, `handler`, or `complete`. These correspond to the GUI toolkit waiting for user activity, executing event-handler code, and completing event-handler code. GUI modules, like the button in Figure 2, are built to accept parameters that are used to constrain transition guards based on the control variable. User interaction with a GUI object is represented by allowing the component of the transition system for that object to make transitions if `control=user`. These transitions then effect the behavior of the appropriate GUI event-handler code. Sequencing of activity within each event-handler is represented as a separate transition system centered around a handler control flow state variable. As with the `control` variable, propositions formed with event-handler control flow variables are used in guards on GUI module transitions. Many event-handlers are small fragments of code whose transition systems under abstraction collapse to be very small.

4.2 Material Safety Data Sheet Display System

The Material Safety Data Sheet (MSDS) display system was developed to satisfy a legal requirement to give employees immediate access to safety data for any material that they might come in contact with. An MSDS gives the constituents of the material and includes health hazards and emergency treatment information. The MSDS also gives the emergency response codes that are displayed in a diamond label to provide information to emergency responders. Users of the MSDS display system can find the appropriate MSDS by entering either the part number, the material name, the MSDS number, the product name, the common name, or the supplier. Because this system is used to meet an OSHA regulation and because the information provided by the system is used for emergency conditions involving hazardous chemicals, it is critical that the system function correctly.

We illustrate system behavior and specifications for a search operation performed by an MSDS end user. Figure 3 illustrates the initial MSDS screen where the user has formulated a search for nitric acid. The user will then click on the search button and the second form in the figure will eventually appear, perhaps with intervening screens to prune the search. Note that the GUI has disabled buttons that allow for searching all names and that viewing/printing is now enabled. This behavior is expressed as CTL formulae which are model checked against the system to verify that the GUI engages in the intended behavior.

The MSDS GUI was implemented using Visual Basic 3.0 along with Robo-HELP to build help screens and OUTSIDE IN to build viewing and printing screens[3]. The system consists of two application screens plus the help and

---

[3] RoboHELP is a registered trademark of Blue Sky Software Corporation. OUTSIDE IN is a registered trademark of Systems Compatibility Corporation.

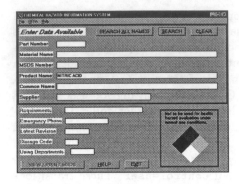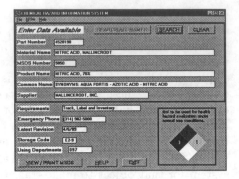

Figure 3: MSDS Query and Data Sheet Screens

view/print screens. There are 6 input and 20 output data fields on the screens and a variety of controls including: 8 buttons, 2 sliders, and 5 menu selections. The following abstractions were used to build the SMV transition system: grouped fields, independent subsystems, and application state. Fields related to text, names, diamond, and substance information were abstracted into separate groups. Help, viewing/printing, and multi-match grid subsystems are independent and were abstracted. Database searches formulated from datasheet queries are abstracted based on the application calls to values of no_match, one_match, and multiple_matches.

Model checking of a collection of twelve CTL specifications that were derived from system requirements was performed. The last three specifications in Figure 4 are a sample of those CTL specifications presented alongside corresponding informal system requirements for the MSDS GUI. The final specification doesn't use the nested until structure because there may be intervening screens and activity between a query and the final datasheet display. The abstract SMV transition system has 16 boolean state variables and 27648 syntactic states. We note that approximately 30% of the functionality of the MSDS system was abstracted away by the independent subsystem abstraction. All model checks returned a true result in under 1 second on a lightly-loaded 167 mhz UltraSPARC with 256 meg of RAM.

4.3 Travel Expense Reporting System

The Travel Expense Reporting System (TERS) aids in the management and tracking of the employee travel process from travel authorization to expense reporting. The system allows travelers to request travel and lodging prior to traveling and to record all expenses after traveling. The system allows supervisors to authorize travel and auditors to access expense reports and confirm their accuracy. The TERS has access to personnel files and as such there are some security concerns regarding access to stored data. A component of the TERS

AG(error.full ->
   A[(!control=user) U
      A[(control=user) U ok.pushed]])
	When an error message is displayed the only available user action is acknowledgement via the 'ok' button.

AG(cancel.pushed & focus=idtraveler ->
   A[(!control=user) U
      A[(control=user) U focus=main]])
	When the cancel button on the identify traveler screen is pressed, control returns to the main menu screen.

AG(dbSearchResult=one_match ->
   A[(!control=user) U
      A[(control=user) U
         (!search.enabled &
            !searchAllNames.enabled)]])
	If a search is done and a match is found, the search and search all names command buttons are not enabled.

AG(!dbSearchResult=no_match ->
   A[(!control=user) U
      A[(control=user) U viewPrint.enabled]])
	If a search returns some match then the view/print command button is enabled.

AG(!dbSearchResult=no_match -> AF (text.full & names.full & substance.full))	When a match is found all fields are filled in.

Figure 4: CTL Specifications for MSDS and TERS Systems

will authenticate end users with username and password. Additional security issues include: actual traveler must approve their own reports regardless of who enters the travel information and only authorized persons have the ability to approve or audit travel information.

The TERS GUI is being implemented using Visual Basic 4.0. The system consists of 30 screens. There are approximately 100 data fields on the screens and a variety of controls including: 40 buttons, 5 list selections, and 30 menu selections. The following abstractions were used to build the SMV transition system: grouped fields, uninterruptable sequences, independent subsystems, and application state.

Model checking of a collection of ten CTL specifications that were derived from system requirements was performed. The first two specifications in Figure 4 are examples of those specifications presented alongside corresponding informal system requirements for the TERS GUI. The abstract SMV transition system has 12 state variables over half of the variables range over domains of 6 or more values. The system has 11 million syntactic states. We note that approximately 80% of the functionality of the TERS system was abstracted away by the independent subsystem abstraction. All model checks returned a true result in under 2 seconds on a lightly-loaded 167 mhz UltraSPARC with 256 meg of RAM.

4.4 Discussion

Our experience in applying abstractions to model checking GUI software has been encouraging. While the MSDS and TERS systems may be similar to other forms-based production GUI systems they do not necessarily represent GUIs in general. It may be the case that other GUIs require more complex specifications and that abstractions may not be as effective as for the systems we considered.

Most of the CTL specifications in this study are relatively simple having two to four temporal operators nested two to three levels deep. The developers of the MSDS and TERS systems formulated these specifications after a 1 semester course in which temporal logic and model checking was a primary topic. We cannot conclude from this study whether the simplicity of the specifications is due to the inexperience of specifiers or whether such specifications are natural partial descriptions of application behavior. In addition, the specifications did not contain existential path quantifiers. Perhaps more complex, context-sensitive GUI systems, such as a web-browser, would require such specifications.

Model checking of the abstract transition systems for the MSDS and TERS was very fast; model check time never exceeded more than a few seconds. Abstraction of the transition systems contributed significantly to this, however, the structure of GUI software may also come into play. A primary contributor to the state-explosion problem in concurrent systems is the interleaving of independent actions in separate system processes. GUIs have very few concurrent activities, and as a consequence, interleavings do not contribute significantly to state space size. This is particularly true of mode-less GUIs which are designed to perform a user requested operation and return to the original GUI state. While there may be many options for different user actions the state space will tend to grow as the sum rather than the product of the number of actions. Perhaps multi-user GUIs in collaborative work applications will exhibit more of the traditional state-explosion.

Selection and application of abstractions is fundamentally a creative process and this is its chief drawback. Focusing on specific software domains can help to address this problem by providing a catalog of abstractions, guidance on when they are applicable, and how they can be applied. Developing and evaluating such catalogs of abstractions, however, is still a significant research problem.

5 Related Work

There has a been a great deal of work on design, development, and validation, e.g., [13], of graphical user interfaces. This work has focused on usability and presentation issues, where the primary approach to validation is prototyping and live-subject testing. The validation of the correctness of the GUI event-handler code is an important practical consideration for which use-case or scenario-based testing appears to be the predominant approach in industry.

State transition systems have been widely studied as a means for specifying user interface systems, e.g., [10, 15]. This work has been focused primarily on the complete specification of the system as a design approach. Given that we view GUI event-handler software as an event-driven system it clearly falls into the category of reactive system [11]. Thus, we can look towards the wealth of research on specification and validation of reactive systems. Much of this work has focused on using temporal logic specifications to describe partial behavior of systems, where a single specification focuses on one aspect of system behavior. Given that our GUI specifications did not require existential quantification we could use a linear time logic. We could also use other specification formalisms such as GIL [7] or QREs [8, 14]. We found that the notion of an interval, bounded by defined start and end states, during which we enforce a pattern of behavior, occured naturally in our collection of specifications. For example, most of the specifications in Figure 4 have an interval-like structure and could be easily stated as GIL formulae or QREs.

In addition to model checking there are a variety of other forms of static analysis that can be used to validate software. Reachability analysis [17], integer necessary conditions analysis [2], equivalence-based analysis [4], and flow analysis [8, 14] have all been applied to verify specifications similar to the ones we consider in this paper. Abstraction has been used in each of these techniques. Use of non-determinism with respect to data values appears in almost all work on reachability and flow analysis. Abstraction in model checking was introduced by Clarke et. al. [3] to analyze very large hardware circuits. The abstractions they used were domain-independent and relied on clever encodings of concrete values for checking specific systems and specifications. Dams [6] has continued the theoretical development of model checking with abstractions. Compositional equivalence-based analysis approaches use a form of abstraction that is similar to our independent subsystem abstraction. Our experience is similar to their results, namely that hiding details internal of components can lead to dramatic reductions in analysis time.

In recent years, there has been an increase in empirical evaluation and case-study of static analysis techniques; some of these have involved model checking with SMV. Corbett's comparative evaluation of deadlock checking techniques for Ada tasking programs [5] automatically constructed weakly preserving SMV transition systems from Ada-like code. In this work, abstractions were encoded into the source code to model data values and branch condition evaluation non-deterministically. Anderson et. al. [1] worked from a system specification rather than source code. Their strategy for generating SMV transition systems included simplifications that non-deterministically model components of system behavior. These simplifications in our terminology are abstractions that weakly preserve ∀CTL. Wing and Vaziri-Farahani [16] studied the potential for model checking using abstractions in the communication protocol domain. They identify three general areas from which abstractions can be extracted: knowledge of the software domain, knowledge of the specification, and problem-specific knowledge. We found that each of these areas provided a significant source of abstractions in the GUI software domain as well. They give intuitive descriptions of five different abstractions used in their case-studies but do not provide a formal description of the information preservation properties of those abstractions.

6 Conclusions

This paper has presented an approach to model checking properties of graphical user interface components of application software using domain-specific abstractions. We developed a collection of abstractions based on structural features of GUI software systems. We identified opportunities to apply these abstractions in two production GUI systems that we studied. The resulting abstract transition systems for these systems preserved the information required to assure correct analysis. These transition systems were small enough that standard model checking technology could produce verification results very rapidly.

We are continuing this work by investigating the extent to which the construction of state transition systems for toolkit-based GUI software can be automated. These toolkits provide well-defined points at which the GUI event-handler software interacts with the toolkit and underlying application. If the semantics of toolkit primitives is well-defined it may be possible to at least partially generate transition systems as a collection of reusable SMV modules for well-known widgets.

We intend to apply the model checking approach outlined in this paper to additional GUI systems. We will study both forms-based database applications as well as more complex multi-user and context-sensitive interfaces to attempt to understand the range of systems for which model checking technology may be a practical validation approach for GUI systems.

Acknowledgements: The authors would like to thank Kristi Hankley and other members of CIS 842 in the Fall of 1996.

References

[1] R. Anderson, P. Beame, S. Burns, W. Chan, F. Modugno, D. Notkin, and J. Reese. Model checking large software specifications. *Software Engineering Notes*, 21(6):156–166, Nov. 1996. Proceedings of the Fourth ACM SIGSOFT Symposium on the Foundations of Software Engineering.

[2] G. Avrunin, U. Buy, J. Corbett, L. Dillon, and J. Wileden. Automated analysis of concurrent systems with the constrained expression toolset. *IEEE Transactions on Software Engineering*, 17(11):1204–1222, Nov. 1991.

[3] E. Clarke, O. Grumberg, and D. Long. Model checking and abstraction. *ACM Transactions on Programming Languages and Systems*, 16(5):1512–1542, Sept. 1994.

[4] R. Cleaveland, J. Parrow, and B. Steffen. The concurrency workbench: A semantics based tool for the verification of concurrent systems. *ACM*

Transactions on Programming Languages and Systems, 15(1):36–72, Jan. 1993.

[5] J. Corbett. Evaluating deadlock detection methods for concurrent software. *IEEE Transactions on Software Engineering*, 22(3), Mar. 1996.

[6] D. Dams. *Abstract Interpretation and Partition Refinement for Model Checking*. PhD thesis, Eindhoven University of Technology, May 1996.

[7] L. K. Dillon, G. Kutty, L. E. Moser, P. M. Melliar-Smith, and Y. S. Ramakrishna. A graphical interval logic for specifying concurrent systems. *ACM Transactions on Software Engineering and Methodology*, 3(2):131–165, Apr. 1994.

[8] M. Dwyer and L. Clarke. Data flow analysis for verifying properties of concurrent programs. *Software Engineering Notes*, 19(5):62–75, Dec. 1994. Proceedings of the ACM SIGSOFT Symposium on the Foundations of Software Engineering.

[9] D. Jackson. Abstract model checking of infinite specifications. In *Proceedings of FME'94 : Industrial Benefit of Formal Methods, Second International Symposium of Formal Methods Europe*, pages 519–531, Oct. 1994. Springer-Verlag.

[10] R. Jacob. Using formal specifications in the design of a human-computer interface. *Communications of the ACM*, 26(4):259–264, Apr. 1983.

[11] Z. Manna and A. Pnueli. *The Temporal Logic of Reactive and Concurrent Systems : Specification*. Springer-Verlag, 1991.

[12] K. McMillan. *Symbolic Model Checking*. Kluwer Academic Publishers, 1993.

[13] B. Myers. User interface software tools. *ACM Transactions on Computer-Human Interaction*, 2(1):64–103, Mar. 1995.

[14] K. Olender and L. Osterweil. Cecil: A sequencing constraint language for automatic static analysis generation. *IEEE Transactions on Software Engineering*, 16(3):268–280, Mar. 1990.

[15] A. Wasserman. Extending state transition diagrams for the specification of human-computer interaction. *IEEE Transactions on Software Engineering*, SE-11(8):699–713, Aug. 1985.

[16] J. Wing and M. Vaziri-Farahani. Model checking software systems : A case study. *Software Engineering Notes*, 20(4):128–139, Oct. 1995. Proceedings of the Third ACM SIGSOFT Symposium on the Foundations of Software Engineering.

[17] M. Young, R. Taylor, D. Levine, K. Nies, and D. Brodbeck. A concurrency analysis tool suite: Rationale, design, and preliminary experience. *ACM Transactions on Software Engineering and Methodology*, 4(1):64–106, Jan. 1995.

Comparing and Combining Software Defect Detection Techniques: A Replicated Empirical Study

Murray Wood, Marc Roper, Andrew Brooks, James Miller

Empirical Foundations of Computer Science (EFoCS)*
Department of Computer Science,
Livingstone Tower,
Richmond Street,
Glasgow G1 1XH,
U.K.

Abstract. This report describes an empirical study comparing three
defect detection techniques: a) code reading by stepwise abstraction,
b) functional testing using equivalence partitioning and boundary value
analysis, and c) structural testing using branch coverage. It is a replication of a study that has been carried out at least four times previously
over the last 20 years. This study used 47 student subjects to apply the
techniques to small C programs in a fractional factorial experimental
design. The major findings of the study are: a) that the individual techniques are of broadly similar effectiveness in terms of observing failures
and finding faults, b) that the relative effectiveness of the techniques depends on the nature of the program and its faults, c) these techniques
are consistently much more effective when used in combination with each
other. These results contribute to a growing body of empirical evidence
that supports generally held beliefs about the effectiveness of defect detection techniques in software engineering.

Keywords: software testing, code reading, code review, functional testing,
structural testing, empirical study, replication.

* email: murray@cs.strath.ac.uk, telephone: +44 (0)141 552 4400

1 Introduction

Detecting defects in program code is a critical activity in software development. The software engineering community generally accepts that defect detection should be based on both testing and inspection techniques. There also appears to be a general acceptance that different techniques should be used in combination as they may find different defects [10]. The motivation behind the work reported here is to find empirical support for this generally accepted view.

Engineering practice must be based on empirical evidence. Within the software engineering community there have been many pleas for more empirical studies [6,3,4] to substantiate claims for software development practices. Recently, the International Software Engineering Research Network (ISERN) has been established, whose aim is to "observe and experiment with technologies, understand their weaknesses and strengths, tailor technologies to the goals and characteristics of particular projects, and package them together with empirically gained experience to enhance their reuse potential in future projects".

The work reported here, performed in the context of ISERN, is a replication of earlier research, originally carried out by Victor Basili and Richard Selby [1], and recently replicated by Erik Kamsties and Chris Lott [7,8]. Replication is a critical component in providing empirical foundations - it is necessary both to validate earlier results and to 'recipe improve' [2]. Recipe improvement is when experimental parameters are varied in a controlled manner, perhaps focusing on specific aspects of previous studies or, alternatively, attempting to generalise earlier findings.

This paper starts by briefly reviewing related work and summarising the key findings to date. Thereafter the design of the experiment comparing structural testing, functional testing and code reading is described. This is followed by a detailed analysis of the experimental results, the key finding of which is that there was an interaction between technique effectiveness and program faults. This leads to an investigation of the effectiveness of different combinations of techniques. The paper concludes by arguing that technique performance depends on the nature of the program and its faults. It provides further empirical evidence that these fundamental techniques should be used in combination.

2 Related Work

The roots of this empirical investigation go back at least two decades to the work of Hetzel [5]. He compared functional testing, code reading and a variation of structural testing ("selective") testing. This experiment used 39 subjects (students and inexperienced programmers) and was based on testing three PL/I programs. His main finding was that functional and "selective" testing were equally effective, with code reading appearing inferior.

This work was built upon by Myers [11] who compared team–based, code "walkthroughs/inspections" with individuals using variations of structural and functional testing. Myer's experiment used 59 professional programmers (averaging 11 years experience). The experiment was based on one PL/I program

— the renowned Naur 'text formatter'. Myers found the three techniques to be of similar effectiveness, that there was "tremendous variability" amongst subjects, and the ability to detect certain types of errors varied from technique to technique.

Myers also investigated theoretical combinations of techniques. Here he found that whilst individuals averaged only 33% fault detection, all pairs averaged 50%.

In the 1980's Basili and Selby [1] compared functional testing using equivalence partitioning and boundary value analysis, structural testing using 100% statement coverage, and code reading using stepwise abstraction. The 74 subjects were a mixture of experienced professionals and advanced students. The four programs studied were written in Fortran or a structured language, Simpl-T. Although Basili and Selby found some evidence that code reading detected more faults, they concluded that each technique had some merit and the effectiveness of the individual techniques depended on the software type.

Selby [14] also investigated all six possible pairwise combinations of the three techniques into hypothetical teams of two. Here he found that, on average, the combinations detected 67.5% of the faults in comparison to an average of 49.8% for individual techniques.

Most recently, Kamsties and Lott [7, 8] have replicated the Basili/Selby experiment. They used a similar experimental design to Basili/Selby, changing the programs, the programming language (to C), and associated faults. They also used a variation of branch coverage (which incorporated additional conditional, loop and relational operator criteria) as the structural testing criteria. The other testing techniques remained unchanged. Kamsties/Lott ran two versions of the replication, both with student subjects (27 subjects and 15 subjects). In terms of percentage faults detected, Kamsties/Lott found no statistical difference between the three techniques in either of the replications. However, they did find that functional testing was the most efficient technique.

A number of significant conclusions are drawn from this review of related research:

- There is no clear, consistent evidence that one defect detection technique is stronger than others, rather the evidence to date suggests that each technique has its own merits;
- The evidence to date suggests that the fundamental techniques are complementary rather than alternatives and as result should be used in combination;

The aim of this replication study is to further investigate these conclusions, and to contribute to the body of empirical evidence that is evolving in this area.

3 Experimental Study

The goals for this study were to replicate the Kamsties/Lott experiment comparing the three common defect detection techniques of code reading, functional testing and structural testing in terms of their effectiveness (percentages of failures observed and faults isolated) and their efficiency (number of failures observed and faults isolated divided by the time required to detect them).

3.1 Instruments

The programs used in training and in the experiment were taken from a replication package produced by Kamsties/Lott [7]. The programs were approximately 200 lines long (excluding blank lines and comments). The first program, `ntree`, implemented an abstract data type, namely a tree with unbounded branching. The second program, `cmdline`, basically displayed the result of parsing a command line. The third program, `nametbl`, implemented another abstract data type, namely a simple symbol table.

The faults used were those provided with the replication package. These faults were mostly seeded by Kamsties/Lott, although it is understood that a few original developer faults are included. The faults were chosen so that programs fail on some inputs only, where a failure may result in no output at all, incorrect output, or a minor problem such as misspelling. There were 8 faults in total in the `ntree` program, 9 in the `cmdline` program, and 8 in the `nametbl` program.

3.2 Treatments

The fault detection techniques were basically the same as those used by Kamsties/Lott and Basili/Selby before them. All three techniques are applied in a two stage process. Firstly, failures are observed, that is the subject looks for observable differences between the program and the specification[1]. Secondly, faults are isolated, that is the subject attempts to identify the exact location of the cause of failure in the program code.

Code reading used the technique of stepwise abstraction [9]. Subjects were initially given a line-numbered program listing. Subjects identify prime subprograms (consecutive lines of code), write a specification for the subprogram, group subprograms and their specifications together, and repeat the process until they have abstracted all the source code, forming their own specification of the program. On completion, they are given the official specification. Failure observation is based on identifying inconsistencies between the derived and official specification.

Functional testing was based on the standard techniques of equivalence partitioning and boundary value analysis [12,13]. Subjects are initially provided with an on-line executable version of the program code and a program specification. Tests cases are derived from the specification, run using the executable, and failures observed in terms of unexpected results.

In structural testing subjects had to achieve as close to 100% branch coverage as possible. (The criteria used by Kamsties/Lott were relaxed as they were considered unrealistic in practical applications.) Students were given the source

---

[1] Two pages of natural language description.

code, without a specification, and access to a testing tool (GCT^2) which reported attained coverage levels. Subjects recorded test data and results. On completion they were given a specification to check the validity of their results. Invalid results correspond to observed failures. Thereafter the fault isolation phase was concerned with finding the sources of observed failures.

3.3 Experimental Design

The experiment combined three programs and three defect detection techniques. The design and analysis of such experiments is dealt with very thoroughly by [15], and the subsequent data analysis has followed the approach described in Sect. 8.6 (p625 et. seq.) of this book.

The design yielded six groups who participated in the experiment as shown in the table below (where *P* refers to program, and an 'x' indicates that the groups' members applied that treatment combination of technique and program):

	Code Reading			Functional Testing			Structural Testing		
	P1	*P2*	*P3*	*P1*	*P2*	*P3*	*P1*	*P2*	*P3*
Group1	x	-	-	-	-	x	-	x	-
Group2	-	x	-	x	-	-	-	-	x
Group3	-	-	x	-	x	-	x	-	-
Group4	x	-	-	-	x	-	-	-	x
Group5	-	x	-	-	-	x	x	-	-
Group6	-	-	x	x	-	-	-	x	-

A further practical constraint arises in this case. Once a program has been used in one phase of the experiment then it effectively becomes public and other subjects may have access to it. For this reason the first phase of the experiment used only program 1, and the second and third phases, programs 2 and 3 respectively. Each phase of the experiment was a week apart and the table below indicates the treatment combinations undertaken by each group organised by time (where *C* represents Code Reading, *F* Functional Testing, and *S* Structural Testing):

	Week 1 *P1*	Week 2 *P2*	Week 3 *P3*
Group1	*C*	*S*	*F*
Group2	*F*	*C*	*S*
Group3	*S*	*F*	*C*
Group4	*C*	*F*	*S*
Group5	*S*	*C*	*F*
Group6	*F*	*S*	*C*

---

[2] Generic Coverage Tool, software developed by Brian Marick and available by anonymous ftp from host cs.uiuc.edu in directory /pub/testing/gct.files

3.4 Procedures

The 47 subjects were honours students enrolled in a practical software engineering class at the University of Strathclyde. The subjects had all completed two years of programming classes (including classes in C programming). The experiments were organised as part of the compulsory coursework for the class and the students were aware that their work was being used for experimental purposes. The students were divided into six groups (as described in the previous section), each group was balanced in terms of student ability, where ability was measured by performance in earlier programming classes. Prior to the experiments the students were given lectures on each of the defect detection techniques together with three 2-hour, supervised training sessions to practice applying each of the techniques.

The live experiments were organised in three 3-hour sessions over three successive weeks. They were organised under exam conditions, prohibiting cooperation between subjects. Subjects could leave early if they completed the tasks within the three hours. Those applying code reading worked in one room, those applying the testing techniques were in separate halves of a laboratory. All rooms were monitored by two staff.

All the subjects' workings were recorded on specially prepared data sheets. All interaction with the computer was also recorded using a scripting environment and questionnaires were used to explore subjects' views of the whole experimental process.

3.5 Independent and Dependent Variables

The experimental design has the two independent variables of defect detection technique and software type. The dependent variables examined in the study were the number of failures observed, the number of faults detected, the time taken to observe failures and the time taken to isolate faults.

3.6 Threats to Validity

The threats to validity in this experiment are identical to those for Kamsties/Lott. Threats to internal validity are unknown factors exerting control over the dependent variables and include:

- Instrumentation effects caused by differences in the programs and their fault profiles.
- Maturation effects arising for subjects learning as the experiment proceeds. These are addressed by manipulating the order in which techniques are applied, as described in Sect. 3.3 above.
- Selection effects due to subject variability is a major problem in software engineering experiments. This was addressed by balancing groups in terms of past examination performance.
- Finally there is the possibility of an observer effect due to the experimental conditions.

Threats to external validity are factors which prevent the generalisation of the results to actual software engineering practice. Once again, these threats are the same as for earlier studies – subjects, programs, faults, fault densities, or techniques may not be representative of software engineering practice. The first four threats are real and can only be addressed by repeated studies using different subjects, programs, faults and fault densities (hence the importance of replication). The techniques are intentionally chosen to be representative of those used in industry. There is some question about the level of industrial usage of the code reading technique employed. Inspection techniques in industry tend to be less formal, but consequently less easily taught, and their successful application requires a significant amount of experience. For this reason it was felt that the subjects would perform better with a technique that is more methodical to apply and hence the code-reading technique was kept.

4 Results

This section examines the main findings of the experiment. In this paper, the only data considered is that related to failure observation. The reason for this is that many subjects failed to complete the fault isolation part of the task and hence the analysis of this data is further complicated. (It is, however, planned to analyse this data in the future.)

4.1 Failure Observation Results

To investigate the impact of the three techniques on failure observation we collected two sets of data — the failures observed and the total time taken. Figures 1, 2 and 3 show the relative effects of the three defect detection techniques on the three programs by plotting, for each failure, the number of subjects finding that failure using a particular technique.[3] From these figures it may be seen that the technique performance varies from fault-to-fault and from program-to-program.

The average number of failures observed per program using each technique is shown in the table below (this is averaged over all subjects and hence includes all three programs which contained 8, 9 and 8 failures respectively):

Technique	Mean	S.D.	N
Code Reading	2.68	1.76	47
Functional Testing	4.60	1.28	47
Structural Testing	4.79	1.69	47

The failure observation rate was calculated by dividing the number of failures found by the time taken (the subjects were aware of the 3-hour time limit for the exercise, but otherwise were not constrained in the amount of time they devoted

---

[3] In these figures the failures are referred to by fault number as there is a one–to–one correspondence.

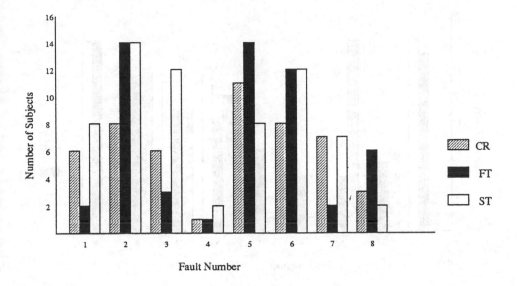

Fig. 1. Program1 (ntree) — Failures Observed by Technique

to failure observation). The rates for the three techniques (number of failures observed per hour, averaged over all subjects) are shown below:

Technique	Mean	S.D.	N
Code Reading	1.06	0.75	47
Functional Testing	2.47	1.10	47
Structural Testing	2.20	0.94	47

4.2 Analysis of Variance

To investigate the significance of the various treatments (programs and techniques) an analysis of variance was carried out based on the percentage of failures observed. The purpose of such an analysis is to try and determine what is causing the effect. The results in the previous section indicate a difference in the performance of the various techniques; but is it a *significant* difference, and is it the technique alone which is causing this difference? A summary of this analysis (which takes into account the non-homogeneity of the group sizes) is given in Table 1.

Referring to Table 1 it can be seen that the F-ratios for Program, Technique *and* Program × Technique are significant. Stated simply, this means that there is a significant interaction between the two treatments which makes it impossible to separate out exactly what is causing the effect. An initial reaction to this might be to consider it as a flaw in the experiment — the three chosen programs were not 'similar' enough. A more considered interpretation is that a technique

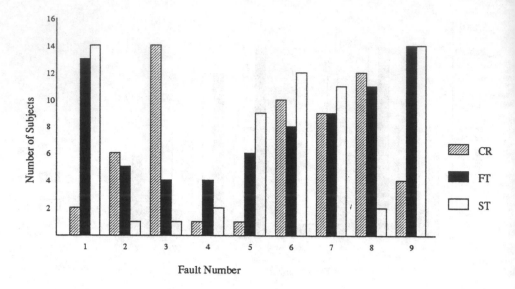

Fig. 2. Program2 (cmdline) — Failures Observed by Technique

Table 1. Summary of Analysis of Variance

Effect	SS_T	df_T	SS_R	df_R	F	Significance Level
Program	17943.45	2	23887.60	88	33.05	< 0.01
Technique	2993.17	2	23887.60	88	5.51	< 0.01
Prog × Tech	7179.12	4	23887.60	88	6.61	< 0.01

does not perform uniformly well over all programs. Remember that a program is a combination of the correct program and the faults (these cannot be separated out) and this is as likely to affect the outcome as the technique. In fact, this phenomenon can be observed in the three bar charts in Sect. 4.1 (Figs. 1, 2 and 3) — no technique appears to perform uniformly well, and there is a visible difference in the total numbers of failures observed in each program.

The drawback of this result is that it is not possible to investigate further any possible significant differences between the defect-detecting capabilities of the three techniques as it is impossible to separate their effect from that of the program.

One additional analysis was carried out with a further set of failure observations not considered in the initial analysis. When performing code reading, several subjects noted faults which they did not observe as failures. In other words, they knew that there was a fault in the program, but were unable to formulate it into an abstraction which was at odds with the specification (this may be either as a result of their lack of practice with the technique, or because

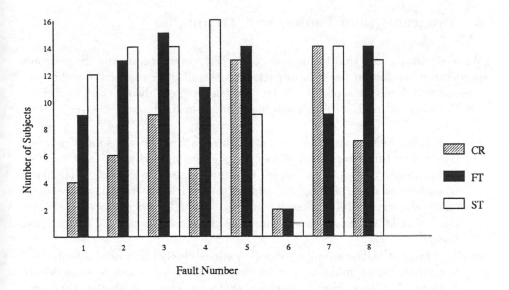

Fig. 3. Program3 (nametbl) — Failures Observed by Technique

the information did not appear in the specification). It was decided to count
these as bona-fide failure observations since they had been discovered during
the failure observation process. An analysis of variance of the data which takes
into account these 'serendipitous' faults discovered in the code reading process
was also carried out and the results were broadly similar to those in Table 1.
(The only difference being that the significance level of the technique dropped
to < 0.05.)

4.3 Summary of Results

The failure to find a significant difference between the techniques is broadly in
line with the results of the related work. One picture which does build up quite
clearly in all the experiments is that all the techniques (or all the testers!) are
quite poor. Many of the authors express disappointment with the total number
of faults found. A further common factor is the variability and unpredictability
of the techniques — no one technique is guaranteed to perform at a particular
rate. The strong message which comes over is that no single technique is best,
that faults themselves impact strongly upon the effectiveness of a technique, and
that to obtain any real effectiveness, a combination of approaches would appear
to be fruitful. It is these ideas that are examined in the next two sections.

5   Programs (and Faults) and Techniques

We have already seen that techniques do not perform uniformly and the program (and hence the faults) have an impact upon the effectiveness of the technique. This section looks at some of the faults where a great disparity in technique performance occurred with a view to explaining this finding.

ntree − fault 3 As may be seen in Fig. 1, this is a fault which seems very sensitive to structural testing, mildly so to code reading and practically invisible to functional testing. It is caused by a missing `malloc` which is triggered when four or more siblings are added to a node in a tree. Any structural tester aiming for 100% branch coverage would be forced to execute this piece of code, whereas this is an unlikely choice of test case for a functional tester.

ntree − fault 4 All techniques performed astonishingly badly on this fault which is a simple typographic error in an output statement. There is some debate as to whether the subjects considered this to be a fault or whether they were simply being unobservant. It is interesting to note that Myers encountered a similar phenomenon.

cmdline − fault 3 Inspection of Fig. 2 reveals that code reading significantly out-performed the other two techniques. The fault is an unused argument to a function which gives an incorrect string comparison in some circumstances. Code readers did well because the function in which the fault occurred was small and the unused argument was easy to spot. Note that a stronger structural testing technique (such as dataflow testing) would have revealed this fault.

cmdline − fault 8 Structural testing performs poorly in this case which misuses a library function to convert a string to an integer (when it should be to a float). Although executed by structural testers, they did not choose the necessary data to observe the failure (some decimal number with a fractional component), whereas functional testers (concentrating on the boundaries of numbers) did so. Code readers were either being vigilant or comparing it with similar code nearby.

cmdline − fault 9 Both functional and structural testing perform well here to reveal a fault which involves an incorrect value being passed to a function. This incorrect value yields a very visible failure in the output. However, the function is located a long way (textually) from the call and so trying to trace the call and maintain the parameter values in mind has obviously proved difficult for code readers.

These are only a fraction of the faults but illustrate the sensitivity of techniques to faults. From this it would seem that dispensing with a defect-detection technique can have disastrous and unpredictable effects. Further work to be pursued in this area includes attempting to devise a classification based upon the sensitivity of faults to the various defect detection techniques.

6   Combining Techniques and Testers

The results of the analysis of variance suggest that there is an interaction between defect detection techniques and program, that the techniques do not perform uniformly across programs and faults. As was discussed in Sect. 4.1, the difference in performance can clearly be seen from the bar charts plotting how many subjects, using each technique, observed each failure.

As the techniques appear to be finding different faults an obvious extension of this work is to follow the earlier research of Myers and Selby and to explore the relative effectiveness of hypothetical teams of testers using combinations of each technique.

Both Myers and Selby explored pairs of testers. It was decided to explore triples formed by taking three subjects applying the same technique and triples involving three subjects each applying a different technique, as well as all possible pairwise combinations of the three techniques. Since it was recorded for each program which failures each tester observed, it was possible to automatically generate pairs and triples of testers combining the same or different techniques.

The permutations investigated were:

- Pairs of code readers.
- Pairs of functional testers.
- Pairs of structural testers.
- One code reader and one functional tester.
- One code reader and one structural tester.
- One structural tester and one functional tester.
- Triples of code readers.
- Triples of functional testers.
- Triples of structural testers.
- One code reader, one functional tester and one structural tester.

All analysis was based on failures observed. The code reading failures include errors observed during reading as well as those identified due to inconsistencies between the abstracted specification and the original specification.

For each of the technique permutations all possible combinations of the 47 subjects were automatically generated. The resulting merged set of observed failures for each combination was then calculated. Thus for program `cmdline` there were 136 pairs of readers, 680 triples of readers, 3808 triples containing a reader, structural and a functional, etc. *Average* failure observation percentages were then calculated for each of the permutations for each of the programs. These are summarised in Table 2. Thus the average percentage of failures observed for individual code readers in program `ntree` was 41.67%, for pairs of code readers was 63.69%, for triples of code readers was 75.77%, and for triples involving a tester applying each of the three techniques was 75.96%. A more visual representation of this data is given in Fig. 6 (where, for example, c represents code reading, cc represents two code readers, cf represents combining code reading and functional testing) where the dramatic effect of combining techniques can be seen clearly.

From this table a number of important observations can be made:

Table 2. Percentage of failures observed by combinations for all programs

Combination	Program		
	ntree	cmdline	nametbl
Individual Code Reading	41.67%	38.56%	50.00%
Individual Functional Testing	45.00%	51.39%	68.75%
Individual Structural Testing	47.79%	53.17%	72.66%
Paired Reading	63.69%	55.88%	69.29%
Paired Functional	58.10%	72.69%	84.69%
Paired Structural	67.83%	63.37%	85.62%
Reading and Functional	63.06%	70.71%	80.89%
Reading and Structural	66.27%	74.60%	83.91%
Structural and Functional	66.72%	71.08%	86.67%
Triple Reading	75.77%	65.23%	79.92%
Triple Functional	65.91%	83.59%	90.07%
Triple Structural	77.59%	68.80%	88.95%
Reading, Functional and Structural	75.96%	83.46%	89.65%

- Across all three programs, there is a general trend of substantial improvement as we move from individuals to pairs to triples.
- The performance of same technique combinations varies substantially from program to program.
- Although code reading is relatively poor as an individual technique it is generally effective when combined with other code readers or with other techniques.
- The best results are *consistently* obtained by combining different techniques (regardless of program) i.e. paired code and functional, paired code and structural, paired functional and structural, and best of all, use of all three techniques combined.

To emphasis the final point, Table 3 compares the *best* single technique performance against the *worst* performing combined pair technique and against all three techniques combined.

Table 3. Comparing best individual technique (failures observed), with worst mixed pair technique, with all three techniques combined. S=Structural Testing, C = Code Reading, F = Functional Testing

	ntree	cmdline	nametbl
best single technique	48% (S)	53% (S)	73% (S)
worst mixed pair	63% (C+F)	71% (C+F)	81% (C+F)
Combination of all 3 techniques	76%	83%	90%

To conclude, these results appear to show the value of combining different techniques, either as pairs, or even better as triples. An important point aris-

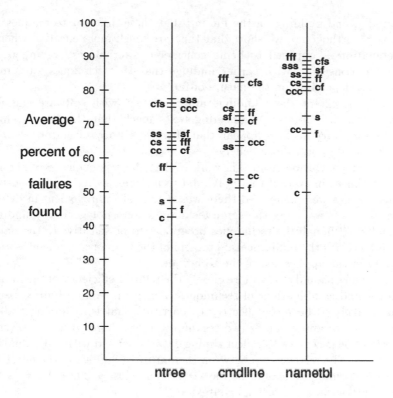

Fig. 4. Percentage of failures observed by combinations

ing from this, also noted by other authors, is that the common perception of techniques detecting certain classes of defect does not necessarily hold. If this was the case then pairing up of a technique would show no improvement. As it is, this pairing shows a substantial improvement in all cases. This demonstrates that while techniques may only be sensitive to certain classes of defect, they are not *reliably* sensitive. That is, there is a variability in the application of the techniques which determines its potency towards a particular fault.

7 Conclusions

The results reported here appear to show that the different techniques have different strengths and weaknesses in terms of the faults that they help to uncover. Their absolute effectiveness as well as their relative effectiveness depends on the nature of the programs and more specifically the nature of the faults in those programs. We argue that this is supported by the significant body of related work which shows no consistent pattern in terms of absolute or relative effectiveness. Rather, as the programs vary so do the results.

Secondly, and building on the finding that these different techniques are to some extent orthogonal, we show that they are much more effective when used in combination as opposed to being considered alternatives. Again, we argue that this is consistent with earlier findings that the techniques vary in their effectiveness depending on the nature of faults.

To a large extent these findings are consistent with software engineering folklore. Standard software engineering texts teach that the basic techniques are complementary. It does appear that there is a body of empirical evidence evolving that supports those beliefs.

The third conclusion from this work is that there is evidence of the fundamental weakness in each of the individual techniques. When subjects using the same techniques were combined there was a general improvement in defect detection. Subjects applying the same techniques were not generally finding the same faults. Although the techniques do appear to be sensitive to the nature of faults there is still the fundamental problem of the human component — subject variability in the application of the technique.

Future work should study more closely the relative efficiency of the individual techniques and combinations of techniques. For example, in a limited period of time is it likely to be more effective to partition that time amongst all three techniques, or to apply one or two techniques more thoroughly? To investigate this it would be necessary to collect timing data associated with individual failure observations. The relationship between the nature of faults and the effectiveness of detection techniques should be looked at more closely. These findings should also be explored in an industrial context.

Acknowledgements

Thanks to Fraser Macdonald for his help in the running of the experiments. Thanks are also due to Erik Kamsties and Chris Lott for their fine example of a replication package for software engineering experiments.

References

1. Victor R. Basili and Richard W. Selby. Comparing the effectiveness of software testing strategies. *IEEE Transactions on Software Engineering*, SE-13(12):1278–1296, December 1987.
2. A. Brooks, J. Daly, J. Miller, M. Roper, and M. Wood. Replication of experimental results in software engineering. Research report EFoCS-17-94, Department of Computer Science, University of Strathclyde, Glasgow, 1995.
3. N. Fenton, S. Pfleeger, and R. Glass. Science and substance: A challenge to software engineers. *IEEE Software*, 11(4):86–95, July 1994.
4. R. Glass. The software research crisis. *IEEE Software*, 11(6):42–47, November 1994.
5. William C. Hetzel. *An Experimental Analysis of Program Verification Methods*. PhD thesis, University of North Carolina, Chapel Hill, 1976.

6. C. Jones. Gaps in the object-oriented paradigm. *IEEE Computer*, 27(6):90–91, June 1994.
7. Erik Kamsties and Christopher Lott. An empirical evaluation of three defect detection techniques. Technical Report ISERN 95-02, Dept. Computer Science, University of Kaiserslautern, May 1995.
8. Erik Kamsties and Christopher Lott. An empirical evaluation of three defect detection techniques. In *Proc. 5th European Software Engineering Conference*, September 1995.
9. Richard C. Linger, Harlan D. Mills, and B.I. Witt. *Structured Programming: Theory and Practice*. Addison-Wesley, 1979.
10. Steve McConnell. *Code Complete*. Microsoft Press, 1993.
11. Glenford J. Myers. A controlled experiment in program testing and code walkthroughs/inspections. *Communications of the ACM*, 21(9):760–768, September 1978.
12. Roger S. Pressman. *Software Engineering - A Practitioners Approach*. McGraw-Hill, 1994.
13. Marc Roper. *Software Testing*. McGraw-Hill, 1993.
14. R. W. Selby. Combining software testing strategies: An empirical evaluation. In *Proc. Workshop on Software Testing*, pages 82–91. IEEE Computer Society Press, July 1986.
15. B. J. Winer. *Statistical Principles in Experimental Design*. McGraw-Hill, 2nd edition, 1971.

Experiences with Criticality Predictions in Software Development

Christof Ebert, Alcatel Telecom, Antwerp, Belgium
christof.ebert@alcatel.be

Abstract: Cost-effective software project management has the serious need to focus resources on those areas with highest criticality. The paper focuses on two areas important for practical application of criticality-based predictions in real projects, namely the selection of a classification technique and the use of the results in directing management decisions. The first part is comprehensively comparing and evaluating five common classification techniques (Pareto classification, classification trees, factor-based discriminant analysis, fuzzy classification, neural networks) for identifying critical components. Results from a current large-scale switching project are included to show practical benefits. Knowing which technique should be applied the second area gains even more attention: What are the impacts for practical project management within given resource and time constraints? Several selection criteria based on the results of a combined criticality and history analysis are provided together with potential decisions.

Keywords: classification, complexity, criticality prediction, data analysis, quality models, software metrics

1. Introduction

Not everything that counts can be counted
and not everything that can be counted counts.
Albert Einstein

Many companies apply techniques of criticality prediction that focus on identifying and reducing release risks. Unfortunately they usually concentrate on testing and rework. However, a fault detected during integration test can cost - with a conservative assumption - 10 times more than the same fault detected during code reading or code inspections [1]. Our goal that is presented in this paper thus is to provide and validate an integrated approach for predicting criticality when it is first visible and therefore reduce late and expensive rework.

One possibility to identify fault-prone modules is a criticality prediction. An analysis of several recent projects revealed the applicability of the Pareto rule: 20 % of the modules are responsible for 80% of the malfunctions of the whole project [4]. These critical modules need to be identified as early as possible, e.g. after coding. By concentrating on these components the effectiveness of code-inspections and module test is increased and less faults have to be found during test phases.

We therefore started with criticality prediction based on complexity-based classification of potentially fault-prone components during design (explanation follows). To achieve feedback for improving predictions the approach is integrated into the development process end-to-end (requirements, design, code, system test, First Office Application, and General Application). Over complex modules are tagged for extra code-inspections and unit testing.

Telecommunication switching systems are among the biggest challenges in current software development because they are distributed both during development time and during runtime. Due to their considerable size (several MLOC), such systems are developed within locally distributed development units by globally operating companies. The Alcatel 1000 S12 is a digital switching system that is currently used in over 40 countries world-wide. It provides a wide range of functionality (small local exchanges, transit exchanges, international exchanges, network service centres, or intelligent networks) and scalability (from small remote exchanges to large local exchanges). Its typical size is about 2.5 MLOC of which a big portion is customised for local network operators. The code used for Alcatel 1000 S12 is realised in Assembler, C and CHILL. In terms of functionality, Alcatel 1000 S12 covers almost all areas of software and computer engineering. This includes operating systems, database management and distributed real-time software.

The organisation responsible for development and integration is registered to the ISO 9001 standard. Typically total staff for development, testing, integration, and field delivery of such a system exceeds 500 software engineers and provides several local releases for different customers per year. Even core development staff at Alcatel (not responsible for integration and field delivery) is distributed over several sites in different European countries. In terms of effort or cost, the share of software is increasing continuously and is currently in the range of 80 %.

The paper is organised as follows. Section 2 presents a brief overview of common complexity-based classification methodologies and their applicability to software quality models. Section 3 provides experimental results to demonstrate the effectiveness of the approach in the area of fault- and change prediction. Application of such criticality prediction models and lessons learned are provided in section 4. Finally, section 5 summarises the results of complexity-based criticality models and provides an outlook on further research options. For this study we are providing data gathered during development and field operation of several releases of the *Alcatel 1000 S12* switching system that cover altogether more than 1000 years of execution time.

2. Complexity-Based Quality Models

Multivariate statistical techniques provide feedback about relationships between components (e.g. factor analysis [16], principal component analysis [2]). Classification techniques help determining outliers (e.g. error-prone components) [3]. Finally, detailed diagrams and tables provide insight into the reasons why distinct components are potential outliers and how to improve them [4]. In this presentation we are focusing on classification techniques.

Criticality prediction is a multifaceted approach taking into account several criteria. One criterion is the analysis of module complexity early in the life-cycle. Other criteria concern the amount of new or changed code in a module, and the amount of field faults a module had in the predecessor project, etc. All these criteria are used to build up a complete criticality prediction model. Based on a ranking list of criticality of all modules used in a build, different mechanisms can be applied to improving quality, namely redesign, code inspections, or module test with high coverage. We will in this first part focus on complexity-based criticality prediction and then enhance the model.

Fig. 1 shows that currently faults are often detected at the end of the development process despite the fact that they had been present since the design phase [1,2,4]. Late fault detection results in costly and time consuming correction efforts, especially when the requirements were misunderstood or a design flaw occurred. On the other hand it is clear that detecting faults earlier yields in advantages towards customer-perceived quality and cost (fig. 2)

Fig. 1: Example for fault detection stream of a CMM level 1 company

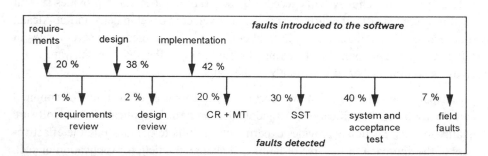

Quality or productivity factors to be predicted during the development of a software system are affected by many product and process attributes, e.g. software design characteristics or the underlying development process and its environment. Quality models are based upon former project experiences and combine the quantification of aspects of software components with a framework of rules (e.g. limits for metrics, appropriate ranges). They are generated by the combination and statistical analysis of product metrics (e.g. complexity metrics) and product or process attributes (e.g. quality characteristics, effort) [4,5,6]. These models are evaluated by applying and comparing exactly those invariant figures they are intended to predict, the process metrics (e.g. effort, fault rate, number of changes since the project started). Iterative repetition of this process can refine the quality models, thus allowing their use as predictors for similar environments and projects. For assessing overall quality or productivity, it is suitable to break it down into its component factors (e.g. maintainability), thus arriving at several aspects of software that can be analysed quantitatively. Typical problems connected to data collection, analysis, and quality modelling are addressed and discussed comprehensively in [4,7].

Fig. 2: Typical benchmark effects of detecting faults earlier in the life cycle

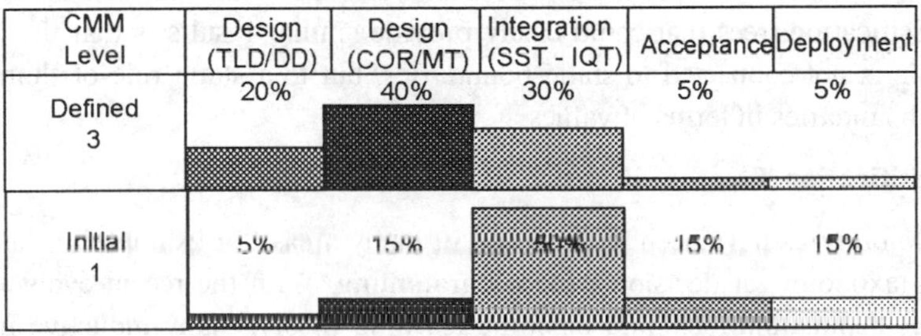

CMM Level	Design (TLD/DD)	Design (COR/MT)	Integration (SST - IQT)	Acceptance	Deployment
Defined 3	20%	40%	30%	5%	5%
Initial 1	5%	15%	50%	15%	15%

Classification or clustering algorithms are mathematical tools for detecting similarities between members of a collection of objects. Classification algorithms can be loosely categorised by the underlying principle (objective function, graph-theoretical, hierarchical) or model type (deterministic, probabilistic, statistical, fuzzy). Information about the objects (e.g. software components) to be analysed is input to classification algorithms in the form of metric vectors. The elements of a metric vector are the measurements of distinct software features that have been chosen as a basis for comparing a specific object to other objects. The output of a classification or clustering algorithm can then be used to classify the objects into subsets or clusters. The classification of metric vectors can be performed with the information about different classes (e.g. faults, change-rate). The training of any classification algorithm using this kind of information is called supervised. If the algorithm classifies the data autonomously the training is unsupervised. We will further focus on supervised learning because quality metrics are provided within training data sets.

Metric vectors assigned to the same cluster are in some sense similar to each other, more so than they are to other metric vectors not assigned to that cluster. Instead of predicting number of faults or changes (i.e. algorithmic relationships) we are considering assignments to groups (e.g. "fault -prone"). While the first goal can be achieved more or less exactly with regression models or neural networks predominantly for finished projects, the latter goal seems to be adequate for predicting potential outliers in running projects, where preciseness is too expensive and unnecessary for decision support. The second part of this section will briefly describe those classification methodologies that are afterwards compared in section 3.

2.1 Pareto Classification

Pareto analysis is a common approach for quick quality analyses. The goal of a Pareto analysis is to identify those 20 % of all components that contribute heavily to all troubles. The principle is hence nicknamed `80:20 rule` because it assumes that the 20 % share is responsible for 80 % of the problems. It is amazing that this simple approach holds in most application domains. Software quality management methods, such as root cause analysis, typically start with identifying the small amount of problems (20 %) that provide the biggest trade-off when resolved. The difference to crisp classification trees that could easily provide similar results is that the classification rule is not connected to static boundaries, but to a static rule of thumb with dynamic boundaries in terms of values.

2.2 Classification Trees

Classification trees have been widely used in many areas, for example in image recognition, taxonomy, or decision table programming. With the recent evolvement of knowledge acquisition tools and machine learning theory, many inductive machine learning systems have been developed for constructing decision trees from the training set of examples (e.g. CART [8]). The trees are based on a set of metrics that are used to classify components according to how likely they are to have certain high-risk properties. They consist of several leaf nodes that contain binary or multivalue decisions to indicate whether a component is likely to be in a certain class based on historical data. Because each leaf considers values of a distinct metric such trees might be composed from a set of production rules. These rules might reflect expert knowledge that is integrated to form a tree. Of course, several leafs in different branches of the tree might consider the same metric with other decisions based on the set of questions asked before. Since these classification trees use multiple metrics simultaneously to identify a particular target class, they can be extended easily to consider other metrics.

2.3 Factor-based Discriminant Analysis

The overall problem of one-dimensional statistical techniques, such as scatter plots or correlation analysis is how to compare all metrics of all components simultaneously. Multidimensional techniques differ from the analysis of variance or standard deviation of a single variable, or from the pairwise relationship between two variables, in a degree that they direct attention to the analysis of correlations of many variables [9]. Multidimensional scaling, factor and cluster analysis are applied to a similarity or distance matrix to obtain one geometrical representation of all relationships implied by the elements of such a matrix. Speaking of objects being "close" implies large similarity and small dissimilarity.

Factor-based discriminant analysis is an instrument to identify structures and suggest possible organisations of the data into meaningful groups [16,9]. Any given metric vector can be considered as a multidimensional space where each software component (e.g. a module) is represented as a point with distinct co-ordinates. We identify as a cluster any subset of the points which is internally well connected and externally poorly connected. The underlying assumption is that objects under investigation may be grouped such that elements residing in a particular group or cluster are, in some sense, more similar to each other than to elements belonging to other groups. Typically the classification consists of two steps. First factor analysis or a principal-components procedure is used for reducing the dimensionality of the metric vector to fewer metrics with orthogonal complexity domains. Discriminant analysis is then used to separate groups of software components according to one selected quality attribute (i.e. changes, fault rate).

2.4 Fuzzy Classification

In the so far mentioned software classification systems, the fuzziness of the knowledge base is ignored because neither predicate logic nor probability-based methods provide a systematic basis for dealing with it [3,10,11]. As a consequence, fuzzy facts and rules are generally manipulated as if they were non-fuzzy, leading to conclusions whose validity is open to question. As a simple illustration of this point, consider the fact [3]: *"If data bindings are between 6 and 10 and cyclomatic complexity is greater than 18 the software component is likely to have errors of a distinct type"*. Obviously the meaning of this - automatically generated - fact is less precise than stated and might be provided by a maintenance expert as a fuzzy fact: *"If data bindings are medium and cyclomatic complexity is large than the software component is likely to have errors of a distinct type."* Fuzzy logic provides a method for representing the meaning of both fuzzy and non-fuzzy predicate modifiers or hedges (e.g. *not, very, much, slightly, extremely*) which permits a system for computing with linguistic variables, that is, variables whose values are words in a natural language [12,13].

Production rules are used to capture both heuristic rules of thumb and formally known relations among the facts in the domain. These rules are represented as if-then-rules that associate conclusions to given antecedents. An example for a production rule is *"if cyclomatic complexity is medium and statement count is medium then the component is error-prone"*. The advantage of production rules obviously lies in the fact that they are a convenient way to represent one's domain knowledge and that they can be augmented easily by adding further rules. The combination of interacting fuzzy rules derived from expert knowledge is called a fuzzy expert system, because it is supposed to model an expert and make his or her knowledge available for non-experts for purposes of diagnosis or decision making [11]. The declarative knowledge of fuzzy expert systems is represented as fuzzy sets and data. The inference engine that controls the application of fitting rules to given data is based on an extension of set-theoretic operators (e.g. and, or, then).

2.5 Neural Network Approaches

To prohibit unnecessary crispness while dealing with approximate knowledge, some recent research has focused towards employing *artificial neural networks* for metric-based decision support [14]. The multilayer perceptron is the most widely applied neural network architecture today. Neural network theory showed that only three layers of neurons are sufficient for learning any (non)linear function combining input data to output data. The input layer consists of one neuron for each complexity metric, while the output layer has one neuron for each quality metric to be predicted. All neurons of the input layer are connected to neurons of a hidden layer whose neurons are connected to all neurons of the output layer. In every neuron of the hidden and the output layers the weighted sums of the previous layer outputs are calculated. These sums are mapped through a non-linear activation function (e.g. sigmoid function). Weights are usually trained with back-propagation algorithms that try to minimise the square error between the desired network output and the actual network output. Multilayer Perceptrons can obviously be tuned by many mechanisms (e.g. number of layers, number of neurons, activation functions, learning algorithm, etc.).

Because neural network based approaches are predominantly result-driven, not dealing with design heuristics and intuitive rules for modelling the development process and its products, and because their trained information is not accessible from outside, they are even less suitable for providing reasons for any result. Neural networks are applied when there are only input vectors (software metric data) and results (quality or productivity data), while no intuitive connections are known between the two sets (e.g. pattern recognition approaches in complicated decision situations). However, neural networks can currently not provide any insight *why* they arrived at a certain decision besides providing result-driven connection weights. It is interesting to note that feedforward neural nets can be approximated to any degree of accuracy by fuzzy expert systems [15], hence offering an approach for classification based on neural fuzzy hybrids.

3. Experiences with Complexity-based Criticality Prediction

It is relatively easy to construct metric-based quality models that happen to classify data of past projects well, because all such models can be calibrated according to quality of fit. The difficulty lies in improving and stabilising models based on historic data that are of value for use in anticipating future outcomes. While working on software for large real-time systems, we had the task of developing a quality model with predictive accuracy. The main interest of these quality models for metric-based software development was in detecting fault-prone modules during the design and providing tailored reliability growth models for release time prediction during several test processes. This report deals with the first aspect.

Training data was taken from several real-time telecommunication projects that had been developed according to a similar design approach. We investigated a selection of 451 modules that had been placed under configuration control since start of coding. The overall size of these modules is in the area of 1 MLOC. Software faults are recorded within the configuration control system for each module together with several complexity metrics based on the *COSMOS* (*ESPRIT* funded) project. The resulting tool is commercially available. *COSMOS* provides a project monitoring system consisting of metrics that are collected throughout the complete development process (e.g. size, cyclomatic complexity, expression compl., statement compl., database access). The architecture of *COSMOS* distinguishes two parts: a parser for different design and coding languages and a set of metrics with abstract metric definitions. It is thus feasible to include other languages into the environment without changing the metrics component.

Evaluation of the classification approaches is based on [1]:
- Low chi-square values which is equal to reduced misclassification errors;
- Comparing the two types of misclassification errors, namely type I errors ("fault-prone components" classified as "uncritical components") and type II errors ("uncritical components" classified as "fault-prone components ").

The goal obviously must be to reduce type I errors at the cost of type II errors because it is less expensive to investigate some components despite the fact that they are not critical compared to labelling critical components as harmless without probing further.

Spearman rank correlation coefficients for the measured complexity metrics (451 modules; $\alpha < 10^{-12}$ for $\rho > 0.3$) against all reported field failures of a digital switching system after over 1000 years of execution time are well below 0.5. Spearman rank correlations among different complexity metrics were above 0.8 for all selected metrics. Such relations between metrics are typical and were studied extensively before [4]. Factor analysis was performed for reducing dimensions of the metric space resulting in three almost orthogonal factors: volume, control and communication. Based on these results we selected six complexity metrics as input values for the prediction models, namely number of (executable) statements, statement complexity, expression complexity, data complexity, depth of nesting (control flow), and data base access (number and complexity of data base accesses). Statement complexity, expression complexity and data complexity are metrics that count the use of distinct statements (e.g. different data types and their use is considered data complexity) according to given hierarchies of individual complexity assignments.

The prediction process was separated into several steps:

1. The modules of a "finished" project where partitioned into three criticality-classes according to the faults that had been reported from field applications: no faults, one fault and more than one fault. The training data set reflected a list of the modules with associated faults.
2. The same list of modules was combined with the complexity metrics of each module.
3. The prediction models were trained with the training data set (complexity metrics and faults) to predict faults as accurately as possible.
4. Validation such as chi-square tests was performed with modules of the same project that had not been used for training (test data). For testing the robustness of different classification methods we treated all project data sets equally despite knowing about the presence of outliers. Compared to other studies [2] we did not eliminate outliers because no common agreement for such filtering exists [4].

The selected prediction model was then used to predict criticality of modules of a new release that at that time was in the subsystem test phase. The result was a small set of modules predicted as most critical that was selected to focus test and review actions on this set instead of all modules.

Applying the five different classification techniques to the switching system data showed almost identical results in terms of overall correct classification of the modules. Table I shows a portfolio of predictions versus reality for the described telecommunication switching system. Notions in quotation marks (in the first column) are the predictions. Instead of common portfolio tables the four values for predictions versus reality are put into single line entries. For example 163 out of the given 200 modules of the test data set (81.5 %) contain zero or one defect, while 37 modules (18.5 %) contain more than 1 defect. This share reflects approximately the 80:20 ratio that is useful for predictions that require rework in terms of redesign or other approaches to improve maintainability.

Applying the Pareto classification (second column) results in a selection of 37 modules that have the biggest volume (i.e. top 20 %). The remaining 163 modules are predicted as having 'few faults'. Now these two groups are compared with reality. 146 modules with few faults and 20 fault-prone modules were classified correctly. 17 modules were misclassified as having few faults (type I error) and another 17 modules were predicted as fault-prone, while belonging to the class of modules with few faults (type II error). Taking these values gives the chi-square result of 38.1.

Factor-based discriminant analysis requires factor analysis for reducing metrics' dimensionality and afterwards discriminant analysis which needs just one learning cycle. This approach therefore is the fastest way for classification. Both classification tree and neural network predictions need several thousand training cycles for optimisation that are performed automatically on workstations or PCs. It was interesting to realise that classification tree results were similar to results from crisp cluster analysis with ten classes, although the latter approach takes almost no computational effort. For neural network classification a three layer perceptron (5, 12, 1 nodes) with backpropagation learning (100000 training cycles; learning rate: 0.5; momentum between 0 and 0.5) showed best results. Fuzzy classification was short-cut to only one given rule system without further optimisation. Therefore the rules (weights = 1) and membership functions (trapezoid and symmetrical) provide good comprehension and portability.

Results showed highest overall correct classification for crisp classification trees (85 % of all modules). Pareto classification (83 % of all modules) and neural network classification (82.5 %) performed slightly worse. Factor-based discriminance analysis and non optimised fuzzy classification finally achieved 81 % correct classifications. Obviously there is no clear winner given this ranking which is due to a number of outliers that either increase type I or type II misclassifications when optimisation of the other area is achieved.

A better indicator for comparing classification techniques is the number of type I misclassifications. Fuzzy classification shows lowest misclassification results with only 8 modules indicated as having few faults while they actually were fault-prone. Chi-square analysis also indicates that fuzzy classification is performing better than the other techniques ($\chi^2 = 52.2$). Automatic optimisation of rules (e.g. more than two input values in one rule) and membership functions would improve these results, however due to intuitiveness of rules we won't discuss such techniques. Residual analysis was not performed because our goal was to predict fault-prone modules and not number of faults. Due to outliers it is intrinsically impossible to optimise one classification method for both types of misclassification errors. Fig. 3 shows a scatterplot of the complete data set (all modules) with faults (vertical axis), volume (horizontal axis), and cyclomatic complexity (shape of dots). Outliers with small complexity and high fault rate can be clearly identified. It is obviously impossible to strive for zero misclassifications because several data sets are overlapping in a sense that they belong to the - intuitively - wrong group according to the delivered error count.

The trade-off of using fuzzy classification and Pareto classification is that this method needs *not necessarily* training (i.e. it could start completely untrained based on design heuristics), thus being more portable to other systems and easier to understand than the three other techniques. We tested this hypothesis with a second project in order to achieve insight in portability of classification techniques without further training. Expert rules and membership functions remained unchanged from the old project which allows application of expert rules as design heuristics. The first classification with data from a follow-on project already provided $\chi^2 = 46.1$ for 200 modules. Pareto classification performed slightly worse ($\chi^2 = 35.7$), while the three remaining classification techniques had a χ^2 below 30.

Fig. 3: Scatterplot of number of faults for modules together with volume and cyclomatic complexity

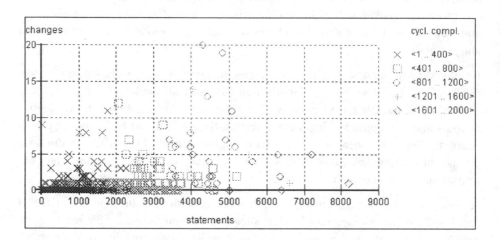

Compared to the other classification techniques fuzzy logic provides a natural conceptual framework for representation of knowledge and inference processes based on knowledge that is imprecise, incomplete or inconsistent. We have to distinguish between uncertainty in the case data and in the knowledge base. In the course of classifying software project and product data we have been discussing the latter case. It is practically unrealistic to deal with automatically generated decision trees or rule sets with crisp thresholds and results without being able to provide intuitive guidance. Since there are some guiding principles for decision support available, we focus on utilising expert-derived, however vague, knowledge that we included in a fuzzy expert system-type classification scheme. If software engineering expert knowledge is available we recommend fuzzy classification before using learning strategies that are only result-driven (e.g. classification trees or mere neural network approaches). However, we see the necessity of such approaches when only few guiding principles are available and sufficient project data can be utilised for supervised learning.

The choice of the proper approach to automatic decision support depends on the problem. To software classification problems, multibranching fuzzy classification provides a more comprehensive solution than crisp decision trees. Such multibranching decision support is based on structures that are not necessarily trees but also networks that resemble expert systems' structures. When these classification schemes are applied to new data sets, the best solution is to provide not only a binary result, but fuzzy attributes that consider those results that lie in between a clear "yes" or "no". We emphasise the necessity of applying fuzzy concepts to the areas of metric-based software project and quality management because subjective and qualitative judgement plays an important role in this area.

A comparison of different classification approaches suitable for metric-based decision support is presented in table II. Results as presented in this table are based on various applications of the five classification techniques to data sets from switching systems. The upper part of this table presents a summary on learning and knowledge representation. The lower part gives the effects of using manipulated data values (i.e. two metrics are highly correlated, one metric is almost random; several data sets contain random values). The remaining two parts of table II provide portability results and a short bibliography for improved orientation.

4. Application in the Development Process

The criticality prediction model is used to identify critical modules for which a code inspection and later a complete module test are indispensable. The most critical of the analysed modules are candidates for a redesign. Other high-ranking modules should have a code inspection a high-coverage in module test.

The linkage of the different criteria together depends on the quality goals and the available budget. A general baseline cannot be provided. Current results indicate, that the amount of new or changed code together with complexity is most important, but the results need to be further investigated. Especially the critical modules which are not inspectable deserve a special treatment.

The process for criticality classification and validation is shown graphically in fig. 4:

1. Provide list of all modules at start of project, during design and after end of module test
2. Provide fault history classification for each module on the lists. A root cause analysis might be added for high ranking faults that allows for a Pareto-based mitigation list.
3. Provide change history classification (i.e. number of compiles or number of deliveries)
4. Provide complexity classification as indicated in previous sections
5. Finalise comprehensive criticality list that takes into account the different inputs from steps 2-4 mapped on the appropriate input list. Before the final rankings are presented to decide on further actions the validity of the lists must be evaluated (e.g. screening on reasonable modules, outliers, potential misleading effects, etc.). The goal of screening is not to filter out what is thought cannot be changed anyway, however to question undesired influences from history. Of course

screening and ranking must primarily ensure that type I prediction errors are lowest feasible.

6. Prepare suggestions based on ranked critical modules. Typical approaches include redesign of few highest ranked modules according to a simultaneous classification (i.e. the top modules must rank high in all three lists simultaneously). Redesign includes reduction of size, improved modularity, etc. Application of thorough module test with C0 coverage > 80 is applied to high runners according to independent classification (i.e. the top modules of all three approaches are grouped). Details of complexity metrics must be investigated for the selected modules to determine redesign approach. In all cases it is typically the different complexity metrics that already indicate which approach in redesign or test should be followed.

7. Validation and improvement of predictions based on post mortem studies with all collected faults and the population of a "real" criticality list. Then the actual fault ranking is compared with the predicted ranking. Reasons for deviations are investigated and used automatic classification approaches are tuned. The rules for screening are improved to ensure that type II prediction errors will be reduced next time.

Fig. 4: Approach for criticality prediction

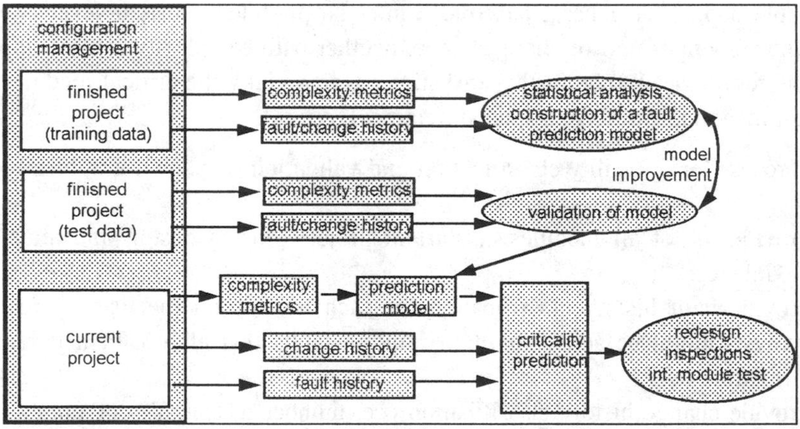

5. Conclusions

We have evaluated several classification techniques as an approach for predicting faults based on code complexity metrics. Given complexity metrics and quality data (fault rates) of several different real-time systems best results were achieved with fuzzy classification. Pareto analysis ('80:20 rule') generally showed good results which clearly underlie its importance as a rule of thumb for easy identification of the top 20 % of critical modules. Complexity-based classification has been applied to the design and testing of telecommunication systems. Its practical use was showed for detecting fault-prone components and assigning additional fault-detection effort. As such the technique proves to be effective in early identification of critical components. It must be emphasised that criticality prediction techniques being used do not attempt to detect all faults. Instead they belong to the set of managerial instruments that try to optimise resource allocation by focusing them on areas with many faults that would affect the utility of the delivered product.

The trade-off of applying complexity-based predictive quality models is estimated based on:
- limited resources are assigned to high-risk jobs or components;
- impact analysis and risk assessment of changes is feasible based on affected or changed complexity;
- grey-box testing strategies are applied to identified high-risk components;
- less customer reported failures (see fig. 2)..

Further research in the area of predictive quality models should focus on the areas:
- Investigation of more projects from different application areas in order to provide fundamental insight in the development of quality models and their influence on different project types. This should include analyses of different approaches for constructing classification schemes (e.g. decision trees) and optimising their accuracy, intelligibility, and reproducibility.
- Model the processes contributing to fault injection, detection and correction (look for example on staffing, late feature changes, corrections affecting complex components, testing strategies and their coverage and distribution over the whole system).
- Coping with noisy data sets for constructing predictive classification systems. Solutions to this problem include robust feature selection and error-estimation during the induction of classification schemes.
- Application to practical software project management based on predictive and dynamic classification models. Derived classification schemes must be combined with IPSE and CM thus providing automatic metric generation for integrated design and test management support.

Acknowledgements
Special thanks are contributed to Th. Liedtke and E. Baisch, Alcatel Telecom for many helpful suggestions while condensing the results.

References
[1] Fenton, N. E. and S.L. Pfleeger: *Software Metrics: A Practical and Rigorous Approach*. Chapman & Hall, London, UK, 1997.
[2] Khoshgoftaar, T.M. et al: Early Quality Prediction: A Case Study in Telecommunications. *IEEE Software*, Vol. 13, No. 1, pp. 65-71, Jan. 1996.
[3] Porter, A. A. und R. W. Selby: Empirically Guided Software Development Using Metric-Based Classification Trees. *IEEE Software*, Vol. 7, No. 3, S. 46-54, Mrc. 1990.
[4] Ebert, C.: Classification Techniques for metric-based software development. *Software Quality Journal*, Vol.5, pp.255-272, 1996.
[5] Kitchenham, B.A., S.G. Linkman and D.T. Law: Critical Review of Quantitative Asessment. *Software Engineering Journal*, Vol. 9, No. 3, pp. 43 - 53, 1994.
[6] Stark, G., R.C. Durst and C.W. Vowell: Using Metrics in Management Decision Making. *IEEE Computer*, Vol. 27, No. 9, pp. 42 - 48, 1994.
[7] Briand, L. C., V. R. Basili, and W. M. Thomas: A Pattern Recognition Approach for Software Engineering Data Analysis. *IEEE Trans. Software Engineering*, Vol. 18, No. 11, S. 931-942, Nov. 1992.
[8] Breiman, L., J.H.Friedman, R.A.Olshen, and C.J.Stone: *Classification and Regression Trees*. Wadsworth, Belmont, CA, 1984.
[9] Dillon, W. R. and M. Goldstein: *Multivariate Analysis-Methods and Applications*. John Wiley & Sons, NY, NY, USA, 1984.
[10] Schneidewind, N. F.: Validating Metrics for Ensuring Space Shuttle Flight Software Quality. *IEEE Computer*, Vol. 27, No. 8, pp. 50 - 57, 1994.
[11] Selby, R. W. and V. R. Basili: Analyzing Error-Prone System Structure. *IEEE Transactions on Software Engineering*, Vol. 17, No. 2, pp. 141-152, 1991.
[12] Ebert, C.: Rule-Based Fuzzy Classification for Software Quality Control. *Fuzzy Sets and Systems*, Vol. 63, pp. 349 - 358, 1994.
[13] Zimmermann, H.-J.: *Fuzzy Set Theory and its Applications*. Kluwer, Boston, 2nd edition, 1991.
[14] Khoshgoftaar, T. and D.L. Lanning: A Neural Network Approach for Early Detection of Program Modules Having High Risk in the Maintenance Phase. *J. Systems and Software*, Vol. 29, pp. 85-91, 1995.
[15] Buckley, J.J. and Y. Hayashi: Neural Nets for Fuzzy Systems. *Fuzzy Sets and Systems*, Vol. 71, pp. 265-276, 1995.
[16] Ebert, C.: Visualization Techniques for Analyzing and Evaluating Software Measures. *IEEE Trans. Software Engineering*, Vol. 18, No. 11, pp. 1029-1034, Nov. 1992.

Table I: Classification Results

200 modules used for testing (163 modules with zero or one faults; 37 modules with more than one fault)	Pareto classification by volume (top 20 %)	crisp classification tree	factor-based discriminance analysis	fuzzy classification	neural network classification
reality: $\leq$ 1 fault: 163 modules (81.5 %)					
prediction: "few faults"	146	149	137	133	149
prediction: "fault -prone" (type II)	17	14	26	30	14
reality: > 1 faults: 37 modules (18.5 %)					
prediction: "few faults" (type I)	17	16	12	8	21
prediction: "fault -prone"	20	21	25	29	16
χ^2	38.1	48.9	42.3	52.2	28.4

Table II: Evaluation of Different Classification Methods

	Pareto classification by volume (top 20 %)	crisp classification tree	factor-based discriminance analysis	fuzzy classification	neural network classification
crisp data values as metric data values	x	x	x	x	x
fuzzy, vague, linguistic data values				x	
algorithmic knowledge representation		(x)	x	(x)	(x)
rule-based knowledge representation	x	x		x	
information represented by *intuitive* rules	x			x	
learning is result-driven (as opposed to design heuristics)	no training	x		(x)*	x
reasons for decisions are given (0, +, ++)	+	++	0	++	0
effects of highly correlated metrics in input training data (0, +, ++)	++	++	++	++	+
effects of uncorrelated metrics in input training data (0, +, ++)	++	+	+	++	0
robustness to outlying data sets during training (0, +, ++)	no training	++*	+	++*	0
portability to data sets from other projects with same design methodology (0, +, ++)	++	+	+	++	0
bibliography for applications and theory	[1]	[3,10]	[2,9,16]	[12,13]	[14]

*   dependent on learning approach or classification algorithm

0   bad results (negative);   +   medium results;   ++   good results (positive)

Validating the Defect Detection Performance Advantage of Group Designs for Software Reviews: Report of a Laboratory Experiment Using Program Code

Lesley Pek Wee Land [†]
l.lau@unsw.edu.au

Chris Sauer [§]
c.sauer@unsw.edu.au

Ross Jeffery [†]
r.jeffery@unsw.edu.au

[†] School of Information Systems
[§] Australian Graduate School of Management, Fujitsu Centre for Managing Information Technology in Organisations

University of New South Wales, Sydney 2052, New South Wales, Australia.

Abstract

It is widely accepted that software development technical reviews (SDTRs) are a useful technique for finding defects in software products. Recent debates centre around the need for review meetings (Porter and Votta 1994, Porter et al 1995, McCarthy et al 1996, Lanubile and Visaggio 1996). This paper presents the findings of an experiment that was conducted to investigate the performance advantage of interacting groups over average individuals and artificial (nominal) groups. We found that interacting groups outperform the average individuals and nominal groups. The source of performance advantage of interacting groups is not in finding defects, but rather in discriminating between true defects and false positives. The practical implication for this research is that nominal groups constitute an alternative review design in situations where individuals discover a low level of false positives.

Keywords: Software Development Technical Review, defect detection, interacting group, nominal group, false positives.

1.   Introduction

Software development technical review (SDTR) stands out as an important technique in the software quality literature. It is generally agreed in the software engineering community that the different types of review (e.g. inspection, walkthrough) have a common purpose in detecting errors in software (Fagan 1976, Yourdon 1989). There are various designs for how to carry out reviews (Kim et al 1995) but there is little empirical evidence to support the relative merits claimed of them.

Most review designs include a group meeting because it is believed that groups perform better than individuals. Until recently, this belief has not been contested. However recent experiments (Votta 1993, Porter and Votta 1994, Porter et al 1995, Lanubile and Visaggio 1996, Siy 1996) have suggested that groups may not be necessary. We suggest in this paper that this conclusion may be premature because it gives too little weight to the importance of false identification of defects.

Empirical SDTR research has focused on a few factors such as defect detection approaches (Porter and Votta 1994, Porter et al 1995, Kamsties and Lott 1995, Basili et al 1996, McCarthy et al 1996) (e.g. scenario-based, ad hoc, checklist-based, perspective-based reading) and cost-benefit issues (Siy 1996). It has explored the performance effects of very specific types of intervention rather than conclusively verify that groups are an effective basis for reviews. Research in behavioural science into the performance of groups in general suggests that the traditional belief in the value of interacting groups may be well founded although the source of their performance advantage is not likely to derive from the group's discovering new defects (Yetton and Bottger 1982, Bottger and Yetton 1988). Behavioural research therefore predicts that the so-called synergy effects of SDTR meetings discovering new defects (Fagan 1976) will be negligible.

We designed and conducted a controlled experiment using 101 undergraduates as subjects. Our main aim was twofold: to test whether interacting groups outperform individuals as is widely assumed, and if so why groups do better.

Our main contribution is the confirmation of interacting group's performance advantage over average individuals as is implied in the normative SDTR literature (Fagan 1976, Freedman and Weinberg 1990, Strauss and Ebenau 1994, Yourdon 1989). However, the source of this advantage is not "synergy" as it is commonly believed. We confirmed that interacting groups do not find significant new defects. Instead, they appear to have the ability to perform defect discrimination.

This paper is structured as follows. Section 2 details the key research questions posed in this paper. We discuss the justifications for them and state the detailed hypotheses tested in this paper. Section 3 explains the experimental design, set-up, conduct, and other relevant issues pertaining to the experiment. The results are described in section 4. Section 5 discusses the results, states the key contributions for this paper and suggests future research direction.

2.   Research Questions

Research into SDTRs comprises normative and empirical work. Normative research has emphasised how to carry out reviews and/or has sought to design improved types of reviews (Fagan 1976, Parnas and Weiss 1987, Freedman and Weinberg 1990, Schneider et al 1992, Gilb 1993, Knight and Myers 1993, Strauss and Ebenau 1994). Empirical research has sought to understand the performance of the different types of review in terms of defect detection effectiveness, cost-benefit, cycle time, and other variables (Votta 1993, Porter and Votta 1994, Porter et al 1995, Lanubile and Visaggio 1996, Siy 1996). Ideally empirical research would evaluate the recommendations of normative research and motivate further improvement.

Hitherto in the quest to increase our knowledge of SDTRs, normative research has not been subject to systematic empirical evaluations.

In this paper, we use a two stage model for software reviews: individual defect detection followed by group defect detection. This model reflects current practice and is assumed in recent experiments (Porter and Votta 1994, Siy 1996). We restrict our interest to review effectiveness as measured by defect detection, and not other variables such as cost-benefit and cycle time. Once the defect detection task is better understood, other factors can gradually be included in future research.

The first and fundamental question in relation to SDTR designs is whether normative research's advocacy of groups for software reviews is justified. It has always been taken for granted that a group will find more defects than an individual reviewer. To our knowledge this has not been rigorously tested in the case of SDTRs. Evidence from the behavioural sciences suggests that an average group of software reviewers will outperform an average individual reviewer (Lorge 1958, Shaw 1981, Yetton and Bottger 1982). This is a significant question to examine because software review groups are known to suffer from process loss, that is the phenomenon by which defects identified by individual reviewers in preparation are not included in the list of defects by the groups (Porter and Votta 1994, Porter et al 1995, Siy 1996). Process loss is common to group performance in all kinds of task (Steiner 1972). We therefore need to empirically confirm that process losses do not outweigh any extra defects identified through holding a group.meeting. Our first research question is therefore:

Research Question 1:
Are groups more effective at software reviews than individuals?

The traditional understanding has been that interacting groups are especially effective as a result of their interactions or synergy (Fagan 1993, Votta 1993). Recent empirical research has found little or no evidence to support this view (Votta 1993, Porter and Votta 1993, Johnson 1996). These research findings show insignificant new defects are discovered as a result of group interaction (often referred to as meeting gains). Moreover, the discovery of process loss in software reviews has led some to challenge the need for multiple reviewers to interact.

These findings of limited or no synergy, together with process loss, are consistent with findings by behavioural researchers for other tasks. Nevertheless, behavioural researchers still find that interacting groups outperform nominal groups (these are groups which do not meet but where individual performances are aggregated). There is therefore the possibility that interacting groups have some other virtue or performance advantage. Sauer et al (1996) argue that this performance advantage in software reviews is the ability of interacting groups to filter out false positives (i.e. defects which are discovered by individuals or groups but which prove not to be true defects) from the true defects discovered by individuals. This is something that nominal groups cannot achieve because there is no provision in the procedure to aggregate individuals' defects and for discriminating between true defects and false positives.

Up to this point, SDTR research has taken little account of false positives. It seems likely that most researchers have assumed that they are unimportant. In fact, findings regarding false positive vary across industrial studies. Votta (1993) finds they account for 1% of the review findings, whereas Siy(1996) finds they account for 22%. False positives are a problem if they occur frequently and have an adverse effect on software quality. Siy's findings, together with evidence from laboratory studies suggest that false positives are a frequent occurrence. They have costs. For example, time can be spent repairing false positives, possibly introducing new defects. The added cost of investigating and reworking the product is hard to quantify. It depends on the type and impact of the false positives on the overall system and the 'repair' if undertaken. We suggest that it is prudent at the current stage of empirical research for review performance to be measured by taking into account both true defects and false positives.

Our discussion indicates that there is no conclusive evidence as to why a group design for software reviews should be preferable to an individual reviewer. Moreover we do not as yet know whether the presumed performance advantage of the group derives from the fact that more than one reviewer is involved or from special aspects of the interaction of the group. Resolving this issue will help us develop empirically justified designs. For example, if the group's advantage lies solely in there being multiple reviewers all applied to the same task, then it would be possible to achieve the same result as an interacting group review more cheaply by using a nominal group design. We therefore pose the next research question:

Research Question 2:
What is the source of the performance advantage of interacting groups?

2.1.   Experimental Hypotheses

Figure 1 shows the relationships between the research questions and the hypotheses presented in this paper. Hypothesis 1.1 is directly motivated from research question 1. It seeks to confirm the basic assumption that a group of reviewers will find more true defects than an average individual reviewer. Disconfirmation would undermine established beliefs in the effectiveness of group reviews.

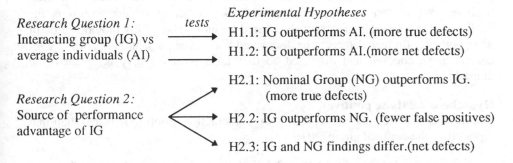

Figure 1: Relationships Between Research Questions and Hypotheses

Hypothesis 1.1 (true defect)

The number of true defects reported by an interacting group (IG) review is greater than that reported by an average individual (AI) group member.

A stronger test of the same basic assumption would use the net defect score. 'Net defect score' combines the true defect and false positive findings, on the assumption that false positives offset the true defect score to some degree. Hence it is a more appropriate reflection of review performance although we lack the empirical knowledge on the extent in which false positives affect the overall review performance. Support for hypothesis 1.2 would give us a stronger indication that interacting groups outperform the average individual.

Hypothesis 1.2 (net defect)

The net defect score of an interacting group (IG) is greater than that of an average individual (AI) group member.

We previously noted that interacting groups suffer from process loss, and that nominal groups avoid this. In helping us to answer research question 2 - finding the source of performance advantage of groups, we compare the relative interacting and nominal groups' performance. Since nominal groups do not suffer from process loss, and because there is evidence that the level of emergent solutions in interacting software review groups is low (Porter and Votta 1994, Porter et al 1995), and in view of the fact that behavioural research is consistent with this, we would expect nominal groups to outperform interacting groups in true defects. Support for hypotheses 1.1, 1.2, and 2.1 would show that although interacting groups outperform the average individual (1.1 and 1.2), they do not outperform nominal groups in terms of true defects (i.e. NG is a better design than IG in terms of true defects). Hence the source of IG advantage is *not* in defect detection.

Hypothesis 2.1 (true defect)

The number of true defects reported by the nominal group (NG) is greater than that reported by the interacting group (IG).

To directly test the importance of interacting groups' ability to filter out false positives, we compare interacting and nominal groups on the number of false positives. We reason that the chief activity of interacting review groups is the "collection" or assembly of defects discovered by individuals. This provides little or no opportunity for new defects to be discovered but it does present an opportunity for defects to be checked and discussed so that false positives may be deleted and eliminated.

Hypothesis 2.2 (false positive)

The number of false positives reported by the interacting group (IG) is less than that reported by the nominal group (NG).

Support for hypotheses 2.1 and 2.2 will show that nominal groups have an advantage over interacting groups on true defects, but that interacting groups have the advantage on false positives. There is currently no indicative evidence as to which will be the stronger effect. We therefore propose that in respect of net defects, either nominal or interacting groups have the advantage.

Hypothesis 2.3 (net defect)
The net defect score of the interacting group (IG) is not the same as that of the nominal group (NG).

3.   The Experiment

A controlled experiment was conducted in June 1995. We used 101 third year undergraduates who acted as the reviewers. All subjects were undertaking the Software Engineering course with the School of Information Systems at the University of New South Wales.

3.1.   Experimental Design

All subjects were required to inspect the same piece of compiled code first as an individual, then followed by a face-to-face group review. Both tasks required them to complete defect forms, from which defect data was taken. Random assignment was used to allocate individuals to groups of three. This ensured that any differences in performance between the individuals and the groups was not due to pre-existing differences between the groups. And hence, we will be able to conclude that our results apply on average, given a large enough sample.

3.1.1.   Variables

The experiment manipulates one *independent variable* — the review design. Each subject was exposed to two treatments: an independent review, followed by a group review. A third review design (nominal group review) was included in the data analysis. These are the review designs considered:

1. *individual review* - reviewers work independently of each other to produce a list of defects each.

2. *interacting group review* - reviewers interact face-to-face in teams of three, using the results of their prior individual reviews to produce a single list of defects for the group.

3. *nominal group review* - reviewers do not interact with one another. This is not a separate activity, its measurement is generated from individual review scores (see below).

The dimensions of *dependent variable* performance are:

1. the number of *true defects*

These defects can be classified using the defect checklist (see section 3.1.3), and need rework by the author(s) of the review product.

2. the number of *false positives*
   These are the non-true defects - 'defects' which require no repair. They can be classified using the defect checklist. The following are not counted as false positives:
   - Syntax errors
     Since the code was already compiled without errors, any reports of syntax errors would not risk being 'reworked' because they would be obvious false positives.
   - Incomprehensible 'defect' descriptions
     These descriptions are ambiguous, too general, unclear, incomplete, insufficient, or illogical.

3. net defect score
   net defect score = the number of true defects – the number of false positives

   In the above, the true defect and false positive data of individuals/groups are directly extracted from the individual/group defect forms (see section 3.1.3). For simplicity, we consider a false positive to be as unsatisfactory as a true defect undiscovered. Hence the negative effect of false positives is reflected in the net defect score by a simple subtraction. The net defect score can be positive, zero or negative (reflecting the fact that a review can potentially either improve or damage the quality of a piece of code).

All dependent variables are operationalised for the review designs as follows:

- *average individual (true defect, false positive and net defect) scores*
  These are calculated for each review team by taking the average of the three individual members' scores, using the same membership as that of interacting groups.

- *interacting group (true defect, false positive and net defect) scores*
  These are obtained as previously discussed above; no further computation is required.

- *nominal group (true defect, false positive and net defect) scores*
  These are calculated by aggregating the scores obtained from the individual members' scores, that is counting the combined list of unique defects (i.e. with duplicates removed). We use the same nominal group memberships as that of interacting groups. This allows direct comparison between nominal and interacting groups.

3.1.2.   Subjects, Training, and Incentives

All subjects had the same training prior to the experiment. They had previously passed the same prerequisite introductory programming course. A one hour lecture was delivered to them a week prior to the experiment, towards the end of the session when the subjects had grasped the basics of the programming language used in the review code, and completed a team project using it. The lecture introduced subjects to SDTRs, the review materials, the purpose of the review tasks[1], and the instructions on how to perform the tasks. Subjects appeared to be attentive during training and most were observed taking notes. Course assessment incentives were presented to the subjects to motivate performance.

3.1.3.   Experimental Materials

Reviewers were given a piece of code and documents (code overview, input and output formats, detailed pseudocode, and flow charts) to aid the review process. Two defect forms F1 and F2 were used to record the individual and group findings, respectively. The review product contained 135 noncommentary lines of COBOL code. The code and the supporting documents were taken from Welburn (1981). Twenty-five defects were inserted in the code, as suggested by two experts of the programming language. The code (seeded with defects) was properly compiled without syntax errors. A defect checklist consisting of guidelines and examples of defect classifications, was modified from Strauss and Ebenau (1994) to make it suitable for the code review.

3.2.   Experimental Validity

Internal validity describes the extent to which the research design permits us to reach causal conclusions about the effect of the independent variable on the dependent variable (Judd et al 1991). We shall consider the following internal validity threats:

Selection Threat

We minimised the differences between individuals in the different treatment groups (i.e. the selection threat) by randomly assigning individual subjects to review teams.

Maturation Threat

Maturation threats are caused by naturally occurring processes within subjects that could cause a change in performance (Judd et al 1991). In this experiment, we sought to minimise any learning effect. Similar training and incentives given to subjects (section 3.1.2) ensured they all started at the same level. The time lag between the individual and group activities was as short as possible to minimise any

---

[1] We encouraged reviewers to find as many defects as possible, but discouraged solution hunting.

interaction between individuals. Since there was no feedback between the individual and group work, there was no learning effect. All the individual forms were collected immediately after the completion of the individual review, before the group activity began, to prevent any illegal changes as a result of the group task. Subjects were only exposed to the review code during the experiment and not before; this was again to prevent them from discussing the code before the experiment The overall maturation threat is hence negligible.

Instrumentation Threat

In this experiment, there is no instrumentation threat caused by changes in the measurement procedures. All the data used in the analysis was taken from the completed defect forms. All individuals and groups used the same individual and group forms respectively, after reviewing the same piece of code using the same supporting documents.

External validity threats limit our ability to generalise our research results to the general software engineering population and other settings. We identify certain possible external validity threats. Firstly, most of the subjects had no commercial programming experience (mean 7 months) or SDTR experience (mean 3 months). While the latter is not that crucial since reviews are not widely used in every organisation, the former poses a real threat. Subjects' lack of expertise in the programming language and experience in commercial programming (which is also indicated by the low proportion of the average number of true defects found) make it hard for us to easily generalise our results to professional software engineers. On the other hand, results of SDTR empirical research do not indicate that professional software engineers perform so much better than student subjects. Myers (1978) who used highly experienced professionals, showed tremendous variability among subjects' performance in terms of defect detection. Other recent works which utilised professional developers showed varying levels of false positive detection: Votta (1993) reported only 1% of issues were false positives, while Siy (1996) reported 22%. The conflicting research findings above inform us that the extent of external validity threat due to the use of student subjects, is not really known, and that this factor does not necessarily invalidate our results.

Secondly, the code may not be representative of real-world code. In our experiment, the application domain of the code (stock-inventory system) is fairly common and familiar to the students. We also attempted to give the subjects a complete set of supporting documents to fully describe the code. Since there is no way of measuring how 'realistic' the code is, it is difficult to overcome this problem. Nevertheless every subject was exposed to the same review code and training. Other aspects of code representativeness relate to its size and complexity. The times taken to complete the individual and group reviews (see sections 3.3) indicate that the code is not too complex or large (see section 3.1.3). There was no indication from our observation of the experiment that the tasks set for the subjects were unmanageable in the given time. This is important so that we know the reviewers were not rushed in the tasks and hence did not miss the detection of any true defects due to a lack of time; otherwise we also risk unnecessary false positive identification and process loss. Hence the issue of how far the representativeness of the code affected the review performance is mitigated.

Finally, the defects in the code were artificially seeded (i.e. they were not naturally occurring) and hence may influence the reviewers' defect detection. These defects were fairly evenly spread across the defect categories, and the code was compiled without any errors. In a professional review setting, true defects of any kind and distribution within the code should be detectable by reviewers; hence the fact that our defects were seeded should not affect the validity of our results.

3.3. Experimental Procedure

The experiment involved two activities as shown in Figure 2. It was carried out during a normal two hour lecture timeslot allocated for the subject. We organised the experiment to be conducted in two lecture theatres close together since the usual lecture venue was not big enough to spread out subjects for the group activity.

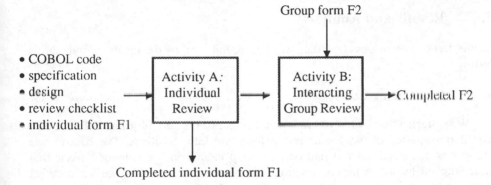

Figure 2: Experimental Procedure

Activity A lasted fifty minutes. Each subject collected a package of the instructions and materials needed to carry out activity A. Then they were randomly seated, well spaced between adjacent subjects. Subjects independently reviewed the code, with the aid of supporting documents (checklist, specification, and design) which were reused for activity B. Subjects were reminded to mark on the piece of code the defects they found so that they could discuss them with their group members during activity B. At the end of activity A, form F1 was collected.

Activity B involved subjects working in groups of three. Group members were not assigned any specific roles, with the exception of the inspector (all members were inspectors) and recorder[2] (chosen by group members). Activity B lasted only about thirty minutes, although it was planned for forty-five minutes to one hour. This was because some subjects began to leave after thirty minutes. Our observation was that

---

[2] The main job of the recorder (in addition to being the inspector) is to record each defect found by the group.

most groups however did appear to have finished after about twenty minutes. This is essential because we did not want the group data to be confounded by the lack of time to complete the task.

In another experiment where we introduced a more disciplined approach to the meeting process, meetings lasted for about 50 minutes (Lau et al 1997). This experiment by contrast imposed no specific constraints on the group process and as such it is not surprising that the meeting duration was shorter. While it would have been desirable to collect data on actual group processes, it was not possible to do so for such a large sample.

Two of the authors and a volunteer colleague were present throughout the experiment to ensure its smooth conduct. In both activities, students were told to feel free to raise any questions about anything they were not clear about. Each activity required the completion of an individual form (F1) and a group form (F2) respectively, where the individual or group reported on the details of each defect found (description, location). Each subject also reported on their experience in commercial programming and reviews.

4.   Results and Analysis

In this section, we discuss how data was coded, followed by the results of hypothesis testing.

4.1.   Data Coding

We collected and coded 101 individual defect forms and 34 group defect forms. The data consisted of two kinds: true defects and false positives. The data of one group was discarded since it had only 2 group members. We counted defects that were implied by the defect descriptions. Sometimes even within the same defect form, duplicate defects were reported. In that case, we counted multiple identifications of the same defect once only. Syntax errors and unclear descriptions were discarded (see section 3.1.1). Hence only true defects and false positives were coded and analysed.

4.2.   Results of Hypotheses

Table 1 summarises the means and standard deviations for all the dependent variables. Table 2 summarises the results of the statistical testing performed for each hypothesis. We used the paired t-test to test all our hypotheses because each dependent variable has these properties: the same number of values derived from the same population (i.e. 33), ratio scales and normal distributions. Normality of data was tested using the Kolmogorov-Smirnov statistic with a Lilliefors significance level. For each variable, the significance level was large enough that it was not unreasonable to assume normal distribution. Furthermore, all the hypotheses specify a direction (i.e. some variable is greater or less than another) and hence the one-tailed test was used (Norušis 1995).

	N	Mean	S. D.
Average Individual (AI)	33		
true defect		5.51	1.79
false positive		3.13	1.66
net defect		2.37	2.21
Interacting Group (IG)	33		
true defect		7.76	2.86
false positive		2.85	2.39
net defect		4.91	3.76
Nominal Group (NG)	33		
true defect		11.91	3.22
false positive		8.64	4.70
net defect		3.27	4.91

Table 1: Means and Standard Deviations of the Dependent Variables

Hypotheses	Results
H1.1: IG outperforms AI in true defects.	p=0.000 (1-tail sig. level)
H1.2: IG outperforms AI in net defects.	p=0.001 (1-tail sig. level)
H2.1: NG outperforms IG in true defects.	p=0.000 (1-tail sig. level)
H2.2: IG finds fewer false positives than NG.	p=0.000 (1-tail sig. level)
H2.3: IG and NG findings differ in net defects.	p=0.036 (2-tail sig. level)

Table 2: Results of Hypothesis Testing

Results of Interacting Group versus Average Individual: Hypotheses 1.1 and 1.2

Hypothesis 1.1 asserts that interacting groups report more true defects than the average individual reviewer. This hypothesis is supported; interacting groups (mean 7.76) significantly outperform the average individual (mean 5.51) by an average of 29% (observed significance level < 0.05). This result is consistent with other results on the performance advantage of groups over individuals (Yetton and Bottger 1982).

Hypothesis 1.2 asserts that interacting groups report more net defects than the average individual reviewer. This hypothesis is supported; interacting groups (mean 4.91) significantly outperform the average individual reviewer (mean 2.37) by an average of 52% (observed significance level < 0.05).

Therefore, interacting groups do outperform the average individual whether or not false positives are taken into account.

Results of Interacting versus Nominal Groups : Hypotheses 2.1 to 2.3

Hypothesis 2.1 asserts that nominal groups report more true defects than interacting groups. This hypothesis is supported; nominal groups (mean 11.91) significantly outperform interacting groups (mean 7.76) by an average of 35% (observed significance level < 0.05). Hence while interacting groups do outperform the average individuals (Hypotheses 1.1 to 1.2), they do not outperform nominal groups in true defects.

Hypothesis 2.2 asserts that interacting groups report fewer false positives than nominal groups. This hypothesis is supported; interacting groups (mean 2.85) significantly outperform nominal groups (mean 8.64) by an average of 67% (observed significance level < 0.05). Although nominal groups outperform interacting groups in terms of true defects (Hypothesis 2.1), interacting groups appear to have the ability to filter out false positives through interaction.

Hypothesis 2.3 asserts that the net defect score reported by interacting groups is not the same as that of nominal groups. This hypothesis is supported; interacting groups (mean 4.91) outperform nominal groups (mean 3.27) by an average of 33% (observed significance level < 0.05). While nominal groups report more true defects (hypothesis 2.1), interacting groups still find more net defects than nominal groups. Hence all our hypotheses were supported.

5.   Discussion and Conclusion

Our results have demonstrated the effectiveness of interacting groups over an individual selected at random. Hence the normative assumption that groups have a performance advantage over individuals is valid.

Next, we showed that the source of an interacting group's advantage is not in finding true defects. The number of new defects first reported by interacting groups (meeting gain) is low, in the range 0 to 4 inclusive, with an average of 0.67 defects. The majority of defects is found in the individual review phase. This result is consistent with other SDTR research (Eick et al 1992, Votta 1993, Porter et al 1995) which reported insignificant meeting gains. Hence this finding discounts the importance of synergy as a source of interacting group advantage contrary to common belief.

In addition, we have also shown that process loss occurs with interacting groups. That is, there are defects discovered by individuals which are not included in the group findings. This is again consistent with both the SDTR and behavioural literatures.

Having ruled out the source of an interacting group's performance advantage in the detection of true defects, we found the performance advantage lies in the interacting group's ability to discriminate between true defects and false positives, thereby filtering out some of the incorrect solutions previously reported by individuals. This finding is new and significant. Previous work in this area has not taken into account false positives when considering net meeting performance (it has only considered the difference between meeting gain and loss in terms of true defects) (Porter and Votta 1994, Porter et al 1995, Lanubile and Visaggio 1996, Siy 1996). This result also supports Johnson et al (1996) who found that nominal groups reported a significantly greater percentage of false positives than those working in real groups when using computer-mediated review software.

Our data is consistent with Siy's (1996) work in terms of false positive findings. We found 26.9% false positives with student subjects, and Siy (1996) found 22% with professional developers, indicating that false positives are not an insignificant issue in practice. Note that in the calculation of net defects, we have opted for unit weighting of both true defects and false positives. This might not be a true reflection of their relative importance. Future research should investigate this further in an industrial setting.

We have also demonstrated that nominal groups are better than interacting groups in finding true defects. Nominal group reviews appear to be an attractive option as an alternative review design, if false positives are not a significant issue in practice. This has practical implications for how software reviews are organised.

Furthermore, we have also shown that although process loss occurs in interacting groups, it is more than compensated for by their ability to discriminate true defects from false positives. So although nominal groups do not suffer from process loss, but because they do not have any provision for defect discrimination, interacting groups still have a performance advantage over nominal groups in terms of net defects.

As process loss has been observed in this and other experiments, future research should investigate its causes and seek ways to reduce it. Possible causes include the fallibility of the recorder and the lack of a disciplined approach to the meeting.

Our results confirm that the two stage defect detection task model used is sound. Although it may not prove to be the only model for reviews, it nevertheless gives us a framework on which to further build our knowledge of SDTRs.

Acknowledgements

We would like to thank all out experimental subjects, and Dr. John D'ambra for allowing time in his classes. Our special thanks to our colleague Benjamin Cheng who kindly helped us conduct the experiment. Finally, we would also like to acknowledge the efforts of our two COBOL experts, John D'ambra and Brian Watts, who gave us invaluable suggestions in setting up the review code.

References

Basili, V. R., Green, S., Laitenberger, O. U., Lanubile, F., Shull, F., Sorumgaard, S., Zelkowitz, M. V., The Empirical Investigation of Perspective-Based Reading, *Journal of Empirical Software Engineering*, 1(2), 1996.

Bottger, P. C., Yetton, P. W., Improving Group Performance by Training in Individual Problem Solving, *Journal of Applied Psychology*, 42, 234-249, 1988.

Eick, S. G., Loader, C. R., Long, M. D., Votta, L. G., Wiel, S. V., Estimating Software Fault Content Before Coding, *14th Proceedings International Conference on Software Engineering*, 59-65, May 11-15, 1992.

Fagan, M. E., Design and Code Inspections to Reduce Errors in Program Development, *IBM Systems Journal*, 15(3), 1976.

Freedman, D. P., Weinberg, G. M., *Handbook of Walkthroughs, Inspections, and Technical Reviews: Evaluating Programs, Projects, and Products*, Third Edition, Dorset House Publishing, 353 West 12th St., New York, NY 10014, 1990.

Gilb, T., Graham, D., *Software Inspection*, Addison-Wesley, 1993.

Jelinski, Z., Moranda, P. B., Applications of a Probability-Based Model to a Code Reading Experiment, *IEEE Symposium on Computer Software Reliability*, New York City, 1973.

Johnson, P. M., Tjahjono, D., Assessing Software Review Meetings: A Controlled Experimental Study Using CSRS, *Technical Report 96-06, Department of Information and Computer Sciences, University of Hawaii*, Honolulu, HI, 96734, USA, 1996.

Judd , C. M., Smith, E. R., Kidder, L. H., *Research Methods in Social Relations*, Sixth Edition, Harcourt Bruce Jovanovich College Publishers, 1991.

Kamsties, E., Lott, C., An Empirical Evaluation of Three Defect Detection Techniques, *Proceedings of 5th European Software Engineering Conference*, September 1995.

Kim, L. P. W., Sauer, C., Jeffery, R., A Framework of Software Development Technical Reviews, *Software Quality and Productivity: Theory, Practice, Education and Training*, Edited by Matthew Lee, Ben-Zion Barta, Peter Juliff, Chapman and Hall, 294-299, IFIP 1995.

Knight, J. C., Myers, A. N., An Improved Inspection Technique, *Communications of the ACM*, 36(11), November 1993.

Lanubile, F., Visaggio, G., Assessing Defect Detection Methods for Software Requirements Inspections Through External Replication, *International Software Engineering Research Network, Technical report ISERN-96-01*, January 1996.

Lau, L. P. W., Sauer, C., Jeffery, R., Validating the Defect Detection Performance Advantage of Group Designs for Software Reviews: Report of a Replicated Experiment, *Centre for Advanced Empirical Software Research Technical Report 96/8*, The University of New South Wales, 1997.

Lorge, I., Fox, D., Davitz, L, Brenner, M., A Survey of Studies Contrasting the Quality of Group Performance and Individual Performance, *Psychological Bulletin*, 55, 337-371, 1958.

McCarthy, P., Porter, A., Harvey, S., Votta, L., An Experiment to Assess Cost-Benefits of Inspection Meetings and their Alternatives: A Pilot Study, *Proceedings of the Third International Software Metrics Symposium, Berlin*, Germany, March 25-26 1996.

Myers, G. J., A Controlled Experiment in Program Testing and Code Walkthroughs/Inspections, *Communications of ACM*, 21(9), September 1978.

Norušis, M. J., *SPSS: SPSS 6.1 Guide to Data Analysis*, Prentice Hall, Englewood, New Jersey 07632, 1995.

Parnas, D. L., Weiss, D. M., Active Design Reviews: Principles and Practices, *The Journal of Systems and Software*, 7, 259-265, 1987.

Porter, A. A., Votta, L. G., An Experiment to Assess Different Defect Detection Methods for Software Requirements Inspections, *Proceedings of the Sixteenth International Conference on Software Engineering*, Sorrento, Italy, May 1994.

Porter, A. A., Votta, L. G., Basili, V. R., Comparing Detection Methods for Software Requirements Inspections: A Replicated Experiment, *IEEE Transactions on Software Engineering*, 21(6), 563-575, June 1995.

Sauer, C., Jeffery, R., Lau, L. P. W., Yetton, P., A Behaviourally Motivated Programme for Empirical Research into Software Development Technical Reviews, *Technical Report 96/5, Centre for Advanced Empirical Software Research, School of Information Systems, University of New South Wales*, Sydney 2052, 1996.

Schneider G. M., Martin, J., Tsai, W. T., An Experimental Study of Fault Detection in User Requirements Documents, *ACM Transactions on Software Engineering and Methodology*, 1(2), April 1992.

Shaw, M. E., *Group Dynamics: The Psychology of Small Group Behaviour*, Third Edition, McGraw-Hill Publishing Company, 1981.

Siy, H. P., *Identifying the Mechanisms Driving Code Inspection Costs and Benefits*, PhD Dissertation, 1996.

Steiner , I. D., *Group Process and Productivity*, Academic Press, New York, 1972.

Strauss, R. G., Ebenau, R. G., *Software Inspection Process*, McGraw-Hill, Inc., 1994.

Votta, L. G., Does Every Inspection Need a Meeting, *Proceedings of the ACM SIGSOFT*, Symposium on Foundations of Software Engineering, December, 1993.

Welburn, T., *Structured COBOL: Fundamentals and Style*, Mayfield Publishing Company, Mitchell Publishing. INC., 1981.

Yetton, P. W., Bottger, P. C., Individual Versus Group Problem Solving: an Experimental Test of a Best-Member Strategy, *Organizational Behavior and Human Performance*, 307-321, June 1982.

Yourdon, E., *Structured Walkthrough*, Fourth Edition, Prentice-Hall, 1989.

Integration of Sequential Scenarios*

Jules Desharnais[1], Marc Frappier[2], Ridha Khédri[1], and Ali Mili[3]

[1] Département d'informatique, Université Laval, Québec, QC, G1K 7P4 Canada,
Jules.Desharnais@ift.ulaval.ca, Ridha.Khedri@ift.ulaval.ca
[2] Département de mathématiques et d'informatique, Université de Sherbrooke,
Sherbrooke, QC, J1K 2R1, Canada, Marc.Frappier@dmi.usherb.ca
[3] Department of Computer Science, University of Ottawa,
Ottawa, ON, K1N 6N5, Canada, amili@csi.uottawa.ca

Abstract. We give a formal relation-based definition of scenarios and
we show how different scenarios can be integrated to obtain a more global
view of user-system interactions. We restrict ourselves to the *sequential*
case, meaning that we suppose that there is only one user (thus, the
scenarios we wish to integrate cannot occur concurrently). Our view of
scenarios is state-based, rather than event-based, like most of the other
approaches, and can be grafted to the well-established specification language **Z**. Also, the end product of scenario integration, the specification
of the functional aspects of the system, is given as a relation; this specification can be refined using independently developed methods. Our
formal description is coupled with a diagram-based, transition-system
like, presentation of scenarios, which is better suited to communication
between clients and specifiers.
Keywords: Scenario, integration, user-system interaction, requirements
elicitation, relational approach, state-based approach.

1   Introduction

The generally accepted meaning [1,7,8,15,18,19,21,24,31,33] of the term *scenario*
is that it is a partial description of the interaction between a user and a computer
system. As such, scenarios have a variety of uses [1,7,8]. Our purpose in using
scenarios is to support requirements elicitation and specification generation.

Traditionally, scenarios have been discussed and used in informal terms, although a number of formal definitions have been proposed recently. Hsia et
al. [19], Kawashita [21], Lustman [25] and Somé et al. [33] use finite automata to
represent scenarios, while Glinz [15] advocates the use of statecharts [16,17] to
this effect; also, Rubin and Goldberg [31] and Dardenne et al. [10] use pre- and
post-conditions on the operations of objects involved in scenarios. In addition to
its traditional benefits, the use of formal methods to specify scenarios offers us
the ability to define the concept of scenario integration, whereby partial scenarios can be combined to produce more global descriptions of the system that we

---

* This research is supported by FCAR (Fonds pour la Formation de Chercheurs et
l'Aide à la Recherche, Québec) and NSERC (Natural Sciences and Engineering Research Council of Canada).

wish to specify [15,21,33]. Formalizing scenarios does not mean rejecting informal scenarios; it simply offers the possibility to move from the informal to the formal at the level of scenarios rather than at the level of the system specification.

Section 2 contains the relational foundations of the approach. Section 3 presents a formal relation-based definition of scenarios, together with a description of an associated diagram-based view of scenarios, better suited to communication between clients and specifiers [15]. Section 4 follows with the definition of integration. Section 5 concludes with a discussion of completeness issues, a comparison with other approaches, and prospects for future developments.

2 Relations

The relational concepts needed to define scenarios and their integration are elementary and can be found in any textbook on dicrete mathematics. Nevertheless, we briefly recall the necessary notions. For more advanced material on relations, see [6,32].

Definition 1. A relation R on a set T is a subset of the cartesian product of T with itself, that is, $R \subseteq T \times T$. Among the possible operations on relations, we select the following[1]:

$$
\begin{aligned}
\text{Union} \quad Q \cup R &\triangleq \{(s, s') \mid (s, s') \in Q \vee (s, s') \in R\} \ , \\
\text{Intersection} \quad Q \cap R &\triangleq \{(s, s') \mid (s, s') \in Q \wedge (s, s') \in R\} \ , \\
\text{Empty relation} \quad \emptyset &\triangleq \{(s, s') \mid \mathsf{false}\} \ , \\
\text{Identity relation} \quad I &\triangleq \{(s, s') \mid s' = s\} \ , \\
\text{Domain} \quad \mathrm{dom}(R) &\triangleq \{s \mid \exists s' : (s, s') \in R\} \ , \\
\text{Range} \quad \mathrm{rng}(R) &\triangleq \{s \mid \exists s' : (s', s) \in R\} \ , \\
\text{Demonic meet} \quad Q \sqcap R &\triangleq (Q \cap R) \\
& \cup \{(s, s') \mid s \notin \mathrm{dom}(R) \wedge (s, s') \in Q\} \\
& \cup \{(s, s') \mid s \notin \mathrm{dom}(Q) \wedge (s, s') \in R\} \ , \\
& \text{defined if } \mathrm{dom}(Q) \cap \mathrm{dom}(R) = \mathrm{dom}(Q \cap R) \ .
\end{aligned}
$$

The name of the demonic meet comes from the fact that it is the meet operator of a refinement semilattice used to give a so-called *demonic semantics* to programming languages [5,11,12]. This is a partial operator; the definedness condition $\mathrm{dom}(Q) \cap \mathrm{dom}(R) = \mathrm{dom}(Q \cap R)$ means that, for any argument in their common domain, Q and R must agree on at least one result. Thus, for instance,

$$
Q \triangleq \{(0,3), (0,4), (1,5)\} \quad \text{and} \quad R \triangleq \{(0,3), (0,6), (2,5)\}
$$

satisfy the condition because, on their common domain ($\{0\}$), they agree on result 3. This is not the case for

$$
Q \triangleq \{(0,3), (0,4), (1,5)\} \quad \text{and} \quad R \triangleq \{(0,5), (0,6), (2,5)\} \ .
$$

---

[1] The symbols used in these equations are: $\triangleq$ (equality by definition), $\vee$ (disjunction), $\wedge$ (conjunction) and $\exists$ (existential quantifier).

When $Q \sqcap R$ is defined, $\mathrm{dom}(Q \sqcap R) = \mathrm{dom}(Q) \cup \mathrm{dom}(R)$. Note that $\mathrm{dom}(Q) \cup \mathrm{dom}(R)$ can be partitioned into three disjoint subsets, namely $\mathrm{dom}(Q) \cap \mathrm{dom}(R)$, $\mathrm{dom}(Q) \setminus \mathrm{dom}(R)$ and $\mathrm{dom}(R) \setminus \mathrm{dom}(Q)$ (the operator $\setminus$ is set difference); this partition corresponds to the three terms in the expression of the demonic meet.

Let Id be a set of variable identifiers and $Values$ be a set of values. A *state* is a function $t : Id \to Values$. A *space* is a set of states. Typically, we define spaces by declarations of the form $x_1{:}D_1, \ldots, x_n{:}D_n$, where $D_1, \ldots, D_n$ are sets. Such a declaration defines a space T such that $Id = \{x_1, \ldots, x_n\}$, $Values = D_1 \cup \ldots \cup D_n$ and $t(x_1) \in D_1, \ldots, t(x_n) \in D_n$ for any $t \in T$. Assuming a fixed ordering of the variable identifiers, a state of $t \in T$ can be given as a tuple $(t_1, \ldots, t_n)$, instead of the longer form $t(x_1) = t_1, \ldots, t(x_n) = t_n$.

Let a space T be defined by the declarations $x{:}\mathbb{N}, y{:}\mathbb{Z}$, where $\mathbb{N}$ is the set of natural numbers and $\mathbb{Z}$ is the set of integers. An example of relation on T is

$$R \triangleq \{((x,y),(x',y')) \mid x' = x^2 \wedge y' = y - x\} \ .$$

We write such a relation under the abbreviated form

$$R = \{x' = x^2 \wedge y' = y - x\} \ ,$$

the convention being that unprimed variables refer to initial values and primed variables refer to final values.

Assume $x, y{:}\mathbb{N}$ and consider the following transition system:

While it is customary in automata theory to refer to vertices of transition systems as states, we will instead use the term *node*, in order to avoid confusion with our definition of state given above (which is consistent with traditional usage in model-oriented specifications [13,27,34]). Each node of the above transition system is labeled with a predicate constraining the state at this node (the predicate is defined by the conjunction of the conditions listed; thus, the predicate labeling the rightmost node is $x > 10 \wedge y < 20$). The arrows of the transition system are labeled with relations (when labeling transition systems with relations, we even omit "{}"). Each arrow determines a relation obtained by combining the label of the arrow with those of the origin and destination nodes. Thus, e.g., the arrow from the node labeled $x < 5$ to the node labeled $x = 5$ corresponds to the relation $\{x < 5 \wedge x' = 5 \wedge y' = x + 1\}$. The relation depicted by the transition system is the union of the relations corresponding to the arrows. For the transition system above, this relation is

$$\{ (x < 5 \wedge x' = 5 \wedge y' = x + 1) \vee (x = 5 \wedge x' < 5 \wedge y' = y)$$
$$\vee (x = 5 \wedge x' > 10 \wedge y' < 20 \wedge y' = y^2)\} \ .$$

Note that the predicates labeling the nodes are disjoint and thus uniquely identify a node. This means that the structure of the graph does not provide any intrinsic control information. Hence, iterating the above relation from a state with $x = 5$ leads to the same sequence of transformations on the variables x and y as starting from the node labeled $x = 5$ and following the arrows in the corresponding transition system. For this to be possible, it suffices that the predicates labeling the nodes be disjoint; the transition systems that we use in the sequel satisfy this constraint.

3 Scenarios

As mentioned in the introduction, a scenario is usually defined as a partial description of the interaction between a human user and a computer. More generally, we consider that a scenario is a partial description of the interaction between an unconstrained system, called *the environment* (a human user being a particular case) and a computer-based system (program), simply called *the system* in the sequel. A scenario indicates *possible actions* of the environment, together with the *desired reaction* of the system. Whence the following definition.

Definition 2. A *scenario* is a triple (T, R_e, R_s), where T is a space, and R_e and R_s are two disjoint relations on T (that is, $R_e \cap R_s = \emptyset$), called the *relation of the environment* and the *relation of the system*, respectively. The relation $R_e \cup R_s$ is called the *relation of the scenario*.

As a running example, we will describe part of a library system (inspired by work done in [13,15,18,21]). The user (the environment) is a library employee. The first scenario that we consider is about the checkout of a book. The informal description of this scenario, given by the client to the specifier, is the following:

The reader comes in. The system is in the initial state of the reader_serv menu. The user enters the name of the reader. If the system does not know this name, then the user either
1. switches to the registration menu or
2. goes back to the initial state of the reader_serv menu (and abandons the operation) or
3. reenters the name correctly.
If the system knows the reader's name, it asks whether the transaction is a checkout or the return of a document. The user may choose to return to the initial state of the reader_serv menu (abondoning the operation) or choose the checkout option. In the latter case, for each document that the reader wants to borrow, the system displays the list of books already loaned to the reader and asks for the code of the new document; the user then enters the code of the borrowed document, the system adds the document to the set of documents borrowed by the reader and also registers who the document is loaned to (so that it is possible to obtain the name of the borrower from a description of the document). The user finally returns the system to the initial state of the reader_serv menu.

From this informal requirement, the specifier determines that the following structures are needed for the formal description of the scenario:

1. A, a set of symbols (an alphabet). In what follows, A^+ denotes the set of nonempty finite sequences of elements of A, and $A^* \triangleq A^+ \cup \{\lambda\}$, where λ is the empty sequence.

2. C, a set of commands. It is assumed that $C \cap A^* = \emptyset$. Below, commands begin with the symbol '@'. These commands are given by the user to navigate the menus.

3. $Readers{:}\,\wp(A^+)$, the set of readers known to the system, where the symbol $\wp$ denotes the power set operator.

4. $r{:}A^+$, a variable used by the system to hold the name of a reader.

5. $Documents{:}\,\wp(A^+)$, the set of documents known to the system.

6. $Loaned\_to{:}\,Documents \mapsto Readers$, a partial function giving the reader a document is loaned to. If a document is not in the domain of $Loaned\_to$, it means that this document is not checked out.

7. $Borrowed\_by{:}\,Readers \rightarrow \wp(Documents)$, a total function giving the set of documents borrowed by a reader.

8. $i{:}A^* \cup C$, an input variable. It is set to a nonempty sequence by the user to transmit information to the system. The system resets it to λ by consuming it.

9. $o{:}A^*$, an output variable. It is set by the system to transmit information to the user. Table 1 displays various output messages, together with the abbreviations used in the sequel.

10. $M{:}A^+$, a variable giving the name of the current menu. It is set by the system.

Table 1. Output messages and their abbreviation

Abbreviations	Messages
name?	Enter the name of the reader
unk; name?	This name is unknown; enter the correct name
co, return?	Is the operation a checkout or a return?
address?	Enter the address
$Borrowed\_by(r)$; doc?	$\langle$List of documents borrowed by $r\rangle$ Enter new document
$Borrowed\_by(r)$; limit	$\langle$List of documents borrowed by $r\rangle$ Your limit is reached

The variables $Readers, r, Documents, Loaned\_to$ and $Borrowed\_by$ are *internal variables*, while i, o and M are *interface variables* of the system. Figure 1 is the transition-system view of this scenario. The nodes of this transition system are labeled with identifiers of the form E_i or S_i; they are also labeled with predicates giving the value of the interface variables at these nodes (e.g., for node E_0, this predicate is $M = $ reader_serv $\land\, i = \lambda \land o = $ name?). Note that the predicates labeling the nodes are all disjoint. To avoid cluttering the diagram, we have

315

adopted the convention that whenever an internal variable is not shown on the arc of a transition, then it is not changed by this transition. For example, the transition from node E_0 to node S_0 represents the relation

$$\{ \ M = \text{reader\_serv} \wedge i = \lambda \wedge o = \text{name?} \wedge M' = M \wedge i' \in A^+ \wedge o' = o$$
$$\wedge \ Readers' = Readers \wedge r' = r \wedge Documents' = Documents$$
$$\wedge \ Loaned\_to' = Loaned\_to \wedge Borrowed\_by' - Borrowed\_by\} \ .$$

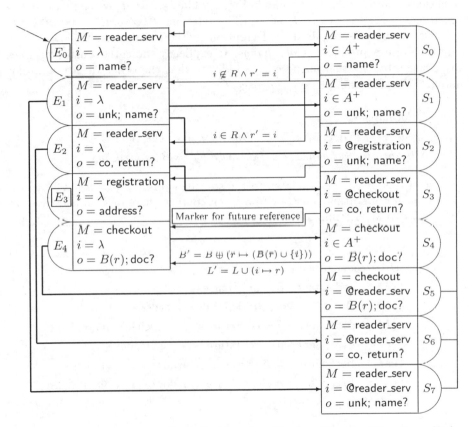

Fig. 1. Checkout scenario (R, B, L abbreviate *Readers, Borrowed_by, Loaned_to*)

At the nodes labeled E_i, the user has to provide some input to the system. As can be seen, the transitions leaving these E nodes affect variable i only. At the nodes labeled S_i, the system reacts to a user action by providing some output and/or changing the menu, by resetting the input to λ, and possibly by changing the value of some internal variable. For finite relations, one could use a different representation by a finite state machine, with transitions labeled by a pair (input of the environment, reaction of the system); however, for our purpose, it is better to represent the actions of the environment and those of the system by disjoint sets of transitions. The notation $(a \mapsto b)$ used in the diagram means the same thing as $\{(a, b)\}$. The notation $f \oplus (a \mapsto b)$, where f is a function, is the function f' defined by $f'(x) = f(x)$ if $x \neq a$ and $f'(a) = b$ (these are $\mathbf{Z}$ notations [13,34]).

The formal description of the Checkout scenario $(T_C, \textit{Checkout}_e, \textit{Checkout}_s)$ now follows. The space T_C is defined by the variables

$$\textit{Readers}, r, \textit{Documents}, \textit{Loaned\_to}, \textit{Borrowed\_by}, i, o, M,$$

whose description was given above. The relation $\textit{Checkout}_e$ corresponds to the transitions from E nodes to S nodes in Fig. 1, while $\textit{Checkout}_s$ corresponds to the transitions from S nodes to E nodes. The relations $\textit{Checkout}_e$ and $\textit{Checkout}_s$ are thus disjoint, as required by Definition 2; their definitions follow. These definitions use a predicate $\textit{OnlyChange}$. It explicitly indicates which variables may change, but its real purpose is to indicate that the other variables do not change. Thus, for example, on the space T_C,

$$\textit{OnlyChange}(M, i, o)$$
$$\Leftrightarrow \textit{Readers}' = \textit{Readers} \wedge r' = r \wedge \textit{Documents}' = \textit{Documents}$$
$$\wedge \textit{Loaned\_to}' = \textit{Loaned\_to} \wedge \textit{Borrowed\_by}' = \textit{Borrowed\_by} \ .$$

The use of this predicate is related to the so-called *frame problem* [4,26], which is the problem of stating succintly in a given context (here determined by a set of variables) that "nothing else changes".

$$\textit{Checkout}_e \tag{1}$$
$$\triangleq \{ (\ (M = \mathsf{reader\_serv} \wedge o = \mathsf{name?} \wedge i' \in A^+)$$
$$\vee (M = \mathsf{reader\_serv} \wedge o = \mathsf{unk; name?}$$
$$\wedge (i' \in A^+ \vee i' = @\mathsf{registration} \vee i' = @\mathsf{reader\_serv}))$$
$$\vee (M = \mathsf{reader\_serv} \wedge o = \mathsf{co, return?} \wedge i' = @\mathsf{checkout})$$
$$\vee (M = \mathsf{reader\_serv} \wedge o = \mathsf{co, return?} \wedge i' = @\mathsf{reader\_serv})$$
$$\vee (M = \mathsf{checkout} \wedge o = \textit{Borrowed\_by}(r); \mathsf{doc?} \wedge i' \in A^+)$$
$$\vee (M = \mathsf{checkout} \wedge o = \textit{Borrowed\_by}(r); \mathsf{doc?} \wedge i' = @\mathsf{reader\_serv}))$$
$$\wedge i = \lambda \wedge \textit{OnlyChange}(i)\}$$

$$\textit{Checkout}_s \tag{2}$$
$$\triangleq \{ (M = \mathsf{reader\_serv} \wedge i \in A^+ \wedge i' = \lambda \wedge r' = i \wedge \textit{OnlyChange}(i, o, r)$$
$$\wedge (o = \mathsf{name?} \vee o = \mathsf{unk; name?})$$
$$\wedge (\ (i \notin \textit{Readers} \wedge o' = \mathsf{unk; name?})$$
$$\vee (i \in \textit{Readers} \wedge o' = \mathsf{co, return?})))$$
$$\vee (M = \mathsf{reader\_serv} \wedge i = @\mathsf{registration} \wedge o = \mathsf{unk; name?}$$
$$\wedge M' = \mathsf{registration} \wedge i' = \lambda \wedge o' = \mathsf{address?} \wedge \textit{OnlyChange}(M, i, o))$$
$$\vee (M = \mathsf{reader\_serv} \wedge i = @\mathsf{checkout} \wedge o = \mathsf{co, return?}$$
$$\wedge M' = \mathsf{checkout} \quad \boxed{\text{Marker for future reference}}$$

$$\land\, i' = \lambda \land o' = \textit{Borrowed\_by}(r); \mathsf{doc}? \land \textit{OnlyChange}(M,i,o))$$
$$\lor\, (M = \mathsf{checkout} \land i \in A^+ \land o = \textit{Borrowed\_by}(r); \mathsf{doc}? \land i' = \lambda$$
$$\land\, \textit{Borrowed\_by}' = \textit{Borrowed\_by} \oplus (r \mapsto (\textit{Borrowed\_by}(r) \cup \{i\}))$$
$$\land\, \textit{Loaned\_to}' = \textit{Loaned\_to} \cup (i \mapsto r)$$
$$\land\, \textit{OnlyChange}(\textit{Loaned\_to}, \textit{Borrowed\_by}, i))$$
$$\lor\, (i = @\mathsf{reader\_serv}$$
$$\land\, (\;(M = \mathsf{checkout} \land o = \textit{Borrowed\_by}(r); \mathsf{doc}?)$$
$$\lor (M = \mathsf{reader\_serv} \land (o = \mathsf{co},\ \mathsf{return}? \lor o = \mathsf{unk};\ \mathsf{name}?)))$$
$$\land\, M' = \mathsf{reader\_serv} \land i' = \lambda \land o' = \mathsf{name}? \land \textit{OnlyChange}(M,i,o))\}$$

In Fig. 1, there is a small arrow pointing to node E_0; this indicates that E_0 is the initial node, as is clear from the narrative of the scenario given by the client. Note also that the identifiers E_0 and E_3 appear in a small box; this indicates that E_0 and E_3 are final nodes of the scenario. The notions of initial and final nodes are not part of the formal definition of scenarios (Definition 2), although they could. One possible usage of this information is assertion propagation. For example, starting from E_0 (or iterating relation $Checkout \overset{\triangle}{=} Checkout_e \cup Checkout_s$ from the corresponding initial states) and exploring all paths to S_6, it is clear that the assertion $r \in Readers$ holds in S_6. This assertion could be explicitly added to S_6 (and to $Checkout_s$), resulting in a relation with a smaller domain, thus leaving more freedom for refinement [5,12,14].

Thus, we have two equivalent views[2] of the Checkout scenario: the transition system view, better suited for communications between the client and the specifier, and the relation view, better suited for formal manipulations.

Note that the graph in Fig. 1 is bipartite: a transition from an E node goes to an S node and vice-versa. One may wonder whether this is the case for any scenario (T, R_e, R_s). A little thinking shows that this need not be the case. The transitions of the environment may be more detailed (e.g., showing the user going for a coffee), thus giving rise to transitions from E nodes to E nodes. Similarly, the behaviour of the system may be more detailed and show some internal transitions. This is probably not a good idea for top level scenarios (arising directly from requirements analysis), but it would be a natural view after some refinements have been carried out.

4 Scenario Integration

Given a set of scenarios, the goal of a specifier is to construct a global scenario integrating the partial scenarios, and to derive the specification of the system from this global scenario. In this section, we first give the definition of scenario integration. Then, we present another library scenario (loan refused because the reader has reached the limit number of books he is allowed to borrow) and we show how to integrate it with the Checkout scenario of the previous section.

---

[2] We have not described the equivalence formally, though.

Definition 3. Let R be a relation on a space T defined by $x_1:D_1,\ldots,x_m:D_m$. Let T' be a space defined by $x_1:D_1,\ldots,x_m:D_m,x_{m+1}:D_{m+1},\ldots,x_n:D_n$. The *expansion* of R to space T' is the relation

$$R\!\uparrow\! T' \triangleq \{((x_1,\ldots,x_m,x_{m+1},\ldots,x_n),(x'_1,\ldots,x'_m,x'_{m+1},\ldots,x'_n)) \mid$$
$$((x_1,\ldots,x_m),(x'_1,\ldots,x'_m)) \in R \wedge x'_{m+1} = x_{m+1} \wedge \ldots \wedge x'_n = x_n\} \ .$$

In other words, the expansion of R to T' is the same as R on the components of T and is the identity on the new components introduced by T'.

Definition 4. Let $S_Q \triangleq (T_Q,Q_e,Q_s)$ and $S_R \triangleq (T_R,R_e,R_s)$ be two scenarios and assume that $(q_1:A_1,\ldots,q_j:A_j,x_1:B_1,\ldots,x_k:B_k)$ are the declarations defining T_Q and that $(r_1:C_1,\ldots,r_l:C_l,x_1:D_1,\ldots,x_k:D_k)$ are those defining T_R (that is, the variables x_i are shared, the others are not). We say that T_Q and T_R are *compatible* if and only if $B_1 = D_1,\ldots,B_k = D_k$ (the shared variables have the same types).

Assume that T_Q and T_R are compatible and let T_P be the space defined by the declarations $(q_1:A_1,\ldots,q_j:A_j,x_1:B_1,\ldots,x_k:B_k,r_1:C_1,\ldots,r_l:C_l)$. The *integration* of S_Q and S_R, denoted by $S_Q \boxplus S_R$, is the scenario (T_P,P_e,P_s), where:

$$P_e \triangleq (Q_e\!\uparrow\! T_P) \cup (R_e\!\uparrow\! T_P) \ ,$$
$$P_s \triangleq (Q_s\!\uparrow\! T_P) \sqcap (R_s\!\uparrow\! T_P) \ .$$

If T_Q and T_R are not compatible or the demonic meet in the expression of P_s is not defined (Definition 1), then it is not possible to integrate S_Q and S_R.

The definition of compatibility could be relaxed; in fact, the declarations could be merged using rules similar to those of **Z** [13] for combining schemas.

The definition of scenario integration can be justified as follows. As in Definition 4, assume that the two scenarios are $S_Q \triangleq (T_Q,Q_e,Q_s)$ and $S_R \triangleq (T_R,R_e,R_s)$, and that $S_P \triangleq (T_P,P_e,P_s) \triangleq S_Q \boxplus S_R$. Before integrating the scenarios, they must be expanded to a common space, by means of an expansion that imposes to the added variables to preserve their value (if this expansion is not appropriate, it means that the original scenarios should be modified to explicitly indicate possible actions on the variables added by the expansion). Recall that a scenario is supposed to describe the possible actions of the environment (relations Q_e and R_e). Thus, scenario S_Q indicates that the actions described by Q_e are possible, and scenario S_R indicates that the actions described by R_e are possible. The relation P_e then simply indicates that the actions described by $(Q_e\!\uparrow\! T_P) \cup (R_e\!\uparrow\! T_P)$ are possible. In other words, integrating scenarios does not constrain the environment. As for integration of the system relations Q_s and R_s, there are two possible situations. Assume that $t \in T_P$:

1. If $t \notin \mathrm{dom}(Q_s\!\uparrow\! T_P)$ and $t \in \mathrm{dom}(R_s\!\uparrow\! T_P)$, this means that, as far as scenario S_Q is concerned, input t is not going to be submitted to the system. However, scenario S_R indicates that it could and specifies how it should be treated (relation R_s). This is why the integrated scenario S_P considers that t can

be submitted to the system, and that it should be treated according to R_s (by definition of $\sqcap$ (Definition 1)). The symmetric situation $t \in \text{dom}(Q_s \uparrow T_P)$ and $t \notin \text{dom}(R_s \uparrow T_P)$ is treated similarly.

2. If $t \in \text{dom}(Q_s \uparrow T_P)$ and $t \in \text{dom}(R_s \uparrow T_P)$, then both S_Q and S_R assert that t can be submitted to the system and they both specify what the reaction of the system should be. The integrated scenario S_P also asserts that t can be submitted to the system and specifies that the possible results must be possible according to both Q_s and R_s (by definition of $\sqcap$). If there is no such result, then the scenarios are contradictory and cannot be integrated.

More details on the use of the demonic meet operator for merging separate specifications can be found in [14]. Note that the operation $\boxplus$ is commutative and associative, by definition of $\cup$ and $\sqcap$, and by the way the space of the integrated scenario is defined.

We now present the Limit-reached scenario. Its informal description follows.

The reader comes in. The system is in the initial state of the reader_serv menu. The user inputs the name of the reader to the system. If the reader's name is known to the system, then the system asks whether the transaction is a checkout or the return of a document. The user chooses the checkout option. If the reader has reached his quota (limit number of books he is permitted to borrow), then the system displays the list of books already loaned to the reader and indicates that the limit is reached. The user then chooses to return to the initial state of the reader_serv menu.

From this description, the specifier determines that a new variable

$$Limit:Readers \rightarrow \mathbb{N}$$

is needed. For any reader $r \in Readers$, $Limit(r)$ is the maximum number of books that may be borrowed by r. Thus, the space T_L of the Limit-reached scenario is defined by the same declarations as that of the Checkout scenario, with the addition of the declaration of $Limit$ (the variable $Loaned\_to$ might be excluded from the space of T_L, since it is not needed; this would not change the result of the integration). The transition-system view of the Limit-reached scenario is given in Fig. 2. The expression $|B(r)|$ denotes the cardinality of the set $B(r)$. We have given the same identifiers to the nodes whose interface variables have the same value in both this scenario and the Checkout scenario of the previous section. These nodes will indeed be identified by the integration operation. However, it must be noted that the specifier should make sure that this is the desired effect (this is quite clear from the understanding we have of the application). If these nodes should not be identified, then another variable should be added to distinguish them (e.g., a variable related to a higher-level menu). The opposite problem might also arise: variables corresponding to the same concept could be given different names in different scenarios (e.g., $Menu$ instead of M). Again, it is the role of the specifier to detect these situations.

The relations $Limit_e$ and $Limit_s$ follow.

320

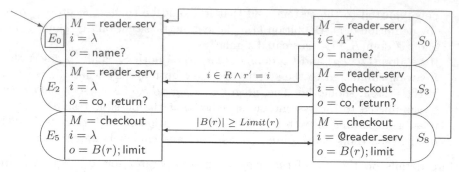

Fig. 2. Limit-reached scenario (R abbreviates *Readers*, B abbreviates *Borrowed_by*)

$Limit_e$ (3)
$$\triangleq \{\; (\; (M = \text{reader\_serv} \land o = \text{name?} \land i' \in A^+)$$
$$\lor (M = \text{reader\_serv} \land o = \text{co, return?} \land i' = @\text{checkout})$$
$$\lor (M = \text{checkout} \land o = Borrowed\_by(r); \text{limit} \land i' = @\text{reader\_serv}))$$
$$\land i = \lambda \land OnlyChange(i)\}$$

$Limit_s$ (4)
$$\triangleq \{\; (M = \text{reader\_serv} \land i \in Readers \land o = \text{name?}$$
$$\land r' = i \land i' = \lambda \land o' = \text{co, return?} \land OnlyChange(i, o, r))$$
$$\lor (M = \text{reader\_serv} \land i = @\text{checkout} \land o = \text{co, return?}$$
$$\land |Borrowed\_by(r)| \geq Limit(r) \land M' = \text{checkout}$$
$$\land i' = \lambda \land o' = Borrowed\_by(r); \text{limit} \land OnlyChange(M, i, o))$$
$$\lor (M = \text{checkout} \land i = @\text{reader\_serv} \land o = Borrowed\_by(r); \text{limit}$$
$$\land M' = \text{reader\_serv} \land i' = \lambda \land o' = \text{name?} \land OnlyChange(M, i, o))\}$$

Next, we proceed to give the result of the integration of the Checkout scenario with the Limit-reached scenario,

CheckoutLimit-reached   (5)
$$\triangleq (T_{CL}, CheckoutLimit_e, CheckoutLimit_s)$$
$$\triangleq (T_C, Checkout_e, Checkout_s) \boxplus (T_L, Limit_e, Limit_s) \quad .$$

The space T_{CL} of the integrated scenario CheckoutLimit-reached is that of the Limit-reached scenario (T_L), since the latter includes all the declarations of the Checkout scenario. Hence, $Limit_e{\uparrow}T_{CL} = Limit_e$ and $Limit_s{\uparrow}T_{CL} = Limit_s$. Even though $Checkout_e{\uparrow}T_{CL} \neq Checkout_e$ because their spaces are different, we can use for $Checkout_e{\uparrow}T_{CL}$ the same expression as for $Checkout_e$ (Equation 1). The reason is that the predicate $OnlyChange(i)$, on the expanded space T_{CL}, now includes the conjunct $Limit' = Limit$, giving the correct expansion.

$CheckoutLimit_e$

$=$ 　　　　⟨ Definition 4, Equation 5 and $Limit_e \!\uparrow\! T_{CL} = Limit_e$ ⟩

$(Checkout_e \!\uparrow\! T_{CL}) \cup Limit_e$

$=$ 　　　　⟨ Equations 1 and 3 ⟩

$\{\ (\ (M = \mathsf{reader\_serv} \land o = \mathsf{name?} \land i' \in A^+)$

　　$\lor\, (M = \mathsf{reader\_serv} \land o = \mathsf{unk;\ name?}$

　　　　$\land\, (i' \in A^+ \lor i' = @\mathsf{registration} \lor i' = @\mathsf{reader\_serv}))$

　　$\lor\, (M = \mathsf{reader\_serv} \land o = \mathsf{co,\ return?} \land i' = @\mathsf{checkout})$

　　$\lor\, (M = \mathsf{reader\_serv} \land o = \mathsf{co,\ return?} \land i' = @\mathsf{reader\_serv})$

　　$\lor\, (M = \mathsf{checkout} \land o = Borrowed\_by(r);\mathsf{doc?} \land i' \in A^+)$

　　$\lor\, (M = \mathsf{checkout} \land o = Borrowed\_by(r);\mathsf{doc?} \land i' = @\mathsf{reader\_serv})$

　　$\lor\, (M = \mathsf{checkout} \land o = Borrowed\_by(r);\mathsf{limit} \land i' = @\mathsf{reader\_serv}))$

$\land\, i = \lambda \land OnlyChange(i)\}$

However, the integration of the system relations is not possible, because the demonic meet of $Checkout_s$ and $Limit_s$ is not defined (see Equation 5 and Definitions 4 and 1). Indeed, one can check, using (2) and (4), that

$$\mathrm{dom}((Checkout_s \!\uparrow\! T_{CL}) \cap Limit_s) = \{M = \mathsf{reader\_serv} \land i \in Readers \land o = \mathsf{name?}\}$$

whereas

$$\mathrm{dom}(Checkout_s \!\uparrow\! T_{CL}) \cap \mathrm{dom}(Limit_s) \qquad\qquad (6)$$
$$= \{\ (M = \mathsf{reader\_serv} \land i \in Readers \land o = \mathsf{name?})$$
$$\lor\, (M = \mathsf{reader\_serv} \land i = @\mathsf{checkout} \land o = \mathsf{co,\ return?}$$
$$\land\, r \in Readers \land |Borrowed\_by(r)| \geq Limit(r))\}$$

(the condition $r \in Readers$ is explicitly added in this expression, although it need not be, since it is implied by the definition of the type of $Borrowed\_by$). The demonic meet is undefined because $Checkout_s$ and $Limit_s$ do not agree on a common output for the following subset of their common domain (Equation 6):

$\{M = \mathsf{reader\_serv} \land i = @\mathsf{checkout} \land o = \mathsf{co,\ return?}$

$\land\, r \in Readers \land |Borrowed\_by(r)| \geq Limit(r)\}$.

The relation $Checkout_s$ requires $o' = Borrowed\_by(r);\mathsf{doc?}$, whereas $Limit_s$ requires $o' = Borrowed\_by(r);\mathsf{limit}$. A verification with the client reveals that his Checkout scenario should include the constraint $|Borrowed\_by(r)| < Limit(r)$ on the transition from S_3 to E_4 (since it is not possible to borrow if the limit is reached). Hence, the words "Marker for future reference" in both Fig. 1 and Equation 2 should be replaced by "$|Borrowed\_by(r)| < Limit(r)$". This also leads to the addition of the variable $Limit$ to the space T_C. It then becomes clear that the Checkout scenario should not modify this variable; this is achieved by keeping the same expressions for $Checkout_e$ and $Checkout_s$ (Equations 1 and 2), since the predicate $OnlyChange$ enforces this constraint. Note that the expression given above for the relation $CheckoutLimit_e$ is still correct. After this modification,

$$\mathrm{dom}(\mathit{Checkout_s}) \cap \mathrm{dom}(\mathit{Limit_s})$$
$$= \{M = \mathsf{reader\_serv} \wedge i \in \mathit{Readers} \wedge o = \mathsf{name?}\}$$
$$= \mathrm{dom}(\mathit{Checkout_s} \cap \mathit{Limit_s}) \quad .$$

On this common domain, $\mathit{Checkout_s}$ and $\mathit{Limit_s}$ have the same images, defined by $r' = i \wedge i' = \lambda \wedge o' = \mathsf{co}$, return? $\wedge \; \mathit{OnlyChange}(i,o,r)$. Using Definition 1, one can check that under this condition,

$$\mathit{CheckoutLimit_s} = \mathit{Checkout_s} \sqcap \mathit{Limit_s} = \mathit{Checkout_s} \cup \mathit{Limit_s} \quad .$$

This is a simple calculation (similar to that of $\mathit{CheckoutLimit_e}$) and we do not present the result. The transition-system view of the CheckoutLimit-reached scenario is given in Fig. 3.

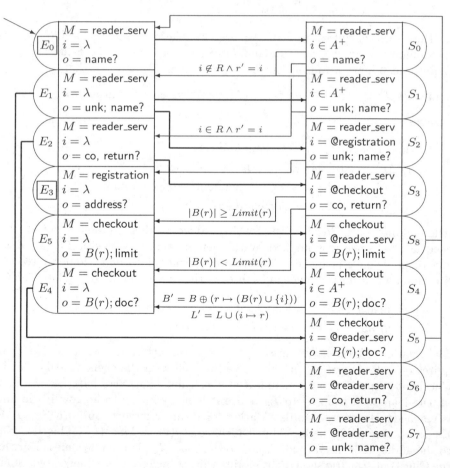

Fig. 3. Integration of the Checkout and Limit-reached scenarios (R, B, L abbreviate *Readers, Borrowed_by, Loaned_to*)

Suppose that the complete set of scenarios describing the environment-system interactions is $S_1, \ldots, S_n$ and let $S \triangleq (T, R_e, R_s) \triangleq S_1 \boxplus \ldots \boxplus S_n$. The *specification of the functional aspects of the system* is the relation R_s. Being a relation, this specification can be refined using independently developed methods [5,11,12,14,27–29]. Note however that R_s is not necessarily the whole specification of the computer system, but might be only part of it. For instance, the scenarios we have used as examples describe user actions at a fairly high level. They do not say how the code of a document or the name of a reader is submitted to the system (typing, optical reading, ...), or how a command is given (control key, menu choice, typing). These details could be made explicit by finer-grained scenarios; these would lead to the design of the user interface. Another aspect is the completeness of the specification R_s with respect to the treatment of possible inputs; this can be determined with the help of the environment relation R_e, since the latter provides the possible inputs.

5   Conclusion

We have described a relational approach to the integration of sequential scenarios, which are scenarios involving a single user. The integration is possible if a certain consistency condition (see Definition 4) is satisfied. In addition to consistency, completeness issues arise: when is the set of scenarios sufficiently large? This depends ultimately on the requirements, but our approach offers several opportunities for detecting possible sources of incompleteness.

1. The environment (the user) is free to do any possible action in a given state. Thus, from any E node (see Fig. 3), there should be a transition to an S node for any possible user action. For example, if the user selects menus with control keys, there should be a transition for the command @registration from every E node. If this is an illegal choice, then the system should answer by a beep to warn the user. The choice of illegal options can also be prevented by forcing the user to choose from a menu. Whatever the approach, the point is that from any E node, one should investigate the consequences of all possible user actions.

2. Every user action should provoke a reaction of the system or allow another user action (no deadlock). If the global scenario is (T, R_e, R_s), this requirement is written formally as $\text{rng}(R_e) \subseteq \text{dom}(R_e \cup R_s)$. The scenario of Fig. 3 does not satisfy this condition: because of the types of *Borrowed_by* and *Loaned_to*, the transition from node S_4 to node E_4 is possible only if $i \in Documents$. However, the user may submit an input $i \notin Documents$ (transition E_4–S_4). Either the user must be prevented from such an input or the system must react to it.

3. The condition $\text{rng}(R_s) \subseteq \text{dom}(R_e \cup R_s)$ should also be satisfied, except for the special case when the system has to terminate. That is, after an action of the system, the user or the system should be able to proceed for another action. Also, infinite loops of the system must be prevented. In this way, the system eventually gives control to the user.

The relational approach presented here is state-oriented and can be grafted to the well-established specification language **Z** [13,34], both for the description of data types and the specification of user-system interactions. This means that the approach integrates the treatment of data and functionality, which is also a major goal of Glinz in [15], whose formalization is based on statecharts [16,17]. Like [15], we can graphically depict the information in a form suitable for client-specifier communications. However, at the moment, this aspect is better developed in the case of statecharts. In particular, statecharts include a notation for concurrency, an issue we have not addressed in this paper; indeed, this is part of our future research. On the other hand, the relational approach allows us to integrate overlapping scenarios, a case forbidden in [15]. The closeness of the notation to that of **Z** means that it should be possible to use the tools that have been developed for **Z**. Of particular interest is the possibility to automatically discover inconsistencies due to undefined demonic meets when integrating scenarios. Although this is in general undecidable (because one has to calculate domains of relations), the relations used in most systems are simple enough for this goal to be achievable. Here, we could benefit of the work of Boiten et al. [3] on the integration of partial specifications in **Z**. Finally, we note that the graphical notation presented in this article is also used by Lamport [23] to associate a picture to a formula of the Temporal Logic of Actions (TLA [22]), another state-based formalism.

With respect to automata-based approaches [19,21,25,33], the relational approach distinguishes itself because data and complex conditions are naturally incorporated in the formalism. Conditions must be added to automata-based formalisms as extensions of the basic formalism (see, e.g., [33]). An advantage of automata-based specifications is the possibility to use a variety of model-checkers to validate their properties. But this is becoming possible with **Z** specifications, by reducing the size of the data types for validation purposes (for instance, simulating a library with only few books and few readers) [9]. Tools such as RELVIEW [2] could also be used for this purpose. Finally, we note that in [33], scenarios include timing constraints; we have not investigated this type of scenarios.

In addition to the treatment of concurrent scenarios, our future research will aim at improving the graphical presentation of scenarios. Complex scenarios could be abstracted as *procedure scenarios* that could be used as atomic entities in higher-level graphs; such a possibility of abstraction is inherently present in statecharts. A capability of abstraction is necessary if the approach is to scale up to systems mith a large number of variables and components. Parnas' tabular representations [20,30] could also be used to foster the systematic analysis of completeness issues. These improvements can be done while keeping the underlying relational representation, which brings rigour in the construction of scenarios and comes with laws for the refinement of system specifications [12,14,27–29].

Acknowledgements

The authors thank the anonymous referees for their helpful comments.

References

1. Benner, K. M., Feather, M. S., Johnson, W. L., Zorman, L. A.: Utilizing Scenarios in the Software Development Process. In Prakash, N., Rolland, C. and Pernici, B., Editors, Information System Development Process, Elsevier Science Publisher B. V., North-Holland (1993) 117–134
2. Berghammer, R., Schmidt, G.: The RELVIEW-System. In Choffrut, C. and Jantzen, M., Editors, STACS 91, 8th Annual Symp. on Theoretical Aspects of Computer Science (Feb. 1991) Hamburg, Germany, Lect. Notes in Comp. Sci. 480, Springer, 535–536
3. Boiten, E., Derrick, J., Bowman, H., Steen, M.: Consistency and Refinement for Partial Specification in Z. In Gaudel, M. C. and Woodcock, J., Editors, FME'96: Industrial Benefit of Formal Methods, 3rd Int. Symp. of Formal Methods Europe, Lect. Notes in Comp. Sci. 1051, Springer (Mar. 1996) 287–306
4. Borgida, A., Mylopoulos, J., Reiter, R.: "...And Nothing Else Changes": The Frame Problem in Procedure Specifications. 15th IEEE Int. Conf. on Software Engineering (May 1993) Baltimore, MD, 303–314
5. Boudriga, N., Elloumi, F., Mili, A.: On the Lattice of Specifications: Applications to a Specification Methodology. Formal Aspects of Computing 4 (1992) 544–571
6. Brink, C., Kahl, W., Schmidt, G., Editors: Relational Methods in Computer Science. Springer (1997)
7. Campbell, R. L.: Will the Real Scenario Please Stand Up? ACM SIGCHI Bulletin 24, 2 (Apr. 1992) 6–8
8. Campbell, R. L.: Categorizing Scenarios: A Quixotic Quest? ACM SIGCHI Bulletin 24, 4 (Oct. 1992) 16–17
9. Damon, C. A., Jackson, D., Jha, S.: Checking Relational Specifications with Binary Decision Diagrams. ACM SIGSOFT Software Engineering Notes 21, 6 (Nov. 1990) 70–80
10. Dardenne, A., van Lamsweerde, A., Fickas, S.: Goal-Directed Requirements Acquisition. Sci. Comput. Programming 20 (1993) 3–50
11. Desharnais, J., Belkhiter, N., Ben Mohamed Sghaier, S., Tchier, F., Jaoua, A., Mili, A., Zaguia, N.: Embedding a Demonic Semilattice in a Relation Algebra. Theoret. Comput. Sci. 149, 2 (Oct. 1995) 333–360
12. Desharnais, J., Mili, A., Nguyen, T. T.: Refinement and Demonic Semantics. In Brink et al. [6], chapter 11, 166–183.
13. Diller, A.: Z: An Introduction to Formal Methods. John Wiley & Sons (1990)
14. Frappier, M., Mili, A., Desharnais, J.: Program Construction by Parts. Sci. Comput. Programming 26, 1–3 (May 1996) 237–254
15. Glinz, M.: An Integrated Formal Model of Scenarios Based on Statecharts. In Fifth European Software Engineering Conference (1995) Lect. Notes in Comp. Sci. 989, Springer, 254–271
16. Harel, D.: Statecharts: A Visual Formalism for Complex Systems. Sci. Comput. Programming 8 (1987) 231–274
17. Harel, D.: On Visual Formalisms. Comm. ACM 31, 5 (May 1988) 514–530
18. Holbrook III, H.: A Scenario-Based Methodology for Conducting Requirements Elicitation. ACM SIGSOFT Software Engineering Notes 15, 1 (Jan. 1990) 95–104
19. Hsia, P., Samuel, J., Gao, J., Kung, D., Toyoshima, Y., Chen, C.: Formal Approach to Scenario Analysis. IEEE Software 11, 2 (Mar. 1994) 33–41
20. Janicki, R., Parnas, D. L., Zucker, J.: Tabular Representations in Relational Documents. In Brink et al. [6], chapter 12, 184–196.

21. Kawashita, I.: Spécification Formelle de Systèmes d'Information Interactifs par la Technique des Scénarios. Master's thesis, Département d'informatique et de recherche opérationnelle, Université de Montréal, Montréal (Nov. 1996)

22. Lamport, L.: The temporal logic of actions. ACM Transactions on Programming Languages and Systems **16** (May 1994) 872–923

23. Lamport, L.: TLA in Pictures. IEEE Transactions on Software Engineering **21**, 9 (Sep. 1995) 768–775

24. Lubars, M., Potts, C., Richter, C.: Developing Initial OOA Models. In 15th IEEE International Conf. on Software Engineering (1993) 255–264

25. Lustman, F.: A Formal Approach to Scenario Integration. Annals of Software Engineering, to appear

26. McCarthy, J., Hayes, P.: Some Philosophical Problems from the Standpoint of Artificial Intelligence. In Melzter, B. and Michie, D., Editors, Machine Intelligence **4**, Edinburgh University Press (1969) 463–502

27. Mili, A.: A Relational Approach to the Design of Deterministic Programs. Acta Informatica **20** (1983) 315–328

28. Mili, A., Desharnais, J., Mili, F.: Relational Heuristics for the Design of Deterministic Programs. Acta Informatica **24**, 3 (1987) 239–276

29. Mili, A., Desharnais, J., Mili, F.: Computer Program Construction. Oxford University Press, New York, NY (1994)

30. Parnas, D. L., Madey, J., Iglewski, M.: Precise Documentation of Well-Structured programs. IEEE Transactions on Software Engineering **20**, 12 (Dec. 1994) 948–976

31. Rubin, K. S., Goldberg, A.: Object Behavior Analysis. Comm. ACM **35**, 9 (Sep. 1992) 48–62

32. Schmidt, G., Ströhlein, T.: Relations and Graphs, Discrete Mathematics for Computer Scientists. EATCS-Monographs on Theoretical Computer Science, Springer (1993)

33. Somé, S., Dssouli, R., Vaucher, J.: From Scenarios to Timed Automata: Building Specifications from Users Requirements. In 2nd Asia Pacific Software Engineering Conference (1995)

34. Spivey, J. M.: Understanding Z: A Specification Language and its Formal Semantics, Cambridge Tracts in Theoret. Computer Science 3, Cambridge Univ. Press, UK (1988)

A View-Oriented Approach to System Modelling Based on Graph Transformation*

Gregor Engels[1], Reiko Heckel[2], Gabi Taentzer[2], Hartmut Ehrig[2]

[1] Leiden University, Dept. of Computer Science, P.O. Box 9512, NL-2300 RA Leiden,
The Netherlands
engels@wi.leidenuniv.nl
[2] Technical University of Berlin, Dept. of Computer Science, Franklinstrasse 28/29,
D-10587 Berlin, Germany
{ehrig, reiko, gabi}@cs.tu-berlin.de

Abstract. The idea of a combined reference model- and view-based specification approach has been proposed recently in the software engineering community. In this paper we present a specification technique based on graph transformations which supports such a development approach. The use of graphs and graph transformations supports an intuitive understanding and an integration of static and dynamic aspects on a well-defined semantical base. On this background, formal notions of view and view relation are developed and the behaviour of views is described by a loose semantics. We define a construction for automatic view integration which assumes that the dependencies between different views are described by a reference model. The views and the reference model are kept consistent manually, which is the task of a model manager. All concepts and results are illustrated at the well-known example of a banking system.

keywords specification language, view, viewpoint, view integration, software process, graph transformation systems

1 Introduction

The most challenging issue of software engineering still is the question how to master the complexity of the development of large software systems. Currently, a variety of approaches try to solve certain aspects of this problem.

One important approach is to reuse well-established pieces of specifications, documentations, and/or software, while developing a new system. While in the beginning the reuse idea was restricted to often needed classes, in the meantime it has become clear that reuse should be tackled on a much greater scale by specialising integrated networks of classes, so-called frameworks [LRP+96].

* Research partially supported by the German Research Council (DFG), the TMR network GETGRATS, and the ESPRIT Basic Research Working Group APPLIGRAPH

Thus, a major research as well as development field is currently the definition of frameworks for various application domains.

Another important approach is based on the observation that, due to the size and the diversity of the planned software system, teams of concurrently working application engineers are needed for the realisation of a software system. For instance, during the requirements specification phase, a team of application engineers with different skills and backgrounds is splitted into subgroups. Each subgroup specifies only that aspect of an interactive software system, which is later seen and used by a certain type of user (role). Thus, modularisation concepts are required, which allow to compose a complete and consistent specification out of possibly overlapping pieces.

In the data base world, but also in the field of software and requirements engineering, one way to obtain this modularisation is the concept of views and view integration. In the data base world it is standard to distinguish between a conceptual model and several external models, which are considered to be individual views of the data base. Each view is a restriction of the conceptual model - the total community user view - to just that portion of interest to that particular user (cf. [Dat79]).

In the software engineering field, the view-oriented approach is known by the notion of viewpoints (cf. [FKN+92]). In contrast to the view integration approach, here is no common integrated model intended. The basic idea is to monitor the relationships between different viewpoints, to detect inconsistencies and to resolve them by interactive support of the user. Relationships between different viewpoints are inferred by the use of common names.

This implies that the different application engineers agree on a certain vocabulary for a specific problem domain before they start to develop their own viewpoint. As all notions within a problem domain are somehow related, a more suited starting point than a long list of notions is a so-called reference model for a problem domain, where basic notions and their interrelations are fixed. This idea of a combined reference model- and view-based specification approach was especially proposed by B. Balzer during his keynote speech at SP'96 (Software Process) (cf. [Bal96]).

In this paper we present a specification technique based on graph transformations which supports such a development approach. We explain this approach informally in Section 2. In Section 3, 4, and 5 we present the formal base of our approach together with illustrating examples. The basic notions of graphs and graph transformation for the modelling of static and dynamic aspects of software systems are presented in Section 3. In Section 4 we give a definition for views of graph transformation systems. Since all different views are required to be based on a common reference model, we are able to present in Section 5 a general construction for view integration. This can be considered as an automatic view integration. Finally in Section 6 we summarise the main ideas and discuss some remaining open problems.

2 Concept of Views and View Integration Using Graph Transformations

Graph grammars and transformations have been introduced as a generalisation of Chomsky grammars on one hand and of term rewriting systems on the other hand about 25 years ago. Meanwhile there is a well-established theory of graph transformations (see e.g., [Roz97]) which has a number of applications to system modelling and software engineering (cf. [Nag96,Zam96,AE96,SWZ95]) based on concrete specification languages and supporting tools (cf. [Sch91,LB93]). The main idea of our specification approach is to model object structures and their interrelationships by graphs and modifying operations by graph transformations. In particular our approach is based on typed graph transformation systems [CEL+96,HCEL96,Rib96] which allow to define a set of graphs by a type (scheme) graph together with type-consistent operations on these graphs. Compared to currently popular object-oriented modelling techniques, typed graph transformation systems really support an integrated modelling of static and dynamic aspects, which goes much further than the use of common names. Nevertheless, it shall be noted that graph transformations in its pure form are not object-oriented. There are, however, class-based extensions (see e.g., [Tae96,Wag97]).

This paper applies typed graph transformation systems for defining the concept of a view that models a certain aspect of the complete system. Thus, a view specifies only partially the structure of the system's state and analogously only partially, what the effect of an operation is. It may be that a view operation, being executed on the system's state, has to be concurrently coupled with operations of other views to ensure a consistent system's state transition. Thus, a view specifies only what at least has to happen on a system's state. In this sense, the semantics of a view can only be a loose one, in contrast to the semantics of the complete model.

The overall specification approach can be sketched as follows (cf. Figure 1). Starting with a common reference model, each application engineer develops his

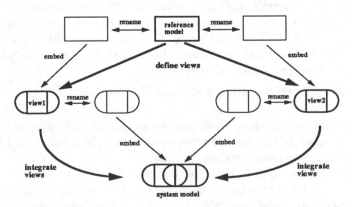

Fig. 1. A view-oriented approach to system modelling.

own viewpoint by extending and refining the reference model appropriately. In the case that different names for the same concept have been used, a renaming step has to be executed by the application engineer. We will explain later that technically spoken, a (partial) specification is called a view on another specification, if a renamed version of the first can be embedded into the second. In a following step, all these views have to be integrated or synchronised in a common system model. We will show in this paper that by following our specification approach, this integration step can be done automatically. This is mainly due to the fact that we assume that the definition of all views is based on the same common reference model.

This basic assumption is in line with above mentioned current approaches in the object-oriented world, where also reference models in the form of domain-specific frameworks are regarded as the desired starting point for any new software development project. But in addition and in contrast to such a framework-based specification approach, we allow that the framework (or reference model) is specialised concurrently by several views.

Following such a view-based specification approach, different forms of possible inconsistencies can be distinguished.

(i) The same concept, e.g. operation, is specified in two different views by using different names.

(ii) The same names are used in two different views denoting semantically different concepts.

In particular, the first form (i) of inconsistency has extensively been investigated in database research, as it is one of the problems which have to be solved during scheme integration (cf. [BLN86]). Instead of trying to identify dependencies between different names, we start with a common reference model of names and their interrelations. In the case that different views want to share the same name for the same concept and this name is not yet contained in the reference model, the reference model has to be extended. In this situation, a model manager is required who mediates between the different view designers and extends the reference model appropriately.

In the second case (ii), two solutions are possible: The two names are kept distinct within the overall specification (for instance, by qualifying them with the view name) or the two names are even rejected by the model manager.

While the above explained two forms of inconsistencies relate to static inconsistencies between specification documents, a third form of inconsistency may occur during executing (or enacting) the system.

(iii) Execution of a view operation violates the constraints defined by another view.

This means that two different views overlap in their specification of the desired system's behaviour. In this case, the two views have to be synchronised to achieve a consistent system's behaviour specification.

Different solutions for (iii) can be distinguished. The viewpoint approach (cf. [FKN+92]) follows an algorithmic approach by checking the effect of operations and triggering update operations to end in a consistent result state. Other specification approaches, like e.g. Z (cf. [Jac95]), follow a descriptive approach, where the application engineer has to integrate different view specifications in an overall specification by additional inter-view constraints. In our approach, we follow a constructive approach, where different views are automatically integrated. This means that two operations from two different views are merged into one operation in the resulting overall system specification. The common underlying reference model indicates and identifies the overlapping part.

This discussion shows that the presented automatic view integration relies on a series of prerequisites. In particular, a human being in the role of a model manager is required to guide and support the integration process. Nevertheless, the construction of the integrated specification will be done automatically.

3 Graph Transformation for System Modelling

In this section, we explain how rule-based graph transformations can be used to model the static and dynamic aspects of software systems in a formal and integrated way. The main concepts are illustrated by a small banking example.

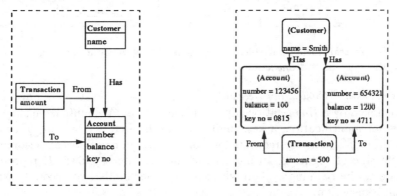

Fig. 2. Example of scheme and instance graphs

Graphs. Graphs and diagrams are often used in software engineering for visualising complex structures. We only mention Entity-Relationship (ER) diagrams and instances in data modelling or class and object diagrams in object-oriented design. Formally, a *graph* consists of a set of vertices V and a set of edges E such that each edge e in E has a source and a target vertex $s(e)$ and $t(e)$ in V, respectively.

Both in ER modelling and OO design graphs occur on two levels, as *scheme graphs* (ER diagram, class diagram) and their *instance graphs* (ER instance, object diagram). Scheme graphs impose structural constraints on its instances by requiring that each instance can be mapped to its scheme in a structure-preserving way. This mapping also provides vertices and edges of the instance graph with their *types*, i.e., the vertices and edges of the scheme graph.

Example. A sample pair of scheme and instance graphs is shown in Figure 2. The scheme graph on the left contains the main object and relationship types.

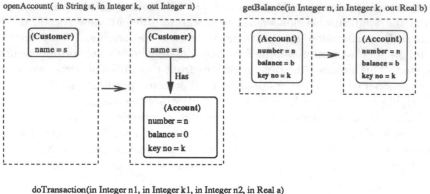

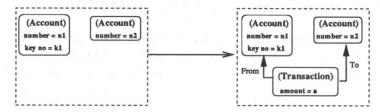

Fig. 3. Graph transformation rules for opening a new account, getting the balance, and starting a transfer transaction.

Object types are *Customer, Account*, and *Transaction*. Customers have a name and are linked by a *Has* relationship to their accounts. Accounts have an account number for identification, a key number for authorised access and, of course, a balance. Transactions are requests for transferring money between accounts. On the right side of Figure 2, an instance of this scheme is shown. It represents a toy state of the banking system where a customer holds two accounts with an ongoing transaction. △

Rule-Based Graph Transformation. State changing operations on graphs are modelled by graph transformations which are specified by *graph transformation rules* $r : L \to R$. They consist of a rule name r and two instance graphs L and R, called *left-* and *right-hand side*, which represent a part of the system's state before and after the operation, that is, the pre– and postcondition of the operation. We assume that the intersection $L \cap R$ is a graph, called the *interface* of r. It contains those items that are read but not deleted by the operation.

Example. The upper left rule in Figure 3 specifies the customer's operation of opening a new account. It requires the customer's name and a key number as input. Then, a *Customer* object with this name is selected from the current state, and a new *Account* object is created together with a *Has* relationship. Balance and key number are set, and an account number is chosen and passed to the customer as output. The *getBalance* rule in the right specifies the operation of reading the balance of an account, and *doTransaction* below creates a transfer transaction. △

More generally, a derivation step $G \stackrel{r}{\Longrightarrow} H$ from G to H using a rule $r : L \to R$ requires that (a renaming of) L occurs as a subgraph in G. Then, $L \setminus R$ is removed from G and $R \setminus L$ is added to the result leading to the derived graph H that contains a renaming of R as a subgraph.[1] Hence we denote by $delete(r)$ the part $L \setminus R$ and by $add(r)$ the part $R \setminus L$. The application deletes and creates exactly what is specified by the rule, i.e., there is an implicit *frame condition* stating that everything that is not rewritten explicitly by the rule is left unchanged.

The same rule can also be interpreted in a more loose way. In this case, it specifies only some part or local view of the changes that affect the current state. Since we are interested in the behaviour of views, we introduce the notion of *graph transition* by dropping the above mentioned frame condition. Like a derivation step, a graph transition $G \overset{r}{\leadsto} H$ from G to H via r requires that L occurs in G. Then, *at least* $delete(r)$ is removed from G and *at least* $add(r)$ is added, but there may be unspecified deletion and addition as well.

For modelling state transitions that are entirely caused by the environment we introduce ϵ-transitions, i.e., transitions using the empty production $\epsilon : \emptyset \to \emptyset$. Such a production specifies no effect, that is, $delete(\epsilon) = add(\epsilon) = \emptyset$. A transition via ϵ allows any change to the current state.

Graph Transformation Systems. A graph transformation system $\mathbf{G} = \langle SG, N, \rho \rangle$ consists of a scheme graph SG, a set of rule names N and a mapping ρ providing for each rule name r a rule $L \to R$ where L and R are instance graphs of SG.

The rules of a graph transformation system can be applied sequentially and/or in parallel leading to sequences of (parallel) derivation steps. These *derivation sequences* form its classical semantics that corresponds to the *closed behaviour* of a non-reactive and fully specified system. The *loose semantics* of

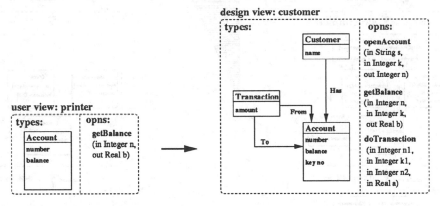

Fig. 4. A graph transformation system modelling the customer's view of a bank with a view relation from an account printer's view.

a graph transformation system $\mathbf{G}$, given by all *transition sequences* in $\mathbf{G}$, represents the *open behaviour* of a system that is embedded in a not completely specified environment.

---

[1] Formally, the occurrences of L in G and R in H are specified by a graph homomorphism $m : L \to G$ and $m^* : R \to H$, called *match* and *comatch* respectively, that allow the renaming of L and R.

334

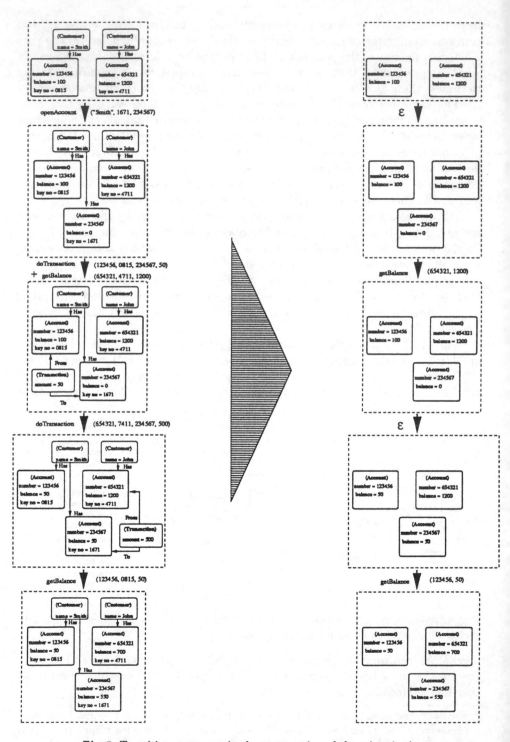

Fig. 5. Transition sequences in the customer's and the printer's view.

Example. A sample graph transformation system modelling a banking system from the customer's point of view is depicted in Figure 4 on the right. The rules are shown in Figure 3. The left-hand side of Figure 5 shows a sample transition sequence modelling the customer's view of some banking operations. After opening the new account "234567" (where the number is provided by the bank), a transfer transaction is ordered by customer Smith. At the same time, customer John asks for the balance of his account. This is modelled by two derivation steps (without unspecified changes) where the second one consists of the parallel application of *doTransaction* and *getBalance*. Thereafter, also customer John starts an order, while the first order is executed by the bank and the result becomes visible for the customers. Thus, the first *Transaction* object disappears without actually being deleted by the *doTransaction* rule, and the balances of the accounts "123456" and "234567" change. These are (from the customer's point of view) unspecified effects, i.e., the third step in the sequence is a true transition. Finally, customer Smith asks for the balance of account "123456" while the second transaction order is executed (which again is a true transition). $\triangle$

4 Views of Graph Transformation Systems

For the integration of views it is essential to specify the intended correspondences between different views by relating a common reference model to each view by a view relation. A view relation allows the renaming and extension of scheme graphs and rules. After the integration, similar view relations are established between a view and the overall system model.

Renaming. In order to allow, for example, the use of different names for the same operation in different views and the reference model, renaming relations are introduced. A *renaming relation* $\mathbf{G} \xleftrightarrow{ren} \mathbf{G'}$ can be seen as a kind of dictionary establishing a one-to-one correspondence between the types, the rule names, and the (vertices and edges of the) rules of two graph transformation systems $\mathbf{G}$ and $\mathbf{G'}$. If x is an item (a type, a rule name, etc.) of $\mathbf{G}$ and x' the corresponding item in $\mathbf{G'}$ we write $x \xleftrightarrow{ren} x'$.

Extension. As anticipated above, a view relation shall be composed of a renaming and an extension. The extension of a rule r_0 by another rule r_1 is modelled by the *subrule relation*. The rule $r_0 : L_0 \to R_0$ is a *subrule* of $r_1 : L_1 \to R_1$, written $r_0 \subseteq r_1$ if the effects of applying the latter extend the effects of applying the first. Formally, this means that $L_0 \subseteq L_1, R_0 \subseteq R_1$ (pre- and post-conditions are extended), $delete(r_0) \subseteq delete(r_1)$ (more is deleted by r_1), and $add(r_0) \subseteq add(r_1)$ (more is added by r_1).

A graph transformation system $\mathbf{G}_1$ *extends* another one $\mathbf{G}_0$, written $\mathbf{G}_0 \subseteq \mathbf{G}_1$, if scheme graph and rule names of $\mathbf{G}_0$ are extended, i.e., $SG_0 \subseteq SG_1$ and $N_0 \subseteq N_1$, and for each rule name $r \in N_0$ the associated rule in $\mathbf{G}_0$ is a subrule of the one in $\mathbf{G}_1$, i.e., $\rho_0(r) \subseteq \rho_1(r)$.

View relation. In order to specify the relation between a view and a system model, a *view relation* has to be specified. A view relation $v = (\mathbf{G}_0 \xleftrightarrow{ren} \mathbf{G}_0^1 \subseteq$

G_1) from G_0 to G_1 is a renaming of G_0 such that G_1 is an extension of the renamed system G_0^1. More abstractly, we write $v : G_0 \to G_1$ and say that G_0 *is a view of* G_1. View relations may be composed by composing the underlying renamings and extensions in a suitable way. This makes it possible to regard a view $v_0 : G_0 \to G_1$ on a view $v_1 : G_1 \to G_2$ as a view $v_0; v_1 : G_0 \to G_2$.

Let's discuss in more detail the relationship between a graph transformation system G_1 and its view G_0.

- A name x_0 of G_0 may change to x_1 in G_1. In order to represent this relationship, a dictionary $G_0 \xleftrightarrow{ren} G_1$ is used containing the entry $x_0 \xleftrightarrow{ren} x_1$ (and $x \xleftrightarrow{ren} x$ for all unchanged names of G_0).
- G_0 may be extended by G_1 by introducing new types or rule names. An item is new in G_1 if it is not listed in the dictionary *ren*. The new types and rules of G_1 are not visible to G_0, i.e., they do not belong to this view.
- A rule r defined in G_0 may be extended in G_1. On the left- and/or right-hand side of r new vertices and edges may be added, while the name of the rule might be the same. This means that the effects of applying r are extended (additional items are deleted and/or added) while the pre- and post-conditions are strengthened.

Example. Figure 4 shows a view *Printer* of the customer's view that shall become a view of the banking system by composition of view relations later on. It models the restricted view of a printer where customers can ask for the balances of their accounts. Such a printer does not know about key numbers and is not able to open new accounts or to order transactions. Hence, the corresponding types and rules are not visible in the printers view. A renaming is not needed.

The printer's view of the sample transition sequence in Figure 5 on the left is shown in the same figure on the right. Recall that, e.g., the step in the user sequence on the left – opening an account – is a derivation step. In the printer's sequence on the right, however, it is seen as an ϵ-transition. The first *getBalance*-transition in the printer's view results from the parallel derivation step using *doTransaction* and *getBalance* in the customer's view. The *doTransaction* rule is hidden in the printer's view but its effects are still visible. $\triangle$

Hence, a view relation $v : G_0 \to G_1$ describes not only a projection of the state graphs of G_1 to G_0 but also a more abstract view of the behaviour of G_1. Notice that derivation sequences (without unspecified effects) are not viewed as derivation sequences in general but as transition sequences, too: The view of a derivation sequence in G_1 may be a transition sequence in G_0.

5 Automatic Integration of Views

In the previous section, view relations were introduced for describing the relationships between views, reference model, and system model. Now, we explain the main technical concept of our approach, the integration of views.

All development starts with the reference model as domain-specific framework. The reference model of the banking system is shown in Figure 8. In the beginning it contains the basic object and relationship types of the banking system (i.e., without the operation *newAccount* that shall be added later on as extension of the reference model). The views *Customer* and *Clerk* are derived independently of each other from the reference model. This results in a situation where the reference model itself forms a view on the two specifications *Customer* and *Clerk*, which are so-called design views on the complete system model.

When integrating the design views to the system model, we have to know which items in the two views represent the same types and operations. Rather then relying on the names of these items, this correspondence is specified by the reference model, i.e., two items are assumed to represent the same concept if and only if they have a common origin. In fact, since view relations allow the renaming of items, this means that developers are free to choose the names in their view according to the preferences of the particular user group.

A situation of two design views G_1 and G_2 based on a reference model G_0 by view relations v_1 and v_2 is shown in Figure 6. The integration of G_1 and G_2 over G_0 will be done in two steps. First, we have to rename the design views so that the renamed views G_1' and G_2' share a name if and only if there is a common origin in the reference model G_0. Then the construction of the integrated system view can be done by componentwise set-theoretical union of G_1' and G_2'. We assume that the names in the design views G_1 and G_2 are disjoint which can be ensured by qualification with the name of the view (like $G_i.name$). The view relations $v_i : G_0 \to G_i$ are given by $G_0 \xleftrightarrow{ren_i} G_0^i \subseteq G_i$ in Figure 6.

Renaming of Views. The system G_1' and the renaming $G_1 \xleftrightarrow{ren_1'} G_1'$ are obtained by extending the renaming $G_0^1 \xleftrightarrow{ren_1} G_0$ to G_1. More precisely, ren_1' agrees with ren_1 on G_0^1, i.e., $ren_1'|_{G_0^1} = ren_1$, and is minimal in the sense that nothing else is renamed, i.e., the renaming is the identity on $G_0 \setminus G_0^1$. The renamed system G_1' becomes an extension of G_0. In a similar way we obtain G_2' with $G_0 \subseteq G_2'$ and $G_2 \xleftrightarrow{ren_2'} G_2'$ by extending the renaming ren_2 to G_2. This renaming is always possible and can be done automatically. Now, the integrated view G_3' can be constructed as union of the renamed views G_1' and G_2' in Figure 6.

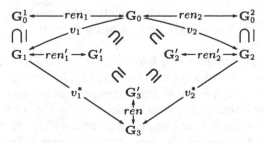

Fig. 6. Integration of the design views G_1 and G_2 to the system model G_3.

Construction of Integrated View. The integrated view $G_3' = \langle SG_3', N_3', \rho_3' \rangle$ is obtained by forming the union of the scheme graphs $SG_3' = SG_1' \cup SG_2'$ and of

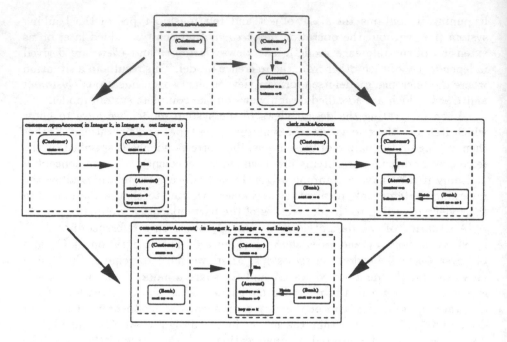

Fig. 7. Synchronisation of the *openAccount* rules.

the sets of rule names $N_3' = N_1' \cup N_2'$ of $\mathbf{G}_1'$ and $\mathbf{G}_2'$, respectively. For the rule $\rho_3'(r')$ associated with a rule name $r' \in N_3'$ we distinguish three cases:

- If $r' \in N_1' \setminus N_2'$ then $\rho_3'(r') = \rho_1'(r')$, i.e., the rule of $\mathbf{G}_1'$ is inherited
- If $r' \in N_2' \setminus N_1'$ then $\rho_3'(r') = \rho_2'(r')$, i.e., the rule of $\mathbf{G}_2'$ is inherited
- If $r' \in N_2' \cap N_1'$ then $\rho_3'(r') = L_1' \cup L_2' \to R_1' \cup R_2'$ where $L_i' \to R_i'$ is the rule associated with r_i' in $\mathbf{G}_i'$ for $i = 1, 2$. The new so-called synchronised rule obtained by componentwise union of left- and right-hand sides models the combined effect of applying these two rules simultaneously.

Then, the integrated view $\mathbf{G}_3'$ may be renamed to $\mathbf{G}_3$ via *ren*. The view relation v_1^* is obtained by composing the view relation $\mathbf{G}_1 \xleftrightarrow{ren'} \mathbf{G}_1' \subseteq \mathbf{G}_3'$ with the renaming *ren* (which is a special view relation as well). In a similar way we obtain view relation v_2^*.

Example. The synchronised rule *common.newAccount* is constructed in Figure 7 as the union of the rules *openAccount* and *makeAccount* of the customer's and the clerk's view. It synchronises the activities that are necessary for creating a new account. The integrated system model *Bank* in Figure 8 also contains the other rules of the customer's and the clerk's view, which are not synchronised. Note that not only the customer's view contains a rule *doTransaction* but also the clerk's view. These two rules are not identified, however, since they have no common source in the reference model. The name conflict is resolved automatically by qualification of the local names with the names of the views. (The qualifications are skipped in the clerk's and customer's view in Figure 8.) On the other hand, the rules *openAccount* and *makeAccount* represent the same op-

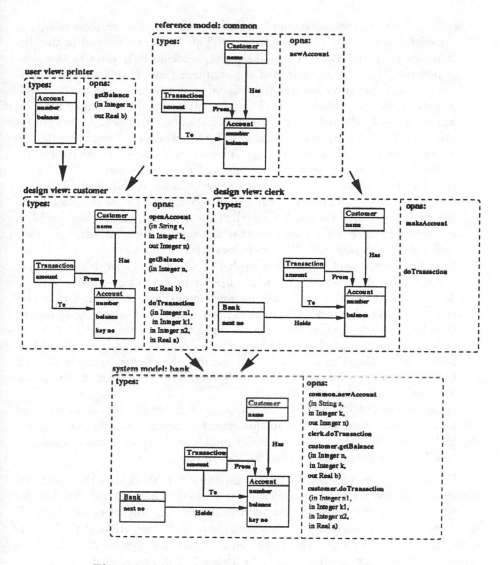

Fig. 8. Integration of the customer's and the clerk's view.

eration (despite their different names) since they both stem from the same rule *common.newAccount*. They are both renamed to *common.newAccount* in the renaming step of the construction. The rule *clerk.doTransaction* is not shown. It describes the execution of a transfer transaction. △

More generally, we may have the following situations:

– It may be the case that "semantically the same" concept is described in G_1 and G_2 using different names (like *openAccount* and *makeAccount* above). This relationship between G_1 and G_2 is only understood (and may be taken into account by the integration) if both names have a common source in the common view G_0 (like *newAccount*). This has to be defined in the dictionaries ren_1 and ren_2. Then, the concept occurs only once in the integrated model, under the name of the common view. If this relationship is not specified, the two concepts are considered as unrelated and are kept separately in the integrated model. This illustrates also the difference between a synchronised rule and the parallel application of two rules. A parallel application of *Customer.openAccount* and *Clerk.makeAccount* would create two distinct new *Account* nodes. The synchronised rule *common.newAccount* realizes that, as desired, only one new account node is created.

- On the other hand, the same name may be used in G_1 and G_2 in order to describe "semantically different" concepts (e.g., *doTransaction* in the customer's and the clerk's view). This does not causes any problem in our approach since we assume that the names are qualified, i.e., *Customer.doTransaction* and *Clerk.doTransaction*.

- In order to represent shared knowledge of G_1 and G_2, which is not yet expressed by the reference model, it has to be extended. This should be done by the model manager. If the reference model is used by more than two views, however, this means that the extra information is also propagated to all other views as well. If this is not desired the reference model has to be kept unchanged and an *abstract view* has to be introduced instead which is also based on the reference model and specifies the sharing between G_1 and G_2. The result is a hierarchy of views. Scenarios of more than two views are discussed in a subsequent paper.

- A similar observation holds if a rule of G_0 is extended in G_1 and G_2 with the same intended meaning. Also in this case, the model manager may suggest to lift this extension to the reference model, or in case of other views, to specify the extension by an abstract view instead.

Example. Figure 9 shows a derivation sequence that models the same operations of Figure 5 from the bank's point of view. The *common.newAccount* operation is a synchronised action of a customer and the clerk. The parallel *Customer.doTransaction* and *Customer.getBalance* operation is performed, while the clerk has an idle step. The second *Customer.doTransaction* and *Customer.getBalance* are complemented by two *Clerk.doTransaction* operations, that take over the formerly (in the customer's view) unspecified effects. Hence, the transitions of the system model are obtained in a compositional way by integrating the transitions of the two design views.   △

341

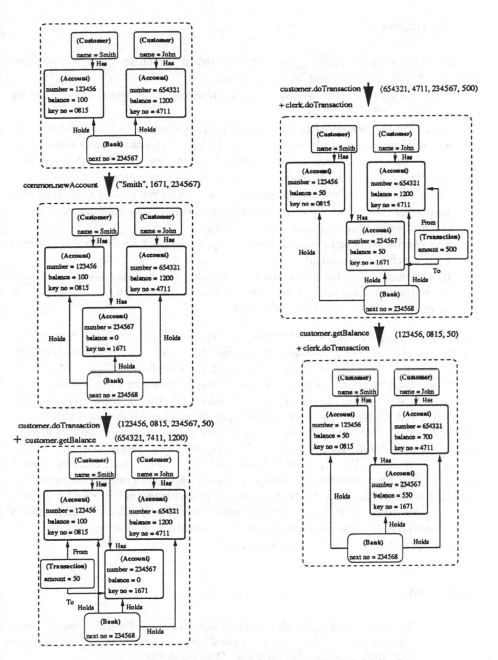

Fig. 9. Derivation sequence in the system view of the bank.

6 Conclusion

In this paper we have presented a view-oriented approach to concurrent system modelling with the following basic features:

- Separate viewpoints of a system are represented by different views sharing a common reference model.
- Each view is represented in an intuitive graphical way, which integrates static and dynamic aspects of the system, and has a sound theoretical base.
- The views are kept consistent by a model manager by extending the reference model whenever new dependencies occur in the development process.
- Using the reference model, consistent views can be integrated automatically.
- In case of more than two views, additional abstract views may have to be introduced leading to a hierarchy of views.
- The specification approach is based on typed graph transformation systems with a rich mathematical theory.
- In addition to the classical semantics of graph transformation systems based on derivation sequences, a new loose semantics is considered which is able to model an open behaviour of a view.

Despite the benefits mentioned above, our view-oriented approach has still to be fully exploited and systematically applied to examples of realistic size. Reference models for different application areas have to be developed. Moreover, views are usually more complex than flat graph transformation systems, i.e., we have to extend our approach by horizontal structuring techniques as considered in [HCEL96] and more powerful operations like rule-based transactions. Also, we have to consider different kinds of constraints, especially temporal logic formulas, in order to specify and verify important (e.g. safety critical) system properties (see [HEWC97]). Last but not least our view-oriented technique must be supported by a specification language based on typed graph transformation systems and corresponding tools. A good candidate for this is PROGRES [Sch91] where a related construction is already used for merging different versions of a document [Wes91]. The relationship of this construction and our approach to view integration has still to be investigated.

References

[AE96]   M. Andries and G. Engels. A hybrid query language for the extended entity relationship model. *Journal of Visual Languages and Computing*, 7(3):321–352, 1996. Special Issue on Visual Query Systems.

[Bal96]   R. Balzer. Current state and future perspectives of software process technology. Keynote Speech, Software Process (SP 96), Brighton, 2-6 December 1996.

[BLN86]   C. Batini, M. Lenzerini, and S. Navathe. A comparative analysis of methodologies for database schema integration. *ACM Computing Surveys*, 18(4):323–364, 1986.

[CEL+96]   A. Corradini, H. Ehrig, M. Löwe, U. Montanari, and J. Padberg. The category of typed graph grammars and their adjunction with categories of derivations. In *5th Int. Workshop on Graph Grammars and their Application to Computer Science, Williamsburg '94, LNCS 1073*, pages 56–74, 1996.

[Dat79]   C.J. Date. *An Introduction to Database Systems*. Addison-Wesley, 1979.

[FKN+92]   A. Finkelstein, J. Kramer, B. Nuseibeh, M. Goedicke, and L. Finkelstein. Viewpoints: A framework for integrating multiple perspectives in system development. *International Journal of Software Engineering and Knowledge Engineering*, 2(1):31–58, March 1992.

[HCEL96]   R. Heckel, A. Corradini, H. Ehrig, and M. Löwe. Horizontal and vertical structuring of typed graph transformation systems. *Math. Struc. in Comp. Science*, 6(6):613–648, 1996. Also techn. report no 96-22, TU Berlin.

[HEWC97]   R. Heckel, H. Ehrig, U. Wolter, and A. Corradini. Integrating the specification techniques of graph transformation and temporal logic. In *Proc. of MFCS'97, Bratislava*, 1997. To appear.

[Jac95]   D. Jackson. Structuring Z specifications with views. *ACM Transactions on Software Engineering and Methodology (TOSEM)*, 4(4):365–389, October 1995.

[LB93]   M. Löwe and M. Beyer. AGG — an implementation of algebraic graph rewriting. In *Proc. Fifth Int. Conf. Rewriting Techniques and Applications, LNCS 690*, pages 451–456. Springer Verlag, 1993.

[LRP+96]   T. Lewis, L. Rosenstein, W. Pree, A. Weinand, E. Gamma, P. Calder, G. Andert, J. Vlissides, and K. Schmucker. *Object-oriented Application Frameworks*. Prentice-Hall, 1996.

[Nag96]   M. Nagl, editor. *Building Tightly Integrated Software Development Environments: The IPSEN Approach*. LNCS 1170, Springer, 1996.

[Rib96]   L. Ribeiro. *Parallel Composition and Unfolding Semantics of Graph Grammars*. PhD thesis, TU Berlin, 1996.

[Roz97]   G. Rozenberg, editor. *Handbook of Graph Grammars and Computing by Graph Transformation, Volume 1: Foundations*. World Scientific, 1997.

[Sch91]   A. Schürr. Progress: A vhl-language based on graph grammars. In *4th Int. Workshop on Graph Grammars and their Application to Computer Science, LNCS 532*. Springer, 1991.

[SWZ95]   A. Schürr, A.J. Winter, and A. Zündorf. Graph grammar engineering with PROGRES. In W. Schäfer and P. Botella, editors, *5th European Software Engineering Conference (ESEC'95), Sitges*, pages 219–234. Springer LNCS 989, September 1995.

[Tae96]   G. Taentzer. Modeling dynamic distributed object structures by graph transformation. *Object Currents*, 1(12), Dec. 1996. http://www.sigs.com/publications/docs/oc/9612/oc9701.f.taentzer.html.

[Wag97]   A. Wagner. *A Formal Object Specification Technique Using Rule-Based Transformation of Partial Algebras*. PhD thesis, TU Berlin, 1997.

[Wes91]   B. Westfechtel. Structure-oriented merging of revisions of software documents. In P. Feiler, editor, *Proc. 3rd Int. Workshop on Software Configuration Management (SCM3) New York*, pages 68–79. ACM Press, 1991.

[Zam96]   A. Zamperoni. GRIDS - graph-based integrated development of software: Integrating different perspectives of software engineering. In *Proc. 18th International Conference on Software Engineering (ICSE)*, pages 48–59. IEEE CS Press, March 25-29 1996.

A Design Framework for Internet-Scale Event Observation and Notification

David S. Rosenblum

Dept. of Info. & Computer Science
University of California, Irvine
Irvine, CA 92697-3425
USA
dsr@ics.uci.edu
http://www.ics.uci.edu/~dsr/

Alexander L. Wolf

Dept. of Computer Science
University of Colorado
Boulder, CO 80309-0430
USA
alw@cs.colorado.edu
http://www.cs.colorado.edu/users/alw/

Abstract

There is increasing interest in having software systems execute and interoperate over the Internet. Execution and interoperation at this scale imply a degree of loose coupling and heterogeneity among the components from which such systems will be built. One common architectural style for distributed, loosely-coupled, heterogeneous software systems is a structure based on event generation, observation and notification. The technology to support this approach is well-developed for local area networks, but it is ill-suited to networks on the scale of the Internet. Hence, new technologies are needed to support the construction of large-scale, event-based software systems for the Internet. We have begun to design a new facility for event observation and notification that better serves the needs of Internet-scale applications. In this paper we present results from our first step in this design process, in which we defined a framework that captures many of the relevant design dimensions. Our framework comprises seven models—an *object model*, an *event model*, a *naming model*, an *observation model*, a *time model*, a *notification model*, and a *resource model*. The paper discusses each of these models in detail and illustrates them using an example involving an update to a Web page. The paper also evaluates three existing technologies with respect to the seven models.

Keywords: design, distributed systems, events, Internet, software engineering

1 Introduction

There is increasing interest in having software systems execute and interoperate over the Internet. Workflow systems for multi-national corporations, multi-site/multi-organization software development, and real-time investment analysis across world financial markets are just a few of the many applications that lend themselves to deployment on an Internet scale. Execution and interoperation at this scale imply a high degree of loose coupling and heterogeneity among the components from which such systems will be built. One common architectural style for distributed, loosely-coupled, heterogeneous software systems is a structure based on event generation, observation and notification. The technology to support this architectural style is well-developed for local area networks (e.g., Field's Msg [31], SoftBench's BMS [13], ToolTalk [17] and Yeast [20]), but it is ill-suited to networks on the scale of the Internet. Hence, new technologies are needed to support the construction of large-scale, event-based software systems for the Internet.

We envision event observation and notification as being an explicit facility provided to software components across the Internet. The facility would have the ability to observe the occurrence of events in components, to recognize patterns among such events, and to notify other, interested components about the (patterns of) event occurrences. This is a fairly simple and intuitive characterization of its requirements. However, this simple characterization masks the richness and complexity of the issues that must be addressed in the design and implementation of the facility. For example,

- To what extent should the facility support recognition of patterns of non-causally related events?
- What architecture will allow the facility to efficiently organize and partition its observation task, to handle notifications to multiple components interested in the same events, and to characterize events involving multiple components?
- Where in the architecture should the facility support event-pattern recognition and event information filtering?

These and many other questions must be carefully addressed in any design and implementation effort.

Recently there have been a small number of proposals and initial prototypes for Internet-scale event facilities, such as the OMG CORBA Event Service [27,28] and the TINA Notification Service [35]. But the definitions of these facilities address only a limited portion of the full problem space. Therefore, we have begun to design a new facility for event observation and notification that better serves the needs of Internet-scale applications.

In this paper we present results from our first step in this design process, in which we defined a framework that captures many of the relevant design dimensions. Our framework comprises seven models:

1. an *object model*, which characterizes the components that generate events and the components that receive notifications about events;
2. an *event model*, which provides a precise characterization of the phenomenon of an event;
3. a *naming model*, which defines how components refer to other components and the events generated by other components, for the purpose of expressing interest in event notifications;
4. an *observation model*, which defines the mechanisms by which event occurrences are observed and related;
5. a *time model*, which concerns the temporal and causal relationships between events and notifications;
6. a *notification model*, which defines the mechanisms that components use to express interest in and receive notifications; and

7. a *resource model*, which defines where in the Internet the observation and notification computations are located, and how resources for the computations are allocated and accounted.

Each of these models has a number of possible realizations. Taken together, these realizations define a seven-dimensional design space for Internet-scale event observation and notification facilities. Of course, these dimensions are not completely independent, because the models are interrelated in various ways. Because of these interrelationships, only a proper subset of the points in this space will correspond to adequate designs for Internet-scale facilities.

The design of an Internet-scale event observation and notification facility will be based upon one or more metaphors for distributed, loosely-coupled computation. Well-known examples of such metaphors include *publish/subscribe*, *client/server*, *electronic mail*, *online transaction processing* and *central dispatch*. The choice of metaphor(s) will bring coherence to the designs of the individual model realizations.

We describe these models fully in Section 3, but first in Section 2 we define more precisely what we mean by the notion of "Internet scale". In Section 4 we evaluate three existing technologies with respect to the design framework, and we conclude in Section 5 with a discussion of our plans for future work.

2   Attributes of Internet Scale

In order to provide an adequate design framework for an Internet-scale event observation and notification facility, we must first fully explore the ramifications of Internet scale. Some attributes of Internet scale will affect more the implementation of the facility rather than its design. An example of such an attribute is the heterogeneity of network elements. For this paper we limit our discussion to those attributes relevant to the design.

The primary distinguishing characteristics of an Internet-scale computer network are the vast numbers of computers in the network and the vast numbers of users of these computers. As a consequence of this, it would be infeasible to employ many kinds of low-level mechanisms that are used to support event observation and notification in a local-area network, such as the following:

- *broadcast mechanisms*, which indiscriminately communicate event occurrences and notifications to all machines on a local network; and

- *vector clocks*, which piggyback onto each message exchanged between the communicating processes of an application a vector timestamp (whose size is linear in the total number of processes in the application), in order to aid the identification of causally-related events.

There are other characteristics of Internet scale that we can identify, and they are consequences of the vast numbers of participants.

One important related characteristic is the worldwide *geographical dispersion* of the computers and their users. As a consequence of geographical dispersion, it becomes necessary to address relativistic issues in multiple observations of the same event. For instance, observers of two events occurring on opposite sides of the world may observe two different orders for those events. Additionally, an application requesting a notification about an event at roughly the same time as, but prior to, the occurrence of the event of interest may or may not be notified about the event.

At the scale of the Internet, the huge numbers of geographically-dispersed computers and users also have a much greater degree of *autonomy* than in local-area networks. Because of this autonomy, issues of resource usage are of greater concern, such as accounting for resource usage for observation and notification computations, placing limits on resource usage, and preventing misuse of resources or intrusiveness on others' usage of resources.

Related to the issue of autonomy is the *security* of the computers and users. Mechanisms and policies must be established that will allow Internet-scale event observation and notification to take place in a manner that is compatible with security mechanisms such as firewalls, and is consistent with the need to enforce access permissions and other protection mechanisms.

Finally, concerns related to *quality of service* obtain much greater visibility at the scale of the Internet. Because of network latencies, outages and other dynamically-varying network phenomena, an Internet-scale event observation and notification facility will have to cope with decreased reliability of observations and notifications, as well as decreased stability of the entities to be observed and notified.

3 Design Framework

In this section we present a design framework for an Internet-scale event observation and notification facility. The framework is organized around the seven models listed in the introduction, each of which focuses on a different domain of concern in the design. Although the framework is general (in the sense of being independent of any particular application domain), we impose certain constraints that we feel are required in order for the facility to support true Internet-scale event observation and notification. And although the framework is quite comprehensive, there are aspects that it does not yet fully address, including considerations of security, quality-of-service and mobility; these are subjects of future work. Note that because the seven models are interrelated, it is necessary to defer the definitions of some concepts until the sections in which their relevant models are given full treatment.

Implicit in the relationships among the seven models is a timeline of activities involved in event observation and notification. We can identify eight such activities, which occur in sequence:

1. *determination* of which events will be made observable;

2. *expression of interest* in an event or pattern of events;

3. *occurrence* of each event;

4. *observation* of each event that occurred;

5. *relation* of the observation to other observations to recognize the event pattern of interest;

6. *notification* of an application that its pattern of interest has occurred;

7. *receipt* of the notification by the application; and

8. *response* of the application to the notification.

We consider the last of these activities to be outside the domain of concern of the event observation and notification facility.

Looking at these activities from a slightly different perspective, our framework distinguishes three separate but related aspects of an event:

1. the *occurrence* of the event itself;

2. the *communication* of the fact of the occurrence to applications that are interested in the event; and

3. *information* about the event, some of which is general for all events (such as the time at which the event was observed), and some of which is specific to the event that occurred.

Two separate but related aspects of the communication include the *observation* of the occurrence and the *notification* of the occurrence. We consider notifications to be independent and unrelated. Any attempt by an application to relate in some way the different notifications it receives is a duplication of, and may be inconsistent with, the functionality of the event observation and notification facility.

3.1 Object Model

The object model for an Internet-scale event observation and notification facility incorporates the usual notion of encapsulation of functionality, which transcends considerations of Internet scale. An *object* can be a processor, storage device, network device, or some other hardware component of the network, as well as any logical entity residing on a hardware component, such as a file, a program, a process, a communication packet, and the like.[1] Humans also fit into this model, in that we assume that they always have computer-based proxy objects working on their behalf. An object supports a set of *operations*, each of which can be *invoked* by some other object. We refer to an object whose operation is invoked as *an object of interest*, and we refer to the object invoking the operation as the *invoker*. An operation may be invoked directly through some apparatus associated with the object, or it may be invoked indirectly as a result of executing some program or software tool. Objects are also the entities that are recipients of notifications about events; we refer to such objects as *recipients*. Note that the object of interest can be an active object and therefore the invoker of its own operations. Note also that the sole purpose of an operation may be to generate an event.

Fig. 1 presents a simple example illustrating the concepts of the object model. The example involves three objects—a Web page object (the object of interest), an object that updates the Web page (the invoker), and an object that receives notifications about the update (the recipient). The operation applied to the object of interest in this case is an *update* operation, which replaces the contents of the Web page with new contents supplied by the invoker.

3.2 Event Model

The event model for an Internet-scale event observation and notification facility incorporates a straightforward notion of event. An *event* is the instantaneous effect of the (normal or abnormal) termination of an invocation of an operation on an object, and it *occurs* at that object's location. An event can be uniquely characterized by the identity of the object of interest involved in the event, the identity of the operation, the

---

[1] While hardware objects and their operations may be of interest to applications such as network managers, in this paper we will concern ourselves solely with applications involving software objects and operations.

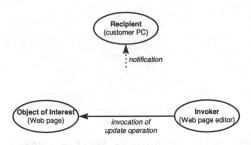

Fig. 1. An Object Model for Web Page Updates.

identity of the invoker, and the time of occurrence of the event.[2]   An event is *observable* if some object other than the object of interest and the invoker can detect the occurrence of the event; it is up to the object of interest to determine which of its events can be observable. We refer to an observing object as an *observer*.

A consequence of this model is that there is a one-to-one correspondence between operation invocations and event occurrences. However, not every event will result in an observation of the event, and not every observation will result in a notification being communicated to some recipient. An event is simply a phenomenon that occurs regardless of whether or not it is observed. In other words, an event "costs" nothing; any costs that are incurred result from observations and notifications.

Another consequence of this model is that events corresponding to the initiation of operation invocations are not associated with the object of interest. Such events are associated instead with the invoker (viewing invocation as an operation on the invoker). This treatment of invocation and termination of an operation is analogous to the distinction between preconditions and postconditions in a formal specification of an operation, where the precondition must be satisfied by the invoker of the operation, while the postcondition must be satisfied by the implementation of the operation.

Looking again at the Web page example, Fig. 2 depicts the event that is the effect of the termination of the update of the Web page. This event is observable, since a Web browser could be used to load the old version of the page prior to the occurrence of the event and the new version after the occurrence.

3.3   Naming Model

Naming is of central importance in any software system [19], and this is especially true of the naming model for an Internet-scale event observation and notification facility, which provides a way of identifying events, as well as the objects, operations and other information associated with events. The naming model is employed to express interest in events and request notifications about events. The realization of a naming model will typically offer a language that can be used to uniquely identify a specific event and to construct expressions whose interpretations are sets of events. In particular, the language will support the (possibly partial) specification of a name, for which there may be multiple matching event occurrences. We use the term *event kind* to refer to the set of event occurrences that can match a name.

---

[2]   The notion of identity is an aspect of the naming model, while the notion of the time of an event occurrence is an aspect of the time model, both of which are discussed below.

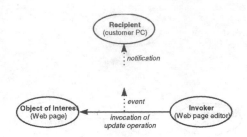

Fig. 2. An Event Model for Web Page Updates.

The designer of an event observation and notification facility will have wide latitude in the choice of realization for the facility's naming model. The two most prevalent classes of naming models are *structure-based* and *property-based*. Structure-based naming models typically employ a hierarchical naming scheme that corresponds to the hierarchical organization of the entities of interest. The state-of-the-art in Internet-scale structure-based naming models is the Universal Resource Locator (URL), which provides a way of locating and accessing Internet resources [3]. URLs could be used as the realization for a facility's naming model, but the URL syntax and semantics would have to be extended to support the naming of additional kinds of objects; work in this direction is the subject of a draft specification for Uniform Resource Identifiers (URIs) [8].

In a property-based naming model, the entities to be named are named declaratively with a description of some property they possess or some predicate they satisfy. The current state-of-the-art in Internet-scale property-based naming models is to be found in Web search engines such as the AltaVista[TM] Search Service, which supports a content-based search mechanism for the location of Web pages.[3]

Fig. 3 returns to the Web page example and depicts a possible syntax for naming the update event. A URL is used in this example to identify the object of interest, while the standard hierarchical Internet domain naming scheme is used in the example to identify the invoker. As was mentioned above, because this same name can be used to refer to all future instances of Web page updates by the invoker, we say that the update of the Web page by the invoker is a particular *kind* of event.

3.4 Observation Model

The observation model for an Internet-scale event observation and notification facility defines the way in which event occurrences and patterns of event occurrences are observed for the purpose of notifying interested recipients. Observation is achieved through a set of observer objects, and it is implemented according to a number of policies that are defined as part of the model:

- an *observation policy*, which defines the mechanism by which observation of an event is achieved;

- an *information policy*, which defines how event-specific information is to be requested and observed;

---

[3] AltaVista is a trademark of Digital Equipment Corporation.

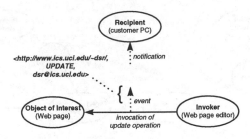

Fig. 3. A Naming Model for Web Pages Updates.

- a *pattern abstraction policy*, which defines what kinds of event patterns can be specified, how observer objects are configured to recognize event patterns, and how event patterns are to be identified for the purposes of requesting notifications about patterns;
- a *partitioning policy*, which defines the way in which observation tasks are partitioned among observers; and
- a *filter policy*, which defines how event-specific information is used to select events for notification.

There are other issues related to event observation that we discuss below as part of the resource model, such as when, where and how observers are created and destroyed.

As a consequence of Internet scale, it may be infeasible for the realization of the observation model to maintain histories of observations. Therefore, some observation policies may preclude the persistence of observations. In other words, under such a policy, a recipient could not receive a notification about an event that occurred prior to the expression of interest in that event. On the other hand, a set of observers embodies a conceptual "registry" for the expression of interest in events by recipients.

There are two classes of observation methods that can be employed for the observation policy: *synchronous observation*, in which the fact of an event occurrence is communicated explicitly to and in synchronization with the observer, and *polling*, in which the observer periodically checks for the occurrence of an event. Synchronous observation can be further subdivided according to whether the invoker communicates with the observer or whether the object of interest does. In all cases the observer eventually communicates a notification synchronously to one or more recipients and/or one or more other observers.

Fig. 4 depicts the Web page example, with synchronous observations obtained from the invoker depicted on the left and synchronous observations from the object of interest depicted on the right. Fig. 5 depicts an observer that uses polling to check for the Web page update event.

The information policy governs how event-specific information is requested, identified and observed. In particular, it must reconcile the desire of a recipient to request specific information about an event occurrence with the ability of an observer to obtain that information. For instance, in the case of the Web page update, a recipient may desire to obtain both the old contents of the Web page and the new contents of the Web page, to enable it to determine what was changed in the update. Thus, the recipient needs a way of expressing interest in both pieces of information so

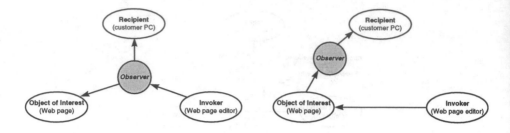

Fig. 4. A Synchronous Observation Model for Web Page Updates.

that the observer can take adequate steps to preserve the old contents prior to the occurrence of the update. In general, it will be unreasonable to support unrestrained requests for access to event-specific information, so the information policy must define precisely what kinds of request it can accommodate. One approach may be for recipients to provide the observer with a function or program that can be used to compute desired information from the object of interest.

The pattern abstraction policy contains a definition of a language for specifying patterns of event kinds of interest. There are a number of suitable candidates for this pattern language, including general-purpose languages and logics such as regular expressions, first-order predicate calculus or temporal logic, as well as more specialized event-oriented languages such as TSL [23,32]. It is common to support *event abstraction* in order to provide a way of naming a pattern of events. Event abstraction is an especially notable feature of process algebras such as CCS [26]. The pattern abstraction policy may support a notion of event abstraction, in which a pattern of observed events is represented by a single abstract event or by a name that is used to refer to the pattern. Note that in order to treat a pattern as a true abstract event, it is necessary for the policy to establish some way of associating an object of interest, an operation and an invoker with the abstract event.

The partitioning policy must address the cardinality relationships among events, observers, and recipients. For events, we can consider a single event, multiple independent events, or a pattern of events. For observers, we can consider a single observer or a cooperating team of observers. For recipients, we can consider a single or multiple recipients. In general, the differences among the possible combinations of cardinality relationships come down to an issue of performance. Factors such as the rate at which events of a particular kind occur or the number and (physical or administrative) distance of recipients, must be understood before the "correct" policy can be chosen. Therefore, an event observation and notification facility should allow flexibility and dynamism in how the observation task is partitioned.

Once a pattern of interesting events has been observed, a notification must be sent to the recipient. Whether that notification actually takes place depends on whether the information associated with the events can pass through any filter that has been established between the observer and the recipient. Notice that we are drawing here an important distinction between event *filters*, which are predicates on the content of associated information, and event *patterns*, which are predicates on the relationships among event occurrences. The filter policy is concerned with the language for expressing filter predicates, and where those predicates get evaluated, either at the

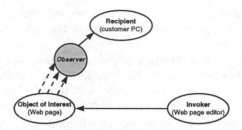

Fig. 5. A Polling Observation Model for Web Page Updates.

observer or at the recipient. For instance, in the Web-page example, a recipient might be interested in only being notified of changes that involve more than 30% of the Web page. A predicate such as this highlights the fact that there is a general dependency between the associated information that is available and the filter predicate that can be expressed. In the example, the percentage of change must be somehow derivable from the information associated with the event.

3.5 Time Model

The theoretical problems of associating times with events in distributed systems and synchronizing clocks across distributed systems are well known (e.g., see Lamport [21]). But as a practical matter, the full ramifications of these issues are yet to be fully understood for networks of Internet scale. As we observe in Section 1, relativistic issues may preclude the use of any deterministic techniques for associating times and causal relationships with events. Internet-scale applications may therefore have to accommodate approximate representations of time, such as assuming the existence of a global clock even though such an assumption may result in inconsistent observations in different frames of reference.

Such issues are the concerns of the time model. An additional choice that must be made in the realization of the time model is the point or points at which times are to be associated with the activities involved in event observation and notification. With a synchronous observation model, either the invoker, the object of interest, or the observer of an event could have the responsibility of associating a time with the event. With a polling observation model, the observer would most naturally associate a time with the event; by necessity, this time would be approximate unless the time of occurrence can be derived from information about the event itself or the object of interest. For patterns of events, it may or may not be desirable to associate a time of occurrence; the time could be the time at which the first event was matched to the pattern or at which the last event was matched.

For the Web page example, the file system of the object of interest will associate a modification time with the new version of the Web page. It should be possible to use this modification time as the time of occurrence for the event.

3.6 Notification Model

The notification model for an Internet-scale event observation and notification facility is concerned with the communication between observers and interested recipients, which was illustrated for the Web page example in Fig. 4 and Fig. 5. In fact, this communication is bi-directional, since it involves, first, the expression of interest by a

354

recipient in a particular pattern of events and, second, the communication of the notification along with any associated information that was requested back to the recipient.

Looking closer at the first direction of communication, we can see that there are essentially two ways in which it can be facilitated. One way is through a pre-existing observer and a request being sent from the recipient to that observer. Another way is to treat the observer as the instantiation of an expression of interest.

Notifications themselves should be seen as independent communications between observers and recipients. This becomes particularly important when there are multiple independent observers involved. Attempts to relate notifications duplicate the job of the event observation facility, which is responsible for recognizing patterns of events.

A final issue related to notification is the lifetime of a recipient's expression of interest. The realization of the notification model must give a recipient the flexibility to specify whether it wants to be notified only upon the *first occurrence* of events matching its pattern of interest, upon *every occurrence*, or according to more complex characterizations such as *every Nth occurrence*.

Note that we could generalize our notification model somewhat to identify a separate *requester* or *broker* object, which establishes a relationship between an observer and a recipient. In other words, event observation and notification need not be initiated by the recipient. This model would accommodate applications that may be interested in forcing notifications to be sent to recipients, such as a software company wanting to notify customer PCs about product updates. The familiar *publish/subscribe* metaphor would be a degenerate case in which the object of interest and the observer together form the publisher, while the broker and recipient together form the subscriber.

3.7   Resource Model

An intriguing way to view an Internet-scale event observation and notification facility is as an architectural style for distributed computation in a wide-area network. We touched upon this idea in Section 1 where we noted that the facility will be designed around one or more distributed computing metaphors. Given that view, one can study the facility in terms of how resources in the network are allocated to carry out its computation. In our design framework this is the domain of the resource model.

The first consideration has to do with the specific architecture chosen within the style. The primary issue here is the computational independence of observers: are observation and notification simply part of the computation associated with invokers, objects of interest, or even recipients, or are they independent computations in their own right? A design that incorporates observation and notification with one of the other computations provides a straightforward answer to the question of which participant incurs the costs of observation and notification. But such a design raises other questions, such as how to share observation and notification tasks. In contrast, if observers are independent computations, then there is greater potential for sharing. This independence, however, raises the question of where those computations take place and which participants are charged for those computations.

Related to the issue of architecture is the issue of managing the initiation and termination of the computations. Of course, invokers, objects of interest, and recipients all exist even in the absence of any event observation and notification tasks. So the resource model is specifically concerned with initiation and termination of observers. If observers are dependent computations, then clearly their lifetimes are tied to the objects within which they operate. If observers are independent computations, then a realization of the event observation and notification facility must provide some form of management mechanism.

3.8 Discussion

It is apparent from the definition of our design framework that considerations of Internet scale influence the seven models to varying degrees. For instance, the object model is very generic and applicable to many kinds of systems, not just those that operate at an Internet scale. But the object model is necessitated by our formulation of the event model, which *is* driven by considerations of Internet scale.

The event model may appear somewhat restrictive, since its characterization in terms of an invocation of an operation on an object implicitly associates each event with a single invoker. Some events, such as meetings, may be more naturally characterized in terms of multiple invokers. But our formulation arises from Internet-scale considerations, since in general it would be infeasible to support the observation of an event involving multiple, Internet-wide invokers. Instead, events involving multiple invokers can be accommodated through event patterns in the observation model. Similarly, in the naming model, property-based naming may work well on an Internet-scale because it may be difficult or impossible to structurally name all events of interest. As we gain more experience with the design of our own facility, we expect to refine our models to incorporate additional constraints reflecting further considerations of Internet scale.

4 Evaluation of Existing Technologies

This section examines the space of existing technologies to determine the extent to which some of these technologies could serve as (the basis for) an Internet-scale event observation and notification facility, as well as to show how the design framework defined in Section 3 can be used to evaluate a candidate technology. A number of technologies are relevant to Internet-scale event observation and notification, and we can classify them as follows:

1. *theoretical models* of distributed clocks [21], vector timestamps [9,25] and partial orders of events [29];

2. *low-level event managers* for operating systems and windowing systems, such as the XView Notifier [16] and the Macintosh™ Toolbox Event Manager [6];[4]

3. the *implicit invocation* design model [10];

4. *languages and systems for event-based specification, analysis and debugging of software*, including Instant Replay [22], Event-Based Behavioral Abstraction [2], TSL [23,32] and Rapide [24];

5. *software buses*, such as Polylith [30], OLE/ActiveX [5] and CORBA [34];

6. *tool integration frameworks*, including Field [31], SoftBench™ [13] and ToolTalk™ [17];[5]

---

[4] Macintosh is a trademark of Apple Computer, Inc.

7. *communication and collaboration systems*, such as electronic mail, electronic bulletin boards, network news services [18], Lotus Notes®, and Corona [15];[6]

8. *software agent technology* (e.g., see Genesereth and Ketchpel [12]);

9. *active database systems*, such as AP5 [7] and Ode [11]; and

10. *event-action systems*, such as Yeast [20] and Amadeus [33].

Below we examine three particular technologies in detail—the Yeast Event-Action System, the CORBA Event Service, and the Network News Transfer Protocol. A more exhaustive evaluation of existing technologies will be the subject of future work.

4.1 Yeast

Yeast (Yet another Event-Action Specification Tool) is a client-server system in which distributed clients register *event-action specifications* with a centralized server, which performs event detection and specification management [20]. Each specification submitted by a client defines a pattern of events that is of interest to the client's application, plus an action that is to be executed in response to an occurrence of the event pattern. The Yeast server triggers the action of a specification once it has detected an occurrence of the associated event pattern. Higher-level applications are built as collections of Yeast specifications. These applications range from simple deadline notifications to comprehensive automation of activities in a software process.

Yeast's object model includes support for predefined object classes and user-defined object classes. Yeast views an event as being a change to the value of an attribute of an object belonging to some object class. An event is named in Yeast's specification language by specifying the object class, object and attribute involved in the event, as well as an expression that the attribute value must satisfy as an indication of the occurrence of the event. Yeast employs a hybrid observation model, using polling to identify occurrences of events involving predefined object classes, and a synchronous announcement mechanism to receive indications of occurrences of events involving user-defined object classes; the observations and specifications handled by one Yeast server are completely independent of those handled by any other Yeast server. For its time model, Yeast assumes the existence of a global clock, and it performs time zone conversions when the client and server are located in different time zones. Yeast's notification mechanism is the KornShell [4]. Communication from client to server is achieved through a number of Yeast client commands, while notification from server to client is achieved by executing the sequence of shell commands specified as the action of a specification. By default, any output produced by the commands of the action is sent by electronic mail to the user who submitted the specification. The Yeast server runs as a single UNIX® process and therefore has all of the computational privileges of the user that spawned the process.[7]

Because Yeast uses the TCP/IP protocol to implement all communication between client and server, it technically qualifies as an Internet-scale event

---

[5] SoftBench is a trademark of Hewlett-Packard Company. ToolTalk is a trademark of Sun Microsystems, Inc. See Barrett et al. for a recent study of event-based integration [1].

[6] Notes is a registered trademark of Lotus Development Corporation.

[7] UNIX is a registered trademark in the United States and other countries, exclusively licensed through X/OPEN Company, Ltd.

observation and notification mechanism. However, the ability of a Yeast server to poll for events is limited to objects it can access in its local area network, typically via network file system services. Network transparency is also limited to a local area network, since at a minimum the client must specify the local network domain of the server with which it wishes to communicate. And although Yeast was designed as a general-purpose event-action system, the existing implementation is suited primarily to observation of operating system-level events in networks of UNIX machines.

4.2   The CORBA Event Service

The Common Object Request Broker Architecture (CORBA) is a general-purpose, Internet-scale software architecture for component-based construction of distributed systems using the object-oriented paradigm [27,34]. The CORBA specification includes specifications for a number of Common Object Services, one of which is the CORBA Event Service [28]. The CORBA Event Service defines a set of interfaces that provide a way for objects to synchronously communicate event messages to each other. The interfaces support a *pull* style of communication (in which the *consumer* requests event messages from the *supplier* of the message) and a *push* style of communication (in which the supplier initiates the communication). Additional interfaces define *channels*, which act as buffers and multicast distribution points between suppliers and consumers. The TINA Notification Service is a similar service defined on top of the CORBA Event Service [35].

The CORBA Event Service lacks support for many aspects of event observation and notification defined in Section 3. The object model is the object model of CORBA, and an event is simply a message that one object communicates to another object as a parameter of some interface method. The specification of the CORBA Event Service does not define the content of an event message, so objects must be pre-programmed with "knowledge" about the particular event message structure that is to be shared between communicating suppliers and consumers. Given this view of events, a naming mechanism is unnecessary, as is an observation mechanism, and any attempt to identify patterns of events is the responsibility of the consumers of event messages. Timestamps can be associated with events, but the meaning of such timestamps is at the discretion of the objects exchanging the event messages. Being a message, an event is its own notification. Computational and other resource related aspects of events are subsumed by those of CORBA as a whole.

In summary, an event as defined by the CORBA Event Service really has no special semantics that distinguish it from any other method call in CORBA. We hope that future refinements of the CORBA specification will address more fully the phenomenon of event occurrences within CORBA applications.

4.3   The Network News Transfer Protocol

The Network News Transfer Protocol (NNTP) is the protocol used to distribute Usenet news articles across the Internet [18]. These articles are organized into a collection of *newsgroups*, each one being set up to support ongoing discussion of a particular topic. Users express interest in a newsgroup by *subscribing* to it. A user can post an article to one or more newsgroups, whereby the article is distributed across a geographical reach specified by the user (although distribution of the articles posted to a newsgroup can be restricted according to policies established by the *administrator* of the newsgroup). As users post replies to articles they read, a *thread* is formed among a set of related articles. At some point an article expires.

One could view the newsgroups, the articles posted to the newsgroups, and the users who post the articles as being the objects recognized by NNTP. One could also view the reading of articles as being the key events, since responding to articles is the primary means by which new articles are generated. NNTP employs a simple hierarchical model for naming newsgroups, with articles numbered sequentially within a newsgroup and users identified by their electronic mail addresses. Except for the distribution specified at the time an article is posted, articles are broadcast indiscriminately across the Internet. This makes observation simply a matter of retaining unexpired articles of a newsgroup for any users who have subscribed to the newsgroup, and with threading being the sole pattern recognition task of the protocol. A notion of time is not required except for the expiration of articles, and it suffices to assume the existence of a global clock for such a purpose. Users are notified about new articles by periodically running a news reading program, which makes available new articles that have been posted to subscribed newsgroups. System administrators may enforce computational limits such as blocking access to or distribution of certain newsgroups, and they may establish expiration policies and storage limits for articles.

NNTP does an excellent job supporting an Internet-scale *publish/subscribe* model of communication. Several elements of NNTP do not quite correspond with our notion of event observation and notification.

5   Conclusion

We have described a design framework for an Internet-scale event observation and notification facility, to support construction of Internet-scale distributed software applications. The framework comprises seven models that address seven different aspects of the design of the facility. We used this framework to evaluate three event observation and notification technologies representative of the state of the art.

We have several plans for future research on this problem. First, we have begun work on a prototype Internet-scale event observation and notification facility that we are studying in the context of the Software Dock, an agent-based architecture for Internet-scale distributed configuration management and deployment [14].

Second, our design framework must better address security, quality-of-service and mobility issues, which could naturally be the subject of additional models in the framework. As we gain experience in designing and constructing an Internet-scale event observation and notification facility, we will refine the models to incorporate lessons learned from our experience. A number of these refinements will likely be made to the observation and notification models, whose realizations will require careful engineering to ensure efficient and reliable operation on an Internet scale. Such refinements might involve the definition of a formal calculus of event operations that would support systematic optimization of the configuration of a network of observers, much in the same way that optimizations are applied to relational database queries in query languages such as SQL. Some operations that the calculus could support include generation, filtering, observation, notification, advertising, publication, subscription and reception.

Another key issue that must be addressed is the formal definition of the semantics of events. It is one thing to declare that a new kind of event is to be observed. However, in order to ensure that all occurrences of the event kind are generated uniformly, it will be necessary to provide a way of formally describing the semantics of the event kind and enforcing the semantics on objects to which they apply.

Finally, it is clear that humans will play different roles in the use of an event observation and notification facility, but it is not yet clear how that role should be embodied in a user interface. The user interface will have to provide some scripting language or graphical means for the declaration of event kinds, the specification of event patterns of interest, and the generation of notifications. An important question to investigate, therefore, is whether the design of the user interface affects the design of all aspects of the facility itself, or whether it can instead be treated simply as just another application built on top of the facility.

Acknowledgments

The authors thank Antonio Carzaniga, Prem Devanbu, Alfonso Fuggetta, Richard Hall, Dennis Heimbigner, André van der Hoek and Dick Taylor for several fruitful discussions on the problem of Internet-scale event observation and notification. We also thank the anonymous referees.

References

[1] D.J. Barrett, L.A. Clarke, P.L. Tarr, and A.E. Wise, "A Framework for Event-Based Software Integration", *ACM Trans. Software Engineering and Methodology*, vol. 5, no. 4, pp. 378–421, 1996.

[2] P.C. Bates and J.C. Wileden, "High-Level Debugging of Distributed Systems: The Behavioral Abstraction Approach", *Journal of Systems and Software*, vol. 3, no. 4, pp. 255–264, 1983.

[3] T. Berners-Lee, L. Masinter, and M. McCahill, "Uniform Resource Locators (URL)", Internet Engineering Task Force, Request for Comments RFC 1738, December 1994.

[4] M.I. Bolsky and D.G. Korn, *The New KornShell Command and Programming Language*, 2nd ed. Upper Saddle River, NJ: Prentice Hall, 1995.

[5] K. Brockschmidt, *Inside OLE*. Redmond, WA: Microsoft Press, 1995.

[6] S. Chernicoff, *Macintosh^{TM} Revealed*, vol. 2: Programming with the Toolbox, 2nd ed. Indianapolis, IN: Hayden Books, 1987.

[7] D. Cohen, "Compiling Complex Database Transition Triggers", *Proc. of SIGMOD '89: 1989 Int'l Conf. on Management of Data*, pp. 225–234, 1989.

[8] R. Daniel and M. Mealling, "Resolution of Uniform Resource Identifiers using the Domain Name System", Internet Engineering Task Force, Internet Draft (Work in Progress) 21 November 1996.

[9] C.J. Fidge, "Logical Time in Distributed Computing Systems", *IEEE Computer*, vol. 24, no. 8, pp. 28–33, 1991.

[10] D. Garlan and D. Notkin, "Formalizing Design Spaces: Implicit Invocation Mechanisms", *Proc. of VDM '91: 4th Int'l Symposium of VDM Europe on Formal Software Development Methods*, Noordwijkerhout, The Netherlands, pp. 31–44, 1991.

[11] N.H. Gehani and H.V. Jagadish, "Ode as an Active Database: Constraints and Triggers", *Proc. of VLDB 91: 17th Int'l Conf. on Very Large Data Bases*, pp. 327–336, 1991.

[12] M.R. Genesereth and S.P. Ketchpel, "Software Agents", *Communications of the ACM*, vol. 37, no. 7, pp. 48–53 and 147, 1994.

[13] C. Gerety, "HP SoftBench: A New Generation of Software Development Tools", *Hewlett-Packard Journal*, vol. 41, no. 3, pp. 48–59, 1990.

[14] R.S. Hall, D. Heimbigner, A. van der Hoek, and A.L. Wolf, "An Architecture for Post-Development Configuration Management in a Wide-Area Network", *Proc. of 1997 Int'l Conf. on Distributed Computing Systems*, Baltimore, MD, pp. 269–278, 1997.

360

[15] R.W. Hall, A. Mathur, F. Jahanian, A. Prakash, and C. Rassmussen, "Corona: A Communication Server for Scalable, Reliable Group Collaboration Systems", *Proc. of CSCW '96 6th Conf. on Computer Supported Cooperative Work*, Boston, MA, pp. 140–149, 1996.

[16] D. Heller, "The XView Notifier", *Unix World*, pp. 123–133, 1990.

[17] A.M. Julienne and B. Holtz, *ToolTalk and Open Protocols: Inter-Application Communication*: Prentice Hall, 1994.

[18] B. Kantor and P. Lapsley, "Network News Transfer Protocol", Internet Engineering Task Force, Request for Comments RFC 977, February 1986.

[19] A. Kaplan and J.C. Wileden, "Formalization and Application of a Unifying Model for Name Management", *Proc. of ACM SIGSOFT '95 Third Symposium on the Foundations of Software Engineering*, Washington, DC, pp. 161-172, 1995.

[20] B. Krishnamurthy and D.S. Rosenblum, "Yeast: A General Purpose Event-Action System", *IEEE Trans. Software Engineering*, vol. 21, no. 10, pp. 845–857, 1995.

[21] L. Lamport, "Time, Clocks and the Ordering of Events in a Distributed System", *Communications of the ACM*, vol. 21, no. 7, pp. 558–565, 1978.

[22] T.J. LeBlanc and J.M. Mellor-Crummey, "Debugging Parallel Programs with Instant Replay", *IEEE Trans. Computers*, vol. C-36, no. 4, pp. 471–482, 1987.

[23] D.C. Luckham, D.P. Helmbold, D.L. Bryan, and M.A. Haberler, "Task Sequencing Language for Specifying Distributed Ada Systems (TSL-1)", *Proc. of PARLE—The Conf. on Parallel Architectures and Languages Europe, Volume II: Parallel Languages*, pp. 444–463, 1987.

[24] D.C. Luckham, J.J. Kenney, L.M. Augustin, J. Vera, D. Bryan, and W. Mann, "Specification and Analysis of System Architecture Using Rapide", *IEEE Trans. Software Engineering*, vol. 21, no. 4, pp. 336–355, 1995.

[25] F. Mattern, "Virtual Time and Global States of Distributed Systems", *Proc. of Parallel and Distributed Algorithms*, pp. 215–226, 1988.

[26] R. Milner, *Communication and Concurrency*. Hemel Hempstead, Hertfordshire, UK: Prentice Hall International, 1989.

[27] Object Management Group, "The Common Object Request Broker: Architecture and Specification", revision 2.0, July 1995.

[28] Object Management Group, "Common Object Services Specification, Volume I", revision 1.0, March 1994.

[29] V. Pratt, "Modeling Concurrency with Partial Orders", *Int'l Journal of Parallel Programming*, vol. 15, no. 1, pp. 33–71, 1986.

[30] J.M. Purtilo, "The POLYLITH Software Bus", *ACM Trans. Programming Languages and Systems*, vol. 16, no. 1, pp. 151–174, 1994.

[31] S.P. Reiss, "Connecting Tools Using Message Passing in the Field Environment", *IEEE Software*, vol. 7, no. 4, pp. 57–66, 1990.

[32] D.S. Rosenblum, "Specifying Concurrent Systems with TSL", *IEEE Software*, vol. 8, no. 3, pp. 52–61, 1991.

[33] R.W. Selby, A.A. Porter, D.C. Schmidt, and J. Berney, "Metric-Driven Analysis and Feedback Systems for Enabling Empirically Guided Software Development", *Proc. of 13th Int'l Conf. on Software Engineering*, pp. 288–298, 1991.

[34] J. Siegel, *CORBA Fundamentals and Programming*. New York, NY: Wiley, 1996.

[35] Telecommunications Information Networking Architecture Consortium, "TINA Notification Service Description", July 1996.

Refining Data Flow Information Using Infeasible Paths*

Rastislav Bodík, Rajiv Gupta, and Mary Lou Soffa

Dept. of Computer Science, University of Pittsburgh, Pittsburgh, PA 15260, USA

Abstract. Experimental evidence indicates that large programs exhibit significant amount of branch correlation amenable to compile-time detection. Branch correlation gives rise to infeasible paths, which in turn make data flow information overly conservative. For example, def-use pairs that always span infeasible paths cannot be tested by any program input, preventing 100% def-use testing coverage. We present an algorithm for identifying infeasible program paths and a data flow analysis technique that improves the precision of traditional def-use pair analysis by incorporating the information about infeasible paths into the analysis. Infeasible paths are computed using branch correlation analysis, which can be performed either intra- or inter-procedurally. The efficiency of our technique is achieved through demand-driven formulation of both the infeasible paths detection and the def-use pair analysis. Our experiments indicate that even when a simple form of intraprocedural branch correlation is considered, more than 2% of def-use pairs in the SPEC95 benchmark programs can be found infeasible.

1 Introduction

Static analysis is an integral component of many software engineering tools. Because static analysis is performed before execution, it is necessarily conservative in its assumptions. One commonly made assumption is that every program path is executable. However, some of the paths may be infeasible in that there is no input for which the paths will be taken. Thus, the static analyzers produce imprecise information.

Imprecision in the analysis information results in undesirable consequences in software engineering applications, particularly in testing and debugging. In path testing, paths may be selected for testing which are, in fact, infeasible. In data flow testing, imprecision may lead to the selection of definition-use (*def-use*) pairs which are impossible to test because they lie on infeasible paths. Considerable effort may be wasted in trying to generate input data, either manually or automatically, that traverses the infeasible paths [9].

Knowledge about infeasible paths can be used to improve the precision of static analyzers because these paths can be excluded from consideration. Although it is impossible to solve the general problem of identifying all infeasible

* Supported in part by Hewlett Packard, the National Science Foundation PYI Award CCR-9157371, and Grant CCR-9402226 to the Univ. of Pittsburgh.

paths, some can be determined by detecting static branch correlation. A conditional branch has *static correlation* along a path if its outcome can be determined along the path from prior statements or branch outcomes at compile time. For example, along a given path, the direction of a branch may be determined from a constant assignment to the variable that is tested in the conditional, or from the outcome of another branch. Experiments show that from 9 to 40 % of conditionals in large programs exhibit correlation that is detectable at compile time [2]. This implies that a significant number of infeasible program paths can be detected prior to program execution.

Although the infeasible path information can be used to sharpen many tools that are based on data flow analysis, it is particularly useful for software engineering applications, including the following:

- The infeasible path information can be directly used by *path testing*. In path testing, the algorithm for selecting paths to be tested can avoid paths found infeasible due to branch correlation and thus reduce the effort to generate test cases. Typically, such algorithms do not consider infeasible paths [7, 16].
- In *def-use testing*, def-use pairs that occur only along infeasible paths can be eliminated from the set of requirements to be covered by test cases. Since 100% test coverage can rarely be achieved on real programs due to presence of infeasible paths, reducing the number of infeasible def-use pairs increases the confidence in regression testing [11] and integration testing [4].
- By avoiding the consideration of infeasible paths during *static slicing* [10, 14, 17], fewer statements are added to the program slice, thus more precisely identifying the potentially erroneous statements.

In this paper we present a static def-use pair analysis technique that avoids identification of infeasible def-use pairs through detection of branch correlation. The technique consists of two algorithms: (1) the detection of branch correlation and identification of infeasible program subpaths, and (2) the def-use pair analysis that excludes def-use pairs spanning the identified infeasible subpaths. (In the remainder of the paper, the terms *infeasible path* and *infeasible def-use pair* refer to paths and pairs, respectively, that are found infeasible by our technique.) Both algorithms are demand-driven, which guarantees good analyzer performance because only nodes that may influence branch correlation or def-use pair computation are visited. Since significantly more correlation can be detected interprocedurally, we have developed both intra- and inter-procedural versions of our analyses.

The algorithm for detection of interprocedural branch correlation was originally developed to support a compiler optimization for the elimination of redundant conditional branches [2]. We extend the correlation detection algorithm in this paper to *identify* shortest infeasible paths and to *label* the control flow graph with these paths. Techniques for static branch correlation detection have also been developed by other researchers [8, 15]. While these techniques can detect correlated branches, they do not identify the shape of infeasible paths, a requirement for eliminating infeasible def-use pairs. Furthermore, only correlation between pairs of branches is detected, which is not sufficient for identifying some infeasible paths that cross multiple conditionals. Finally, only correlation along paths that do not cross procedure boundaries is considered in these techniques.

Improving the precision of data flow analysis by reducing the impact of infeasible paths has also been considered by Holley and Rosen [13]. In their framework, a data flow problem is solved by considering paths feasible under a given set of assertions on variable values. Since this approach tracks the entire program state that *might* determine the outcome of a conditional branch, it necessarily collects assertions not contributing to the correlation. The size of the program state to be maintained by the analysis makes this technique impractical for detection of a meaningful class of static correlation. Our demand-driven approach examines only values that are relevant to the computation of the branch predicate. Thus, in practice, our approach is more efficient and, in particular, more suitable for use in a software engineering environment because, during maintenance, the program change would drive the process of re-analysis.

The remainder of the paper is organized as follows. In Section 2 we present the demand-driven analysis for identifying infeasible paths. In Section 3, the infeasible path information is used to develop the improved def-use analysis. The interprocedural def-use pair analysis algorithm is in Section 4. The experiments are summarized in Section 5 and the conclusion is in Section 6.

2 Infeasible Paths

We first present the technique to identify infeasible paths and then show in the next section how this information is used to compute more precise def-use pairs. Infeasible paths analysis consists of two steps, each covered in the following two subsections: a) detecting branch correlation and identifying infeasible paths, and b) determining and labeling shortest infeasible paths.

2.1 Detection of branch correlation

A conditional branch exhibits *correlation* if along some paths its outcome is implied by the outcome of other conditionals or by prior program statements, such as assignments to the variable tested in the conditional. The correlation is *static* if this dependence exists along the *correlated path* for any program input and can be determined at compile time. In the presence of correlation, some program paths are not executable because, along the correlated paths leading to the conditional, control will always take either the true or the false direction.

Definition 1. Let b be a conditional branch with predicate expression p and c be a path from the start of the program to the true (false) out-edge of the node b. Path c is **infeasible** if the predicate p always evaluates to false (true) when the control reaches node b along the path c.

The duality between infeasible and correlated paths allows us to determine the shape and extent of infeasible paths using a branch correlation analysis. We have recently developed such analysis to support the elimination of interprocedurally redundant conditional branches [2]. Here we summarize its intraprocedural version; please refer to [2] for details of the interprocedural correlation analysis.

The goal of the analysis is to find paths along which the outcome of branches can be determined from *assertions* generated by other program statements. Our algorithm determines the infeasible paths by detecting correlation of each conditional separately. Given a conditional b with predicate expression p (e.g., x>0), we find the infeasible paths in a demand-driven fashion by raising at b a query containing the expression p and propagating it backwards in the flow graph until the query is resolved along all paths. The query is resolved at nodes where the value of the expression p carried within the query can be determined from the assertions generated in the node. We identified four sources of useful assertions:

1. a *constant assignment* to a variable may imply a particular direction of the conditional.
2. a prior *conditional branch* may *subsume* the branch predicate p. The prior conditional generates on its out-edges assertions on the variable tested in its predicate, and these assertions may suffice to evaluate p.
3. *type conversion*. For example, unsigned integers converted to signed integers will always have non-negative values.
4. *pointer dereferencing*. The value of a pointer after it is used to access a memory cell must be non-zero, otherwise an exception would have been raised.

The query can be resolved to one of three answers. If the assertions generated at a node are sufficient to evaluate the expression p, the query is answered to either **TRUE** or **FALSE**. The query is resolved to **UNDEF** at a node that makes the outcome of p unknown at compile time, such as at the procedure entry node or a relevant **read** statement. If the query cannot be answered at a node, it is raised at its predecessors. Propagating the query to predecessors may involve symbolic *query substitution* due to an assignment to a variable from the expression p.

The paths along which the propagation of the query resulted in a **TRUE** (**FALSE**) answer correspond to infeasible paths. These paths start at the nodes where the query was resolved and end at the false (true) out-edge of the analyzed branch, respectively. We identify the shapes of these infeasible paths by propagating forward the answers obtained at the resolution nodes. After forward propagation of answers, each query raised at a node can obtain multiple answers, each corresponding to a different set of paths.

In summary, the algorithm has two steps, shown in Fig. 1. The backward query propagation algorithm of the first step is based on the demand-driven analysis framework in [3]. The algorithm finds correlation for a single conditional node b. Line 1 removes from $Q[n]$ all queries raised during the previous invocation of the algorithm. The initial query q_b holds the branch predicate expression and is raised at all predecessors of b at line 2. Starting from the predecessor of the analyzed conditional node b, lines 3–10 process all nodes at which a query was raised. The array $A[n, q]$ stores the set of answers for a query q at a node n.

Step 1: Detect correlation of conditional branch b with predicate $v < c$

1   initialize $Q[n]$ to $\{\}$ at each node n; set *worklist* to $\{\}$
      raise the initial query $q_b = (v < c)$ at each predecessor of b
2   **for** each $m \in \text{Pred}(b)$ **do raise_query**$(m, \textbf{substitute}(b, q_b))$
3   **while** *worklist* not empty **do**
4   remove pair (node n, query q) from *worklist*
          assume unknown outcome of b at procedure entry
5   **if** n is entry node of a procedure **then** $A[n, q] :=$ UNDEF
        else – – *attempt to answer q using assertions generated at n*
6   *answer* := **resolve**(n, q)
7   **if** *answer* $\in \{$TRUE, FALSE, UNDEF$\}$ **then** $A[n, q] := \{$*answer*$\}$
8   **else for** each $m \in \text{Pred}(n)$ **do raise_query**$(m, \textbf{substitute}(n, q))$
9   **end if**
10   **end while**

    Procedure raise_query(node n, query q)
      raise q at n unless previously raised there (terminate analysis of loops)
11   **if** $q \notin Q[n]$ **then** add q to $Q[n]$; add pair (n, q) to *worklist*
    end

Step 2: Identify correlated paths of conditional branch b

    start from immed. succ. of nodes where any query was resolved in lines 5 or 7
12   *worklist* $:= \{\text{Succ}(n) : n \in R\}$, where $R := \{n : $ a query was resolved at node $n\}$
    raise the initial query at the analyzed branch, to collect final answers
13   add the initial query $q_b = (v < c)$ to $Q[b]$
14   **while** *worklist* not empty **do**
15   remove a node n from *worklist*
        determine answers for each query that was not propagated backward
16   **for** each query q from $Q[n]$ s.t. q was *not* resolved at node n **do**
          collect all answers to query q from all predecessors of n
17   **for** each $m \in \text{Pred}(n)$ **do** add $A[m, \textbf{substitute}(n, q)]$ to $A[n, q]$
18   **if** value of $A[n, q]$ changed in line 17 **then** add $\text{Succ}(n)$ to *worklist*
19   **end for**
20   **end while**

Fig. 1. Intraprocedural static correlation analysis.

A query raised at procedure entry node resolves to UNDEF because nothing can be concluded about the outcome of the analyzed branch (lines 5). At any other node n, the function **resolve** determines if assertions on n exist that evaluate the predicate expression. If no answer can be concluded, the query is propagated to predecessors, possibly modified by the call to **substitute** due to symbolic substitution in the predicate expression. The algorithm terminates when all queries are resolved. In Step 2, query answers are propagated forward in lines 12–20.

2.2 Marking shortest infeasible paths

To make the def-use pairs analysis aware of the detected infeasible paths, we mark the paths on the flow graph. The marking can be compared to placing finite-length threads on the graph, with the meaning that any program path which fully includes any thread is infeasible. While we are not enumerating all infeasible paths, all of them can be identified from the infeasible-path markings.

Labeling of the flow graph with an infeasible path is achieved through placing of *start*, *end*, and *present* marks on flow graph edges. The three marks identify the edges where a path begins, the edge where it ends, and all the edges the path follows, respectively. The marks are implemented as unique integers; they are stored on each control flow edge in three corresponding sets that identify the start, end, and present marks of the infeasible paths that cross the edge.

The placement of marks is derived from the answers to queries collected during identification of infeasible paths (Step 2 in Fig. 1). Along each infeasible path in the graph there will be a sequence of queries with answers **TRUE** or **FALSE** such that the queries were raised in response to one another starting from the conditional. A pair (*query, answer*) can thus serve to uniquely identify an infeasible path from its start to the end. Each query-answer pair is assigned a unique small integer to facilitate efficient bit-vector operations. This integer id identifies the path using the start, end, and present sets maintained on graph edges. Due to predicate expression symbolic substitution carried out by the correlation analysis, while tracing the path it may be necessary to switch from $(q, answer)$ to $(q', answer)$ at a node where the query q was changed into q'.

Because the infeasible paths identified by the correlation detection extend from the correlated branch all the way to the source of the correlation, they are not the *shortest infeasible paths*. The start of each infeasible path can be delayed in the forward direction, as specified by the definition below.

Definition 2. An infeasible path $p = e_{i_1}.e_{i_2} \ldots e_{i_n}$ is a **shortest infeasible** path if the subpath $e_{i_2} \ldots e_{i_n}$ is not infeasible.

Determining shortest infeasible paths maximizes the number of def-use pairs that can be excluded during def-use analysis because more def-use pairs can span shorter infeasible paths. The central idea behind placing the start mark is that, if a query at a node n has a single answer, then the start of the corresponding path can be delayed past n because only infeasible paths enter n. However, if a query has multiple answers at n, the start must precede n because some feasible paths may pass through n. Thus the start mark is placed at the edge where the query has a single answer but the destination node of the edge has multiple answers to the query. The marks for the shortest infeasible paths leading to branch b are placed in Step 3 (Fig. 2). The end marks are always placed in the out-edges of the conditional branch (lines 21–23). The present marks are placed at all nodes where a query was raised (lines 28–29). Throughout the remainder of the paper, the term infeasible path refers to the shortest infeasible path.

The algorithm we have presented can be used to exhaustively compute infeasible paths or to incrementally update infeasible path information. Following

---

Step 3: Label CFG with shortest infeasible paths that end at branch b

```
21   let e_t, e_f be the true and false out-edges of b
22   if TRUE ∈ A[b, q_b] then end[e_t] := (q_b, t)
23   if FALSE ∈ A[b, q_b] then end[e_f] := (q_b, f)
24   for each node n visited during correlation analysis (Step 1) do
25       for each query q ∈ Q[n] do
26           q' := substitute(n, q)
27           for each edge e = (m, n) do
28               if TRUE ∈ A[m, q'] then add (q', t) to present[e]
29               if FALSE ∈ A[m, q'] then add (q', f) to present[e]
                 shortest paths start where two different answers meet
30               if (A[m, q'] = {TRUE} or A[m, q'] = {FALSE})
                 and |A[n, q']| > 1 then add (q', A[m, q']) to start[e]
31           end for
32       end for
33   end for
```

Fig. 2. Marking infeasible paths on the control flow graph.

a program change, the infeasible paths for only those branch exits that may be affected by program changes need to be recomputed. Consider a statement n at which the set of path marks *present* is not empty. Any modification to n or insertion of new statements in n will require the infeasible paths included in the *present* set to be recomputed.

The example in Fig. 3 shows the infeasible and shortest infeasible paths that end at the true and false exits of the conditional node 7, and at the false exit of the node 10. We use regular expression notation to denote the paths. A subpath of the form [p] indicates that the subpath p is optionally included in the path, while a subpath of the form (p)$*$ indicates that p may be repeated zero or more times. The variable names below each node number denote the predicate expression from the query raised at that node. For example, w for the node 7 means that the query has the form ($w = 5$). Consider the computation of the infeasible paths for node 7. Using the algorithm in Fig. 1 (Step 1), node 3 is identified as a constant definition that makes the false exit of node 7 impossible. The infeasible paths that start at node 3 are 3 4 5 6 (14 10 11 13 6)$*$ 7. After path marking (Fig. 2, Step 3), the paths 4 5 6 (14 10 11 13 6)$*$7 are identified as the shortest infeasible paths. Thus no path going through the out-edge of node 4 can take the false exit of node 7. Also during the analysis of node 7, the copy assignment in node 9 changes the query from ($v = 5$) to ($w = 5$), with the result that node 1 is identified as a node that makes the true exit of node 7 impossible. The resulting infeasible paths from node 1 are 1 2 [3 4] 5 6 7 8 9 (10 11 13 6 14)$*$ 10 11 13 6 7. The shortest infeasible paths exclude 1 2 [3 4] because it is guaranteed that at node 5, the value of w is still the constant 1. The infeasible paths for the false exit of node 10 are also shown in the figure.

368

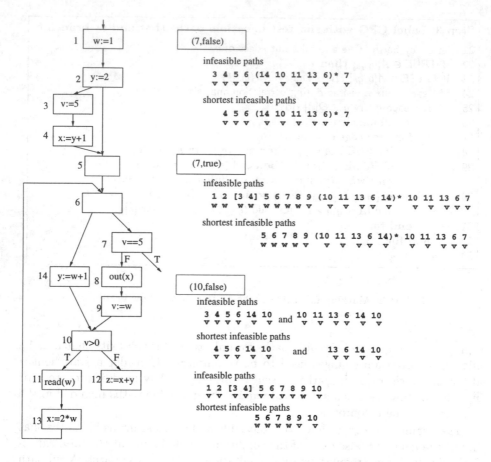

Fig. 3. An example of intraprocedural infeasible paths.

3 Def-Use Analysis

The previous section described how infeasible paths are identified and marked on the control flow graph. In this section we present a data flow analysis method that provides refined data flow information by tracing the infeasible paths and excluding def-use pairs that are formed exclusively along infeasible paths.

Def-use pairs are determined by solving the data flow problem of reaching definitions. Given the set of definitions that reach a node, we can determine def-use pairs for all of the uses in the node. Traditional data flow analysis conservatively assumes that all program paths are executable and computes the data flow information as a meet operation along all paths. To refine the result of the analysis, we strengthen the definition of a def-use pair: if all paths between a definition and a use contain an infeasible path, then this def-use pair is infeasible and is excluded from the set of def-use pairs found by the analysis.

Definition 3. Given a definition d and a use u of a variable v, (d, u) is a **def-use pair** iff a path p_{du} from d to u exists such that v is not redefined along p_{du} and p_{du} does not contain any infeasible path.

To exclude infeasible reaching definitions, we associate with the data flow information of each reaching definition (traditionally, a single bit in a data flow vector) information about infeasible paths that have been encountered in the propagation of the reaching definition. We call these paths *infeasible paths in progress*. When the propagation of a reaching definition d encounters the start mark of an infeasible path, we remember the path in the propagated data flow information in order to trace the encountered path. When d reaches the end mark of the path without previously leaving the path, we can remove d from further consideration, as d has traversed an infeasible path. However, when d leaves the infeasible path before its end mark is reached, the tracing information about the path is removed from the data flow information because the path is no longer in progress, and d is propagated further.

Reaching definitions can be computed either using an exhaustive data flow algorithm (such as iterative) [1] or using a demand-driven algorithm [3]. In an exhaustive algorithm, the reaching definitions are computed for all variables at all nodes. In the demand-driven algorithm, the reaching definitions for each variable used in a node are computed. Recent studies have demonstrated that demand-driven algorithms take less time and space to compute reaching definitions than exhaustive ones, even when the computation of all def-use pairs is required [4, 12]. We present in this paper the demand-driven version of def-use analysis.

The demand-driven algorithm is presented in Fig. 4. It computes def-use pairs for a variable v used at a node u. Similar to the demand-driven algorithm in Fig. 1, the algorithm raises a query at the use node u and propagates it backward through the graph until a reaching definition of v is encountered or until the query is discarded due to having followed an infeasible path. Removing the query ensures that when a definition of v is encountered by a query, only a feasible def-use pair is recorded. To determine when a query can be safely discarded, a set of paths in progress are carried with each query and are updated by the algorithm as the query traverses paths marks.

The initial query is formed and raised at lines 2–3. The query has a single component, *ipp*, the set of infeasible paths in progress. Initially, this set is empty. Note that, since the propagation proceeds in the opposite direction as in the exhaustive analysis, the *end* mark is considered to be the start of the path. Line 6 considers each propagated query. Function **resolve** updates the *ipp* information for the query and determines if a reaching definition has been encountered. Line 8 discards the query if an infeasible path in progress ends at the edge e. Lines 9 to 14 update the tracing information. Lines 15–19 record a new def-use pair and terminate propagation of the query if a definition has been reached. Procedure **raise_query** performs the *meet* data flow function for the *ipp* information. While the problem of reaching definitions is a *may*-problem, the set *ipp* computes a *must*-problem; a path in progress is preserved at a control flow meet point only if it was in progress in each query that reached the meet point. As in every

Procedure Demand_Driven_Def-Use_Analysis (var v, node u)

$Q[n] = nil$ means no query for var v and use u was raised at n,
$Q[n] \neq nil$ stores infeasible paths that are in progress for the query
1   initialize $Q[n]$ to nil at each node n; set *worklist* to $\{\}$
Initial query carries an empty set of paths in progress:
2   form the initial query $q_{v,u} = (\{\})$
3   **for** each edge $e = (m, u)$ **do raise_query**$(e, q_{v,u})$
4   **while** *worklist* not empty **do**
5   remove pair (node n, query q) from *worklist*
6   **for** each edge $e = (m, n)$ **do raise_query**(e, q)
7   **end while**
end

Function resolve(edge $e = (m, n)$, query (ipp))

Terminate query propagation if query followed an infeasible path:
8   **if** $ipp \cap start[e] \neq \{\}$ **then return** nil
Remove paths in progress that are no longer followed:
9    $ipp := ipp \cap present[e]$
Add paths in progress that are started at edge e:
10    $ipp := ipp \cup end[e]$
Rename paths in progress due to query substitution at node m:
11   **for** each $q \in ipp$ **do**
12   remove q from ipp
13   add **substitute**(m, q) to ipp
14   **end for**
Terminate propagation if m defines v:
15   **if** node m defines v **then**
16   add def-use pair (m, u) to *DEF-USE*
17   **return** nil
18   **end if**
19   **return** (ipp)
end

Procedure raise_query(edge $e = (m, n)$, query $q = (ipp)$)

20    $q' := $ **resolve**(e, q)
nil is returned when q not to be propagated across e
21   **if** $q' \neq nil$ **then**
22   **if** $Q[m] = nil$ **then** $Q[m] := ipp$
Preserve only paths that are in progress along all merging paths:
23   **else** $Q[m] := Q[m] \cap ipp$
If merge in line 23 removed a path in progress, re-raise query:
24   **if** $Q[m]$ changed **then** add pair $(m, (Q[m]))$ to *worklist*
25   **end if**
end

Fig. 4. Intraprocedural demand-driven def-use analysis.

distributive data flow problem, this conservative merge of data flow information provides efficiency of the analysis but may prevent detection of some infeasible def-use pairs when multiple infeasible paths contribute to the infeasibility of the def-use pair. In the algorithm, the query is propagated further (in line 24) when it is raised at the node for the first time (line 22) or when a path previously in progress at node m has been removed at line 23.

For the example in Fig. 3, our analysis detects three less def-use pairs than the traditional def-use analysis. In response to a query raised at the use of x in node 8, our def-use analysis excludes the def-use pair $(4, 8)$ because the propagated query is removed at the edge $(4, 5)$. This edge is the start of the infeasible path that ends at the false exit of node 7. The def-use pair $(4, 12)$ on variable x is excluded due to the first infeasible path leading to the false exit of node 10. Finally, the def-use pair $(2, 12)$ on y is excluded due to the infeasible path that leads to the true exit of node 7.

The demand-driven algorithm which finds the definitions reaching a given use is also useful for determining more precise *program slices* [17]. By repeated application of this algorithm, the data slice corresponding to a given statement node can be easily computed. Due to the refined def-use analysis, this algorithm computes smaller slices than traditional slicing algorithms.

Time complexity. The cost of our technique can be divided between the infeasible paths analysis and the def-use analysis. The cost of the former is dominated by Step 1 in Fig. 1. In our experiments, the pattern of analyzed conditionals was restricted to branches that compare a variable with a constant (e.g., x<10) and the only statements on which we performed symbolic substitutions of the propagated predicate expression were copy assignments (e.g., x:=y). Under these restrictions, the cost to find infeasible paths leading to a single branch is $O(NV)$, where N is the number of nodes in the program CFG, and V is the number of program variables. All infeasible paths can be found in $O(N^2V)$ steps.

The cost of finding all def-use pairs for a single use is bounded by $O(NI)$, where I is the maximum number of infeasible paths that cross a node. The value of I bounds the number of times a query can be re-raised on a single node (line 24 in Fig. 4) because the value of $Q[n]$ can be monotonically decreased at most I times (line 23). All def-use pairs can thus be found in $O(N^2I)$ steps. While in the worst case $I = O(N^2V)$, we observed in our experiments, that I was never higher than 75 and averaged below 2.01 (see Table 2, columns *present*).

4   Interprocedural Analysis

Both infeasible path analysis and def-use analysis can be extended to operate across procedure boundaries. When implementing a practical def-use analyzer, it is however not required to develop both techniques interprocedurally. Obviously, interprocedural def-use analysis can benefit from purely intraprocedural infeasible paths. Combining interprocedural infeasible paths analysis with intraprocedural def-use pair analysis appears even more attractive: by examining the calling context of each procedure, interprocedural correlation detection may discover strictly intraprocedural infeasible paths, which will benefit intraprocedural def-use analysis, typically employed in def-use testing. In the remainder of this section we describe the interprocedural versions of both infeasible path analysis and the def-use analysis.

Detecting infeasible paths. The interprocedural version of infeasible path analysis from Fig. 1 is based on the algorithm in [2]. The extension is based on propagating queries between callers and callees and maintaining appropriate procedure summary nodes. The infeasible path marking algorithm in Fig. 2 does not require changes.

Interprocedural Reaching Definitions. The extension of the def-use analysis requires the elimination of reaching definitions that occur exclusively along infeasible interprocedural paths. This may affect not only interprocedural but also intraprocedural def-use pairs. For example, at a call site node, a reaching definition may be killed along one path through the called procedure but may reach the procedure exit along the other possible path through the callee. If the latter path is found infeasible by interprocedural analysis, this interprocedural exclusion of the reaching definition may eliminate an intraprocedural def-use pair in the calling procedure.

The extension involves the introduction of procedure summary nodes, which are computed independently of the calling context. The summary node of a procedure maps a variable and a specific set of infeasible paths in progress (ipp) to the set of reaching definitions generated within the procedure. Due to the many possible subsets of the ipp set, the amount of information to be stored in the summary node is significant. However, since only a fraction of a summary node will likely be referenced, we present in this section the demand-driven def-use analysis based on [3], which achieves efficiency by computing only the needed subset of each summary node.

In the context of query-based analysis, the purpose of summary node is to cache for each query raised on the exit of a procedure the answers to the query that were found within the procedure and its callees. In our reaching definitions analysis, each query is associated with the analyzed variable v and the set of infeasible paths ipp encountered during propagation of the query. Therefore, the summary node maps a procedure exit node x, a variable v, and the set of paths ipp to: (1) RD, the set of reaching definitions from the procedure that are feasible *given* the paths in ipp, (2) *transp*, the boolean variable indicating whether the query propagated to the procedure entry (*transp* is true if there is a feasible path through the procedure with no definition of v), and (3) ipp', the set of paths that are in progress for the query at the procedure entry, if *transp* = *true*. The summary node entry $SN[x, v, ipp]$ is thus a triple (RD, *transp*, *ipp*).

The algorithm in Fig. 5 extends its intraprocedural counterpart with the functionality to compute on demand the summary nodes. Whenever a query is about to enter a procedure exit node, the summary node is looked up for a previously cached result. If the lookup fails, the summary node entry is computed by raising at the procedure exit an identical query, which is however marked as a special, *summary node query*. This query never leaves the scope of its procedure;

Procedure Demand_Driven_Def-Use_Analysis (var v, node u)

```
1       initialize Q[n] to nil at each node n; set worklist to {}
2       form the initial query q_{v,u} = ({}, nil)
3       for each edge e = (m, u) do raise_query(e, q_{v,u})
4       while worklist not empty do
5           remove pair (node n, query q = (ipp, sn)) from worklist
            case n is call site node:
                let x be callee's exit node and s be summary node entry SN[x, v, q.ipp]
6               if s = nil then
                    summary node (SN) lookup failed, create a new SN entry
7                   s := ({}, false, {})
                    raise SN query to compute the new entry
8                   raise_query((x, n), (ipp, s))
9               end if
                use information cached in the SN entry
10              add s.RD to DEF-USE
11              if s.transp then for each e = (m, n) raise_query(e, (s.ipp, q.sn))
            case n is procedure entry node:
                record information into SN entry
12              if q is summary node query (ipp, s) then s.transp := true; s.ipp := ipp
13              for each call site m of the procedure do
14                  if q is standard query or q ∈ Q[m] then raise_query((m, n), q)
15              end for
            otherwise :
16              for each edge e = (m, n) do raise_query(e, q)
            end case
17      end while
        end
```

Fig. 5. Interprocedural demand-driven def-use analysis.

its only task is to compute the cached summary node entry. To support both standard and summary node queries, the algorithm represents a query with a pair (ipp, sn), where sn is a pointer to the summary node entry that is being computed by the query. The initial query is created at line 2, where the *nil* value of the sn pointer signifies that this is a standard query (i.e., one that does not compute a summary node). If the summary node lookup fails in line 6, a new summary node entry $SN[x, v, ipp]$ is created in line 7 and the computation of the entry is initiated by raising the summary node query in line 8. The *transp* and *ipp* fields of the entry are recorded in line 12. Line 14 raises the query in all callers, restricting the scope of summary node queries to the procedure. The procedures **resolve** and **raise_query** from Fig. 4 are unchanged, except that line 16 may now add the reaching definitions to the RD set of the summary node entry. An example of interprocedural infeasible paths is shown in Fig. 6.

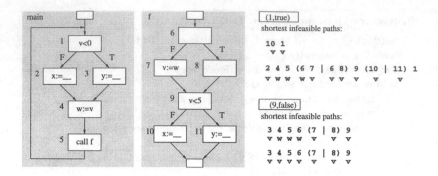

Fig. 6. An example of interprocedural infeasible paths.

5 Experimental Results

To measure the cost and benefit of our analysis technique, we implemented the algorithms in our interprocedural compiler which is based on the lcc compiler [6]. In this section, we compare the traditional *intra*procedural def-use analysis with *two* configurations of our technique: the *intra*procedural def-use analysis utilizing a) *intra*procedural and b) *inter*procedural infeasible paths analysis.

The experiments were performed on the integer benchmarks from the SPEC95 suite. All benchmarks are real application programs and, as Table 1 shows, are of considerable size. The first three columns list the number of source lines, the number of procedures defined in the program, and the number of external library procedures. Columns 4 and 5 list the total number of nodes in the interprocedural control flow graph of the program and the number of conditional nodes in the graph.

In both the intra- and inter-procedural versions of our infeasible paths analysis, we considered only conditionals whose predicate expressions p was of the form $(v \text{ relop } c)$, where v is a scalar variable and c is a constant. About 45% of program conditionals were analyzable under this restricted pattern. Given a predicate p of this form, we found those infeasible paths to p along which the outcome of p can be determined from a prior constant assignment or a prior conditional branch, which are the first two types of the static assertions described in Section 2. Another implementation restriction was that the function **substitute** used in Fig. 1 performed query substitution only on copy assignments of the form $v := w$. Our infeasible path detection technique, however, supports the analysis of arbitrary predicate expressions and is limited only by the capabilities of the symbolic evaluation routines in the compiler.

The effectiveness of our branch correlation analysis is described in the last group of columns in Table 1. The column **analyzable** describes what percentage of all conditionals in the graph were analyzed by the analysis, given the restrictions mentioned above. The columns **corr-P** and **corr-I** give the number of conditionals that have some correlation, detected using intra- and inter-procedural infeasible paths analyses, respectively. For each conditional node with correla-

benchmark program	source lines	procedures		nodes		correlation [% of cond]		
		defined	library	all	cond	analyzable	corr-P	corr-I
099.go	29 246	372	11	36 283	5 304	31.1	11.1	14.6
124.m88ksim	19 915	252	35	20 616	2 431	57.9	13.1	24.0
129.compress	1 934	24	6	942	92	61.8	7.9	27.0
130.li	7 597	357	26	9 600	878	30.2	6.4	19.2
132.ijpeg	31 211	467	30	25 420	2 355	46.1	6.2	9.2
134.perl	26 871	276	66	46 891	5 628	28.6	6.7	9.4
147.vortex	67 202	923	63	96 380	9 646	59.2	8.5	40.5

Table 1. The benchmarks: program size and amount of correlated branches.

benchmark program	*present*				analysis steps [k]			def-use pairs		
	max-P	avg-P	max-I	avg-I	tradit	inf-P	inf-I	tradit	elim-P	elim-I
099.go	27	0.29	75	0.86	1 465	1 758	1 781	43 737	910	921
124.m88ksim	17	0.06	74	1.23	322	349	410	12 415	400	506
129.compress	5	0.00	19	0.02	6.6	6.9	7.3	651	0	0
130.li	26	0.02	41	0.63	65	70	72	5 061	198	209
132.ijpeg	12	0.04	19	0.10	608	642	647	17 930	110	115
134.perl	30	0.47	60	0.77	3 467	4 769	4 980	123 295	2 460	2 476
147.vortex	28	0.51	46	2.01	3 996	5 252	5 836	93 282	3 135	3 389

Table 2. The costs and results of our def-use analysis.

tion, there is at least one infeasible path. The number of correlated conditionals is given as a percentage of all conditional nodes.

The comparison of the traditional def-use analysis and our def-use analysis is given in the last three columns of Table 2. Both analyses were restricted to intraprocedural def-use pairs and each call site node was assumed to be a definition of each global variable. Column **tradit** gives the number of def-use pairs found by the traditional def-use analysis. The columns **elim-P** and **elim-I** give the number of pairs that were eliminated by our def-use analysis, using the intra- and inter-procedural infeasible paths analyses, respectively. With intraprocedural infeasible paths, we are able to eliminate 2.2% of def-use pairs, on an average. Some additional pairs can be removed when interprocedural infeasible paths analysis is used. While this may appear to be a small amount, knowing these infeasible def-use pairs will significantly strengthen the confidence in the testing level of a program. Assume that a def-use testing of a program achieved 97% testing coverage. After the infeasible def-use pairs are removed from consideration, the testing coverage of the program will be over 99%, without expending additional testing effort. We should also point out that, while using interprocedural infeasible paths enables elimination of only a small additional amount of def-use pairs, these def-use pairs are extremely difficult to confirm as infeasible manually because the calling context of procedures must be carefully examined, as reported in [5].

Table 2 also presents the cost of our analysis. Since the set of infeasible paths *ipp* is best implemented by a bit vector, we are interested in the maximum and average size of the *present* marking sets, across all edges in the control flow graph. These values are reported in the first four columns, separately for the intra- and inter-procedural infeasible paths. The low average values suggest that many edges in the graph contain no infeasible paths markings. Note that when the *ipp* set and all three mark sets are empty at lines 8–14 in Fig. 4, these statements can be bypassed, resulting in query processing time that is equivalent to that of the traditional def-use analysis. Next, we report the number of steps performed by the considered demand-driven def-use analyses, measured in the number of times a query was removed from the worklist at line 5 in Fig. 4. We report the amount of work for the traditional def-use analysis (which was also implemented as a demand-driven analyzer) and for the two versions of our def-use analysis (columns 5 to 7). We can observe that infeasibility-aware analysis does not require significantly more steps to terminate than the traditional def-use analysis.

6 Conclusion and Future Work

We have presented a method for improving the accuracy of def-use pair analysis. Our technique consists of two parts. First, program paths that are infeasible due to branch correlation are detected and marked on the flow graph. Second, the def-use analysis is modified to be aware of the infeasible paths, with the goal of excluding def-use pairs that occur exclusively along such infeasible paths. The infeasible path analysis uses assertions known at compile time from the program text alone, e.g, from constant assignments.

To provide more precise def-use pairs and, consequently, slices during run-time analysis and debugging, our technique can take advantage of available dynamic information and identify infeasible paths that are specific to a given program execution. These *dynamic* infeasible paths can be detected if our analysis is provided with a small amount of run-time information collected inexpensively at user-defined breakpoints. It is sufficient to record at each breakpoint the value of those variables that contribute to evaluation of branch predicates. This subset of variables can be identified for each node by our analysis prior to program execution.

In the future, we will extend the def-use data flow analysis to define a general data flow framework in which other data flow problems can be computed more accurately using the infeasible paths information. We will also perform experiments to determine exactly what pattern of predicate expressions should be considered to detect a large majority of statically detectable infeasible paths.

References

1. A.V. Aho, R. Sethi, J.D. Ullman, *Compilers, Principles, Techniques, and Tools*, Addison-Wesley, 1986.
2. R. Bodik, R. Gupta, and M.L. Soffa, "Interprocedural Conditional Branch Elimination," *Proceedings of the ACM SIGPLAN '97 Conference on Programming Language Design and Implementation*, June 1997.
3. E. Duesterwald, R. Gupta, and M.L. Soffa, "Interprocedural Data Flow Analysis on Demand," *The 22nd Annual ACM SIGPLAN-SIGACT Symposium on Principles of Programming Languages*, pages 37-48, San Francisco, California, January 1995.
4. E. Duesterwald, R. Gupta, and M.L. Soffa, "A Demand-Driven Analyzer for Data Flow Testing at the Integration Level," *International Conference on Software Engineering*, Berlin, Germany, March 1996.
5. P.G. Frankl, E.J. Woycker, "An Applicable Family of Data Flow Testing Criteria," *IEEE Transactions on Software Engineering*, pages 1483-1498, Vol. 14, No. 10, October 1988.
6. C. Fraser and D. Hanson, *A Retargetable C Compiler: Design and Implementation*, Benjamin/Cummings, 1995.
7. H.N. Gabow, S.N. Maheshwari, L.J. Osterweil, "On Two Problems in the Generation of Program Test Paths," *IEEE Transactions on Software Engineering*, Vol. SE-2, No. 3, pages 227–231, September 1976.
8. R. Gupta and P. Gopinath, "Correlation Analysis Techniques for Refining Execution Time Estimates of Real-Time Applications," *11th IEEE Workshop on Real-Time Operating Systems and Software*, pages 54-58, Seattle, Washington, May 1994.
9. R. Gupta and M.L. Soffa, "Employing Static Information in the Generation of Test Cases," *Journal of Software Testing, Verification and Reliability*, Vol. 3, No. 1, pages 29-48, December 1993.
10. R. Gupta and M.L. Soffa, "Hybrid Slicing: An Approach for Refining Static Slices Using Dynamic Information," *ACM SIGSOFT Third Symposium on the Foundations of Software Engineering*, pages 29-40, Washington, DC, October 1995.
11. R. Gupta, M.J. Harrold, and M.L. Soffa, "An Approach to Regression Testing using Slicing," *Conference on Software Maintenance*, pages 299-308, Orlando, Florida, November 1992.
12. S. Horwitz, T. Reps, and M. Sagiv, "Demand Interprocedural Data Flow Analysis," *ACM SIGSOFT Third Symposium on the Foundations of Software Engineering*, Washington, DC, October 1995.
13. L.H. Holley and B.K. Rosen, "Qualified Data Flow Problems," *IEEE Transactions on Software Engineering*, Vol. SE-7, NO.1, January 1981
14. J.R. Lyle and M. Weiser, "Automatic Program Bug Location by Program Slicing," *Proc. Second IEEE Symposium on Computers and Applications*, pages 877-883, June 1987.
15. F. Mueller and D.B. Whalley, "Avoiding conditional branches by code replication," *Proceedings of the ACM SIGPLAN '95 Conference on Programming Language Design and Implementation, SIGPLAN Notices*, 30(6):56–66, June 1995.
16. H.S. Wang and S.R. Hsu, "A Generalized Optimal Path-Selection Model for Structural Program Testing," *The Journal of Systems and Software*, Vol. 10, pages 55–63, 1989.
17. M. Weiser, "Program Slicing," *IEEE Transactions on Software Engineering*, Vol. SE-10, No. 4, pages 352–357, July 1984.

Feasible Test Path Selection by Principal Slicing*

István Forgács[1] and Antonia Bertolino[2]

[1] Computer and Automation Institute, Hungarian Academy of Sciences, XI. Kende
u. 13-17, Budapest, Hungary
[2] Istituto di Elaborazione della Informazione, Consiglio Nazionale delle Ricerche, via
S. Maria, 46, 56126 Pisa, Italy

Abstract. We propose to improve current path–wise methods for automatic test data generation by using a new method named *principal
slicing*. This method statically derives program slices with a near *minimum number of influencing predicates*, using both control and data flow
information. Paths derived on principal slices to reach a certain program
point are therefore very likely to be feasible. We discuss how our method
improves on earlier proposed approaches, both static and dynamic. We
also provide an algorithm for deriving principal slices. Then we illustrate
the application of principal slicing to testing, considering a specific test
criterion as an example, namely branch coverage. The example provided
is an optimised method for automated branch testing: not only do we
use principal slicing to obtain feasible test paths, but also we use the
concept of spanning sets of branches to guide the selection of each next
path, which prevents the generation of redundant tests.

Keywords: automatic test data generation, ddgraph, influencing predicates,
PDG, principal definition, slicing

1 INTRODUCTION

The problem addressed in this paper is how to select some program path from
the entry to a certain point (or to some certain points) of a given program
module. This problem is common to all white–box test methods, specifically, to
coverage criteria [2], both control flow– and data flow–based, to domain [19],
and to fault-based (for example mutation) testing [6], in the unit test phase of
software.

White–box approaches are more usefully applied to evaluate the adequacy of
the exercised test set (e.g., wrt the achieved branch coverage in branch testing,
or the mutation score in mutation testing), and to decide whether testing can
be stopped. However, in a case which is quite common the test set is deemed
inadequate, and so more tests have to be selected to improve test adequacy. In

* Reseach was supported in part by Hungarian National Foundation, grants 7314,
023307, by Soros Foundation, and in part by OLOS HCM Network under EC
Contract No. CHRX-CT94-0577.

such a situation, the test criterion (e.g., branch coverage or mutation) is used to guide the selection of new tests. Generally speaking, each newly selected test will require the determination of a program path to be executed (e.g., to an as yet not covered branch in branch testing, or to the location of the syntactic change of an as yet not killed mutant). Determining a suitable path is the task we consider here.

The difficulty of this task is in how to determine a *feasible* path, i.e., a path that is executable under some input data. As is well known, feasible path selection is undecidable in general [18].

Dynamic techniques proceed by attempts and, when they succeed, provide directly the input data which exercise the selected path. In the *goal-oriented* approach [12], some "goal" nodes to be traversed in the program flowgraph are given. A test input is selected randomly, and the associated program path is analyzed. If this path excludes a goal node, the branch "responsible" for the undesired execution is identified. Function minimization search algorithms are then used to find new input data which alter the flow of control so that the "good" branch is followed instead. This iterative search either leads to an input under which all the goal nodes are traversed, or fails (i.e., no appropriate test data for these goal nodes are found). The *chaining approach* [7] is an extension of the goal-oriented approach, in which data flow information is also used. If the goal-oriented approach fails because of a given predicate p, a new sequence of nodes (event sequence) is generated for which the desired branch on p can be executed. Event sequences are generated so that the data flow (definition use pairs) of each new event sequence is different from earlier failed event sequences.

A completely different approach to overcome the path feasibility problem consists of selecting paths with a low number of predicates, through the use of static analysis techniques. This approach follows from the very intuitive concept that the shorter a path is, the more likely it is that it is feasible. This has also been empirically validated. Yates and Malevris [20] investigated 642 generated control paths. They showed that the probability of feasible paths in a program decays exponentially with the number of traversed predicates. For paths in which the number of traversed predicates is greater than five, the number of infeasible paths exceeds the number of feasible paths. Therefore, a good path selection method should select paths so that the number of traversed predicates is as low as possible.

Heuristics have been proposed to select paths according to this principle, e.g., in [3], [21]. However, all the methods proposed so far to find such "short" paths only consider control flow information, while data flow dependencies are ignored. Indeed, the testers' main aim is generally not to execute a specific path, but rather to reach one (or more) selected program point(s). In order to satisfy this goal, what actually should be minimised is not the total number of predicates in the entire path, but the number of predicates which are actually determinant to reach that(those) point(s). We call these determinant predicates *influencing predicates*. Those predicates which do not affect the selected predicate, the *non–influencing predicates*, need not be considered for path selection.

Consequently, we propose a new approach for selecting feasible test paths. This approach consists of selecting those paths which reach a specified program point with a number of influencing predicates that is as low as possible. To do this, we introduce a new method called *principal slicing*, which supplies a program slice to a specified program instruction with an almost *minimum number of influencing predicates*.

A slice [17] [13] is a program segment which contains all and only those statements that might affect a set of specified variables at a given program point. Intuitively, in our new method principal slices are generated so that an appropriately derived set of program statements is traversed during program execution. In this way we can get a program segment which is smaller than the slice which would be obtained without having to traverse the appropriate set of statements, and yet still yields the property of a slice. Assuming that the appropriate statements are executed, the principal slice contains all and only those statements that might affect a set of variables referenced at a given program point. All other program parts can be removed, thus reducing the number of predicates to be then considered during the phase of input data generation.

Our method improves on earlier static methods, in that these, being based exclusively on control flow analysis, only select the shortest route on the entire program flowgraph. By contrast, based on data flow analysis, we first obtain a principal slice which may contain far fewer predicates than the original program and then we can more easily derive a test path on the flowgraph of this reduced module.

Finally, our method also improves on dynamic methods for path selection, in that principal slicing explicitly includes specific techniques for finding a set of flowgraph nodes such that a path traversing such nodes is very likely to be feasible. In contrast, the goal-oriented approach and its extension of the chaining approach select arbitrary program paths with respect to the influencing predicates. Our method is thus more comprehensive.

In the next section we provide the necessary background. In Section 3, after a brief introduction to (static and dynamic) slicing techniques, we describe the method of principal slicing, and provide an algorithm to derive principal slices. Then, in Section 4, an example of an application of our method to branch testing is given. In this example, we combine principal slicing with the concept of spanning sets of entities for coverage testing criteria [14]. Spanning sets help to reduce and estimate the number of test cases needed to satisfy a given coverage criterion. Finally, the conclusions of our investigation are drawn in Section 5.

2   BACKGROUND

The control flow of a program module M is typically represented on a digraph $G(M)$, called a flowgraph. A digraph $G = (N, A)$ consists of a set N of nodes and a set A of arcs, where an arc $e = (T(e), H(e))$ is an ordered pair of *adjacent* nodes, called *Tail* and *Head* of e, respectively. What changes from one author's flowgraph to another's is the mapping from program elements (instructions and predicates) to flowgraph elements (arcs and nodes). We shall use a flowgraph model called a *ddgraph* [3]. A program basic block (i.e., an uninterruptible sequence of program statements) is mapped onto a ddgraph arc, while a divergence or a junction in the program control flow is mapped onto a ddgraph node (with outdegree or indegree ≥ 2, respectively). In some cases, an arc is introduced that does not correspond to a program block, but nevertheless represents a possible course of the program control flow (e.g., the implicit *else* part of an *if* statement). A program branch corresponds to a ddgraph arc leaving a node with outdegree ≥ 2. Note that, by construction, a ddgraph does not contain *procedure nodes*, i.e., nodes with just one arc entering *and* just one arc leaving them. Formally, a *ddgraph* $G = (N, A, e_0, e_k)$ consists of a digraph with two distinguished arcs e_0 and e_k, which are the unique entry arc and the unique exit arc, respectively. For each node $n \in N$, except $T(e_0)$ and $H(e_k)$, $(indegree(n) + outdegree(n)) > 2$ (while $indegree(T(e_0)) = 0$ and $outdegree(T(e_0)) = 1$, $indegree(H(e_k)) = 1$ and $outdegree(H(e_k)) = 0$).

As an example, ddgraph $G(Example)$, corresponding to the simple program *Example* in Figure 1, is shown in Figure 2.

A path $p = (e_0, e_1..., e_k)$ in a ddgraph is a finite sequence of adjacent arcs. A path is simple if all its nodes are distinct. A *control path* is any path in $G(M)$, while a *program path* is a path that has been actually executed on M for a given input.

Considering a module M, the use of a variable v in an instruction u and a definition for v in an instruction d form a *du pair* if the value of v defined in d can potentially be used in u. For this case we say that u is *directly data dependent* on d. Instruction u is *data dependent* on instruction d if there is a sequence $I_1, I_2, ..., I_k$ $(k > 1)$ of instructions, such that $d = I_1$, $u = I_k$, and I_{i+1} is directly data dependent on I_i for $1 \leq i \leq k - 1$. Another type of dependence is control dependence. An instruction I_p is *control dependent* on an instruction I_r if every program path beginning with entry and ending with I_p traverses I_r, I_r has at least two successors, and there is a control path through I_r that does not include I_p.

The *program dependence graph* for module M, denoted by PDG, is a digraph whose arcs are labelled. The nodes of PDG represent individual program instructions in M; in addition, there is an "enter" node. Some other nodes may be added to PDG (see [8] for details). An arc in the PDG represents either a control or a data dependence. The source of a control dependence arc is the enter node or a predicate node. Control arcs are labelled according to the result of the predicate. For example, the two branches of an *if* statement are labelled with *True* (*then* part) or *False* (*else* part). For *case* predicates, a different number is attached to each branch. Examples of PDGs can be seen in Figure 5.

In this paper we investigate intraprocedural dependencies, i.e., modules with no procedure calls. The modules are structured programs. Data types are not limited, thus array and pointer types are not excluded.

382

```
procedure Example
  read(y,z)              (0)
  x = z * 2              (1)
  if z > 0 then          (a)
      w = z              (2)
  else
      w = y              (3)
  endif
  if y > 0 then          (b)
      x = 10             (4)
  else
      x = x - 10         (5)
      while w < y do     (c)
         w = w + 2       (6)
      endwhile
  endif
  if z + y > 10 then     (d)
      x = y + 2          (7)
  else
      y = w + 2          (8)
      x = x + w * 2      (9)
  endif
  if x = 0 then          (e)
      write(y)           (10)
  endif
endprocedure
```

Fig. 1. A program module

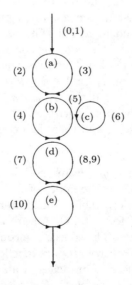

Fig. 2. A ddgraph

3 PRINCIPAL SLICING

3.1 Slicing Overview

Program (or *static*) slicing, originally defined by Weiser in [17], is a method for decomposing programs into segments. In Weiser's concept, a slice consists of an executable program segment involving all statements and predicates that might affect a set V of variables at a program instruction I. The pair $C_s = (I, V)$ is said to be a *slicing criterion*. In some cases [8], it is assumed that the variables in the set V are referenced at program instruction I.

A different slicing method is called *dynamic* slicing [13]. A slicing criterion for dynamic slicing is a triple $C_d = (x, I^q, V)$, in which x is the selected input, I^q denotes an instruction I at an execution position q, and V is a set of variables (because an instruction I may be executed several times, the qth time instruction I is executed is referred to as the qth execution position of I and referred to as I^q). Intuitively, a dynamic slice is an executable program segment whose behavior is identical to the original program with respect to a given execution position for a specified input.

Static and dynamic slicing differ in that a dynamic slicing criterion is defined with respect to a given input x, i.e., the program M is actually executed along a program path associated with x. In contrast, static slicing assumes arbitrary program paths in a reduced sub-program of M. A second difference is that the static slicing criterion requires a program instruction I, while dynamic slicing entails specifying a given execution point of that instruction. Dynamic slicing leads to smaller slices than static slicing [10].

Slicing has many applications in software engineering, e.g., algorithmic debugging, differencing and integration, testing, reverse engineering, and maintenance. An extensive overview of program slicing techniques and applications is provided in [10].

3.2 Intuition for Principal Slicing

In this paper we use slicing to improve automatic test data generation for pathwise test strategies. Specifically, we consider the problem of selecting a suitable program path reaching a certain point of a given program module.

For the following discussion, without loss of generality, let the program point to be reached be q, where q is a predicate from which a branch to be traversed forks. We also refer to this predicate as the *current predicate*.

We observe that those predicates which have no effect on the current predicate q can be neglected. A predicate p has no effect on another predicate q if under any input the result (*true, false*) of q is the same for both for the original program and the one which whould be obtained by removing p and all the statements (transitively) control dependendent on p. Depending on whether they affect the current predicate or not, predicates are referred to either as *influencing predicates* or as *non-influencing predicates* with respect to q.

If we apply static slicing the influencing predicates are unambiguously determined. However, considering dynamic slicing, the influencing predicates strongly depend on the program path actually executed. In fact, in a chosen program path a definition may be redefined without it having been used or may not be traversed at all, and thus it has no influence on q. If such a definition was control dependent on a predicate, then q may also be independent of this predicate. Thus, this non-influencing predicate can be ignored when an input has to be determined for the chosen program path although it may contain the non-influencing predicate. Therefore, instead of searching for a minimum number of predicates from the entry to a given predicate q, we should determine *the minimum number of influencing predicates* between these two nodes.

The question now is: how can we construct a slice that contains as few influencing predicates as possible? By applying static slicing, we would obtain a very inefficient result, since (as explained above) a program path might contain far fewer influencing predicates than a path selected arbitrarily from the static slice. Applying dynamic slicing is inefficient as well, because again we may find dynamic slices that contain many more influencing predicates than others. In addition, our final objective is precisely to find an input which executes a selected program instruction. Assuming that a priori we have such an input (as would be required by the dynamic slicing criterion) is a tautology. In conclusion, we would need to develop a method that is static, yet which finds and removes as many non-influencing predicates as possible.

This paper introduces a new slicing method, referred to as *principal slicing*, which results in a slice with an almost minimum number of influencing predicates. As we will show, one way to do this is to find a suitable set of *principal definitions* in the program to be traversed at any program execution. A principal definition can be any definition that, if executed, reduces the number of influencing predicates. Traversing *the principal instructions* containing these principal definitions ensures that (hopefully many) predicates have no influence on the current predicate. Thus, if we determine these principal definitions effectively, we can get a slice containing an almost minimum number of influencing predicates.

For instance, let us consider the module in Fig. 1. Let the current predicate be (e). Then, the definition of variable x in (7) is a principal definition that is worth considering. In fact, if, in order to reach (e), we select to traverse (7), then only predicate (d) is influencing wrt current predicate (e) since predicates (a), (b) and (c) do not affect it. On the other hand if we select the *else* branch from (d), then there are at least three influencing predicates: (a), (b) and (d). We will show in the next section how principal definitions can be found using data flow analysis.

By comparison, the static slice for $C_s = ((e), \{x\})$ would contain the whole procedure except instructions (8) and (10); thus all the predicates are influencing.

Hence, principal slicing consists of two steps: i) determining an effective set of principal instructions Q; and ii) reducing the program module M to a slice M' on which we select program paths traversing all the instructions in Q. The method is static, in that we determine the principal instructions and module M' prior to program execution.

Definition *Principal Slicing*

A principal slicing criterion is a triple $C_p = (Q, I, V)$, in which Q is a set of principal instructions to be traversed, I is the target instruction and V is the set of variables that are referenced at the instruction I. A principal slice of a program module M on slicing criterion C_p is any syntactically correct and executable module M' obtained by removing zero or more statements from M, so that M' contains all the statements that might affect the elements of V at I, provided that any program path selected from M' always traverses all the elements in Q. The expression "always traverses" means that if $r \in Q$ is within a loop, then r is traversed for each iteration of the loop.

Note that for principal slicing, V is a set of variables referenced at I as in [8]. This requirement is sufficient for our purposes, and makes slice determination easier. Also note that there may be control paths that exclude an $r \in Q$, but we only select program paths that include *all* the elements in Q.

Let us compare principal slicing to both static and dynamic slicing. The main difference between principal and static slicing is that principal slicing requires some instructions to be traversed during the program execution, while static slicing does not. Both require static analysis of programs. Dynamic slicing differs from principal slicing as follows: (a) dynamic slicing requires program execution prior to slicing, while principal slicing does not; (b) in this way, dynamic slices contain instructions along one program path, instead of a set of possible paths as principal slices do; (c) a principal slicing criterion requires an instruction at which the original program should be sliced, while dynamic slicing requires an execution position of a given instruction. Based on this comparison, one may think that dynamic slicing leads to smaller slices (i.e., with fewer predicates) than principal slicing. This is not so. Obviously, an optimal algorithm for principal slice determination does not exist, therefore dynamic slices containing fewer predicates may exist. Other dynamic slices, however, might contain more predicates. Since the goal of principal slicing is to find principal definitions which lead to slices with an (almost) minimum number of influencing predicates, we believe that principal slices contain fewer influencing predicates than an average dynamic slice.

3.3 An Algorithm for Principal Slice Determination

In this section we give an algorithm for determining principal slices. The key part of this algorithm is the determination of Q, i.e., of the principal instructions to be traversed.

Let us recall that we are assuming that the instruction in C_p is q, or, the current predicate. A first step is to search for (in order to remove them) those predicates that do not affect q for arbitrary inputs. This can be obtained by applying "standard" techniques of static slicing [17], [15]. When the static slice has been determined, the PDG of the sliced program is constructed as a starting point for the subsequent analysis. In the remainder of this section, PDG will refer to the procedure dependence graph of the sliced module (rather than of the original).

The central issue is what other slice simplifications are possible. If we select a priori a set of "good" paths traversing the current predicate, then some more predicates can be removed. Indeed, along some paths the effect of some definitions does not arise. This can happen in two cases.

- Case 1: a definition is redefined and thus does not affect q, although there may exist another path along which this definition (transitively) influences the predicate.
- Case 2: a definition is not traversed by the selected path.

Let us first concentrate on Case 1. If a definition d_2^x of variable x always redefines another definition d_1^x of the same variable, d_1^x can be ignored. We refer to the latter as a *substitutable definition*. For a definition being substitutable, we have both static and dynamic conditions to be satisfied, i.e., the first condition is applied during the (static) derivation of the principal slice, while the second is considered for the selection of the test input. Case 1 is satisfied when both static and dynamic conditions hold. The static condition is that whenever d_2^x is traversed, it prevents any possible effect of d_1^x on q, that is to say traversing d_2^x should avoid any possible use of definition d_1^x in an assignment or a predicate statement (a write statement, for instance, would produce no effect). This is a necessary condition in order to exclude any program path in which u^x actually uses the value defined by d_1^x.

To check whether this condition holds, we use flow analysis after PDG reduction. For each definition d_p^x of every variable x in the sliced module, we consider the corresponding node m in PDG and take the node n from which there is a control arc to m in the PDG. Since every execution should traverse the principal definitions, non-executable nodes and arcs can be deleted. First, all the control arcs leaving n and having a different label than the one entering m can be deleted from the PDG. We repeatedly go backward along control arcs analysing each traversed node n_i in similar way, i.e., all outgoing control arcs with different labels than the one by which n_i is reached can be deleted from the PDG. Next, during a forward process the nodes (and their incoming and outgoing arcs) with no entering control arcs are also removed. This process is repeated, i.e., each node for which the entering control arcs is missing is deleted with all its entering and leaving arcs. In this analysis, we mark the deleted nodes for subsequent use.

After deleting the non-executable nodes, we get a reduced program (in the form of a reduced PDG). A simple data flow analysis of this reduced program determines the substitutable definitions. Really, all those definitions d_s^x for which there does not exist any du pair can be substituted by definition d_p^x, since these definitions do not affect any part of the program assuming that the principal definition is traversed.

The dynamic condition requires that a principal definition d_2^x should always be traversed at every possible iteration. It is not enough for d_2^x to be executed once after executing d_1^x. Namely, if at some iteration d_2^x is not traversed, but a du pair (d_1^x, u^x) is covered, u^x can influence the current predicate, even after d_2^x has been executed in a subsequent iteration.

Obviously, the static and dynamic conditions illustrated above are sufficient but not necessary.

To summarise, the procedure for determining all the substitutable definitions d_i^x for a given (principal) definition d_p^x (according to the static condition) is depicted in Figure 3.

```
procedure SubstitutableDefinitions
   input(PDG: PDG of static slice; q: current predicate;
         d_p^x:principal definition)
   output(Subst(d_p^x) = the set of substitutable defs for d_p^x )
      Subst(d_p^x) = ∅
      reduce PDG eliminating non-executable nodes and arcs for d_p^x
      mark removed PDG nodes for d_p^x
      derive reduced G'(M)          {G'(M) is the ddgraph related to the
                                     reduced PDG}
      for each definition d_i^x do
         if  there exists a du pair (d_i^x, u^x) for any u^x
            then SubstOK = false else SubstOK = true endif
         if SubstOk then insert d_i^x into Subst(d_p^x) endif
      endfor
endprocedure
```

Fig. 3. Procedure SubstitutableDefinitions

Using procedure SubstitutableDefinitions we may collect a set *Subst* (which may be empty) of substitutable definitions for each definition in a given module M. Those definitions yielding a not empty *Subst* set are the principal definitions. Principal definitions are contained in principal instructions. However, principal instructions may be located in different paths. The next step is therefore to group together the principal definitions whose instructions are located along the same path. For instance, for module *Example* in Fig. 1, procedure SubstitutableDefinitions finds two principal definitions. The first is (7) which may substitute (4) and (5), the second is (4) which substitutes (1). Since (4) and (7) may be in the same path we have only one list $Q =< (7), (4) >$.

More in general, we derive ordered sets, or *lists*, of principal instructions located along the same path in Postorder. To do this, we can use the results of the earlier principal definition analysis. We investigate principal definitions in Postorder. The first definition d_1 is inserted into a first list Q_1. Next, definition d_2 is investigated as follows. If d_2 reaches[3] d_1, then they are on the same path and d_2 is also inserted into Q_1; otherwise, d_2 is put into a new list. Any new element is inserted behind the last element of the list, the order of the elements within one class is thus Postorder. This method is repeated, i.e., for each principal definition d_i all the already formed lists are investigated. If d_i reaches the last element d_k in a class, then it is inserted into this list. If there is no suitable list

---

[3] Note that "reaches" here corresponds to graph reaching, rather than "reaching" definitions.

for the insertion of d_i, then a new list may be created in the following way. We investigate every element in each list (bottom-up) until we find a d_j such that d_i reaches d_j. If such a definition exists, then d_i and all the definitions in the list from the first to d_j are inserted into the new list. If no new list is formed in this way, then a new one with the unique element d_i is created.

Now we have a set of principal definitions collected into a number num of lists, whereby all the definitions in a list can be traversed by the same path. The final step of the principal slicing algorithm is the reduction of the PDG, based on the principal definition lists. Each list gives rise to a different principal slice, so we can derive a number num of principal slices.

We process the lists one by one. Let Q be the list considered. We can eliminate two types of nodes from the PDG (they correspond to the two cases in which a definition has no effect on the current predicates, as explained earlier). Informally, we can eliminate: Case 1) all the nodes corresponding to substitutable definitions for the principal definitions in Q; and Case 2) all the nodes corresponding to branches that are not executed because the principal instructions in Q are traversed (e.g., the *else* part of an *if* statement, where the *then* part corresponds to a principal definition).

PDG reduction according to Case 2) has already been considered when we discussed the removal of the non-executable nodes introducing procedure `SubstitutableDefinitions`. When there are several principal definitions in the list Q considered, all non-executable nodes for each principal definition are deleted. We now discuss Case 1) in more detail.

We consider the elements in Q from the first to the last (remember that this corresponds to a Postorder selection of principal instructions). For each principal definition in Q, we consider the associated set of substitutable definitions, or rather the set of nodes in PDG representing the substitutable definitions. All these nodes, with their incoming and outgoing arcs, are deleted from the PDG. After this, each node (with its incoming arcs) that has no outgoing arcs (but originally had some in the PDG) is repeatedly deleted from the PDG until there are no such nodes. Whenever a substitutable definition is also a principal definition, then the substitutable definition is removed from the analyzed class. If a list is modified, then it is compared to the as yet not processed lists and equivalent lists (if any) are removed.

As a result of the above reduction, we get a principal slice PS for the current predicate in the form of a reduced PDG. From the reduced PDG and the original module, the program segment corresponding to the principal slice can be derived. Note that since the principal slicing method involves subalgorithms (for example, du pair determination) that are safe but not precise, we only obtain a slice with a near minimum number of influencing predicates. For this slice, we can then determine a path from entry to the current predicate (e.g., one containing a near minimum number of predicates, using static methods based on control flow analysis). Let us refer to this path as p_{min}. We may construct p_{min} for each list Q_i and obtain a set of paths (for instance we may consider them ordered by increasing sizes). Very plausibly, some of them are feasible.

The listing of the described algorithm for generating the principal slices for the current predicate q is depicted in Fig. 4.

```
program PrincipalSlices
   input(M: program module; q: current predicate)
   output(PS: set of pairs [PDG_i of a principal slice, list Q_i
                                 of principal instructions] )
   begin
   derive G(M)
   compute  static slice S for M
   derive PDG (with labels)
   PS = ∅
   for each definition d_j^x in PDG do   {d_j^x is a possible principal
                                          definition of x}
      call SubstitutableDefinitions(M,q,d_j^x)   { it derives Subst(d_j^x)}
   endfor
   group principal definitions d_j^x into lists Q_1,..., Q_num
   for i = 1 to num do
      select list Q_i of principal definitions
      reduce PDG to PDG_i by eliminating:
         all the marked non-executable nodes,
         all the substitutable nodes for each d_j^x ∈ Q_i and then transitively
         all nodes that have no leaving arcs
      PS = PS ∪ {[PDG_i,Q_i]}
   endfor
endprogram
```

Fig. 4. Program PrincipalSlices

Algorithm `PrincipalSlices` is now illustrated by applying it to Fig. 1 for criterion $C_p=(< (7),(4) >, (e), \{x\})$ (the list $Q =< (7),(4) >$ has been previously derived by procedure `SubstitutableDefinitions`). First we process (7). PDG reduction for (7) removes (9) as a non-executable node and (4), (5) as substitutable nodes. Thus as yet not processed principal definition (4) is removed from Q. Deleting (9) involves the removal of (6) and (transitively) of (c). Ignoring (4) and (5) (in addition to (6) and (c)), (b) can also be removed. Removing (c), (6) and (9) involves the deletion of (2) and (3) and then transitively of (a). Finally, since (5) is deleted, (1) can also be removed obtaining a principal slice only consisting of lines (0),(d), (7) and (e). Thus, for this example, using principal slicing we can see that only one predicate actually needs to be satisfied to generate a test path reaching instruction (10), precisely predicate (d)$=z + y > 10$. By contrast, existing static approaches [3, 21], which only use control flow analysis, could only select a "short" control path by taking the *then* branch at predicate (b) (i.e., only avoiding predicate (c)).

The PDGs for the original and the sliced programs are shown in Fig. 5.a and 5.b.

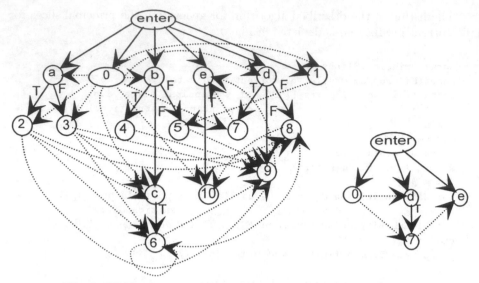

Fig. 5. PDG *a* for procedure Example and *b* for its principal slice

We omit here the complexity analysis of algorithm `PrincipalSlices` because some steps of the algorithm can be realized in different ways resulting in different precision. On the other hand, we observe that our algorithm leads to an exponential improvement of feasible path determination, therefore any polynomial algorithm is efficient, and any step of `PrincipalSlices` can be realized by polynomial subalgorithms.

4 FEASIBLE TEST PATH SELECTION FOR BRANCH COVERAGE

In this section we illustrate the application of principal slicing to white–box testing. To do this we choose as an example a particular criterion, specifically branch coverage, for two reasons. Firstly, branch coverage is certainly the best suited white–box criterion for exemplificative purposes, because it is well known and very intuitive. It requires that each branch alternative in the program control flow is executed at least once. Secondly, branch testing is widely used in industry, and is accepted as the "minimum mandatory testing requirement" for the unit test phase by major software companies [2]. Hence, the proposed example procedure may be of interest to software test practitioners who wish to improve branch test automation.

The procedure described is not only an example of using principal slicing, but it also provides an optimized method for the automatic generation of a test suite satisfying the branch coverage criterion. The latter statement is justified by the fact that we use the concept of *spanning sets* of entities for coverage criteria, recently introduced in [14].

Coverage test criteria require that a set E_c of entities of the program (control or data) flow is covered by the executed tests. A spanning set UE is a subset of E_c with the following properties:
i) a test suite which covers all the entities in this subset UE will cover all the entities E_c in the program (control or data) flow, and
ii) it is a minimum subset of E_c with property i), i.e., any subset of E_c having property i) above has cardinality at least $|UE|$.

In particular, for the branch coverage criterion the entities to be covered are represented by arcs in the program ddgraph, and there exists only one spanning set of arcs for a given ddgraph. A test suite covering all the arcs in the spanning set will also cover all the arcs in the ddgraph, and no smaller subset of arcs exists with this property. Two different methods for deriving a spanning set of arcs for the branch coverage criterion are given in [3] and in [14], respectively.

In Figure 6 we present the procedure FIND-A-TEST-SUITE-FOR-BRANCH-COVERAGE (FTSBC) which finds a set of test inputs to cover a set of arcs CA in a given program ddgraph G. The set CA can correspond either to the whole set of program branches, or to the set of branches as yet not covered by the already executed tests. Below, we discuss some steps of this procedure needing further explanation.

```
procedure FIND-A-TEST-SUITE-FOR-BRANCH-COVERAGE
input (G: program ddgraph; CA: set of ddgraph arcs to be covered)
output (T: set of test data covering CA)
begin
  T = ∅; {T, initially empty, will return the test suite found}
1. derive the spanning set UE of arcs for program ddgraph G;
2. CUA = CA ∩ UE;
3. select an arc U_i ∈ CUA;
4. derive a set of principal slices PS_i for predicate T(U_i);
5. repeat
     (a) select a slice S^i_j in PS_i;
     (b) derive a path p^i_j over S^i_j and look for an input t^i_j which executes p^i_j
     until a t^i_j has been found or there are no more slices to be processed;
6. T = T ∪ {t^i_j}; {assuming a t^i_j was found}
7. execute the program on t^i_j and monitor the set of arcs A_i exercised by
   t^i_j;
8. CUA = CUA - CUA ∩ A_i;
9. if CUA = ∅ then return(T) else goto 3;
endprocedure.
```

Fig. 6. Procedure FTSBC

Step 3: Procedure FTSBC finds test cases one at a time. Once the spanning set of arcs has been found, we need to choose an as yet not covered arc in it to be processed next. We would like to use a selection heuristic which reduces the effort of generating test inputs in the further steps of FTSBC. To this end, we observe the following points: i) the required time of steps 4 and 5 of procedure FTSBC increases with the number of predicates between the entry arc and the selected arc U_i; and ii) a test path covering the selected arc U_i may in general cover more arcs in the spanning sets after U_i. Therefore, we choose to select an arc U_i from the set of as yet not covered arcs CUA so that U_i is "close" to the program entry (i.e., the subpath from the entry to this arc has a low number of predicates). A detailed procedure can be found in [3].

Step 4: Once a U_i has been selected, we can use the program *PrincipalSlices* from the previous section with $T(U_i)$ as the current predicate for deriving a set of principal slices.

Step 5: Hence, we select a principal slice, for instance the slice S^i_{small} that has the smallest number of predicates. However, there may be several paths over this slice. We select a path p^i_{short} from these paths such that the number of predicates along it is near minimum. To do this we can apply one of the methods in the literature, e.g., [3], [21]. We can also apply one of the methods in the literature (either symbolic execution [4] [9] or execution oriented approach [11]) to find an input that executes such a path. Considering that path p^i_{short} has a near minimum number of influencing predicates (because of both principal slicing and path minimization process), these methods have high chances of success.

The remaining steps of the procedure are straighforward.

A practical question arises with loops. Usually, the shortest paths over principal slices iterate loops zero times. However in some cases, though zero iteration of some loops is feasible, this doesn't happen if several loops are present and have to be combined. In these cases, our method would lead to infeasible paths, at least at the beginning of the analysis. To avoid this, we can modify both the ddgraph and the PDG of the module to be tested such that we force the execution of at least one iteration for the loops (except possibly for the current predicate). Considering structured programs this transformation can easily be done. The resulting principal slice can be then converted back based on the original module.

In the example provided, principal slicing is used to derive a path to reach a certain point. We observe that the `PrincipalSlices` algorithm can easily be adjusted to find paths which traverse more than one given point, as would be required for instance to cover a given du pair in data flow testing. In this case, we find a principal slice to the last (i.e., the nearest to the exit arc) point and initialise each list Q_i with the set of the other points to be reached (this would require also to modify the insertion procedure in order to preserve Postorder). In fact, this is sufficient to guarantee that all of them are traversed by any path in the derived principal slices.

5 CONCLUSIONS

In this paper a new method for selecting feasible program paths has been introduced. Previous methods either considered only control flow information, such as the static selection of shortest paths [21], [3] and the goal-oriented approach [12], or used data flow without any optimization [7]. As statistically validated [20], feasible paths can be found with a much higher probability along paths traversing fewer predicates. By applying our new method of principal slicing, paths with almost minimum number of influencing predicates can be found such that both control and data flow are considered.

Principal slicing is a general method for test data generation since it finds the best potentially feasible paths in any program. This is the basis for every automatic path–wise test data generation tool, independently of which testing criterion is applied. Thus, by applying principal slicing, automated branch, data flow, and even constraint-based testing can be improved.

Another advantage of principal slicing is that all path realisation methods can use it. This means that after the selection of a very likely feasible path, both symbolic execution and function minimization methods can be applied.

We have also provided an optimised procedure for automating branch coverage testing, using principal slicing and the concept of a spanning set of branches. The procedure derives a minimal test suite (since we use the spanning set of branches to guide test path selection, we avoid redundant tests) in an effective way (since the paths are derived over principal slices with a near minimum number of influencing predicates, the test paths found are very likely to be feasible).

An interesting observation is that the concept of principal slicing provides an appealing generalization of program slicing, in the following sense. Static slices, involving *any statement* that affects a given predicate at a certain instruction, and dynamic slices, involving influencing statements along *just one* path (pertaining to a specified input), can be seen as two extreme approaches to perform program slicing. In between, one could imagine several other slicing methods, yielding slices which involve a set of paths which is smaller than for static slices and larger than for dynamic slices. These methods could be based on specific criteria depending on the objective the slice is being constructed for. In other words, one could tailor and optimise program reduction to one's specific needs, in a sort of *special–purpose* slicing. There have been some proposals in the literature. Venkatesh [16] has introduced *quasi–static* slicing, in which values of some of the inputs are fixed, while values of other are arbitrary. This can be used for program understanding. Agrawal et. al. [1] introduced *relevant slices* for incremental regression testing. Relevant slices are dynamic slices determined as follows: (1) select an input and execute the program; (2) assume that any statement in the program may be modified. A relevant slice contains all the influencing statements that may be traversed if (1) and (2) hold.

In our case, principal slicing derives a special-purpose slice which is optimised to facilitate *feasible* path generation for path-wise testing. We have discussed how, with regard to this objective, principal slices are more suitable than both static and dynamic slices and how their use in test input generation improves on earlier approaches.

References

1. H. Agrawal, J.R. Horgan, E.W. Krauser and S.A. London. Incremental regression testing, *Proc. of the 1993 IEEE Conf. on Software Maintenance*, Montreal, Canada, 348-357 (1993)
2. B. Beizer. *Software Testing Techniques, Second Edition.* Van Nostrand Reinhold, New York. 1990.
3. A. Bertolino and M. Marré. Automatic generation of path covers based on the control flow analysis of computer programs. *IEEE Trans. on Software Eng.*, 20(12):885–899, (1994).
4. L. A. Clarke. A system to generate test data and simbolically execute programs. *IEEE Trans. on Software Eng.*, 2(3):215-222, (1976).
5. R. Conradi, Experience with FORTRAN VERIFIER - A tool for documentation an error diagnosis of FORTRAN-77 programs *Proc. 1st European Software Engineering Conference*, Strasburg, France 8-11 Sept. 263-275 Springer Verlag LNCS 289 (1987)
6. R. A. DeMillo and A.J. Offutt. Constraint–based automatic test generation. *IEEE Trans. on Software Eng.*, 17(9):900–910, (1991).
7. R. Ferguson and B. Korel. The chaining approach for software test data generation. *ACM Trans. on Software Eng. and Meth.*, 5(1):63-86, (1996)
8. S. Horwitz, T. Reps and D. Binkley. Interprocedural slicing using dependence graphs. *ACM Trans. Progr. Lang. Syst.*, 12(1):26–61, (1990).
9. W. E. Howden. Symbolic testing and the DISSECT symbolic evaluation system. *IEEE Trans. on Software Eng.*, 3(4):266–278, (1977).
10. M. Kamkar. An overview and comparative classification of program slicing techniques. *Journal of Systems and Software*, 31(3):197-214, (1995)
11. B. Korel. Automated software test data generation. *IEEE Trans. on Software Eng.*, 16(8):870–879, (1990).
12. B. Korel. Dynamic method for software test data generation. *J. Softw. Testing Verif. Reliab.* 2(4):203-213, (1992)
13. B. Korel and J. Laski. Dynamic slicing of computer programs. *Journal of Systems and Software*, 13(3):187–195, (1990)
14. M. Marré and A. Bertolino. Reducing and estimating the cost of test coverage criteria. In *Proc. ACM/IEEE Int. Conf. Software Eng. ICSE-18*, pages 486–494, Berlin, Germany, March 1996.
15. K.J. Ottenstein and L.M. Ottenstein. The program dependence graph in a software development environment. *ACM SIGPLAN Notices*, 19(5):177-184, (1984)
16. G.A. Venkatesh. The semantic approach to program slicing *Proc. of the ACM SIGPLAN'91 Conference on Programming Language Design and Implementation* Toronto, Canada, 107-119 (1991)
17. M. Weiser. Program slicing. *IEEE Trans. on Software Eng.*, 10(4):352–357, (1984).
18. E. Weyuker. Translatability and decidability questions for restricted classes of program schemas. *SIAM Journal on Computers*, 8(4):587–598, (1979)
19. L. J. White and E. I. Cohen. A domain strategy for computer program testing. *IEEE Trans. on Software Eng.*, 6(3):247–257, (1980).
20. D. F. Yates and N. Malevris. Reducing the effects of infeasible paths in branch testing. *ACM SIGSOFT Software Engineering Notes*, 14(8):48–54, (1989).
21. D. F. Yates and N. Malevris. The effort required by LCSAJ testing: an assessment via a new path generation strategy. *Software Quality J.*, 4(3):227–242, (1995).

Cryptographic Verification of Test Coverage Claims

Prem Devanbu & Stuart G. Stubblebine

AT&T Labs — Research
180 Park Ave.
Florham Park, NJ 07932-0971, USA
{prem, stubblebine}@research.att.com

Abstract. The market for software components is growing, driven on the "demand side" by the need for rapid deployment of highly functional products, and on the "supply side" by distributed object standards. As components and component vendors proliferate, there is naturally a growing concern about quality, and the effectiveness of testing processes. White box testing, particularly the use of coverage criteria, is a widely used method for measuring the "thoroughness" of testing efforts. High levels of test coverage are used as indicators of good quality control procedures. Software vendors who can demonstrate high levels of test coverage have a credible claim to high quality. However, verifying such claims involves knowledge of the source code, test cases, build procedures etc. In applications where reliability and quality are critical, it would be desirable to verify test coverage claims without forcing vendors to give up valuable technical secrets. In this paper, we explore cryptographic techniques that can be used to verify such claims. Our techniques have some limitations; however, if such methods can be perfected and popularized, they can have an important "leveling" effect on the software market place: small, relatively unknown software vendors with limited resources can provide credible evidence of high-quality processes, and thus compete with much larger corporations.

1 Introduction

As the size, functionality, and complexity of software applications increase (*e.g.* the Microsoft Office^{TM} products are in the range of $O(10^6)$ lines) vendors seek to break applications into components (spell checkers, line breakers, grammar checkers etc.). Distributed component standards such as CORBA, ubiquitous networking, portable object-oriented platforms such as Java are also additional drivers of this trend. The prospect of achieving lower costs *and* higher quality with off-the-self (COTS) components has wide attraction: recently a committee appointed by the National Research Council in the USA (See [8], pp 71-76) has discussed the reuse of COTS software in nuclear power plants.

All these trends now drive a vibrant market for software components. The cost of entry into this market is low, and small vendors can be players. As the number and types of components proliferate, and smaller, newer vendors enter the market, there is a natural concern about quality. Traditionally, systems with stringent quality requirements undergo a rigorous verification process, often under the auspices of third party *verification agents* [1, 18, 19]. One common testing technique used is *white box* testing; the goal is to ensure that a system has been adequately exercised during testing. In this approach, an abstraction of the system (*e.g.*, a control flow graph) is used to identify the parts of the system that need to be exercised. Each of these parts is called a *coverage point*, and the entire set is the *coverage set*. When a suite of tests can exercise the entire coverage set, it is called a *covering test suite* with respect to this coverage set. One popular criterion for adequate test coverage is that a preponderance of the basic blocks in the control flow graph have been exercised. Typically, an instrumented version of the system is used to measure test coverage by keeping records of the blocks that are executed. We can abstract the situation as follows.

There is a system X, with source code S, out of which a (shipped) binary B_s is built. Also, from the source S, we can generate a coverage set C_γ (for some coverage criterion γ) as follows:

$$C_\gamma = c_1, c_2, \ldots c_n$$

Each of the c_i's refer to a coverage point. To cover these coverage points, it is necessary to develop a covering test suite T_γ that can exercise the coverage set for the criterion γ:

$$T_\gamma = t_1, t_2, \ldots t_m$$

such that for any given coverage point c, there is a t such that the execution of test t hits c. This is verified by first building an appropriately instrumented binary B_γ, and running the test suite T_γ.

A vendor who undertakes the cost of developing an adequate set T_γ for some stringent γ can reasonably expect that the system is less likely to fail[1] in the field due to undetected faults in in system X [15]. Often, in fields with exacting reliability requirements (such as transportation, telecommunications, energy or health) software users demand high quality standards, and expect vendors to use testing processes that achieve high levels of coverage with stringent coverage criteria. In such situations, in order to establish that the requirements have been achieved, a vendor may balk at giving a customer access to the entire source code, and all the test scripts so that coverage can be verified. The current approach is to use a third party who is trusted by both the vendor and customer to operate according to well defined procedures. Typically, these procedures restrict the third party from revealing the source code. In either case, there are considerable risks, delays, and/or expense involved for the vendor; these may be acceptable in some situations, and not in others. Indeed a given situation (where test coverage has to be verified) comprising of a vendor, a piece of software and a customer can be analyzed by considering the following issues.

---

[1] Providing, of course, that the system passes the tests!

1. How much information (source code, coverage set, test scripts etc.) is the vendor willing to reveal?
2. Is there a third party trusted by both the vendor and the customer?
3. How much time/money can be spent on test coverage verification?
4. To what level of confidence does the customer want to verify test coverage?

These questions represent different goals, which are sometimes conflicting; any practical situation will surely involve trade-offs. Different trade-offs will be acceptable under different circumstances. This paper describes one set of possible solutions that cover some typical cases; we certainly have not covered all the possibilities.

Much of the work described in this paper is aimed at reducing the amount of information that the vendor has to disclose, *viz.*, source code, symbol tables, and (particularly) the test cases. Source code is clearly the most valuable information; even the symbol table, which is typically embedded in the binary, can also be a valuable aid to reverse engineering. A large and exhaustive set of test scripts is also valuable information regardless of whether the source code or symbol table is known. Generating such a test set involves careful analysis of the requirements, as well as familiarity with the design and implementation of the system. While the most typical functions of the system may be widely known, a complete set of test cases would have to exercise unusual situations, create various feature interactions, cause exceptions to be raised etc. A comprehensive consideration of all these special cases is a valuable piece of intellectual property that demands protection. Indeed, there are vendors who make it their business to develop and sell comprehensive test suites [16, 26]. Our goal is to protect this information, while allowing the vendor to make credible test coverage claims.

Caveats and Assumptions. First, we assume that vendors are strongly motivated by market forces[2] to provide the highest quality software. Our goal is to *allow vendors to face this market demand for high quality software by providing customers with credible evidence of high quality software practices, while reducing disclosure of intellectual property.*

Second, coverage testing (like any other testing method) is not perfect. All faults may not be revealed by testing every coverage point. Vendors may contrive to create test sets that achieve coverage while concealing faults. Coverage levels may also be artificially boosted by adding spurious code. These issues are dealt with greater detail in Section 7, and some strategies for dealing with these problems are suggested; however, a significant practical disincentive to such practices is the market demand for high quality software, and the high cost of cancelled sales, refunds and/or fixing bugs in the field. Third, we make the usual assumption that all parties involved in coverage verification protocols have access to a test oracle[27] that decides, at low cost, whether the output for any test case is right or not.

---

[2] Different kinds of software sell in different markets, so quality needs do differ. For example, software components used in servers need to be of much higher quality than software used in clients

Finally, we have little to say about techniques for defeating reverse engineering; our focus is more to protect the secrecy of the largest possible number of test cases (which represent a significant investment by the vendor), while allowing the use of common methods for repelling reverse engineering, *viz.*, shipping only binaries without symbol tables. Without a physically protected hardware platform, a determined adversary can reverse-engineer a good deal of information about software. Techniques and tools to support reverse engineering are an area of active research. In fact, previous research [2, 4, 20, 24] demonstrates how control-flow graphs, profile information, compiler-generated binary idioms, and even slices can be derived by analyzing and instrumenting binaries. De-Compilation (converting binary to source code) and binary porting (converting binaries from one machine architecture to another) are typical goals of binary analysis. We say more on this in the conclusion.

We employ several different cryptographic techniques in this paper. We begin with a brief description of these techniques; readers familiar with cryptography may skim this section.

2 Summary of Cryptographic Methods

Different combinations of customers, vendors and software require different solutions. In this paper, we apply several cryptographic techniques to address some common scenarios that may arise in practice. We now briefly describe the techniques we have used in our work; more complete descriptions can be found in [23]. All of these techniques are used to build assurance in the customer ($\mathcal{C}$) that the vendor($\mathcal{V}$) has high test coverage, while attempting to protect $\mathcal{V}$'s secrets. Our work is somewhat related to the notion of zero-knowledge protocols (ZKP). Zero-knowledge protocols are designed to allow a prover to demonstrate knowledge of a secret while revealing no information about the secret. ZKP are based on a challenge-response regime. We use a similar idea: a skeptical $\mathcal{C}$ challenges $\mathcal{V}$ to provide test cases, given a particular part of a system; with appropriate responses, the $\mathcal{C}$ develops confidence in $\mathcal{V}$'s claims about test coverage. Unlike ZKP's however, our approach actually reveals *some* information. The thrust of this work has been to reduce the amount of information revealed. For the descriptions that follow, we use some public/private key pairs: assume $K_{\mathcal{P}}^{-1}$ is a good private signing key for the individual $\mathcal{P}$ and $K_{\mathcal{P}}$ is the corresponding public signature verification key for the lifetime of the test coverage verification process.

1. **Cryptographic Signatures**. Given a datum δ, $\sigma_{K_{\mathcal{P}}^{-1}}(\delta)$ is a value representing the signature of δ by $\mathcal{P}$, which can be verified using $K_{\mathcal{P}}$. $\sigma_{K_{\mathcal{P}}^{-1}}(\delta)$ is typically just an encrypted hash value of δ. Given δ, the signature can be verified using $K_{\mathcal{P}}$. This is a way for $\mathcal{P}$ to "commit" to a datum in an irrevocable manner.

2. **Trusted Third Party**. If there is a trusted third party (denoted by $\mathcal{T}$) that can act as a "buffer" between $\mathcal{C}$ and $\mathcal{V}$, $\mathcal{T}$ can use information supplied by $\mathcal{V}$

to assure C about V's testing practices, while protecting V's secrets. T can be relied upon both to protect V's secrets, and operate fairly, without bias. Note that T can certify a datum δ by appending the signature $\sigma_{K_T^{-1}}(\delta)$.

3. **Trusted Tools.** To verify any type of white box coverage, it is necessary to provide information extracted from source files. Tools (trusted by all parties involved) that extract exactly the information required for coverage verification, and adjoin a cryptographic signature with a published key, can be used to extract trusted coverage information providing the tools are not tampered with; later, we address limitations of using trusted tools.

4. **Random Sampling.** Consider an adverserial situation where a party P_a claims that a proportion ρ of the members of a set σ have a property π, and P_a is willing to reveal the proof that π holds for only *some* members of σ. A skeptical party P_b can choose a member σ_i, of this set at random, and challenge P_a to demonstrate that $\pi(\sigma_i)$ holds. After several such trials, P_a can estimate ρ subject to confidence intervals. This technique can be used to estimate test coverage levels.

5. **Autonomous Pseudo-Random Sampling.** The random challenges discussed above can be performed by P_a herself, using a published pseudo-random number generator G with a controlled seed. If G can be trusted by adversaries to produce a fair random sample, P_a can publish a credible, self-verified estimate of ρ. Notice that successive fragments of a very long hash string produced by a one-way hash function can also be used to generate samples.

3   Exploring the Problem

To explore this problem, we exhibit a series of methods that are applicable in different situations as we discussed earlier.

We start with the basic third party method, that is the currently used approach to verifying test coverage while simultaneously protecting a vendor's secrets. We then gradually introduce cryptographic techniques to protect the vendor V's secrets while simultaneously making it difficult for V to cheat. Our focus of security is not at the session layer but at the application layer. Thus we assume the testing protocols occur over secure channels[3] such as those provided by Secure Socket Layer (SSL [13]). In the following scenarios, V refers to the vendor who claims to have achieved γ test coverage on a system X, and C refers to the skeptical customer who wants to be convinced.

Basic Third Party Method

1. V sends T, a trusted third party, the source code S, and the test suite T_γ, and a description of the coverage criterion γ.
2. T builds B_γ from S, and constructs the coverage set C_γ.

---

[3] Such facilities provide message integrity, confidentiality, and participant authentication.

3. $\mathcal{T}$ runs the test suite T_γ against B_γ and verifies that the suite hits the coverage set.
4. $\mathcal{T}$ tells $\mathcal{C}$ that the γ coverage criterion for X has been met by the test suite T_γ.
5. $\mathcal{V}$ ships B_s to $\mathcal{C}$, with the claim that $\mathcal{T}$ has verified coverage.

This approach is weakened by some questionable assumptions. First, there may not be a trusted third party acceptable to both $\mathcal{T}$ and $\mathcal{C}$, and to whom $\mathcal{V}$ is willing to to reveal the source and the test suite. There may be a commercial incentive for $\mathcal{T}$ to exploit this information in some legal or undetectable ways; a truly trustworthy $\mathcal{T}$ may be hard to find. Second, $\mathcal{T}$ has to replicate $\mathcal{V}$'s entire build apparatus, (*viz.,* compilers, libraries, and auxiliary tools) and execute the build (which may be complex). There is also a glaring weakness: $\mathcal{V}$ could have sent an older, well tested version to $\mathcal{T}$, and ship a newer version of X, with additional, untested functionality to $\mathcal{C}$ (One way to avoid this problem is to have $\mathcal{T}$ also build an *uninstrumented* binary version of X, from the same source, sign it, and have this be the version that $\mathcal{V}$ ships to her customers). Finally, there is a subtle and inevasible attack whereby $\mathcal{V}$ can try to find "fault-hiding" test cases, which we discuss later[4] (Section 7).

The *Basic Method* requires significant effort of $\mathcal{T}$. This will probably increase $\mathcal{V}$'s costs and cause delays. However, this method can be used when there is a suitable $\mathcal{T}$, the costs are acceptable, and $\mathcal{C}$ wants an accurate estimate of test coverage. Indeed it is the main current method used for test coverage verification [18]. It would be better if $\mathcal{V}$ could just ship $\mathcal{T}$ the binary and not the source. This gives $\mathcal{V}$ a few opportunities to cheat, some of which can be addressed; the remaining ones may sometimes be acceptable. This is the motivation for the next section.

3.1 Simple Binary Patching approaches

We now explore some approaches that use just the binary to verify test coverage claims. Note that we usually mean binaries built with full symbol tables, i.e., compiled with the "-g" option in most C compilers; the issue of eliminating (or abridging to the extent possible) this symbol table is visited in the next section. *Protocol 1*

1. From S, $\mathcal{V}$ constructs the system B_s and the set of coverage points C_γ.
2. $\mathcal{V}$ sends $\mathcal{T}$: B_s, C_γ and the test suite T_γ, with the locations in the source files corresponding the coverage points.
3. $\mathcal{T}$ uses a binary instrumentation tool, either interactive *e.g.,* a debugger, or batch-oriented (*e.g.,* ATOM [25], EEL [20]) to instrument B_s, using the line number/file information sent by $\mathcal{T}$, and the symbol table information embedded in B_s. For example, a debugger can set break points at the appropriate locations (e.g., line numbers in files).

---

[4] All the protocols we describe in this paper are subject to this attack, although there are mitigating considerations.

4. $\mathcal{T}$ runs the test suite T_γ against the instrumented binary, and verifies coverage level. For example, the debugger can be set to delete each break point when "hit". The coverage level is verified by the number of remaining breakpoints.
5. $\mathcal{T}$ signs the file B_s (perhaps after extracting the symbol table from B_s) and sends $\sigma_{K_\mathcal{T}^{-1}}(B_s)$ to $\mathcal{V}$.
6. $\mathcal{V}$ verifies the signature on $\sigma_{K_\mathcal{T}^{-1}}(B_s)$, using $K_\mathcal{T}$; then, $\mathcal{V}$ sends B_s and $\sigma_{K_\mathcal{T}}(B_s)$ to $\mathcal{C}$.

This method improves upon the *Basic Method* in a few ways: first, the source is not revealed to $\mathcal{T}$. Second, $\mathcal{T}$ does not recreate $\mathcal{V}$'s build environment. Third, $\mathcal{T}$ works with the shipped version of the software, so he can directly "sign" it after he has verified the coverage claims. Finally, $\mathcal{T}$'s work is reduced; rather than building instrumented and uninstrumented versions, he only has to instrument the binary, which is not harder than the link phase of a build. So presumably, *Protocol* 1 would be cheaper, faster and less error-prone than the *Basic Method*.

A major weakness in *Protocol* 1 is that $\mathcal{V}$ is trusted to build an accurate coverage set C_γ. $\mathcal{V}$ can cheat and build a smaller coverage set, and thus convince $\mathcal{C}$ that he has a higher test coverage than he really does. However, he may have difficulties if he ships faulty software while falsely claiming high levels of test coverage. If the software fails frequently in the field, he could be called upon to reveal the source code to a trusted third party, and prove that his coverage analysis was accurate, and that the shipped binary was built with the same source code.

Even so, $\mathcal{V}$ still has to reveal a lot to $\mathcal{T}$: the entire coverage set and the entire test set. If X is a very popular and/or difficult system to build, this information may be very valuable, and $\mathcal{T}$ may quietly sell this information to $\mathcal{V}$'s competitors. The next protocol reduces the amount of information $\mathcal{V}$ has to reveal, while not increasing $\mathcal{V}$'s opportunities to cheat;
Protocol 2

1. $\mathcal{V}$ builds B_s from S, creates C_γ, $\sigma_{K_\mathcal{V}^{-1}}(i, C_\gamma(i))$, for $i = 1 \ldots | C_\gamma |$. and $\sigma_{K_\mathcal{V}^{-1}}(i, C_\gamma(i), t_i, r_i)$, for $i = 1 \ldots | C_\gamma |$. t_i is the corresponding test case[5], and r_i is a random number inserted to confound attacks which attempt to guess the content before it is revealed.
2. $\mathcal{V}$ sends $\mathcal{T}$ all the above signatures and B_s.
3. $\mathcal{T}$ challenges $\mathcal{V}$ with some small number l of the coverage points.
4. For each challenge, $\mathcal{V}$ reveals $C_\gamma(i), t_i$, and r_i. $\mathcal{T}$ can cross-check with the signatures delivered above.
5. $\mathcal{T}$ uses the coverage point location information, instruments B_s and runs the supplied test case to check coverage.
6. $\mathcal{T}$ signs the binary and sends $\sigma_{K_\mathcal{T}^{-1}}(B_s)$ to $\mathcal{V}$.
7. $\mathcal{T}$ archives the testing procedure including all the information sent in step 2.

[5] Or a string indicating the lack of a test case for this coverage point.

8. $\mathcal{V}$ ships $(B_s, \sigma_{K_{\mathcal{T}}^{-1}}(B_s))$ to $\mathcal{C}$.

We shall discuss the commitments in step 1 presently; for now, we focus on steps 3-5. Here $\mathcal{T}$ randomly picks a small number of challenges to $\mathcal{V}$. This method betters *Protocol* 1 in one important way: $\mathcal{V}$ reveals only *some* coverage points, and *some* tests. Since $\mathcal{V}$ cannot predict which coverage points $\mathcal{T}$ will pick, he must prepare tests to cover most of them. $\mathcal{V}$ packages the test cases with the corresponding coverage point, and a random number; this discourages $\mathcal{T}$ from brute-force searching for test cases and coverage points using the signatures from step 1; he reveals these on being challenged. With a small number of random challenges, $\mathcal{T}$ can bound $\mathcal{V}$'s test coverage. If $\mathcal{V}$'s responses cover a proportion p_s of $\mathcal{T}$'s challenges, $\mathcal{T}$ can estimate $\mathcal{V}$'s actual coverage p (using Hoeffding's version of Chernoff bounds for the "positive tail" of a binomial distribution, see [17], pp 190-191):

$$P(p_s - p \geq \epsilon) \leq e^{\frac{-n\epsilon^2}{2p(1-p)}} \ when \ p \geq 0.5 \qquad (1)$$

For a 95% confidence level, we can bound ϵ:

$$e^{\frac{-n\epsilon^2}{2p(1-p)}} \leq 0.05$$

$$\epsilon = \sqrt{\frac{2ln(\frac{1}{0.05})p(p-1)}{n}}$$

Clearly, as n goes up, $\mathcal{T}$ gains confidence in his estimate p_s. Thus, at the 95% confidence level, $\mathcal{T}$ can reasonably conclude that an estimate of $p = 0.95$ is no more than 0.09 *too high* with about 25 samples. Experimental work [15, 21] indicates that branch coverage levels in the range of 80-90% have a high likelihood of exposing faults in the software. Estimated coverage levels in this range can give a customer high confidence that the $\mathcal{V}$'s testing has exposed a good number of faults. So it is in $\mathcal{V}$'s interest to allow $\mathcal{T}$ the largest possible number of challenges, with a very high expected p. Clearly, this will incent $\mathcal{V}$ to achieve very high coverage levels. It is also important to keep in mind that this "random sampling" places limits on the accuracy of $\mathcal{T}$'s estimate of $\mathcal{V}$'s test coverage; essentially, we are trading off the amount of information disclosed for $\mathcal{T}$. In cases where this trade-off is acceptable, this technique is applicable.

There is a threat to the validity of the confidence level calculation described above: the sampling process is not really a series of independent events. Executions of coverage points (blocks, branches, or functions) are often strongly correlated. Detailed discussions are omitted here for brevity; some approaches are discussed in more detail in [6]; In a later section, we discuss the possibility of committing ahead of time to a coverage level; this avoids sampling difficulties.

Now we return to the two sets of commitments (signatures) in step 1. The first set reveals a signature on each element of the coverage set and the corresponding test case; $\mathcal{T}$ needs only to know the actual coverage points for his challenges. $\mathcal{V}$ pads each signature computation with a random number to securely hide the association of the test case and the coverage point for the unchallenged coverage points. The second set of signatures, on the unpadded coverage points, can be used to check that the coverage points are indeed different. Vendors do have the ability ship the software with a spurious (smaller) coverage set; this attack can be dealt with by providing the vendor with trusted coverage analysis tool ensconced in a physically secure device with an embedded secret key that can sign its output. Details are omitted here for brevity, and can be found in [6, 7].

Finally, this approach involves the disclosure of the symbol table along with the binary; the table is needed by debuggers to set break points. This disclosure can be avoid by shipping the actual memory address of the instrumentation point, and using a tool that insert a break point given a binary address. Such tools can also be embedded in a physically secure device. Details are can be found in [6].

3.2 Eliminating coverage analysis tools

Such physically secured analysis tools, however, are not yet available; we now suggest an approach to eliminate the dependence on the source altogether. However, there are complications with this approach. In the verification protocol listed below, we use basic-block coverage as an illustration; this approach can be extended to some other coverage models. The approach used here depends upon analysis of the binary, which $\mathcal{T}$ has access to. Given an instruction at an arbitrary location in the binary, and a knowledge of the instruction set of the architecture, it is possible to bound the basic block containing that instruction. This property can be used for verifying basic block coverage.

Protocol 3

1. $\mathcal{V}$ sends to $\mathcal{T}$ the binary B_s, and $\sigma_{K_v^{-1}}(i, C_\gamma(i), t_i, r_i)$, *for* $i = 1 \ldots | C_\gamma |$.
2. $\mathcal{T}$ chooses a random location, l, within the binary.
3. $\mathcal{V}$ reveals the corresponding test case, coverage point, and random pad.
4. $\mathcal{T}$ can set a breakpoint at l using his favorite instrumentation technique, and execute the test to verify the coverage.
5. Repeat the above steps for the desired number of challenges and proceed as before.

With this approach, we don't need to analyze source code to determine the set of coverage points Here, $\mathcal{T}$ (presumably) chooses random points in the executable, and it is up to $\mathcal{V}$ to provide the coverage evidence. This can be done by $\mathcal{V}$, since he has access to both the binary symbol table and the source code. Given a machine address, $\mathcal{V}$ can identify the corresponding source line easily, using a debugger (*e.g.,* with gdb, the "info line *addr*" will translate a given machine address to a source file and line number). If the $\mathcal{V}$ has previously developed a good covering test set, and verified his coverage levels, he can readily identify the specific covering test using the file/line number and data from his coverage verification process.

However, there are several difficulties with this approach; they all have to do with "testability" of the binary. Finding test cases to cover a given location in a binary can be harder than with source code, specially when:

1. the location occurs in code generated by the compiler in response to a complex source language operator (e.g, inlined constructors or overloaded operators in C++); this code may contain control flow not present in the source, or when

2. it occurs in unreachable code generated by the compiler, or when,

3. it occurs in off-the-shelf (OTS) software incorporated by vendor in his product, for which the vendor has no tests;

There are approaches to dealing with some of these issues. Generated code often corresponds to idioms; this information can be used to find test cases. Sometimes generated code may contain additional control flow that represent different cases that can occur in the field, and V can legitimately be expected to supply covering test cases. When the generated code is genuinely unreachable [22], V can claim it as such, and supply source code that C can compile to create similar binaries. Occurrences of dead code in the binary are really bugs in the compiler, and are likely to be rare.

Even when a challenge happens to fall within the bounds of an OTS binary, V has several options for test coverage verification. If the OTS is a well-known, reputable, piece of public domain software, he can simply identify the software, and C can download the software and do a byte-comparison. Even if the OTS in not public, signatures can be obtained from V_{ots}, the vendor, for comparison. If the OTS is not well known, but has been independently subject to test coverage verification, then evidence of this verification can be provided to C. Another approach is for V to relay challenges to V_{ots}, who may be able to handle them, and pass her responses back to C.

Binary-based random challenges can be performed without revealing source code, or symbol tables, and without resorting to trusted tools; the trade-off here is that the mapping to source code may be non-trivial for some parts of the binary; for this and other reasons, it may be hard to construct an exercising test case. As binary de-compilation tools [3] mature and become more widely available, they can be used by customers to build confidence about areas of the binary that V claims to be non-testable for the reasons listed above.

4 Towards Eliminating the trusted third party

All the approaches described above rely upon a trusted third party ($\mathcal{T}$). However, it may sometimes be undesirable to use $\mathcal{T}$, for reasons of economy or secrecy.

A naive approach to eliminating $\mathcal{T}$ would be for V to rerun the verification protocols described above with each software buyer. This is undesirable. First, repeating the protocol with each buyer is expensive and slow. Second, V would reveal information to different, potentially adverserial parties who might collude to reverse engineer secrets about B_s. Third, since a potentially adverserial buyer is involved, there is a risk that the challenge points might be deliberately chosen to expose the most valuable information about V's software. For example, if $\mathcal{T}$ was forced to reveal (on a challenge from a customer c_1) some test cases that pertained to handling some unusual or difficult case in the input domain, other customers might collude with c_1 to probe other points in the same area of the binary to expose $\mathcal{V}$'s implementation/design strategies for dealing with some difficult cases.

Re-examining *Protocols* $1 \ldots 3$ listed in the previous section, it becomes clear that the main role played by $\mathcal{T}$ is choosing the challenge coverage points; we eliminate his role using autonomous pseudo-random sampling.

Protocol 4

1. $\mathcal{V}$ prepares the binary B_s, and $\sigma_{K_{\mathcal{V}}^{-1}}(i, C_\gamma(i), t_i, r_i)$, *for* $i = 1 \ldots \mid C_\gamma \mid$.
2. $\mathcal{V}$ computes a well-known, published one-way hash function of B_s to yield a *location control string*, $\mathcal{L}$. Successive byte groups of $\mathcal{L}$ are used to derive locations $l^1, \ldots, l^j$.
3. For each l_i, $\mathcal{V}$ reveals the test cases, random numbers and coverage points; call each revelation $\mathcal{R}_i$.
4. After some set of challenges l_i, $\mathcal{V}$ stops, and packages the $\mathcal{R}_i$'s and the $\sigma_{K_{\mathcal{V}}^{-1}}(i, C_\gamma(i), t_i, r_i)$'s, along with his release of B_s
5. $\mathcal{C}$ verifies test coverage by repeating the generation of the location control string, and checking the corresponding revelations by $\mathcal{V}$ for coverage.

Protocol 4 offers several advantages. We have eliminated the "middleman", $\mathcal{T}$, thus saving time and money. This approach is also advantageous where secrecy is involved. Instead of $\mathcal{T}$, a one-way hash function now drives the choice of the challenges. $\mathcal{V}$ cannot control the value of the string S_{vc}; a customer can easily verify the value of the location control string using the delivered software and the public hash function. Furthermore, there is no need for $\mathcal{V}$ to repeat this process with each customer. There is no risk that customers might collude and pool information.

There is, however a plausible risk in the above scenario: since $\mathcal{V}$ has control over the input to the hash string, he could automatically repeat the following:

1. Compute $\mathcal{L} = hash(B_s)$.
2. If a very large subset of the resulting locations $l_1 \ldots l_n$ are not covered, stop. Otherwise,
3. Generate another binary B_{s1} by padding B_s with null instructions. Go to step 1

This amounts to repeated Bernoulli trials drawn from the set of coverage points; after some trials, $\mathcal{V}$ could find an $\mathcal{L}$ that artificially boosts his coverage ratio. To avoid this attack, we need a way to "monitor" his trials. In [6] we describe an approach involving the use of a simple, fully automated trusted server to register trials; this allows a customer to monitor every trial made by a vendor, and appropriately bound the confidence intervals on the coverage estimate. Details are omitted for brevity.

5 Committing and Enforcing an Upper Bound on Test Coverage

The protocols described up to this point have a weakness: V may get lucky and demonstrate a higher test coverage then he actually has. This is inherent to challenges based on random sampling. We now describe a technique that requires the vendor to assert an upper bound on test coverage. This technique can be used in conjunction with any of the protocols described above. With this approach, the vendor can be caught cheating if he is called upon to reveal a test case corresponding to a coverage point which he did not account for as a untested coverage point. However, the vendor is not forced to reveal potentially sensitive information about exactly which coverage points have no test cases. We present the technique here as a series of steps that can be interleaved into the protocols described above.

1. V commits to untested coverage points by sending $Hash(i, r_i, C_i), i = 1 \ldots N_{nt}$ for each coverage point not tested (where r_i is chosen at random by V). Using this, the C or T can compute the upper bound on test coverage claims.
2. When the vendor is called upon to reveal a test point for which it does not have a test case, the vendor reveals r_i and i, the reference to the particular hash in the first step. The tester can recompute the hash of the tuple i, r_i, and C_i and compare it to the commitment of the untested coverage points.
3. If testing results with numbers higher than the coverage claims, the results are decreased to the upper bound.

In step 1, V commits to all the coverage points which are admittedly not covered by test cases. From this information C (or T, as the case might be) can determine an upper bound on the actual coverage ratio. For example, in the case of Protocol 4, C can determine the coverage set by analysis of the binary; if the size of this set is N_{cs}, he can bound the coverage ratio as

$$\frac{N_{cs} - N_{nt}}{N_{cs}}$$

Step 1 can be done at the same time as the first step in (*e.g.,*) Protocols 4. Step 2 above is basically an extension to the random challenge step in many of the protocols. Given a random challenge, the vendor may or may not have a test case; if he does, the protocols work as described earlier. In the case where there is no test case, he reveals r_i and i, thus "checking off" one of the uncovered coverage points committed in step 1. If V is unable to reveal a test case, or an r_i, i pair, he is caught in a lie. Finally, in Step 3 above, the tester can compare his estimate from the random sample to the *a priori* upper bound computed above.

In this technique, V makes a clear claim about the proportion of tests he has coverage for, and the total number of tests. The purpose of the random trials therefore is not to narrow the confidence intervals around an *estimate* the value of the coverage ratio, but just to make sure $\mathcal{V}$ is not lying. With each trial, there is a probability that he will be caught; this increases with the number of trials. To model this analytically, assume that there are N total coverage points, and $\mathcal{V}$ is lying about l of those. i.e., for l of those he has no coverage points for, but he is trying to pretend he does. Denote the fraction $\frac{l}{N}$ by f. On any one trial, the chance that he will be caught is f, and that he will sneak through is $1 - f$. After n trials, the probability that he will escape is $(1 - f)^n$ If we bound this above by ϵ, we can bound n as follows:

$$n \leq \frac{log\ \epsilon}{log\ (1 - f)}$$

It behooves $\mathcal{V}$ to provide many trials to build confidence that he is not lying. Note that the value of the coverage ratio is always what the vendor says it is—the confidence value refers to $\mathcal{C}$'s subjective probability of $\mathcal{V}$'s veracity, i.e., the likelihood that $\mathcal{V}$ would have been caught trying to cheat. Such an event will seriously damage a vendor's credibility; most vendors may not be willing to tolerate even a small chance of being caught, and thus would be cautious about misrepresenting the coverage ratio. If $\mathcal{V}$ tried to cheat on even 5% of the cases, with 20 trials, there is a 50% chance of exposure. For many vendors, this may be intolerable. We expect that this approach should provide $\mathcal{C}$ with a more accurate coverage estimate.

6 Disclosure Concerns

We now return to the key first issue in the list of desiderata in Section 1, How much of $\mathcal{V}$'s valuable technical secrets do our techniques reveal?

At a minimum, $\mathcal{V}$ has to ship the binary B_s. Simply from the binary (even without a symbol table) an adverserial customer $\mathcal{C_A}$ can construct a good deal of information by static analysis: the control flow graph, the size of the data space, the number of functions/entry points etc. A limited amount of static control & data dependency analysis is even possible. Indeed, tools like EEL [20] can perform much of this analysis. In addition, by instrumentation, and dynamic analysis. $\mathcal{C_A}$ can detect which paths of the control path are activated for different input conditions. Some recent work by Ball & Larus [2] show how it is possible to trace and profile control flow path execution using just the binary. Additional information can be gained by tracing memory references and building dynamic slices. Given the degree of information that can be reconstructed, it is important to evaluate carefully if the approaches listed above yield additional opportunities for $\mathcal{C_A}$.

First, assume that the symbol table is stripped from the delivered binary B_s. During the verification process, whether driven by $\mathcal{T}$ or not, the only additional information revealed in response to challenges are the relevant coverage points and the applicable test cases. The coverage points, if based on the binary, can be independently generated by $\mathcal{C_A}$ or $\mathcal{T}$; the only additional information is the test case, and its connection to this coverage point. *A priori*, the value of this information is difficult to estimate. Important factors include the manner in which the test cases are supplied, the resulting behavior of the system, etc. Test cases could be supplied in the form of source code or ASCII input (which might be very revealing) or in the form of binary objects or binary data (which could be more difficult to interpret). As far as the verification protocol is concerned, the only relevant behavior is that the selected challenge coverage point be exercised; however, there may be additional behaviour that reveals information to the adversary.

In the best case, if the relevant test case reflects a fairly "typical" type of usage, then the information given away is minimal; presumably C_A would very likely find this out during his attacks using dynamic analysis. However, if the test case reflects an unusual circumstance, and the test case is delivered in a manner transparent to C_A, then some valuable information about unusual but important design and requirements details of B_s may be revealed. The risk of such an exposure is traded-off against the ability to verify test coverage.

The delivery of test cases to C_A, particularly the tests that somehow embody valuable proprietary information is an important issue that remains to be addressed: Can we deliver test cases in a way that protect V's secrets, while still exhibiting test coverage?

Now we relax the assumption that the symbol table is stripped out. While it is possible to verify test coverage without the symbol table, there are some difficulties (discussed above) associated with omitting it. In several of the protocols we listed above, we assumed that the symbol table was included in the binary shipped to the verifier. Clearly, the symbol table offers additional opportunities for C_A to reconstruct information. Some standard obfuscation techniques such as garbling the symbolic names would be helpful. But in general, the advantages of omitting the symbol table may override the resulting difficulties.

7 Coverage Verification Limitations

There are limitations to the type of coverage that can be verified with our protocols. Any protocol that hides source code from the verifier (Protocols 1 and 2) is limited by the available binary instrumentation facilities, and by the testability of the binary (which we discussed earlier). For simplicity, in the above discussion, we have assumed basic block coverage, since it very simple to check *e.g.*, with a debugger. If a far more stringent coverage is desired, such as *all paths* [11] then a tool based on [2] could be used to monitor the various paths during coverage verification. However, this level of coverage testing is extremely rare in practice.

Another limitation is the manner in which the challenge coverage points are selected. The discussion above again assumes "single point" type of coverage criteria (*e.g.* basic block or statement coverage). Other criteria, such as *all d-u paths*[6] involve pairs of statements. We have not addressed *d-u path* coverage; for

---

[6] A d-u path is a control flow path from the definition of a variable to its use, free of additional definitions of the same variable.

practical software, particularly in the context of heap memory usage, there are formidable obstacles to using this type of coverage. Our protocols can, however, be adapted to branch coverage, with suitable extensions to the instrumentation tools and to our random sampling protocol. Thus, to adapt Protocols 3 and 4 to branch coverage: first, a random location in the binary is chosen; then, the bounding basic block is found; at this point, if entry point of this basic block has a conditional branch, a coin is flipped to determine the direction of this branch; now, $\mathcal{V}$ can be challenged for a covering test case. With a suitable instrumentation facility, the binary can be instrumented and coverage verified.

It should be noted here that while coverage testing has widely used in industry, some researchers dispute the effectiveness of whitebox (or "clearbox") coverage methods. Most recent empirical work [15, 21] has found that test sets with coverage levels in the range of of 80-90% have a high chance of exposing failures. Earlier work [10] had yielded inconclusive results; however, the programs used in [10] were substantially smaller than [15, 21]. On the analytic front, rigorous probabilistic models of the relationship between increasing white-box coverage and the likelihood of fault detection have been developed [9, 12]. However, no known testing process is perfect; all known methods, white box or black box *will let some faults slip!* The best current experimental work [15, 21] suggests that high levels of white box test coverage can guarantee high levels of fault detection. However, since white box testing is not perfect, there are several complications. Given a coverage point that has faults, there may be several test cases that exercise that point. Some of these test cases will expose faults, but others may not. Consider a particular coverage point c, which has a fault f. When $\mathcal{V}$ generates a covering set of test cases, assume he finds a test τ which just happens to not expose the fault f. Since his software tests correctly, he will simply supply this test case along with the (faulty) delivered program. No malice is intended: coverage testing is imperfect, the vendor honestly delivered a program with a fault that just happened to slip by.

Now consider the case where the test case chosen by $\mathcal{V}$ happens to expose the fault. $\mathcal{V}$ now has two choices. He can fix the fault, or he can cheat: he can try to find a different test case τ^*, which covers c but does not expose a fault. The incentive for $\mathcal{V}$ to cheat depends on several factors: the likelihood the fault will occur in the field, the market conditions for the software (how many copies can he sell, for how long?), the cost of fixing the software, and the difficulty of finding a fault-hiding (but c-covering) test case τ^*. In most cases, it will probably be best to fix the fault. In the absolute worst case, assuming that the nature of the fault and the business conditions really motivate $\mathcal{V}$ to cheat, the cost finding such a τ^* depends on the distribution of failure-causing input within the subdomain of the input that causes the coverage point c to be exercised. If $\mathcal{V}$ is lucky, the failure region is small and well isolated within this input partition; he may succeed in finding a covering test case that is fault hiding. On the other hand, if the fault is provoked by many inputs from the subdomain of the input that exercises c, then $\mathcal{V}$ may have to read the code carefully (or spend a lot of time randomly sampling the input partition) to find such a τ^*; in this case, it may be easier to simply fix the problem. Finally, this method of attack (finding covering test cases that hide the fault) is not specific to the cryptographic techniques we have described; even the third party coverage certification method that is currently used is vulnerable.

We can favorably bias the situation by encouraging vendors to provide (and commit to) more than one test case per coverage point. The more tests a vendor provides for a coverage point, the less likely it is that *all* these tests are fault-hiding. A random search for fault-covering cases in the corresponding input partition is not likely to work; it becomes necessary to understand the nature of the fault, and carefully construct several examples that exercise that coverage point, but hide the fault. As this effort increases, so does the incentive for V to simply fix the fault. The more test cases V can provide[7] for each coverage point, the less likely it is that he is hiding a fault in that coverage point.

Another difficulty inherent in coverage analysis is the opportunity to *pad*. Vendors can add spurious code which introduces additional control flow. Such code can be designed to be readily covered, thus artificially boosting coverage. It is not feasible to determine if this has been done. The only way to totally avoid this problem insist upon 100% coverage for some criteria; padding becomes irrelevant. For some criteria 100% coverage may be feasible for a medium-sized component; since such coverage levels are indicators of thorough testing, there may be market incentives that push vendors to achieve such a level. A series of coverage levels for increasingly stronger criteria, starting at and gradually decreasing from 100%, would be a desirable goal. Another approach to discourage padding is to demand explanations when challenge points are uncovered by tests. A vendor can voluntarily build confidence that he hasn't padded by making large number of pseudo random choices among his uncovered set and providing explanations for why they are not covered, and describing the conditions under which the points would be executed. Such conditions had better be highly unusual and difficult to create; if they are not, the vendor could be expected to provide a test case. If a large number of such disclosures are made, the vendor would be at risk of embarrassment by subsequent revelation that the coverage point was executed under less uncommon circumstances. A large number of such disclosures can build confidence that points do not remain uncovered simply as a result of padding. Again, another powerful disincentive to excessive padding is the vendor's inherent desire to produce high-quality software, and thus avoid costs of refunds, cancelled sales and extra update releases.

To summarize, our work rests on the assumption (again, supported by [15, 21]) that comprehensive coverage testing tends to expose faults, and on the assumption that vendors will most often find it more profitable to fix faults exposed by a covering test (rather than searching for a test that covers but hides faults). In the worst case, when the difficulty of fixing the faults exceeds the difficulty of finding test cases to hide the fault, and V expects the faults in question are rare enough so that he can collect enough revenue before the fault

---

[7] The test cases do not all have to be revealed; they could be hidden as a hash value, and revealed only upon a (random) challenge.

is exposed in in the field, then he may be tempted to find a hiding test case. By encouraging vendors to reveal many test cases for each coverage point, we can decrease the incentive to hide faults. But even in this worst case, the use of these techniques can provide customers with the justified belief that the vendors have every incentive and the means to find and fix all but the ones that are very unusual and/or difficult to fix. Padding is another problem; 100% coverage is the best way to preclude the chance of padding. We have suggested some ways that vendors can provide evidence that they did not pad; we are actively pursuing better ways of determining if padding has occurred.

In any case, during practical use of the protocol, it is important for both customers and vendors to be mindful of the suspected limitations of white box coverage testing. Additional black-box and/or acceptance testing will often be needed.

Protocol id	Reveals source code	Reveals symbol table	Reveals all test cases	Reveals entire coverage set	Uses trusted third party	Comments
Basic	yes	yes	yes	yes	yes	
1	no	yes	yes	yes	yes	a
2	no	yes	no	no	yes	a,d
3	no	no	no	no	yes	b,d
4	no	no	no	no	no	b,c,d

a Vendor can cheat by building a spurious coverage set.
b Verifying test coverage on binary, rather than source, complicates finding test cases. Binary analysis tools may help build C's confidence.
c Vendor can try to cheat by performing repeated trials by padding the binary (but countermeasures are available).
d Vendor's coverage level can only be estimated, subject to confidence levels; however, the "upper bound" technique described in Section 5 is applicable.

Table 1. Characteristics of the various protocols.

8 Conclusion

We have shown a set of protocols that can be used to verify test coverage, while protecting information valuable to the vendor and simultaneously reducing the vendor's ability to cheat. The results are summarized in Table 7. These protocols use various techniques such as trusted third parties, trusted tools, signatures, random challenges, and "autonomous" random challenges. These techniques can be used in different combinations, depending on the needs of the customer and the vendor. Combinations other than the ones we have presented are possible. For example, in Protocol 2, rather than using a third party to generate the challenges, the vendor could use a location control string like that used in Protocol 4 to generate the challenges.

Some of our techniques are compatible with a widely used method for repelling reverse engineering, which is shipping binaries without source code or a symbol table. The only additional vendor information that our techniques need reveal are a small proportion of test cases. While it is possible to conceive of reverse engineering countermeasures that may not be compatible with our techniques, we believe that we can adjust our methods to be compatible with countermeasures that may complicate reverse engineering, such as the introduction of additional static control flow, additional dynamic control flow, or even certain other approaches that involve dynamically decrypting code prior to execution; we are actively exploring these issues.

Finally, we note that "self-validated" approaches (if they can be perfected) that verify testing effectiveness may have an important *leveling* effect on the software market. Notice that our protocols impose a modest overhead on developers who already have achieved high levels of test coverage: with the self-validated approach of Protocol 4, the developer simply runs an autonomous random sampling of his coverage points; his (pre-existing) test coverage data points to the relevant tests to be revealed. Much of this can be automated, and we are constructing supporting tools based on GENOA [5]. Using such methods, any vendor, without the help of a trusted third party, and at relatively low overheads, can provide a credible claim that their software quality control is stringent, while disclosing only a minimal amount of information. This enables small and unknown vendors to compete effectively (on the basis of perceived quality) with very large vendors with established brand names. It is our hope that such approaches, as they are perfected and widely adopted, will engender a creative "churn" in the software market place, to the ultimate benefit of the consumer. Gannon [14] has pointed out a significant potential application of this work: customers with stringent quality requirements, such as the nuclear industry [8] need to obtain good evidence of good software quality control practices, prior to "dedicating" COTS software for use in control systems. Our techniques can be used to obtain such evidence while protecting important intellectual property.

Acknowledgements We are grateful to Naser Barghouti, Alex Borgida, Mary Fernandez, Richard Kemmerer, Douglas McIlroy, Dewayne Perry, Robert Schapire, Elayne Weyuker, Pamela Zave, and the anonymous reviewers for valuable comments and technical input.

References

1. Delta Software Testing (accredited by Danish Accreditation Authority-DANAK). http://www.delta.dk/se/ats.htm.
2. T. Ball and J. Larus. Efficient path profiling. In *Micro '96*. IEEE Press, December 1996.
3. C. Cifuentes. Partial automation of an integrated reverse engineering environment for binary code. In *Third Working Conference on Reverse Engineering*, 1996.

4. C. Cifuentes and J. Gough. Decompilation of binary programs. *Software Practice and Experience*, July 1995.

5. P. Devanbu. Genoa- a language and front-end independent source code analyzer generator. In *Proceedings of the Fourteenth International Conference on Software Engineering*, 1992.

6. P. Devanbu and S. G. Stubblebine. Cryptographic verification of test coverage claims. *Available from the authors*, May 97.

7. P. Devanbu and S. G. Stubblebine. Software engineering with trusted hardware. *Unpublished Manuscript, available from the authors*, June 97.

8. D. M. Chapin *et al. Digital Instrumentation and Control System in Nuclear Power Plants.* National Academy Press, 1997.

9. P.G. Frankl, R. Hamlet, B. Littlewood, and L. Strigini. Choosing a testing method to deliver reliability. In *Proceedings of the 19th International Conference on Software Engineering (To Appear)*. IEEE Computer Society, 1997.

10. P.G. Frankl and S. N. Weiss. An experimental comparison of the effectiveness of branch testing and data flow testing. *IEEE Transactions on Software Engineering*, August 1993.

11. P.G. Frankl and E. J. Weyuker. An applicable family of data flow testing criteria. *IEEE Transactions on Software Engineering*, August 1988.

12. P.G. Frankl and E. J. Weyuker. A formal analysis of the fault-detecting ability of testing methods. *IEEE Transactions on Software Engineering*, March 1993.

13. A. Freier, P. Karlton, and P. Kocher. The ssl protocol, version 3.0 (internet draft), March 1996.

14. John Gannon. Personal conversation, April 1997.

15. M. Hutchins, H. Foster, T. Goradia, and T. Ostrand. Experiments on the effectiveness of dataflow- and controlflow-based test adequacy criteria. In *Proceedings of the 16th International Conference on Software Engineering*. IEEE Computer Society, May 1994.

16. Plum Hall Inc. http:/www.plumhall.com.

17. M. J. Kearns and U. V. Vazirani. *An Introduction to Computational Learning Theory*. MIT Press, 1994.

18. National Software Testing Labs. http://www.nstl.com.

19. Software Testing Labs. http://www.stlabs.com.

20. J. Larus and E. Schnarr. Eel: Machine-independent executable editing. In *ACM SIGPLAN PLDI*. ACM Press, 1995.

21. Y. Malaiya, N. Li, J. Bieman, R. Karcich, and B. Skibbe. Software test coverage and reliability. Technical report, Colorado State University, 1996.

22. Doug McIlroy. Personal e-mail communication, 1996.

23. Alfred J. Menezes, Paul C. van Oorschot, and Scott A. Vanstone. *Handbook of Applied Cryptography*. CRC Press, 1996.

24. N. Ramsey and M. Fernandez. Specifying representations of machine instructions. *ACM Transactions on Programming Languages and Systems*, 1997.

25. A. Srivastava and A. Eustace. Atom: A tool for building customized program analysis tools. Technical Report 1994/2, DEC Western Research Labs, 1994.

26. Applied Testing and Technology Inc. http://www.aptest.com.

27. E. J. Weyuker. On testing non-testable programs. *The Computer Journal*, 25(4):465–470, 1982.

A C++ Data Model Supporting Reachability Analysis and Dead Code Detection

Yih-Farn R. Chen, Emden R. Gansner, Eleftherios Koutsofios

AT&T Labs - Research, 180 Park Ave., Florham Park, NJ 07932, USA
{chen,erg,ek}@research.att.com
http://www.research.att.com/info/{chen,erg,ek}

Abstract. A software repository provides a central information source for understanding and reengineering code in a software project. Complex reverse engineering tools can be built by analyzing information stored in the repository without reparsing the original source code. The most critical design aspect of a repository is its data model, which directly affects how effectively the repository supports various analysis tasks. This paper focuses on the design rationales behind a data model for a C++ software repository that supports reachability analysis and dead code detection at the declaration level. These two tasks are frequently needed in large software projects to help remove excess software baggage, select regression tests, and support software reuse studies. The language complexity introduced by class inheritance, friendships, and template instantiations in C++ requires a carefully designed model to catch all necessary dependencies for correct reachability analysis. We examine the major design decisions and their consequences in our model and illustrate how future software repositories can be evaluated for completeness at a selected abstraction level. Examples are given to illustrate how our model also supports variants of reachability analysis: impact analysis, class visibility analysis, and dead code detection. Finally, we discuss the implementation and experience of our analysis tools on a C++ software project.

1 INTRODUCTION

There has been a growing trend [25][1][24] in building software repositories to help maintain structure information of existing legacy code. A software repository provides a central information source for understanding and reengineering code in a software project. While many variants of repository-based systems have been constructed, there is not a clear agreement on how the repository should be organized. One popular approach is to store variants of abstract syntax trees in the repository, such as those used in Reprise[23], ALF[20], Genoa[9], Cobol/SRE[21], PRODAG[22], Aria[10], and Rigi[18] in the IBM program understanding project[2]. Because of the nature of the representations, tree traversal routines are frequently used to generate various abstractions.

The other popular approach, which was adopted in the construction of the C/C++ Information Abstraction Systems[4][7][15] and in XREFDB[17], is to structure the repository as a relational database so as to reuse the large body of existing database technology. Complex reverse engineering tools can be built by composing queries without reanalyzing the original source code. In this approach, the most critical design component of a repository is its data model, which directly affects how effectively the repository supports various analysis tasks.

This paper focuses on the design of a data model for a C++ software repository that, among other goals, supports reachability analysis and dead code detection, two tasks that are frequently needed in large software projects. They serve as the basis for various reverse engineering tasks, such as detecting unnecessary include files[27], performing selective regression testing[8], and computing objective software reuse metrics[6]. This paper also examines how we use our model to implement reachability analysis and its variants (including dead code detection) in the context of the C++ programming language.

Researchers have found it frustrating to compare reverse engineering tools even on simple criterion such as how well they extract function call graphs[19]. The difficulty arises because different underlying models of these tools give different interpretations on what a function call means. On the other hand, the ability for a repository to support complete reachability analysis as defined in this paper is an objective criterion, for a selected abstraction level, that programmers and researchers can use to compare different repository implementations.

A complex, object-oriented language such as C++ makes constructing a data model adequate for reachability analysis a complicated and delicate process. In addition to the entities and relationships found in typical procedural languages, C++ introduces such additional relationships as inheritance, friendship, access adjustments and template instantiation, which affect the analysis in various ways. As an example, Figure 1 shows what we expect to obtain from a simple query like

Find all C++ entities reachable from the class `Pool`.

`Pool` is a class in a C++ components library developed in AT&T that manages a set of same-size memory blocks. In Figure 1, boxes are used for functions, diamonds for types, and ovals for variables. Class inheritance relationships are shown in dashed lines, friendships in dotted lines, and all other relationships in solid lines. This picture reveals several key relationships used in C++ reachability analysis:

- *containment relationship*: between `Pool` and `Pool::alloc()`
- *friendship relationship*: between `Pool` and `Pool_element_header`
- *inheritance rationship*: between `Pool` and `Block_pool_ATTLC`
- *reference relationship*: between `Pool::purge` and `Pool::head`

These relationships and the template instantiation relationship will be examined in detail when we discuss our C++ model.

This paper is organized as follows. We start by presenting our C++ data model and explain the rationales behind many design decisions. We then discuss how the model supports various flavors of reachability analysis in C++

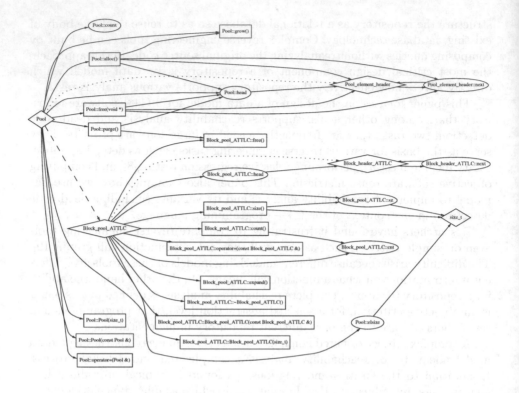

Fig. 1. The reachability graph of the class `Pool`

programs, followed by a description of our implementation and an experience report on some sample C++ code we collected from a C++ software project. Finally, we discuss our future plans for the C++ software repository and research opportunities.

2 A C++ DATA MODEL

Our C++ data model is formulated using Chen's entity-relationship modeling[3] and it supports both C and C++ programming languages. We consider a C or C++ program as a collection of source entities referring to each other, an entity representing a static, syntactic construct such as a macro, a type, a function or a variable. Since our focus is on creating a *complete* data model that supports reachability analysis and dead code detection, we need to provide a clear definition on *completeness*:

> *Completeness:* A data model M on a programming language L is considered *complete* if, for any two entities a and b in the model, a dependency

relationship $a \to b$ also exists in M when one of the following two conditions holds:

- $C1$: if the *compilation* of the entity a depends on the existence of a declaration of the entity b.
- $C2$: if the *execution* of the entity a depends on the existence of the entity b.

For example, if a is a source file that includes a header file b, then $a \to b$ should be captured according to $C1$. Similarly, if a is a variable initialized with a macro b, or a class that inherits from class b, or a template class instantiated from class template b, then $a \to b$ should exist as well because a cannot be compiled without a declaration of b.

On the other hand, if a function a calls or refers to a function b, even if b is not declared (as is allowed in some C programs and shell scripts), then $a \to b$ should exist in the model according to $C2$. For a discussion on conditions required (*well-defined memory* and *well-bounded pointer*) for static analysis tools to capture such relationships, directly or indirectly, refer to the TestTube paper[8].

A model that satisfies the completeness criterion allows us to define *reachable entity set* and *dead entity set* in the following way:

Reachable Entity Set: A reachable entity set $R(a)$ is the set of entities reachable from an entity a through standard closure computations on the dependency relationships in the model.

Source Entity Set: A source entity set S is simply the set of all entities in a program according to the model.

Dead Entity Set: A dead entity set $D(r)$ is simply the difference between $R(r)$ and S, where r is the entity that serves as the starting point of the program execution. $D(r)$ is the set of program entities that are not needed for the compilation or execution of the program.

The first design choice we have to make in designing a *complete* model is the entity granularity. There are several possibilities, moving from coarser to finer granularity:

- *file:* This is the granularity used by most source code control systems such as RCS[26] and configuration management tools such as *nmake*[12].
- *top-level declaration:* This creates entities for all constructs not defined within function bodies, *plus* the nested components of any entity representing a type. This level could be expanded to include entities for all declarations.
- *atomic:* This models all program information, down to the level of statements and expressions. It captures the complete static syntactic and semantic information of the program. This is used by syntax-directed editors, and is the basis of many commercial software browsers and debuggers.

Each choice has its own consequences. For example, the file granularity does not allow dead entity declarations in a source file to be detected, while the declaration granularity implies that questions concerning detailed flow control cannot be answered. In addition, as the granularity becomes finer, the size of the repository and the time of queries can be prohibitive for real software projects. Whatever entity granularity is selected, all relationships among entities at that level of abstraction must be captured in the repository in order for reachability analysis to be complete and accurate.

Our model uses the granularity of top-level declarations. This includes entities for types, functions, variables, macros and files. We feel that this level provides adequate information for the vast majority of analyses pertaining to issues of software engineering, while avoiding the excessive overhead of finer granularities. It captures the principal structural artifacts of a program, especially those used across modules and classes.

Our C++ model significantly expands and cleans up an earlier model proposed in [15]. In particular, we have added support for template-related entities and relationships, and enforce consistent reference relationships in nested class declarations. Both are required for complete reachability analysis.

In the following, we first discuss the basic attributes shared by all C++ entities and then discuss additional attributes that are required for each entity kind. Many of these attributes are used to modify the behaviors of variants of reachability analysis.

2.1   Common Entity Attributes

The attributes that are shared by all C++ (and C) entities in our model include *unique id, entity kind, entity name, source file, location, definition/declaration flag*, and *checksum*, a numeric value associated with the entity's contents. All C++ entities, including functions, variables, types, macros, and files, have these common attributes.

Note that even such a simple model, without additional attributes discussed later, already implies that several queries are possible:

- count entities: we can count the number of entities of each *kind*.
- search entities: we can find out if an entity with a certain pattern exists in the database.
- retrieve entity source: we can retrieve and view the source code of each entity by using the *source file* and *location* attributes. This is useful if software entities are to be rearranged or packaged for reuse.
- detect entity changes: With two versions of a database, we can find out the lists of entities that are deleted, added, or changed from the old version to the new by examining their corresponding checksums.

For example, a query like "*count the number of deleted function definitions from version 1 to version 2*" can easily be handled by a difference database, which has an additional entity attribute that specifies whether an entity is deleted, added, or changed.

2.2 Principal Entities

The entities for types, functions and variables form the basis for most significant program analyses. In addition, C++ allows the constructs to be declared as members inside classes and structs. We call these entities *principal entities*, which require three additional attributes:

- *scope*: A member can be either *private*, *protected*, or *public*. The scope of a non-member entity is either *extern* (global scope) or *static* (file scope). The scope of an entity affects *visibility analysis* discussed later.
- *parent*: This attribute records the parent class or struct of a member, if any.
- *subkind*: In C++, a type entity can be a class template, template class, typedef, struct, class, union or an enum. A function entity can be a function template, template function, or just a regular one. Instead of creating an entity kind for each of these variations, we use this attribute to distinguish among them.

Since a type can be a class template or an instantiated template class, an additional attribute *type param* is necessary to store the formal parameters in the former case and actual parameters in the latter case. For example, the following shows a class template Map and an instance of it retrieved from one of our C++ databases for standard C++ headers:

```
<class S, class T>Map
Map<Set_of_Bag_hashval, unsigned int>
```

Similarly, a function can be a function template, an instantiated template function, or a regular function. We need an additional attribute *function param* to store the template or actual arguments. The following example shows both the function template declaration and a template function of remove instantiated with a String type:

```
<class T>remove(T * arry, int sz, const T & val)
remove(String *, int, const String &)
```

The definition of C++ limits what a model can provide concerning templates. The macro nature of templates in the language, with non-lexical scoping of free identifiers, means that some relationships simply cannot be resolved at the point of definition. Given this, our model supports various attributes, such as formal template parameters, and containment relationships in templates, such as those between a parent class template and its member function templates, but largely forgoes more complete analysis of template definitions[1]. On the other hand, when a template is used, i.e. instantiated, all the relationships involving the template class or function are captured.

Note that the kind and subkind fields are useful in determining whether some operations are applicable. For example, a tool that detects unnecessary include

---

[1] We could extend the model to provide entities for the components (e.g., member functions and variables) of a class template, but even this is problematic, as the types associated with these entities may well involve unresolvable type identifiers.

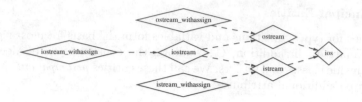

Fig. 2. Class inheritance structure of the `iostream` library

files need only be applied to file entities, while *visibility analysis*, discussed later, can only be applied to classes and their members.

2.3 C++ Relationships

There are several possible relationships in C++: inheritance, friendship, containment, instantiation, and reference relationships. We examine each relationship in detail and explain how it affects reachability analysis.

Inheritance Relationship Figure 2 shows the inheritance structure of the C++ `iostream` library. Note that if an entity refers to `iostream_withassign`, then it also depends on `iostream`, `ostream`, `istream`, and `ios` for compilation. An inheritance relationship can be *private, protected*, or *public*. Also, an inheritance relationship can be *virtual*. Two additional attributes are created to handle these variations: *protection kind* and *virtual flag*. The *protection kind* attribute affects the visibility analysis described later.

Friendship Relationship There is a friendship relationship from *class A* to *class B* if *class B* declares *class A* as a friend. The relationship direction is set this way because members in *class A* may access members in *class B* and therefore depend on *class B* as far as the direction of reachability analysis is concerned. For example, `ios` depends on `Iostream_init` in the following piece of code because members of `ios` are allowed to access members of `Iostream_init`.

```
static class Iostream_init {
        static int         stdstatus ;
        static int         initcount ;
        friend class       ios ;
public:
        Iostream_init() ;
        ~Iostream_init() ;
} iostream_init ;
```

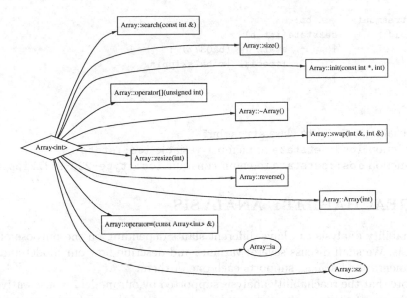

Fig. 3. Containment relationships between `Array<int>` and its members

Containment Relationship There is a containment relationship between every parent class or struct and a member. For example, Figure 3 shows that there are 10 member functions (boxes) and two member variables (ovals) contained in the template class `Array<int>`.

Containment relationships may or may not be walked through depending on the purpose of the reachability analysis . We shall elaborate on this in the next section.

Instantiation Relationship An instantiation relationship exists if entity A is an instance of template B. A depends on B for compilation and linking. For example, the template class `set<int>` is an instance of the class template `<class T>set` and the template function `sort(String *,int)` is an instance of `<class T>sort(T* arry, int sz)`.

Reference Relationship Formally, a reference relationship exists between entity A and entity B if (a) it is not one of the above relationships, and (b) entity A refers to entity B in its declaration or definition. Again, entity A cannot be compiled and linked without the declaration or definition of entity B. The following example shows several reference relationships:

```
class ios {
    ...
    enum        { skipping=01000, tied=02000 } ;
```

```
streambuf*      bp;
void            setstate(int b)
                {       state |= (b&0377) ;
                        ispecial |= b&~skipping ;
                }
        ...
};
```

- variable ios::bp to class streambuf
- function ios::setstate to member variable ios::state
- function ios::setstate to enum constant ios::type-230-9::skipping[2]

3   REACHABILITY ANALYSIS

Reachability analysis can have different slants depending on the purpose of the analysis. We shall discuss several variants and describe how our model and the implementation, *Acacia*, supports each one of them.

Note that the reachability analysis supported by our model is conservative, in that the set of entities returned may be a superset of the minimal closure based on the actual source. This follows from the fact that we are only capturing static syntactic information concerning top-level declarations. For example, an analysis of a program at the expression level may indicate that a call to a function only occurs in a branch that is never executed, and hence the function is never called, whereas Acacia would report the function as needed. Based on our experience, this appears to be reasonable for typical software engineering tasks.

3.1   Forward Reachability Analysis

Forward reachability analysis, which computes *Reachable Entity Set* as defined earlier, is the basis for detecting dead code, packaging reusable software entities, and computing software reuse metrics.

For many tasks, computing the simple transitive closure is sufficient. In some cases, such as software reuse, the task also requires computing certain indirect relations by doing selective reverse reachability computations. For example, class member declarations cannot exist on their own for compilation and therefore we must also capture the *containing* parent declarations. In general, the model explicitly or implicitly contains complete reachability information, so that indirect relations can be generated using appropriate queries over the database.

Figure 4 shows the first three layers of C++ entities transitively reachable from the main function in a sample program. The complete closure set includes 134 functions, 17 types, and 72 variables and is too large to fit on a single page.

Note that there is an *instantiation relationship* between Array<int> and <class Type>Array. Also, while ostream::operator <<(const char*) is considered referenced by main, the class ostream itself is not. We have two choices, depending on the purpose of reachability analysis:

---

[2] type-230-9 is a surrogate name created for the anonymous enum type.

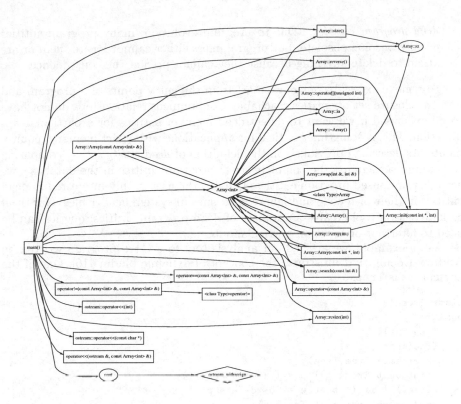

Fig. 4. The first three layers of C++ program entities reachable from `main`

software reuse: In this case, the parent of `ostream::operator <<(const char*)`, `ostream`, is considered referenced. We then include the forward reachability analysis on `ostream` in the closure. While this process may include some class members that are not used in a particular application, we assume that a class should be treated as a unit[3].

– *dead code detection*: This is discussed next.

3.2 Dead Code Detection

Many large software projects suffer from a syndrome called *excess baggage* that has one or more of the following symptoms:

– *unnecessary include files:* Many declarations in the header files are never used, but are compiled repeatedly for the source file that includes them.

---

[3] If space is an issue, the analysis can be modified to only include class member functions that are used in the given program.

– *dead program entities:* Due to program evolution, many program entities usually become obsolete, but programmers either cannot locate them or are afraid to delete anything because they cannot predict the consequences.

To remove excess baggage, we start from the entry points of a program and find the closure set of entities reachable. Containment relationships do not have to be expanded if we want to detect dead member entities for a particular application. This is sometimes critical for applications with strict memory requirements. As described previously in the definition of *dead entity set*, by comparing the closure set against the complete set of program entities in the database, we get a list of unused program entities. Usually, the user is only interested in dead entities in their own code and ignore dead ones in system header files. Our dead code detection tool creates a database of dead program entities; queries can be used to filter out or focus on particular subsets.

As an example, we applied our analysis tool to a C++ program written by Andrew Koenig that illustrates the concept of dynamic binding[16]. One of the key classes is `Tree`:

```
class Tree {
public:
    Tree(int);
    Tree(char*,Tree);
    Tree(char*,Tree,Tree);
    Tree(const Tree& t){ p = t.p; ++p->use; }
    ~Tree() { if (--p->use == 0) delete p; }
    void operator=(const Tree& t);
private:
    friend class Node;
    friend ostream& operator<< (ostream&, const Tree&);
    Node* p;
};
```

We would like to determine if the sample test program (shown below) exercises all member entities in the `Tree` class.

```
main()
{
  Tree t = Tree ("*", Tree("-", 5), Tree("+", 3, 4));
  cout << t << "\n";
  t = Tree ("*", t, t);
  cout << t << "\n";
}
```

While it may not be immediately obvious for some users, this small test program does exercise all member functions of `Tree`, including the destructor, which is called implicitly on the local variable t just before the function exits.

On the other hand, if we replace the test driver with the following piece of code:

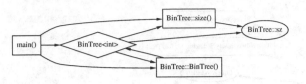

Fig. 5. Impact Analysis: C++ entities that depend on `BinTree:sz` directly or indirectly

```
main()
{
  Tree t = Tree (5);
  cout << t << "\n";
}
```

then the dead code analysis tool reports that the following three member functions of `Tree` are not exercised by the new test driver:

```
Tree::Tree(const Tree &)
Tree::Tree(char *, Tree)
Tree::Tree(char *, Tree, Tree)
```

3.3 Impact Analysis

Before software changes are made, it is frequently desirable to find all program entities that potentially can be affected. Impact analysis, or reverse reachability analysis, allows programmers to find all program entities that depend on an entity directly or indirectly. For example, Figure 5 shows that if `BinTree::sz` is changed, then all the other entities in the graph potentially can be affected. Such an impact analysis is the basis for selecting regression tests[8] after a change is made in the source code.

3.4 Visibility Analysis

It is frequently necessary to determine what member variables and functions in a class inheritance hierarchy are visible to a derived class. For example, to find all member functions, variables, and types visible to class `BinaryNode` in Koenig's example[16], we can perform a reachability analysis on the containment relationships in the inheritance tree starting from `BinaryNode` and limit the search to members of the proper scope. All members in `BinaryNode` are obviously visible to itself; all *public* and *protected* members from `Node` are also visible because `BinaryNode` has a *public* inheritance relationship with `Node`, but the *private* member variable of `Node` (`Node::use`) is not included. On the other hand, `Node` is a friend of `Tree` and therefore all members of `Tree` are visible to `Node`, but none of them are visible to `BinaryNode` because friendship cannot be inherited. Figure 6 shows the result obtained.

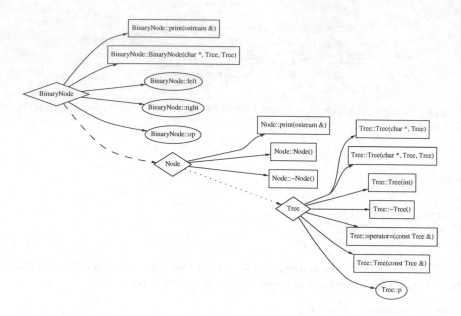

Fig. 6. Visibility analysis of `BinaryNode` and `Node`. The subgraph in the lower right is visible only to members of `Node`, not `BinaryNode`. A dashed edge represents an inheritance relationship, while a dotted edge represents a friendship relationship.

4   IMPLEMENTATION

We have implemented a system called Acacia that implements the data model described above. This system consists of a collection of tools for analyzing C++ source, plus an instantiation of the CIAO software visualization system[5] based on our C++ model. Acacia uses `cql`[13] for query and closure computations, and `dot`[14] for automatic graph layouts. In this section, we briefly describe the implementation of the major components in Acacia.

4.1   Repository Creation

We built the C++ database extraction tool using the Edison Design Group's (EDG)[11] compiler front end. The front end preprocesses, parses, and type-checks the source, producing a fairly detailed representation, essentially corresponding to a high-level abstract syntax tree, in an intermediate language. In addition to dynamic semantic information, this representation also contains declaration, file and source data. This latter detail is crucial for constructing a source level view of the code.

Given the intermediate language representation, the extraction tool traverses the data structure to generate entities for all source items that are not nested within a function scope. After creating the entities, the extraction tool then performs a second pass over the intermediate language representation to generate the required relationships. For C++, this analysis must record implicit uses, such as calls to copy constructors, destructors, and assignment or cast operators, that are not syntactically evident but are generated due to C++ semantics.

The extraction tool produces a repository based on the information within a single source file, analogous to a compiler's producing a single object file corresponding to a single source file. A second tool in the Acacia suite plays a role analogous to the linker, which combines multiple object files into a single executable image. In Acacia, this tool combines the individual repositories into a single repository representing an entire program or subsystem. This integration largely involves replacing references to declarations with references to the corresponding definition, if found.

Since the analysis in Acacia is performed at the source code level, the use of an imported library, without access to its source code, limits the completeness and accuracy of the analysis. Library interfaces, typically specified in source include files, can provide much of the relevant entity and relation information. By the nature of a library, most direct relationships involve external code using something in a library, and not the other way around. When the library does access an entity from a higher level, such as a call-back function, this usually involves the higher level providing a pointer to this entity. Since we cannot analyze how this entity is used within the library, we can only make the conservative assumption that it is used. In the cases when external libraries are involved for which Acacia repositories are not available, definition entities will not exist. In this case, all references to differing declarations of a single entity are replaced by a reference to a single, representative declaration entity.

4.2 Instantiation of CIAO for C++

The query and visualization subsystem of Acacia is built by constructing a C++ instance of the CIAO system[5] using an *instance compiler* that takes a specification file for a new language or document type and generates the complete query and visualization environment automatically.

The specification file has five sections:

- *schema*: It maps our data model to the physical *cql*[13] database schema by enumerating the entity and relationship fields. Typically, a field is either an integer or string, but a data type of *entity pointer* allows an entity record to refer to another entity. For example, the *parent type* field of a member entity stores the entity id of its parent class.
- *database view*: This section defines how different entity and relationship records are to be presented as a query result in CIAO's database mode. Each entity kind can have a customized format. For example, the printed name of a member entity is *parent_name::member_name*. If an entity is a template

instance, the template arguments are attached after the name. Otherwise, the name is just the plain name of the entity. This is important in C++ since it is very common to have members of the same or different classes to share a common name due to operator overloading, redefining of inherited methods, etc.

- *source view*: The third section defines what fields are needed to locate the source file and position within that file where an entity appears. A standard CIAO source view tool can use these pointers to output the actual text.
- *graph view*: The fourth section defines how to represent each entity and relationship when CIAO displays the results of a query as a graph. Entities are represented as nodes of various shapes, colors, and fonts. Relationships are represented as edges of various edge styles and colors.
- *GUI front end*: The fifth section defines the appearance and functionality of the graphical front end. It also defines which queries are appropriate for each kind of entity. For example, in the C instance of CIAO, the query *incl* is marked as only being appropriate for file entities.

Our specification file for C++ consists of only 284 lines. The complete suite of query, visualization, and generic reachability analysis tools in Acacia was generated from this specification file. Only dead code detection and visibility analysis tools require special *cql*[13] query code to handle customized closure computations.

5   PERFORMANCE AND EXPERIENCE

This section examines speed and storage requirements of our tools on some sample test code and reports our experience in applying Acacia to a C++ software project.

5.1   Storage Requirements and Speed

To evaluate the storage requirements and speed of our C++ database generator, we compared it to our local C++ compiler, which is also based on EDG's front end.

The sample C++ source program consists of 1525 lines of C++ code (including header files), with a total size of 42.3 KB. It took 1.47 CPU seconds (sys time + user time) to compile this program on an SGI Challenge L server (with four 200 MHZ MIPS R4400 processors)running IRIX 5.3. Our C++ database generator spent 1.51 seconds on the same piece of code. So its speed is roughly comparable to the C++ compiler. The database consists of 756 entity and 796 relationship records with a total size of 94.9 KB, which is roughly 2.2 times the size of the program source. This storage and speed overhead is rather low compared to many CASE vendor tools that we have seen and is acceptable to the software projects that we have been working with inside AT&T.

429

5.2 Experience on a C++ Software Subsystem

This C++ software subsystem is part of a telecommunications system. The software subsystem was merged from two previous and similar projects and is expected to have a significant amount of unnecessary code.

The system consists of 202 source files and a total of 41,821 lines of C++ code. The C++ database we generated consists of 2,878 C++ functions, 3,208 variables, and 791 types, which include 276 C++ classes. There are no templates used in this project. The program database consists of 7,649 entity records (definitions and declarations), and 9,260 relationships. The size of the database is 1.02 MB.

We picked a user-defined class that deals with alarm transmission and ran the reachability analysis tool to see how large its closure set can be. The result shows that it can reach 241 entities, including 92 functions, 20 types, and 117 variables, defined or declared in 11 separate source files. All these entities must be collected just for the alarm transmission class to compile if it is to be reused in a different project. The closure computation took only 1.58 CPU seconds to run on a desktop SGI Indy (150 MHZ R4400 processor) running IRIX 5.3.

As an example of impact analysis, we ran a reverse reachability analysis to find out how many C++ entities would be directly or indirectly affected if we change the implementation of a function that gets an application message. The reverse closure consists of 332 entities, including 217 functions, 35 variables, and 39 types distributed in 40 different files. The reverse closure computation took only 2.50 cpu seconds to run on the same SGI desktop.

These results show how difficult it might be, without the assistance of automatic analysis tools, for a programmer to reuse a software component or to track down how far-reaching the impact of a software change could be.

6 SUMMARY AND FUTURE WORK

The growing body of C++ code and its language complexity have been presenting challenging maintenance tasks and generating research opportunities in the software engineering community. Reachability analysis is the fundamental building block that supports many complex analysis tasks such as dead code detection, software reuse, and selective regression testing. This paper presents the data model of a C++ software repository and discusses how design decisions made in our C++ model affect variants of reachability analysis. It is crucial that the model be complete at the selected level of abstraction so that the analysis can be performed accurately. Efforts in our implementation of Acacia were greatly reduced due to two factors: the use of an EDG's mature compiler front end and the new instance compiler that generates the complete query and visualization environment from a small specification file. Due to the entity granularity and tradeoffs we selected, the performance and storage overhead of our implementation is quite acceptable to real software projects. We feel our work and experience on the C++ model can benefit future repository builders for other object-oriented languages such as Java, Eiffel or Ada 95.

7   AVAILABILITY

Acacia is available for experiments to educational institutions. Please visit

   http://www.research.att.com/sw/tools/Acacia

for information on how to obtain the package.

References

1. R. S. Arnold. Software Reengineering: A Quick History. *Commun. ACM*, 37(5):13–14, May 1994.
2. E. Buss, R. D. Mori, W. Gentleman, J. Henshaw, J. Johnson, K. Kontogianis, E. Merlo, H. Müller, J. Mylopoulos, S. Paul, A. Prakash, M. Stanley, S. TIlley, J. Troster, and K. Wong. Investigating Reverse Engineering Technologies for the CAS Program Understanding Project. *IBM Systems Journal*, 33(3):477–500, 1994.
3. P. P. Chen. The Entity-Relationship Model – Toward a Unified View of Data. *ACM Transactions on Database Systems*, 1(1):9–36, Mar. 1976.
4. Y.-F. Chen. Reverse engineering. In B. Krishnamurthy, editor, *Practical Reusable UNIX Software*, chapter 6, pages 177–208. John Wiley & Sons, New York, 1995.
5. Y.-F. Chen, G. S. Fowler, E. Koutsofios, and R. S. Wallach. Ciao: A Graphical Navigator for Software and Document Repositories. In *International Conference on Software Maintenance*, pages 66–75, 1995.
6. Y.-F. Chen, B. Krishnamurthy, and K.-P. Vo. An Objective Reuse Metric: Model and Methodology. In *Fifth European Software Engineering Conference*, 1995.
7. Y.-F. Chen, M. Nishimoto, and C. V. Ramamoorthy. The C Information Abstraction System. *IEEE Transactions on Software Engineering*, 16(3):325–334, Mar. 1990.
8. Y.-F. Chen, D. Rosenblum, and K.-P. Vo. TestTube: A System for Selective Regression Testing. In *The 16th Internation Conference on Software Engineering*, pages 211–220, 1994.
9. P. Devanbu. Genoa—a language and front-end independent source code analyzer generator. In *Proceedings of the Fourteenth International Conference on Software Engineering*, pages 307–317, 1992.
10. P. Devanbu, D. Rosenblum, and A. Wolf. Generating Testing and Analysis Tools with Aria. *ACM Trans. Software Engineering and Methodology*, 5(1):42–62, 1996.
11. Edison Design Group. http://www.edg.com.
12. G. Fowler. A Case for make. *Software – Practice and Experience*, 20:35–46, June 1990.
13. G. Fowler. cql – A Flat File Database Query Language. In *USENIX Winter 1994 Conference*, pages 11–21, Jan. 1994.
14. E. R. Gansner, E. Koutsofios, S. C. North, and K.-P. Vo. A Technique for Drawing Directed Graphs. *IEEE Transactions on Software Engineering*, pages 214–230, Mar. 1993.
15. J. Grass and Y. F. Chen. The C++ Information Abstractor. In *The Second USENIX C++ Conference*, Apr. 1990.
16. A. Koenig. An Example of Dynamic Binding in C++. *Journal of Object-Oriented Programming*, 1(3), Aug. 1988.

17. M. Lejter, S. Meyers, and S. P. Reiss. Support for Maintaining Object-Oriented Programs. *IEEE Transactions on Software Engineering*, 18(12):1045–1052, Dec. 1992.

18. H. Müller, M. A. Orgun, S. TIlley, and J. S. Uhl. A Reverse Engineering Approach to Subsystem Structure Identification. *Journal of Software Maintenance*, 5(4):181–204, 1993.

19. G. Murphy, D. Notkin, and E.-C. Lan. An Emprical Study of Static Call Graph Extractors. In *The 18th International Conference on Software Engineering*, pages 90 – 99, 1996.

20. R. Murray. A Statically Typed Abstract Representation for C++ Programs. In *Proceedings of the USENIX C++ Conference*, pages 83–97, Aug. 1992.

21. J. Q. Ning, A. Engberts, and W. Kozaczynski. Automated Support for Legacy Code Understanding. *Commun. ACM*, 37(5):50–57, May 1994.

22. D. Richardson, T. O'Malley, C. Moore, and S. Aha. Developing and Integrating PRODAG in the Arcadia Environment. In *Fifth ACM SIGSOFT Symp. Software Development Environments*, pages 109–119, Dec. 1992.

23. D. Rosenblum and A. Wolf. Representing Semantically Analyzed C++ Code with Reprise. In *USENIX C++ Conference Proceedings*, pages 119–134, Apr. 1991.

24. D. Sharon and R. Bell. Tools that Bind: Creating Integrated Environments. *IEEE Software*, 12(2):76–85, Mar. 1995.

25. I. Thomas. PCTE Interfaces: Supporting Tools in Software-Engineering Environments. *IEEE Software*, 6(6):15–23, Nov. 1989.

26. W. F. Tichy. RCS-a system for version control. *Software – Practice and Experience*, 15(7):637–654, July 1985.

27. K. P. Vo and Y.-F. Chen. Incl: A Tool to Analyze Include Files. In *Summer 1992 USENIX Conference*, pages 199–208, June 1992.

The Use of Program Profiling for Software Maintenance with Applications to the Year 2000 Problem [*]

Thomas Reps,[†] Thomas Ball,[‡] Manuvir Das,[†] and James Larus[†]

Abstract. This paper describes new techniques to help with testing and debugging, using information obtained from path profiling. A path profiler instruments a program so that the number of times each different loop-free path executes is accumulated during an execution run. With such an instrumented program, each run of the program generates a path spectrum for the execution—a distribution of the paths that were executed during that run. A path spectrum is a finite, easily obtainable characterization of a program's execution on a dataset, and provides a behavior signature for a run of the program.

Our techniques are based on the idea of comparing path spectra from different runs of the program. When different runs produce different spectra, the spectral differences can be used to identify paths in the program along which control diverges in the two runs. By choosing input datasets to hold all factors constant except one, the divergence can be attributed to this factor. The point of divergence itself may not be the cause of the underlying problem, but provides a starting place for a programmer to begin his exploration.

One application of this technique is in the "Year 2000 Problem" (*i.e.*, the problem of fixing computer systems that use only 2-digit year fields in date-valued data). In this context, path-spectrum comparison provides a heuristic for identifying paths in a program that are good candidates for being date-dependent computations. The application of path-spectrum comparison to a number of other software-maintenance issues is also discussed.

1. Introduction

The world faces cataclysmic breakdown at the turn of the millennium!

While this alarm may be old news to anyone who was present at the turn of the last millennium, there are significant reasons for residents of the (first) world to be concerned this time around: Because many computer programs use only two digits to record year values in date-valued data, they may process a year value of 00 as 1900 in cases where 2000 was intended. If the intended value is 2000—such as when 00 represents the value of the current year in a computation performed after the calendar rolls over on January 1, 2000—then a faulty computation may be carried out. Because computations can involve dates in the future, the phenomenon can occur well before the calendar rolls over on January 1, 2000. For example, if the (approximate) age of someone born in 1956 were calculated for January 1, 2000, he would appear to be $00 - 56 = -56$ years old! If the program tries to use the value -56 to index into a life-expectancy table, the program will either fetch a bogus life-expectancy value or quit with an error (depending on whether the run-time system catches "index-out-of-bounds" errors). In both cases, the system functions improperly. In general, such behavior can have serious—even life-threatening—consequences. This problem and a variety of other date-related problems that will show up with increasing frequency around January 1, 2000 are known collectively as the "Year 2000 Problem" (Y2K problem).

---

[*]This work was supported in part by NSF under grants CCR-9625667, MIP-9625558, and NYI Award CCR-9357779 (with support from HP and Sun), and by DARPA (monitored by ONR under contracts N00014-92-J-1937 and N00014-97-1-0114, and by Wright Laboratory Avionics Directorate under grant #F33615-94-1-1525).

The Wisconsin Alumni Research Foundation is in the process of seeking patent protection for the ideas described herein.

[†]Computer Sciences Department, University of Wisconsin, 1210 W. Dayton St., Madison, WI 53706. E-mail: {reps, manuvir, larus}@cs.wisc.edu.

[‡]Lucent Technologies, 1000 E. Warrenville Road, P.O. Box 3013, Naperville, IL 60566-7013. E-mail: tball@research.bell-labs.com.

In July 1996, the first author was asked by the Defense Advanced Research Projects Agency (DARPA) to help them plan a project aimed at reducing the impact of the Y2K problem on the Department of Defense. DARPA was particularly interested in whether there were "any techniques in the research community that could be applied to the Y2K problem and have impact beyond present commercial Y2K products and services".

The most exciting of the ideas that turned up concerns a method for using path profiling as a heuristic to locate some of the sites in a program where there are problematic date manipulations. It works as follows:

> In path profiling, a program is instrumented so that the number of times each different loop-free path executes is accumulated during an execution run. With such an instrumented program, each run (or set of runs) of the program generates a path spectrum for the execution—a distribution of the paths that were executed. Path spectra can be used to identify paths in a program that are good candidates for being date-dependent computations by finding differences between path spectra from execution runs on pre-2000 data and post-2000 data. By choosing input datasets to hold all factors constant except the way dates are used in the program, any differences in the spectra obtained from different execution runs can be attributed to date-dependent computations in the program. Differences in the spectra reveal paths along which the program performed a new sort of computation during the post-2000 run, as well as paths—and hence computations—that were no longer executed during the post-2000 run.

With some further analysis of the spectra, for each such path that shows up in the spectral difference, it is possible to identify the shortest prefix that distinguishes it from all of the paths in the other path set.

Of course, the path-spectrum-comparison technique is not guaranteed to uncover all sites of date manipulations. No technique can do this; all one can hope for are good heuristics. However, because path-spectrum comparison involves a different principle from the principles that lie behind the heuristics used in commercial Y2K tools, it should be a good complement to current techniques.

The path spectrum-comparison technique is actually applicable to a much wider range of software-maintenance problems than just the Y2K problem. In particular, the problem of how to carry out adequate execution tests is a huge problem for software developers, and will still be with us long past the year 2000. As discussed in Section 6, the path-spectrum-comparison technique offers new perspectives on testing, on the task of creating test data, and on what tools can be created to support program testing.

Note that the idea of comparing path spectra to identify possible execution errors is a completely different use of path profiling in program testing from another use that has been proposed for path profiles in program testing, namely as a criterion for evaluating the coverage of a test suite [21,13,7,15].

The remainder of the paper is organized into six sections: Section 2 provides background on the Y2K problem. Section 3 describes the use of run-time profiling to locate date-dependent paths and their shortest distinguishing prefixes. Section 4 summarizes the key insights behind recent work that makes it possible to carry out path profiling in an efficient manner, as well as an alternative technique for locating shortest distinguishing prefixes of path-spectrum differences. Section 5 describes our implementation of a tool based on these ideas, as well as the results of our preliminary experience with the tool. Section 6 discusses other applications of the technique to a broader range of software-maintenance problems. Section 7 discusses related work.

2. The Year 2000 Problem

In addition to the rollover problem with two-digit year fields, the phrase "Year 2000 Problem" has come to mean a whole host of date-related problems that will eventually crop up, many of which strike around the turn of the millennium. For example, leap years come every four years, except for centuries, except for centuries divisible by 400. Thus, the year 2000 is, in fact, a leap year. However, some programs implement the exception, but not the exception to the exception. Such a bug could cause havoc in financial transactions (*e.g.*, by causing failures in computer-driven trading) and military maneuvers (*e.g.*, by causing logistical planning failures). UNIX systems are also subject to date-representation rollover problems, most of which occur later in the 21st century.[1]

For both date-representation rollover problems and leap-year bugs, it is necessary to find the code that declares and manipulates date-valued variables, rewrite it, and test the modifications. Unfortunately, dates are hidden in programs. "Date" is not a data-type in most programming languages, and so heuristics must be developed for identifying the locations where date-valued data is manipulated. Even when a language does have a "date" data-type, there is nothing to forbid programmers from creating or encoding "raw" dates that are embedded in data of other data types, such as character strings.

Much of the problem is in administrative computing: purchasing and billing records, maintenance and inventory records, payrolls, and the like. However, all of the world-wide infrastructure that incorporates automated components could conceivably be affected, including telephone and electrical power systems, industrial plants, nuclear power plants, defense early-warning systems, logistics and planning systems, and weapons systems. Cost estimates for correcting the various date problems run as high as $600 billion world-wide [8], $300 billion in the U.S., $30 billion for the Federal government, and $10 billion for the Department of Defense—not to mention an estimated $1 trillion in legal fees in the aftermath.

The Y2K problem is in large part a management problem: There are enormous difficulties that must be addressed by any organization that faces the Y2K problem, including battling for adequate resources (*e.g.*, financial, equipment, and staffing), inventorying an organization's custom programs and COTS ("commercial off-the-shelf") programs, and coordinating the deployment of "renovated" systems (which may have to interoperate with systems, including those of other companies, that have not yet been renovated). However, there are serious technical problems as well, including program-analysis methods for determining the sites at which date-manipulation code occurs, code- and data-transformation algorithms, post-renovation testing, and the technical challenges of coping with interoperating renovated and unrenovated systems.

The techniques described in this paper are relevant to two of these problems: (i) determining the sites at which date-manipulation code occurs, and (ii) post-renovation testing.

Because the leverage that tools for the Y2K problem can provide is limited by their accuracy for locating the places in a piece of code where dates are employed, the date-location issue is crucial to the creation of effective tools for correcting date-manipulation problems. Two techniques for locating dates are used in present commercial products:

(1)   Some date-manipulation sites can be identified by the places where a program makes certain calls to the operating system, for example, to retrieve the current date. This method is accurate, but does not identify all the date-manipulation sites in the program. For instance, the variable into which the current date has been placed can be manipulated elsewhere in the program, or its contents can be assigned to another variable. In addition, other date values can be read in from files, from across the network, or from interactive user input.

(2)   Other date-manipulation sites can be identified by exploiting any conventions that programmers may have used for naming the variables in the program. Automatic string-searching tools are used to search the source code—or alternatively, just the identifiers in a tokenized version of the source code—with respect to patterns that reflect such conventions, for example, "*date*", "*gmt*", "*yy*", etc. (where "*" is a wild-card symbol that means "match any substring").

After these techniques have been used to identify candidate sites at which dates are manipulated, this information can be "amplified", via searching and slicing [20,12,9,14] operations, to find other potential locations of problems.

3. Path Profiling and the Year 2000 Problem

In path profiling, a program is instrumented so that the number of times different paths of the program execute is accumulated during an execution run. Typically, the paths of interest are loop-free intraprocedural paths. The distribution of paths from an execution of the program is called a *path profile* or a *path spectrum*. We are sometimes just interested in Boolean information (which paths were executed? which were not?), but other times we are interested in the frequencies with which paths were executed. This corresponds to considering a path spectrum as either a set of paths or a multi-set of paths, respectively.

---

[1]Overflow in the UNIX *time* function occurs on Tuesday, January 19, 2038 at 03:14:08 UTC.

The observation underlying our technique for applying program profiling to the Y2K problem is that differences between path spectra obtained from different runs of a program can be used to identify paths that are good candidates for being date-dependent computations. By choosing input datasets to hold all factors constant except the way dates are used in the program, any differences in the path spectra from different execution runs can be attributed to date-dependent computations in the program. In particular, one would obtain path spectra from execution runs of the program in which the program is run on pre-2000 data and post-2000 data (or data that is likely to bring to light whatever "date vulnerability" we are trying to test). By comparing the two path spectra, paths along which the program performed a new sort of computation during the post-2000 run can be identified, as well as paths—and hence computations—that were no longer executed during the post-2000 run.

Our thesis is that this technique provides a good heuristic for identifying date-dependent computations. The basis for this belief is that a path spectrum provides an approximate characterization of the program's behavior, in the following sense:

> The program's execution paths serve as representatives for a set of execution states: Consider the set of all possible execution states of the form (pt, σ), where σ is a store value and pt is not an arbitrary program point, but one occurring at the beginning of a path p that the profiler is prepared to tabulate. In terms of characterizing the program's execution behavior, two execution states (pt, σ_1) and (pt, σ_2) are "similar" if they both cause the program to proceed from pt along execution path p. Path p serves as a representative of this equivalence class of similar execution states.

Differences in the path spectra obtained during two runs of a program on different inputs indicate differences in the (equivalence classes of) execution states encountered, and hence are a reflection of differences in the program's behavior due to the differences in the input. In the case of runs using pre- and post-2000 data, differences in the path spectra must therefore reflect changed behavior due to date-dependent computations.

Of course, this only holds in one direction: Not all differences in behavior due to date-dependent computations will necessarily show up as differences in the (equivalence classes of) execution states encountered.

Example. Consider the program fragment shown in Figure 1, which reads and processes data from a database of customer information. (This fragment does not contain any cycles, but might appear as part of a loop in a larger program. Path profiling in programs with loops is typically carried out by considering loop-free segments of the program. See Section 4.1 or reference [4] for more discussion of this issue.)

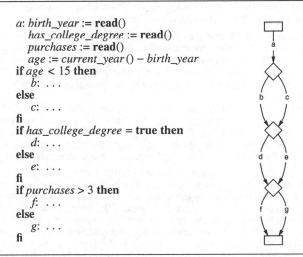

```
a: birth_year := read()
   has_college_degree := read()
   purchases := read()
   age := current_year() − birth_year
if age < 15 then
   b: ...
else
   c: ...
fi
if has_college_degree = true then
   d: ...
else
   e: ...
fi
if purchases > 3 then
   f: ...
else
   g: ...
fi
```

Figure 1. A program fragment that reads and processes data from a database of customer information, and its control-flow graph.

For purposes of this example, assume that years are represented with only two digits and that no person recorded in the database who is younger than fifteen years old possesses a college degree. Because of the latter assumption, no path from a pre-2000 run can begin with the prefix $[a,b,d]$.

Now consider a post-2000 run (*e.g.*, a simulated post-2000 run in which the system clock has been set ahead so that *current_year*() returns a value representing a year in the future, say 00, representing the year 2000), and suppose that the program reads in data about someone born in 1956 who possesses a college degree: The initialization code in region *a* would set *age* to $00 - 56 = -56$; because the test $-56 < 15$ evaluates to true, region *b* would be executed; because the person possesses a college degree, region *d* would be executed; finally, either region *f* or *g* would be executed. In either case, the program performs a faulty computation: The path executed is a path that should only be executed when a record is encountered for a person younger than fifteen who possesses a college degree. Because no such paths are ever executed during the pre-2000 run, the path-spectrum-comparison technique would detect the fact that the program performed a new sort of computation during the post-2000 run.

In addition, other anomalies may be detected: The pre-2000 run could very well execute paths with the prefix $[a,c]$. Because in the post-2000 run the value of *age* is always negative, the post-2000 run would never execute such paths.

The following table shows path spectra that might be accumulated during pre-2000 and post-2000 execution runs (assuming that the fragment occurs in a loop, so that it is executed multiple times):

Run	Paths Executed							
	$[a,b,d,f]$	$[a,b,d,g]$	$[a,b,e,f]$	$[a,b,e,g]$	$[a,c,d,f]$	$[a,c,d,g]$	$[a,c,e,f]$	$[a,c,e,g]$
pre-2000			•	•	•	•	•	•
post-2000	•	•	•	•				

These spectra show clearly that the pre-2000 and post-2000 behavior of the program is not the same: Paths $[a,b,d,f]$ and $[a,b,d,g]$ occur in the post-2000 run, but do not occur in the pre-2000 run; paths $[a,c,d,f]$, $[a,c,d,g]$, $[a,c,e,f]$, and $[a,c,e,g]$ occur in the pre-2000 run, but do not occur in the post-2000 run. □

Each path in a path spectrum represents a sequence of edges in the program's control-flow graph. From two path spectra, *new_spectrum* and *old_spectrum*, the path-spectrum-comparison technique reveals paths of *new_spectrum* that are not found in *old_spectrum*, and vice versa. Given a path of *new_spectrum* (resp., *old_spectrum*) that does not occur in *old_spectrum* (*new_spectrum*), we can determine the shortest prefix of the path that distinguishes it from all of the paths in *old_spectrum* (*new_spectrum*). For the Y2K problem, such path prefixes furnish a programmer with even more precise information about what contributes to the differences in behavior between the pre-2000 and post-2000 runs:

- Let *p* be an execution path that was executed during the post-2000 run but not during the pre-2000 run. By finding the shortest prefix of *p* that is not a prefix of any path executed during the pre-2000 run, we identify the critical portion of *p* that represents a new sort of computation (or state-transformation pattern) performed during the post-2000 run. The programmer can focus on this prefix of *p* to locate the date-dependent code, which very likely needs to be rewritten.
- Similarly, let *q* be an execution path that was executed during the pre-2000 run but not during the post-2000 run. The shortest prefix of *q* that is not a prefix of any path executed during the post-2000 run identifies the critical portion of *q* that represents a computation (state-transformation pattern) no longer performed during the post-2000 run. Again, the programmer can focus on this prefix of *q* to locate the date-dependent code.

Example. In the example program discussed earlier, paths $[a,b,d,f]$ and $[a,b,d,g]$ of the post-2000 run do not occur in the pre-2000 run. For both paths, the shortest prefix that is not a prefix of any path executed during the pre-2000 run is $[a,b,d]$. In asking the question "Why is the path $[a,b,d]$ executed during the post-2000 run?", the programmer would be led to ask the question "How can it be that *age* is less than 15 and *has_college_degree* is true?", which would in turn lead him to the statement that computes *age* as a function of *current_year*().

Conversely, paths $[a,c,d,f]$, $[a,c,d,g]$, $[a,c,e,f]$, and $[a,c,e,g]$ of the pre-2000 run do not occur in the post-2000 run. For all of these paths, the shortest prefix that is not a prefix of any path executed during the post-2000 run is [a,c]. In this case, the programmer would be led to ask the question "Why is the path [a,c] never executed during the post-2000 run? That is, why is the value of *age* always less than 15 during the post-2000 run?" Again, the programmer is led to the statement that computes *age* as a function of *current_year* (). □

One can find the shortest prefix of a path *p* that is not a prefix of any executed path in a spectrum *S* using a trie structure on *S* [16]: The first edge of *p* that "deviates from the trie" identifies the edge at which *p* veers into "unknown territory", and the prefix of *p*, up to and including this edge, is the shortest prefix of *p* that distinguishes *p* from *S*.

Example. The solid arrows in the diagram below show the trie for the pre-2000 spectrum.

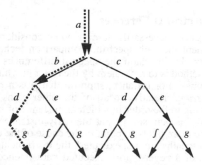

The dotted edges show path [a,b,d,g] (which occurs during the post-2000 run). The shortest prefix of [a,b,d,g] that is not a prefix of any path executed during the pre-2000 run is [a,b,d]. □

3.1. Thresholding

Rather than concentrating on paths *p* that are executed in *new_spectrum* but not in *old_spectrum* (or vice versa), we may wish to gather information from a path *p'* that is executed a different number of times in the two spectra. Usually, we would be interested in a path *p'* that is executed frequently in *new_spectrum* but not in *old_spectrum*, or vice versa. Perhaps some threshold ratio, say 100 to 1, would be used to identify "interesting paths". For instance, in the example from Section 3, suppose the database did contain a few records for people younger than fifteen years old in possession of a college degree. In this case, the differences between the pre- and post-2000 runs would show up as the post-2000 run appearing to process a large multiple of the number of such records processed by the pre-2000 run.

In this situation, we would again be interested in understanding which prefix distinguishes path *p'* from the paths in *old_spectrum*. To do this, we merely remove *p'* (temporarily) from the *old_spectrum* path set, and then perform the normal path-comparison operation on *p'* with respect to *old_spectrum* (*e.g.*, via a trie on *old_spectrum* or by the alternative technique described in Section 4.2).

It is important that the over-threshold paths be removed from *old_spectrum* only one at a time. The reason is that the over-threshold paths in *old_spectrum* may share prefixes in common. If all of the over-threshold paths were removed from *old_spectrum* simultaneously, and the path comparison carried out against the resulting spectrum, an incorrect set of shortest distinguishing prefixes could be reported.

3.2. Other Uses of Path Profiling for the Year 2000 Problem

In addition to its utility for "date prospecting" in the Y2K problem, the path-spectrum-comparison technique also has the potential to help out with two other important issues that are part of the Y2K problem: (i) determining whether COTS components (*i.e.*, libraries) or COTS tools have date problems, and (ii) testing renovated code:

(i)   COTS software is usually distributed without source code, as an object-code file or as an executable file. (Executables are usually distributed without symbol-table or relocation information, as well.) Because it is possible to perform the instrumentation necessary for obtaining path spectra on object-code files and executable files [10,19,11], the path-spectrum-comparison technique is one of the few methods we are aware of that can be used to identify date-manipulation problems in programs for which source code is not available: Differences between pre-2000 and post-2000 spectra would be an indication that a piece of COTS software may have a Y2K problem.

Of course, in this scenario the lack of access to the source code prevents one from actually fixing the Y2K problem. However, the manufacturer can presumably make use of the information that the path-spectrum-comparison technique brings to light about suspicious paths through the object code.

(ii) A correctly renovated system should have similar path spectra from execution runs on pre-2000 data and post-2000 data. Remaining path-spectrum differences could indicate that a Y2K problem still exists in the renovated system.

3.3. Prioritization of Spectral Differences

Not all path-spectrum differences necessarily deserve equal consideration by the user. For this reason, it is useful to augment the path-spectrum-comparison technique with a prioritization method for establishing an order in which the spectral differences should be brought to the attention of the user. One method is to rank them by the order in which paths were executed (in one of the two execution runs). For instance, suppose that p is a path in *new_spectrum* that does not occur in *old_spectrum*. Relative to all of the other paths in this category, p's rank would be established according to the order in which an instance of p was executed for the first time. The reasoning behind this heuristic is that the early instances of behavioral differences between the two runs may be more likely to point to the cause of the underlying problem.

To track the order in which paths are first executed, the instrumented code could use a global counter: Each time the end of a never-before-executed path is encountered (*i.e.*, each time a path count is set from 0 to 1), the counter's value would be recorded with the path, and the counter incremented.

3.4. Why Not Node Profiling or Edge Profiling?

A comparison process similar to that described above could be carried out using pairs of spectra created using node profiling or edge profiling. However, in general, these variations on the idea are not likely to produce as good results as when spectra from path profiles are used.

By considering what happens during different post-2000 execution runs, the example from Figure 1 can be used to illustrate that path-spectrum comparison is able to distinguish more behavioral differences than either node-spectrum comparison or edge-spectrum comparison. First, note that a pre-2000 run can exercise all edges of the example program's control-flow graph (*i.e.*, regions a, b, c, d, e, f, and g). This is not the case for some post-2000 runs. For instance, for runs during which the system clock is set so that *current_year*() returns a value in the range 00 to 14 (representing a year in the range 2000 to 2014), the value of *age* will always be less than 15, and thus region c will never be executed. For these runs, node-spectrum comparison and edge-spectrum comparison would both detect a behavioral difference between the pre- and post-2000 runs (as would path-spectrum comparison).

In contrast, if the system clock is set so that *current_year*() returns a value greater than or equal to 15 (representing 2015 or later), we again have a situation in which all nodes and edges are able to be executed. In particular, when a record for a person born in the year 2000 is processed during a year-2015 run, the initialization code in region a will set *age* to $15 - 00 = 15$, the test *age* < 15 will evaluate to false, and region c will be executed. Thus, pre-2000 and post-2015 runs can exercise all edges of the example program's control-flow graph, and hence neither node-spectrum comparison nor edge-spectrum comparison would detect any differences in behavior between these runs. However, as in the 2000 to 2014 runs, if the program reads in data about someone born in 1956 who possesses a college degree, the program will follow a path that should only be executed when a record is encountered for a person younger than fifteen who possesses a college degree: The initialization code in region a would set *age* to $15 - 56 = -41$; because the test $-41 < 15$ evaluates to true, region b would be executed; because the person possesses a college degree, region d would be executed; finally, either region f or g would be executed. Because no such paths are ever executed during the pre-2000 run, the path-spectrum-comparison technique *would* detect the fact that the program performed a new sort of computation during the post-2015 run. This example shows that, in general, path-spectrum comparison is able to distinguish more behavioral differences than either node-spectrum comparison or edge-spectrum comparison.

What is the significance of this for the Y2K problem, in general? For node-spectrum comparison and edge-spectrum comparison to detect behavioral differences between execution runs on pre-2000 data and post-2000 data, the post-2000 run either has to exercise a completely new part of the program, or completely fail to exercise some part of the program that was exercised during the pre-2000 run. In contrast, with the path-spectrum-comparison technique, it is possible to detect behavioral differences even if exactly the same nodes and edges are exercised during the two runs (as long as different paths are exercised). Execution of the same nodes and edges can give rise to different sets of paths if the *correlations between branches* are different in the different runs. Consequently, of the three techniques, the path-spectrum-comparison technique provides the highest-fidelity test for identifying date-dependent computations.[2]

4. Efficient Path Profiling

The path-spectrum-comparison technique is not tied to any particular path-profiling method. Furthermore, there are a wide variety of options in how one performs the instrumentation required to gather information about what paths execute. Instrumentation can be performed at any one of a number of levels:

- At the source-code level, as a source-to-source transformation.
- As part of compilation, by extending a compiler to use its intermediate representations for the purpose of determining where to introduce instrumentation instructions.
- As an object-code-level transformation, by modifying object-code files (such as UNIX ".o" files).
- As a post-loader transformation, by modifying executable files (such as UNIX "a.out" files) [10,19,11].

One could even use different instrumentation methods on different parts of the system.

Although any method for generating path profiles could be used, it is only recently that methods have been devised for obtaining path profiles with acceptable overheads [4,2]. In particular, Ball and Larus report that execution-time overheads on the order of only 30–40% can be achieved with their method for collecting path profiles [1]. Their work relies on a particular method for numbering the paths in the program, the main points of which are described in Section 4.1. When the paths in path profiles are reported using this numbering scheme, an alternative technique for interpreting path spectra can be used to identify the shortest prefix of a path in *new_spectrum* that is not a prefix of any executed path in *old_spectrum* (or vice versa). This is described in Section 4.2.

4.1. The Ball-Larus Scheme for Numbering Paths

The Ball-Larus path-numbering scheme applies to an acyclic control-flow graph with a unique source node *Start* and a sink node *Exit*. Control-flow graphs that contain cycles are modified by a preprocessing step to turn them into acyclic graphs:

> Every cycle must contain one backedge, which can be identified using depth-first search. For each backedge $w \rightarrow v$, add edges $Start \rightarrow v$ and $w \rightarrow Exit$ to the graph. Then remove all of the backedges from the graph.

The resulting graph is acyclic. In terms of the ultimate effect of this transformation on profiling, the result is that we go from having an infinite number of unbounded-length paths in the control-flow graph to having a finite number of bounded-length paths. A path p in the original graph that proceeds several times around a loop will, in the profile, contribute "execution counts" to several smaller acyclic paths whose concatenation makes up p. In particular, the paths from *Start* to *Exit* in the modified graph correspond to acyclic paths in the original graph

---

[2]Path-spectrum comparison subsumes node-spectrum comparison and edge-spectrum comparison in the sense that all behavioral differences identified by node-spectrum comparison and edge-spectrum comparison will also be identified by path-spectrum comparison, but not vice versa. Path-spectrum comparison subsumes node-spectrum comparison and edge-spectrum comparison in a second sense, as well. Node profiling and edge profiling can be considered to be degenerate cases of path profiling: edge profiling is the case where the paths tabulated are all of length 1; node profiling is the case where the paths tabulated are all of length 0.

(where following the edge *Start* → *v* that was added to the modified graph corresponds to following backedge *w* → *v* in the original graph and beginning a new path at *v*, and following the edge *w* → *Exit* that was added to the modified graph corresponds to ending the path in the original graph at *w*).

In the discussion below, when we refer to the "control-flow graph", we mean the transformed (*i.e.*, acyclic) version of the graph.

The Ball-Larus numbering scheme labels the control-flow graph with two quantities:

(1) Each *node V* in the control-flow graph is labeled with a value, *num_paths_from* (*V*), which indicates the number of paths from *V* to the control-flow graph's *Exit* node.

(2) Each *edge* in the control-flow graph is labeled with a value derived from the *num_paths_from* quantities.

For expository convenience, we will describe these two aspects of the numbering scheme as if they are generated during two separate passes over the graph. In practice, the two labeling passes can be combined into a single pass.

In the first labeling pass, nodes are considered in reverse topological order. The base case involves the *Exit* node: It is labeled with 1, which accounts for the path of length 0 from *Exit* to itself. In general, a node *W* is labeled only after all of its successors W_1, W_2, $\cdots$, W_k are labeled. When *W* is considered, *num_paths_from* (*W*) is set to the value $num\_paths\_from(W_1) + \cdots + num\_paths\_from(W_k)$, as indicated in the diagram below:

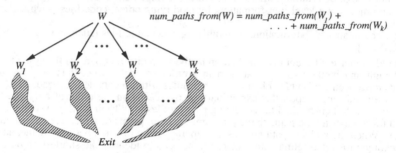

$$num\_paths\_from(W) = num\_paths\_from(W_1) + \\ \ldots + num\_paths\_from(W_k)$$

The goal of the second labeling pass is to arrive at a numbering scheme for which, for every path from *Start* to *Exit*, the sum of the edge labels along the path corresponds to a *unique* number in the range [0 .. *num_paths_from* (*Start*) − 1]. That is, we want the following properties to hold:

(1) Every path from *Start* to *Exit* is to correspond to a number in the range [0 .. *num_paths_from* (*Start*) − 1].

(2) Every number in the range [0 .. *num_paths_from* (*Start*) − 1] is to correspond to some path from *Start* to *Exit*.

Again, the graph is considered in reverse topological order. The general situation is shown below:

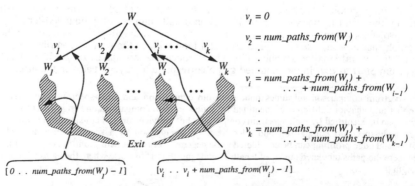

$$v_1 = 0$$
$$v_2 = num\_paths\_from(W_1)$$
$$\vdots$$
$$v_i = num\_paths\_from(W_1) + \\ \ldots + num\_paths\_from(W_{i-1})$$
$$\vdots$$
$$v_k = num\_paths\_from(W_1) + \\ \ldots + num\_paths\_from(W_{k-1})$$

$[0 \, . \, . \, num\_paths\_from(W_1) - 1]$ $[v_i \, . \, . \, v_i + num\_paths\_from(W_i) - 1]$

At this stage, we may assume that all edges along paths from each successor of W, say W_i, to

Exit have been labeled with values so that the sum of the edge labels along each path corresponds to a unique number in the range [0 .. *num_paths_from* (W_i) – 1]. Therefore, our goal is to attach a number v_i on edge $W \to W_i$ that, when added to numbers in the range [0 .. *num_paths_from* (W_i) – 1], distinguishes the paths of the form $W \to W_i \to \cdots \to Exit$ from all paths from W to *Exit* that begin with a different edge out of W.

This goal can be achieved by generating numbers $v_1, v_2, \cdots, v_k$ in the manner indicated in the above diagram: The number v_i is set to the sum of the number of paths to *Exit* from all successors of W that are to the left of W_i:

$$v_i = \sum_{j=1}^{i-1} num\_paths\_from\,(W_j).$$

This "reserves" the range [v_i .. v_i + *num_paths_from* (W_i) – 1] for the paths of the form $W \to W_i \to \cdots \to Exit$. The sum of the edge labels along each path from W to *Exit* that begins with an edge $W \to W_j$, where $j < i$, will be a number strictly less than v_i. The sum of the edge labels along each path from W to *Exit* that begins with an edge $W \to W_m$, where $m > i$, will be a number strictly greater than v_i + *num_paths_from* (W_i) – 1.

Example. Returning to the example used in Section 3, Figure 2 shows how the control-flow graph of the program fragment that reads and processes data from a database of customer information would be annotated. Each box is annotated with the number of paths from that node to the final node of the fragment; each edge is annotated with the number that would be assigned by the edge-numbering scheme described above.

Note that the sum of the edge labels along each path from the beginning to the end of the graph falls in the range [0 .. 7], and that each number in the range [0 .. 7] corresponds to exactly one such path. □

The final step is to instrument the program, which involves introducing a counter variable and appropriate increment statements to accumulate the sum of the edge labels as the program executes along a path.

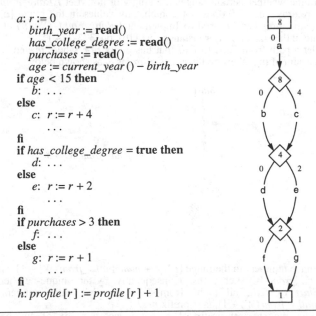

```
a: r := 0
    birth_year := read()
    has_college_degree := read()
    purchases := read()
    age := current_year () – birth_year
if age < 15 then
    b: ...
else
    c:  r := r + 4
       . . .
fi
if has_college_degree = true then
    d: ...
else
    e:  r := r + 2
       . . .
fi
if purchases > 3 then
    f:  ...
else
    g:  r := r + 1
       . . .
fi
h: profile [r] := profile [r] + 1
```

Figure 2. The instrumented version of the program fragment that reads and processes data from a database of customer information, and the program's annotated control-flow graph.

Example. The instrumented version of the program's source code is shown on the left in Figure 2. Statements that increment counter *r* have been introduced so that at the end of the fragment its value indicates which path through the fragment was executed. This value is then used to increment the appropriate element of array *profile*, which maintains the frequency distribution of paths executed. (Alternatively, *profile* could maintain just a Boolean indicator of whether the path is ever executed.) □

Several additional techniques are employed to reduce the runtime overheads incurred. These exploit the fact that there is actually a certain amount of flexibility in the placement of the increment statements [3,4].

Profiles obtained from the instrumented program can be displayed in the fashion shown below, where paths are arranged on the *x*-axis according to the path number, and the *y*-axis is used to indicate either the execution frequency or just a Boolean indicator of whether the path was executed at all. The spectra discussed in Section 3 would be displayed as follows:

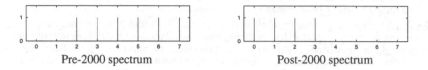

Pre-2000 spectrum   Post-2000 spectrum

4.2. An Alternative Technique for Identifying Problematic Path Prefixes

Suppose that *p* is a path in *new_spectrum* that does not occur in *old_spectrum*. This section describes how to exploit the Ball-Larus path-numbering scheme for the purpose of finding the shortest prefix of *p* that is not a prefix of any executed path in *old_spectrum*. (If *p* is a path in *old_spectrum* that does not occur in *new_spectrum*, then flip the roles of *old_spectrum* and *new_spectrum* in what follows.) Instead of using a trie structure on *old_spectrum*, an index structure that supports range queries is built on *old_spectrum*, and a sequence of queries is issued to determine whether certain ranges are empty or not. Let *IsRangeEmpty* (S,a,b) be an operation that returns true if *S* does not contain any values in the range [*a* .. *b*], inclusive. (Standard data structures can be used to implement *IsRangeEmpty* (S,a,b) efficiently, *i.e.*, in time logarithmic in the size of *S*. For instance, see [16], pp. 373-374.)

Now consider a path from *Start* to *Exit* that has prefix *pre*, where *pre* ends at node *W*, and suppose that the sum of the labels on the edges of *pre* is *c*, as shown below:

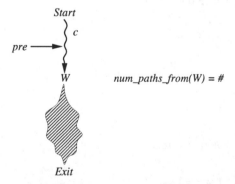

All such paths have numbers in the range [*c* .. *c* + *num_paths_from* (*W*) − 1], and there are precisely *num_paths_from* (*W*) such paths. Consequently, by the unique-numbering property of paths from *Start* to *Exit*, all paths from *Start* to *Exit* with numbers in the range [*c* .. *c* + *num_paths_from* (*W*) − 1] have prefix *pre*.

The search for the shortest prefix of *p* that is not a prefix of any executed path in *old_spectrum* is carried out as follows. As above, suppose that *p* is a path from *Start* to *Exit* that has prefix *pre*, where *pre* ends at node *W*, and that the sum of the labels on the edges of *pre* is *c*. Suppose further that we have already searched from *Start* to node *W* and have not yet found the edge that distinguishes *p* from the paths of *old_spectrum*:

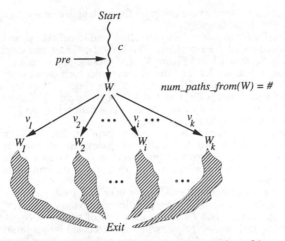

(When the search is initiated, $W = Start$, pre is the empty path, and $c = 0$.)

Assume that path p continues from W along edge $W \rightarrow W_i$, which is labeled with the value v_i (i.e., p has prefix $pre \parallel (W \rightarrow W_i)$, where "$\parallel$" denotes path concatenation). We need to know if any of the paths in $old\_spectrum$ also have prefix $pre \parallel (W \rightarrow W_i)$. Again, by the unique-numbering property of paths from $Start$ to $Exit$, the paths in the graph from $Start$ to $Exit$ that have prefix $pre \parallel (W \rightarrow W_i)$ are exactly the paths with numbers in the range $[c + v_i \, .. \, c + v_i + num\_paths\_from(W_i) - 1]$. Thus, to determine if any of the paths in $old\_spectrum$ have prefix $pre \parallel (W \rightarrow W_i)$, we need to perform the test

$$IsRangeEmpty(old\_spectrum, \; c + v_i, \; c + v_i + num\_paths\_from(W_i) - 1).$$

If this test is true, then W is the branch statement at which p veers into "unknown territory" (along the edge $W \rightarrow W_i$). Otherwise, we continue the search at node W_i using the path prefix $pre \parallel (W \rightarrow W_i)$ and path-prefix value $c + v_i$.

The running time for this method of identifying the shortest prefix of a path in $new\_spectrum$ that does not occur in $old\_spectrum$ is not strictly comparable to the time used by the trie method discussed in Section 3. However, the asymptotic worst-case running time for building the range-query structure is better than the worst-case running time needed to build the trie, and the worst-case space usage of the range-query method is also better than the worst-case space usage of the trie method. For both methods, suppose that we are given an unsorted list of the paths executed in $old\_spectrum$. Let $|old\_spectrum|$ denote the size of $old\_spectrum$ (i.e., the number of paths in $old\_spectrum$).

- The time required to build a trie structure for $old\_spectrum$ is proportional to the sum of the number of edges in the paths in $old\_spectrum$. (Note that this is potentially much greater than $|old\_spectrum|$, which is simply the number of paths in $old\_spectrum$.) In the worst case, storing the trie could require space proportional to the sum of the number of edges in the paths in $old\_spectrum$. The time needed to determine the shortest distinguishing prefix pre of a path p is proportional to the number of edges in the answer: $|pre|$.
- The time required to build a range-query structure for $old\_spectrum$ is proportional to $|old\_spectrum| \cdot \log |old\_spectrum|$, and the space needed to hold the range-query structure is proportional to $|old\_spectrum|$. The time needed to determine the shortest distinguishing prefix pre of a path p is proportional to $|pre| \cdot \log |old\_spectrum|$.

5. Implementation and Preliminary Results

We built a prototype system, called DYNADIFF, that implements the path-spectrum-comparison technique, and carried out several preliminary experiments with it. DYNADIFF runs under Solaris on Sun SPARCstations. It uses Tcl/Tk to implement a graphical user interface, and Larus's implementation of the Ball-Larus path-profiling algorithm as the underlying machinery for generating path spectra. The path profiler instruments executable files, so programs can be written in any language (as long as the compiler for the language obeys certain calling conventions) or even in a mixture of languages.

The goal of DYNADIFF's user interface is to allow one to collect up, and perform difference operations on, collections of path profiles. The DYNADIFF user can display path profiles as spectra (as shown in Section 4.1 and Figure 4). (At present, we are not using the thresholding technique described in Section 3.1, and the system treats each path profile as merely a set of paths; that is, the frequency counts of the number of times each path executed is ignored. Thus, an executed path in a spectrum is displayed as a stick of height 1.) Spectra have links back to the source code: Clicking on the stick that represents a path brings up an *emacs* window with the elements of the path displayed in a special color.

DYNADIFF is organized around the notions of *profiles* and *workspaces*: Collections of profiles can be selected and placed in named workspaces. Because we are interested in path-spectrum differences, when path profiles from a workspace are displayed as spectra, each spectrum shows only paths that were executed in at least one of the profiles of the workspace but not in all of the profiles.

As part of calling up spectrum differences, the user forms sub-partitions of the profiles in a workspace. The profiles in a workspace are partitioned into three groups, which we will call *A*, *B*, and *Other*. (That is, *A*, *B*, and *Other* are each sets of profiles.) Spectrum differences are displayed by showing path sticks for paths that are executed by all profiles in *A*, but not by some profile in *B*, and vice versa. Clicking on one of the path sticks brings up an *emacs* window with the statements of the last edge of the shortest distinguishing prefix of the path displayed in one special color, the rest of the shortest distinguishing prefix displayed in a second special color, and the rest of the elements of the path displayed in a third special color.

```
cal(m, y, p, w)
char *p;
{
    register d, i;
    register char *s;
    int foo = 0;

    s = p;
    d = jan1(y);
    mon[2] = 29;
    mon[9] = 30;
    switch((jan1(y+1)+7-d)%7) {
        case 1:    /* non-leap year */
            mon[2] = 28;
            break;
        default:   /* 1752 */
            mon[9] = 19;
            break;
        case 2:    /* leap year */
            foo = foo + 1;    /* Statement added so that something in the leap-year case */
            break;            /* could be highlighted */
    }
    for(i=1; i<m; i++)
        d += mon[i];
    d %= 7;
    s += 3*d;
    . . .
```

Figure 3. The code displayed in *Times-BoldItalic*, **Helvetica-Bold**, and Times-Bold indicates a path that was executed during a run with input *"cal 2 1992"*, but not during a run with input *"cal 2 1997"*. The code shown in *Times-BoldItalic* and **Helvetica-Bold** indicates the shortest prefix of the path that distinguishes it from all paths of the *"cal 2 1997"* run. The code shown in **Helvetica-Bold** indicates the last edge of the shortest distinguishing prefix (*i.e.*, switch((jan1(y+1)+7-d)%7) → foo = foo + 1;).

One experiment that we carried out with DYNADIFF was aimed at testing the ability of path-spectrum comparison to identify leap-year calculations. This experiment involved the UNIX *cal* utility, which, given a month and a year as input, prints the calendar for that month. The *cal* program does not actually have a leap-year problem: It calculates correctly that the year 2000 is a leap year. However, because our goal was merely to determine whether path-spectrum comparison would be able to identify leap-year calculations, this did not matter—we tested the method's sensitivity to leap-year calculations by comparing spectra from leap years and non-leap years. Path spectra obtained from runs that we expected would involve leap-year calculations (*e.g.*, from inputs like "*cal 2 1992*", "*cal 2 1996*", etc.) were compared against spectra obtained from runs that we expected not to involve leap-year calculations (*e.g.*, "*cal 2 1997*", "*cal 2 1998*", etc.).

For example, in a trial with workspace-partition *A* consisting of the profile from a run with input "*cal 2 1992*" and *B* consisting of the profile from a run with input "*cal 2 1997*", there was

- One path that was executed during the run with input "*cal 2 1992*", but not during the run with input "*cal 2 1997*".
- One path that was executed during the run with input "*cal 2 1997*", but not during the run with input "*cal 2 1992*".

Figure 3 shows the path that was executed during the run with input "*cal 2 1992*", but not during the run with input "*cal 2 1997*", as well as the shortest prefix of the path that distinguishes it from all paths of the "*cal 2 1997*" run. To understand the code shown in Figure 3, it helps to know that the routine "jan1" receives a year value as its parameter, and returns a number in the range [0 .. 6] that represents the day of the week on which January 1 falls that year. The values 0 through 6 correspond to Sunday through Saturday, respectively. The switch statement chooses one of three cases, depending on the difference (in terms of number of days of the week) between jan1(y) and jan1(y+1). The switch value is 1 in the case of an ordinary, non-leap year; 2 in the case of a leap year; and 5, represented by the default case, in 1752, the year that England and the Colonies shifted from the Julian to the Gregorian calendar. The default case is used to make a minor adjustment to one of the program's internal tables, which has an effect elsewhere on how the calendar for September 1752 is created.

Figure 3 also illustrates a small glitch due to the fact that the path profiler we used instruments executable files. The program shown in Figure 3 has an additional statement, "foo = foo + 1;" that we added in "case 2" of the switch statement. With the original program, in which "case 2" was empty, we were initially confused by the path that DYNADIFF highlighted. No part of "case 2" was highlighted, and we did not at first recognize that the path actually did go into that branch of the switch statement. The reason for this was that the current version of DYNADIFF uses information generated by the compiler to map from addresses in executable files to lines in the source code. Our confusion was caused by the fact that the compiler had not generated any instructions for the empty case, and so DYNADIFF did not have the information it needed to highlight "case 2". In Figure 3, the statement "foo = foo + 1;" was added so that something existed in the body of "case 2" that could be highlighted. (If DYNADIFF were to perform path profiling via source-code instrumentation, it would not have this problem.)

A second experiment that we carried out with DYNADIFF was aimed at testing the ability of path-spectrum comparison to identify date-rollover problems. The test involved a version of *ncftp*, a file-transfer utility. As in the first experiment, the standard version of the program does not, in fact, have a Y2K problem—so we introduced one, by arranging for all year values that the program manipulates to be in the range [00 .. 99]! The results are presented in Figure 4, which shows the path spectra obtained from six runs of the date-sensitive version of the program. The six runs processed input data associated with different years. Note how the path spectra change as we cross the year 2000 boundary, but are almost completely stable on either side of it.

Similar results were obtained in two other experiments that we carried out: As we would expect, the path spectra for the UNIX *cal*[3] and *rcs* utilities change as we cross the transition point when the UNIX *time* function overflows (*i.e.*, 03:14:08 UTC, Tuesday, January 19, 2038).

---

[3]When *cal* is invoked with no arguments, it prints the calendar of the current month. The current month is determined via a call on the UNIX *time* function. Just after *time* overflows, *cal* prints the calendar for December 1901.

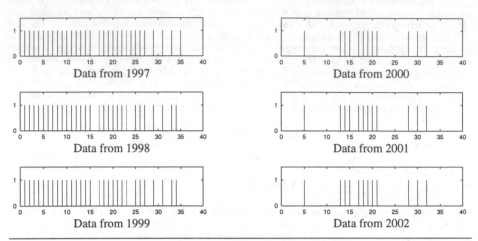

Figure 4. Path spectra from six runs of a date-sensitive version of *ncftp*.

6. Other Applications in Software Maintenance

The path-spectrum-comparison technique is actually applicable to a much wider range of problems that arise in software maintenance than just the Y2K problem. A number of other ways to enlist path-spectrum comparison in the cause of providing better help for software-maintenance problems are described below.

Testing

The application of path-spectrum comparison to the Y2K problem involves comparing path spectra from different execution runs. The principle is that "information about possible date-dependent computations can be obtained by comparing path spectra from execution runs on pre-2000 data and post-2000 data". This is essentially a testing strategy, although one of a novel kind. The Y2K problem is also just one example of a problem to which this kind of testing strategy can be applied.

In broadest terms, the general principle can be stated as follows:

A path spectrum is a finite, easily obtainable characterization of a program's execution on a dataset, and provides a behavior signature for a run of the program. When different runs of a program produce different path spectra, the spectral differences can be used to identify paths in the program along which control diverges in the two runs. By choosing input datasets to hold all factors constant except one, any such divergence can be attributed to this factor. The point of divergence itself may not be the cause of the underlying problem, but provides a starting place for a programmer to begin his exploration.

This principle offers new perspectives on testing, on the task of creating test data, and on what tools can be created to support program testing.

This approach to testing is a new variant of white-box testing, which we propose to call "I/B testing", for "Input/Behavior" testing, by analogy with I/O testing. In contrast to I/O testing, I/B testing can reveal possible problems—by finding path-spectrum differences—even when the output of an execution run is correct.

The effectiveness of path-spectrum comparison for uncovering errors depends on how good the two input datasets are at eliciting different behaviors during the different runs. For instance, the results in the Y2K problem depend on how well the input data stimulates different behaviors during the pre-2000 and post-2000 runs. This raises a number of questions. Two of them—analogs of well-known issues that arise with conventional testing methods, and left open here for future research—are: "How does one design pairs of input sets that are likely to cause errors to be revealed via spectral differences?" and "How does one evaluate the quality of a suite of input-set pairs?"

Testing is a huge problem for software developers, and will be with us long past the year 2000. We believe that the path-spectrum-comparison technique holds the promise of providing a useful adjunct to conventional methods for testing whether programs are functioning properly (and debugging them when they are malfunctioning).

Systems that Warn of Possible Errors Within Themselves

As described thus far, the spectra that are compared come from different runs of a program. However, the underlying principle is simply that "information about possible execution problems can be obtained by comparing two spectra". The spectra do not necessarily have to be from different runs of the program. All we care about is that there are two spectra to be compared (and that the spectra provide some sort of behavior signature). The spectra could be obtained from two or more runs (as in the application of the technique to the Y2K problem); however, there are situations in which it would be meaningful to compare spectra obtained during a single run.

Two situations in which this would be useful are: (i) when a system is being tested, and (ii) in a system that warns of possible errors within itself. In both cases, the idea is to have the system compare each path executed by the program with the paths executed so far. When a new path is discovered (i.e., when the path is executed for the first time) the program would signal that a possibly erroneous computation has just occurred—i.e., to warn the user or system tester that the program has just gone down a possibly bad path. (The system could issue the warning directly to the user, to a dialog box, to the console window, or to a log file.)

Such information (e.g., perhaps the last few such paths reported) could provide important clues that would help in tracking down a bug once a symptom comes to the attention of the user. Of course, one would want to wait until the program had run for a while before starting to issue such warnings, but after a break-in or warm-up period it would begin to be useful to gather such information.

Testing Which Parts of a System are Affected by a Modification

Another variation on path-spectrum comparison could be used to support the testing of bug fixes and other small changes to a system. The goal here would be to understand whether the only behavioral changes introduced by the modification were to the intended parts of the system. The idea is to use path-spectrum comparison as a heuristic method for understanding the magnitude of behavioral changes between two versions of a program.

In this context, the comparison that needs to be carried out is somewhat different from what has been discussed earlier: Instead of comparing spectra from two runs of the *same* program on *different* data, one would compare spectra from two runs of a (slightly) *different* program on the *same* data. As before, the premise that "states are similar if they proceed down the same path" provides the justification for why it makes sense to be comparing path spectra (even though they now come from execution runs of *different* programs).

Of course, one expects there to be differences between the two spectra obtained from the two versions of the program. For example, one would expect to see differences on the input that elicits the bug in the original program. The purpose of comparing the path spectra would be to obtain information about the extent of actual changes in behavior. One wants to make sure that a small change in the program text does not lead to radical changes in the behavior. The behavior of most of the unmodified parts of the system should be unaffected by a modification. The programmer can use the information obtained from path-spectrum comparison to develop an understanding of the actual magnitude of behavioral differences that a bug fix introduces.

In order to carry out comparisons between paths from two different programs, a concordance between paths in the old program and paths in the new program would be needed. The instrumentation strategy used affects how difficult it is to provide such a concordance: It would not be too hard to establish a correspondence between paths in the old and new programs when source-code instrumentation is used, but would be much more difficult when instrumentation is carried out on object-code files or executable files.

Testing for Inconsistent Data

Another potential application of path-spectrum comparison is to the "data hygiene" problem. The goal here is to identify data in a database or file that is contaminated, or inconsistent with the assumptions about the data that the program relies on. Our hypothesis is that some contaminated data items will cause the program to take unusual paths through the code (but ones that do not actually crash the system). Presumably the percentage of contaminated data is low; thus, the idea behind using path-spectrum comparison is to use information about infrequently executed paths to identify possibly contaminated data in the database. Any peculiar paths (*i.e.*, paths with count 1 or low relative frequency in the path spectrum) when the program is run against the database would be taken as a signal that the program was processing possibly contaminated data. To actually identify the contaminated data, one would need the instrumented program to gather some additional information in order to link the low-frequency paths back to the inputs that were most recently read in at the times the path was executed.

7. Related Work

This paper has described new techniques to help with testing and debugging, using information obtained from path profiling. Our work is based on the idea of comparing path spectra from different runs of the program to identify paths in the program along which control diverges in the different runs. The path-spectrum-comparison technique is a completely different way of using path profiling in the context of program testing from another use that has been proposed in the past, namely as a criterion for evaluating the coverage of a test suite [21,13,7,15]. The question of whether there is any hope of using the path-coverage criterion in practice has often been raised. The published results of Ball and Larus suggest that the answer to this question is "no". They report that some of the SPEC benchmarks had approximately $10^9 - 10^{11}$ paths, of which only 10^4 were ever executed on a given run [4]. Although not all of the possible paths are necessarily feasible, it could be necessary to run $10^5 - 10^7$ tests (and probably far more) to achieve a high degree of coverage.

Because our goal is different—our aim is to use spectral differences to identify paths in the program that represent changed behavior in the different runs—our use of path profiling to support program testing does not run afoul of the "high-number-of-paths/low-coverage-per-run" issue. This is not to imply that our use of path profiling does not come equipped with its own set of problems. On the contrary: The effectiveness of the path-spectrum comparison for testing depends on how good two test sets are at eliciting different behaviors during execution, and the question of how one designs pairs of input sets that are likely to cause errors to be revealed has been left open for future research.

The Docket project has explored ways to use information obtained from testing and dynamic analysis, including information about paths traversed during execution, in tools to support program comprehension [5]. One application of the Docket toolset addressed the problem of extracting "business rules" from programs [17]—*i.e.*, high-level requirements on how input data is to be processed, expressed in terms of the application domain (*e.g.*, "to be billed after delivery the customer must have a credit rating of at least satisfactory, otherwise, the customer must pay on delivery" [18]). Information about an input/output value pair, the types of the input and output values, and the path through the program that was executed is used to generate several candidate assertions (*viz.* possible "business rules") that characterize the I/O transformation.

There is a distant relationship between some of the techniques proposed in Section 6 and previous work on testing and debugging:

- Relative debugging allows programmers to compare the execution behaviors of multiple instances of the same program [1]. The setting for relative debugging is the porting of code (usually Fortran) from one platform (hardware/OS) to another. Because of differences in hardware and/or numerical libraries, the *same* program may exhibit different behaviors on different platforms. With relative debugging, the programmer places assertions in the source code, which are then checked against one another as the two programs execute in parallel on the different platforms. The debugger takes care of the details of inserting breakpoints and comparing data structures across the two executions. When a substantial difference in behavior is found (*i.e.*, an assertion is violated), the programmer is notified. Relative debugging also supports runtime comparison of a modified program to an older reference program.
- Dependences between tests and program entities have been used to implement selective regression testing in the TestTube system [6]. In this case, there are two different versions of a program, and dependence information gathered from previous tests is used to determine whether a test needs to be rerun on the new version.

Acknowledgements

We are grateful for the helpful comments of K. Baxter, B. Carlson, J. Field, S. Horwitz, T. Taft, and D. Weise.

References

1. Abramson, D., Foster, I., Michalakes, J., and Sosic, R., "Relative debugging: A new methodology for debugging scientific applications," *Commun. of the ACM* **39**(11) pp. 68-77 (Nov. 1996).
2. Bala, V., "Low overhead path profiling," Tech. Rep., Hewlett-Packard Labs (1996).
3. Ball, T., "Efficiently counting program events with support for on-line queries," *ACM Trans. Program. Lang. Syst.* **16**(5) pp. 1399-1410 (Sept. 1994).
4. Ball, T. and Larus, J., "Efficient path profiling," in *Proc. of MICRO-29*, (Dec. 1996).
5. Benedusi, P., Benvenuto, V., and Tomacelli, L., "The role of testing and dynamic analysis in program comprehension supports," pp. 149-158 in *Proc. of the Second IEEE Workshop on Program Comprehension*, (July 8-9, 1993, Capri, Italy), ed. B. Fadini and V. Rajlich,IEEE Comp. Soc. Press, Wash., DC (July 1993).
6. Chen, Y.-F., Rosenblum, D.S., and Vo, K.-P., "TestTube: A system for selective regression testing," in *Proc. of the Sixteenth Int. Conf. on Softw. Eng.*, (May 16-21, 1994, Sorrento, Italy), IEEE Comp. Soc. Press, Wash., DC (1994).
7. Clarke, L.A., Podgurski, A., Richardson, D.J., and Zeil, S.J., "A comparison of data flow path selection criteria," pp. 244-251 in *Proc. of the Eighth Int. Conf. on Softw. Eng.*, IEEE Comp. Soc. Press, Wash., DC (1985).
8. Gartner Group, *Year 2000 Problem Gains National Attention*, Gartner Group, Stamford, CT (April 1996). (See URL http://www.gartner.com/aboutgg/pressrel/pry2000.html.)
9. Horwitz, S., Reps, T., and Binkley, D., "Interprocedural slicing using dependence graphs," *ACM Trans. Program. Lang. Syst.* **12**(1) pp. 26-60 (Jan. 1990).
10. Johnson, S.C., "Postloading for fun and profit," pp. 325-330 in *Proc. of the Winter 1990 USENIX Conf.*, (Jan. 1990).
11. Larus, J.R. and Schnarr, E., "EEL: Machine-independent executable editing," *Proc. of the ACM SIGPLAN 95 Conf. on Programming Language Design and Implementation*, (La Jolla, CA, June 18-21, 1995), *ACM SIGPLAN Notices* **30**(6) pp. 291-300 (June 1995).
12. Ottenstein, K.J. and Ottenstein, L.M., "The program dependence graph in a software development environment," *Proc. of the ACM SIGSOFT/SIGPLAN Softw. Eng. Symp. on Practical Software Development Environments*, (Pittsburgh, PA, Apr. 23-25, 1984), *ACM SIGPLAN Notices* **19**(5) pp. 177-184 (May 1984).
13. Rapps, S. and Weyuker, E.J., "Selecting software test data using data flow information," *IEEE Trans. on Softw. Eng.* **SE-11**(4) pp. 367-375 (Apr. 1985).
14. Reps, T., Horwitz, S., Sagiv, M., and Rosay, G., "Speeding up slicing," *SIGSOFT 94: Proc. of the Second ACM SIGSOFT Symp. on the Found. of Softw. Eng.*, (New Orleans, LA, Dec. 7-9, 1994), *ACM SIGSOFT Softw. Eng. Notes* **19**(5) pp. 11-20 (Dec. 1994).
15. Roper, M., *Software Testing*, McGraw-Hill, New York, NY (1994).
16. Sedgewick, R., *Algorithms*, Addison-Wesley, Reading, MA (1983).
17. Sneed, H.M. and Ritsch, H., "Reverse engineering programs via dynamic analysis," pp. 192-201 in *Proc. of the IEEE Working Conf. on Reverse Engineering*, (May 21-23, 1993, Baltimore, MD), IEEE Comp. Soc. Press, Wash., DC (May 1993).
18. Sneed, H.M. and Erdos, K., "Extracting business rules from source code," pp. 240-247 in *Proc. of the Fourth IEEE Workshop on Program Comprehension*, (Mar. 29-31, 1996, Berlin, Germany), ed. V. Rajlich, A. Cimitile, and H.A. Mueller,IEEE Comp. Soc. Press, Wash., DC (Mar. 1996).
19. Srivastava, A. and Eustace, A., "ATOM: A system for building customized program analysis tools," *Proc. of the ACM SIGPLAN 94 Conf. on Programming Language Design and Implementation*, (Orlando, FL, June 22-24, 1994), *ACM SIGPLAN Notices* **29**(6) pp. 196-205 (June 1994).
20. Weiser, M., "Program slicing," *IEEE Trans. on Softw. Eng.* **SE-10**(4) pp. 352-357 (July 1984).
21. Woodward, M.R., Hedley, D., and Hennell, M.A., "Experience with path analysis and testing of programs," *IEEE Trans. on Softw. Eng.* **SE-6**(3) pp. 278-286 (May 1980).

Reduction and Slicing of
Hierarchical State Machines*

Mats P.E. Heimdahl and Michael W. Whalen

University of Minnesota, Institute of Technology
Department of Computer Science, 4-192 EE/CS Bldg.
Minneapolis, MN 55455

Abstract. Formal specification languages are often criticized for being difficult to understand, difficult to use, and unacceptable by software practitioners. Notations based on state machines, such as, Statecharts, Requirements State Machine Language (RSML), and SCR, are suitable for modeling of embedded systems and eliminate many of the main drawbacks of formal specification languages. Although a specification language can help eliminate accidental complexity, the inherent complexity of many of today's systems inevitably leads to large and complex specifications. Thus, there is a need for mechanisms to simplify a formal specification and present information to analysts and reviewers in digestible chunks.

In this paper, we present a two tiered approach to slicing (or simplification) of hierarchical finite state machines. We allow an analyst to simplify a specification based on a *scenario*. The remaining behavior, called an *interpretation* of the specification, can then be sliced to extract the information effecting selected variables and transitions.

To evaluate the effectiveness and utility of slicing in hierarchical state machines, we have implemented a prototype tool and applied our slicing approach to parts of a specification of a large avionics system called TCAS II (Traffic alert and Collision Avoidance System II).

1 Introduction

Formal specification languages are often criticized for being difficult to understand, difficult to use, and unacceptable by software practitioners. Notations based on state machines, such as, Statecharts [2–4], Requirements State Machine Language (RSML) [12,13], and SCR [8–10], are suitable for modeling of embedded systems and eliminate many of the main drawbacks of formal specification languages. State-based languages are based on familiar concepts, have intuitive syntax and semantics, and help in reducing the perceived complexity of a formal specification. A suitable language syntax and semantics alone, however, cannot overcome the problems caused by inherent system complexity. Although a specification language can help eliminate accidental complexity, the inherent complexity of many of today's systems inevitably leads to large and complex

* This work has been partially supported by NSF grants CCR-9624324 and CCR-9615088, and University of Minnesota Grant in Aid of Research 1003-521-5965.

specifications. Thus, there is a need for mechanisms to simplify a formal specification and present information to analysts and reviewers in digestible chunks.

In this paper, we present a two tiered approach to slicing (or simplification) of hierarchical finite state machines. We allow an analyst to simplify a specification based on a *scenario*. The remaining behavior, called an *interpretation* of the specification, can then be sliced to extract the information effecting selected variables and transitions. The simplified model has the same behavior as the original specification for the reduced input domain defined by the scenario. The objective is for the reduced specification to be significantly smaller than the original specification and to help analysts and domain experts to understand and validate the model.

To evaluate the effectiveness and utility of slicing in hierarchical state machines, we have implemented a prototype tool and applied our slicing approach to a specification of a large avionics system called TCAS II (Traffic alert and Collision Avoidance System II). We used our slicing tool to help clarify a set of questions we have asked ourselves during previous investigations. In this case study, the reduction results were very helpful and slicing of RSML specifications seems to have great potential.

1.1 Background

In a previous investigation, the Irvine Safety Research Group, under the leadership of Dr. Nancy Leveson, developed a requirements specification language called the Requirements State Machine Language (RSML) suitable for the specification of safety-critical embedded control systems [12, 13]. To make RSML suitable as a requirements specification language usable by all stake-holders in a specification effort, the syntax and semantics of RSML were developed with readability, understandability, and ease of use in mind. The usefulness of the language was demonstrated through the successful development of a requirements specification for a large commercial avionics system called TCAS II (Traffic alert and Collision Avoidance System II) [12, 13]. Furthermore, we have developed a collection of automated analysis procedures that check an RSML specification for desirable properties such as completeness, consistency, and determinism [7] and we have explored the possibility of provably correct code generation from RSML specifications [11].

However, even if requirements specifications are readable, understandable, and can be shown to be complete and consistent, the sheer size and complexity of many systems make the specifications difficult to understand and review. For example, a table in an SCR specification typically spans multiple pages and table sizes of 14 pages or more are not uncommon [8]. In RSML, tables are used differently and the table sizes are kept much smaller so that tables always fit on one single page [13]. Nevertheless, a specification for a complex system will, due to inherent system complexity, inevitably grow large and through its size hinder readability. Since manual inspection is an effective way of validating a specification to the customers real needs, readability, understandability, and clarity of a specification document are of utmost importance. Therefore, tools and techniques to help reduce the complexity of a large specification are needed.

To aid in the review and inspection of specifications based on hierarchical state machines we are currently investigating the feasibility of *specification slicing* as a tool for specification understanding. We have focused on hierarchical state machines since they, in our opinion, are the most viable formalism for the class of systems we are interested in, namely reactive embedded control systems.

1.2 Program Slicing

Weiser introduced the concept of slicing as a means of simplifying programs to aid in debugging and identification of program fragments suitable for parallel execution [17]. A program slice is a projection of a program, which is smaller and potentially more comprehensible than the original program. Traditionally, program slicing is based on variables and statements. A slice consists of the statements that potentially effect the value of a particular variable at a given statement. Today, program slicing is used to reduce the complexity of a program and is successfully used in debugging, program comparison, testing, and maintenance.

Formal specifications provide a concise, mathematically well defined description that details the intended behavior of a system. Yet formal specifications often contain so much information that they overwhelm a reader and make the specifications less useful. Oda and Akari [14], and Chang and Richardson [1] have extended slicing to formal specifications expressed in Z. Their techniques were designed to help alleviate the readability problems in Z specifications. Both techniques are based on a traditional definition of slicing and calculates slices based on the use of a variable in a Z schema post-condition.

Slicing high-level specifications is in some aspects quite different from slicing programs. First, in state-based models variables are not the only entity we want to use as a basis for calculating a slice. Meaningful state-based specifications without variables are quite common during the early stages of the specifications effort. For example, if the focus of the specification effort is on the modal aspects of a system, input and output variables may not be defined until later in a project. In this case, the transitions between states are the focus of attention and we should be able to construct a slice containing the parts of the specification that effect a specific transition (or set of transitions).

Second, in the early stages of development, specifications are often incomplete and inconsistent. For example, the events and actions in a state-based specification may not be fully defined, and the specification may be internally inconsistent. Thus, a slicing approach must be able to work with incomplete and inconsistent models.

Sloane and Holdsworth extended the concept of slicing to a generalized marking of a program's abstract syntax tree [15]. This generalization allows (1) slicing of programs without statements and variables, and (2) slicing based on criteria other than the use of a variable at a given statement. Their approach enables slicing based on, for example, call graphs, object structure, and type dependencies. We also base our approach to reduction and slicing of hierarchical state machines on a marking of the abstract syntax tree. Therefore, it is similar to Sloane's and Holdsworth's approach.

1.3 Motivation

When reviewing and or inspecting a specification, we are interested in answering questions about the behavior of the specification. For example, during our work with TCAS II, we asked questions such as "When do we downgrade a threat that has stopped reporting altitude?" and "How do we treat an intruder that is considered to be on the ground?".

Most questions regarding a specification involve an action, as in, downgrading an intruder that is considered to be a threat, and a specific scenario, such as, when the intruder has stopped reporting altitude. To help answer questions of this type we provide a two tiered approach to specification reduction.

First, we allow the analyst to reduce an RSML specification based on the specific scenario of interest. Our tool accepts a *reduction scenario* that is used to reduce the specification to contain only the behaviors that are possible when the operating conditions defining the reduction scenario are satisfied. We call such a reduced specification the *interpretation* of the specification under this scenario.

Second, we allow the analyst to slice the interpretation based on different entities in the model to highlight, for example, the portions of the specification effecting the value of an output variable or the information effecting whether a specific transition can be taken.

In this paper we report on our first experiences with reduction and slicing of RSML specifications. To evaluate the feasibility of state machine slicing and to get some early feedback on our approach, we have applied our slicing technique to parts of the TCAS II requirements specification. Initial results show that the slicing approach is very useful and would have helped us answer a set of questions we encountered in previous investigations. Naturally, more experimentation is needed, but these initial results are promising and show that slicing of state based specifications provides many benefits for specification readability and understandability.

The next section gives a brief description of the syntax and semantics of RSML. The testbed we have used in this work is introduced in Section 3. Section 4 describes our approach to slicing of RSML specifications and Section 5 discusses our experiences from a case study. Section 6 provides concluding remarks.

2 Requirements State Machine Language (RSML)

RSML was developed as a requirements specification language for embedded systems. The language is based on hierarchical finite state machines and is similar to David Harel's Statecharts[2, 5]. For example, RSML supports parallelism, hierarchies, and guarded transitions which originated in Statecharts (Figure 1).

One of the main design goals of RSML was readability and understandability by non computer professionals such as, in our case, pilots, air frame manufacturers, and FAA representatives. During the TCAS project, we discovered that the guarding conditions required to accurately capture the requirements were often complex. The prepositional logic notation traditionally used to define these conditions did not scale well to complex expressions and quickly became unreadable. To overcome this problem, we decided to use a tabular representation of disjunctive normal form (DNF) that we call AND/OR tables (see Figure 2 for an example from the TCAS II requirements). The far-left column of the AND/OR table lists the logical phrases. Each of the other columns is a conjunction of those phrases and contains the logical values of the expressions. If one of the columns is

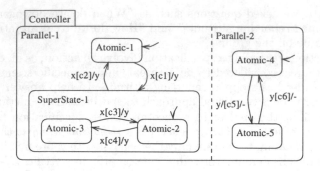

Fig. 1. An example of an hierarchical state machine.

Transition(s): | Potential-Threat | $\longrightarrow$ | Other-Traffic |

Location: Other-Aircraft ▷ Intruder-Status$_{s-136}$

Trigger Event: Air-Status-Evaluated-Event$_{e-279}$
Condition:

$$OR$$

Alt-Reporting$_{s-101}$ **in state** Lost	T	T	.	.	T	T	.	.	.	.
RA-Mode-Cancelled$_{m-218}$	.	.	T	T	.	.	T	T	.	.
Alt-Reporting$_{s-101}$ **in state** No	.	.	T	T	.	.	T	T	.	.
Other-Bearing-Valid$_{v-130}$	F	.	F	.	F	.	F	.	.	.
Other-Range-Valid$_{v-117}$ = True	.	F	.	F	.	F	.	F	.	.
Potential-Threat-Range-Test$_{m-214}$	T	T	T	T	F	F	F	F	.	.
Potential-Threat-Condition$_{m-213}$	.	.	.	.	.	.	.	.	F	.
Proximate-Traffic-Condition$_{m-216}$	.	.	.	.	T	T	T	T	F	.
Threat-Condition$_{m-224}$	.	.	.	.	.	.	.	.	F	.
Other-Air-Status$_{s-101}$ **in state** On-Ground	.	.	.	.	.	.	.	.	.	T

(rows 4–9 grouped by "AND")

Output Action: Intruder-Status-Evaluated-Event$_{e-279}$

Fig. 2. A transition definition from TCAS II with the guarding condition expressed as an AND/OR table.

true, then the table evaluates to true. A column evaluates to true if all of its elements are true. A dot denotes "don't care." To further increase the readability of the specification, we introduced many other syntactic conventions in RSML. For example, we allow expressions used in the predicates to be defined as mathematical functions (e.g., Other-Tracked-Relative-Alt-Rate$_{f\text{-}246}$), and familiar and frequently used conditions to be defined as macros (e.g., Threat-Condition$_{m\text{-}224}$)[1]. A macro is simply a named AND/OR table defined elsewhere in the document. Naturally, the state machine in a real system is never as simple as in Figure 1. As an example of a realistic model, a part of the state machine modeling an intruding aircraft in TCAS II can be seen in Figure 4.

Formally, the behavior of a finite-state machine can be defined using a next-state relation. In RSML, this relation is modeled by the transitions between states and the sequencing of events. Thus, one can view a graphical RSML specification as the definition of the mathematical next-state relation F. In short, an RSML specification is a mapping from a set of states (called the set of all configurations – $Config$) representing the states in the graphical model and a set of variables (V) representing the input and output variables in the model to new states and variables. Thus, the next state relation F is a mapping $C \mapsto C$, where $C \subseteq (Config \times V)$. For a rigorous treatment of formal foundation of RSML the reader is referred to [7]. A detailed description of the graphical notation can be found in [13].

3 Testbed Specification

To evaluate the effectiveness of our approach and to better understand the effect of slicing on a large real world RSML specification, we applied our tool to the TCAS II RSML model. To introduce the reader to our case study, we provide a short overview of TCAS II.

3.1 TCAS II

TCAS is a family of airborne devices that function independently of the ground-based air traffic control (ATC) system to provide collision avoidance protection for commercial aircraft and larger aircraft. TCAS II provides traffic advisories and recommended escape maneuvers (resolution advisories) in a vertical direction to avoid conflicting aircraft.

In this paper, we will use examples from the part of the collision avoidance system (CAS) in TCAS II that classifies intruding aircraft as Other-Traffic, Proximate-Traffic, Potential-Threats, or Threats. In the CAS logic, the states of two main components are modeled: our own aircraft and other aircraft.

Own-Aircraft: Figure 3 shows the expanded Own-Aircraft portion of the CAS model. Effective-SL (sensitivity level) controls the dimensions of the protected airspace around own aircraft.

---

[1] The subscript is used to indicate the type of an identifier (f for functions, m for macros, and v for variables) and gives the page in the TCAS II requirements document where the identifier is defined.

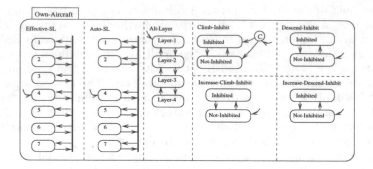

Fig. 3. Model of Own-Aircraft

There are two primary means that CAS uses to determine Effective-SL: ground-based selection and pilot selection. When the pilot selects an automatic sensitivity selection mode, CAS selects sensitivity level based on the current altitude of own aircraft (defined in the Auto-SL state machine).

Alt-Layer effectively divides vertical airspace into layers (e.g., Layer-3 is approximately equal to the range 20,000 feet to 30,000 feet). Alt-Layer and Effective-SL are used in the determination other aircraft threat classification (see Figure 4).

Other-Aircraft: The model of an intruding aircraft can be seen in Figure 4. In short, the top-level state machine reflects whether a particular Other-Aircraft is currently being tracked or not.

The Intruder-Status state within Tracked reflects the current classification of Other-Aircraft (Other-Traffic, Proximate-Traffic, Potential-Threat, and Threat). When an intruder is classified as a threat, a two-step process is used to select a Resolution Advisory (RA). The first step is to select a sense (Climb or Descend). The CAS logic computes the predicted vertical separation for both climb and descend maneuvers, and selects the sense that provides the greater vertical separation.

The second step in selecting an RA is to select the strength of the advisory. The least disruptive vertical rate maneuver that will still achieve safe separation is selected. For a more complete description of TCAS II and how it was modeled using RSML the reader is referred to [13].

4 Specification Slicing

During our work with static analysis [6, 7] we identified questions regarding the behavior of TCAS II where some tool support to aid in answering the questions would have been helpful. The questions were seldom related to output variables. Instead, we wanted to know how the specification behaved when, for example, an intruding aircraft was declared to be on the ground or when an intruding aircraft stopped reporting altitude. Thus, our slicing approach was defined to help an analyst answer questions that we know are common from experience. Typical questions we encountered can be seen in Table 1.

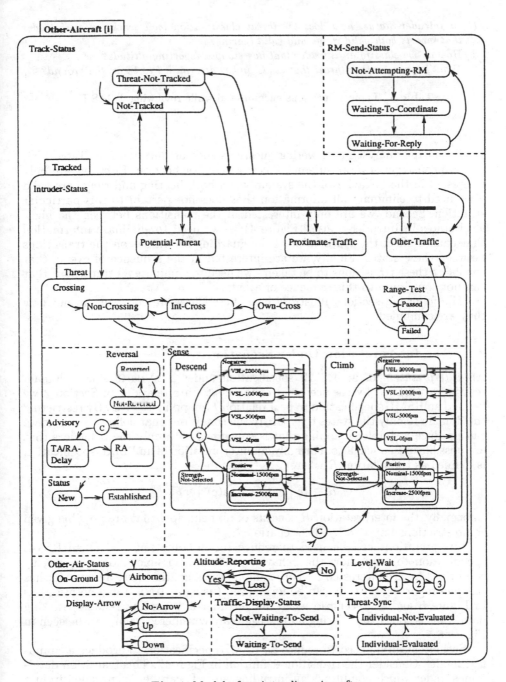

Fig. 4. Model of an intruding aircraft

1. *In Intruder-Status, how does the threat classification logic work for an intruder that reports both valid range and valid bearing?*
2. *How do we classify an intruder that has stopped reporting altitude?*
3. *What happens with a threat that lands and is determined to be on the ground?*

Table 1. Typical questions encountered while reviewing TCAS II.

To aid the analyst in answering questions such as question 1 in Table 1 we need to construct several different slices of the specification. First, we are only interested in the behavior of the system when both bearing and range are valid – we need to eliminate all information that does not pertain to this particular situation. Second, we are only interested in the transitions between the high-level states in Intruder-Status (Figure 4)[2] – we need to eliminate information that cannot effect the truth value of the guarding conditions on the transitions between these states. Finally, we are interested in the sequence of events that can cause these transitions to be taken - we need to eliminate all transitions that can not contribute to this sequence of events.

The following sections illustrate how these slices are constructed and how they are combined.

4.1 The Interpretation Under Scenario *s*

An *interpretation* of an RSML specification under a *scenario s* is a domain restriction (defined by the scenario) of the next state relation. In Section 2 we defined an RSML specification to be a relation F mapping $C \mapsto C$. By restricting the domain to only the states that satisfy the conditions that define a scenario we can produce a simpler mapping that is concerned with only the behaviors that are possible in this scenario. Formally, an interpretation of an RSML specification is defined as the relation R where

$$R \equiv \{ c \mid c \in C \ \wedge \ s(c) \ \} \lhd F$$

Informally, the interpretation R consists of all behaviors that are possible given the restrictions imposed by the scenario s [3].

Interpretations can be used to reduce (or in some sense slice) an RSML specification to only show the behaviors that are possible under the specific conditions we are interested in. For example, the scenario where an intruder has stopped reporting altitude can be formalized (using AND/OR table notation) as in Figure 5 and the scenario where an intruder is providing reliable tracking data, that is, both the bearing and altitude are considered valid, can be seen in Figure 6.

Scenarios can be used to reduce an RSML specification to produce a simplified model. Consider the transition definition in Figure 2. This transition determines under which conditions an intruding aircraft can be downgraded from a

---

[2] The states involved in threat classification are Other-traffic, Proximate-Traffic, Potential-Threat, and Threat.

[3] The notation $S \lhd R$ is borrowed from Z [16] and defines a relation that relates a to b iff R relates a to b and a is a member of S.

Reduction Scenario: Not-Reporting-Altitude

$$\begin{matrix} A \\ N \\ D \end{matrix} \quad \boxed{\text{Alt-Reporting}_{s\text{-}101} \ \textbf{in state } \text{No}} \quad \boxed{\text{T}}$$

Fig. 5. An intruder has stopped reporting altitude expressed as an AND/OR table.

Reduction Scenario: Valid-Tracking

$$\begin{matrix} A \\ N \\ D \end{matrix} \quad \boxed{\begin{matrix} \text{Other-Bearing-Valid}_{v\text{-}130} = \text{Valid} \\ \text{Other-Range-Valid}_{v\text{-}133} = \text{Valid} \end{matrix}} \quad \boxed{\begin{matrix} \text{T} \\ \text{T} \end{matrix}}$$

Fig. 6. An intruder reporting reliable tracking data expressed as an AND/OR table.

Transition(s): $\boxed{\text{Potential-Threat}} \longrightarrow \boxed{\text{Other-Traffic}}$

Location: Other-Aircraft ▷ Intruder-Status$_{s\text{-}136}$

Trigger Event: Air-Status-Evaluated-Event$_{e\text{-}279}$

Condition:

OR

R.A-Mode-Cancelled$_{m\text{-}218}$	T	T	T	T	·	·
Alt-Reporting$_{s\text{-}101}$ **in state** No	T	T	T	T	·	·
Other-Bearing-Valid$_{v\text{-}130}$	F	·	F	·	·	·
Other-Range-Valid$_{v\text{-}117}$ = True	·	F	·	F	·	·
Potential-Threat-Range-Test$_{m\text{-}214}$	T	T	F	F	·	·
Potential-Threat-Condition$_{m\text{-}213}$	·	·	·	·	F	·
Proximate-Traffic-Condition$_{m\text{-}216}$	·	·	T	T	F	·
Threat-Condition$_{m\text{-}224}$	·	·	·	·	F	·
Other-Air-Status$_{s\text{-}101}$ **in state** On-Ground	·	·	·	·	·	T

(rows grouped by AND on the left)

Output Action: Intruder-Status-Evaluated-Event$_{e\text{-}279}$

Fig. 7. The transition definition sliced based on the reduction scenario Not-Reporting-Altitude in Figure 5

Transition(s): | Potential-Threat | $\longrightarrow$ | Other-Traffic |

Location: Other-Aircraft ▷ Intruder-Status$_{s\text{-}136}$

Trigger Event: Air-Status-Evaluated-Event$_{e\text{-}279}$
Condition:

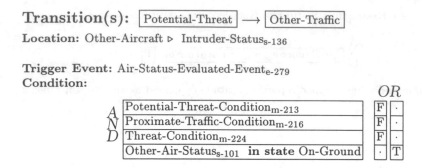

Output Action: Intruder-Status-Evaluated-Event$_{e\text{-}279}$

Fig. 8. The transition definition sliced based on the scenario Valid-Tracking in Figure 6.

Potential-Threat (indicating that an intruder is close and that a traffic advisory should be issued to the pilot) to Other-Traffic (indicating that an intruder is considered to be irrelevant and no information about the intruder is presented to the pilot). Under normal circumstances, a potential threat is only downgraded to other traffic if it is not considered to be a potential threat, nor a threat or in proximity (captured in column 9 of Figure 2). However, there are many exceptions for abnormal operating conditions, for example, when an intruder stops reporting altitude. These exceptions make the threat detection logic quite complex and obfuscates the specification. If we construct an interpretation of the specification based on the scenario named Not-Reporting-Altitude in Figure 5, we get a simpler transition definition (Figure 7) telling us how TCAS downgrades a non-altitude reporting intruder. The scenario Not-Reporting-Altitude requires the state machine Alt-Reporting to be in state No. Since the state machine Alt-Reporting (Figure 4) by definition can only be in one state at the time, all columns in Figure 2 requiring Alt-Reporting to be in a state other than No can be eliminated (columns 1, 2, 5, and 6 can be eliminated).

If we are only interested in the normal operating condition where we have reliable tracking data from an intruding aircraft, we can construct an interpretation based on the scenario named Valid-Tracking in Figure 6. This interpretation almost eliminates the guarding condition (Figure 8) and we can more clearly see how TCAS operates under normal conditions.

Construction of Interpretations: As mentioned in Section 4, our slicing algorithms are based on a marking of the abstract syntax tree. In a previous investigation we developed an RSML parser as a part of an analysis environment for RSML [7]. This parser has been modified to allow us to mark the abstract syntax tree based on various slicing criteria.

A reduction scenario is used to mark the infeasible columns in each AND/OR table. A column is infeasible if any of the truth values in the column (recall that a column represents a conjunction) contradicts the scenario. We have implemented a collection of decision procedures to determine if the predicates constituting a column contradict a scenario. The current decision procedures cover predicates expressed over enumerated variables and over the states in the model. The decision procedures do not cover predicates over integer and real variables. These limitations are discussed in more detail below.

After the infeasible columns have been marked they are removed from the table. Furthermore, after the columns have been removed, any rows consisting of all don't care are removed since those rows are now superfluous. If a table is left with no remaining columns, the guarding condition defined by the table cannot be satisfied in this scenario. After all tables have been reduced, the transitions with unsatisfiable guarding conditions are eliminated from the model. The remaining specification constitutes the interpretation of the specification under the scenario.

Limitation: Our current implementation of the reduction algorithm only allows the definition of the scenarios to contain predicates over enumerated variables and over the states in the specification. Since simplification of a table involves determining if two predicates contradict each other, we have limited our approach to predicates where the decision procedures are relatively easy to implement. We are currently extending the decision procedures to handle a wider range of predicates. However, extending the algorithm to handle the full range of predicates in the RSML syntax is not possible since the language allows both linear and non-linear arithmetic in predicate definitions. The interested reader is referred to [7] for a detailed discussion about how the expressive power of RSML effects static analysis.

4.2 Data Flow Slices

To help answering the questions in Table 1, it is not enough to construct the interpretation of the specification under a reduction scenario. In general, few transitions are completely eliminated in an interpretation, most transitions are still satisfiable and cannot be removed from the model. Thus, in addition to constructing an interpretation, we are interested in knowing what parts of the state machine that effect a particular transition or variable we are interested in. We need to construct a slice based on the *data dependency* of the guarding condition on the transition.

To discover the data dependencies for a guarding condition, we perform a graph traversal of an RSML specification. A partial version of the static data dependency graph for the elements of an RSML specification can be seen in Figure 9. The solid lines represent data dependencies and the dotted lines represent a parent child (is-a) relationship between the elements. To discover the data dependencies for a given node in the graph, we traverse all of the nodes below it in the data dependency graph. For example, a transition is data-dependent on its guarding condition, which in its turn is dependent on an AND/OR table. Eventually, all aspects of the system are dependent on the system's current state, constants, and variable values (the gray roundtangles).

To illustrate our approach, consider the set of transitions between the top-level states in Intruder-Status (Figure 4). We are interested in answering the first question in Table 1. Thus, we have first constructed an interpretation based

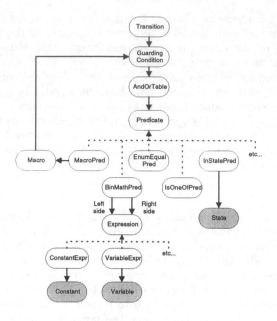

Fig. 9. Data dependencies

on the scenario in Figure 6. The transition between Potential-Threat and Other-Traffic (Figure 2) is in this interpretation reduced to the table in Figure 8. Many other transitions in the model exhibit similar reductions for the same scenario.

To construct the data-flow slice for this transition we simply mark all entities (states, macros, functions, variables, and constants) that can directly or indirectly effect the truth value of the reduced guarding condition. The unmarked entities in the specification cannot effect the behavior of the transition and can safely be removed from the specification.

4.3 Control Flow Slices

The slice constructed based on the data dependencies only shows us what information is needed to determine *if* a transition can be taken. It does not tell us *when* the transition can be taken. To determine this, we need to construct a slice based on the control flow in the specification. In RSML, the order in which state machines are evaluated is based on the events and actions on the transitions (see Section 2). Thus, to determine when a transition can be taken we need to construct a slice that shows all the parts of the specification that are involved in the generation of the trigger event on the transition. For example, the transition in our example is triggered by the Air-Status-Evaluated-Event (Figure 8) so all transitions with this event as an action (all transitions that can generate this event) must be included in our control slice. In this case, the event is generated by the transitions in the state machine Other-Air-Status. This process is now repeated for the transitions just added to the slice. The algorithm is terminated when we reach transitions that are triggered by the receipt of an input from an external source (the event is not generated from within the RSML model).

The construction of the control slices is also based on a simple marking of the abstract syntax tree.

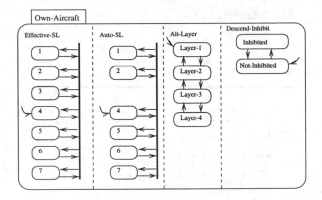

Fig. 10. Model of Own-Aircraft reduced

As mentioned above, a slice is identifies by the set of tagged entities in the abstract syntax tree. By using a different tag for each slice, it is trivial to combine slices using standard set operations (union, intersection, and set complement), For example, the combined slice needed to fully answer question 1 in Table 1 consists of the union of all data flow and control flow slices for all transitions between the high-level states in Intruder-Status (Figure 4). The states and transitions in this slice are shown in Figures 10 and 11.

In summary, our approach to slicing of hierarchical state machines allows an analyst to reduce a specification based on a scenario. We call such a reduced specification the interpretation of the specification under the scenario. The interpretation can then iteratively be sliced based on data-flow and control-flow information. The slices can be arbitrarily combined using standard set operations to construct a combined slice containing the information of interests.

5 Case Study

To evaluate the effectiveness of our approach and to better understand the effect on a large real world RSML specification, we applied our tool to the most complex part of the TCAS II RSML model. This section discusses some metrics we used to evaluate the reduction capability and discusses our experiences.

5.1 Evaluation Criteria

In traditional program slicing, the effectiveness of a slicing algorithm is easily evaluated by comparing, for example, the number of statements in the slice to the number of statements in the original program. In hierarchical state machines, however, there is no established way of evaluating a slice. In fact, there are no established metrics to measure the size and complexity of a state machine.

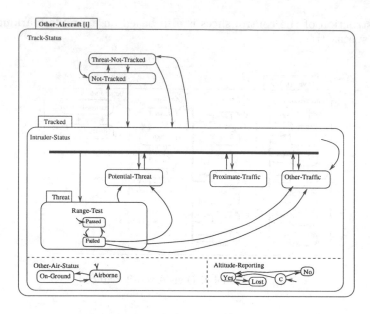

Fig. 11. Model of an intruding aircraft

Measures such as number of reachable states, number of named states, or number of transitions are reasonable, but the correlation between these metrics and the difficulty of understanding a specification is unknown. Nevertheless, in an attempt to make a reasonably objective evaluation of the effectiveness of our approach, we use some metrics to measure the reduction of the specification. We have chosen to measure number of transitions, perceived table size, and effective table size.

Number of transitions: The number of transitions in the model is easily counted and the metric is a reasonable and intuitive measure of the difficulty of understanding a model.

Perceived table size: The perceived size of a table is defined to be the table height (the number of rows in the table) times the table width (the number of columns). This metric indicates the complexity of a single table shown on one page. Naturally, to fully understand a table one may have to trace macros through several layers of indirection and this added complexity is captured in our third metric.

Effective table size: The use of macros reduces the perceived size of a table since much of the complexity of the guarding condition is hidden in the macros. The complexity added through macro indirection is captured by the effective table size. The effective size of a table is defined to be the perceived size of the table with all macro references recursively expanded.

As an absolute measure of the complexity of a state machine these metrics may have little value, there is no evidence that a state machine with 200 transitions is harder to understand than one with 100 transitions. Nevertheless, as measure of the *relative complexity* between the original specification and the reduced model produced by our reduction tool the metrics make intuitive sense. Intuitively, if a model with 40 transitions is reduced to a model with 20 transitions, it is easier to understand and review.

5.2   Reduction Results

We applied our tool to the transitions defining the behavior of state machine Tracked in Figure 4. We used reduction scenarios based on questions (for example, the questions in Table 1) encountered during previous investigations related to TCAS II. Thus, we believe the reduction scenarios are representative of scenarios that would be used during reviews and inspections of an RSML model. This section summarizes the main observations from this limited case study.

Table size: The reduction scenarios we used provided significant reductions in the tables effected by the criteria. A typical example is the reductions of the transition from Potential-Threat to Other-Traffic discussed in Section 4.

Most of our reduction criteria were related to the classification of an intruding aircraft as a Threat, Potential-Threat, Proximate-Traffic, or Other-Traffic. The perceived size of the conditions guarding these transitions ranged from 1 to 80^4 before reduction and ranged from 0 to 40 after reduction. Subjectively, these reductions helped clarify some issues regarding threat classification (as illustrated by the reductions of the transition in Figure 2).

The effective size of the transitions involved in threat classification ranged from approximately 10^8 to 10^{10} when all macro references were expanded. The effective size after reduction ranged from 0 to 10^8 based on the same set of reduction criteria as in the previous paragraph. These numbers led to two observations. First, we were surprised when we got an indication of the true complexity of the guarding conditions in the threat detection logic. This complexity is effectively hidden by the macro abstractions in RSML. Some guarding conditions involved more that 100 predicates and would be nearly impossible to capture without the use of macros.

Second, the effective size metric does not tell us much about the readability of a real-world specification—all the metric indicates is that this model is very large. Focusing on the size of individual tables seems to be a better gauge of readability, small tables seem to be easy to understand regardless of how many macros and levels of indirection are used. Nevertheless, to accurately determine the effect of slicing on the readability of RSML specifications we need to conduct controlled readability studies. Such studies are in the planning stages.

Transitions: When constructing an interpretation, the number of transitions in the model was not effected to the extent we had hoped. Some interpretations produced useful elimination of transitions, for example, all transitions upgrading an intruding aircraft to a threat are unsatisfiable if the intruder is declared to be on the ground, but as a whole most transitions were still satisfiable under the reduction scenarios we applied. On the other hand, after an analyst has selected a subset of the transitions for closer study, the data flow slices and control flow slices eliminated large unrelated parts of the specification. The simplification is

---

[4] 8 columns by 10 rows.

clearly illustrated in the difference between Figure 4 and Figure 11. Nevertheless, all the questions we had compiled were related to the threat detection encapsulated in Intruder-Status. Thus, all data flow and control flow slices produced similar results. We are currently in the process of slicing TCAS II based on a multitude of data-flow and control-flow criteria, for example, slices based on the data dependencies for all output variables and all transitions. We are collecting data and we hope to be able to present an empirical study of the reduction capabilities in a large real world application shortly.

6 Conclusion

In this paper we described an approach to reducing an RSML specification based on a reduction scenario in conjunction with traditional program slicing techniques. Our approach is two tiered. First, we allow an analyst to simplify a specification based on a *scenario*. As scenario is some operating condition the under which we are interested in inspecting or reviewing a specification. Second, the remaining specification, called an *interpretation* of the specification, is sliced based on data-flow and control-flow information to extract the parts of the specification effecting selected variables and transitions.

To evaluate the effectiveness of the approach, we implemented a prototype tool and applied it to a specification for a large avionics system called TCAS II. We used the tool to slice the specification to help us answer a set of questions we have asked ourselves during previous investigations. In this case study, the reduction results were very helpful and the approach seems to have great potential. The reduction scenarios provided significant reductions in the tables relevant to answer the question and the data-flow and control-flow slices eliminated large parts of, for these questions, irrelevant information.

Although the slices helped clarify and simplify the model, we have not yet collected sufficient empirical data regarding the reduction capabilities in hierarchical state machines. The metrics we used in the case study are inadequate. The perceived size of a table is a very simplistic metric and the effective size of a table (the size of a table with all macro references expanded) only told us that guarding conditions are very complex, but did not aid much in the evaluation of the reduction capability of the slicing approach. New metrics and controlled readability studies are needed to objectively evaluate the effect of slicing in hierarchical state machines.

Finally, the approach to specification slicing outlined in this paper is not limited to RSML specifications. The approach is general enough to apply to all languages based on state machines using guarded transitions. From our experiences in this investigation, we are convinced that specification slicing holds great potential in areas such as requirements development, requirements inspections, and visual requirements verification. Specification languages such as SCR [8] would benefit from the same simplification mechanisms and we strongly encourage tool developers to include such a mechanism in future versions of their tools.

References

1. J. Chang and D.J. Richardson. Static and dynamic specification slicing. In *Proceedings of the Fourth Irvine Software Symposium*, April 1994.

2. D. Harel. Statecharts: A visual formalism for complex systems. *Science of Computer Programming*, 8:231–274, 1987.

3. D. Harel, H. Lachover, A. Naamad, A. Pnueli, M. Politi, R. Sherman, A. Shtull-Trauring, and M. Trakhtenbrot. Statemate: A working environment for the development of complex reactive systems. *IEEE Transactions on Software Engineering*, 16(4):403–414, April 1990.

4. D. Harel and A. Naamad. The STATEMATE semantics of Statecharts. *ACM Transactions on Software Engineering and Methodology*, vol-5(4):293–333, October 1996.

5. D. Harel and A. Pnueli. On the development of reactive systems. In K.R. Apt, editor, *Logics and Models of Concurrent Systems*, pages 477–498. Springer-Verlag, 1985.

6. M. P.E. Heimdahl and N.G. Leveson. Completeness and Consistency Analysis of State-Based Requirements. In *Proceedings of the 17th International Conference on Software Engineering*, pages 3–14, April 1995.

7. M. P.E. Heimdahl and N.G. Leveson. Completeness and Consistency Analysis of State-Based Requirements. *IEEE Transactions on Software Engineering*, TSE-22(6):363–377, June 1996.

8. C. L. Heitmeyer, , R.D. Jeffords, and B. L. Labaw. Consistency checking of SCR-style requirements specifications. *ACM Transactions on Software Engineering and Methodology*, vol-5(3):231–261, July 1996.

9. C. L. Heitmeyer, B. L. Labaw, and D. Kiskis. Consistency checking of SCR-style requirements specifications. In *Proceedings of the International Symposium on Requirements Engineering*, March 1995.

10. K. L. Heninger. Specifying software for complex systems: New techniques and their application. *IEEE Transactions on Software Engineering*, 6(1):2–13, January 1980.

11. D.J. Keenan and M.P.E. Heimdahl. Code generation from hierarchicl state machines. In *Proceedings of the International Symposium on Requirements Engineering*, 1997.

12. N. G. Leveson, M. P.E. Heimdahl, H. Hildreth, J. Reese, and R. Ortega. Experiences using Statecharts for a system requirements specification. In *Proceedings of the Sixth International Workshop on Software Specification and Design*, pages 31–41, 1991.

13. N. G. Leveson, M. P.E. Heimdahl, H. Hildreth, and J. D. Reese. Requirements specification for process-control systems. *IEEE Transactions on Software Engineering*, 20(9):694–707, September 1994.

14. T. Oda and K. Araki. Specification slicing in formal methods of software engineering. In *Proceedings of the Seventeenth International Computer Software and Applications Conference*, November 1993.

15. A.M. Sloane and J. Holdsworth. Beyond traditional program slicing. In *Proceedings of the International Symposium on Software Testing and Analysis*, pages 180–186, January 1996.

16. J.M. Spivy. *The Z Notation: A Reference Manual.* Prentice-Hall, 1992.

17. M. Weiser. Program slicing. *IEEE Transactions on Software Engineering*, SE-10(4):352–357, July 1984.

A Pattern-Based Application Generator for Building Simulation

Martin Schuetze, Jan Peter Riegel, Gerhard Zimmermann
Computer Science Department
University of Kaiserslautern, Germany

Abstract:
This paper describes a domain-specific software development method based on object-oriented modeling, design patterns, and code generation principles. The example domain is building simulation, however, the approach is general and may be applied to other domains as well. Patterns are used to describe how the simulation objects interact. Code-templates associated with every pattern are used to generate the final application code. The method can be applied to generate large families of customized application frameworks from variations of the models. This is particularly useful for domains where applications have to exist in individually tailored versions for every project.

1. Introduction

In this paper, we describe a domain-specific software development method based on code generation from object-oriented application models. The static aspects of applications are defined in terms of object types, relations, and attributes, as it can be found in most CASE methods (e.g. the Booch Method /Boo91/ or OMT /RBP91/). The techniques to generate code for the static aspects of applications are well-known and will not be described here (see for example /ARS97/). The way the objects interact, as well as their domain-specific operations, are defined with design patterns which provide the 'glue' between objects or even between partial models. Code for operations and interaction of the application's objects is then generated from the glue. Therefore, our method combines techniques for code generation as used in application generators with the design pattern approach /GHJ95/ (see also section 5). In the following, we will focus on the partial formalization of design patterns as well as on the code generation phase, both implemented in a system called PSiGene (*P*attern-Based *Si*mulator *Gene*rator).

Application Domain

PSiGene was developed within the MOOSE[1] project, mainly to support building control system designers in testing their applications by providing a highly customized, real-time building simulation framework. It is necessary to trade accuracy for speed when large buildings are simulated. At the same time, the simulation should be carried out at different levels of abstraction, incorporating different physical effects. Last but not least, the model of the simulator should be defined by the system designer (which is an software engineer), not by simulation experts. The simulation objects should be

---

1. *M*odel Based *O*bject-*O*riented *S*oftware Generation *E*nvironment, see /ASS95, ARS97/: MOOSE is a framework for model-driven code generation. It consists of a central database for different types of models, a set of model editors, and several code generators for different software components.

identical to 'real world' building objects and control artifacts. It seemed impossible to support all requirements optimally with one fixed simulation library. Therefore, we have chosen a generator approach to create customized and optimized building simulators from object-oriented models and from design patterns defining object interaction and domain specific operations.

Our method is not bound to any particular domain, while instantiations of the method (i.e. instantiations of model editors and generators) are domain specific.

Goals

PSiGene was developed with the following goals in mind:

❑ Easy integration of domain-specific functions with object-oriented models:
Modeling of the simulator should take place on the object type level, simulation methods and operations should be encapsulated as far as possible.

❑ Clear distinction between 'objects' and 'operations':
Because the class model of the simulation objects may change from application to application, it is useful to divide the simulation objects from the simulation methods and link both together using domain specific patterns.

❑ Generation of large portions of code for a specific application domain:
For a limited domain, we are able to set up powerful models with strict semantics. In our case, we deal with models and well-defined simulation methods for certain aspects of building physics. For these models, it is possible to generate large portions of the code automatically.

❑ Support of reuse on a medium granularity scale:
While our overall method ensures reuse of complete application designs as well as code reuse, the patterns should represent what /GHJ93/ calls reusable micro-archi tectures. The reuse takes place every time a pattern is connected to appropriate objects.

❑ A flexible way to create customized frameworks:
The output of PSiGene is a highly application specific simulation framework, optimized for one simulation purpose. By this example, our approach shows that reuse of large software components, the frameworks, can effectively be supported by code generators in conjunction with pattern-based models.

The rest of this paper is structured as follows: section 2 discusses object models, patterns, and frameworks. In section 3, we show how we define patterns for PSiGene. Section 4 describes the generator, and section 5 discusses related approaches. The paper concludes with a discussion oft the benefits and limitations of our approach in section 6.

2. Modeling with Patterns

Within our MOOSE system, an application is defined as a set of interacting components. Consequently, the model of the application also consists of several component models, each describing one aspect of the application's structure and behavior. The component models and their elements are connected by what we call the 'glue' of the application.

For PSiGene, we support the following component modeling notations: class models are used to define the structure of the application. This notation is quite similar to those used by other OOD techniques. At the same time, it is used to express libraries on the modeling level, for example a real-time simulation kernel. The set of initial objects is defined by an object model. We use an architectural CAD editor to provide simulation objects. A finite state machine model is used to express dynamic behavior other than hard coded in the pattern's code templates.

The glue is provided by model aggregation, by ordinary relations, by aggregation relations, by inheritance, and by a set of design patterns as described in the next section. The design patterns define the interaction between objects and encapsulate fragments of the simulator's functionality. They also contain code templates for the generation of simulation methods.

The use of patterns is closely related to the use of frameworks and the reuse of design provided by frameworks. Most authors /GHJ95, Pre95/ emphasize the documentation aspect of patterns: patterns help to adapt frameworks (and of course to create 'good' designs) by stating how the objects of a framework can be customized and integrated, and by describing the interaction between those objects. PSiGene produces a building simulation framework which may be used stand-alone or in other applications such as smart building control software. By using patterns, the coupling and interaction between simulation objects (and between kernel and simulation objects) can be defined on the modeling level while the implementation details are left open to the generator (e.g. linking a thread to a simulation object by delegation or by inheritance). At the same time, the usage of patterns as a glue between the simulation objects allows us to define what quality of service is needed for the current simulation problem, simply by instantiating the appropriate patterns. The generator may then, based on the class model and the patterns, choose from a variety of code templates for the implementation. This leads to the generation of powerful, optimized, and customized frameworks which exactly fulfill the application's needs.

The process of generating a simulator with MOOSE/PSiGene is shown in figure 1. The user specifies the class model of the application. At this time, necessary libraries will already be available as MOOSE class models. The ADT (abstract data type) generator of MOOSE automatically creates a complete class hierarchy for the class model with all create/destroy/access methods.

After setting up the class model, the simulation problem is specified by applying the appropriate, predefined simulation patterns: the patterns are bound to elements of the model (see also figure 3). Due to the descriptive nature of the patterns, the user may find that some classes, attributes, or relations are missing. This leads to a cycle of alternately modifying the object model and applying patterns. After finishing this process, PSiGene will link simulation methods to the classes.

The set of initial objects is specified with a standard architectural CAD editor. After transforming the CAD drawing into corresponding objects defined by the class model, these objects can be used by PSiGene to optimize the simulation methods and by the simulation framework to form a complete executable.

Our method can also be applied to related domains, like building control, if the appropriate patterns are provided.

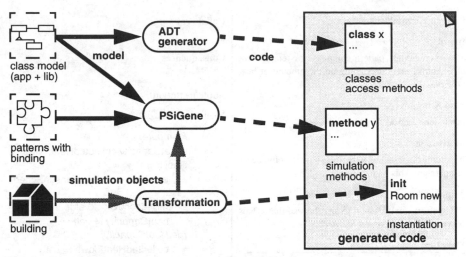

Fig. 1   Simulator Development with MOOSE/PSiGene

3. Catalog of Patterns

The catalog of patterns we use within PSiGene as well as their textual description is very much influenced by the work of the "gang of four" /GHJ95/ while the graphical notation and the binding was inspired by the work of Pree /Pre95/. But in contrast to these two approaches, we had to further formalize the pattern description in order to allow code generation from instantiated patterns. This means that we had to define the interface of the patterns formally as well as the code templates from which the source code of the application is constructed. We set up a pattern catalog where every pattern is structured as shown in figure 2. Every catalog entry defines the context where the pattern can be used, as well as the problems addressed and their solution. It has a *Name* and is classified by an *Intent*. Many parts like *Motivation* and *Applicability* are self-explanatory, however, they are written with the application domain in mind so that the information here are very concrete and closely related to the function/behavior associated with the pattern. The *Structure* is defined graphically, so that the user has a direct feeling for the context the pattern may be used in.

The patterns are bound to the application's class model by binding formal pattern parameters to objects, attributes, relations, and methods of the class model. The *Participants* part defines these formal parameters. In contrast to other pattern catalogs, this interface is described by **name:type** pairs. The **name** is used internally by a pattern to reference an element, the **type** defines types of elements that can be bound to the name. Examples are **target:Object** or **volume:Attribute**. Currently, PSiGene supports the following types: **Object, Attribute, Relation, Method**, and **Expression**.

The *Implementation* part contains, for every target language, code templates for the pattern which are used by the generator (see section 4). This part is needed for the implementor of the pattern catalog only. The user of PSiGene does not need the *Implementation* part as the system does all the necessary implementation work.

Some of the patterns currently implemented in PSiGene (see table 1) are nearly identical to more abstract patterns presented in other catalogs, some are domain- and appli-

472

Pattern ThermalMass

Intent

The ThermalMass pattern computes the temperature of a thermal mass depending on the amount of heat affecting the...

Also Known As

Simulation thermischer Masse /1/

Motivation

A volume has to act as a thermal mass to compute its temperature. This pattern works...

Applicability

This pattern can be bound to any thermal mass. This is typically a room or a thick wall...

Structure

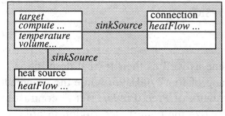

Participants

- *target:Object*
  Object to bind pattern to.

- *temperature:Attribute*
  Last computed temperature.

- *volume:Attribute*
  Volume of the thermal mass.

- *compute:Method*
  Does the calculation cycle once.

...

Collaborations

...

Consequences

...

Implementation

Smalltalk-Code-Templates

```
{compute}
| heatCapacity collectedHeatFlows
timeNow |
    timeNow := Scheduler simSched

simMillisecondClockValue.
    heatCapacity := self
{getHeatCapacity}.
    collectedHeatFlows := self
            {collectHeatFlows}.
    self
{calculateTemperature}WithCapacity:
            heatCapacity
        withHeatFlows:
collectedHeatFlows
        while: (timeNow - self

{timeOfLastComputation}).
    self {timeOfLastComputation}:
timeNow.
```

...

Related Patterns

Thermal Exchange

Fig. 2   Pattern example (abbreviated)

cation specific adaptations of well-known patterns. Examples are *SingleIndirection* and *ContinuousComputation* which roughly correspond to *Adapter* and *Mediator* from /GHJ95/. In addition, we derived some highly domain dependent patterns from prototype building simulators, for example *ThermalMass* (figure 2) which describes the thermal calculation of a volume with respect to heat sources and connections to other volumes.

The patterns and the catalog form a pattern system /BMR96/: every pattern provides just a partial solution to the simulation problem. In order to form a working simulator, all patterns must work together (e.g. *ThermalMass* must cooperate with *ThermalJunction*, *ThermalExchange*, and *ContinuousComputation*). This problem is addressed in two steps: first of all, all patterns are able to work together with certain other patterns by construction. Second, the formal interface definition of the patterns is used to ensure that all bindings are complete and correct.

Table 1: Some available patterns from the catalog

Category	Name	Intent
Physical Effects	ThermalMass	calculate walls or rooms thermally
	ThermalJunction	calculate the heat exchange through different materials
	ThermalExchange	calculate the transition from gas to solids and vice versa
	Radiator	Calculate heating installation
Simulator Control	ContinuousComputation	simulate continuous time domain problems
	EventTriggeredComputation	discrete event simulation
	Sensor	monitor values
	Actuator	modify values
	UpdateControl	react on changes
	ConcurrentProcess	compute concurrently
Structural Adaptation	SingleIndirection	transport values from one object to another
	DistributedSum	gather and add up different values
	MethodAlias	map between names

The complete catalog is divided into three categories: patterns for the calculation of physical effects (e.g. *ThermalMass*), patterns to control the simulator (e.g. *ContinuousComputation*), and patterns to deal with different structures in the class model (e.g. *SingleIndirection*). The purpose of the catalog is to document the available patterns and their usage for the user of PSiGene. An implemented version of the catalog is used within PSiGene as described in the next section.

4. Pattern-Based Generator

All patterns provided by the catalog are realized within PSiGene as VisualWorks classes. The implementation ignores the informal parts of the pattern description (e.g. *Intent*) and emphasizes the *Participants* as well as the *Implementation* part. The implemented patterns are descendants of a common superclass *AbstractPattern*. This class provides the protocol needed to bind patterns, to generate code, and to create error reports for the user. As with ordinary classes, patterns may be either abstract or concrete. Abstract patterns provide just a partial protocol, for example the code templates may be missing. Patterns may be arranged in an inheritance hierarchy if specializations of general patterns are needed. Also, patterns may aggregate other patterns in order to use their services. Technically, this means a pattern may bind other patterns to the class model. For these reasons, the pattern class hierarchy within PSiGene is not identical with the patterns from the catalog: in particular, there are some smaller patterns (or idioms), which do not appear in the catalog, but which are aggregated by other, more complex patterns within PSiGene.

PSiGene assumes that the class model for the simulator is already implemented (by the ADT generator, see figure 1). Nevertheless, this class model and eventually the simulation objects are inputs to the generator, too (figure 1). The generation of simulation code is then divided into two phases, which are performed automatically, without manual intervention:

In the binding phase, an instance of a pattern class is created for every pattern bound to the simulator's class model. In this phase, no code is generated. The set of all instances can then be checked for completeness, based on the formal parameters defined by each pattern. A report is generated for the user of PSiGene. This report includes information about missing and wrong bindings for every single pattern instance so that errors in the binding description can easily be identified and corrected.

In the generation phase, all pattern instances are asked to generate code for the objects they are bound to. There is no 'master generator': each pattern instance is responsible for its own code portion (by providing a code generation method), making the generation process flexible and easily extendible.

The main task of the generation phase is to select, personalize and instantiate the code templates of all pattern instances. PSiGene supports multiple code templates for every method to be implemented. The first step during code generation is therefore the selection of the right template, based on the pattern binding information and the class model. The code must then be personalized by replacing generic code fragments (macros) with the information derived from their actual binding. After that, the code has to be instantiated, for example by adding a method to the target class the pattern is bound to.

Code templates are defined as source code fragments with macros for the necessary adaptations (see figure 2). The macros are placed in braces. They may be used for simple elements like variable names, but they may also represent more complex code fragments like loops, which is important for optimizations.

A very simple pattern binding example is shown in figure 3. A room needs to know the amount of heat q from all radiators. The pattern *DistributedSum*, based on its binding, is used to install a simple method in class *Room* which performs the calculation. The simplified generation method for *DistributedSum* looks as follows:

```
generateCode
        | macroText |
  ...
        macroText := self perform: #sumTemplate.
        macroText replaceMacrosUsing: self macrosAndElements.
        self putMethod: (self elementAtMacro: 'sum')
             withSource: macroText
             to: (self elementAtMacro: 'target').
```

For more complex patterns, the generation method selects the kind of code linking (see below), performs optimizations, assembles methods from smaller fragments, compiles finite state machine definitions, and aggregates other patterns. If the class model does

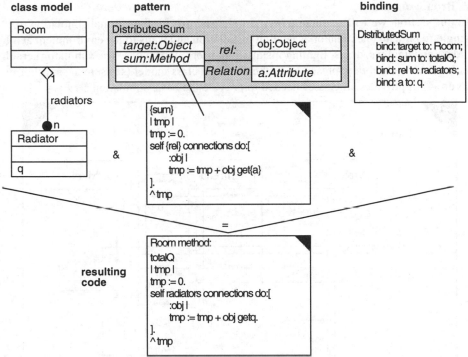

Fig. 3   Simple pattern binding and code generation example

not match to the pattern's *Structure*, a special set of patterns is used to transport information to the desired objects.

The code may be linked to the simulation objects in three different ways:

❑ Inheritance:

An additional superclass is added to the simulation object's class. This is the easiest way to link the simulation code. But it has some drawbacks: the inherited code is generic and can not be optimized for the simulation object. Multiple inheritance may impose some problems and is not available in all languages.

❑ Delegation:

An instance of a special pattern-implementing class is created. This also does not permit individual code optimizations. But it can avoid problems related with multiple inheritance. The *ContinuousComputation* pattern uses this technique to provide multi-threading capabilities for simulation objects.

❑ Code injection:

The code is installed within the simulation object's class. This allows powerful optimizations of the code for individual classes, but may lead to a large amount of code if a single pattern is instantiated many times. Nevertheless, this is the most common way to create code within PSiGene.

Which method exactly is used depends on the target language, the kind of pattern, and on the context of the pattern usage. The decision is made by the code generator.

A Brief Example

In this section, we will examine a very simple example for the thermal simulation of a single room with one radiator as heating installation and walls to the environment at all sides (no windows, doors, lighting installation, users, and so on). The simulator kernel is available as a library, presented to the user as a class model (see screen snapshot in figure 4). It provides all classes needed to provide the basic simulation services.

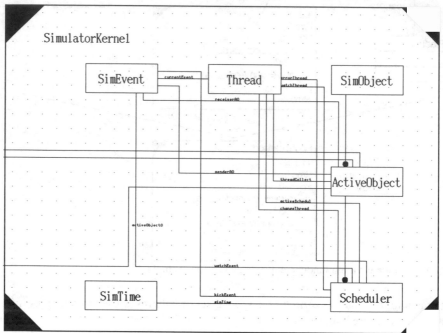

Fig. 4   Screen snapshot of the simulator kernel library

The first step one has to do in order to create a generator is the definition of the class model for the simulation objects. In this case, we primarily need a room, a representation of a wall and a surface between room and walls (modeled as a sequence of layers), see screen snapshot in figure 5. This figure shows the object types and the object relations. Lines with a dot at the end denote inheritance. Object attributes are not displayed graphically. Let's assume that attributes are assigned 'reasonably'. Lines leaving the diagrams to the right are relations to the simulator kernel from figure 4. This model is input to the ADT generator of MOOSE, which in turn creates the complete class hierarchy with all attribute and relation access functions.

In a second step, the user has to select the appropriate patterns from the catalog (which is not supported by PSiGene) and has to specify the pattern bindings. At the moment, this is done textually, but we are currently implementing a graphical binding editor which will allow the user to bind patterns directly to the class model. This editor will include the possibility to check the pattern bindings and to display wrong bindings on

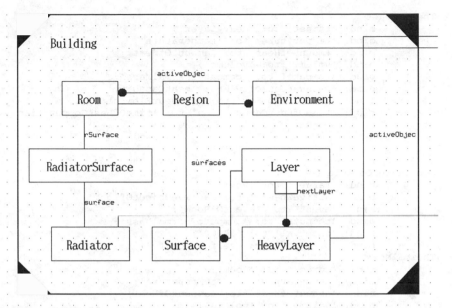

Fig. 5 Screen snapshot of the example's simulation object class model

the screen, which we hope will greatly simplify the process of setting up correct bindings. A part of the example's bindings can be seen in the following code fragment:

```
"----- RadiatorSurface -----"
ThermalJunction
        bind: 'target' to: 'RadiatorSurface';
        bind: 'area' to: 'area';
        bind: 'thermalResistance' to: 'thermalResistance';
        bind: 'getTemperature' to: 'temperature';
        bind: 'getThermalResistance' to: 'getThermalResistance';
        bind: 'getHeatFlowFor' to: 'getHeatFlowFor';
        bind: 'neighbouringObject' to: 'surface'.
"----- Radiator -----"
ContinuousComputation
        bind: 'target' to: 'Radiator';
        bind: 'activeObject' to: 'activeObjectOfRadiator';
        bind: 'event' to: 'eventOfRadiator';
        bind: 'compute' to: 'computeRTemp';
        bind: 'interval' to: '10000'; "calc every 10000ms"
        bind: 'priority' to: 'self priority'.
...
"----- Surface -----"
..... in principle like RadiatorSurface
"----- HeavyLayer -----"
...
ContinuousComputation
        bind: 'target' to: 'HeavyLayer';
        bind: 'activeObject' to: 'activeObjectOfHeavyLayer';
        bind: 'event' to: 'eventOfHeavyLayer';
        bind: 'compute' to: 'computeThermalMass';
        bind: 'interval' to: '30000';
        bind: 'priority' to: 'self priority'.
```

```
ThermalMass
          bind: 'target' to: 'HeavyLayer';
          bind: 'temperature' to: 'temperature';
          bind: 'amountOfHeat' to: 'amountOfHeat';
          bind: 'volume' to: 'volume';
          bind: 'compute' to: 'computeThermalMass';
          bind: 'getHeatCapacity' to: 'heatCapacity';
          bind: 'getHeatFlowFor' to: 'getHeatFlowFor';
          bind: 'timeOfLastComputation' to: 'timeOfLastComputation'.
...
"----- Layer -----"
...
"----- Room -----"
ContinuousComputation
          bind: 'target' to: 'Room';
          bind: 'activeObject' to: 'activeObjectOfRoom';
          bind: 'event' to: 'eventOfRoom';
          bind: 'compute' to: 'computeThermalMass';
          bind: 'interval' to: '30000';
          bind: 'priority' to: 'self priority'.
ThermalMass
          bind: 'target' to: 'Room';
          bind: 'temperature' to: 'temperature';
          bind: 'amountOfHeat' to: 'amountOfHeat';
          bind: 'volume' to: 'volume';
          bind: 'compute' to: 'computeThermalMass';
          bind: 'getHeatCapacity' to: 'heatCapacity';
          bind: 'getHeatFlowFor' to: 'getHeatFlowFor';
          bind: 'timeOfLastComputation' to: 'timeOfLastComputation'.
DistributedSum
          bind: 'target' to: 'Room';
          bind: 'sum' to: 'getHeatFlowFor';
          bind: 'rel' to: '#(surfaces rSurface)';
          bind: 'access' to: 'getHeatFlowFor'.
...
```

Let's take a closer look at one of the bindings: for class *Room*, the pattern *Continuous-Computation* is bound to several methods, attributes and relations. The *target* for the pattern is the class *Room* itself. The *activeObject* (from the kernel library, implementing multiple threads) can be found following the *activeObjectOfRoom*-Relation, *event* is handled in a similar manner. The method that needs to be *compute*d is named *computeThermalMass*, the reactivation *interval* is 30000ms. Process *priority* is standard priority.

As one can see from the binding code fragment, the patterns serve as glue between different simulation objects, defining their interaction (e.g. the *ThermalMass* pattern bound to *Room* and, via *DistributedSum*, also bound to *Surface* and *RadiatorSurface*), and they serve as glue between the simulation objects and the simulator kernel classes (e.g. the *ContinuousComputation* pattern bound to *Room* and to kernel's *ActiveObject* via *activeObjectOfRoom*).

In the next step, simulation code is generated. PSiGene reads the class model for the simulator kernel and the example classes (see figures 4 and 5) and the pattern bindings. For every pattern instantiated in the bindings, it creates an instance of the pattern class implemented within PSiGene. When all patterns are instantiated, the resulting set of instances is checked for completeness and correctness. Afterwards, the generation method is called for every pattern instance, which in turn creates the application code. For the pattern *ContinuousComputation* bound to class *Room*, this means that two methods are generated, an *init* method called by the constructor, and an *establish* method, which activates the periodic computation and looks as follows:

```
establish
            |aThread|
            ... "some initializations"
            "create Thread:"
            aThread:= Thread createThread:
            [      :currentEvent|
                self computeThermalMass.
                (self eventOfRoom instance)
                        timestamp: currentEvent timestamp + 30000;
                        deadline: currentEvent deadline + 30000;
                        send.
            ] atPriority: self priority.
            "register Thread within ActiveObject:"
            self activeObjectOfRoom instance addThread: aThread
                reactOn: #activate.
            self eventOfRoom instance send.
```

All parts of the method where template macros were replaced with the actual bindings by the generator are underlined. For this simple example, code generation means simply macro replacement. However, PSiGene is also able to create much more complex code (for example, to compile finite state machine definitions into methods), or to perform more elaborate macro replacements, for example to eliminate loops over sets if it is known in advance that the cardinality of the set is exactly one.

5. Related Work

This work is closely related to works in the area of application generators and pattern-based design strategies.

Our approach shares with application generators (e.g. UI builders, simulation systems) that it is always optimized for one domain. However, we rely on object-oriented modeling and the pattern approach and we believe that our method in itself is usable in many domains, only concrete manifestations of the method are domain dependent. In contrast to many application generators (for example from the simulation domain), we don't use domain specific modeling languages (such as discrete event simulation languages) because we wanted the user of our method to be an expert in object-oriented design, not in simulation techniques.

Code generation in PSiGene is a one-step approach. There are other approaches to code generation, based on program transformation (see for example GenVoca /BST94/ or CIP /GoH85/). There, an abstract program is transformed to implemented code by a sequence of refinement steps. The input for these types of generators is usually more abstract than our models. However, the goals of this approach (in terms of productivity gains, reuse potential, scalability, and optimizations) are the same. Although GenVoca has a different focus (component based), we share its basic principles (see /BST94/): generation from subsystem building blocks, standardized interfaces, and parameterization.

At the moment, many people experiment with pattern-based design methods and with design patterns. We share with these approaches the idea of having a design catalog, capturing good design in general /GHJ95/ or domain specific knowledge (see examples in /CoS95/). Also, some people discuss pattern languages or pattern systems in order to make patterns work together. A discussion of pattern systems, as well as a complete system, can be found in /BMR96/. As far as we know, not much work has been done in automatically generating code from pattern descriptions. In /BFV96/, an approach is described which creates some code from a partially automated, WWW-based pattern catalog. However, this approach does not reach the amount of integration of object-oriented structure models and connected patterns as our approach does.

Finally, there is at least one approach which uses design patterns for the same purpose as we do: in the DEMETER project /Lie96/, objects and operations are kept separate and design patterns are used to adapt to different object-oriented structure models. Operations can be performed on objects even if the model changes. This approach does not use code generators, the mapping is performed at runtime.

6. Discussion of our Approach

Our application domain, building simulation, has two characteristics we exploited for the development of our method. First of all, we wanted to be able to generate large families of building simulators with different requirements, as stated in the introduction. Therefore, a generator based approach was feasible. Second, in this domain, we find a limited number of primitive operations and interacting objects, like solving differential equations, executing methods periodically, controlling objects with finite state machines, doing discrete event simulation, and so on; these operations stay always the same, they are just combined in different ways. Exactly these recurring design problems of combining the right operations in the right way were put into the patterns.

Setting up the pattern catalog is a difficult task: on one hand we would like to have patterns as abstract and powerful as possible. On the other hand, every pattern should be as flexible as possible regarding its usability for different class structures. We always have to find the right tradeoff between these points, as a powerful pattern, involving many classes and relations, depends very much on a certain class structure. This limits the possibility of using the pattern in a wide variety of situations and with different class models. There is no general rule of how to set up the pattern catalog. At the moment, we try to deal with this problem by allowing to define complex, specialized patterns hierarchically from smaller, flexible patterns.

The patterns were gained by a sequence of hand coded simulator prototypes which we developed. Therefore, the code generated by PSiGene is comparable to handwritten code. This is valid for the code length as well as for the performance. While experienced programmers might be able to write better code because of very 'local' optimizations, PSiGene does it's job as good as average programmers. The overall code quality is still better, because the generator produces no programming errors, given that the patterns are correct. If a code template should have errors, fixing it can be done in minutes.

While it took nearly the same time to implement PSiGene as it took to implement one of the simulator prototypes, productivity gains dramatically using PSiGene. We conducted an experiment where we produced a thermal building simulator by hand and with PSiGene. Class model (about 15 classes) and functionality, as well as the used physical abstractions were the same. The designers had comparable skills and knowledge. It took three weeks to implement the simulator by hand, using the ADT generator (figure 1). Using PSiGene, setting up the bindings (about 20 pattern instantiations from about 10 different patterns) took one day. Both simulators came up with about 5000 lines of code. Of course, this comparison only holds as long as we always find the required patterns. Installing a new pattern is done in minutes, however, developing a new pattern may take significant time, depending on its purpose.

Changing simulation requirements, e.g. changing the physical abstraction for walls, is also a matter of minutes, as long as the required patterns are present. For the hand coded version, it takes significant time to do the same.

There are some limitations of our approach: first of all, the user is restricted to a limited pattern catalog. The approach tends to produce large pattern catalogs with small patterns (in order to use the patterns for different class structures, see above), making the modeling less abstract. Here, it takes skilled pattern writers to find the right level of abstraction. Our approach develops its abilities best when the required code has a certain generic potential. If nearly every method is unique, we can not profit from instantiating the same pattern many times. Although modeling takes place on a rather abstract level, specifying the pattern bindings is still a complex and creative task: building simulation does not come for free. Last not least, we have (up to now) no possibility to debug pattern bindings. Finding errors in the bindings other than syntactical ones may be a hard task. It would be desirable to debug patterns graphically on the binding level, but further research is needed to find a satisfying solution.

Nevertheless, we believe that our approach is useful in many domains, particularly those where the characteristics are the same as mentioned above. If we take a look at table 1, we will find that primarily patterns of the 'Physical Effects' category are restricted to building simulation. Other Patterns like *ConcurrentProcess* or *Actuator* could very well be used for different problem domains like control systems. Here, the transition to the new domain would probably be straight forward. We are currently extending PSiGene to handle distributed systems and building control systems. Other technical application domains might match our approach as well.

7. Conclusions

We presented the PSiGene approach to generate application code for one domain from object-oriented models and patterns. Because object types and operations are kept separate and are connected via patterns, the code generator is very flexible with respect to changing class models and different patterns. Experiments showed that about 10 patterns (with about 20 instantiations) are sufficient to specify a framework for thermal building simulation. Every additional physical effect takes another 5 to 10 patterns. This shows that even for complex simulation problems the number of patterns and instances is quite moderate.

Because the major part of reuse takes place while adapting existing models and combining them with patterns, the potential of our method develops best when used in environments where the underlying models and/or requirements are rapidly changing and where the characteristics of our application domain (see section 6) are met, like many technical domains. This is particularly true for environments where applications have to exist in customized versions for every project.

Our pattern catalog is much more concrete than other catalogs and can not be used for all design problems in other domains. However, some of our patterns are just domain specific adaptations of more general patterns, and we believe that domain specific pattern catalogs are an effective way to support the designer.

All in all, our approach leads to an efficient way of generating code for certain types of applications. All code generators within MOOSE (and therefore also PSiGene) are aware of manually written code: MOOSE/PSiGene can be combined with traditional OOD methods and manual extensions can be made wherever required. We believe that our tool is an effective help to application designers and programmers.

References

/ASS95/   J. Altmeyer, B. Schürmann, M. Schütze: "Generating ECAD Framework Code from Abstract Models", Proceedings of the Design Automation Conference '95, San Francisco, California, 1995

/ARS97/   J. Altmeyer, J.P. Riegel, B. Schürmann, M. Schütze, G. Zimmermann, "Application of a Generator-Based Software Development Method Supporting Model Reuse", Proc. CAiSE*97, Barcelona, 1997

/BFV96/   F.J. Budinsky, M.A. Finnie, J.M. Vlissides, P.S. Yu: „Automatic code generation from design patterns", IBM Systems Journal, Vol. 35, No. 2, 1996 (http://www.almaden.ibm.com/journal/sj/budin/budinsky.html)

/BMR96/   F. Buschmann, R. Meunier, H. Rohnert, P. Sommerlad, M. Stal: "Pattern-Oriented Software Architecture - A System Of Patterns", John Wiley & Sons, Chichester, 1996

/BST94/   D. Batory, V. Singhal, J. Thomas, S. Dasari, B. Geraci, M. Sirkin: „The GenVoca Model of Software-System Generators", IEEE Software, September 94, 1994

/Boo91/   G. Booch: "Object-Oriented Design with Applications", The Benjamin/Cummings Publishing Company, 1991

/CoS95/   J. O. Coplien, D.C. Schmidt: "Pattern Languages of Program Design", Addison-Wesley, 1995

/GHJ93/   E. Gamma, R. Helm, R. Johnson, J. Vlissides: "Design Patterns: Abstractions and Reuse of Object-Oriented Design", Proc. ECOOP '93, 1993

/GHJ95/   E. Gamma; R. Helm; R. Johnson; J. Vlissides: "Design Patterns", Addison-Wesley, 1995

/GoH85/   G. Goos, J. Hartmanis, eds.: "The Munich Project CIP", Vol. I, Springer Verlag, 1985

/Lie96/   K.J. Lieberherr: "Adaptive Object-Oriented Software: The Demeter Method with Propagation Patterns", PWS Publishing Company, Boston, 1996

/Pre95/   W. Pree: "Design Patterns for Object-Oriented Software Development", ACM Press, Addison-Wesley, 1995

/RBP91/   J. Rumbaugh; M. Blaha; W. Premerlani; F. Eddy; W. Lorensen: „Object-Oriented Modeling and Design", Prentice Hall, Englewood Cliffs, N.J., 1991

/SSA95/   M. Schütze, B. Schürmann, J. Altmeyer: "Generating Abstract Datatypes with Remote Access Capabilities", in "Electronic Design Automation Frameworks; Volume 4" , F. J. Rammig, F. R. Wagner (eds.), Chapman & Hall, 1995

Executable Connectors: Towards Reusable Design Elements*

Stéphane Ducasse and Tamar Richner

Software Composition Group, Institut für Informatik (IAM), Universität Bern
(ducasse,richner)@iam.unibe.ch
http://iamwww.unibe.ch/~(ducasse,richner)/

Abstract. The decomposition of a software application into components and connectors at the design stage has been promoted as a way to describe and reason about complex software architectures. There is, however, surprisingly little language support for this decomposition at implementation level. Interaction relationships which are identified at design time are lost as they get spread out into the participating entities at implementation. In this paper, we propose first-class connectors in an object-oriented language as a first step towards making software architecture more explicit at implementation level. Our connectors are run-time entities which control the interaction of components and can express a rich repertoire of interaction relationships. We show how connectors can be reused and how they enhance the reuse of components.

1 Introduction

In modeling software architectures Allen and Garlan distinguish between implementation relationships and interaction relationships of software modules or components: "Whereas the implementation relationship is concerned with how a component achieves its computation, the interaction relationship is used to understand how that computation is combined with others in the overall system" [AG94]. Allen and Garlan propose a formal model for software design that makes explicit the interaction relationships between components using the abstraction of connector.

Describing software architectures in terms of interaction relationships between components brings us closer to a compositional view, and hence a more flexible or open view of an application [ND95]. First-class connectors allow us to view an application's architecture as a composition of independent components. We gain in flexibility, since each component could engage in a number of different agreements, increasing the reuse potential of individual components. Separating connectors from the components also promotes reuse and refinement of typical interaction relationships. It opens the possibility of the refinement of connectors and the construction of complex connectors out of simpler ones.

* This research is supported by the Swiss National Science Foundation, grant MHV 21-41671.94 (to T.R.) and project grant 2000-46947.96

But whereas implementation relationships use the primitive abstractions of a programming language such as procedure or method call, interaction relationships are rarely captured by programming language constructs. In this sense, traditional object-oriented languages provide little support for explicit representation of software architecture. Class hierarchies are the only design elements visible at the implementation level - but they represent inheritance relationships, and do not reflect an application's architecture. In contrast, interaction relationships, such as coordination and synchronization of a group of objects collaborating to achieve a task, manifest themselves as patterns of message exchanges. Such patterns of communication have a logical and conceptual identity at the design level but this identity is lost when we move from design to implementation as the information about such collaborations is spread out amongst the participating objects. The loss of this information makes the resulting application opaque with respect to its architecture: the design is no longer apparent, making the application difficult to understand, to re-use and to re-engineer.

A first step towards making an application's architecture more explicit at the code level is to enable the localization of information about interactions in an application's code. In this paper we propose one solution: enriching object-oriented languages with an explicit connector construct. As in [AG94], our connectors are first-class objects which represent the interaction relationships between components. Our contribution, however, is to provide connectors at the *implementation level*: our connectors are run-time entities that not only describe, but actually control inter-component communication. Note that we are not proposing a new object-oriented language. Rather, by presenting our model, FLO [1], we show how the traditional object model can be extended to provide explicit connectors between components and show that the reification of such entities promotes reuse of components as well as of typical interactions.

The paper is structured as follows: in section 2 we discuss the problem of language support for explicit connectors. Section 3 presents the basic concepts and notation for representing connectors in FLO. Sections 4 and 5 illustrate our approach with some examples and section 6 discusses implementation issues. Section 7 gives an overview of related work. Finally, section 8 concludes with a discussion - evaluating our contribution and pointing to directions for future work.

2 Language Support for Explicit Connectors

Our work is based on the recognition that relations between components are as important as the components themselves. Providing a construct for explicitly specifying interactions between components addresses the following common software problems:

Inability to localize interaction information: loss of design information.
Some of the design of the application is lost during the implementation since

---

[1] The FLO model is an extension of the ObjVlisp model [Coi87] and is implemented in a CLOS-like language and in Smalltalk.

we cannot localize information about interactions. This is most evident when we try to re-engineer an application. Program code contains little of the interaction relationships identified at design time, making reverse engineering a much more difficult task.

Mixing of concerns: impediment to reuse. Logically, components should have an identity independent of the different interactions in which they could engage. When no connector construct is available, component behavior includes the connector behavior, making for less reusable components. Providing a connector entity at implementation level allows abstraction and factorization of all the information about a connection and also allows for the reuse of typical interaction relationships.

To address the first problem, interaction relationships should be represented by an *explicit* construct, as in [AG94]. This is in contrast to approaches of enriching component interfaces with protocols which capture interaction information [YS94], and to the approach of Darwin [MDEK95], where the connection of components is defined as the binding of services and is found *inside* the definition of a composite component. To address the second problem, components and connectors should be independent of each other - more specifically, although connectors must specify the kinds of components which they connect, components should not be aware of the relationships in which they may engage. This is in contrast to the composition-filters approach of [AWB+94], where object interfaces must be modified to allow them to engage in new kinds of interactions, and to the approach of *gluons* [Pin93], where objects must address the mediating gluon in order to collaborate with each other.

Given these basic properties, we first present specific issues which must be addressed in providing language support for such connectors, then summarize the design choices made in our approach.

2.1 Requirements for First-Class Connectors

Connector Specification. Is a connector a user-defined abstraction or is it represented by a fixed abstraction? How can connectors be specified?

Range of abstractions. A connector should be a user-defined abstraction, permitting us to represent a large range of interaction relationships, rather than restricting us to a fixed set of abstractions or mechanisms, as can be found in certain environments (e.g. pipe/filter systems). To allow a larger range of relationships to be described, a connector should be able to connect more than just two participants. A connector specification should define the kinds of participants which may engage in the interaction abstractly, in terms of the interface of those participants.

Specification process. A connector should first be defined *abstractly* then later instantiated with the actual participants. We should be able to define a connector *incrementally* - that is, a new connector could be defined from existing ones by modifying or combining connector definitions. Finally, we would like to be able to define *generic* connectors, to allow for the reuse of typical interaction relationships.

Connector Lifetime. Is a connector a dynamic entity which can be created and destroyed, or is it active throughout the application or throughout the lifetime of its participants? How is a connection activated and terminated?

Lifetime. Since it is natural that interactions between entities are formed and dissolved dynamically, a connector should be a dynamic entity which can be created to manage an interaction and destroyed when that interaction is no longer required.

Activation and Termination. A connector should be activated and terminated in such a way that the participants themselves need not be aware of the connection.

Connector behavior. What kinds of relationships can be expressed with a connector? What expressive power do connectors require to represent these relationships?

Kinds of Relationships. Connectors should be used to specify all the information relating to the interaction of components, including data conversion [AWB+94], interface adaptation [YS94], synchronization and coordination [FA93] and other patterns of collaboration and cooperation.

Expressive power required. In representing the communication behavior in relationships such as those given above, we depend on the basic communication paradigm of the language in which the connectors are implemented. As a general rule, however, we consider it important for expressive power that connectors not only be able to coordinate communication as do *synchronizers* [FA93], but also to enforce state changes in the participants.

Formal Properties. Can compatibility of a component with a connector be checked? Can we give certain guarantees on the behavior of a composition?

Ideally we would like to have a formal notion of compatibility and substitutability so that we know exactly what kinds of components can participate in a connection, and which kinds of components can replace each other as participants. Furthermore, we would like to be able to prove certain connector properties (e.g. deadlock freedom) [AG94].

2.2   Connectors in FLO

FLO is an extension of the object-oriented model with first-class connectors. Connectors in FLO are user-defined: they are first defined abstractly, then instantiated. They can be specified incrementally and, in some cases, as generic constructs. They are dynamically created and destroyed, with components remaining unaware of the connectors in which they participate. Connectors allow for the specification of a large range of relationships – they observe and control the communication between participants and can also enforce state changes in the participants. FLO is based on a *sequential* object-oriented model: we do not yet seek, therefore, to represent synchronization and coordination mechanisms which require concurrency for their expression. Our approach provides a *descriptive* and *executable* notation for connectors, in contrast to Allen and Garlan [AG94], who present a notation for connectors which has descriptive and analytical properties. FLO's connectors can provide a basic test at connector instantiation to check if the participants indeed provide the required interface, but our approach does not, at present, formalize the notion of compatibility. In the next section we present the basic concepts of FLO's connectors in greater detail.

3 FLO's Basic Concepts and Notation

3.1 Component

In the object-oriented programming context, we consider that a component is an object or a grouping of objects. A grouping of objects can be realized using inheritance, aggregation or connectors, the only restriction being that a component should provide as an interface a set of method selectors and signatures[2]. A component's interface is then basically a set of signatures as in CORBA IDL [OMG95] and does not provide a formal description of the relationships between its different methods as do the augmented interfaces proposed by [YS94].

3.2 Connector

Connector Specification. A connector in FLO is a special object that connects components, called its *participants*. A component can participate in more than one connector. A connector is specified by a connector template, which describes all the information representing the connection between the participants by specifying how message exchanges influence the behavior of the participants. We call this specification the *dynamic behavior* of the connector. A component can participate in a connection as long as it provides an interface compatible to a *role* required by the connector. Roles are specified by variable names in the connector template declaration, but they are implicitly defined in the dynamic behavior of the connector; a role is the set of method selectors on a participant which will be intercepted or invoked by the connector, so it is a subset of a component's interface. This will be clarified further in the discussion of the dynamic behavior of a connector.

```
(defConnector  connectorAB  (:roleA :roleB)    ; a list of role names
    :inherit ((...))              ; a list of ancestors
    :var                          ; some connector variables
    :behavior                     ; interaction rules of connector
)
```

Abstraction, incremental definition, and generic connectors. Connectors are first specified abstractly by defining a connector template, then instantiated by specifying the actual participants. This abstraction of the behavior of a connector is useful for incrementally defining new connectors. A new connector template can

---

[2] FLO is implemented on untyped languages such as CLOS, so a signature is only a list of symbols representing formal arguments of a method.

be defined from existing connector templates by adding new interaction rules or by combining connector definitions (see example in section 5.2).

Moreover, FLO provides *generic* connectors in certain cases. A generic connector template specifies a connection schema which can then be instantiated to generate a new connector template by specifying the abstract interfaces with the effective component interfaces (see example in section 4.2).

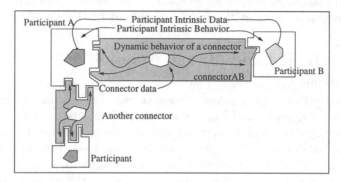

Fig. 1. Connectors and components.

Connector Lifetime. A connector, like other objects, has a lifetime - it is created, during its lifetime it controls the communication between entities and it can be destroyed. Different kinds of actions can be associated to these three distinct phases of the connector's lifetime:

> **creation.** Some actions are mandatory at connection creation time. For example, a component could be initialized before being connected with others components. A connector can also refuse to create the connection, depending on specified criteria - that is, the connector would be destroyed without moving on to the next phase.
>
> **active connection.** During the connection, a connector intercepts the method invocations of the participants and ensures that the specification of the connection is met. For example, a connector can forbid messages according to certain conditions, or send new messages to other participants [AWB+94]. This behavior is specified in a connector template definition by interaction rules (see dynamic behavior below).
>
> **destruction.** Some actions can be specified when a connector is removed. A component can be informed, for example, of the closing of the connection.

Connector Behavior.

Dynamic behavior. The behavior of a connector is defined by means of a set of *interaction rules* which specify how the messages received by participant objects should be controlled: is the message allowed? Under which conditions? Does the reception of a message imply the sending of other messages? We call this the *context* of a message reception.

The rules for specifying the dynamic behavior possess the following simplified syntax, their semantics differing only according to the rule operator.

Rule	::=	Filter Operator Context
Filter	::=	Selector Rolename List-Of-Calling-Args
Context	::=	Message$^+$
Message	::=	Selector Rolename Args
Operator	::=	`implies` | `permitted-if` | `corresponds`

The *filter* of a rule specifies which messages (method selector with calling arguments) should be intercepted for which kinds of participants, given by *rolename*. The *operator* defines the semantics of the rule and gives meaning to the *context* of the rule. Three operators: `implies`, `permitted-if` and `corresponds` are predefined[3] in FLO. Finally, the *context* of the rule specifies the execution of messages: a list of method invocations on participants. Note here that in order for a component to participate in a connector it must provide in its interface all the selectors which are associated to its rolename in the interaction rules.

These rules allow us to specify three different kinds of semantics:

Propagation is specified using the `implies` operator. After the reception and the execution of a message, some other messages, named *compensating messages* are sent to the sender object or to other participants.

Inhibition is specified using the `permitted-if` operator. The received message is only executed if a condition, named a *guard*, is satisfied[4]. The context part is then a boolean expression giving the condition for which the execution is permitted.

Delegation is specified by the `corresponds` operator. Instead of the received message being executed a new message is sent to some of the participants.

Here we see that, in contrast to event-based connectors like Mediators [SN92], FLO's connectors can *forbid* method execution, and that, in contrast to Synchronizers [FA93], FLO's connectors can *invoke* methods on controlled components.

Special operations. The fact that a connector is an object means that its behavior is represented by means of methods, some of which can be specialized to adapt the connector behavior. Because of space limitations, we do not present here special methods linked to the creation phase of a connector and to the dynamic aspect of managing groups of participants.

As FLO has an open implementation [KdRB91], different methods defining a *meta object protocol* allow the complete connector behavior to be adapted. However, as these aspects concern the modification of the language itself and

---

[3] However, FLO has an open implementation language [Duc97b] and its meta-object protocol allows for the definition of new operators.

[4] In case the condition is false, a default value is sent to notify the caller.

should not concern an application developer, they are out of the scope of this paper (see [Duc97b] for more information).

In summary, a connector is a run-time entity in which information about interaction (data and behavior) between components is stored. Data represents the state of the interaction, e.g. which component has received or sent a message. Connector behavior represents behavior specific to the interaction of the participants. A connector is then an appropriate place to specify all the information which is particular to an interaction: in addition to specifying constraints on message exchanges when components collaborate to achieve a task, connectors are also the right place to define conversion of data and to adapt or enrich component interfaces (see example of section 5).

Having summarized the main properties of FLO's connectors, we now present some examples. These allow us to demonstrate how connectors are defined, to illustrate their properties and to show how connectors can be reused.

4   Ensuring Exclusion

We first show how a connector template is defined and discuss connector properties, then show how FLO provides generic connectors.

4.1   Connector Definition

We show how a template can be defined for connectors which enforce exclusion between a set of components (in a sequential setting) – that is, which allows only one component to be active at any time.

Let us suppose that we have simple components – buttons – each of which provides `select` and `deselect` methods. Moreover, following the same constraint given in [Frø94], these buttons are constructed so that each button cannot receive the same message twice. We make this assumption here only because it allows us to provide a shorter code example.

A reactive solution. To specify an exclusion situation among components, a connector is defined which ensures that as soon as a new component is selected the previous one is deselected. Another schema is presented in [Frø94], where a component can be selected only if no other component is already selected[5]. This connector requires only one kind of participant, so the list of roles is given as a set of identical role names.

In the following examples, FLO's global constructs are represented using bold font to distinguish them from other expressions that are specific to the defined connector. The keyword **connector** represents the connector itself - that is, the instantiation of the connector template.

---

[5] The presented solution sends message to the other participant object, hence the reactive adjective.

```
1  (defConnector  reactive-exclusion  (set-of :buttons)
2  :var ((active? :initform #f  :accessor active?)    ; two connector
3        (last-button-selected  :accessor selected))    ; variables
4  :behavior
5   (((deselect  :buttons-receiver) implies (set! active? connector #f))
6     ; a button is deselected, connector state is adapted
7    ((select   :buttons-receiver) implies-before
8       (when (active? connector) (deselect (selected connector))))
9     ; before a button is selected, deselect the previous one selected
10   ((select   :buttons-receiver) implies
11      (set! active? connector #t)
12      (set! selected connector   :buttons-receiver))))
13     ; a button is selected, connector state is adapted
14 ; end of behavior definition
15 (defmethod action-before-effective ((connector  reactive-exclusion)
                                        args)
16   (for-each deselect (give-participant connector :buttons)))
17     ; before creating the connector, all the buttons are deselected
```

This template definition is an abstract definition of an exclusion schema between buttons or any other components that provide the same interface. Once defined this connector template can be instantiated on different sets of buttons as shown below (lines 17 and 18), resulting in two independent connectors. The interface required for participants of this connector is that each participant provide the methods **select** and **deselect**.

```
17  (define re1 (make   reactive-exclusion :buttons (list b1 b2 b3)))
18  (define re2 (make   reactive-exclusion :buttons (list b4 b5 b6)))
```

Properties. The *reactive-exclusion* connector template groups all the information related to the connection.

- Line 1 :buttons is a variable representing the role of the component. The set-of keyword specifies that several components can take this role in the connector and defines a role-group.
- Lines 2 and 3 define two variables: active? that indicates if one button of the group is selected and last-button-selected that represents the last selected button. These variables possess initial values and accessors. As in a class/instances model, each instantiated connector possesses its own set of variable values.
- Lines 5 to 13 specify how messages should be controlled to ensure that only one button is selected. When a new button is selected, the currently selected button, if there is one, will be deselected[6].
- Lines 14 and 15 specify the actions that should be performed when the connector is created. Here all buttons should be deselected. The method

---

[6] The implies-before allows for the definition of the action performed before the execution of the controlled method, here the deselection of the last selected component. Using it ensures real exclusion.

action-before-effective invokes the deselect method on all the participants associated with the rolename :buttons using the give-participant
method defined for all connectors. However, a connector can also check if
the participants are in the right state to be connected and the creation of a
connector can be refused according to certain criteria.

The fact that connectors are entities separate from components provides
important benefits - connector information is no longer spread across component
code. In this example, for instance, buttons do not need to keep track of the last
selected button in their own select and deselect methods, as would be the
case with traditional object-oriented languages. This increases the reusability of
components, making their code clearer and simpler. A connector can thus be
understood at code level as a logical unit and carries an important part of the
design decisions down to the implementation level.

4.2   Generic Connectors

FLO allows for the definition of *generic* connector templates, currently with
some restrictions. A generic connector template defines a general connection
schema that can be instantiated to create a specific connector template for a
particular context. Generic connector templates are defined in terms of generic
interfaces that are then *instantiated* with real component interfaces. For example,
a generic connector template is defined as shown in the code below (lines 1 to 12)
and then instantiated in case of buttons (lines 13 to 15). The resulting connector
template is identical to the *reactive-exclusion* connector template in section 4.1.

```
1  (defGenericConnector  generic-reac-excl  (set-of :components)
2  :var ((active? :initform #f  :accessor active?)
3       (anchor  :accessor anchor))
4  :behavior
5  (((action1  :components-receiver) implies (set! active? connector #f))
6    ((action2  :components-receiver) implies-before
7        (when (active? connector) (action2 (anchor connector))))
8    ((action2  :components-receiver) implies
9        (set! active? connector #t)
10       (set! anchor connector  :components-receiver))))
11 (defmethod action-before-effective ((connector  generic-reac-excl) args)
12      (for-each action2 (give connector :components)))
```

```
13 (defConnector  reactive-exclusion-between-buttons14
14   :is generic-reac-excl :with-participants component = buttons
15   :with-methods action1 = select, action2 = deselect)
```

```
16  (make  reactive-exclusion-between-buttons :buttons (list b1 b2 b3))
```

A generic connector template describes a general pattern of communication
between components in terms of abstract interfaces. The use of generic connectors allows for the reuse of complex connector templates that need only be

defined once. The definition of generic connectors in FLO is at present limited to specific cases - to those cases when the context of a rule is independent of the filter. That is, the context of an interaction rule should not use the arguments of the controlled message. Future improvements of the FLO implementation will take into account these problems and propose a way to manipulate calling arguments.

5 A kind of Client-Server Connector

In this example we show a connector in which participants play different roles, and demonstrate how a new connector can be defined from existing connectors. For the sake of exposition, our example is a rather simplified schema of a client-server relationship between tools. It allows us, however, to illustrate that connectors in FLO can forbid message execution according to specified criteria, in contrast to *mediators* [SN92], or to implementations of the MVC model [KP88] or the Observer design pattern [GHJV94], which only propagate messages.

Suppose that we have a simple calculator component that generates new data when the method `computes-new-value` is invoked, and we would like to display the calculated data on a graph displayer that displays a limited number of values on x-y axes, and has a method for displaying a value (`add-new-value`) and one for removing a value by clicking on the display (`remove-one-value`). We want to express that each value computed by the calculator should be displayed by the graph displayer - this means in particular that if the graph displayer is full (method `free-variables?`) a new value should not be computed. An additional constraint is that the format of the calculator result values is not compatible with the format required by the displayer, so the values must be converted.

5.1 Connector between Calculator and Graph Displayer.

The following connector definition ensures that all the constraints mentioned above are satisfied:

```
1 (defConnector   calculator-displayer  (:calculator :displayer)
2                       ;two distinct participants
3  :behavior
4  (((compute-new-value  :calculator val) implies
5       (add-new-value :displayer (convert connector val result)))
6     ; when a new value is computed, the displayer is aware
7     ; the value is converted to be understood by the displayer
8   ((compute-new-value  :calculator val) permitted-if
9     (free-variables? :displayer))))
10 ; computing a new value is only possible if the displayer can display it
11 ; end of behavior definition
12  (defmethod convert ((connector  calculator-displayer) v1 v2)
13     (list (from-float-to-pixels v1) (from-float-to-pixels v2))
14       ; a conversion  from two floats to a list of two pixels
```

The keyword **result** at line 5 represents the value returned by the controlled method, here the method `compute-new-value`. The connector template above can be instantiated as follows:

```
17 (define c (make calculator))
18 (define d (make displayer  :x 120  :y 200))
19 (define calc-disp (make  calculator-displayer
20                          :calculator c :displayer d :x 50 :y 70))
```

This example illustrates that, in contrast to the MVC model [KP88] or the Observer design pattern [GHJV94], which are design descriptions, a connector actually *controls* the message exchange between participants, ensuring the integrity of the design. Here, the calculator cannot produce a new value if the displayer is not in the appropriate state.

Distinct roles. In this example, the connector requires participants that play different roles. Here two roles are defined – a calculator which provides a method called `compute-new-value` and a displayer which provides the methods `add-new--value`, `free-variables?`, `specify-axes` and `clear-variables`.

A place to define connector behavior. A connector allows for the definition of connection information, one aspect of which is data conversion. Line 5 specifies that the result of the call to the calculator should be converted before sending the `add-new-value` method to the displayer. Whereas with traditional object-oriented languages this conversion would be included in the interface of the component, with a new conversion method being added for each new interaction, here the conversion is a method, called `convert`, local to the connector itself (lines 12 and 13). The components themselves need not provide such a conversion method - since a component should not be required to anticipate its possible connection with other incompatible components.

5.2 Reusing and Composing Connectors

We now show how connector templates can be composed to create new templates. Suppose that we want to visualize with a new grapher, called *history*, all the values calculated by the calculator. In addition we would like that when a user selects a vertex in the first graph displayer the corresponding value is highlighted in the history graph. We assume that the history grapher provides a way to change the color of a value (methods `find-values` and `change-color`).

There are different possibilities to implement this new connection. We can define a separate connector template and instantiate from it a new connector which links the history grapher to the graph displayer and to the calculator, retaining the existing connector which links the calculator to the graph displayer. Or we can define a connector template for a connector which links all three components to each other (see figure 2), thus no longer requiring the existing connector. We now present these two solutions.

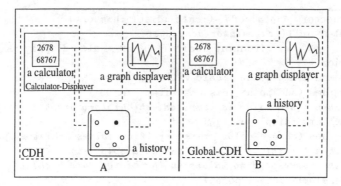

Fig. 2. Two possibilities for defining a new connector: (A) Addition of a separate connector and (B) Derivation of a global connector from the previous definition.

Adding a separate connector. We define a separate connector template called *CDH* as shown below (lines **1** to **11**) and instantiate it (line **13**) on the previous components (i.e. the graph displayer and the calculator) plus the new one (i.e. the history graph). For the sake of simplicity, we assume now that the returned values of the calculator are compatible with the history graph. There are now two independent connectors: *cdh*, instantiated from template *CDH* (line **13**), and *calc-disp*, instantiated from template *calculator-displayer*. It is possible to remove one without being concerned about the other one, and the variable names (`:calc`, `:displ` and `:history`) are also independent. The displayer should provide two new methods: `select` and `deselect`.

```
1 (defConnector  CDH  (:calc :displ :history)
2  :behavior
3  (((compute-new-value  :calc val)
4     implies (add-point :history val result)))
5     ; when a new value is computed, the history graph adds it
6   ((select  :displ point)
7     implies (change-color :history (find-values  :history point))
8        ; when a point is selected in the displayer,
9        ; the corresponding values in the history are highlighted
10  ((deselect  :displ point)
11    implies (change-color :history (find-values  :history point)))))
```

```
12 (define h (make history))
13 (define cdh (make CDH :displ d :calc c :history h))
```

Connector Inheritance. Instead of having two separate connectors, it is possible to define by inheritance one connector template which manages the connections described by *CDH* and *calculator-displayer* (figure B in figure 2). Here we can enrich the *calculator-displayer* connector template with new interaction rules as shown in lines **1** to **11** or use multiple inheritance between connector templates *CDH* and *calculator-displayer* (lines **13** to **16**).

```
1  (defConnector   Global-CDH  (:calc :displ :history)
2    :inherit-from (( calculator-displayer
3                        (rename :calculator as :calc :display as displ)))
3    :behavior
4      (((compute-new-value  :calc val)
5        implies (add-point :history val result)))
6        ; when a new value is computed, the history graph displays it
7      ((select  :displ point)
8        implies (change-color  :history (find-values  :history point))
9        ; when a point is selected in the displayer,
10       ; the corresponding values in the history are highlight
11     ((deselect  :displ point)
12       implies (change-color  :history (find-values  :history point)))))
```

```
13  (defConnector   Global-CDH  (:calc :displ :history)
14    :inherit-from (( calculator-displayer
15                        (rename :calculator as :calc :display as displ))
16                    ( CDH)))
```

The last template definition is equivalent to the previous one. This last example shows that the inheritance mechanism provides a way to rename the variable representing the role of the participants. It also shows that when two connector templates are composed to give a new connector template through multiple inheritance, the roles of the participants are composed to give a new role.

6 Implementation Issues

The FLO model is based on full message passing control as offered by reflexivity and the open aspect of languages like CLOS [KdRB91,DBFP95] or Smalltalk [GR89]. Few object-oriented languages offer message passing control. Preprocessing the code, as used in Synchronizer [FA93] or OpenC++ [Chi95], can be a solution to introduce such control of message passing. Another approach is to use an implicit invocation mechanism that can be easily added to any language [NGGS93]. However, this solution does not allow full message passing control because implicit invocation cannot support inhibition or redirection of messages.

The connectors described in this paper are fully implemented in CLOS, and a new version is under development in Smalltalk at the University of Berne (see http://iamwww.unibe.ch/~ducasse/). Moreover, we are now evaluating the introduction of reflexive facilities into Java [Gol97] to support connectors.

7 Related Work

Allen and Garlan propose a formal approach to connectors which is independent of object-oriented languages, their main motivation being to formalize software architectures in general [AG94]. Their formalism allows one to reason about the compatibility of a component's interface, or *port*, with a connector's *role*, and to prove properties such as deadlock-freedom of a connector. Whereas component ports in [AG94] are processes, our ports are just sets of methods. Our connectors have a dynamic behavior part, specified by interaction rules, which corresponds to Allen and Garlan's connector *glue*, but the *role* part of our connectors is implicitly defined in a connector specification as explained in section 3.2. Furthermore, though FLO's connectors can provide a basic test at connector instantiation to check if the participants provide the required interface, our approach does not, at present, formalize the notion of compatibility.

In contrast to Allen and Garlan's formal approach, our contribution is to provide an *executable* notation for connectors: connectors which not only describe component relationships, but also enforce them. *Contracts* [HHG90] are design formalisms used to express cooperation between objects, but they describe rather than enforce the constraints on the message exchange between participants. Also, many design patterns [GHJV94] can be expressed using connectors - in this way retaining and enforcing design decisions at implementation level.

The problem of providing a language construct to express and also control interaction relationships has been approached from a variety of angles. Pintado [Pin93] proposes *gluons* to mediate object collaborations. His approach emphasizes collaborations between objects as client-server protocols, and does not allow for the specification of more general patterns of collaboration, in particular for ones where no server is required, such as the example in section 4. Similarly, components in Darwin [MDEK95] interact through services required and services provided, so that the unit of connection is basically a binding of services of two components. In the Composition-Filters approach of SINA [AWB$^+$94], Abstract Communication Types are proposed for enforcing invariant behavior among objects. But, object interfaces must be modified before an object can engage in a new kind of interaction — an impediment to the reuse of components in new contexts.

Yellin and Strom [YS94] represent interaction relationships using protocols specified in the object's interface. When two components are functionally compatible, but their interface protocols are not compatible *adaptors* are used to translate the interfaces. Adaptors are connector-like constructs but in the context of augmented interfaces they require a limited expressive power and can represent only two-party relationships.

Sullivan and Notkin [SN92] separate connectors from the components at the implementation level by providing *mediators*, proposed to facilitate tool integration. Our connectors are close to mediators in the sense that they are based on an implicit message passing mechanism which allows components to remain truly independent [SG96]. In contrast to mediators, however, our connectors are explicit programmable entities which not only relay messages, but can forbid message delivery, redirect messages or send compensating messages to the participants.

Frølund and Agha [FA93] propose *synchronizers* for multi-object coordination in a concurrent language. Synchronizers are similar to our connectors but there is a main difference between the two approaches. A synchronizer only updates its own state on receiving a message from a participant, but it cannot itself send messages to its participants and alter their state. A synchronizer only coordinates communication. Our connector is, in this sense, more active - it can enforce state changes in the participants by sending messages to components.

8   Conclusions

We have proposed first-class connectors in a sequential object-oriented language as dynamic user-defined abstractions which coordinate and control component communication. We consider FLO's connectors a powerful construct for expressing interaction between components and for structuring software in a way which gives equal importance to relationships and to the components they relate. Our contribution is to provide a descriptive and executable notation for connectors and thus enable the localization of information about interaction of components at the level of implementation.

We have also shown how connectors themselves can be reused: through inheritance or through generic connectors which describe schematic interaction relationships, and have argued that the presence of connectors promotes the reuse of components in new contexts.

Executable connectors are a first step towards the goal of making software architecture more explicit at implementation. Connectors enrich the design vocabulary and carry some design information to the application code. They do not, on their own, lead to better designs, but they are an aid in the codification and enforcement of design idioms (e.g. design patterns [Duc97a]). We further plan to investigate the use of connectors in enforcing more general design constraints, as in architectural styles [SG96]. We see this use of connectors as a contribution to the goal of composing applications from existing software artefacts.

We plan to pursue our work on connectors in three main directions:

Genericity. In particular, improving generic connectors by developing constructs to manipulate calling arguments and by introducing parameters for connectors which would allow generic connectors to be instantiated with code fragments to tailor a generic interaction schema to a particular context.

Concurrency. We are currently extending our approach to concurrent object-oriented languages with active objects. A connector is then an entity that synchronizes concurrent objects and controls their communication. This leads us to introduce new kinds of operators to handle different synchronization schemes.

Formal approach. The current approach lacks a formalization of component-connector compatibility and of component substitutability. To formalize these notions we may need to revise our notion of component interface and connector role, perhaps in the line of augmented interfaces proposed in [YS94].

9   Acknowledgments

We are grateful to Oscar Nierstrasz for his encouragement and advice, and for many helpful comments on the manuscript. Our thanks also to Serge Demeyer, Theo Dirk Meijler, Markus Lumpe and the anonymous referees for their comments on an earlier draft.

References

[AG94]   R. Allen and D. Garlan. Formal connectors. Cmu-cs-94-115, Carnegie Mellon University, Mar. 1994.

[AWB+94]   M. Aksit, K. Wakita, J. Bosch, L. Bergmans, and A. Yonezawa. Abstracting object interactions using composition filters. In *Object-Based Distributed Programming (ECOOP'93 workshop)*, LNCS 791, pp. 152–184, 1994.

[Chi95]   S. Chiba. A Metaobject Protocol for C++. In *OOPSLA'95*, pp. 285–299, 1995.

[Coi87]   P. Cointe. Metaclasses are first Class: The ObjVlisp Model. In *OOPSLA'87 Proceedings*, pp. 156–165, October 1987.

[DBFP95]   S. Ducasse, M. Blay-Fornarino, and A. Pinna. A Reflective Model for First Class Dependencies. In *OOPSLA'95*, pp. 265–280, 1995.

[Duc97a]   *Message Passing Abstractions as Elementary Bricks for Design Pattern Implementation*, 1997. Language Support for Design Patterns and Frameworks ECOOP'97 Int. Workshop.

[Duc97b]   S. Ducasse. *Intégration réflexive de dépendances dans un modèle à classes*. PhD thesis, Université de Nice-Sophia Antipolis, 1997.

[FA93]   S. Frølund and G. Agha. A Language Framework for Multi-Object Coordination. In *ECOOP'93*, LNCS 707, pp. 346–360, 1993.

[Frø94]   S. Frølund. *Constraint-Based Synchronization of Distributed Activities*. PhD thesis, University of Illinois at Urbana-Champaign, 1994.

[GHJV94]   E. Gamma, R. Helm, R. Johnson, and J. Vlissides. *Design Patterns: Elements of Reusable Object-Oriented Software*. Addison-Wesley, 1994.

[Gol97]   M. Golm. Design and implementation of a meta architecture for java. Master's thesis, IMMD at F.A. University, Erlangen-Nuernberg, 1997.

[GR89]   A. Goldberg and D. Robson. *Smalltalk-80: The Language*. Addison-Wesley, 1989.

[HHG90]   R. Helm, I. Holland, and D. Gangopadhyay. Contracts. Specifying compositions in object-oriented systems. In *OOPSLA'90*, pp. 169–180, 1990.

[KdRB91]   G. Kiczales, J. des Rivieres, and D. G. Bobrow. *The Art of the Metaobject Protocol*. MIT Press, 1991.

[KP88]   G. Krasner and S. T. Pope. A cookbook for using the Model-View-Controller user interface paradigm in Smalltalk-80. *JOOP*, Aug. 1988.

[MDEK95]   J. Magee, N. Dulay, S. Eisenbach, and J. Kramer. Specifying distributed software architectures. In *Proc. ESEC'95, LNCS 989*, pp. 137–153, 1995.

[ND95]   O. Nierstrasz and L. Dami. Component-oriented software technology. In *Object-Oriented Software Composition*, pp. 3–28. Prentice Hall, 1995.

[NGGS93]   D. Notkin, D. Garlan, W. G. Griswold, and K. Sullivan. Adding Implicit Invocation to Languages: Three Approaches. In *Proc. ISOTAS'93, LNCS 742*, pp. 487–510, 1993.

[OMG95]   OMG. *The common object request broker: architecture and specification*, 1995. Revision 2.0.

[Pin93]   X. Pintado. Gluons: a support for software component cooperation. In *Proc. ISOTAS'93*, LNCS 742, pp. 43–60, 1993.

[SG96]   M. Shaw and D. Garlan. *Software Architecture: Perspectives on an Emerging Discipline*. Prentice-Hall, 1996.

[SN92]   K. Sullivan and D. Notkin. Reconciling environment integration and software evolution. *Trans. on Software Engineering and Methodology*, 1(3):228–268, July 1992.

[YS94]   D. M. Yellin and R. E. Strom. Interfaces, Protocols, and the Semi-Automatic Construction of Software Adaptors. In *Proc. of OOPSLA'94*, pp. 176–190, 1994.

Expressing Code Mobility in Mobile UNITY

Gian Pietro Picco[1,2], Gruia-Catalin Roman[2], and Peter J. McCann[2]

[1] Dipartimento di Automatica e Informatica, Politecnico di Torino,
C.so Duca degli Abruzzi 24, 10129 Torino, Italy
picco@polito.it
[2] Department of Computer Science, Washington University,
Campus Box 1045, One Brookings Drive, Saint Louis, MO 63130-4899, USA
[roman | mccap]@cs.wustl.edu

Abstract. Advancements in network technology have led to the emergence of new computing paradigms that challenge established programming practices by employing weak forms of consistency and dynamic forms of binding. Code mobility, for instance, allows for invocation-time binding between a code fragment and the location where it executes. Similarly, mobile computing allows hosts (and the software they execute) to alter their physical location. Despite apparent similarities, the two paradigms are distinct in their treatment of location and movement. This paper seeks to uncover a common foundation for the two paradigms by exploring the manner in which stereotypical forms of code mobility can be expressed in a programming notation developed for mobile computing. Several solutions to a distributed simulation problem are used to illustrate the modeling strategy for programs that employ code mobility.
Keywords. Code mobility, UNITY, Mobile UNITY, coordination, mobile computing, mobile code languages.

1 Introduction

Code mobility is defined informally as the capability, in a distributed application, to dynamically reconfigure the binding between code fragments and the location where they are executed [2]. *Mobile code languages (MCLs)* [12,11] provide specialized abstractions and run-time support capabilities designed to support various forms of code mobility. They assume that hosts and communication links are part of a highly dynamic global computing platform, where the application code can move freely among the computing nodes. This *network centric* style of computing is at the center of the emerging mobile code languages.

For a comprehensive survey of MCLs, the reader is directed to [5] which reviews a number of existing languages and attempts to extract their essential features. The unit of mobility, that in [5] is called *executing unit*, is implemented differently in different languages, but can be thought of as a process in an operating system or a thread in a multithreaded environment. *Strong mobility* allows executing units to move their code and their *execution state* to a different site. *Weak mobility* allows an executing unit at a site to be bound dynamically to freshly initialized code coming from a different site.

By and large, these developments fall outside the traditional concerns of distributed computing since much of the existing work on models, algorithms, proof systems, methodologies, and impossibility has been carried out assuming networks with a fixed topology and static binding between the application code and the hosts where it is being executed. In contrast, MCLs enable more dynamic solutions to distributed computing problems, such as design paradigms that encompass new forms of interaction among the components of a distributed application. Relating these new paradigms to previous research on distributed computing is the main theme of this paper.

The model we use in our study is called *Mobile UNITY* [7,10], an extension of work by Chandy and Misra on UNITY [4]. Mobile UNITY provides a programming notation that captures the notion of mobility and transient interactions among mobile nodes and includes an assertional-style proof logic. The model adheres to the minimalist philosophy of the original UNITY, supports text-based reasoning about programs, and focuses only on essential abstractions needed to cope with the presence of mobility. As we use this model to examine mobile code paradigms, the fundamental goal is to determine whether Mobile UNITY by itself is adequate to this modeling task.

The remainder of this paper is structured as follows. Section 2 describes a simplified version of a distributed simulation problem and introduces standard UNITY via a centralized solution. Section 3 presents a distributed solution to the problem using the client-server paradigm. In doing so, it also provides the reader with a gentle introduction to Mobile UNITY. Section 4 introduces basic concepts relevant to code mobility, provides some background information, and presents mobile code solutions to the distributed simulation problem. They illustrate our strategies for modeling mobile code in Mobile UNITY and are modeled after the taxonomy of mobile code design paradigms found in [2]. Finally, Section 5 explores some of the issues raised by this investigation.

2 A Distributed Simulation Problem

In this section we present an example that will be used for illustration purposes throughout the remainder of the paper and as a vehicle to introduce the reader to the UNITY notation. The example is inspired by the work of Chandy and Misra who provided a formal characterization and solution for a distributed simulation problem [3]. The basic idea is to simulate the behavior of a physical system such as an electronic circuit on a network of computing nodes which communicate asynchronously and in the absence of global shared memory. Physical entities are allocated to nodes across the network and simulated according to their expected behavior. The nodes must communicate among themselves in order to simulate the interactions normally occurring among the physical components (e.g., passing a signal from one gate to the next) and also in order to preserve the correct temporal relationships among the actions associated with the various simulated entities. It is the latter aspect of the problem which is central to its solution. For this reason, in our simplified version we focus strictly on the temporal aspects of the problem and ignore any other interactions among the components. In other words, we assume that each simulated entity executes at most one action at a time in a deterministic manner and does not interact with any other entities being simulated at other nodes. However, because the simulation may be monitored by some external agent while in progress, the ordering of actions in time must be consistent with those occuring in the simulated system. These simplifying assumptions would be realistic, for instance, when particle movement is simulated in the absence of collisions.

The behavior of each node is very simple. A *local timer* holds the time value at which the next local action is to be executed. The action can be executed only when all nodes participating in the simulation reach that particular time, i.e., all actions scheduled for earlier times have been executed. The notion of *global virtual time (GVT)*, whose value is defined as the minimum among the values of all local timers, formalizes the intuitive idea that the simulation reached a particular point in time. In a centralized solution to the problem, such as the UNITY solution appearing later in this section, the value of the GVT can be stored in a variable and can be updated by examining the value of each local timer. In a distributed solution, each node has to discover the GVT value by communicating with other participating nodes.

A system is modeled by a set of N processes, indexed from 0 to $(N-1)$. Each process $P(i)$ has an associated local timer, $t(i)$. The GVT T is defined as the minimum of all the local timers, i.e., $T = \langle min\ i : 0 \leq i \leq N - 1 :: t(i) \rangle$[1]. The scheduling criterion used by a process to update its timer is embodied in the definition of the function $f_i(t(i), T, z)$ where $t(i)$ denotes the value for a local timer, T denotes the GVT value, and z identifies the simulation mode, e.g., a parameter of the physical components. The definition captures the following requirements:

1. The local timer cannot change if it is ahead of the GVT.
2. The local timer, if permitted, can only increase, i.e., actions are always scheduled in the future.
3. The value of a local timer can never be behind the GVT. For such cases the function f is undefined.

In this section, we discuss a solution for the distributed simulation problem that uses the UNITY notation described in [4]. In the UNITY program shown in Fig. 1, the **declare** section contains variable declarations. The array t contains the value of the local timer for each process i. T stores the current value for the GVT and z represents the simulation mode. The **initially** section contains a set

---

[1] The three-part notation $\langle$ op *quantified_variables* : *range* :: *expression* $\rangle$ is borrowed from UNITY and will be used throughout the paper. It is defined as follows: The variables from *quantified_variables* take on all possible values permitted by *range*. If *range* is missing, the first colon is omitted and the domain of the variables is restricted by context. Each such instantiation of the variables is substituted in *expression* producing a multiset of values in which **op** is applied. In the case above, it is equivalent to $min\{t(i) \mid 0 \leq i \leq N - 1\}$.

```
Program DistributedSimulation
    declare
        t : array of integer [] T, z : integer
    initially
        ⟨[] i :: t(i) = 0⟩ [] T, z = 0. z
    assign
        SimulationWork(t)
    [] T := ⟨min i :: t(i)⟩
    [] ⟨[] i :: t(i) := fᵢ(t(i), T, z)⟩
    [] z := d(T)
end
```

Fig. 1. Standard UNITY solution for the distributed simulation problem.

of predicates, separated by the symbol [], which define the allowed set of initial states. Uninitialized variables will assume an arbitrary value belonging to their declared type. All local timers $t(i)$ are initialized to zero and T is initialized consistently. The simulation mode z is initialized to some default initial value, $\bar{z}$. The **assign** section is the core of the program. It consists of a set of assignment statements that specify the program behavior. Program execution starts in the state described in the **initially** section and evolves as a non-deterministic, fair interleaving of statements—in an infinite execution of the program each statement is executed infinitely often. The first statement computes the current GVT as the minimum among the values of the local timers, and stores it in T. The second statement is a set of asynchronous assignments each updating the local timer for a corresponding process $P(i)$. Due to the definition of f, the update is performed only when the timer value is equal to the value of T, otherwise it has no effect on T. The statement is defined using the three-part notation with [] as a quantifier, hence it is equivalent to N assignments separated by [] and executed non-deterministically and independently. If we wanted to specify synchronous execution instead, we could have used || in place of []. Note also that, because of fair execution, each of the assignments separated by [] is non-deterministically interleaved with the one computing the GVT. In some fair execution, it could happen for all the $t(i)$ to be updated before the new GVT is computed. In this case, T actually represents a lower bound for the GVT value, and the T parameter used as an argument for function f is actually an approximation of the GVT. The details about the behavior of processes are irrelevant. In this solution, we abstract them into a function $SimulationWork(t)$, which will be dropped in the other solutions. Finally, the value of the simulation mode is updated dynamically according to the definition of a function $d(T)$ whose details are left out.

3 A Client-Server Solution in Mobile UNITY

Although the solution presented in Fig. 1 is formally correct, it is not acceptable from a design point of view because every variable appears to be *shared* and, in particular, the GVT is shared among all processes—which has been explicitly forbidden by the statement of the problem. In addition, it is not apparent that the local timers are associated with processes, and the program text does not even capture explicitly the notion of independent processes. In this section we show a client-server solution that does not employ shared variables and makes explicit the location and encapsulation embodied in each process. In doing this, we will introduce Mobile UNITY, which will be used in Section 4 to describe the distributed solutions exploiting code mobility.

In the *Client-Server (CS)* paradigm, a server component exports a set of services. The client component, at some point in its execution, lacks some of the resources needed to proceed with its computation. The resources are located on the server host and they are accessed by the client by interacting with the server through message passing. The interaction specifies the service that needs to be invoked on the server in order to access the resources.

As in our earlier centralized solution, we will ignore the internal simulation steps except for their effect on the advancement of the local timers. Each process must calculate an estimate T of the GVT to determine whether the next step in its local simulation is allowed. For correctness, this estimate should never exceed the real GVT, otherwise a process might take a step even when its timer value is in the future with respect to some other component. The distributed solutions presented in this and the following sections must compute a lower bound on the GVT without using statements like $T := \langle \min i :: t(i) \rangle$ which imply centralized access to the local timers of each component. The client-server solution of Fig. 2 provides for such distribution by breaking up the system into a single server and a set of clients. The server contains an array τ which attempts to maintain the global state of all the local timer values from each of the clients. This array is updated via asynchronous message passing, and therefore may sometimes contain old values of the local timers. A new estimate for the GVT is calculated at the server and returned to waiting clients again via asynchronous message passing. Figure 2 is illustrative of the new structuring conventions provided by Mobile UNITY. The first line provides the system name, *DSClientServer*. Next are a set of program definitions the first of which, *P(i)*, will serve as the code executed by each client and is parameterized by a single index representing the client number. The second, *Server*, has no such parameter. The program definitions are treated as types that are instantiated in the **Components** section. The program instances listed there are considered to be the running components of a distributed computation. In this example, the **Components** section instantiates one client for every value of i in the appropriate range, and a singleton *Server* instance. Each component has a distinct name: the clients, because they are indexed, and the server, because it is instantiated only once.

Note that each program definition begins with a line like **Program** *name* **at** λ. This denotes that each program exists at a specific physical or logical location denoted by the distinguished program variable λ. Each program contains a predicate in its **initially** section that gives the initial position of the component. We assume the existence of a function Location() that returns the initial position of each component based on an address which is either a client number or the constant SERVER. Each program may also contain code in its **assign** section that reads or modifies the position of the component. An assignment to λ mod-

```
System DSClientServer
    Program P(i) at λ
        declare
            t, z : integer [] T : integer ∪ {⊥} [] RQ : request ∪ {⊥}
        initially
            t, z = 0, z [] T = ⊥ [] λ = Location(i) [] RQ = ⊥
        assign
            [] t, T := fᵢ(t, T, z), ⊥              if def(T)
            [] RQ := ⟨SERVER,CS, MINSERV, t⟩      if ¬def(RQ) ∧ ¬def(T)
            [] T, RQ := RQ ↑ 4, ⊥                 if RQ ↑ 1 = i
    end
    Program Server at λ
        declare
            T : integer ∪ {⊥} [] τ : array of integer [] q : array of (request ∪ {⊥})
        initially
            T = ⊥ [] ⟨|| j :: τ(j) = 0⟩ [] ⟨|| j :: q(j) = ⊥⟩ [] λ = Location(SERVER)
        assign
            ⟨[] j :: τ(j), q(j) ↑ 2 := q(j) ↑ 4, WAIT⟩   if q(j) ↑ 1 = SERVER ∧ q(j) ↑ 2 ≠ WAIT⟩
            [] T := ⟨min k :: τ(k)⟩                       if ⟨∃ j :: q(j) ↑ 2 = WAIT⟩ ∧ ¬def(T)
            [] ⟨|| j :: q(j), T := ⟨j, ⊥, ⊥, T⟩, ⊥       if def(T) ∧ q(j)' ↑ 2 = WAIT⟩
    end
    Components
        ⟨[] i :: P(i)⟩ [] Server
    Interactions
        Server.q(i) := P(i).RQ                    when ¬def(Server.q(i)) ∧
                                                      serviceRequest(CS, MINSERV, i)

        [] P(i).RQ, Server.q(i) := Server.q(i), ⊥   when serviceReady(i)
end
```

Fig. 2. Client-Server solution for the distributed simulation problem.

els actual migration of the component through some physical or logical address space.

Throughout this paper, we will leave the type of λ unspecified. The type may be determined by the characteristics of a particular problem domain and needs to be specified only to the extent necessary to the respective application. We will make much more use of λ in later examples that, in contrast to *DSClientServer*, actually do contain mobile components, and where the connectivity among components depends on their dynamically changing locations.

In standard UNITY, there is no notion of changing connectivity among the programs making up a composed system, and two variables with the same name in different programs are considered shared throughout execution of the system. All variables of a Mobile UNITY component are considered local to that component. When dealing with a collection of instantiated components, a specific instance variable is referenced by prepending the name of the variable with the name of the program in which it appears. For example, the variables t and z of the program *P(1)* have the fully qualified names $P(1).t$, and $P(1).z$. These fully qualified names should be used when carrying out formal reasoning about the behavior of the system, although we will sometimes leave off the program name when the context is clear.

Because variables are local, no communication can take place among components without the presence of interaction clauses spanning the scope of components. These appear in the **Interactions** section, and serve to provide implicit communication and coordination among the components. The two interaction clauses given in Fig. 2 allow for communication between each client and the

```
clientAddress = ⟨Set n : 0 ≤ n ≤ N − 1 :: n⟩
address = {{SERVER} ∪ clientAddress}
opName = {CS,REV,COD}
opStatus = {WAIT}
request = ⟨address, opName ∪ opStatus ∪ {⊥}, serviceName ∪ {⊥}, integer⟩
serviceRequest(j :  opName, k :  serviceName, i :  clientAddress) ≡
    P(i).RQ ↑ 1 = SERVER ∧ P(i).RQ ↑ 2 = j ∧ P(i).RQ ↑ 3 = k
serviceReady(i :  clientAddress) ≡ Server.q(i) ↑ 1 = i
```

Fig. 3. Macro definitions used in the example systems. Allowed values for each data element are represented as sets.

server. We assume that the index i is instanced over the appropriate range. Note that these clauses look like ordinary UNITY assignment statements, except that they use the keyword **when** in place of the keyword **if**. Also, because they are not internal to some component, they may reference variables of any component, using the naming conventions given above. For example, the first interaction clause provides asynchronous message transfer from the client message buffer $P(i).RQ$ to the server message buffer $Server.q(i)$, when the server buffer is empty and there is a valid request message waiting in the client buffer:

$$Server.q(i) := P(i).RQ \quad \textbf{when } \neg def(Server.q(i)) \wedge$$
$$\text{serviceRequest}(\text{CS}, \text{MINSERV}, i)$$

The second interaction transfers a reply back to the client and empties the server buffer, when the reply is ready:

$$P(i).RQ, Server.q(i) := Server.q(i), \bot \quad \textbf{when } \text{serviceReady}(i)$$

Semantically, these two statements are treated like ordinary assignment statements, and we assume that execution consists of a fair interleaving of all assignment statements of each component as well as these "extra statements" in the **Interactions** section.

The meaning of the macros used in the guards of the interactions is shown in Fig. 3. These macros will be used throughout the remaining examples. A **request** is a tuple consisting of four elements. We denote the tuple by enclosing it in angle brackets and separating its four elements by commas. We use the field index operator ↑ to access individual fields of a record, e.g., $P(i).RQ \uparrow 1$ represents the **address** field of the request variable $P(i).RQ$. This field is used to denote the destination of the message, and must be either a client index or the constant SERVER. The second field is used to denote the paradigm used to deliver the service, and must be an **opName**, which is one of CS for Client-Server, REV for Remote Evaluation, or COD for Code On Demand, with the meaning defined later. This field may also represent the status of the request with an **opStatus**, if the server is in the process of constructing a reply. The third field denotes the specific service requested, which in the case of the client-server solution is specified by the client to be MINSERV, which indicates that the client wants an estimate of the minimum local time across all clients. This field is always MINSERV in the client-server example, but we provide it because a server, in general, may provide multiple services. This field will take on a different value for the Code On Demand example presented later. The fourth and final field of a request must be an integer data item, which the client uses to transmit its current value of t to the server. With this in mind, the reader can see that the predicate serviceRequest checks to see that the message buffer of client i contains a message destined for the SERVER, with the opName and serviceName given. The predicate serviceReady checks the $Server.q(i)$ buffer for a message destined for client i.

Now we examine the inner workings of each component, as given by the **assign** section of each program definition. The assignment statements in the client program $P(i)$ look very much like the ones in the centralized solution *DistributedSimulation* presented in Section 2, except that now the variable t occurs once in each component instead of appearing as global arrays of values: we now use $P(i).t$ in place of $t(i)$. Also, T appears once in each program instead of being globally declared. Note that the simulation mode $P(i).z$, in contrast to the centralized solution, is initialized statically for each component and does not change during simulation execution. This is done for the sake of simplicity and clarity. In the Code On Demand solution presented later, we will compute this value dynamically. Otherwise, the statement to update the local simulation time $P(i).t$ is the same as before, except that the estimated GVT variable $P(i).T$ is simultaneously set to $\perp$ when an update to the local time is made. Throughout the example, the notation $\mathsf{def}(v)$ denotes the predicate $v \neq \perp$, i.e., the variable v is defined. This is used in the guard of the update to the local timer, and signals the fact that the client needs a new value of T before it can proceed with another simulation step. The new estimate of GVT is computed in the server at the request of the client, and the request is made by the third statement in the program $P(i)$, which writes a request record to the message buffer $P(i).RQ$.

Once the assignment to $P(i).RQ$ has taken place, the first interaction clause is enabled. Its guard makes use of the macro serviceRequest, which is a predicate that detects the presence of a valid request. After the interaction is enabled it is eventually executed, which asynchronously transmits the request to the server.

The *Server* program consists of three groups of assignments. The first processes input requests by updating the array $Server.\tau$ with the local time sent by the client. The second computes a new estimate of the GVT based on the current values in $Server.\tau$, if some client request is waiting in a buffer. The third takes the estimate and constructs a reply message to all waiting clients, clearing the estimate. Once the reply has been written to $Server.q(i)$, the second interaction clause is enabled. Its guard makes use of the macro serviceReady, which is a predicate that detects the presence of a valid reply. After the interaction is enabled it is eventually executed, which asynchronously transfers the reply back to the client. The fourth assignment statement of $P(i)$ processes the reply by updating the local GVT estimate $P(i).T$ and clearing the request buffer.

The client-server example does not exercise all the features of Mobile UNITY. A Mobile UNITY system can contain more powerful interaction clauses, such as the specification of *transient shared variables*. These are variables of one component that are dynamically bound to variables of another component in a location-dependent manner. Any assignments to one of the variables are considered to propagate atomically to the other, while the two variables are bound. This allows the designer to express location-dependent consistency, i.e., when components are "near" each other, a high degree of consistency is maintained due to the availability of a high bandwidth, low latency communication channel. When components move apart, only a low degree of consistency would be possible for good performance in the face of decreased or non-existent bandwidth. The Mobile UNITY specification of this sharing could be written as:

$$Server.q(i) \approx P(i).RQ \quad \textbf{when } Server.\lambda = P(i).\lambda$$

which states that the request buffer of client i should be shared with $Server.q(i)$ when the two components are at the same place. In the case of a network of workstations, location would be the IP address of the machine, for instance.

While a pair of transiently shared variables are disconnected, they may take on different values, because assignments to one are not immediately propagated to the other. This may present a problem when the variables are later reconnected. Mobile UNITY allows for the specification of an **engage** value, which is assigned atomically to both variables immediately upon a transition of the **when** predicate from false to true. We may want to specify, for instance, that the message buffer will take on the value present at the server when a new process arrives—e.g., because implementation details of inter-process shared memory make it more efficient for the buffers to be allocated in a single block, and thus placed on the server. We would write this as

$$Server.q(i) \approx P(i).RQ \quad \textbf{when } Server.\lambda = P(i).\lambda$$
$$\textbf{engage } Server.q(i)$$

Similarly, a pair of **disengage** values may be specified that are assigned atomically to the variables when they become disconnected:

$$Server.q(i) \approx P(i).RQ \quad \textbf{when } Server.\lambda = P(i).\lambda$$
$$\textbf{engage } Server.q(i)$$
$$\textbf{disengage } Server.q(i), \perp$$

Note that if no **engage** value is specified, the variables will remain in an inconsistent state after sharing takes effect until the first assignment is propagated. If no **disengage** value is specified, the variables will retain the values they had before the variables are disconnected. Later examples will make extensive use of transient sharing, including one-way sharing, where updates are propagated in one direction but not the reverse. This is expressed as above except with an $\leftarrow$ in place of $\approx$, pointing in the same direction as updates are to be propagated.

To accommodate shared variables, as well as other forms of component interaction, Mobile UNITY makes certain adjustments to the standard UNITY operational model. Because the updates to shared variables must happen in the same atomic step as an assignment, but sharing is specified separately from the (possibly many) assignments that may change the value of a variable, Mobile UNITY has a two-phased operational model where the first phase is an ordinary assignment statement and the second is responsible for propagating changes to shared variables. We call the statements that execute in the second phase *reactive statements*, and they are denoted in the text of a Mobile UNITY program by the use of **reacts-to** in place of **if**. Mobile UNITY also allows for global constraints on the execution of statements, called **inhibit** clauses. These serve to strengthen the guard on a statement and can express scheduling constraints that may not be expressible using only local state information. A third construct, the *transaction*, is used for specifying a sequence of statements that are executed as a unit with respect to other, non-reactive statements. Together, these primitives provide a powerful notation for expressing inter-component interaction in a highly decoupled and dynamic way, although for the purposes of this paper, we will express our solutions using only shared variables. The reader should keep in mind that transient sharing is really a shorthand notation for a set of reactive statements. Further information, including a proof logic that has been developed to match the new operational model, can be found in [7].

4 Mobile Code Design Paradigms

The idea behind code mobility is not new, as witnessed by the work of Stamos et al. [6] and Black et al. [1]. Nevertheless, these technologies were conceived mostly to provide operating system support on a LAN, while MCLs explicitly target large scale distributed systems—like the Internet.

On the Internet, client-server is the most used paradigm for the development of applications. In this paradigm, the application code is statically bound to the client and server hosts and the binding cannot be changed during the execution of the distributed application. Each interaction between the client and the server makes use of the communication infrastructure through message passing or some higher level mechanism like remote procedure call (RPC). Mechanisms that actually hide the location of components from the application programmer are also being considered, e.g., CORBA [9].

By contrast, in MCLs component locations are not hidden. Location is explicitly handled by the programmer who is able to specify *where* the computation of a given code fragment must take place. This capability leads to new paradigms for the design of distributed applications where the interaction between client and server is no longer constrained to exchanging simple, non-executable data via the network. For example, a portion of the client may move in order to bypass the communication infrastructure and to achieve local interaction with the server. This may improve performance by reducing latency and may increase dependability by avoiding problems inherent to partial failures.

The essential features of the interaction patterns found in MCLs can be characterized by considering the kinds of pairwise interactions that are possible between two software design components located on different hosts. In [2], Remote Evaluation (REV), Mobile Agent (MA), and Code on Demand (COD) are identified as the key mobile code design paradigms. A schematic view of all the paradigms appears in Fig. 4.

In the following solutions the GVT is always computed by a single component, like in the CS solution, and its value is communicated back to the processes $P(i)$. Thus, we continue to refer to components $P(i)$ as *clients* of the process computing the GVT, whether they are mobile or not. Furthermore, as in the CS solution we assume that the value for the simulation mode z is computed statically. We will relax this assumption when we describe a solution based on the COD paradigm.

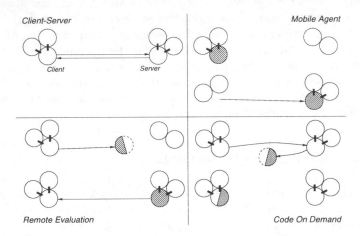

Fig. 4. Mobile code design paradigms. Components are identified by circles, and bindings between components are identified by black rectangles connecting circles. A component can be thought of as being composed of code, data state (holding data local to the component), and control state (holding information about its run-time execution). Grayed components participate in migration. Half-grayed dashed circles represent migration of a portion of a component, i.e., the code, or code plus the data state. Such portions can be used to create a new component, like in REV, or to augment an already existing component, like in COD. Arrows indicate network traffic, i.e., calls, return values, and code movement.

4.1 Remote Evaluation

The *Remote Evaluation* paradigm can be regarded as a variation of the CS paradigm where the server component offers its computational power and resources, like the server in a CS paradigm, but does not provide any application specific service. In the REV paradigm the client provides the code constituent for a component that will be instantiated on the server and bound there to the resources it needs to access. Eventually, a result will be sent back to the client component via a message, like in a CS paradigm. Hence, the REV paradigm leverages off the flexibility provided by the server, instead of relying on a fixed functionality. The REV paradigm is inspired by work on the REV [6] system, which extends remote procedure call with one additional parameter containing the code to execute on the server. Among recent MCLs, the paradigm is supported natively in TACOMA, Agent Tcl, Facile, and M0.

In the solution shown in Fig. 5, the client components $P(i)$ behave similarly to the ones in the *DSClientServer* system. Besides computing a new local timer,

```
System DSRemoteEvaluation
    Program P(i) at λ
        declare
            t, z : integer [] T : integer ∪ {⊥} [] RQ : request ∪ {⊥}
        initially
            t, z = 0, z [] T = ⊥ [] λ = Location(i) [] RQ = ⊥
        assign
            [] t, T := f_i(t, T, z), ⊥                    if def(T)
            [] RQ := ⟨SERVER,REV, MINSERV, ⊥⟩            if ¬def(RQ) ∧ ¬def(T)
            [] T, RQ := RQ ↑ 4, ⊥                        if RQ ↑ 1 = i
    end
    Program Min(i) at λ
        declare
            t : integer  [] T : integer ∪ {⊥} [] τ : (array of integer) ∪ {⊥} [] q : request ∪ {⊥}
        initially
            t, T = 0, ⊥ [] τ = ⊥ [] q = ⊥ [] λ = Location(i)
        assign
            τ(i) := t                    if def(τ)
            [] T := ⟨min k :: τ(k)⟩      if def(τ)
            [] q := ⟨i, ⊥, ⊥, T⟩         if τ(i) = t ∧ T = ⟨min k :: τ(k)⟩
    end
    Program Server at λ
        declare
            τ : array of integer [] q : array of (request ∪ {⊥}) []
        initially
            ⟨|| j :: τ(j) = 0⟩ [] ⟨|| j :: q(j) = ⊥⟩ [] λ = Location(SERVER)
    end
    Components
        ⟨[] i :: P(i)⟩ [] Server [] ⟨[] i :: Min(i)⟩
    Interactions
        Min(i).t ← P(i).t                    when Min(i).λ = P(i).λ
                                             engage P(i).t
        [] Min(i).λ := Server.λ              when Min(i).λ = P(i).λ ∧
                                                 serviceRequest(REV, MINSERV, i)
        [] Min(i).τ ≈ Server.τ              when Min(i).λ = Server.λ
                                             engage Server.τ
                                             disengage [], Server.τ
        [] Min(i).q ≈ Server.q(i)           when Min(i).λ = Server.λ
                                             engage ⊥
        [] P(i).RQ, Server.q(i)[, Min(i).λ] := Server.q(i), ⊥[, P(i).λ]    when serviceReady(i)
end
```

Fig. 5. Remote Evaluation solution for the distributed simulation problem.

clients can also request the execution of a service that computes the new GVT estimate, provided that the old GVT estimate has been already consumed during an earlier timer update and that a message request has not yet been sent. The corresponding reply message is eventually collected and its fields are checked to verify that the recipient's and receiver's addresses match. In this case, the new estimate becomes defined and available for the assignment that updates the timer, while the message buffer is reset to enable further requests—just like in the CS solution. The key difference between the two solutions is the second parameter in the message request

$$RQ := \langle \text{SERVER},\text{REV}, \text{MINSERV}, \bot \rangle \quad \text{if } \neg\text{def}(RQ) \wedge \neg\text{def}(T),$$

specifying that the code for the service named MINSERV must be sent to the *Server*'s location, where its execution exploits bindings with *Server*'s resources. In contrast with the CS solution, the request message is not delivered to the message buffer of the *Server*. Its presence within the client buffer enables subsequent code migration. The code for service MINSERV is described by the program

Min(i) and is structured in three steps: update of the global state maintaned in *Server.τ* with the timer value of the corresponding client *P(i)*, computation of the new GVT, and communication of the results to the client. All these steps can take place only when *Min(i)* and *Server* are co-located. In this situation, the statement

$$Min(i).\tau \approx Server.\tau \quad \textbf{when } Min(i).\lambda = Server.\lambda$$
$$\textbf{engage } Server.\tau$$
$$\textbf{disengage } \bot, \ Server.\tau$$

in the **Interactions** section specifies a transient sharing between the representation of the global state *τ* owned by *Min(i)* and *Server*. Upon departure, the **disengage** clause voids the value of *τ* in *Min(i)*, thus preventing execution of any statement within this component while it is not at the *Server*'s location. Upon a subsequent arrival, the *τ* values owned by the two components are reconciled by the **engage** clause, which assigns to *Min(i).τ* the up-to-date *τ* value kept on *Server*. Updating a client's timer value stored in *τ* is made possible by the interaction

$$Min(i).t \leftarrow P(i).t \quad \textbf{when } Min(i).\lambda = P(i).\lambda$$
$$\textbf{engage } P(i).t$$

which specifies that the timer value in a client *P(i)* is shared with the one in the corresponding *Min(i)*—as long as they are co-located. Upon departure of *Min(i)* from *P(i)*'s location, *Min(i)* will retain the current value[2] of *t*, which will be used at the *Server* location to update of the global state. The actual code migration happens when

$$Min(i).\lambda := Server.\lambda$$
$$\textbf{when } \mathsf{serviceRequest}(\mathrm{REV}, \mathrm{MINSERV}, i) \wedge Min(i).\lambda = P(i).\lambda$$

is eventually executed after a client has sent a message request.

At this point, it is worth noting how, in contrast with the CS solution, the REV request does not contain information that needs to be passed to the *Server*. However, in both solutions the action of putting a message in the request buffer *RQ* can be regarded as modeling the invocation of a communication primitive, which enables actions in the underlying run-time support. In the CS solution, these actions are represented by the transfer of the message to the *Server*; in the REV solution, the actions encompass migration of the *Min(i)* component to the *Server*'s location. Hence, in both solutions the client component is given a uniform interface (the request buffer) to the rest of the system, whose details are handled within the **Interactions** sections—thus modeling the run-time support for communication provided by implementations of RPC and of the REV [6] system. Analogous considerations hold for the output buffer of *Server*. In the REV solution,

---

[2] Mobile code languages implement parameter passing either explicitly by referring to input parameters and code using RPC-like primitives or implicitly by attaching to the procedure to be executed remotely the portion of data space needed for remote computation [5]. We chose the second alternative, in order to illustrate how to dynamically establish and remove bindings among variables in Mobile UNITY.

$$Min(i).q \approx Server.q(i) \quad \textbf{when } Min(i).\lambda = Server.\lambda$$
$$\textbf{engage } \perp$$

models the fact that *Min(i)* is somewhat given access to the communication facilities co-located on the *Server*; the last interaction, in turn, models the actual transfer of information provided by the underlying run-time support. Note that in our REV solution the *Server* does not provide any service, except for offering a name space in which each *Min(i)* can have access to the global state by sharing τ and to the communication facilities by sharing the message buffer q.

Finally, in the last statement of the system the message replies pending in the output queue are sent to the corresponding client. This is accomplished as in the CS solution, except for the assignment

$$[Min(i).\lambda := P(i).\lambda] \quad \textbf{when } \mathsf{serviceReady}(i).$$

This statement is enclosed in square brackets to highlight the fact that it is not a direct consequence of the REV paradigm, yet is needed because of the way Mobile UNITY is currently defined. The REV paradigm involves migration of a copy of a component's code. After that, a message containing the result of the computation on the server is sent back to the client, and what happens to the code remaining on the server is left to the implementation. On the other hand, in the **Component** section of the solution presented we create statically N components which are initialized with their own data and control state. These components are unique in the system, consequently they must return to the client's location in order to become available for another message request—dynamic instantiation of components is not yet available in Mobile UNITY. This issue will be revisited in Section 5.

4.2 Mobile Agent

In the *Mobile Agent* paradigm, the client needs to access some of the resources that are located on the server and, like in the REV paradigm, it owns the necessary know-how to use such resources. In contrast with the REV paradigm, the client sends a whole component that is already being executed on the client host, together with its data and control state. Bindings to resources on the client host are voided and replaced by the new bindings to resources on the server host. The component, once arriving on the server host, resumes execution as if no migration took place. Typically, this step is repeated many times by the same component, which consequently is able to visit a number of hosts on behalf of the client without requiring interaction with it. The MA paradigm is supported natively by languages exploiting strong mobility, like Telescript and Agent Tcl.

Figure 6 shows a Mobile UNITY system designed using the MA paradigm. As in the CS solution, the client processes *P(i)* can increment the timer value, consuming the local estimate for GVT—which prevents further timer increments until a new estimate becomes available. In contrast with the CS solution, no handling of message requests is needed. The location of each client is initialized to a given value, which cannot be changed. The *Server* component, in turn, is

```
System DSMobileAgent
    Program P(i) at λ
        declare
            t, z : integer [] T : integer ∪ {⊥}
        initially
            t, z = 0, ≡ [] T = ⊥ [] λ = Location(i)
        assign
            t, T := f_i(t, T, z), ⊥     if def(T)
    end
    Program Server at λ
        declare
            t, T : integer ∪ {⊥} [] τ : array of integer [] pos : clientAddress
        initially
            t, T = ⊥, ⊥ [] ⟨|| j :: τ(j) = 0⟩ [] λ = Location(pos)
        assign
            τ(pos) := t
         [] T := ⟨min k :: τ(k)⟩
         [] λ, pos := Location(pos + 1 mod N), pos + 1 mod N    if t = τ(pos) ∧
                                                                 ; T = ⟨min k :: τ(k)⟩
    end
    Components
        ⟨[] i :: P(i)⟩ [] Server
    Interactions
        P(i).T ← Server.T        when P(i).λ = Server.λ
                                 engage Server.T
     [] Server.t ← P(i).t        when P(i).λ = Server.λ
                                 engage P(i).t
end
```

Fig. 6. Mobile Agent solution for the distributed simulation problem.

initially co-located with an arbitrarily chosen client and changes explicitly its location during execution in order to visit all clients in a round-robin fashion. The *Server* carries with it the global state of all local timers, which is updated with the timer value of a client *P(i)* while the two components are co-located. The *Server* is also responsible for computing a new GVT value. However, the update of the global state and the computation of the GVT can happen in any order, because the *Server* cannot depart until both the values are up-to-date. The actions performed by the components above are coordinated by the transient variable sharing defined in the **Interactions** section. The GVT estimate and the local timer belonging to the client *P(i)* are shared with their analogues within the *Server*, as long as the two components are co-located:

$$P(i).T \leftarrow Server.T \quad \textbf{when } P(i).\lambda = Server.\lambda$$
$$\textbf{engage } Server.T$$
$$Server.t \leftarrow P(i).t \quad \textbf{when } P(i).\lambda = Server.\lambda$$
$$\textbf{engage } P(i).t$$

The last statement in *Server*, which modifies explicitly the location λ of the component, exercises the **engage** clause of the second interaction. Upon departure, absence of a **disengage** clause guarantees that both the client and the *Server* retain their value for the timer and the GVT. Upon arrival at the next location, the **engage** clause specified in the second read-only shared variable definition guarantees that *as soon as* the two components become co-located, they share the same value for the local timer. The **engage** clause in the first interaction guarantees that the GVT value computed by *Server* on the previous client is communicated to $P(i)$. In general, this value will be changed by the recomputation of the minimum of all timers, which will take into account the current value of the local timer in $P(i)$. Nevertheless, if this timer has not changed since the last visit, the corresponding value in τ remains unchanged and the GVT computed on the previous client—and already communicated to $P(i)$—is still valid and does not need to be recomputed. Hence, in this case the third statement in *Server* is enabled and allows *Server* to depart immediately, without waiting for execution of the two other statements. As an aside, note that disengagement of values, movement, and subsequent re-engagement form a single, atomic action.

4.3 Code On Demand

The *Code On Demand* paradigm is gaining in popularity mainly due to the success of the Java language. In this paradigm, a component on a host performs some kind of computation on its local resources. When it recognizes that a portion of the know-how needed to perform the computation is lacking, the know-how is retrieved from some host on the network. The retrieved code augments the one already present in the client component and new bindings may be established on the client host. The COD paradigm is natively supported in Java through the class loader feature, and in Tcl derivates through the unknown function. In both cases, the programmer can determine the actions to be performed by the run-time support whenever a name cannot be resolved locally. In particular, these actions may encompass retrieval of the corresponding code from a remote site.

We present the solution exploiting the COD paradigm by enhancing the CS solution shown earlier. In the system shown in Fig. 7, clients $P(i)$ are augmented with some statements that enable them to request the code needed to compute dynamically the simulation mode. The requests are issued when a given condition is established, which is modeled by the assignment setting the variable *static* to *false*. This variable is *true* initially, thus the clients initially behave like the ones in *DSClientServer*, which use the initial value $\bar{z}$ for the simulation mode. When *static* becomes *false*, the client is enabled to issue a request

$$RQ := \langle \text{SERVER}, \text{COD}, \text{DYNMODE}, \bot \rangle \quad \textbf{if } \neg\text{def}(RQ) \wedge static = false$$

in order to make the code for the service DYNMODE available to $P(i)$. This code is contained in program $Dyn(i)$, which simply contains an assignment to update the simulation mode by evaluating the function $d(T)$—provided that the GVT estimate is currently defined in $P(i)$. We assume that, once the simulation mode is computed dynamically, it can no longer be reverted to a statically determined value. The *Server* component is left unmodified with respect to the CS solution, while N components $Dyn(i)$ are instantiated in the **Components** section—for reasons similar to those explained for the REV solution. Within the **Interactions** section, the last two statements are unchanged and manage the message exchanges needed to compute the GVT estimate in the a CS paradigm. In turn, the statement

$$Dyn.\lambda, \ P(i).static := P(i).\lambda, \bot$$
$$\textbf{when } Dyn(i).\lambda = Server.\lambda \wedge \text{ serviceRequest}(\text{COD}, \text{DYNMODE}, i)$$

```
System DSCodeOnDemand
   Program P(i) at λ
      declare
         t, z : integer [] T : integer ∪ {⊥} [] static : boolean ∪ {⊥} [] RQ : request ∪ {⊥}
      initially
         t, z = 0, z̄ [] T = ⊥ [] λ = Location(i) [] static = true [] RQ = ⊥
      assign
         [] static := false                              if def(static)
         [] t, T := f_i(t, T, z), ⊥                      if def(T)
         [] RQ := ⟨SERVER,CS, MINSERV, t⟩                if ¬def(RQ) ∧ ¬def(T)
         [] T, RQ := RQ ↑ 4, ⊥                           if RQ ↑ 1 = i
         [] RQ := ⟨SERVER,COD, DYNMODE, ⊥⟩              if ¬def(RQ) ∧ static = false
   end
   Program Dyn(i) at λ
      declare
         z : integer [] T : integer ∪ {⊥}
      initially
         λ = Location(SERVER)
      assign
         z := d(T)      if def(T)
   end
   Program Server at λ
      declare
         T : integer ∪ {⊥} [] τ : array of integer [] q : array of (request ∪ {⊥})
      initially
         T = ⊥ [] ⟨|| j :: τ(j) = 0⟩ [] ⟨|| j :: q(j) = ⊥⟩ [] λ = Location(SERVER)
      assign
         ⟨[] j :: τ(j), q(j) ↑ 2 := q(j) ↑ 4, WAIT⟩    if q(j) ↑ 1 = SERVER ∧ q(j) ↑ 2 ≠ WAIT
         [] T := ⟨min k :: τ(k)⟩                        if ⟨∃ j :: q(j) ↑ 2 = WAIT⟩ ∧ ¬def(T)
         [] ⟨|| j :: q(j), T := ⟨j, ⊥, ⊥, T⟩, ⊥        if def(T) ∧ q(j) ↑ 2 = WAIT⟩
   end
   Components
      ⟨[] i :: P(i)⟩ [] Server [] ⟨[] i :: Dyn(i)⟩
   Interactions
      Dyn.λ, P(i).static := P(i).λ, ⊥                 when Dyn(i).λ = Server.λ ∧
                                                          serviceRequest(COD, DYNMODE, i)
      [] P(i).z ← Dyn(i).z                            when P(i).λ = Dyn(i).λ
                                                          engage P(i).z
      [] Dyn(i).T ← P(i).T                            when P(i).λ = Dyn(i).λ
                                                          engage P(i).T
      [] Server.q(i) := P(i).RQ                       when ¬def(Server.q(i)) ∧
                                                          serviceRequest(CS, MINSERV, i)
      [] P(i).RQ, Server.q(i) := Server.q(i), ⊥       when serviceReady(i)
end
```

Fig. 7. Code On Demand solution for the distributed simulation problem.

satisfies a code request issued by a client $P(i)$ by changing the location of the corresponding component $Dyn(i)$. Furthermore, it prevents further changes in the way z is computed by setting *static* to undefined—which permanently disables the statement issuing the request. Finally,

$$P(i).z \leftarrow Dyn(i).z \qquad \textbf{when } P(i).\lambda = Dyn(i).\lambda$$
$$\textbf{engage } P(i).z$$
$$Dyn(i).T \leftarrow P(i).T \qquad \textbf{when } P(i).\lambda = Dyn(i).\lambda$$
$$\textbf{engage } P(i).T$$

specify the bindings established between $P(i)$ and $Dyn(i)$ when they are co-located. The **engage** clauses initialize the values of z and T in $Dyn(i)$ with the corresponding values in $P(i)$. As in the REV solution, we are forced to instantiate statically multiple components from the same program, instead of migrating the code and instantiating components only when and if needed. This and other issues raised by the solutions presented so far will be discussed in the next section.

5 Conclusions

Mobile UNITY is a new model of distributed computing specialized for mobile computation, i.e., for systems in which components travel through space, compute in a decoupled fashion, and communicate opportunistically when co-located. Mobile UNITY provides a notation system for capturing mobility and an assertional proof logic. Research on Mobile UNITY has shown that a small number of constructs suffice to express transitive forms of transient data sharing and transient synchronization. Restricted forms of these proposed interaction constructs appear to have efficient implementations and more abstract and powerful interaction constructs can be built from the basic forms. In addition, the Mobile UNITY proof logic has been tentatively evaluated in the verification of the Mobile IP protocol [8]. Against this background of promising technical developments, this paper raised a simple question: Can Mobile UNITY model in straightforward manner the kinds of interactions that take place in applications involving mobile code?

The investigative style of this paper is empirical. We started with established mobile code paradigms and sought out corresponding Mobile UNITY solutions. As expected, the decoupled style of computation promoted by Mobile UNITY appears to be a good match for the realities of mobile code.

The **Interactions** section was able to encapsulate appropriately the communication taking place between components. Asynchronous data transfer had a direct counterpart in Mobile UNITY and code movement was easily expressed by the same mechanisms by which components change location. Because the only notion of blocking in Mobile UNITY is busy waiting, blocking for responses to requests was naturally captured by tagging relevant variables as being unavailable (undefined) and strengthening the guards of related statements to check for availability of data. In several cases we used the fact that a variable was no longer available as the trigger for generating a request in the first place—this led to elegant separation between actions embedded in the application program and those supplied by the run-time support. Finally, the transient sharing constructs offered a good solution for the data binding process that needs to take place when a mobile code fragment arrives at a new location. Since the mobile code is treated as a program having its own internal state, the movement of code can be accompanied by data movement. The **engage** feature of transient variable sharing encapsulates the binding process while the **disengage** plays a role in implementing policies that define how much state information maybe carried along by a departing code fragment. When a piece of code carries no data state, for instance, the disengagement reinitializes all its shared variables.

The only possible mismatch identified by this case study has to do with dynamic instantiation of code segments. In the REV solution, for instance, there is no need to "return" the code being evaluated as we do in our example. New

518

fresh copies can be sent each time and several copies may co-exist on different servers. In Mobile UNITY, however, the set of components making up a system is fixed. Further research is needed to evaluate this issue.

Acknowledgements This paper is based upon work supported in part by the National Science Foundation under Grant No. CCR-9217751. Any opinions, findings, and conclusions or recommendations expressed in this paper are those of the authors and do not necessarily reflect the views of the National Science Foundation. Gian Pietro Picco was partially supported by Centro Studi e Laboratori Telecomunicazioni S.p.A., Italy.

References

1. A. Black, N. Hutchinson, E. Jul, and H. Levy. Fine-Grained Mobility in the Emerald System. *ACM Transactions on Computer Systems*, 6(1), February 1988.
2. A. Carzaniga, G.P. Picco, and G. Vigna. Designing Distributed Applications with Mobile Code Paradigms. In R.N. Taylor, editor, *Proceedings of the 19th International Conference on Software Engineering*, 1997.
3. K.M. Chandy and J. Misra. Distributed Simulation: A Case Study in Design and Verification of Distributed Programs. *IEEE Transaction on Software Engineering*, 5(5):440–452, September 1979.
4. K.M. Chandy and J. Misra. *Parallel Program Design*. Addison-Wesley, 1988.
5. G. Cugola, C. Ghezzi, G.P. Picco, and G. Vigna. Analyzing Mobile Code Languages. pages 93–111. In [12].
6. J.W. Stamos and D.K. Gifford. Remote Evaluation. *ACM Transactions on Programming Languages and Systems*, 12(4):537–565, October 1990.
7. P.J. McCann and G-.C. Roman. Mobile UNITY: A Language and Logic for Concurrent Mobile Systems. Technical Report WUCS-97-01, Dept. of Computer Science, Washington University, St.Louis, 1996.
8. P.J. McCann and G-.C. Roman. Mobile UNITY Coordination Constructs Applied to Packet Forwarding for Mobile Hosts. Technical Report WUCS-96-15, Dept. of Computer Science, Washington University, St.Louis, 1996. To appear at the 2nd *Intl. Conf. on Coordination Models and Languages*, Berlin, September 1-3, 1997.
9. Object Management Group. *CORBA: Architecture and Specification*, August 1995.
10. G-.C. Roman, P.J. McCann, and J.Y. Plun. Mobile UNITY: Reasoning and Specification in Mobile Computing. Technical Report WUCS-96-08, Dept. of Computer Science, Washington University, St.Louis, 1996. To appear in *ACM Transactions on Software Engineering and Methodology*.
11. K. Rothermel and R. Popescu-Zeletin, editors. *Mobile Agents*, volume 1219 of *Lecture Notes on Computer Science*. Springer-Verlag, 1997.
12. J. Vitek and C. Tschudin, editors. *Mobile Object Systems: Towards the Programmable Internet*, volume 1222 of *Lecture Notes on Computer Science*. Springer-Verlag, 1997.

Incremental Development for AXE 10

Even-André Karlsson* and Lars Taxen**

1. Introduction

The telecommunication market is changing very rapidly mainly because of two forces: The deregulation with the entering of many new operators, leading to more competition and the proliferation of new technology, e.g. mobile communications, intelligent networks etc. This market change has put a demand on the suppliers to be more reactive and flexible to the market needs, i.e. shorter lead-times and more flexibility in handling late and changing requirements. This is a very challenging change considering the size, complexity and in service performance (up-time) requirements of telecommunication systems. Ericsson has met this challenge by applying incremental development in many large projects. Incremental development has been supported by an adaptation of Ericsson's existing development processes. In this paper we briefly describe what we mean by incremental development, and the Incremental Development Method Package developed by Ericsson Utvecklings AB, who is responsible for Ericsson's AXE 10 development process, Medax.

2. What are increments?

An increment is a well-defined, testable and rather independent functionality in the final system. An increment is preferably a feature offered to the customer. A group of increments is packaged in a build which together form a new executable system. The sequence of builds will provide a system with growing functionality. Usually the projects are organized in 3-6 internal builds with 1-2 month intervals before the system is finally delivered to the customer and put into operation, but we also have examples of intermediate deliveries to the customer.

3. Customer benefits

Incremental development provides:

- Customer focus by emphasizing the customer features. The customer can also provide feedback on the intermediate builds.
- Requirements flexibility by allowing changes to features in later builds and also keeping the feature focus during each build.
- Reduced risks by having a system with gradually growing functionality.
- Early feedback through each build, both to the customer as well as to the designers. In particular the continuous system test activity with feedback to design has proven beneficial for the final performance and quality of the system.
- Shorter lead-time by overlap and thus concurrent work between different builds.

4. Construction planning

A carefully prepared construction plan is essential for a successful incremental development project. The construction planning process determines the possible increments,

* Q-Labs, S-22 370 Lund, email: Even-Andre.Karlsson@q-labs.se
**Ericsson Utvecklings AB, S-125 25 Älvsjö, email: Lars.Taxen@uab.ericsson.se

allocates them to builds and schedules the builds as well as the individual increments in time. The process is designed to satisfy:

- Gradually detailing in planning through the earlier phases of the project.
- Distribution of responsibility, both horizontally from total project to teams and vertically between subsystems.
- Adaptation of the model and processes to the specific needs of each projects.

5. Incremental Development Method Package

The Incremental Development Method Package contains the following elements:

- Incremental Development for AXE 10 - general description
- Incremental Development for AXE 10 - wall-chart
- Definition and Planning of Increments, work instruction
- Preparing the Increment Specification Documents, work instruction
- Configuration Management in Incremental Development, work instruction
- Incremental Development with Medax and Current Tools, work instruction
- Increment Dependency Matrix, document instruction
- AD (Build)-Plan, document instruction
- Functional Anatomy Description, document instruction
- Increment Task Specification, document instruction
- OH-slides and Teacher's Guide

In addition the following documents are provided:

- Incremental Development—Guidelines and Experiences
- Incremental Development and PROPS (Ericsson's project management process)

This package was developed in cooperation with several pilot projects, and was released for general use late 1996. It is based on experiences from about 10 incremental development projects.

The method package has been supported by a series of seminars during its introduction. The largest one attracted 90 people, and was a three days seminar with the first day focusing on the methods, the second day covering project experiences and the last day work-groups looking into special aspects of incremental development, e.g. daily builds, project planning and tracking, configuration management, tool support, etc.

6. Experiences

Incremental development is now becoming a standard way to develop projects within Ericsson, and we have experiences from projects ranging in size from small to very large (e.g. two million man-hours spread over 20 sites). Since incremental development is a very flexible concept we still see a lot of variations in how projects choose increments, but the ID method package gives a common reference. We are also now starting to collect the first set of serious adaptations of the package, which will provide valuable feedback to the second version of the package which is planned for 1998. We are also working on tools support to help projects with the construction planning, follow-up and build. The general experience with incremental development at Ericsson is very positive and most projects have experienced several of the benefits mentioned in section three.

The Tale of Two Projects — Abstract

Dewayne E. Perry[1] and Lawrence G. Votta[2]

[1] Bell Laboratories, Murray Hill, NJ 07974, USA
[2] Bell Laboratories, Naperville IL 60566, USA

We have two hypotheses that we want to demonstrate in this study: organization is not independent of process, and process is not independent of technology. Clearly, one can imagine cases where organizational issues can be separated from process issues. Similarly, there are levels of abstraction where aspects of process are independent of particular technologies. In general, the three should be considered as interrelated and interdependent. We show the validity of our claims in the discussions of the two case studies below.

We have selected these two projects for the following reasons: they have executed a complete cycle of development, they have well-documented post mortems of their experience, and they have the requisite quantitative data. We measure product development projects using three interrelated, macroscopic variables by which: cost, quality, and time interval. In our analysis we focus primarily on time interval, with some consideration given to quality, and emphasize the contrast between the prevailing process, organizational and technological development structure and the one implemented in each of the case studies.

The Y0 Packet Features Development is composed of four features with a total code size is 54.6 thousand noncommentary source lines (KNSCL), a total staff size of 39.8 and a total number of faults at delivery to the first customer of 12. The goal was to reduce the development interval from 16 to 12 months, while maintaining or slightly improving the quality of the product. The fault density, as delivered to the first customer, is the measure of the product quality.

The standard development [3] results from an assembly line like approach to developing software. At each stage a major milestone is defined. Throughput was increased by making one organization responsible for each stage, but at the cost of many handoffs which are costly in time and quality, and are difficult to coordinate. The unit of planning is one month and is the result of balancing the need for tight coordination required to control interval with many organizational handoffs and the cost of tracking the process.

The Y0 development process altered these factors. Instead of a functional organization approach, a team approach was used to minimize handoffs. This solution mitigates the monthly intervals, as well, because the team does not need as much formal review. The milestones were more naturally matched to the structure of the Y0 features and the team's talents. This allowed the team to exploit characteristics of the problem making the entire development less prone to fault insertion.

---

[3] Joseph S. Colson, Jr., and Edward M. Prell.: Total Quality Management for a Large Software Project. AT&T Technical Journal 71:3 (May/June 1992) 48-56

The FNMS-R3 software development [4] was an enhanced release of 45 KNCSL of C++ on a base of 140KNCSL undertaken by about 25 people and consisted of three major features and a number of minor features. The previous release (FNMS-R2) took about 16 months to complete. The process was too unresponsive to customer needs and the products were too unstable in the field.

The development schedule was mapped out and used as the management plan directing the development process. The general intent was to support incremental development. Except for a one day high level design review and an external architecture review of the FNMS-R1 architecture, there were no design reviews or code inspections. Moreover, there was no formal unit testing and only minimal integration testing (with no clear exit criteria). Documentation was done after the fact — while the product was being soaked at a field site.

The organization was structured functionally: systems engineering, development, and system test. Problems that arose from the separation of these functions included: interface problems; lack of support in reviewing requirements in a timely manner; an inactive MR review board; and status meetings which were reduced to fighting fires and managing crises.

The FNMS-R3 development process altered four things in order to achieve their goals. 1) They added some standard quality gate techniques. 2) They decreased interval time by decoupling features that could be developed in parallel. 3) They changed from a functional to an interdisciplinary team organization. The teams were empowered to be responsible for their features from feature specification through integration. 4) Within the individual feature developments, team members were encouraged to do as much in parallel as possible.

The results of these changes were as follows. 1) The cycle time was reduced by about 25% to 12 months. 2) Decoupling features enabled short features to be implemented and delivered very quickly. One of the major features was delivered three months ahead of the other two features. 3) Defects were removed earlier with very few problems encountered after integration testing. 4) The team organization increased the effectiveness of the development process with team members assuming various roles that were previously in different functions. Moreover, the team approach significantly increased the effectiveness.

Thus, both the development interval and the product quality were increased by effectively exploiting the structure of the organization and the technology of the product, and introducing sound software engineering techniques.

Both projects display the same strong trends even though they were done in very different parts of the business, in different kinds of software developments, and in different geographic locations. Both projects had an organizational structure of strongly empowered teams, understood the technology at a fundamental level, and used some innovative software engineering technology. Without these organizational structures and the technology exploitations, neither of these projects would have achieved the resulting level of success.

---

[4] H. T. Yeh.: Re-Engineering a Software Development Process for Fast Delivery - Approach & Experiences. Proceedings of the First International Conference on the Software Process (Redondo Beach, CA, October 1991) 106-112

Analysis of Software Architectures in High and Low Volume Electronic Systems, industrial experience report

J. Henk Obbink, Philips Research
Prof. Holstlaan 4, 5656 AA Eindhoven, The Netherlands
obbink@natlab.research.philips.com

Introduction

Philips is a world wide operating electronics company. The electronic systems of Philips can be roughly divided into two main segments. The first segment is called low volume electronics and is covered by professional business groups. The second segment is called high volume electronics and is addressed by consumer business groups. Increasingly these systems are becoming software intensive. The required measures that must be undertaken by a company to cope with this shift are twofold.

- Software process improvement issues. In the past few years a lot of attention has been given to SPI activities, based upon the SEI CMM model [2].
- Improvement of the software product architecture.

In this paper we will present the initial results of employing an architectural framework proposed by D. Soni et. al. [1] to analyse various SW architectures in both high and low volume electronic systems inside the Philips Company.

Overview of the Soni Paper and Model

The Soni model [1] is the result of an extensive investigation of the practise of the handling/describing of SW architecture of industrial applications inside the Siemens company. The premise was that software architecture is concerned with capturing the structures and the relationships among the elements both within and between structures. The study involved discussions with architects and engineers, and reading of design documents, and part of the source code. They observed for most systems a distinction between architecture for the product-specific and the platform software. The latter usually provides a virtual machine or an infrastructure. For both parts of the software different structures were used at different stages of the development process. The model indicates that software architectures describe how a system is decomposed into components, and their interconnections, communications and interactions. Furthermore, based upon common practice, the model distinguishes 5 related, but different views on the software. They are:

- The conceptual architecture: the major design elements and their relationships.
- The module (interconnection) architecture: functional decomposition and layers.
- The code architecture: organisation of source code, binaries and libraries.
- The execution architecture: dynamic structure.
- The hardware architecture: hardware components and their connections.

Industrial Examples studied

As a first step towards architecture improvement applications of the Soni ideas have been performed within Philips. The first two are Low Volume: Medical Application (MED) and a Video on Demand System (VOD). The last three are High Volume: Audio system, a TV system, and settopbox software. Not all the mentioned architectures were found during our investigations. The table below lists our findings.

System	Size	Conceptual	Module	Execution	Code
MED	Very Large	+[1]	+	+	+
VOD	Medium	[2]	+[3]	+	+
Audio	Small	[4]	+	+	+[5]
TV	Large	[6]	+	+	+
Settopbox	Medium/Large	+	+	+	[7]

Conclusions and lessons learned

This paper reported about work in progress. One of the main findings is that the Soni ideas, although originated within the Siemens company, are also useful within Philips. We came to similar conclusions as Soni et. al. [1] and particularly we found it difficult to pinpoint the conceptual architecture. Explicit relationships between the various architectures were not always made clear. The most clear is the relationship between module and code architectures. This determined often the relationships between the module and execution architectures, but in general they are difficult to find and in many cases implicit. The similarities and differences among the various systems are surprising. In particular, there appears to be no standard way of representing the various architectures. For each of the individual cases the work has resulted in a much better understanding of the software architectures. In the past these architectures, were either implicit, hidden and scattered over many documents, or only known by the experts. By explicitly extracting them and modelling them from various viewpoints it has become easier to share the relevant architectural knowledge with the non-SW architects (HW-Architects, System Architects, Product Managers, etc.) in the organisation.

References

[1]   D. Soni, R.L. Nord and C. Hofmeier, Software Architecture in Industrial Applications, Proceedings ICSE'95, the 17th International Conference on Software Engineering, Seattle, Washington, 1995.

[2]   Humphrey, W.S., Managing the Software Process, Addison-Wesley, 1989, ISBN no: 0-201-18095-2

---

1. Mirrors the execution architecture
2. Difficult to identify a single one. Several candidates mentioned
3. Mirrors the execution architecture
4. No specific one used
5. Mirrored module architecture
6. A kind of software chassis was used in earlier documents, not used during development
7. Not available at the moment of writing, because G+4 is still under development

Towards an Adaptation of the Cocomo Cost Model to the Software Measurement Theory

A. Idri   B. Griech   A. El Iraki

ENSIAS, BP. 713, Agdal, Rabat, Maroc. email: idri@emi.ac.ma

Abstract:When the COCOMO cost model was published in the beginning of the eighties, software measurement was not grounded on solid theoretical foundations. This has been achieved until the nineties by Fenton ond others. Thus, it is not surprising that some of the concepts defined or used in the COCOMO model are somewhat incompatible with the software measurement theory. In this work, we mainly stress some of the incompatibilities and propose alternaive ways to avoid them.

Introduction

Estimating the work-effort and the schedule required to develop a software system is one of the most critical activities in managing software projects. In order to make accurate estimations and avoid gros misestimations, several techniques are used within companies. The actually most popular work-effort estimation techniques are the algorithmic models such as COCOMO [Boe 81], IBM-FSD [Wal 77], and function points analysis [Alb 83] [Mat 94].

This paper concerns the COCOMO model and especially its intermediate version Instead of many investigations aiming to calibrate, enhance or reformulate the initial vesrion [Miy 85] [Mar 91] [Gul 91], our goal in this work is rather to check whether or not the concepts handled in COCOMO obey to the emerging measurement theory and to propose solutions to the problems encountered.

Classification of the 15 cost Driver Attributes

In addition to the software size and project mode attributes, The intermediate COCOMO takes into account 15 others cost driver attributes which are generally related to the software environment. These 15 attributes are grouped in four major categories (Product, Computer, Personnel, or Project). According to the taxonomy defined in [Fen 91], We can distinguish three major types of software entities (Product, Resource, and Process). So, we propose a new calssification of the COCOMO cost driver . This classification has been achieved after a deep analysis. Many interesting remarks can be deduced.

Arithmetic mean and Linear Interpolation Problems

Each attribute was measured by [Boe 81] using a rating scale of 6 qualitative values. The empirical relations established by [Boe 81] for assigning the effort multipliers to each attribute allows us to conclude that the scale type is *ordinal* [Fen 91] [She 93] Indeed, for a given COCOMO attribute, each effort multiplier associated with a particular rating is obtained from the four effort multipliers of the detailed version using a weighted arithmetic mean. The problem hear is that, according to software measurement theory, this kind of weighted arithmetic mean is not meaningfully unlesse the scale is at least of *interval* type [Fen 91]. We can however, meaningfully use the median for *ordinal* scales as we have mathematically proved.

Unlike the aritmetic mean, there is more than one method for computing the median of a series of data. Furthemore, the results obtained from such methods may differ significantly. We have investigated three differnet methods for the calculation of the median. Only two of them has been retained.

There is another problem in the COCOMO. That is the use of linear interpolation on data which are measured on *ordinal* scales. This can not be used unless the scale is at least an *interval* type. Unfortunately, as we have stressed earlier, the sclaes used in COCOMO are not of such type. From a careful analysis of the initial COCOMO database, it appears that the linear interpolation formula was applied 36 times and 22 projects among 63 were concerned. We have noticed that for four project the anomaly is less important. Hence, the new database contains only 45 projects.

Validation

We validate the effort multipliers abtained from the second and third methods against the retained projects. This validation consists in comparing the accuracy of these two methods. Exactly like in COCOMO, five quantities are used for the appreciation of the degree of accuracy . The third method provides the best accuracy than the second.

Conclusion and Future Works

In this work, some alternative ways has been proposed to ensure the correctness of the computations used in COCOMO. Otherwise, many aspects of the COCOMO model reamins incompatible with this theory (the measure of the software size KDSI, Ideal Effort Multiplier, etc.).

After this investigation of the COCOMO model, our main goal is to build a software cost model for estimating Moroccan software projects. At the present, we are still in an early stage where we are performing inquiries within software companies.

Bibliography

[Alb 83] Albrecht A. J, Gaffney J. E, 'Software Function, Source Lines of Code, and Development Effort Prediction: A Software Science Validation'. IEEE, Transactions on Software Engineering, Vol SE-9, No. 6, Nov. 1983, pp. 639-647.

[Fen 91] Fenton N., Software Metrics, A Rigorous Approach'. Chapman&Hall, 1991.

[Gul 91] Gulezian R, 'Reformulating and Calibrating COCOMO'. Journ. Sys. Soft., vol. 16, 1991, pp.235-242.

[Mar 91] Marwane R, Mili A, 'Building tailor-made software cost model: Intermediate TUCOMO'. Inf. Soft. Techno., vol 33(3), Apr. 1991, pp. 232-238.

[Mat 94] Matson J. E, Barrett B. E, Mellichamp J. M, 'Software Development Cost Estimation Using Function Points'. IEEE, Vol. 20, No. 4, April, 1994, pp. 275-287.

[Miy 85] Miyazaki Y, Mori K, 'COCOMO evaluation and tailoring'. In Proc. Eighth Int. Conf. Software Engineering, London, UK, Aug. 1985, pp. 292-299.

[She 93] Shepperd N, Ince D, 'Derivation and Validation of software metrics'. Oxford Science Publication, 1993.

[Wal 77] Walston C. E, Felix A. P, 'A Method of Programming Measurement and Estimation'. IBM Systems Journal, Vol 16, No. 1, 1977.

Formalizing Software Architectures: An Industrial Experience

Petre Dini, Amina Belkhelladi, *and* Walcélio L. Melo
Centre de recherche informatique de Montréal
1801, McGill College Street, #800
Montreal, (Qc), H3A 2N4, Canada
{dini I abelkhel I wmelo}@crim.ca

Introduction

A software architecture identifies collections of functional modules shared by a *family of products*, but does not analyze the specific algorithms used into such modules. To offer a formal basis for describing software architectures, system descriptions must provide useful documentation adapted to architectural views, e.g. conceptual, modules interconnection, execution, and code [2]. The *conceptual view* of a software architecture (CSA) is made at the early phases of a software system life-cycle, providing a high-level description of a software system [5]. A CSA, once well-defined and documented, can be useful for software engineers for communicating with each other, for deriving the remaining architectural views, or for V&V (Verification and Validation) purposes. The CSA is also useful in checking the consistency and completeness of the software architecture, and thus, taking corrective actions before low level design and implementation activities are performed [1]. Conceptual view helps us derive a static configuration of the system, leading to the *execution architecture*.

In order to document and specify different aspects of software architectures, we have proposed a combination of informal object-oriented analysis and design methods, model-oriented formal languages, and already existing S/W specification languages. The rationale is to combine a graphical representation, which is intuitive and user friendly, with constraints expressed as first-order predicates to precise the interfaces of objects involved in different types of interactions. We have used a multiparadigm approach which combines concepts from OMT [6], Object-Z, and Conic [4], called MODL. MODL extends OMT with notions of pre-conditions, post-conditions, and invariants offered by Object-Z. Additionally, MODL integrates the concept of ports and configuration families (subsystems) provided by Conic. We have used MODL to describe the architecture of a data emulation software. The main purpose is to define a precise documentation, identify commonalities between similar products, and combine these commonalities to build a *generic architecture*. By doing so, we intend to enhance the *reuse* at the earlier phases of the software development lifecycle. The validation work was done within the project EPAC that is a two years long R&D project involving 2.5 man/year. EPAC has defined different research and development topics with the goal of enhancing the quality of emulation software systems, such as reusability, maintainability, and extensibility.

An Overview of MODL

We will present in the following the process to produce the desired software architecture in a sequential way. Obviously, the different steps may be performed iteratively because of refinement and reworking between each of them, according to the knowledge acquisition process. Based on knowledge from domain engineering, conceptual and execution architectures are inferred.

STEP 1. Based on the analysis of several products of the same family, their appropriate documentation, public information on similar products, discussions with domain experts, users of such products, vendors and manufactures, a collection of data is gathered. So, we are able to identify relevant information of a family of products. At this point, the distinction between objects, operations, and attributes is not yet clarified. We use the Object-Z type specification technique to declare discovered information. This approach allows us to know in a precise way the domain-specific vocabulary (terms), and to continuously add other terms or types.

STEP 2. Classify identified information in objects, attribute, operations, abstract types, predicate constraints, or invariants. The goal is to identify potential object classes, attributes specific to certain classes, as well as the distribution of operations to objects. At this point, it is possible that certain operations or properties will not be identified as belonging to already classified terms. STEP1 can be re-applied to reclassify some terms, or it can be iterated in order to highlight missing concepts and terms. The information obtained from this step are specified using OMT or Object-Z.

STEP 3. Represent graphically the conceptual architecture, using decisions derived from STEP2. We use information from STEP2, and the documentation of existing legacy systems of the considered product family. The main goal of this step is the identification of object relationships, such as the inheritance, specializations, aggregations, and particular views on the potential objects.

STEP 4. Specify the structure and behavior for each component. Document each component identified as a class (type) in STEP 3. The operations must be properly assigned to these types. It is suitable to prescribe pre- and post-conditions, as well as several invariants or textual denotations. It is important that activation conditions for all operations identified at STEP 3 be defined for each operation. An Object-Z schema is specified for each class built in STEP3. Some schemes can be designed for only capture some aspects, which are not necessarily objects. Then, schemes can be composed to obtain an appropriate OMT class.

STEP 5. Identify different interaction scenarios within a subsystem, the object interfaces through these scenarios take place, as well as constraints on these interactions. The purpose is to identify activation conditions of all operations identified in STEP 2, and behavioral dependencies between objects identified and specified in the previous steps. This implies the identification of sources of all activation events discovered in STEP 4. We represent interaction scenarios by cooperation relations [3], as introduced below, to obtain a more precise expression than OMT. However, OMT graphical representation diagrams can be used. OMT allows this representation in a graphical manner, but it is difficult to represent other types of constraints, i.e. invariants or state instances. We use Object-Z to specify more precisely these aspects.

STEP 6. Specify detailed scenarios between subsystems through inter-system events. This allows to extend the system on well-defined interactions interfaces, detect dependencies between subsystems, and favors the reuse of already identified components. Scenarios are built using OMT, since in Object-Z it is difficult to prescribe event dependencies. We use the notion of typed interface which has been previously introduced, and create particular types of interactions according to these interfaces between. Systems are clusterized in subsystems, which communicate with each other or with their environment across boundary objects.

Lessons learned

During our work several information favoring the derivation of generic architectures have been identified. In addition, we have been able to identify reusable concepts for a family of data emulation modules. Common operations, interactions, and scenarios (interaction patterns), which can be considered as commonalities of all emulation types, have also been identified. The resulting specification seems to be more rigorous, allowing one ensuring a better and safer transition to the implementation.

However, the marriage between Object-Z, Conic, and OMT is not so straightforward. First, OMT favors the graphical representation, but several problems related to object composition, especially when considering subsystems, remain. It is difficult to build scenarios in Object-Z, and an external operation (e.g. NOTIFY) will be useful to express notifications sent to the emulation managers. The training and learning formal languages, i.e. Object-Z, is effort consuming. However, to improve the system specification, a trade-off between informal and formal requirements is necessary. Some weaknesses are due to the immaturity of the language Object-Z, which was not concerned to cover all aspects related to object-oriented architecture requirements. Conic is object-based, and does not provide neither compositions of interactions, nor inheritance. Consequently, the issues related to the object composition must be enhanced to capture dynamic properties in the object-oriented approach.

References

[1]   Courtois, P.-J., Parnas, D.L. 1995. Documentation for Safety Critical Software, *Proceedings of 15th International Conference on Software Engineering*, Baltimore, Maryland, May 1993, pp. 315-323

[2]   Dini, P., Ramazani, D., Bochmann, v. G. 1995. Formal and Informal in Balanced System Specifications, *The International Conference on Balanced Systems, BASYS'95*, Vitoria, Brasil, June 1995.

[3]   Dini, P. 1997. Automatic Reconfiguration Management in Networks and Distributed Systems, Ph.D. Thesis, University of Montreal, January 1997.

[4]   Magee, J. et al.1989. Constructing Distributed Systems in Conic. *IEEE Tr. on SE*, vol. 15, no. 6, June 1989, pp. 663-675.

[5]   Shaw, M. 1994. Making Choices: A Comparison of Styles for Software Architecture, *School of Computer Science, Carnegie Mellon University*, Pittsburg PA, May 1994.

[6]   Rumbaugh, J., Blaha, M., Premerlani, W., Eddy, F., Lorensen, W. 1991. *Object-Oriented Modeling and Design*, Prentice-Hall, Inc., 1991.

Panel Session

Chair: Mehdi Jazayeri (Technische Universität Wien, Austria)

Software Engineering - Old Problems, New Problems, and Unsolved Problems

Panelists: *Barry Boehm*
             Tom Gilb
             David Parnas
             Tom Maibaum
             John Rushby and others

For someone who has been around the software engineering field, many ideas being discussed today seem uncomfortably familiar. Some people confront any new proposal with a comment like, "Oh, we used to do that" or "This is not new, we have always done it this way." Is it true that there are no new ideas or is it that old problems change as technologies change and require new solutions? I have asked the distinguished panelists to look back in time and consider the following:

1. Name up to three real problems facing software engineering today.

2. Did these problems exist in the old days or are they new?

3. Name up to three important software engineering problems that have been solved.

4. Name some nonproblems that people are working on today. Were these always nonproblems?

Author Index

Springer
and the
environment

At Springer we firmly believe that an international science publisher has a special obligation to the environment, and our corporate policies consistently reflect this conviction.

We also expect our business partners – paper mills, printers, packaging manufacturers, etc. – to commit themselves to using materials and production processes that do not harm the environment. The paper in this book is made from low- or no-chlorine pulp and is acid free, in conformance with international standards for paper permanency.

Lecture Notes in Computer Science

For information about Vols. 1–1238

please contact your bookseller or Springer-Verlag

Vol. 1275: E.L. Gunter, A. Felty (Eds.), Theorem Proving in Higher Order Logics. Proceedings, 1997. VIII, 339 pages. 1997.

Vol. 1276: T. Jiang, D.T. Lee (Eds.), Computing and Combinatorics. Proceedings, 1997. XI, 522 pages. 1997.

Vol. 1277: V. Malyshkin (Ed.), Parallel Computing Technologies. Proceedings, 1997. XII, 455 pages. 1997.

Vol. 1278: R. Hofestädt, T. Lengauer, M. Löffler, D. Schomburg (Eds.), Bioinformatics. Proceedings, 1996. XI, 222 pages. 1997.

Vol. 1279: B. S. Chlebus, L. Czaja (Eds.), Fundamentals of Computation Theory. Proceedings, 1997. XI, 475 pages. 1997.

Vol. 1280: X. Liu, P. Cohen, M. Berthold (Eds.), Advances in Intelligent Data Analysis. Proceedings, 1997. XII, 621 pages. 1997.

Vol. 1281: M. Abadi, T. Ito (Eds.), Theoretical Aspects of Computer Software. Proceedings, 1997. XI, 639 pages. 1997.

Vol. 1282: D. Garlan, D. Le Métayer (Eds.), Coordination Languages and Models. Proceedings, 1997. X, 435 pages. 1997.

Vol. 1283: M. Müller-Olm, Modular Compiler Verification. XV, 250 pages. 1997.

Vol. 1284: R. Burkard, G. Woeginger (Eds.), Algorithms — ESA '97. Proceedings, 1997. XI, 515 pages. 1997.

Vol. 1285: X. Jao, J.-H. Kim, T. Furuhashi (Eds.), Simulated Evolution and Learning. Proceedings, 1996. VIII, 231 pages. 1997. (Subseries LNAI).

Vol. 1286: C. Zhang, D. Lukose (Eds.), Multi-Agent Systems. Proceedings, 1996. VII, 195 pages. 1997. (Subseries LNAI).

Vol. 1287: T. Kropf (Ed.), Formal Hardware Verification. XII, 367 pages. 1997.

Vol. 1288: M. Schneider, Spatial Data Types for Database Systems. XIII, 275 pages. 1997.

Vol. 1289: G. Gottlob, A. Leitsch, D. Mundici (Eds.), Computational Logic and Proof Theory. Proceedings, 1997. VIII, 348 pages. 1997.

Vol. 1290: E. Moggi, G. Rosolini (Eds.), Category Theory and Computer Science. Proceedings, 1997. VII, 313 pages. 1997.

Vol. 1291: D.G. Feitelson, L. Rudolph (Eds.), Job Scheduling Strategies for Parallel Processing. Proceedings, 1997. VII, 299 pages. 1997.

Vol. 1292: H. Glaser, P. Hartel, H. Kuchen (Eds.), Programming Languages: Implementations, Logigs, and Programs. Proceedings, 1997. XI, 425 pages. 1997.

Vol. 1294: B.S. Kaliski Jr. (Ed.), Advances in Cryptology — CRYPTO '97. Proceedings, 1997. XII, 539 pages. 1997.

Vol. 1295: I. Prívara, P. Ružička (Eds.), Mathematical Foundations of Computer Science 1997. Proceedings, 1997. X, 519 pages. 1997.

Vol. 1296: G. Sommer, K. Daniilidis, J. Pauli (Eds.), Computer Analysis of Images and Patterns. Proceedings, 1997. XIII, 737 pages. 1997.

Vol. 1297: N. Lavrač, S. Džeroski (Eds.), Inductive Logic Programming. Proceedings, 1997. VIII, 309 pages. 1997. (Subseries LNAI).

Vol. 1298: M. Hanus, J. Heering, K. Meinke (Eds.), Algebraic and Logic Programming. Proceedings, 1997. X, 286 pages. 1997.

Vol. 1299: M.T. Pazienza (Ed.), Information Extraction. Proceedings, 1997. IX, 213 pages. 1997. (Subseries LNAI).

Vol. 1300: C. Lengauer, M. Griebl, S. Gorlatch (Eds.), Euro-Par'97 Parallel Processing. Proceedings, 1997. XXX, 1379 pages. 1997.

Vol. 1301: M. Jazayeri, H. Schauer (Eds.), Software Engineering - ESEC/FSE'97. Proceedings, 1997. XIII, 532 pages. 1997.

Vol. 1302: P. Van Hentenryck (Ed.), Static Analysis. Proceedings, 1997. X, 413 pages. 1997.

Vol. 1303: G. Brewka, C. Habel, B. Nebel (Eds.), KI-97: Advances in Artificial Intelligence. Proceedings, 1997. XI, 413 pages. 1997. (Subseries LNAI).

Vol. 1304: W. Luk, P.Y.K. Cheung, M. Glesner (Eds.), Field-Programmable Logic and Applications. Proceedings, 1997. XI, 503 pages. 1997.

Vol. 1305: D. Corne, J.L. Shapiro (Eds.), Evolutionary Computing. Proceedings, 1997. X, 313 pages. 1997.

Vol. 1307: R. Kompe, Prosody in Speech Understanding Systems. XIX, 357 pages. 1997. (Subseries LNAI).

Vol. 1308: A. Hameurlain, A M. Tjoa (Eds.), Database and Expert Systems Applications. Proceedings, 1997. XVII, 688 pages. 1997.

Vol. 1309: R. Steinmetz, L.C. Wolf (Eds.), Interactive Distributed Multimedia Systems and Telecommunication Services. Proceedings, 1997. XIII, 466 pages. 1997.

Vol. 1310: A. Del Bimbo (Ed.), Image Analysis and Processing. Proceedings, 1997. Volume I. XXII, 722 pages. 1997.

Vol. 1311: A. Del Bimbo (Ed.), Image Analysis and Processing. Proceedings, 1997. Volume II. XXII, 794 pages. 1997.

Vol. 1312: A. Geppert, M. Berndtsson (Eds.), Rules in Database Systems. Proceedings, 1997. VII, 214 pages. 1997.

Vol. 1313: J. Fitzgerald, C.B. Jones, P. Lucas (Eds.), FME '97: Industrial Applications and Strengthened Foundations of Formal Methods. Proceedings, 1997. XIII, 685 pages. 1997.

Vol. 1314: S. Muggleton (Ed.), Inductive Logic Programming. Proceedings, 1996. VIII, 397 pages. 1997. (Subseries LNAI).

Vol. 1315: G. Sommer, J.J. Koenderink (Eds.), Algebraic Frames for the Perception-Action Cycle. Proceedings, 1997. VIII, 395 pages. 1997.

Vol. 1317: M. Leman (Ed.), Music, Gestalt, and Computing. IX, 524 pages. 1997. (Subseries LNAI).

Vol. 1320: M. Mavronicolas, P. Tsigas (Eds.), Distributed Algorithms. Proceedings, 1997. X, 333 pages. 1997.

Vol. 1321: M. Lenzerini (Ed.), AI*IA 97: Advances in Artificial Intelligence. Proceedings, 1997. XII, 459 pages. 1997. (Subseries LNAI).

Vol. 1324: C. Peters, C. Thanos (Ed.), Research and Advanced Technology for Digital Libraries. Proceedings, 1997. X, 423 pages. 1997.